Plato

Selections From the Dialogues of Plato

With Introd. and Notes by John Purves, and a Pref. by B. Jowett

Plato

Selections From the Dialogues of Plato
With Introd. and Notes by John Purves, and a Pref. by B. Jowett

ISBN/EAN: 9783337007720

SELECTIONS

FROM

THE DIALOGUES OF PLATO

J. PURVES

London

HENRY FROWDE

OXFORD UNIVERSITY PRESS WAREHOUSE

7 PATERNOSTER ROW

Clarendon Press Series

SELECTIONS

FROM THE DIALOGUES OF

PLATO

WITH INTRODUCTIONS AND NOTES

BY

JOHN PURVES, M.A.

FELLOW OF BALLIOL COLLEGE

AND

A PREFACE

BY THE

REV. B. JOWETT, M.A.

MASTER OF BALLIOL COLLEGE
REGIUS PROFESSOR OF GREEK IN THE UNIVERSITY OF OXFORD

Oxford

AT THE CLARENDON PRESS

1883

PREFACE.

THE extracts from Plato which have been brought together in this volume were selected by Mr. Purves and myself several years ago. But, with this slight exception, he alone is the author of the book, to which by his wish I contribute a short preface. As through inadvertence the selection has been announced under our joint names, it is necessary that I should make this disclaimer.

This little work is not designed, like Ritter and Preller's book of extracts, to be an ' Historia Philosophiae e fontium locis contexta.' The object of the editor has been literary rather than philosophical. He has not attempted to set forth the philosophy of Plato in regular order, though in any selection from Plato something of his idealism may be expected to appear. He would be far from wishing to encourage any premature study of philosophy. But before the time has arrived for abstract thought, the young scholar may with advantage make himself acquainted with the style of Plato in its most perfect form; he may gather choice flowers of poetry and fancy; he may grow familiar with the wonderful portrait of the Silenus Socrates (Symp. 215 A), who is the central figure of the Platonic dialogues. Some part of the meaning may slumber in his ear: but he will fill his mind with beautiful passages while the imagination is strongest and the memory most retentive. And when hereafter he reads them in their context, and a new light is thrown upon the page, he will ' rejoice in recognizing ' his old friends : he will return to them with increased interest, perceiving that there was more in them than he thought (Rep. iii. 402 A).

It is the misfortune of all books of extracts that they take the gems out of their setting, and therefore do a kind of injustice to a great writer. The higher beauty and excellence of any writing is necessarily impaired in detached passages. When the fruit is plucked from the tree and put into our hands, there is a loss of freshness or fragrance. But the objection is more than counterbalanced by the advantage of introducing youth at an early age to the writings of a master. The very fragments of Plato have a finish and perfection to which no modern writings can compare. They are fruits which even the youthful scholar perceives to be of a different flavour from Xenophon or Lucian. Living as he did at the convergence of two literary periods, Plato may be truly called at once ' the last of the poets and the first of prose writers.' As Cicero says of his Dialogues, though not himself an imitator of them, ' Poema magis putandum quam comicorum poetarum.' Plato alone of all writers, ancient or modern, has imparted to philosophy the glory of style.

Everything is best learned at the right time and in the natural order. As Aristotle tells us, in a well-known passage of the Nicomachean Ethics (I. i. §§ 5–8), ' the young man is not a good hearer of Ethics.' He may think too much as well as too little. The Socratic 'pang of philosophy,' that is to say, the fascination of abstract ideas, may easily interfere with the growth of the mind in youth or in early manhood. Poetry, language, physical science, mathematics, the works of great writers—Greek, Latin, or English—are a much better basis of education than metaphysical philosophy. They are 'the land of health' in which Plato would have the youth of his city reared: where beauty, 'the effluence of fair works, will visit the eye and ear, and insensibly, like a fresh breeze from a purer region, will draw the soul, even in childhood, into harmony with the beauty of reason.' (Rep. iii. 401 C.) '... He who has received this true education of the inner being will most shrewdly perceive omissions or faults in art and nature, and with a true taste, while he praises and rejoices over and receives into his soul the good, he will justly blame and hate the bad, now in the days of his youth, even before he knows the reason of them.' Whereas the tendency in young men to abstract thought is apt to wither the imagination and to dry up the interest in facts. There is a danger, as Plato also foresaw (Rep. vii. 539 B), 'lest they should taste the dear delight too early ... and get into a way, violently and speedily, of not believing anything which they believed before, ... like puppy dogs, eager to tear and pull at all who come near them. But when a man begins to be older he will no longer be guilty of such insanity.'

We reject then any notion of making this book an introduction to the system of Plato. Yet there are a few points to which the reader's attention may be called, with the view of removing misconceptions, and of making intelligible and interesting what would otherwise appear fanciful and un-meaning. These points are :

    (i.) The dramatic character of the Platonic dialogue.

    (ii.) The popular and half poetical conception of the Platonic ideas.

    (iii.) The true origin and meaning of them.

(i.) The Dialogues of Plato exhibit philosophy in the form of a drama. Socrates is the protagonist or chief actor; around him are ranged the inferior persons upon whom he exercises his magic art of dialectic. There is the statesman, the general, the rhetorician, the poet, the man of the world, the geometrician, the ingenuous youth, the philosopher of a former generation, who are detained by the spell which Socrates exerts over them, and made to give an account of themselves and their callings. There are Sophists, great and small, who, unlike Socrates, are ready to sell the gift of knowledge for money. There is the contrast of different ages and of different pursuits or professions ; above all, of sophistry or pretended knowledge with truth or real knowledge. The true knowledge never is, but is always on the point of being, discovered ; as if Socrates thought that the search after truth was a greater good than the possession of it. Yet the enquirer never loses hope, but is ready to renew the argument on another day with untiring energy. The different states of Hellas,—Athens, Crete, Lacedaemon, Elis, Leontini, Cyrene, Elea, furnish interlocutors, and give something of a local colouring to several of the dialogues. Elaborate studies are made of the two great Sophists, Gorgias and Protagoras, who, although secretly ridiculed, are treated with an outward respect befitting their name and fame.   A greater and more genuine admiration is shown towards Parmenides, 'venerable and awful' (Theaet. 183 E).   Anaxagoras is spoken of with mixed feelings; he was the former master of Socrates, who had been wonderfully delighted at his first utterance of the word 'mind,' and not less disappointed by the inconsistent use which he made of it (Phaedo 97; cp. Arist. Met. i. 4. § 5; also Cratyl. 409).   For some reason or other Heracleitus and his disciples, and also probably Democritus, whose name is not mentioned, are represented in ludicrous and repulsive colours (Soph. 240).   One of the most amusing passages in Plato is the description of the Heracleiteans, or 'patrons of the flux,' who, 'in accordance with their text-books, are always in motion, . . . who grow up anyhow and get their inspiration anywhere, each one of them saying of his neighbour that he knows nothing,' etc. (Theaet. 180; cp. Cratyl. 402).

The dialogues open with chance remarks, as of friends meeting and renewing acquaintance, not with any formal statement of a philosophical thesis.   The scene and the occasion are generally described in the beginning of the dialogue, and sometimes alluded to in the course of it. The plane-tree on the little stream of the Ilissus in the Phaedrus (229): the family circle of Cephalus at the Piraeus (Rep. i. 328), whither Socrates and his disciples had gone by invitation to witness the torch race: the banquet at the house of Agathon, to which the Master came perfumed and sandalled (Symp. i. 134): the reunion of philosophers and their followers which Callias had assembled round him (Prot. *init.*): the opening of the Parmenides, in which that

rather perplexing discourse is said to be recited by the youth
Antiphon, who had given up philosophy for horses—these
and many similar prefaces carry the art of description to
the highest point.   They are as graphic as any modern
narrative of Fielding or Defoe.   ' O Socrates, you can easily
invent tales of Egypt or of any other country,' is the natural
exclamation of one of his auditors (Phaedr. 275 B).   Several
of the greatest dialogues, such as the Theaetetus, Phaedo,
Republic, Parmenides, are narrated dramas; a form which
has been adopted, apparently, with the view of enabling the
writer to introduce descriptive remarks.   Thus in the
Phaedo many beautiful traits are thrown in by the narrator,
such as the calmness of Socrates amid the cries of the
women (60) and the tears of his own disciples : the manner
in which he ' used ' to play with the locks of Phaedo (89 B) :
the dejection of the company at the temporary failure of the
argument (88 C) : the regard for others and regardlessness
of self which is displayed by Socrates in his last hours (116,
117).   These little circumstances could not have been com-
municated to us had there been no eyewitness of the scene.

All the characters are only playthings in the hands of
Socrates, who by his superior power elicits from them any
conclusion which he pleases.   He has talked all his life, and
never was overcome by any man in an argument (Symp.
213 E).   It may be remarked that in the later dialogues,
especially in the Sophist, Politicus, and Laws, the dramatic
character becomes feebler, and Socrates either disappears, as
in the Laws, or is subordinated to other unknown persons,
as in the Sophist and Politicus, apparently because Plato felt
that he was passing out of the sphere of Socratic teaching

into another region of thought. But in the dialogues which are most perfect in form, such as the Protagoras, Euthydemus, Phaedo, Phaedrus, Symposium, Theaetetus, Republic, Socrates is the centre of the argument. The rest of the company are either delighted auditors (Symp. 215 C), or the victims around whom he slowly and surely winds his toils (cp. Rep. i. 345, 349, Gorgias 461–481).

The character of Socrates himself is exhibited by Plato in a great variety of lights; no other man ever equalled or approached this wonderful mortal : First, in his outward appearance and behaviour, as he describes himself in the Theaetetus and is described by Alcibiades in the Symposium —the man-midwife who brought to the birth the thoughts of men (Theaet. 149); the Silenus mask, which, when opened, revealed the images of gods within (Symp. 215 A); the flute-player and Satyr Marsyas, who drew men after him by the power of his voice; the gad-fly given by God to the Athenian people, which, like a noble steed tardy in its motions owing to its very size, was stung by him into life (Apol. 30 E). He is not one 'who has seen many cities,' which was the fond fancy of later ages respecting the old philosophers, who were deemed to be 'learned in all the wisdom of the Egyptians.' His desires are all bounded by Athens and the Piraeus. As he tells us in the Phaedrus (230 C), 'he searched into his own strange nature,' wanting to know 'whether he was a wonder more complicated and swollen with passion than the serpent Typho, or a creature of a gentler and simpler sort, to whom nature has given a diviner and lowlier destiny.' To such a mind the fairest scenes of outward nature had no beauty or interest. 'The men who dwell in the city were his teachers, not the trees nor the country.' During his whole life he had quitted Athens three times only, once when he was present at the battle of Delium, again when he went on a military expedition to Potidaea, and once again to Amphipolis (Apol. 28 E, Symp. 219–221). Of his early years nothing is known to us: though for a time he was a hearer of Anaxagoras, no previous thinker left any mark upon him. Obeying the inspiration of his own mind, 'whither the word within him led he followed' (Rep. iii. 394 D). From early manhood to old age he passed his time in argument and conversation with his fellow-citizens.

To the Athenians his teaching and behaviour appeared strange: nor to ourselves does he seem always perfectly rational. He would stand for a day and a night lost in ecstasy: this strange condition had overtaken him in the camp at Potidaea; and some 'Ionians out of curiosity brought out their mats and slept in the open air, that they might watch him and see whether he would remain all night. There he stood until the following morning, and with the return of light he offered up a prayer to the sun and went his way' (Symp. 220). At a banquet he was the best of company, and able to drink more wine than any other guest without becoming intoxicated, though generally the most abstemious of men (Symp. 214 A). At the battle of Delium after the defeat he seemed to 'keep his head' better than the generals, and went about the field of battle 'stalking like a pelican and rolling his eyes,' as was his manner, according to Aristophanes (Sym. 221 B, Arist. Clouds 361 [1]), when walking

---

[1] ὅτι βρενθύει τ' ἐν ταῖσιν ὁδοῖς καὶ τὠφθαλμὼ παραβάλλει.

in the streets of Athens; at the same time he made it clear to everybody that they had better not meddle with him (Symp. 221). The singularity of his character seemed also to go beyond the ordinary limits of human nature. Though he was always talking to his fellow-men, there was a mystery about him which they were unable to penetrate. He might appear to be the most rational of men; but there was like-wise in him a supernatural or irrational or divine element. He said that he had a sign from heaven, which never com-manded him (see Apology 31 C, 40 A) to do or say anything, but often forbade him to go out of the house, it might be, or to make a speech in his own defence, and where there was no interference he went on with what he was about (Apology 40 B). He especially notes that on the occasion of his trial, when there 'had come upon him what is generally thought to be the last and worst evil, the oracle made no sign of opposition, either when he was leaving his home or when he was ascending the tribune, or while he was speaking, at anything which he was intending to say.' This internal monitor which forbade, but never commanded, was called in after ages the 'Demon of Socrates,' but by Plato, and therefore probably by Socrates himself, was always spoken of in the neuter as the 'Divine Sign' (τὸ δαιμόνιον σημεῖον), which, as he says, had rarely, if ever, been granted to any other (Rep. vi. 496 C). He speaks of it always in the most familiar manner as an undoubted fact, but without pretending that it revealed to him any mysteries or com-municated to him any general truths or principles, or even gave reasons for the prohibitions which it imposed upon him.

The strange being who went about in the streets of Athens talking to his fellow-citizens was a puzzle to other men as well as to himself. He was the most humble and also the most self-asserting of human beings: the wisest, always professing to be the most ignorant: the most sceptical and also the most religious: the ugliest and the most fascinating. Around him were gathered his disciples and friends; all who were curious in the pursuit of knowledge were attracted by an irresistible impulse. In a city numbering twenty or thirty thousand families, there was probably no one to whom he was not known, and in his long life he must have become acquainted with nearly every Athenian citizen. Any day he might be seen barefoot (Phaedrus 229 A) and meanly clad; yet also on some rare occasion he would be met by an admiring disciple, gay and sandalled and fresh from the bath, on his way to a banquet (Symp. 174 A). The snub-nose and projecting eyes (Theaet. 143 E, 144 D) would have been at once recognized even by a stranger passing him in the street. In the group which surrounded him would be found the greatest men of Athens—the magnificent Callias, who had spent more money on the Sophists than all other Athenians (Apol. 20 A); Alcibiades the favourite, and yet the terror, of the Athenian people, the 'young lion whom they should either never have reared or never have banished from his native city' (Arist. Ran. 1431); Critias and Charmides, traitors of a deeper dye and still more dishonoured in history; Xenophon, the leader of the ten thousand; Plato, the great genius in whose writings his own words were to live; probably Aristophanes, who may have gone to parody and caricature, yet, according to Plato, remained into the morning hours whilst Socrates was discoursing of the unity of tragedy and comedy (Symp. *sub fin.*); Agathon the tragic writer, and others, such as Meno the Thessalian nobleman, Callicles the Athenian 'man of the world,' Evenus, poet and sophist, Aristodemus the shadow or inseparable attendant, Apollodorus the 'madman,' whose ways were known to them all and who is present both at the banquet and in the prison scene—these all might be drawn by the bait of his discourse, to use his own image, 'like hungry cattle following the bough,' all round Athens and into the neighbouring country (Phaedrus 230 E). And wherever he was, the conversation came round sooner or later from the trifling talk of the market-place to the concerns of a man's soul (Laches 178 E).

The Dialogues of Plato represent a few fragments of the infinite discourses which Socrates, out of his abundance, poured forth daily to the crowd of Athenian citizens who followed him in his walks. He assumes in them the character of a learner rather than of a teacher partly out of irony, but he also seems to have believed that knowledge could only be attained by the united efforts of his own mind with that of others. Theaetetus, as he says, is 'the bag' out of which he produces arguments. Though at times overmastered by his own wild humour (Cratylus 396), he has a very serious purpose, which is to convert the world, not by preaching, but by talking to them. He is at the same time a delightful companion; the play of fancy mingles with the deep things of philosophy. He is also the politest of men, and knows how to make cutting and disagreeable remarks in the most courteous and well-bred manner. Towards the

Sophists and towards all his opponents he is full of deference; he cannot be too civil to Thrasymachus in the Republic. Even in the Euthydemus, which of all the Platonic dialogues is the most humorous, Socrates, amid a perfect storm of cries and laughter, keeps his countenance to the end of the dialogue. The mask at length clings to the face; the irony becomes reality when he professes in the Apology (30 A) to have a divine mission, which is that of proving to his contemporaries that they know nothing. As Christian teachers have sought to convince the world of sin, so he sought to convince men of ignorance and error. His assumed deference for others may be described as a sort of parody of the Christian virtue, humility. He seems to have supposed that this duty of teaching, or rather of refuting error, was imposed upon him by the Oracle of Delphi, which declared him to be the wisest of men (Apol. 21). For what could the oracle mean by such a declaration? He was conscious that he knew nothing; and he must refute the God by finding some one who knew more than himself. But there was no one: and so he concluded at last that he was wiser than other men, because he alone knew that he knew nothing; they were ignorant of their very ignorance. If we translate his meaning into the phraseology of a later age (for the intellect and the will were not yet distinguished in the time of Plato), we might say that it was an intellectual rather than a moral change which he wanted to effect. To him virtue was knowledge; if a man knew what was right he would certainly do it. His mission was analogous to that of a Christian Apostle, not the same with it. Like St. Paul, he would have said, 'Woe is me, if I speak not the truth which has been committed to me.' But the subject of his preaching would have been not the conversion of the heart, but the enlightenment of the intellect.

He tells us that the detection of pretended knowledge was to the listeners extremely amusing, though to those upon whom he exercised his art, in the highest degree irritating. For forty or fifty years he was a teacher and also a satirist of men, going from one class to another in the hope of obtaining true knowledge, but only finding the greatest professors to be the most shallow (Apol. 22). He made enemies of them all: at length the odium which accumulated against him became too great, and he was put to death. The wonder is not that the Athenians should have at last grown impatient of him, but that they should have endured him so long.

(ii, iii.) The true character of the teaching of Socrates is best illustrated by his own oft-repeated profession, to which allusion has just been made, 'That he knew nothing of himself, but only brought to the birth the thoughts of others' (Theaet. *init.*). In modern language he may be said to have taught men to think for themselves. He did not merely bring knowledge to them from without,—that might be the employment of sophists or schoolmasters : he sought to create in them a new sense, to implant an eye of the soul 'more precious far than ten thousand bodily eyes' (Rep. vii. 527 E), which might guide them through the maze of phenomena. He turned outwards into the light of consciousness the truths which were implicit or latent in them ; he drew conclusions from premises which were already acknowledged by them. They were in the habit of calling one another good and bad, just and unjust; but what was just in one place or at one time or to some one person was deemed unjust at another time or place or to some other person. Socrates would have them pass out of this half-lighted world of contradiction and appearance into the sphere of absolute knowledge: they were to ask, not what is just at Athens or Lacedaemon, but what is right and just everywhere and at all times. Thus men began to acquire 'moral ideas as distinct from legal and political—universal principles liberated from particulars of sense. The clouds of mythology passed away; and firm land appeared.

In a well-known passage of Aristotle (Metaph. xii. 4) there are said to be two things of which the discovery may be truly attributed to Socrates: (i) Induction; and (ii) General Definitions. He means by the first the process of eliciting from one or more instances the general notion which is common to them all. From things known, things unknown were inferred, what was implied became explicit, what was latent and unconscious was brought out into the light of consciousness—this was the process of dialectic. When by methods of comparison and rejection a general notion had been obtained, another question arose, 'how this general notion was to be defined;' or rather the two processes went on together until a definition or description was obtained, which was no longer open to objection. The making of such definitions, e. g. of courage, temperance, friendship, knowledge, etc., is the aim of several of the earlier Platonic Dialogues. The question ' What is justice?'

is the thesis proposed, and partly answered, in the first four books of the Republic.

The General Definitions of Socrates reappear as the Ideas of Plato. In the pre-Socratic age mankind were struggling towards new modes of conception. The persons of mythology, the abstractions of number, the four elements, began to acquire a new significance to them. These seemed to supply the universal form of which they were in so much need; they were opposed to the 'seemings' of opinion, to the 'fleeting particulars' of sense. One generation or school of philosophy was engaged in realizing the meaning of the words 'being and not being,' first and most indispensable of abstractions: another in eliciting out of opposites the simple ideas of relation and motion. The conception of numbers, no longer, as in the childhood of the world, identified with outward objects, but separated from them, now became the great Organon of nature and a symbol of things higher still. He who first uttered the word 'mind' (Anaxagoras) appeared to be 'a sober man among drunkards' (Arist. Met. i. 3). By a great mental effort of some philosopher, each of these notions was for the first time conceived: they were repeated with endless iteration by his disciples (Theaet. 179 D): at length the word of the Master diffused by his school passed into language, never afterwards to lose its place in human thought. A whole philosophy was contained in a few enigmatic sentences; as Plato says in the Sophist (243 A), 'the ancients went on their way rather regardless of whether people like ourselves understood them or not.' (There are modern as well as ancient philosophers to whom this remark may be applied.)

Nor was it to be expected that when first discovered the true nature of ideas or universals would be perfectly understood even by Socrates himself. To Plato they seemed to exist apart from the things which we see in a heaven of their own, and to partake of the Divine. They were unchangeable, but the world was full of shadows always coming and going,—dull and imperfect reflections or expressions of something beyond themselves; and in each individual there was contained an element or seed of the ideal. As Plato represented the matter: A bed or any other work of art could only be made after the pattern of a bed existing previously in the artist's mind: this pattern could not have been derived from beds which are seen, for it was more perfect than they, and must therefore have been recovered by recollection from a former world (Rep. x. 596, Meno 82, 86, Phaedo 73–77). According to one view numbers were interposed between ideas and visible things (Arist. Metaph. A 6); they were the intermediate links by which the two were connected. And as the visible itself was only a shadow in this lower world it had also a shadow of its own. Thus arose four kinds or degrees of knowledge to which four classes of objects corresponded, (1) things in themselves, gathered up into the Idea of Good, which is the Divine essence and first and final cause of them: (2) numbers and relations of number: (3) objects of sense which are the outward aspects or shadows or reflections of the ideas ordered and distinguished by number: (4) the shadows of such objects which are the fancies and creations of man, the world of poets and mythologers twice removed from the true, said also in a figure to ' be seen by a light from behind on the wall of a cave or den,' as the ideas are by the light of the sun or the idea of good. (Rep. vi. 509 ff.; vii. 514 ff.; x. 597, 602.)

This is what may be called the popular theory of the Platonic ideas, gathered chiefly from the Republic, the Phaedo, and the Meno. And it is against this form of them that the assaults of Aristotle are mainly directed, first in the Ethics, and then with greater minuteness of detail in the Metaphysics. All his objections, which are innumerable, may be summed up under two or three heads. First, how can there be any difference between the idea and the object of sense? *e. g.* between the idea of a house or bed and the actual house or bed? For the idea is nothing when separated from individual objects: a mere word, to which no meaning can be attached. Secondly, who can show any relation between them? The ideas are in their world, and we in ours : they are always either absolutely the same or absolutely different. Thirdly, is there any use in such transcendental speculations?

This refutation of Plato might be regarded as conclusive, if the theory itself is taken in a literal sense. But the ideas of Plato are really poetry or imagery, and cannot be stereotyped in any single form, as the Platonists and Peripatetics of a later generation appear to have supposed. They are sometimes ideals, sometimes realities : they take the form of numbers : they become logical abstractions : they are one or many, personal or impersonal, accordingly as they are viewed in different aspects. Sometimes, as in the Symposium, they vanish in poetry and fancy; or, as in the Phaedo, Meno, Phaedrus, they are supposed to be recovered from a former state of existence, still enveloped in poetical fancy; or, as in the Timaeus, they are personified; or, as in the Republic, they become a single idea or principle, which is termed the Idea of Good, or they are exhibited under the celebrated image of the sunlight and the den in which the human spirits are confined: while in the Theaetetus and Parmenides they are subjected to a criticism more searching than that of Aristotle, until nothing any longer remains of them. These various modes of representing the 'idea' are not parts of a system, but are the ever-changing aspects of the same philosophical tendency. Under all these forms Plato is seeking to realize the opposition of mind and sense, of νούμενα and phenomena. One thought underlies them all—the truth of universals.

In the later dialogues of Plato, especially in the Sophist and Politicus, a further advance is made. The fanciful and inconsistent language disappears; and he is seriously occupied with the attempt to connect ideas, not with phenomena, but with one another. Among his contemporaries there were some who said that 'no subject was true of any predicate,' a thesis which renders knowledge of any kind impossible: they were met by another school who maintained the equally untenable proposition that 'all might be asserted of all.' To us these conflicting theories are equally absurd, and yet they were both deeply rooted in the previous philosophy of Hellas. Plato endeavours to find a middle way between them. Not without difficulty he arrives at the conclusion which to us appears self-evident, 'that some things can be asserted of others, but not all of all.' This is probably the furthest point to which he carried his speculation respecting the Ideas. He nowhere clearly explains how they were related to phenomena; but he is at least satisfied that they are connected with each other. The ideas which he had once conceived to exist in isolation he is now able to regard as the links or moments of a system of knowledge.

It is a mistake to regard Plato as the poet-philosopher who produced 'out of the depths of his consciousness' any fancies which occurred to him. In all his writings he is struggling with the problems of his age, striving to give expression to ideas 'which were in the air,' seeking to harmonize conflicting philosophies, or to attain a purer ether which was beyond and above them. Those who think of him as a 'dreamer' only, or as wanting in common sense, or as 'the author of nearly every erroneous notion which has since crept into philosophy,' may be invited to reflect on a few passages of his writings:—'If you think more about things and less about words you will be richer as you grow older in wisdom' (Politicus 261 E). (Compare such expressions as 'the long and difficult language of facts' (ib. 278 C), or 'learning of every nature which was gifted with any special power, and was able to contribute some special experience to the store of wisdom' (ib. 272 B)). Or let him consider the meaning of the following words in the sphere of politics:—'Man should be well advised that he is only one of the animals, and the Hellene in particular should be aware that he himself was the author of the distinction between Hellene and Barbarian, and that the Phrygian would equally divide mankind into Phrygians and Barbarians, and that some intelligent animal, such as a crane, might go a step further, and divide the animal world into cranes and all other animals' (Plato, Introduction to Engl. Transl. of Politicus, vol. iv. p. 528). Or once more:— 'This is and ever will be the best of sayings, *That the useful is the noble, and the hurtful is the base*' (Rep. v. 457 B). Are these the words of a dreamer? Has modern philosophy ever got much beyond them?

If, stripping off the many-coloured garment in which Plato has enveloped his ideas, we seek, after the manner of Aristotle, to reduce them to their logical skeleton, the meaning and import of them may be conveniently summed up under two heads:—

(1) The first great effort of Plato was to realize abstractions or universals. He wanted to define and explain them, and also to divide and distinguish them from one another. At this point the philosophy of Plato touches that of Aristotle and Socrates. All three alike sought to divide the whole into its parts. But whereas Aristotle and Socrates, like ourselves, regard the idea as existing in outward objects, or in the mind itself, to Plato the ideas acquired such an intensity and reality, that they, for a time at least, became separated both from the mind and from external objects. They might be compared in a figure to lights or stars shining in some far-off heaven. They are not ideas, but impersonal Gods, ordered by a Supreme Being, or Idea of Good. They could hardly be seen in the atmosphere of light and beauty which surrounded them. To this poetical enthusiasm there was nothing really corresponding but the deep consciousness of the truth of universal ideas and their importance in the world of philosophy.

(2) When ideas were separated from the mind and from objects of sense, another difficulty began to appear. How were they related to each other? Existing in a world of their own, how can they be either distinguished or connected? The mere assertion that the 'One is Many' and the 'Many are One' did not answer the great question of analysis and synthesis, which also pressed upon Plato in his later years: not only, 'how could the whole be resolved into its parts?' but, 'how could the parts be reunited into a whole?' questions which had to be answered both in the concrete and in the abstract (Philebus 15, 16). In the Philebus he approaches this difficulty: in the Sophist he proceeds to the solution of it. From the heaven of ideas in which he had been wandering he now returns to the ground of experience. He shows that there is a natural connection and correlation of ideas:—'Many cannot be one, nor being become not being, but unity may also be the same, and being can exist in relation.' The difficulty, which to Plato was real and great, is hardly perceptible to ourselves, and the solution would be regarded by every one as a matter of common sense. Thus the idea of Plato may be said to end in a truism.

These are some of the steps by which the human intellect has attained its reasoning and reflecting powers. Socrates and Plato and Aristotle may be deemed to have invented for mankind new implements in the world of mind as powerful as the wedge, the pulley, the lever, in the material world. The progress of mathematics has always been recognized as the great source of improvements in mechanics, and as the greatest instrument of physical knowledge. Yet the beginnings of mathematics had even a greater power in giving form to the mind itself: they taught men how the many might also be one; and they furnished the type of unchanging knowledge. He who first invented the conception of a cause may be said to have created a power in the world analogous to that of the greatest physical discoveries of any age. To enlarge on this wonderful chapter of the human mind which the early Greek philosophy presents to us, would be beyond the scope of this preface. But we cannot too soon recognize the truth (1) that the wisest of men are limited by the conditions of the age in which they live; and (2) that the highest effort of philosophy in one generation may become the common sense of the next.

TABLE OF SELECTIONS.

THE numbers given in the margin of the Greek text are those of the pages of Stephanus. The edition of Stephanus (Henri Estienne) is in three volumes ; but, the name of the dialogue being given, the number of the volume is superfluous. Each page is divided into five parts by the letters A B C D E placed down the margin. This convenient mode of reference is universally employed. The exact point at which each page and division begins may be found in the folio edition of Stallbaum.

The words *supra* and *infra* in the notes indicate that the place quoted is to be found in the Selections.

The order of the passages is that of the Dialogues in Mr. Jowett's translation, the words of which are occasionally borrowed in the notes.

SELECTIONS FROM PLATO.

CHARMIDES.

[155 E—158 E.]

A Headache.

῞Ομως δὲ αὐτοῦ ἐρωτήσαντος εἰ ἐπισταίμην τὸ τῆς
κεφαλῆς φάρμακον, μόγις πως ἀπεκρινάμην ὅτι ἐπισταίμην. Τί οὖν, ἦ δ' ὅς, ἐστίν ; Καὶ ἐγὼ εἶπον ὅτι αὐτὸ
μὲν εἴη φύλλον τι, ἐπῳδὴ δέ τις ἐπὶ τῷ φαρμάκῳ εἴη, ἣν
5 εἰ μέν τις ἐπᾴδοι ἅμα καὶ χρῷτο αὐτῷ, παντάπασιν ὑγιᾶ
ποιοῖ τὸ φάρμακον· ἄνευ δὲ τῆς ἐπῳδῆς οὐδὲν ὄφελος
εἴη τοῦ φύλλου. Καὶ ὅς, Ἀπογράψομαι τοίνυν, ἔφη, παρὰ
σοῦ τὴν ἐπῳδήν. Πότερον, ἦν δ' ἐγώ, ἐάν με πείθῃς 156
ἢ κἂν μή ; Γελάσας οὖν, Ἐάν σε πείθω, ἔφη, ὦ
10 Σώκρατες. Εἶεν, ἦν δ' ἐγώ· καὶ τοὔνομά μου σὺ ἀκριβοῖς ;
Εἰ μὴ ἀδικῶ γε, ἔφη· οὐ γάρ τι σοῦ ὀλίγος λόγος ἐστὶν
ἐν τοῖς ἡμετέροις ἡλικιώταις, μέμνημαι δὲ ἔγωγε καὶ παῖς
ὢν Κριτίᾳ τῷδε ξυνόντα σε. Καλῶς γε σύ, ἦν δ' ἐγώ,
ποιῶν· μᾶλλον γάρ σοι παρρησιάσομαι περὶ τῆς ἐπῳδῆς,
15 οἷα τυγχάνει οὖσα· ἄρτι δ' ἠπόρουν, τίνι τρόπῳ σοι B
ἐνδειξαίμην τὴν δύναμιν αὐτῆς. ἔστι γάρ, ὦ Χαρμίδη,
τοιαύτη οἷα μὴ δύνασθαι τὴν κεφαλὴν μόνον ὑγιᾶ ποιεῖν,
ἀλλ' ὥσπερ ἴσως ἤδη καὶ σὺ ἀκήκοας τῶν ἀγαθῶν ἰατρῶν,
ἐπειδάν τις αὐτοῖς προσέλθῃ τοὺς ὀφθαλμοὺς ἀλγῶν,

B

λέγουσί που, ὅτι οὐχ οἷόν τε αὐτοὺς μόνους ἐπιχειρεῖν 20
τοὺς ὀφθαλμοὺς ἰᾶσθαι, ἀλλ' ἀναγκαῖον εἴη ἅμα καὶ τὴν
κεφαλὴν θεραπεύειν, εἰ μέλλοι καὶ τὰ τῶν ὀμμάτων εὖ
C ἔχειν· καὶ αὖ τὸ τὴν κεφαλὴν οἴεσθαι ἄν ποτε θεραπεῦσαι
αὐτὴν ἐφ' ἑαυτῆς ἄνευ ὅλου τοῦ σώματος πολλὴν ἄνοιαν
εἶναι. ἐκ δὴ τούτου τοῦ λόγου διαίταις ἐπὶ πᾶν τὸ σῶμα 25
τρεπόμενοι μετὰ τοῦ ὅλου τὸ μέρος ἐπιχειροῦσι θεραπεύειν
τε καὶ ἰᾶσθαι. ἢ οὐκ ἤσθησαι ὅτι ταῦτα οὕτω λέγουσί τε
καὶ ἔχει; Πάνυ γε, ἔφη. Οὐκοῦν καλῶς σοι δοκεῖ
λέγεσθαι καὶ ἀποδέχει τὸν λόγον; Πάντων μάλιστα,
ἔφη.   30
D   Κἀγὼ ἀκούσας αὐτοῦ ἐπαινέσαντος ἀνεθάρρησά τε, καί
μοι κατὰ σμικρὸν πάλιν ἡ θρασύτης ξυνηγείρετο, καὶ
ἀνεζωπυρούμην. καὶ εἶπον Τοιοῦτον τοίνυν ἐστίν, ὦ
Χαρμίδη, καὶ τὸ ταύτης τῆς ἐπῳδῆς. ἔμαθον δ' αὐτὴν ἐγὼ
ἐκεῖ ἐπὶ στρατείας παρά τινος τῶν Θρᾳκῶν τῶν Ζαλ- 35
μόξιδος ἰατρῶν, οἳ λέγονται καὶ ἀπαθανατίζειν. ἔλεγε δὲ
ὁ Θρᾷξ οὗτος, ὅτι ταῦτα μὲν ἰατροὶ οἱ Ἕλληνες, ἃ νῦν
δὴ ἐγὼ ἔλεγον, καλῶς λέγοιεν· ἀλλὰ Ζάλμοξις, ἔφη,
E λέγει ὁ ἡμέτερος βασιλεύς, θεὸς ὤν, ὅτι ὥσπερ ὀφθαλμοὺς ἄνευ κεφαλῆς οὐ δεῖ ἐπιχειρεῖν ἰᾶσθαι οὐδὲ κεφαλὴν 40
ἄνευ σώματος, οὕτως οὐδὲ σῶμα ἄνευ ψυχῆς, ἀλλὰ τοῦτο
καὶ αἴτιον εἴη τοῦ διαφεύγειν τοὺς παρὰ τοῖς Ἕλλησιν
ἰατροὺς τὰ πολλὰ νοσήματα, ὅτι τὸ ὅλον ἀγνοοῖεν οὗ δέοι
τὴν ἐπιμέλειαν ποιεῖσθαι, οὗ μὴ καλῶς ἔχοντος ἀδύνατον
εἴη τὸ μέρος εὖ ἔχειν. πάντα γὰρ ἔφη ἐκ τῆς ψυχῆς 45
ὡρμῆσθαι καὶ τὰ κακὰ καὶ τὰ ἀγαθὰ τῷ σώματι καὶ παντὶ
τῷ ἀνθρώπῳ, καὶ ἐκεῖθεν ἐπιρρεῖν ὥσπερ ἐκ τῆς κεφαλῆς
157 ἐπὶ τὰ ὄμματα. δεῖν οὖν ἐκεῖνο καὶ πρῶτον καὶ μάλιστα
θεραπεύειν, εἰ μέλλει καὶ τὰ τῆς κεφαλῆς καὶ τὰ τοῦ
ἄλλου σώματος καλῶς ἔχειν. θεραπεύεσθαι δὲ τὴν ψυχὴν 50

ἔφη, ὦ μακάριε, ἐπῳδαῖς τισί· τὰς δ᾽ ἐπῳδὰς ταύτας τοὺς
λόγους εἶναι τοὺς καλούς. ἐκ δὲ τῶν τοιούτων λόγων ἐν
ταῖς ψυχαῖς σωφροσύνην ἐγγίγνεσθαι, ἧς ἐγγενομένης
καὶ παρούσης ῥᾴδιον ἤδη εἶναι τὴν ὑγίειαν καὶ τῇ κεφαλῇ
55 καὶ τῷ ἄλλῳ σώματι πορίζειν. διδάσκων οὖν με τό τε
φάρμακον καὶ τὰς ἐπῳδάς, Ὅπως, ἔφη, τῷ φαρμάκῳ B
τούτῳ μηδείς σε πείσει τὴν αὑτοῦ κεφαλὴν θεραπεύειν,
ὃς ἂν μὴ τὴν ψυχὴν πρῶτον παράσχῃ τῇ ἐπῳδῇ ὑπὸ σοῦ
θεραπευθῆναι. καὶ γὰρ νῦν, ἔφη, τοῦτ᾽ ἔστι τὸ ἁμάρτημα
60 περὶ τοὺς ἀνθρώπους, ὅτι χωρὶς ἑκατέρου ἰατροί τινες
ἐπιχειροῦσιν εἶναι. καί μοι πάνυ σφόδρα ἐνετέλλετο μήτε
πλούσιον οὕτω μηδένα εἶναι μήτε γενναῖον μήτε καλόν,
ὃς ἐμὲ πείσει ἄλλως ποιεῖν. ἐγὼ οὖν—ὤμοσα γὰρ αὐτῷ, C
καί μοι ἀνάγκη πείθεσθαι—πείσομαι οὖν, καὶ σοί, ἐὰν
65 μὲν βούλῃ κατὰ τὰς τοῦ ξένου ἐντολὰς τὴν ψυχὴν πρῶτον
παρασχεῖν ἐπᾷσαι ταῖς τοῦ Θρᾳκὸς ἐπῳδαῖς, προσοίσω
τὸ φάρμακον τῇ κεφαλῇ· εἰ δὲ μή, οὐκ ἂν ἔχοιμεν ὅ τι
ποιοῖμέν σοι, ὦ φίλε Χαρμίδη.

Ἀκούσας οὖν μου ὁ Κριτίας ταῦτ᾽ εἰπόντος, Ἕρμαιον,
70 ἔφη, ὦ Σώκρατες, γεγονὸς ἂν εἴη ἡ τῆς κεφαλῆς ἀσθένεια
τῷ νεανίσκῳ, εἰ ἀναγκασθήσεται καὶ τὴν διάνοιαν διὰ D
τὴν κεφαλὴν βελτίων γενέσθαι. λέγω μέντοι σοι ὅτι
Χαρμίδης τῶν ἡλικιωτῶν οὐ μόνον τῇ ἰδέᾳ ἐδόκει διαφέρειν, ἀλλὰ καὶ αὐτῷ τούτῳ οὗ σὺ φῂς τὴν ἐπῳδὴν ἔχειν·
75 φῂς δὲ σωφροσύνης. ἦ γάρ; Πάνυ γε, ἦν δ᾽ ἐγώ. Εὖ
τοίνυν ἴσθι, ἔφη, ὅτι πάνυ πολὺ δοκεῖ σωφρονέστατος
εἶναι τῶν νυνί, καὶ τἄλλα πάντα, εἰς ὅσον ἡλικίας ἥκει,
οὐδενὸς χείρων ὤν. Καὶ γάρ, ἦν δ᾽ ἐγώ, καὶ δίκαιον,
ὦ Χαρμίδη, διαφέρειν σε τῶν ἄλλων πᾶσι τοῖς τοιούτοις·
80 οὐ γὰρ οἶμαι ἄλλον οὐδένα τῶν ἐνθάδε ῥᾳδίως ἂν ἔχειν E
ἐπιδεῖξαι, ποῖαι δύο οἰκίαι συνελθοῦσαι εἰς ταὐτὸν τῶν

Ἀθήνησιν ἐκ τῶν εἰκότων καλλίω ἂν καὶ ἀμείνω γεννή-
σειαν ἢ ἐξ ὧν σὺ γέγονας. ἥ τε γὰρ πατρῷα ὑμῖν οἰκία,
ἡ Κριτίου τοῦ Δρωπίδου, καὶ ὑπ' Ἀνακρέοντος καὶ ὑπὸ
Σόλωνος καὶ ὑπ' ἄλλων πολλῶν ποιητῶν ἐγκεκωμιασμένη 85
158 παραδέδοται ἡμῖν, ὡς διαφέρουσα κάλλει τε καὶ ἀρετῇ
καὶ τῇ ἄλλῃ λεγομένῃ εὐδαιμονίᾳ, καὶ αὖ ἡ πρὸς μητρὸς
ὡσαύτως· Πυριλάμπους γὰρ τοῦ σοῦ θείου οὐδεὶς τῶν ἐν
τῇ ἠπείρῳ λέγεται καλλίων καὶ μείζων ἀνὴρ δόξαι εἶναι,
ὁσάκις ἐκεῖνος ἢ παρὰ μέγαν βασιλέα ἢ παρ' ἄλλον τινὰ 90
τῶν ἐν τῇ ἠπείρῳ πρεσβεύων ἀφίκετο. σύμπασα δὲ αὕτη
ἡ οἰκία οὐδὲν τῆς ἑτέρας ὑποδεεστέρα. ἐκ δὴ τοιούτων
B γεγονότα εἰκός σε εἰς πάντα πρῶτον εἶναι. τὰ μὲν οὖν
ὁρώμενα τῆς ἰδέας, ὦ φίλε παῖ Γλαύκωνος, δοκεῖς μοι οὐδένα τῶν προγόνων καταισχύνειν· εἰ δὲ δὴ καὶ πρὸς σωφρο- 95
σύνην καὶ πρὸς τἆλλα κατὰ τὸν τοῦδε λόγον ἱκανῶς πέ-
φυκας, μακάριόν σε, ἦν δ' ἐγώ, ὦ φίλε Χαρμίδη, ἡ μήτηρ
ἔτικτεν. ἔχει δ' οὖν οὕτως. εἰ μέν σοι ἤδη πάρεστιν, ὡς λέγει
Κριτίας ὅδε, σωφροσύνη καὶ εἰ σώφρων ἱκανῶς, οὐδὲν ἔτι
σοι ἔδει οὔτε τῶν Ζαλμόξιδος οὔτε τῶν Ἀβάριδος τοῦ Ὑπερ- 100
C βορέου ἐπῳδῶν, ἀλλ' αὐτό σοι ἂν ἤδη δοτέον εἴη τὸ τῆς
κεφαλῆς φάρμακον· εἰ δ' ἔτι τούτων ἐπιδεὴς εἶναι δοκεῖς,
ἐπαστέον πρὸ τῆς τοῦ φαρμάκου δόσεως. αὐτὸς οὖν μοι
εἰπέ, πότερον ὁμολογεῖς τῷδε καὶ φῂς ἱκανῶς ἤδη σωφροσύνης μετέχειν ἢ ἐνδεὴς εἶναι; Ἀνερυθριάσας οὖν ὁ 105
Χαρμίδης πρῶτον μὲν ἔτι καλλίων ἐφάνη—καὶ γὰρ τὸ
αἰσχυντηλὸν αὐτοῦ τῇ ἡλικίᾳ ἔπρεψεν,—ἔπειτα καὶ οὐκ
ἀγεννῶς ἀπεκρίνατο· εἶπε γὰρ ὅτι οὐ ῥᾴδιον εἴη ἐν τῷ
παρόντι οὔθ' ὁμολογεῖν οὔτε ἐξάρνῳ εἶναι τὰ ἐρωτώμενα.
D ἐὰν μὲν γάρ, ἦ δ' ὅς, μὴ φῶ εἶναι σώφρων, ἅμα μὲν 110
ἄτοπον αὐτὸν καθ' ἑαυτοῦ τοιαῦτα λέγειν, ἅμα δὲ καὶ
Κριτίαν τόνδε ψευδῆ ἐπιδείξω καὶ ἄλλους πολλούς, οἷς

δοκῶ εἶναι σώφρων, ὡς ὁ τούτου λόγος· ἐὰν δ᾽ αὖ
φῶ καὶ ἐμαυτὸν ἐπαινῶ, ἴσως ἐπαχθὲς φανεῖται. ὥστε
115 οὐκ ἔχω ὅ τί σοι ἀποκρίνωμαι. Καὶ ἐγὼ εἶπον ὅτι
μοι εἰκότα φαίνει λέγειν, ὦ Χαρμίδη. καί μοι δοκεῖ,
ἦν δ᾽ ἐγώ, κοινῇ ἂν εἴη σκεπτέον, εἴτε κέκτησαι εἴτε
μὴ ὃ πυνθάνομαι, ἵνα μήτε σὺ ἀναγκάζῃ λέγειν ἃ μὴ E
βούλει, μήτ᾽ αὖ ἐγὼ ἀσκέπτως ἐπὶ τὴν ἰατρικὴν τρέπωμαι.
120 εἰ οὖν σοι φίλον, ἐθέλω σκοπεῖν μετὰ σοῦ· εἰ δὲ μή, ἐᾶν.
Ἀλλὰ πάντων μάλιστα, ἔφη, φίλον, ὥστε τούτου γε
ἕνεκα, ὅπῃ αὐτὸς οἴει βέλτιον σκέψασθαι, ταύτῃ σκόπει.

LYSIS.

[207 D—210 D.]

Why do people put trust in us, and like us?

Ἐπεχείρουν δὴ μετὰ τοῦτο ἐρωτᾶν ὁπότερος δικαι-
ότερος καὶ σοφώτερος αὐτῶν εἴη. μεταξὺ οὖν τις προσελθὼν ἀνέστησε τὸν Μενέξενον, φάσκων καλεῖν τὸν παι-
δοτρίβην· ἐδόκει γάρ μοι ἱεροποιῶν τυγχάνειν. ἐκεῖνος
5 μὲν οὖν ᾤχετο· ἐγὼ δὲ τὸν Λύσιν ἠρόμην, Ἦ που, ἦν δ᾽
ἐγώ, ὦ Λύσι, σφόδρα φιλεῖ σε ὁ πατὴρ καὶ ἡ μήτηρ;
Πάνυ γε, ἦ δ᾽ ὅς. Οὐκοῦν βούλοιντο ἄν σε ὡς εὐδαιμονέ-
στατον εἶναι. Πῶς γὰρ οὔ; Δοκεῖ δέ σοι εὐδαίμων E
εἶναι ἄνθρωπος δουλεύων τε καὶ ᾧ μηδὲν ἐξείη ποιεῖν ὧν
10 ἐπιθυμοῖ; Μὰ Δί᾽ οὐκ ἔμοιγε, ἔφη. Οὐκοῦν εἴ σε φιλεῖ
ὁ πατὴρ καὶ ἡ μήτηρ καὶ εὐδαίμονά σε ἐπιθυμοῦσι γενέσθαι, τοῦτο παντὶ τρόπῳ δῆλον ὅτι προθυμοῦνται ὅπως
ἂν εὐδαιμονοίης. Πῶς γὰρ οὐχί; ἔφη. Ἐῶσιν ἄρα σε
ἃ βούλει ποιεῖν, καὶ οὐδὲν ἐπιπλήττουσιν οὐδὲ δια-
15 κωλύουσι ποιεῖν ὧν ἂν ἐπιθυμῇς; Ναὶ μὰ Δί᾽ ἐμέ γε, ὦ

Σώκρατες, καὶ μάλα γε πολλὰ κωλύουσιν. Πῶς λέγεις ;
ἦν δ' ἐγώ. βουλόμενοί σε μακάριον εἶναι διακωλύουσι
208 τοῦτο ποιεῖν ὃ ἂν βούλῃ ; ὧδε δέ μοι λέγε. ἢν ἐπιθυμήσῃς
ἐπί τινος τῶν τοῦ πατρὸς ἁρμάτων ὀχεῖσθαι λαβὼν
τὰς ἡνίας, ὅταν ἁμιλλᾶται, οὐκ ἂν ἐῷέν σε ἀλλὰ δια- 20
κωλύοιεν ; Μὰ Δί' οὐ μέντοι ἄν, ἔφη, ἐῷεν. Ἀλλὰ
τίνα μήν ; Ἔστι τις ἡνίοχος παρὰ τοῦ πατρὸς μισθὸν
φέρων. Πῶς λέγεις ; μισθωτῷ μᾶλλον ἐπιτρέπουσιν ἢ
σοὶ ποιεῖν ὅ τι ἂν βούληται περὶ τοὺς ἵππους, καὶ
B προσέτι αὐτοῦ τούτου ἀργύριον τελοῦσιν ; Ἀλλὰ τί μήν ; 25
ἔφη. Ἀλλὰ τοῦ ὀρικοῦ ζεύγους, οἶμαι, ἐπιτρέπουσί σοι
ἄρχειν, κἂν εἰ βούλοιο λαβὼν τὴν μάστιγα τύπτειν, ἐῷεν
ἄν. Πόθεν, ἦ δ' ὅς, ἐῷεν ; Τί δαί ; ἦν δ' ἐγώ· οὐδενὶ
ἔξεστιν αὐτοὺς τύπτειν ; Καὶ μάλα, ἔφη, τῷ ὀρεοκόμῳ.
Δούλῳ ὄντι ἢ ἐλευθέρῳ ; Δούλῳ, ἔφη. Καὶ δοῦλον, 30
ὡς ἔοικεν, ἡγοῦνται περὶ πλείονος ἢ σὲ τὸν υἱόν, καὶ
C ἐπιτρέπουσι τὰ ἑαυτῶν μᾶλλον ἢ σοί, καὶ ἐῶσι ποιεῖν
ὅ τι βούλεται, σὲ δὲ διακωλύουσι. καί μοι ἔτι τόδε εἰπέ.
σὲ αὐτὸν ἐῶσιν ἄρχειν σεαυτοῦ, ἢ οὐδὲ τοῦτο ἐπιτρέπουσί
σοι ; Πῶς γάρ, ἔφη, ἐπιτρέπουσιν ; Ἀλλ' ἄρχει τις 35
σου ; Ὅδε, παιδαγωγός, ἔφη. Μῶν δοῦλος ὤν ; Ἀλλὰ
τί μήν ; ἡμέτερός γε, ἔφη. Ἡ δεινόν, ἦν δ' ἐγώ,
ἐλεύθερον ὄντα ὑπὸ δούλου ἄρχεσθαι. τί δὲ ποιῶν αὖ
οὗτος ὁ παιδαγωγός σου ἄρχει ; Ἄγων δήπου, ἔφη,
εἰς διδασκάλου. Μῶν μὴ καὶ οὗτοί σου ἄρχουσιν, οἱ 40
D διδάσκαλοι ; Πάντως δήπου. Παμπόλλους ἄρα σοι
δεσπότας καὶ ἄρχοντας ἑκὼν ὁ πατὴρ ἐφίστησιν. ἀλλ'
ἄρα ἐπειδὰν οἴκαδε ἔλθῃς παρὰ τὴν μητέρα, ἐκείνη σε
ἐᾷ ποιεῖν ὅ τι ἂν βούλῃ, ἵν' αὐτῇ μακάριος ᾖς, ἢ περὶ τὰ
ἔρια ἢ περὶ τὸν ἱστόν, ὅταν ὑφαίνῃ ; οὔ τι γάρ που 45
διακωλύει σε ἢ τῆς σπάθης ἢ τῆς κερκίδος ἢ ἄλλου του

τῶν περὶ ταλασιουργίαν ὀργάνων ἅπτεσθαι. Καὶ ὃς
γελάσας, Μὰ Δία, ἔφη, ὦ Σώκρατες, οὐ μόνον γε διακωλύει, ἀλλὰ καὶ τυπτοίμην ἂν εἰ ἁπτοίμην. Ἡράκλεις, E
50 ἦν δ' ἐγώ, μῶν μή τι ἠδίκηκας τὸν πατέρα ἢ τὴν μητέρα ;
Μὰ Δί' οὐκ ἔγωγε, ἔφη.

Ἀλλ' ἀντὶ τίνος μὴν οὕτω σε δεινῶς διακωλύουσιν
εὐδαίμονα εἶναι καὶ ποιεῖν ὅ τι ἂν βούλῃ, καὶ δι' ἡμέρας
ὅλης τρέφουσί σε ἀεί τῳ δουλεύοντα καὶ ἑνὶ λόγῳ ὀλίγου
55 ὧν ἐπιθυμεῖς οὐδὲν ποιοῦντα ; ὥστε σοι, ὡς ἔοικεν, οὔτε
τῶν χρημάτων τοσούτων ὄντων οὐδὲν ὄφελος, ἀλλὰ πάντες αὐτῶν μᾶλλον ἄρχουσιν ἢ σύ, οὔτε τοῦ σώματος οὕτω 209
γενναίου ὄντος, ἀλλὰ καὶ τοῦτο ἄλλος ποιμαίνει καὶ θεραπεύει· σὺ δὲ ἄρχεις οὐδενός, ὦ Λύσι, οὐδὲ ποιεῖς οὐ
60 δὲν ὧν ἐπιθυμεῖς. Οὐ γάρ πω, ἔφη, ἡλικίαν ἔχω, ὦ
Σώκρατες. Μὴ οὐ τοῦτό σε, ὦ παῖ Δημοκράτους, κωλύῃ,
ἐπεὶ τό γε τοσόνδε, ὡς ἐγῷμαι, καὶ ὁ πατὴρ καὶ ἡ μήτηρ
σοι ἐπιτρέπουσι καὶ οὐκ ἀναμένουσιν ἕως ἂν ἡλικίαν ἔχῃς.
ὅταν γὰρ βούλωνται αὐτοῖς τινὰ ἀναγνωσθῆναι ἢ γραφῆ
65 ναι, σέ, ὡς ἐγῷμαι, πρῶτον τῶν ἐν τῇ οἰκίᾳ ἐπὶ τοῦτο B
τάττουσιν. ἦ γάρ ; Πάνυ γ', ἔφη. Οὐκοῦν ἔξεστί σοι ἐνταῦθ' ὅ τι ἂν βούλῃ πρῶτον τῶν γραμμάτων γράφειν καὶ
ὅ τι ἂν δεύτερον· καὶ ἀναγιγνώσκειν ὡσαύτως ἔξεστι. καὶ
ἐπειδάν, ὡς ἐγῷμαι, τὴν λύραν λάβῃς, οὐ διακωλύουσί
70 σε οὔθ' ὁ πατὴρ οὔθ' ἡ μήτηρ ἐπιτεῖναί τε καὶ ἀνεῖναι ἣν
ἂν βούλῃ τῶν χορδῶν, καὶ ψῆλαι καὶ κρούειν τῷ πλήκτρῳ.
ἢ διακωλύουσιν ; Οὐ δῆτα. Τί ποτ' ἂν οὖν εἴη, ὦ Λύσι,
τὸ αἴτιον ὅτι ἐνταῦθα μὲν οὐ διακωλύουσιν, ἐν οἷς δὲ C
ἄρτι ἐλέγομεν κωλύουσιν ; Ὅτι, οἶμαι, ἔφη, ταῦτα μὲν
75 ἐπίσταμαι, ἐκεῖνα δ' οὔ. Εἶεν, ἦν δ' ἐγώ, ὦ ἄριστε.
οὐκ ἄρα τὴν ἡλικίαν σου περιμένει ὁ πατὴρ ἐπιτρέπειν
πάντα, ἀλλ' ᾗ ἂν ἡμέρᾳ ἡγήσηταί σε βέλτιον αὑτοῦ

φρονεῖν, ταύτῃ ἐπιτρέψει σοι καὶ αὐτὸν καὶ τὰ αὑτοῦ. Οἶμαι
ἔγωγε, ἔφη.   Εἶεν, ἦν δ' ἐγώ. τί δέ; τῷ γείτονι ἆρ' οὐχ
ὁ αὐτὸς ὅρος ὅσπερ τῷ πατρὶ περὶ σοῦ; πότερον οἴει 80
D αὐτὸν ἐπιτρέψειν σοι τὴν αὑτοῦ οἰκίαν οἰκονομεῖν, ὅταν
σε ἡγήσηται βέλτιον περὶ οἰκονομίας ἑαυτοῦ φρονεῖν, ἢ
αὐτὸν ἐπιστατήσειν; 'Εμοὶ ἐπιτρέψειν οἶμαι. Τί δ'; 'Αθη-
ναίους οἴει σοι οὐκ ἐπιτρέψειν τὰ αὑτῶν, ὅταν αἰσθά-
νωνται ὅτι ἱκανῶς φρονεῖς; "Εγωγε.   Πρὸς Διός, ἦν δ' 85
ἐγώ, τί ἄρα ὁ μέγας βασιλεύς; πότερον τῷ πρεσβυτάτῳ
υἱεῖ, οὗ ἡ τῆς 'Ασίας ἀρχὴ γίγνεται, μᾶλλον ἂν ἐπιτρέ-
ψειεν ἑψομένων κρεῶν ὅ τι ἂν βούληται ἐμβαλεῖν εἰς τὸν
E ζωμόν, ἢ ἡμῖν, εἰ ἀφικόμενοι παρ' ἐκεῖνον ἐνδειξαίμεθα
αὐτῷ ὅτι ἡμεῖς κάλλιον φρονοῦμεν ἢ ὁ υἱὸς αὐτοῦ περὶ 90
ὄψου σκευασίας; 'Ημῖν δῆλον ὅτι, ἔφη.   Καὶ τὸν μέν γε
οὐδ' ἂν σμικρὸν ἐάσειεν ἐμβαλεῖν· ἡμᾶς δέ, κἂν εἰ βουλοίμεθα δραξάμενοι τῶν ἁλῶν, ἐῴη ἂν ἐμβαλεῖν.   Πῶς
γὰρ οὔ; Τί δ' εἰ τοὺς ὀφθαλμοὺς ὁ υἱὸς αὐτοῦ ἀσθενοῖ,
ἆρα ἐῴη ἂν αὐτὸν ἅπτεσθαι τῶν ἑαυτοῦ ὀφθαλμῶν, μὴ 95
210 ἰατρὸν ἡγούμενος, ἢ κωλύοι ἄν; Κωλύοι ἄν.   'Ημᾶς
δέ γε εἰ ὑπολαμβάνοι ἰατρικοὺς εἶναι, κἂν εἰ βουλοίμεθα
διανοίγοντες τοὺς ὀφθαλμοὺς ἐμπάσαι τῆς τέφρας, οἶμαι,
οὐκ ἂν κωλύσειεν, ἡγούμενος ὀρθῶς φρονεῖν.   'Αληθῆ
λέγεις. 'Αρ' οὖν καὶ τἆλλα πάντα ἡμῖν ἐπιτρέποι ἂν 100
μᾶλλον ἢ ἑαυτῷ καὶ τῷ υἱεῖ, περὶ ὅσων ἂν δόξωμεν αὐτῷ
σοφώτεροι ἐκείνων εἶναι; 'Ανάγκη, ἔφη, ὦ Σώκρατες.

Οὕτως ἄρα ἔχει, ἦν δ' ἐγώ, ὦ φίλε Λύσι, εἰς μὲν
B ταῦτα ἃ ἂν φρόνιμοι γενώμεθα, ἅπαντες ἡμῖν ἐπι-
τρέψουσιν, "Ελληνές τε καὶ βάρβαροι καὶ ἄνδρες καὶ γυ- 105
ναῖκες, ποιήσομέν τε ἐν τούτοις ὅ τι ἂν βουλώμεθα, καὶ
οὐδεὶς ἡμᾶς ἑκὼν εἶναι ἐμποδιεῖ, ἀλλ' αὐτοί τε ἐλεύθεροι
ἐσόμεθα ἐν αὐτοῖς καὶ ἄλλων ἄρχοντες, ἡμέτερά τε ταῦτα

ἔσται· ὀνησόμεθα γὰρ ἀπ' αὐτῶν. εἰς ἃ δ' ἂν νοῦν μὴ
110 κτησώμεθα, οὔτε τις ἡμῖν ἐπιτρέψει περὶ αὐτὰ ποιεῖν τὰ
ἡμῖν δοκοῦντα, ἀλλ' ἐμποδιοῦσι πάντες καθ' ὅ τι ἂν δύ-
νωνται, οὐ μόνον οἱ ἀλλότριοι, ἀλλὰ καὶ ὁ πατὴρ καὶ ἡ C
μήτηρ καὶ εἴ τι τούτων οἰκειότερόν ἐστιν, αὐτοί τε ἐν
αὐτοῖς ἐσόμεθα ἄλλων ὑπήκοοι, καὶ ἡμῖν ἔσται ἀλλότρια·
115 οὐδὲν γὰρ ἀπ' αὐτῶν ὀνησόμεθα. συγχωρεῖς οὕτως ἔχειν ;
Συγχωρῶ. Ἆρ' οὖν τῳ φίλοι ἐσόμεθα καί τις ἡμᾶς φι-
λήσει ἐν τούτοις, ἐν οἷς ἂν ὦμεν ἀνωφελεῖς ; Οὐ δῆτα,
ἔφη. Νῦν ἄρα οὐδὲ σὲ ὁ πατὴρ οὐδὲ ἄλλος ἄλλον οὐδένα φιλεῖ, καθ' ὅσον ἂν ᾖ ἄχρηστος. Οὐκ ἔοικεν, ἔφη.
120 Ἐὰν μὲν ἄρα σοφὸς γένῃ, ὦ παῖ, πάντες σοι φίλοι καὶ D
πάντες σοι οἰκεῖοι ἔσονται· χρήσιμος γὰρ καὶ ἀγαθὸς ἔσει·
εἰ δὲ μή, σοὶ οὔτε ἄλλος οὐδεὶς οὔτε ὁ πατὴρ φίλος ἔσται
οὔτε ἡ μήτηρ οὔτε οἱ οἰκεῖοι. οἷόν τε οὖν ἐπὶ τούτοις,
ὦ Λύσι, μέγα φρονεῖν, ἐν οἷς τις μήπω φρονεῖ ; Καὶ
125 πῶς ἄν ; ἔφη. Εἰ δ' ἄρα σὺ διδασκάλου δέει, οὔπω
φρονεῖς. Ἀληθῆ. Οὐδ' ἄρα μεγαλόφρων εἶ, εἴπερ ἄφρων
ἔτι. Μὰ Δία, ἔφη, ὦ Σώκρατες, οὔ μοι δοκεῖ.

LACHES.

[182 D—184 A.]

A Professor of Arms.

ΛΑ. Ἀλλ' ἔστι μέν, ὦ Νικία, χαλεπὸν λέγειν περὶ
ὁτουοῦν μαθήματος, ὡς οὐ χρὴ μανθάνειν· πάντα γὰρ
ἐπίστασθαι ἀγαθὸν δοκεῖ εἶναι. καὶ δὴ καὶ τὸ ὁπλιτικὸν
τοῦτο, εἰ μέν ἐστι μάθημα, ὅπερ φασὶν οἱ διδάσκοντες, E
5 καὶ οἷον Νικίας λέγει, χρὴ αὐτὸ μανθάνειν· εἰ δ' ἔστι
μὲν μὴ μάθημα, ἀλλ' ἐξαπατῶσιν οἱ ὑπισχνούμενοι, ἢ

μάθημα μὲν τυγχάνει ὄν, μὴ μέντοι πάνυ σπουδαῖον,
τί καὶ δέοι ἂν αὐτὸ μανθάνειν; Λέγω δὲ ταῦτα περὶ αὐτοῦ εἰς τάδε ἀποβλέψας, ὅτι οἶμαι ἐγὼ τοῦτο, εἴ τι ἦν,
οὐκ ἂν λεληθέναι Λακεδαιμονίους, οἷς οὐδὲν ἄλλο μέλει 10
ἐν τῷ βίῳ ἢ τοῦτο ζητεῖν καὶ ἐπιτηδεύειν, ὅ τι ἂν μα-
183 θόντες καὶ ἐπιτηδεύσαντες πλεονεκτοῖεν τῶν ἄλλων περὶ
τὸν πόλεμον. εἰ δ' ἐκείνους ἐλελήθει, ἀλλ' οὐ τούτους γε
τοὺς διδασκάλους αὐτοῦ λέληθεν αὐτὸ τοῦτο, ὅτι ἐκεῖνοι
μάλιστα τῶν Ἑλλήνων σπουδάζουσιν ἐπὶ τοῖς τοιούτοις 15
καὶ ὅτι παρ' ἐκείνοις ἄν τις τιμηθεὶς εἰς ταῦτα καὶ παρὰ
τῶν ἄλλων πλεῖστ' ἂν ἐργάζοιτο χρήματα, ὥσπερ γε καὶ
τραγῳδίας ποιητὴς παρ' ἡμῖν τιμηθείς. τοιγάρτοι ὃς ἂν
οἴηται τραγῳδίαν καλῶς ποιεῖν, οὐκ ἔξωθεν κύκλῳ περὶ
B τὴν Ἀττικὴν κατὰ τὰς ἄλλας πόλεις ἐπιδεικνύμενος περι- 20
έρχεται, ἀλλ' εὐθὺς δεῦρο φέρεται καὶ τοῖσδ' ἐπιδείκνυσιν.
εἰκότως. τοὺς δὲ ἐν ὅπλοις μαχομένους ἐγὼ τούτους ὁρῶ
τὴν μὲν Λακεδαίμονα ἡγουμένους εἶναι ἄβατον ἱερὸν καὶ
οὐδὲ ἄκρῳ ποδὶ ἐπιβαίνοντας, κύκλῳ δὲ περιιόντας αὐτὴν καὶ πᾶσι μᾶλλον ἐπιδεικνυμένους, καὶ μάλιστα τού- 25
τοις οἳ κἂν αὐτοὶ ὁμολογήσειαν πολλοὺς σφῶν προτέρους
εἶναι πρὸς τὰ τοῦ πολέμου.

C   Ἔπειτα, ὦ Λυσίμαχε, οὐ πάνυ ὀλίγοις ἐγὼ τούτων
παραγέγονα ἐν αὐτῷ τῷ ἔργῳ, καὶ ὁρῶ οἷοί εἰσιν.
ἔξεστι δὲ καὶ αὐτόθεν ἡμῖν σκέψασθαι· ὥσπερ γὰρ 30
ἐπίτηδες οὐδεὶς πώποτ' εὐδόκιμος γέγονεν ἐν τῷ πολέμῳ
ἀνὴρ τῶν τὰ ὁπλιτικὰ ἐπιτηδευσάντων. καίτοι εἴς γε
τἆλλα πάντα ἐκ τούτων οἱ ὀνομαστοὶ γίγνονται, ἐκ τῶν
ἐπιτηδευσάντων ἕκαστα· οὗτοι δ', ὡς ἔοικε, παρὰ τοὺς
ἄλλους οὕτω σφόδρα εἰς τοῦτο δεδυστυχήκασιν. ἐπεὶ καὶ 35
D τοῦτον τὸν Στησίλεων, ὃν ὑμεῖς μετ' ἐμοῦ ἐν τοσούτῳ
ὄχλῳ ἐθεάσασθε ἐπιδεικνύμενον καὶ τὰ μεγάλα περὶ αὐτοῦ

λέγοντα ἃ ἔλεγεν, ἑτέρωθι ἐγὼ κάλλιον ἐθεασάμην ἐν τῇ
ἀληθείᾳ ὡς ἀληθῶς ἐπιδεικνύμενον οὐχ ἑκόντα. προσβα-
40 λούσης γὰρ τῆς νεὼς ἐφ' ᾗ ἐπεβάτευε, πρὸς ὁλκάδα τινά,
ἐμάχετο ἔχων δορυδρέπανον, διαφέρον δὴ ὅπλον ἅτε καὶ
αὐτὸς τῶν ἄλλων διαφέρων. τὰ μὲν οὖν ἄλλα οὐκ ἄξια
λέγειν περὶ τἀνδρός, τὸ δὲ σόφισμα τὸ τοῦ δρεπάνου τοῦ E
πρὸς τῇ λόγχῃ οἷον ἀπέβη. μαχομένου γὰρ αὐτοῦ ἐνέσχετό
45 που ἐν τοῖς τῆς νεὼς σκεύεσι καὶ ἀντελάβετο. εἷλκεν οὖν
ὁ Στησίλεως βουλόμενος ἀπολῦσαι, καὶ οὐχ οἷός τ' ἦν· ἡ
δὲ ναῦς τὴν ναῦν παρῄει. τέως μὲν οὖν παρέθει ἐν τῇ
νηὶ ἀντεχόμενος τοῦ δόρατος· ἐπεὶ δὲ δὴ παρημείβετο ἡ
ναῦς τὴν ναῦν καὶ ἐπέσπα αὐτὸν τοῦ δόρατος ἐχόμενον,
50 ἠφίει τὸ δόρυ διὰ τῆς χειρός, ἕως ἄκρου τοῦ στύρακος 184
ἀντελάβετο. ἦν δὲ γέλως καὶ κρότος ὑπὸ τῶν ἐκ τῆς
ὁλκάδος ἐπί τε τῷ σχήματι αὐτοῦ, καὶ ἐπειδὴ βαλόντος
τινὸς λίθῳ παρὰ τοὺς πόδας αὐτοῦ ἐπὶ τὸ κατάστρωμα
ἀφίεται τοῦ δόρατος, τότ' ἤδη καὶ οἱ ἐκ τῆς τριήρους
55 οὐκέτι οἷοί τ' ἦσαν τὸν γέλωτα κατέχειν, ὁρῶντες αἰωρού-
μενον ἐκ τῆς ὁλκάδος τὸ δορυδρέπανον ἐκεῖνο. ἴσως μὲν
οὖν εἴη ἄν τι ταῦτα, ὥσπερ Νικίας λέγει· οἷς δ' οὖν ἐγὼ
ἐντετύχηκα, τοιαῦτ' ἄττα ἐστίν.

PROTAGORAS.

[310 A—316 A.]

The Gathering of the Sophists.

Τῆς παρελθούσης νυκτὸς ταυτησί, ἔτι βαθέος ὄρθρου,
Ἱπποκράτης ὁ Ἀπολλοδώρου υἱός, Φάσωνος δὲ ἀδελφός,
τὴν θύραν τῇ βακτηρίᾳ πάνυ σφόδρα ἔκρουε, καὶ ἐπειδὴ B
αὐτῷ ἀνέῳξέ τις, εὐθὺς εἴσω ᾔει ἐπειγόμενος, καὶ τῇ

φωνῇ μέγα λέγων, Ὦ Σώκρατες, ἔφη, ἐγρήγορας ἢ καθ- 5
εύδεις ; Καὶ ἐγὼ τὴν φωνὴν γνοὺς αὐτοῦ, Ἱπποκράτης,
ἔφην, οὗτος· μή τι νεώτερον ἀγγέλλεις ; Οὐδέν γ᾽, ἦ δ᾽
ὅς, εἰ μὴ ἀγαθά γε. Εὖ ἂν λέγοις, ἦν δ᾽ ἐγώ· ἔστι δὲ τί,
καὶ τοῦ ἕνεκα τηνικάδε ἀφίκου ; Πρωταγόρας, ἔφη, ἥκει,
στὰς παρ᾽ ἐμοί. Πρώην, ἔφην ἐγώ· σὺ δὲ ἄρτι πέπυσαι ; 10
C Νὴ τοὺς θεούς, ἔφη, ἑσπέρας γε. Καὶ ἅμα ἐπιψηλα-
φήσας τοῦ σκίμποδος ἐκαθέζετο παρὰ τοὺς πόδας μου,
καὶ εἶπεν· Ἑσπέρας δῆτα, μάλα γε ὀψὲ ἀφικόμενος ἐξ
Οἰνόης. ὁ γάρ τοι παῖς με ὁ Σάτυρος ἀπέδρα· καὶ δῆτα
μέλλων σοι φράζειν, ὅτι διωξοίμην αὐτόν, ὑπό τινος 15
ἄλλου ἐπελαθόμην. ἐπειδὴ δὲ ἦλθον καὶ δεδειπνηκότες
ἦμεν καὶ ἐμέλλομεν ἀναπαύεσθαι, τότε μοι ἀδελφὸς λέγει,
ὅτι ἥκει Πρωταγόρας. καὶ ἔτι μὲν ἐνεχείρησα εὐθὺς παρὰ
D σὲ ἰέναι, ἔπειτά μοι λίαν πόρρω ἔδοξε τῶν νυκτῶν εἶναι·
ἐπειδὴ δὲ τάχιστά με ἐκ τοῦ κόπου ὁ ὕπνος ἀνῆκεν, εὐθὺς 20
ἀναστὰς οὕτω δεῦρο ἐπορευόμην. Καὶ ἐγὼ γιγνώσκων
αὐτοῦ τὴν ἀνδρίαν καὶ τὴν πτοίησιν, Τί οὖν σοι, ἦν δ᾽
ἐγώ, τοῦτο ; μῶν τί σε ἀδικεῖ Πρωταγόρας ; Καὶ ὃς γελάσας, Νὴ τοὺς θεούς, ἔφη, ὦ Σώκρατες, ὅτι γε μόνος
ἐστὶ σοφός, ἐμὲ δὲ οὐ ποιεῖ. Ἀλλὰ ναὶ μὰ Δία, ἔφην 25
ἐγώ, ἂν αὐτῷ διδῷς ἀργύριον καὶ πείθῃς ἐκεῖνον, ποιήσει
E καὶ σὲ σοφόν. Εἰ γάρ, ἦ δ᾽ ὅς, ὦ Ζεῦ καὶ θεοί, ἐν τούτῳ
εἴη· ὡς οὔτ᾽ ἂν τῶν ἐμῶν ἐπιλίποιμι οὐδὲν οὔτε τῶν
φίλων. ἀλλ᾽ αὐτὰ ταῦτα καὶ νῦν ἥκω παρὰ σέ, ἵνα ὑπὲρ
ἐμοῦ διαλεχθῇς αὐτῷ. ἐγὼ γὰρ ἅμα μὲν καὶ νεώτερός 30
εἰμι, ἅμα δὲ οὐδὲ ἑώρακα Πρωταγόραν πώποτε οὐδ᾽ ἀκήκοα
οὐδέν· ἔτι γὰρ παῖς ἦ, ὅτε τὸ πρότερον ἐπεδήμησεν.
ἀλλὰ γάρ, ὦ Σώκρατες, πάντες τὸν ἄνδρα ἐπαινοῦσι
καὶ φασι σοφώτατον εἶναι λέγειν. ἀλλὰ τί οὐ βαδί-
311 ζομεν παρ᾽ αὐτόν, ἵνα ἔνδον καταλάβωμεν ; καταλύει 35

δ', ὡς ἐγὼ ἤκουσα, παρὰ Καλλίᾳ τῷ Ἱππονίκου· ἀλλ'
ἴωμεν. Καὶ ἐγὼ εἶπον· Μήπω γ', ὦ 'γαθέ, [ἐκεῖσε ἴωμεν,]
πρῷ γάρ ἐστιν, ἀλλὰ δεῦρο ἐξαναστῶμεν εἰς τὴν αὐλήν,
καὶ περιιόντες αὐτοῦ διατρίψωμεν, ἕως ἂν φῶς γένηται·
40 εἶτα ἴωμεν. καὶ γὰρ τὰ πολλὰ Πρωταγόρας ἔνδον δια-
τρίβει, ὥστε, θάρρει, καταληψόμεθα αὐτόν, ὡς τὸ εἰκός,
ἔνδον.

Μετὰ ταῦτα ἀναστάντες εἰς τὴν αὐλὴν περιῇμεν. Καὶ B
ἐγὼ ἀποπειρώμενος τοῦ Ἱπποκράτους τῆς ῥώμης διε-
45 σκόπουν αὐτὸν καὶ ἠρώτων, Εἰπέ μοι, ἔφην ἐγώ, ὦ Ἱππόκρατες, παρὰ Πρωταγόραν νῦν ἐπιχειρεῖς ἰέναι, ἀργύριον
τελῶν ἐκείνῳ μισθὸν ὑπὲρ σεαυτοῦ, ὡς παρὰ τίνα ἀφιξό-
μενος καὶ τίς γενησόμενος; ὥσπερ ἂν εἰ ἐπενόεις παρὰ
τὸν σαυτοῦ ὁμώνυμον ἐλθὼν Ἱπποκράτη τὸν Κῷον, τὸν
50 τῶν Ἀσκληπιαδῶν, ἀργύριον τελεῖν ὑπὲρ σαυτοῦ μισθὸν
ἐκείνῳ, εἴ τίς σε ἤρετο, Εἰπέ μοι, μέλλεις τελεῖν, ὦ Ἱππό- C
κρατες, Ἱπποκράτει μισθὸν ὡς τίνι ὄντι; τί ἂν ἀπεκρίνω;
Εἶπον ἄν, ἔφη, ὅτι ὡς ἰατρῷ. Ὡς τίς γενησόμενος; Ὡς
ἰατρός, ἔφη. Εἰ δὲ παρὰ Πολύκλειτον τὸν Ἀργεῖον ἢ Φει-
55 δίαν τὸν Ἀθηναῖον ἐπενόεις ἀφικόμενος μισθὸν ὑπὲρ σαυτοῦ τελεῖν ἐκείνοις, εἴ τίς σε ἤρετο, Τελεῖν τοῦτο τὸ ἀργύριον ὡς τίνι ὄντι ἐν νῷ ἔχεις Πολυκλείτῳ τε καὶ Φειδίᾳ;
τί ἂν ἀπεκρίνω; Εἶπον ἂν ὡς ἀγαλματοποιοῖς. Ὡς τίς
δὲ γενησόμενος αὐτός; Δῆλον ὅτι ἀγαλματοποιός. Εἶεν,
60 ἦν δ' ἐγώ· παρὰ δὲ δὴ Πρωταγόραν νῦν ἀφικόμενοι ἐγώ D
τε καὶ σὺ ἀργύριον ἐκείνῳ μισθὸν ἕτοιμοι ἐσόμεθα τελεῖν
ὑπὲρ σοῦ, ἂν μὲν ἐξικνῆται τὰ ἡμέτερα χρήματα καὶ τούτοις πείθωμεν αὐτόν,—εἰ δὲ μή, καὶ τὰ τῶν φίλων προσ-
αναλίσκοντες. εἰ οὖν τις ἡμᾶς περὶ ταῦτα οὕτω σφόδρα
65 σπουδάζοντας ἔροιτο, Εἰπέ μοι, ὦ Σώκρατές τε καὶ Ἱππόκρατες, ὡς τίνι ὄντι τῷ Πρωταγόρᾳ ἐν νῷ ἔχετε χρήματα

E τελεῖν ; τί ἂν αὐτῷ ἀποκριναίμεθα ; τί ὄνομα ἄλλο γε
λεγόμενον περὶ Πρωταγόρου ἀκούομεν, ὥσπερ περὶ Φειδίου
ἀγαλματοποιὸν καὶ περὶ Ὁμήρου ποιητήν ; τί τοιοῦτον
περὶ Πρωταγόρου ἀκούομεν ; Σοφιστὴν δή τοι ὀνομάζουσί 70
γε, ὦ Σώκρατες, τὸν ἄνδρα εἶναι, ἔφη. Ὡς σοφιστῇ ἄρα
ἐρχόμεθα τελοῦντες τὰ χρήματα ; Μάλιστα.   Εἰ οὖν καὶ
312 τοῦτό τίς σε προσέροιτο, Αὐτὸς δὲ δὴ ὡς τίς γενησόμενος
ἔρχει παρὰ τὸν Πρωταγόραν ; Καὶ ὃς εἶπεν ἐρυθριάσας—
ἤδη γὰρ ὑπέφαινέ τι ἡμέρας, ὥστε καταφανῆ αὐτὸν γενέ- 75
σθαι—Εἰ μέν τι τοῖς ἔμπροσθεν ἔοικε, δῆλον ὅτι σοφιστὴς
γενησόμενος.   Σὺ δέ, ἦν δ᾽ ἐγώ, πρὸς θεῶν, οὐκ ἂν
αἰσχύνοιο εἰς τοὺς Ἕλληνας αὐτὸν σοφιστὴν παρέχων ;
Νὴ τὸν Δία, ὦ Σώκρατες, εἴπερ γε ἃ διανοοῦμαι χρὴ λέγειν.   Ἀλλ᾽ ἄρα, ὦ Ἱππόκρατες, μὴ οὐ τοιαύτην ὑπολαμ- 80
B βάνεις σου τὴν παρὰ Πρωταγόρου μάθησιν ἔσεσθαι, ἀλλ᾽
οἵαπερ ἡ παρὰ τοῦ γραμματιστοῦ ἐγένετο καὶ κιθαριστοῦ
καὶ παιδοτρίβου ; τούτων γὰρ σὺ ἑκάστην οὐκ ἐπὶ τέχνῃ
ἔμαθες, ὡς δημιουργὸς ἐσόμενος, ἀλλ᾽ ἐπὶ παιδείᾳ, ὡς τὸν
ἰδιώτην καὶ τὸν ἐλεύθερον πρέπει.   Πάνυ μὲν οὖν μοι 85
δοκεῖ, ἔφη, τοιαύτη μᾶλλον εἶναι ἡ παρὰ Πρωταγόρου
μάθησις.

Οἶσθα οὖν ὃ μέλλεις νῦν πράττειν, ἤ σε λανθάνει ; ἦν
δ᾽ ἐγώ.   Τοῦ πέρι ; Ὅτι μέλλεις τὴν ψυχὴν τὴν σαυτοῦ
C παρασχεῖν θεραπεῦσαι ἀνδρί, ὡς φῄς, σοφιστῇ· ὅ τι δέ 90
ποτε ὁ σοφιστής ἐστι, θαυμάζοιμ᾽ ἂν εἰ οἶσθα.   καίτοι εἰ
τοῦτ᾽ ἀγνοεῖς, οὐδὲ ὅτῳ παραδίδως τὴν ψυχὴν οἶσθα, οὔτ᾽
εἰ ἀγαθῷ οὔτ᾽ εἰ κακῷ πράγματι.   Οἶμαί γ᾽, ἔφη, εἰδέναι·
Λέγε δή, τί ἡγεῖ εἶναι τὸν σοφιστήν ; Ἐγὼ μέν, ἦ δ᾽ ὅς,
ὥσπερ τοὔνομα λέγει, τοῦτον εἶναι τὸν τῶν σοφῶν ἐπιστή- 95
μονα.   Οὐκοῦν, ἦν δ᾽ ἐγώ, τοῦτο μὲν ἔξεστι λέγειν καὶ
D περὶ ζωγράφων καὶ περὶ τεκτόνων, ὅτι οὗτοί εἰσιν οἱ τῶν

σοφῶν ἐπιστήμονες. ἀλλ᾽ εἴ τις ἔροιτο ἡμᾶς, τῶν τί
σοφῶν εἰσὶν οἱ ζωγράφοι ἐπιστήμονες, εἴποιμεν ἄν που
100 αὐτῷ, ὅτι τῶν πρὸς τὴν ἀπεργασίαν τὴν τῶν εἰκόνων, καὶ
τἆλλα οὕτως. εἰ δέ τις ἐκεῖνο ἔροιτο, Ὁ δὲ σοφιστὴς
τῶν τί σοφῶν ἐστί; τί ἂν ἀποκριναίμεθα αὐτῷ; ποίας
ἐργασίας ἐπιστάτης; Τί ἂν εἴποιμεν αὐτὸν εἶναι, ὦ Σώκρατες, ἢ ἐπιστάτην τοῦ ποιῆσαι δεινὸν λέγειν; Ἴσως
105 ἄν, ἦν δ᾽ ἐγώ, ἀληθῆ λέγοιμεν, οὐ μέντοι ἱκανῶς γε,
ἐρωτήσεως γὰρ ἔτι ἡ ἀπόκρισις ἡμῖν δεῖται, περὶ ὅτου
ὁ σοφιστὴς δεινὸν ποιεῖ λέγειν· ὥσπερ ὁ κιθαριστὴς
δεινὸν δήπου ποιεῖ λέγειν περὶ οὗπερ καὶ ἐπιστήμονα, E
περὶ κιθαρίσεως· ἢ γάρ; Ναί. Εἶεν· ὁ δὲ δὴ σοφιστὴς
110 περὶ τίνος δεινὸν ποιεῖ λέγειν; ἢ δῆλον ὅτι περὶ οὗπερ
καὶ ἐπίσταται; Εἰκός γε. Τί δή ἐστι τοῦτο, περὶ οὗ αὐτός
τε ἐπιστήμων ἐστὶν ὁ σοφιστὴς καὶ τὸν μαθητὴν ποιεῖ;
Μὰ Δί᾽, ἔφη, οὐκέτι ἔχω σοι λέγειν.

Καὶ ἐγὼ εἶπον μετὰ τοῦτο· Τί οὖν; οἶσθα εἰς οἶόν 313
115 τινα κίνδυνον ἔρχει ὑποθήσων τὴν ψυχήν; ἢ εἰ μὲν τὸ
σῶμα ἐπιτρέπειν σε ἔδει τῳ, διακινδυνεύοντα ἢ χρηστὸν
αὐτὸ γενέσθαι ἢ πονηρόν, πολλὰ ἂν περιεσκέψω, εἴτ᾽
ἐπιτρεπτέον εἴτε οὔ, καὶ εἰς συμβουλὴν τούς τε φίλους ἂν
παρεκάλεις καὶ τοὺς οἰκείους, σκοπούμενος ἡμέρας συχνάς·
120 ὃ δὲ περὶ πλείονος τοῦ σώματος ἡγεῖ, τὴν ψυχήν, καὶ ἐν
ᾧ πάντ᾽ ἐστὶ τὰ σὰ ἢ εὖ ἢ κακῶς πράττειν, χρηστοῦ ἢ
πονηροῦ αὐτοῦ γενομένου, περὶ δὲ τούτου οὔτε τῷ πατρὶ
οὔτε τῷ ἀδελφῷ ἐπεκοινώσω οὔτε ἡμῶν τῶν ἑταίρων οὐ- B
δενί, εἴτ᾽ ἐπιτρεπτέον εἴτε καὶ οὐ τῷ ἀφικομένῳ τούτῳ
125 ξένῳ τὴν σὴν ψυχήν, ἀλλ᾽ ἑσπέρας ἀκούσας, ὡς φῄς, ὄρ-
θριος ἥκων περὶ μὲν τούτου οὐδένα λόγον οὐδὲ συμβουλὴν
ποιεῖ, εἴτε χρὴ ἐπιτρέπειν σαυτὸν αὐτῷ εἴτε μή, ἕτοιμος
δ᾽ εἶ ἀναλίσκειν τά τε σαυτοῦ καὶ τὰ τῶν φίλων χρήματα,

ὡς ἤδη διεγνωκώς, ὅτι πάντως συνεστέον Πρωταγόρᾳ, ὃν
οὔτε γιγνώσκεις, ὡς φῄς, οὔτε διείλεξαι οὐδὲ πώποτε, 130
C σοφιστὴν δ᾽ ὀνομάζεις, τὸν δὲ σοφιστήν, ὅ τί ποτε ἔστι,
φαίνει ἀγνοῶν, ᾧ μέλλεις σαυτὸν ἐπιτρέπειν; Καὶ ὃς
ἀκούσας, Ἔοικεν, ἔφη, ὦ Σώκρατες, ἐξ ὧν σὺ λέγεις.
Ἆρ᾽ οὖν, ὦ Ἱππόκρατες, ὁ σοφιστὴς τυγχάνει ὢν ἔμπορός τις ἢ κάπηλος τῶν ἀγωγίμων, ἀφ᾽ ὧν ψυχὴ τρέφεται; 135
φαίνεται γὰρ ἔμοιγε τοιοῦτός τις. Τρέφεται δέ, ὦ Σώκρατες, ψυχὴ τίνι; Μαθήμασι δήπου, ἦν δ᾽ ἐγώ. καὶ
ὅπως γε μή, ὦ ἑταῖρε, ὁ σοφιστὴς ἐπαινῶν ἃ πωλεῖ ἐξα-
πατήσῃ ἡμᾶς, ὥσπερ οἱ περὶ τὴν τοῦ σώματος τροφήν,
D ὁ ἔμπορός τε καὶ κάπηλος. καὶ γὰρ οὗτοί που ὧν ἄγουσιν 140
ἀγωγίμων οὔτε αὐτοὶ ἴσασιν ὅ τι χρηστὸν ἢ πονηρὸν περὶ
τὸ σῶμα, ἐπαινοῦσι δὲ πάντα πωλοῦντες, οὔτε οἱ ὠνούμενοι παρ᾽ αὐτῶν, ἐὰν μή τις τύχῃ γυμναστικὸς ἢ ἰατρὸς
ὤν. οὕτω δὲ καὶ οἱ τὰ μαθήματα περιάγοντες κατὰ τὰς
πόλεις καὶ πωλοῦντες καὶ καπηλεύοντες τῷ ἀεὶ ἐπιθυ- 145
μοῦντι ἐπαινοῦσι μὲν πάντα ἃ πωλοῦσι, τάχα δ᾽ ἄν τινες,
ὦ ἄριστε, καὶ τούτων ἀγνοοῖεν ὧν πωλοῦσιν ὅ τι χρηστὸν
E ἢ πονηρὸν πρὸς τὴν ψυχήν· ὡς δ᾽ αὕτως καὶ οἱ ὠνούμενοι
παρ᾽ αὐτῶν, ἐὰν μή τις τύχῃ περὶ τὴν ψυχὴν αὖ ἰατρικὸς
ὤν. εἰ μὲν οὖν σὺ τυγχάνεις ἐπιστήμων τούτων τί χρη- 150
στὸν καὶ πονηρόν, ἀσφαλές σοι ὠνεῖσθαι μαθήματα καὶ
παρὰ Πρωταγόρου καὶ παρ᾽ ἄλλου ὁτουοῦν· εἰ δὲ μή, ὅρα,
314 ὦ μακάριε, μὴ περὶ τοῖς φιλτάτοις κυβεύῃς τε καὶ κιν-
δυνεύῃς. καὶ γὰρ δὴ καὶ πολὺ μείζων κίνδυνος ἐν τῇ τῶν
μαθημάτων ὠνῇ ἢ ἐν τῇ τῶν σιτίων. σιτία μὲν γὰρ καὶ 155
ποτὰ πριάμενον παρὰ τοῦ καπήλου καὶ ἐμπόρου ἔξεστιν
ἐν ἄλλοις ἀγγείοις ἀποφέρειν, καὶ πρὶν δέξασθαι αὐτὰ εἰς
τὸ σῶμα πιόντα ἢ φαγόντα, καταθέμενον οἴκαδε ἔξεστι
συμβουλεύσασθαι, παρακαλέσαντα τὸν ἐπαΐοντα, ὅ τι τε

160 ἐδεστέον ἢ ποτέον καὶ ὅ τι μή, καὶ ὁπόσον καὶ ὁπότε·
ὥστε ἐν τῇ ὠνῇ οὐ μέγας ὁ κίνδυνος. μαθήματα δὲ οὐκ
ἔστιν ἐν ἄλλῳ ἀγγείῳ ἀπενεγκεῖν, ἀλλ᾽ ἀνάγκη, καταθέντα Β
τὴν τιμήν, τὸ μάθημα ἐν αὐτῇ τῇ ψυχῇ λαβόντα καὶ
μαθόντα ἀπιέναι ἢ βεβλαμμένον ἢ ὠφελημένον. ταῦτα
165 οὖν σκοπώμεθα καὶ μετὰ τῶν πρεσβυτέρων ἡμῶν· ἡμεῖς
γὰρ ἔτι νέοι ὥστε τοσοῦτο πρᾶγμα διελέσθαι. νῦν μέντοι,
ὥσπερ ὡρμήσαμεν, ἴωμεν καὶ ἀκούσωμεν τοῦ ἀνδρός,
ἔπειτα ἀκούσαντες καὶ ἄλλοις ἀνακοινωσώμεθα· καὶ γὰρ
οὐ μόνος Πρωταγόρας αὐτόθι ἐστίν, ἀλλὰ καὶ Ἱππίας ὁ
170 Ἠλεῖος—οἶμαι δὲ καὶ Πρόδικον τὸν Κεῖον—καὶ ἄλλοι C
πολλοὶ καὶ σοφοί.

Δόξαν ἡμῖν ταῦτα ἐπορευόμεθα. ἐπειδὴ δὲ ἐν τῷ
προθύρῳ ἐγενόμεθα, ἐπιστάντες περί τινος λόγου διελεγόμεθα, ὃς ἡμῖν κατὰ τὴν ὁδὸν ἐνέπεσεν· ἵν᾽ οὖν μὴ
175 ἀτελὴς γένοιτο, ἀλλὰ διαπερανάμενοι οὕτως ἐσίοιμεν,
στάντες ἐν τῷ προθύρῳ διελεγόμεθα, ἕως συνωμολογή-
σαμεν ἀλλήλοις. δοκεῖ οὖν μοι, ὁ θυρωρός, εὐνοῦχός τις,
κατήκουεν ἡμῶν, κινδυνεύει δὲ διὰ τὸ πλῆθος τῶν σοφισ- D
τῶν ἄχθεσθαι τοῖς φοιτῶσιν εἰς τὴν οἰκίαν. ἐπειδὴ γοῦν
180 ἐκρούσαμεν τὴν θύραν, ἀνοίξας καὶ ἰδὼν ἡμᾶς, Ἔα, ἔφη,
σοφισταί τινες· οὐ σχολὴ αὐτῷ. καὶ ἅμα ἀμφοῖν τοῖν
χεροῖν τὴν θύραν πάνυ προθύμως ὡς οἷός τ᾽ ἦν ἐπήραξε.
καὶ ἡμεῖς πάλιν ἐκρούομεν· καὶ ὃς ἐγκεκλειμένης τῆς θύρας
ἀποκρινόμενος εἶπεν, Ὦ ἄνθρωποι, ἔφη, οὐκ ἀκηκόατε,
185 ὅτι οὐ σχολὴ αὐτῷ; Ἀλλ᾽, ὦ ᾽γαθέ, ἔφην ἐγώ, οὔτε παρὰ
Καλλίαν ἥκομεν οὔτε σοφισταί ἐσμεν, ἀλλὰ θάρρει·
Πρωταγόραν γάρ τοι δεόμενοι ἰδεῖν ἤλθομεν. εἰσάγγειλον Ε
οὖν. μόγις οὖν ποτὲ ἡμῖν ἄνθρωπος ἀνέῳξε τὴν θύραν.

Ἐπειδὴ δὲ εἰσήλθομεν, κατελάβομεν Πρωταγόραν ἐν
190 τῷ προστῴῳ περιπατοῦντα, ἑξῆς δ᾽ αὐτῷ συμπεριεπάτουν

ἐκ μὲν τοῦ ἐπὶ θάτερα Καλλίας ὁ Ἱππονίκου καὶ ὁ ἀδελ-
315 φὸς αὐτοῦ ὁ ὁμομήτριος, Πάραλος ὁ Περικλέους, καὶ
Χαρμίδης ὁ Γλαύκωνος, ἐκ δὲ τοῦ ἐπὶ θάτερα ὁ ἕτερος
τῶν Περικλέους Ξάνθιππος καὶ Φιλιππίδης ὁ Φιλομήλου
καὶ Ἀντίμοιρος ὁ Μενδαῖος, ὅσπερ εὐδοκιμεῖ μάλιστα τῶν 195
Πρωταγόρου μαθητῶν καὶ ἐπὶ τέχνῃ μανθάνει, ὡς σοφιστὴς ἐσόμενος. τούτων δὲ οἱ ὄπισθεν ἠκολούθουν ἐπακούον-
τες τῶν λεγομένων, τὸ μὲν πολὺ ξένοι ἐφαίνοντο, οὓς
ἄγει ἐξ ἑκάστων τῶν πόλεων ὁ Πρωταγόρας, δι᾽ ὧν διεξέρχεται, κηλῶν τῇ φωνῇ ὥσπερ Ὀρφεύς, οἱ δὲ κατὰ τὴν 200
Β φωνὴν ἕπονται κεκηλημένοι· ἦσαν δέ τινες καὶ τῶν
ἐπιχωρίων ἐν τῷ χορῷ. τοῦτον τὸν χορὸν μάλιστα
ἔγωγε ἰδὼν ἥσθην, ὡς καλῶς εὐλαβοῦντο μηδέποτε ἐμ-
ποδὼν ἐν τῷ πρόσθεν εἶναι Πρωταγόρου, ἀλλ᾽ ἐπειδὴ
αὐτὸς ἀναστρέφοι καὶ οἱ μετ᾽ ἐκείνου, εὖ πως καὶ ἐν 205
κόσμῳ περιεσχίζοντο οὗτοι οἱ ἐπήκοοι ἔνθεν καὶ ἔνθεν,
καὶ ἐν κύκλῳ περιιόντες ἀεὶ εἰς τὸ ὄπισθεν καθίσταντο
κάλλιστα.

Τὸν δὲ μετ᾽ εἰσενόησα, ἔφη Ὅμηρος, Ἱππίαν τὸν
C Ἠλεῖον, καθήμενον ἐν τῷ κατ᾽ ἀντικρὺ προστώῳ ἐν θρόνῳ· 210
περὶ αὐτὸν δ᾽ ἐκάθηντο ἐπὶ βάθρων Ἐρυξίμαχός τε ὁ Ἀκου-
μενοῦ καὶ Φαῖδρος ὁ Μυρρινούσιος καὶ Ἄνδρων ὁ Ἀνδρο-
τίωνος καὶ τῶν ξένων πολῖταί τε αὐτοῦ καὶ ἄλλοι τινές.
ἐφαίνοντο δὲ περὶ φύσεώς τε καὶ τῶν μετεώρων ἀστρονο-
μικὰ ἄττα διερωτᾶν τὸν Ἱππίαν, ὁ δ᾽ ἐν θρόνῳ καθήμενος 215
ἑκάστοις αὐτῶν διέκρινε καὶ διεξῄει τὰ ἐρωτώμενα.

Καὶ μὲν δὴ καὶ Τάνταλόν γε εἰσεῖδον. ἐπεδήμει
D γὰρ ἄρα Πρόδικος ὁ Κεῖος, ἦν δὲ ἐν οἰκήματί τινι, ᾧ πρὸ
τοῦ μὲν ὡς ταμιείῳ ἐχρῆτο Ἱππόνικος, νῦν δὲ ὑπὸ τοῦ
πλήθους τῶν καταλυόντων ὁ Καλλίας καὶ τοῦτο ἐκκενώσας 220
ξένοις κατάλυσιν πεποίηκεν. ὁ μὲν οὖν Πρόδικος ἔτ

κατέκειτο, ἐγκεκαλυμμένος ἐν κωδίοις τισὶ καὶ στρώμασι
καὶ μάλα πολλοῖς, ὡς ἐφαίνετο· παρεκάθηντο δὲ αὐτῷ ἐπὶ
ταῖς πλησίον κλίναις Παυσανίας τε ὁ ἐκ Κεραμέων καὶ
225 μετὰ Παυσανίου νέον τι ἔτι μειράκιον, ὡς μὲν ἐγῷμαι,
καλόν τε κἀγαθὸν τὴν φύσιν, τὴν δ' οὖν ἰδέαν πάνυ καλός. Ε
ἔδοξα ἀκοῦσαι ὄνομα αὐτῷ εἶναι 'Αγάθωνα. τοῦτ'
οὖν τὸ μειράκιον καὶ τὼ 'Αδειμάντω ἀμφοτέρω, ὅ τε Κή-
πιδος καὶ ὁ Λευκολοφίδου, καὶ ἄλλοι τινὲς ἐφαίνοντο.
230 περὶ δὲ ὧν διελέγοντο οὐκ ἐδυνάμην ἔγωγε μαθεῖν ἔξωθεν,
καίπερ λιπαρῶς ἔχων ἀκούειν τοῦ Προδίκου—πάσσοφος
γάρ μοι δοκεῖ ἀνὴρ εἶναι καὶ θεῖος,—ἀλλὰ διὰ τὴν βαρύ-
τητα τῆς φωνῆς βόμβος τις ἐν τῷ οἰκήματι γιγνόμενος
ἀσαφῆ ἐποίει τὰ λεγόμενα.

ION.

[533 C—535 A.]

The Poet inspired by the Gods.

ΣΩ. Καὶ ὁρῶ, ὦ Ἴων, καὶ ἔρχομαι γέ σοι ἀποφαινό-
μενος ὅ μοι δοκεῖ τοῦτο εἶναι. ἔστι γὰρ τοῦτο τέχνη μὲν D
οὐκ ὂν παρὰ σοὶ περὶ 'Ομήρου εὖ λέγειν, ὃ νῦν δὴ ἔλεγον,
θεία δὲ δύναμις ἥ σε κινεῖ, ὥσπερ ἐν τῇ λίθῳ ἣν Εὐρι-
5 πίδης μὲν Μαγνῆτιν ὠνόμασεν, οἱ δὲ πολλοὶ 'Ηρακλείαν.
καὶ γὰρ αὕτη ἡ λίθος οὐ μόνον αὐτοὺς τοὺς δακτυλίους
ἄγει τοὺς σιδηροῦς, ἀλλὰ καὶ δύναμιν ἐντίθησι τοῖς δα-
κτυλίοις ὥστ' αὖ δύνασθαι ταὐτὸν τοῦτο ποιεῖν ὅπερ ἡ
λίθος, ἄλλους ἄγειν δακτυλίους, ὥστ' ἐνίοτε ὁρμαθὸς μακ- E
10 ρὸς πάνυ σιδηρῶν δακτυλίων ἐξ ἀλλήλων ἤρτηται· πᾶσι
δὲ τούτοις ἐξ ἐκείνης τῆς λίθου ἡ δύναμις ἀνήρτηται. οὕτω

δὲ καὶ ἡ Μοῦσα ἐνθέους μὲν ποιεῖ αὐτή, διὰ δὲ τῶν ἐνθέων
τούτων ἄλλων ἐνθουσιαζόντων ὁρμαθὸς ἐξαρτᾶται. πάντες
γὰρ οἵ τε τῶν ἐπῶν ποιηταὶ οἱ ἀγαθοὶ οὐκ ἐκ τέχνης ἀλλ᾽
ἔνθεοι ὄντες καὶ κατεχόμενοι πάντα ταῦτα τὰ καλὰ λέ- 15
γουσι ποιήματα, καὶ οἱ μελοποιοὶ οἱ ἀγαθοὶ ὡσαύτως,
534 ὥσπερ οἱ κορυβαντιῶντες οὐκ ἔμφρονες ὄντες ὀρχοῦνται,
οὕτω καὶ οἱ μελοποιοὶ οὐκ ἔμφρονες ὄντες τὰ καλὰ μέλη
ταῦτα ποιοῦσιν, ἀλλ᾽ ἐπειδὰν ἐμβῶσιν εἰς τὴν ἁρμονίαν
καὶ εἰς τὸν ῥυθμόν, καὶ βακχεύουσι καὶ κατεχόμενοι, ὥσ- 20
περ αἱ βάκχαι ἀρύτονται ἐκ τῶν ποταμῶν μέλι καὶ γάλα
κατεχόμεναι, ἔμφρονες δὲ οὖσαι οὔ, καὶ τῶν μελοποιῶν ἡ
ψυχὴ τοῦτο ἐργάζεται ὅπερ αὐτοὶ λέγουσι. λέγουσι γὰρ
δήπουθεν πρὸς ἡμᾶς οἱ ποιηταὶ ὅτι ἀπὸ κρηνῶν μελιρρύτων
B ἐκ Μουσῶν κήπων τινῶν καὶ ναπῶν δρεπόμενοι τὰ μέλη 25
ἡμῖν φέρουσιν ὥσπερ αἱ μέλιτται, καὶ αὐτοὶ οὕτω πετό-
μενοι. καὶ ἀληθῆ λέγουσι· κοῦφον γὰρ χρῆμα ποιητής
ἐστι καὶ πτηνὸν καὶ ἱερόν, καὶ οὐ πρότερον οἷός τε ποιεῖν
πρὶν ἂν ἔνθεός τε γένηται καὶ ἔκφρων καὶ ὁ νοῦς μηκέτι
ἐν αὐτῷ ἐνῇ· ἕως δ᾽ ἂν τουτὶ ἔχῃ τὸ κτῆμα, ἀδύνατος πᾶς 30
ποιεῖν ἐστὶν ἄνθρωπος καὶ χρησμῳδεῖν. ἅτε οὖν οὐ τέχνῃ
ποιοῦντες καὶ πολλὰ λέγουσι καὶ καλὰ περὶ τῶν πραγμά-
C των, ὥσπερ σὺ περὶ Ὁμήρου, ἀλλὰ θείᾳ μοίρᾳ τοῦτο μόνον
οἷός τε ἕκαστος ποιεῖν καλῶς ἐφ᾽ ὃ ἡ Μοῦσα αὐτὸν ὥρμη-
σεν, ὁ μὲν διθυράμβους, ὁ δὲ ἐγκώμια, ὁ δὲ ὑπορχήματα, 35
ὁ δ᾽ ἔπη, ὁ δ᾽ ἰάμβους· τὰ δ᾽ ἄλλα φαῦλος αὐτῶν ἕκαστός
ἐστιν. οὐ γὰρ τέχνῃ ταῦτα λέγουσιν ἀλλὰ θείᾳ δυνάμει,
ἐπεί, εἰ περὶ ἑνὸς τέχνῃ καλῶς ἠπίσταντο λέγειν, κἂν
περὶ τῶν ἄλλων ἁπάντων. διὰ ταῦτα δὲ ὁ θεὸς ἐξαιρού-
μενος τούτων τὸν νοῦν τούτοις χρῆται ὑπηρέταις καὶ τοῖς 40
D χρησμῳδοῖς καὶ τοῖς μάντεσι τοῖς θείοις, ἵνα ἡμεῖς οἱ
ἀκούοντες εἰδῶμεν ὅτι οὐχ οὗτοί εἰσιν οἱ ταῦτα λέγοντες

οὕτω πολλοῦ ἄξια, οἷς νοῦς μὴ πάρεστιν, ἀλλ' ὁ θεὸς
αὐτός ἐστιν ὁ λέγων, διὰ τούτων δὲ φθέγγεται πρὸς ἡμᾶς.
45 μέγιστον δὲ τεκμήριον τῷ λόγῳ Τύννιχος ὁ Χαλκιδεύς,
ὃς ἄλλο μὲν οὐδὲν πώποτ' ἐποίησε ποίημα ὅτου τις ἂν
ἀξιώσειε μνησθῆναι, τὸν δὲ παίωνα ὃν πάντες ᾄδουσι,
σχεδόν τι πάντων μελῶν κάλλιστον, ἀτεχνῶς, ὅπερ αὐτὸς
λέγει, εὕρημά τι Μοισᾶν. ἐν τούτῳ γὰρ δὴ μάλιστά μοι
50 δοκεῖ ὁ θεὸς ἐνδείξασθαι ἡμῖν, ἵνα μὴ διστάζωμεν, ὅτι οὐκ E
ἀνθρώπινά ἐστι τὰ καλὰ ταῦτα ποιήματα οὐδὲ ἀνθρώπων,
ἀλλὰ θεῖα καὶ θεῶν, οἱ δὲ ποιηταὶ οὐδὲν ἄλλ' ἢ ἑρμηνεῖς
εἰσι τῶν θεῶν, κατεχόμενοι ἐξ ὅτου ἂν ἕκαστος κατέχηται.
ταῦτα ἐνδεικνύμενος ὁ θεὸς ἐξεπίτηδες διὰ τοῦ φαυλοτάτου
55 ποιητοῦ τὸ κάλλιστον μέλος ᾖσεν. ἢ οὐ δοκῶ σοι ἀληθῆ 535
λέγειν, ὦ Ἴων ;

ΙΩΝ. Ναὶ μὰ τὸν Δία, ἔμοιγε· ἅπτει γάρ πώς μου
τοῖς λόγοις τῆς ψυχῆς, ὦ Σώκρατες, καί μοι δοκοῦσι θείᾳ
μοίρᾳ ἡμῖν παρὰ τῶν θεῶν ταῦτα οἱ ἀγαθοὶ ποιηταὶ
60 ἑρμηνεύειν.

APOLOGY.

[The whole.]

The Defence of Socrates before his Judges.

Ὅ τι μὲν ὑμεῖς, ὦ ἄνδρες Ἀθηναῖοι, πεπόνθατε ὑπὸ 17
τῶν ἐμῶν κατηγόρων, οὐκ οἶδα· ἐγὼ δ' οὖν καὶ αὐτὸς
ὑπ' αὐτῶν ὀλίγου ἐμαυτοῦ ἐπελαθόμην· οὕτω πιθανῶς
ἔλεγον. καί τοι ἀληθές γε, ὡς ἔπος εἰπεῖν, οὐδὲν
5 εἰρήκασι. μάλιστα δὲ αὐτῶν ἓν ἐθαύμασα τῶν πολλῶν
ὧν ἐψεύσαντο, τοῦτο ἐν ᾧ ἔλεγον ὡς χρὴ ὑμᾶς εὐλαβεῖ-

Β σθαι, μὴ ὑπ' ἐμοῦ ἐξαπατηθῆτε, ὡς δεινοῦ ὄντος λέγειν.
τὸ γὰρ μὴ αἰσχυνθῆναι, ὅτι αὐτίκα ὑπ' ἐμοῦ ἐξελεγχθή-
σονται ἔργῳ, ἐπειδὰν μηδ' ὁπωστιοῦν φαίνωμαι δεινὸς
λέγειν, τοῦτό μοι ἔδοξεν αὐτῶν ἀναισχυντότατον εἶναι, 10
εἰ μὴ ἄρα δεινὸν καλοῦσιν οὗτοι λέγειν τὸν τἀληθῆ
λέγοντα· εἰ μὲν γὰρ τοῦτο λέγουσιν, ὁμολογοίην ἂν
ἔγωγε οὐ κατὰ τούτους εἶναι ῥήτωρ. οὗτοι μὲν οὖν,
ὥσπερ ἐγὼ λέγω, ἤ τι ἢ οὐδὲν ἀληθὲς εἰρήκασιν· ὑμεῖς
δ' ἐμοῦ ἀκούσεσθε πᾶσαν τὴν ἀλήθειαν. Οὐ μέντοι μὰ 15
Δί', ὦ ἄνδρες Ἀθηναῖοι, κεκαλλιεπημένους γε λόγους,
ὥσπερ οἱ τούτων, ῥήμασί τε καὶ ὀνόμασιν, οὐδὲ κεκο-
C σμημένους, ἀλλ' ἀκούσεσθε εἰκῇ λεγόμενα τοῖς ἐπιτυ-
χοῦσιν ὀνόμασι· πιστεύω γὰρ δίκαια εἶναι ἃ λέγω, καὶ
μηδεὶς ὑμῶν προσδοκησάτω ἄλλως· οὐδὲ γὰρ ἂν δήπου 20
πρέποι, ὦ ἄνδρες, τῇδε τῇ ἡλικίᾳ, ὥσπερ μειρακίῳ
πλάττοντι λόγους εἰς ὑμᾶς εἰσιέναι. καὶ μέντοι καὶ
πάνυ, ὦ ἄνδρες Ἀθηναῖοι, τοῦτο ὑμῶν δέομαι καὶ παρί-
εμαι· ἐὰν διὰ τῶν αὐτῶν λόγων ἀκούητέ μου ἀπολογουμένου, δι' ὧνπερ εἴωθα λέγειν καὶ ἐν ἀγορᾷ ἐπὶ τῶν 25
τραπεζῶν, ἵνα ὑμῶν πολλοὶ ἀκηκόασι, καὶ ἄλλοθι, μήτε
D θαυμάζειν μήτε θορυβεῖν τούτου ἕνεκα. ἔχει γὰρ οὑτωσί.
νῦν ἐγὼ πρῶτον ἐπὶ δικαστήριον ἀναβέβηκα, ἔτη γεγονὼς
ἑβδομήκοντα· ἀτεχνῶς οὖν ξένως ἔχω τῆς ἐνθάδε λέξεως.
ὥσπερ οὖν ἂν εἰ τῷ ὄντι ξένος ἐτύγχανον ὤν, ξυνε- 30
γιγνώσκετε δήπου ἄν μοι, εἰ ἐν ἐκείνῃ τῇ φωνῇ τε καὶ
18 τῷ τρόπῳ ἔλεγον, ἐν οἷσπερ ἐτεθράμμην, καὶ δὴ καὶ νῦν
τοῦτο ὑμῶν δέομαι δίκαιον, ὥς γ' ἐμοὶ δοκῶ, τὸν μὲν
τρόπον τῆς λέξεως ἐᾶν—ἴσως μὲν γὰρ χείρων, ἴσως δὲ
βελτίων ἂν εἴη—, αὐτὸ δὲ τοῦτο σκοπεῖν καὶ τούτῳ τὸν 35
νοῦν προσέχειν, εἰ δίκαια λέγω ἢ μή· δικαστοῦ μὲν γὰρ
αὕτη ἀρετή, ῥήτορος δὲ τἀληθῆ λέγειν.

Πρῶτον μὲν οὖν δίκαιός εἰμι ἀπολογήσασθαι, ὦ ἄνδρες
Ἀθηναῖοι, πρὸς τὰ πρῶτά μου [ψευδῆ] κατηγορημένα
40 καὶ τοὺς πρώτους κατηγόρους, ἔπειτα δὲ πρὸς τὰ ὕστερα
καὶ τοὺς ὑστέρους. Ἐμοῦ γὰρ πολλοὶ κατήγοροι γεγό- B
νασι πρὸς ὑμᾶς, καὶ πάλαι πολλὰ ἤδη ἔτη καὶ οὐδὲν
ἀληθὲς λέγοντες· οὓς ἐγὼ μᾶλλον φοβοῦμαι ἢ τοὺς ἀμφὶ
Ἄνυτον, καίπερ ὄντας καὶ τούτους δεινούς. ἀλλ' ἐκεῖνοι
45 δεινότεροι, ὦ ἄνδρες, οἳ ὑμῶν τοὺς πολλοὺς ἐκ παίδων
παραλαμβάνοντες ἔπειθόν τε καὶ κατηγόρουν ἐμοῦ μᾶλλον
οὐδὲν ἀληθές, ὡς ἔστι τις Σωκράτης, σοφὸς ἀνήρ, τά
τε μετέωρα φροντιστὴς καὶ τὰ ὑπὸ γῆς ἅπαντα ἀνεζητη-
κὼς καὶ τὸν ἥττω λόγον κρείττω ποιῶν. οὗτοι, ὦ ἄνδρες
50 Ἀθηναῖοι, οἱ ταύτην τὴν φήμην κατασκεδάσαντες, οἱ C
δεινοί εἰσί μου κατήγοροι· οἱ γὰρ ἀκούοντες ἡγοῦνται
τοὺς ταῦτα ζητοῦντας οὐδὲ θεοὺς νομίζειν. ἔπειτά εἰσιν
οὗτοι οἱ κατήγοροι πολλοὶ καὶ πολὺν χρόνον ἤδη κατηγο-
ρηκότες, ἔτι δὲ καὶ ἐν ταύτῃ τῇ ἡλικίᾳ λέγοντες πρὸς
55 ὑμᾶς, ἐν ᾗ ἂν μάλιστα ἐπιστεύσατε, παῖδες ὄντες, ἔνιοι
δ' ὑμῶν καὶ μειράκια, ἀτεχνῶς ἐρήμην κατηγοροῦντες
ἀπολογουμένου οὐδενός· ὃ δὲ πάντων ἀλογώτατον, ὅτι
οὐδὲ τὰ ὀνόματα οἷόν τε αὐτῶν εἰδέναι καὶ εἰπεῖν, πλὴν D
εἴ τις κωμῳδιοποιὸς τυγχάνει ὤν. ὅσοι δὲ φθόνῳ καὶ δια-
60 βολῇ χρώμενοι ὑμᾶς ἀνέπειθον, οἱ δὲ καὶ αὐτοὶ πεπεισμένοι ἄλλους πείθοντες, οὗτοι πάντες ἀπορώτατοί εἰσιν·
οὐδὲ γὰρ ἀναβιβάσασθαι οἷόν τ' ἐστὶν αὐτῶν ἐνταυθοῖ
οὐδ' ἐλέγξαι οὐδένα, ἀλλ' ἀνάγκη ἀτεχνῶς ὥσπερ σκια-
μαχεῖν ἀπολογούμενόν τε καὶ ἐλέγχοντα μηδενὸς ἀπο-
65 κρινομένου. Ἀξιώσατε οὖν καὶ ὑμεῖς, ὥσπερ ἐγὼ λέγω,
διττούς μου τοὺς κατηγόρους γεγονέναι, ἑτέρους μὲν
τοὺς ἄρτι κατηγορήσαντας, ἑτέρους δὲ τοὺς πάλαι, οὓς E
ἐγὼ λέγω. καὶ οἰήθητε δεῖν πρὸς ἐκείνους πρῶτόν με

ἀπολογήσασθαι· καὶ γὰρ ὑμεῖς ἐκείνων πρότερον ἠκούσατε κατηγορούντων, καὶ πολὺ μᾶλλον ἢ τῶνδε τῶν ὕστε- 70 ρον.

Εἶεν· ἀπολογητέον δή, ὦ ἄνδρες Ἀθηναῖοι, καὶ ἐπι-
19 χειρητέον ὑμῶν ἐξελέσθαι τὴν διαβολήν, ἣν ὑμεῖς ἐν πολλῷ χρόνῳ ἔσχετε, ταύτην ἐν οὕτως ὀλίγῳ χρόνῳ. βουλοίμην μὲν οὖν ἂν τοῦτο οὕτω γενέσθαι, εἴ τι ἄμεινον 75 καὶ ὑμῖν καὶ ἐμοί, καὶ πλέον τί με ποιῆσαι ἀπολογού- μενον· οἶμαι δὲ αὐτὸ χαλεπὸν εἶναι, καὶ οὐ πάνυ με λανθάνει οἷόν ἐστιν. ὅμως δὲ τοῦτο μὲν ἴτω ὅπῃ τῷ θεῷ φίλον, τῷ δὲ νόμῳ πειστέον καὶ ἀπολο- γητέον. 80

Ἀναλάβωμεν οὖν ἐξ ἀρχῆς, τίς ἡ κατηγορία ἐστίν, ἐξ
B ἧς ἡ ἐμὴ διαβολὴ γέγονεν, ᾗ δὴ καὶ πιστεύων Μέλητός με ἐγράψατο τὴν γραφὴν ταύτην. Εἶεν· τί δὴ λέγοντες διέβαλλον οἱ διαβάλλοντες; ὥσπερ οὖν κατηγόρων τὴν ἀντωμοσίαν δεῖ ἀναγνῶναι αὐτῶν. Σωκράτης ἀδικεῖ 85 καὶ περιεργάζεται ζητῶν τά τε ὑπὸ γῆς καὶ οὐράνια, καὶ τὸν ἥττω λόγον κρείττω ποιῶν, καὶ
C ἄλλους ταὐτὰ ταῦτα διδάσκων. Τοιαύτη τίς ἐστι· ταῦτα γὰρ ἑωρᾶτε καὶ αὐτοὶ ἐν τῇ Ἀριστοφάνους κωμῳ- δίᾳ, Σωκράτη τινὰ ἐκεῖ περιφερόμενον, φάσκοντά τε 90 ἀεροβατεῖν καὶ ἄλλην πολλὴν φλυαρίαν φλυαροῦντα, ὧν ἐγὼ οὐδὲν οὔτε μέγα οὔτε σμικρὸν πέρι ἐπαΐω. καὶ οὐχ ὡς ἀτιμάζων λέγω τὴν τοιαύτην ἐπιστήμην, εἴ τις περὶ τῶν τοιούτων σοφός ἐστι· μή πως ἐγὼ ὑπὸ Μελήτου τοσαύτας δίκας φύγοιμι· ἀλλὰ γὰρ ἐμοὶ τούτων, ὦ ἄνδρες 95
D Ἀθηναῖοι, οὐδὲν μέτεστι. μάρτυρας δ' αὐτοὺς ὑμῶν τοὺς πολλοὺς παρέχομαι, καὶ ἀξιῶ ὑμᾶς ἀλλήλους διδάσκειν τε καὶ φράζειν, ὅσοι ἐμοῦ πώποτε ἀκηκόατε διαλεγομένου· πολλοὶ δὲ ὑμῶν οἱ τοιοῦτοί εἰσι. φράζετε οὖν ἀλλήλοις,

100 εἰ πώποτε ἢ σμικρὸν ἢ μέγα ἤκουσέ τις ὑμῶν ἐμοῦ περὶ
τῶν τοιούτων διαλεγομένου· καὶ ἐκ τούτου γνώσεσθε ὅτι
τοιαῦτ' ἐστὶ καὶ τᾶλλα περὶ ἐμοῦ ἃ οἱ πολλοὶ λέγουσιν.

Ἀλλὰ γὰρ οὔτε τούτων οὐδέν ἐστιν, οὐδέ γ' εἴ τινος
ἀκηκόατε ὡς ἐγὼ παιδεύειν ἐπιχειρῶ ἀνθρώπους καὶ
105 χρήματα πράττομαι, οὐδὲ τοῦτο ἀληθές. ἐπεὶ καὶ τοῦτό Ε
γέ μοι δοκεῖ καλὸν εἶναι, εἴ τις οἷός τ' εἴη παιδεύειν
ἀνθρώπους ὥσπερ Γοργίας τε ὁ Λεοντῖνος καὶ Πρόδικος ὁ
Κεῖος καὶ Ἱππίας ὁ Ἠλεῖος. τούτων γὰρ ἕκαστος, ὦ
ἄνδρες, [οἷός τ' ἐστὶν] ἰὼν εἰς ἑκάστην τῶν πόλεων
110 τοὺς νέους, οἷς ἔξεστι τῶν ἑαυτῶν πολιτῶν προῖκα
ξυνεῖναι ᾧ ἂν βούλωνται, τούτους πείθουσι τὰς ἐκείνων
ξυνουσίας ἀπολιπόντας σφίσι ξυνεῖναι χρήματα διδόντας 20
καὶ χάριν προσειδέναι. ἐπεὶ καὶ ἄλλος ἀνήρ ἐστι Πάριος
ἐνθάδε σοφός, ὃν ἐγὼ ᾐσθόμην ἐπιδημοῦντα· ἔτυχον γὰρ
115 προσελθὼν ἀνδρὶ ὃς τετέλεκε χρήματα σοφισταῖς πλείω
ἢ ξύμπαντες οἱ ἄλλοι, Καλλίᾳ τῷ Ἱππονίκου. τοῦτον
οὖν ἀνηρόμην—ἐστὸν γὰρ αὐτῷ δύο υἱέε—Ὦ Καλλία, ἦν
δ' ἐγώ, εἰ μέν σου τὼ υἱέε πώλω ἢ μόσχω ἐγενέσθην,
εἴχομεν ἂν αὐτοῖν ἐπιστάτην λαβεῖν καὶ μισθώσασθαι, ὃς
120 ἔμελλεν αὐτὼ καλώ τε κἀγαθὼ ποιήσειν τὴν προσήκουσαν Β
ἀρετήν· ἦν δ' ἂν οὗτος ἢ τῶν ἱππικῶν τις ἢ τῶν γεωρ-
γικῶν· νῦν δ' ἐπειδὴ ἀνθρώπω ἐστόν, τίνα αὐτοῖν ἐν νῷ
ἔχεις ἐπιστάτην λαβεῖν; τίς τῆς τοιαύτης ἀρετῆς, τῆς
ἀνθρωπίνης τε καὶ πολιτικῆς, ἐπιστήμων ἐστίν; οἶμαι
125 γάρ σε ἐσκέφθαι διὰ τὴν τῶν υἱέων κτῆσιν. ἔστι τις,
ἔφην ἐγώ, ἢ οὔ; Πάνυ γε, ἦ δ' ὅς. Τίς, ἦν δ' ἐγώ, καὶ
. ποδαπός; καὶ πόσου διδάσκει; Εὔηνος, ἔφη, ὦ Σώκρατες, Πάριος, πέντε μνῶν. Καὶ ἐγὼ τὸν Εὔηνον ἐμα-
κάρισα, εἰ ὡς ἀληθῶς ἔχει ταύτην τὴν τέχνην καὶ οὕτως C
130 ἐμμελῶς διδάσκει. ἐγὼ οὖν καὶ αὐτὸς ἐκαλλυνόμην τε

καὶ ἡβρυνόμην ἄν, εἰ ἠπιστάμην ταῦτα· ἀλλ' οὐ γὰρ
ἐπίσταμαι, ὦ ἄνδρες Ἀθηναῖοι.

Ὑπολάβοι ἂν οὖν τις ὑμῶν ἴσως, Ἀλλ', ὦ Σώκρατες, τὸ σὸν τί ἐστι πρᾶγμα; πόθεν αἱ διαβολαί σοι αὗται
γεγόνασιν; οὐ γὰρ δήπου σοῦ γε, οὐδὲν τῶν ἄλλων 135
περιττότερον πραγματευομένου, ἔπειτα τοσαύτη φήμη τε
καὶ λόγος γέγονεν, [εἰ μή τι ἔπραττες ἀλλοῖον ἢ οἱ πολ-
λοί]. λέγε οὖν ἡμῖν, τί ἐστιν, ἵνα μὴ ἡμεῖς περὶ σοῦ αὐ-
D τοσχεδιάζωμεν. Ταυτί μοι δοκεῖ δίκαια λέγειν ὁ λέγων,
κἀγὼ ὑμῖν πειράσομαι ἀποδεῖξαι, τί ποτ' ἔστι τοῦτο ὃ 140
ἐμοὶ πεποίηκε τό τε ὄνομα καὶ τὴν διαβολήν. ἀκούετε δή.
καὶ ἴσως μὲν δόξω τισὶν ὑμῶν παίζειν, εὖ μέντοι ἴστε·
πᾶσαν ὑμῖν τὴν ἀλήθειαν ἐρῶ. Ἐγὼ γάρ, ὦ ἄνδρες Ἀθηναῖοι, δι' οὐδὲν ἄλλ' ἢ διὰ σοφίαν τινὰ τοῦτο τὸ ὄνομα
ἔσχηκα. ποίαν δὴ σοφίαν ταύτην; ἥπερ ἐστὶν ἴσως ἀν- 145
θρωπίνη σοφία. τῷ ὄντι γὰρ κινδυνεύω ταύτην εἶναι σο-
φός· οὗτοι δὲ τάχ' ἄν, οὓς ἄρτι ἔλεγον, μείζω τινὰ ἢ
E κατ' ἄνθρωπον σοφίαν σοφοὶ εἶεν, ἢ οὐκ ἔχω τί λέγω,
οὐ γὰρ δὴ ἔγωγε αὐτὴν ἐπίσταμαι, ἀλλ' ὅστις φησὶ ψεύδεταί τε καὶ ἐπὶ διαβολῇ τῇ ἐμῇ λέγει. καί μοι, ὦ ἄν- 150
δρες Ἀθηναῖοι, μὴ θορυβήσητε, μηδὲ ἂν δόξω τι ὑμῖν
μέγα λέγειν· οὐ γὰρ ἐμὸν ἐρῶ τὸν λόγον, ὃν ἂν λέγω,
ἀλλ' εἰς ἀξιόχρεων ὑμῖν τὸν λέγοντα ἀνοίσω· τῆς γὰρ ἐμῆς,
εἰ δή τίς ἐστι σοφία καὶ οἵα, μάρτυρα ὑμῖν παρέξομαι
τὸν θεὸν τὸν ἐν Δελφοῖς. Χαιρεφῶντα γὰρ ἴστε που. οὗ- 155
21 τος ἐμός τε ἑταῖρος ἦν ἐκ νέου, καὶ ὑμῶν τῷ πλήθει
ἑταῖρός τε καὶ ξυνέφυγε τὴν φυγὴν ταύτην καὶ μεθ' ὑμῶν
κατῆλθε. καὶ ἴστε δὴ οἷος ἦν Χαιρεφῶν, ὡς σφοδρὸς ἐφ'
ὅ τι ὁρμήσειε. καὶ δή ποτε καὶ εἰς Δελφοὺς ἐλθὼν ἐτόλ-
μησε τοῦτο μαντεύσασθαι,—καί, ὅπερ λέγω, μὴ θορυ- 160
βεῖτε, ὦ ἄνδρες· ἤρετο γὰρ δή, εἴ τις ἐμοῦ εἴη σοφώτε-

ρος. ἀνεῖλεν οὖν ἡ Πυθία μηδένα σοφώτερον εἶναι. καὶ
τούτων πέρι ὁ ἀδελφὸς ὑμῖν αὐτοῦ οὑτοσὶ μαρτυρήσει,
ἐπειδὴ ἐκεῖνος τετελεύτηκεν.

165 Σκέψασθε δὴ ὧν ἔνεκα ταῦτα λέγω· μέλλω γὰρ ὑμᾶς B
διδάξειν, ὅθεν μοι ἡ διαβολὴ γέγονε. ταῦτα γὰρ ἐγὼ
ἀκούσας ἐνεθυμούμην οὑτωσί, Τί ποτε λέγει ὁ θεός, καὶ
τί ποτε αἰνίττεται; ἐγὼ γὰρ δὴ οὔτε μέγα οὔτε σμικρὸν
ξύνοιδα ἐμαυτῷ σοφὸς ὤν· τί οὖν ποτὲ λέγει φάσκων
170 ἐμὲ σοφώτατον εἶναι; οὐ γὰρ δήπου ψεύδεταί γε· οὐ γὰρ
θέμις αὐτῷ. καὶ πολὺν μὲν χρόνον ἠπόρουν, τί ποτε λέγει, ἔπειτα μόγις πάνυ ἐπὶ ζήτησιν αὐτοῦ τοιαύτην τινὰ
ἐτραπόμην. ἦλθον ἐπί τινα τῶν δοκούντων σοφῶν εἶναι,
ὡς ἐνταῦθα, εἴ πέρ που, ἐλέγξων τὸ μαντεῖον καὶ ἀπο- C
175 φανῶν τῷ χρησμῷ ὅτι Οὑτοσὶ ἐμοῦ σοφώτερός ἐστι, σὺ
δ᾽ ἐμὲ ἔφησθα. διασκοπῶν οὖν τοῦτον—ὀνόματι γὰρ
οὐδὲν δέομαι λέγειν, ἦν δέ τις τῶν πολιτικῶν, πρὸς ὃν
ἐγὼ σκοπῶν τοιοῦτόν τι ἔπαθον, ὦ ἄνδρες Ἀθηναῖοι—
καὶ διαλεγόμενος αὐτῷ, ἔδοξέ μοι οὗτος ὁ ἀνὴρ δοκεῖν
180 μὲν εἶναι σοφὸς ἄλλοις τε πολλοῖς ἀνθρώποις καὶ μάλιστα
ἑαυτῷ, εἶναι δ᾽ οὔ. κἄπειτα ἐπειρώμην αὐτῷ δεικνύναι,
ὅτι οἴοιτο μὲν εἶναι σοφός, εἴη δ᾽ οὔ. ἐντεῦθεν οὖν τούτῳ D
τε ἀπηχθόμην καὶ πολλοῖς τῶν παρόντων, πρὸς ἐμαυτὸν
δ᾽ οὖν ἀπιὼν ἐλογιζόμην ὅτι Τούτου μὲν τοῦ ἀνθρώπου
185 ἐγὼ σοφώτερός εἰμι· κινδυνεύει μὲν γὰρ ἡμῶν οὐδέτερος
οὐδὲν καλὸν κἀγαθὸν εἰδέναι, ἀλλ᾽ οὗτος μὲν οἴεταί τι
εἰδέναι οὐκ εἰδώς, ἐγὼ δέ, ὥσπερ οὖν οὐκ οἶδα, οὐδὲ
οἴομαι. ἔοικα γοῦν τούτου γε σμικρῷ τινι αὐτῷ τούτῳ
σοφώτερος εἶναι, ὅτι ἃ μὴ οἶδα οὐδὲ οἴομαι εἰδέναι. ἐν-
190 τεῦθεν ἐπ᾽ ἄλλον ᾖα τῶν ἐκείνου δοκούντων σοφωτέρων
εἶναι, καί μοι ταὐτὰ ταῦτα ἔδοξε· καὶ ἐνταῦθα κἀκείνῳ E
καὶ ἄλλοις πολλοῖς ἀπηχθόμην.

Μετὰ ταῦτ᾽ οὖν ἤδη ἐφεξῆς ᾖα, αἰσθανόμενος μὲν καὶ λυπούμενος καὶ δεδιὼς ὅτι ἀπηχθανόμην, ὅμως δὲ ἀναγκαῖον ἐδόκει εἶναι τὸ τοῦ θεοῦ περὶ πλείστου ποιεῖσθαι· 195 ἰτέον οὖν, σκοποῦντι τὸν χρησμὸν τί λέγει, ἐπὶ ἅπαντας τούς τι δοκοῦντας εἰδέναι. καὶ νὴ τὸν κύνα, ὦ ἄνδρες 22 Ἀθηναῖοι,—δεῖ γὰρ πρὸς ὑμᾶς τἀληθῆ λέγειν—ἦ μὴν ἐγὼ ἔπαθόν τι τοιοῦτον. οἱ μὲν μάλιστα εὐδοκιμοῦντες ἔδοξάν μοι ὀλίγου δεῖν τοῦ πλείστου ἐνδεεῖς εἶναι ζητοῦντι 200 κατὰ τὸν θεόν, ἄλλοι δὲ δοκοῦντες φαυλότεροι ἐπιεικέστεροι εἶναι ἄνδρες πρὸς τὸ φρονίμως ἔχειν. δεῖ δὴ ὑμῖν τὴν ἐμὴν πλάνην ἐπιδεῖξαι, ὥσπερ πόνους τινὰς πονοῦντος, ἵνα μοι καὶ ἀνέλεγκτος ἡ μαντεία γένοιτο. Μετὰ γὰρ τοὺς πολιτικοὺς ᾖα ἐπὶ τοὺς ποιητὰς τούς τε τῶν τραγῳ- 205 B διῶν καὶ τοὺς τῶν διθυράμβων καὶ τοὺς ἄλλους, ὡς ἐνταῦθα ἐπ᾽ αὐτοφώρῳ καταληψόμενος ἐμαυτὸν ἀμαθέστερον ἐκείνων ὄντα. ἀναλαμβάνων οὖν αὐτῶν τὰ ποιήματα, ἅ μοι ἐδόκει μάλιστα πεπραγματεῦσθαι αὐτοῖς, διηρώτων ἂν αὐτοὺς τί λέγοιεν, ἵν᾽ ἅμα τι καὶ μανθάνοιμι παρ᾽ αὐτῶν. 210 αἰσχύνομαι οὖν ὑμῖν εἰπεῖν, ὦ ἄνδρες, τἀληθῆ· ὅμως δὲ ῥητέον. ὡς ἔπος γὰρ εἰπεῖν, ὀλίγου αὐτῶν ἅπαντες οἱ παρόντες ἂν βέλτιον ἔλεγον περὶ ὧν αὐτοὶ ἐπεποιήκεσαν. ἔγνων οὖν καὶ περὶ τῶν ποιητῶν ἐν ὀλίγῳ τοῦτο, ὅτι οὐ C σοφίᾳ ποιοῖεν ἃ ποιοῖεν, ἀλλὰ φύσει τινὶ καὶ ἐνθουσιά- 215 ζοντες, ὥσπερ οἱ θεομάντεις καὶ οἱ χρησμῳδοί· καὶ γὰρ οὗτοι λέγουσι μὲν πολλὰ καὶ καλά, ἴσασι δὲ οὐδὲν ὧν λέγουσι· τοιοῦτόν τί μοι ἐφάνησαν πάθος καὶ οἱ ποιηταὶ πεπονθότες. καὶ ἅμα ᾐσθόμην αὐτῶν διὰ τὴν ποίησιν οἰομένων καὶ τἆλλα σοφωτάτων εἶναι ἀνθρώπων, ἃ οὐκ 220 ἦσαν. ἀπῇα οὖν καὶ ἐντεῦθεν, τῷ αὐτῷ οἰόμενος περιγεγονέναι, ὧπερ καὶ τῶν πολιτικῶν.

Τελευτῶν οὖν ἐπὶ τοὺς χειροτέχνας ᾖα· ἐμαυτῷ γὰρ

ξυνῄδειν οὐδὲν ἐπισταμένῳ, ὡς ἔπος εἰπεῖν, τούτους δέ γ' D
225 ᾔδειν ὅτι εὑρήσοιμι πολλὰ καὶ καλὰ ἐπισταμένους. καὶ
τούτου μὲν οὐκ ἐψεύσθην, ἀλλ' ἠπίσταντο ἃ ἐγὼ οὐκ
ἠπιστάμην καί μου ταύτῃ σοφώτεροι ἦσαν. ἀλλ', ὦ ἄνδρες Ἀθηναῖοι, ταὐτόν μοι ἔδοξαν ἔχειν ἁμάρτημα, ὅπερ
καὶ οἱ ποιηταί, καὶ οἱ ἀγαθοὶ δημιουργοί· διὰ τὸ τὴν
230 τέχνην καλῶς ἐξεργάζεσθαι ἕκαστος ἠξίου καὶ τἆλλα
τὰ μέγιστα σοφώτατος εἶναι, καὶ αὐτῶν αὕτη ἡ πλημμέ-
λεια ἐκείνην τὴν σοφίαν ἀπέκρυπτεν· ὥστ' ἐμὲ ἐμαυτὸν
ἀνερωτᾶν ὑπὲρ τοῦ χρησμοῦ, πότερα δεξαίμην ἂν οὕτως E
ὥσπερ ἔχω ἔχειν, μήτε τι σοφὸς ὢν τὴν ἐκείνων σοφίαν
235 μήτε ἀμαθὴς τὴν ἀμαθίαν, ἢ ἀμφότερα ἃ ἐκεῖνοι ἔχουσιν
ἔχειν. ἀπεκρινάμην οὖν ἐμαυτῷ καὶ τῷ χρησμῷ, ὅτι μοι
λυσιτελοῖ ὥσπερ ἔχω ἔχειν.

Ἐκ ταυτησὶ δὴ τῆς ἐξετάσεως, ὦ ἄνδρες Ἀθηναῖοι,
πολλαὶ μὲν ἀπέχθειαί μοι γεγόνασι καὶ οἶαι χαλεπώταται 23
240 καὶ βαρύταται, ὥστε πολλὰς διαβολὰς ἀπ' αὐτῶν γεγονέναι, ὄνομα δὲ τοῦτο λέγεσθαι, σοφὸς εἶναι. οἴονται
γάρ με ἑκάστοτε οἱ παρόντες ταῦτα αὐτὸν εἶναι σοφόν,
ἃ ἂν ἄλλον ἐξελέγξω· τὸ δὲ κινδυνεύει, ὦ ἄνδρες, τῷ
ὄντι ὁ θεὸς σοφὸς εἶναι, καὶ ἐν τῷ χρησμῷ τούτῳ τοῦτο
245 λέγειν, ὅτι ἡ ἀνθρωπίνη σοφία ὀλίγου τινὸς ἀξία ἐστὶ
καὶ οὐδενός· καὶ φαίνεται τοῦτ' οὐ λέγειν τὸν Σωκράτη,
προσκεχρῆσθαι δὲ τῷ ἐμῷ ὀνόματι, ἐμὲ παράδειγμα
ποιούμενος, ὥσπερ ἂν εἰ εἴποι ὅτι Οὗτος ὑμῶν, ὦ ἄνθρω- B
ποι, σοφώτατός ἐστιν, ὅστις ὥσπερ Σωκράτης ἔγνωκεν
250 ὅτι οὐδενὸς ἄξιός ἐστι τῇ ἀληθείᾳ πρὸς σοφίαν. ταῦτ'
οὖν ἐγὼ μὲν ἔτι καὶ νῦν περιιὼν ζητῶ καὶ ἐρευνῶ κατὰ
τὸν θεόν, καὶ τῶν ἀστῶν καὶ τῶν ξένων ἄν τινα οἴωμαι
σοφὸν εἶναι· καὶ ἐπειδάν μοι μὴ δοκῇ, τῷ θεῷ βοηθῶν
ἐνδείκνυμαι ὅτι οὐκ ἔστι σοφός. καὶ ὑπὸ ταύτης τῆς

ἀσχολίας οὔτε τι τῶν τῆς πόλεως πρᾶξαί μοι σχολὴ 255
C γέγονεν ἄξιον λόγου οὔτε τῶν οἰκείων, ἀλλ' ἐν πενίᾳ
μυρίᾳ εἰμὶ διὰ τὴν τοῦ θεοῦ λατρείαν.

Πρὸς δὲ τούτοις οἱ νέοι μοι ἐπακολουθοῦντες, οἷς
μάλιστα σχολή ἐστιν, οἱ τῶν πλουσιωτάτων, αὐτόματοι χαίρουσιν ἀκούοντες ἐξεταζομένων τῶν ἀνθρώπων, 260
καὶ αὐτοὶ πολλάκις ἐμὲ μιμοῦνται, εἶτα ἐπιχειροῦσιν ἄλλους ἐξετάζειν· κἄπειτα, οἶμαι, εὑρίσκουσι πολλὴν ἀφθονίαν οἰομένων μὲν εἰδέναι τι ἀνθρώπων, εἰδότων δὲ ὀλίγα
ἢ οὐδέν. ἐντεῦθεν οὖν οἱ ὑπ' αὐτῶν ἐξεταζόμενοι ἐμοὶ
D ὀργίζονται, ἀλλ' οὐχ αὑτοῖς, καὶ λέγουσιν ὡς Σωκράτης 265
τίς ἐστι μιαρώτατος καὶ διαφθείρει τοὺς νέους· καὶ ἐπειδάν τις αὐτοὺς ἐρωτᾷ, ὅ τι ποιῶν καὶ ὅ τι διδάσκων,
ἔχουσι μὲν οὐδὲν εἰπεῖν, ἀλλ' ἀγνοοῦσιν, ἵνα δὲ μὴ δοκῶσιν ἀπορεῖν, τὰ κατὰ πάντων τῶν φιλοσοφούντων πρό-
χειρα ταῦτα λέγουσιν, ὅτι τὰ μετέωρα καὶ τὰ ὑπὸ γῆς, 270
καὶ θεοὺς μὴ νομίζειν, καὶ τὸν ἥττω λόγον κρείττω ποιεῖν.
τὰ γὰρ ἀληθῆ, οἶμαι, οὐκ ἂν ἐθέλοιεν λέγειν, ὅτι κατά-
δηλοι γίγνονται προσποιούμενοι μὲν εἰδέναι, εἰδότες δὲ
E οὐδέν. ἅτε οὖν, οἶμαι, φιλότιμοι ὄντες καὶ σφοδροὶ καὶ
πολλοί, καὶ ξυντεταγμένως καὶ πιθανῶς λέγοντες περὶ 275
ἐμοῦ, ἐμπεπλήκασιν ὑμῶν τὰ ὦτα καὶ πάλαι καὶ σφο-
δρῶς διαβάλλοντες. ἐκ τούτων καὶ Μέλητός μοι ἐπέθετο
καὶ Ἄνυτος καὶ Λύκων, Μέλητος μὲν ὑπὲρ τῶν ποιητῶν
ἀχθόμενος, Ἄνυτος δὲ ὑπὲρ τῶν δημιουργῶν καὶ τῶν
24 πολιτικῶν, Λύκων δὲ ὑπὲρ τῶν ῥητόρων. ὥστε ὅπερ ἀρ- 280
χόμενος ἐγὼ ἔλεγον, θαυμάζοιμ' ἂν εἰ οἷός τ' εἴην ἐγὼ
ὑμῶν ταύτην τὴν διαβολὴν ἐξελέσθαι ἐν οὕτως ὀλίγῳ χρόνῳ οὕτω πολλὴν γεγονυῖαν. Ταῦτ' ἐστιν ὑμῖν, ὦ ἄνδρες
Ἀθηναῖοι, τἀληθῆ, καὶ ὑμᾶς οὔτε μέγα οὔτε σμικρὸν
ἀποκρυψάμενος ἐγὼ λέγω οὐδ' ὑποστειλάμενος. καί τοι 285

οἶδα σχεδὸν ὅτι τοῖς αὐτοῖς ἀπεχθάνομαι. ὃ καὶ τεκμήριον, ὅτι ἀληθῆ λέγω καὶ ὅτι αὕτη ἐστὶν ἡ διαβολὴ ἡ ἐμὴ
καὶ τὰ αἴτια ταῦτά ἐστι. καὶ ἐάν τε νῦν ἐάν τε αὖθις B
ζητήσητε ταῦτα, οὕτως εὑρήσετε.

290 Περὶ μὲν οὖν ὧν οἱ πρῶτοί μου κατήγοροι κατηγόρουν αὕτη ἔστω ἱκανὴ ἀπολογία πρὸς ὑμᾶς· πρὸς δὲ
Μέλητον τὸν ἀγαθόν τε καὶ φιλόπολιν, ὥς φησι, καὶ
τοὺς ὑστέρους μετὰ ταῦτα πειράσομαι ἀπολογεῖσθαι. αὖθις γὰρ δή, ὥσπερ ἑτέρων τούτων ὄντων κατηγόρων, λά-
295 βωμεν αὖ τὴν τούτων ἀντωμοσίαν. ἔχει δέ πως ὧδε· Σωκράτη φησὶν ἀδικεῖν τούς τε νέους διαφθείροντα καὶ θεοὺς
οὓς ἡ πόλις νομίζει οὐ νομίζοντα, ἕτερα δὲ δαιμόνια
καινά. τὸ μὲν δὴ ἔγκλημα τοιοῦτόν ἐστι· τούτου δὲ τοῦ C
ἐγκλήματος ἐν ἕκαστον ἐξετάσωμεν. Φησὶ γὰρ δὴ τοὺς
300 νέους ἀδικεῖν με διαφθείροντα. ἐγὼ δέ γε, ὦ ἄνδρες Ἀθηναῖοι, ἀδικεῖν φημὶ Μέλητον, ὅτι σπουδῇ χαριεντίζεται,
ῥᾳδίως εἰς ἀγῶνας καθιστὰς ἀνθρώπους, περὶ πραγμάτων
προσποιούμενος σπουδάζειν καὶ κήδεσθαι, ὧν οὐδὲν τούτῳ
πώποτε ἐμέλησεν. ὡς δὲ τοῦτο οὕτως ἔχει, πειράσομαι
305 καὶ ὑμῖν ἐπιδεῖξαι.

Καί μοι δεῦρο, ὦ Μέλητε, εἰπέ, Ἄλλο τι ἢ περὶ
πολλοῦ ποιεῖ, ὅπως ὡς βέλτιστοι οἱ νεώτεροι ἔσονται ;
Ἔγωγε. Ἴθι δὴ νῦν εἰπὲ τούτοις, τίς αὐτοὺς βελτίους D
ποιεῖ ; δῆλον γὰρ ὅτι οἶσθα, μέλον γέ σοι. τὸν μὲν γὰρ
310 διαφθείροντα ἐξευρών, ὡς φής, ἐμὲ εἰσάγεις τουτοισὶ καὶ
κατηγορεῖς· τὸν δὲ δὴ βελτίους ποιοῦντα ἴθι εἰπὲ καὶ
μήνυσον αὐτοῖς, τίς ἐστιν. ὁρᾷς, ὦ Μέλητε, ὅτι σιγᾷς καὶ
οὐκ ἔχεις εἰπεῖν ; καί τοι οὐκ αἰσχρόν σοι δοκεῖ εἶναι καὶ
ἱκανὸν τεκμήριον οὗ δὴ ἐγὼ λέγω, ὅτι σοι οὐδὲν μεμέλη-
315 κεν ; ἀλλ' εἰπέ, ὦ 'γαθέ, τίς αὐτοὺς ἀμείνους ποιεῖ ; Οἱ
νόμοι. Ἀλλ' οὐ τοῦτο ἐρωτῶ, ὦ βέλτιστε, ἀλλὰ τίς E

ἄνθρωπος, ὅστις πρῶτον καὶ αὐτὸ τοῦτο οἶδε, τοὺς νόμους·
Οὗτοι, ὦ Σώκρατες, οἱ δικασταί. Πῶς λέγεις, ὦ Μέλητε; οἶδε τοὺς νέους παιδεύειν οἷοί τέ εἰσι καὶ βελτίους
ποιεῖν; Μάλιστα. Πότερον ἅπαντες, ἢ οἱ μὲν αὐτῶν, 320
οἱ δ' οὔ; Ἅπαντες. Εὖ γε νὴ τὴν Ἥραν λέγεις, καὶ
πολλὴν ἀφθονίαν τῶν ὠφελούντων. τί δὲ δή; οἶδε οἱ
25 ἀκροαταὶ βελτίους ποιοῦσιν, ἢ οὔ; Καὶ οὗτοι. Τί δὲ
οἱ βουλευταί; Καὶ οἱ βουλευταί. Ἀλλ' ἄρα, ὦ Μέλητε,
μὴ οἱ ἐν τῇ ἐκκλησίᾳ, [οἱ ἐκκλησιασταί,] διαφθείρουσι τοὺς 325
νεωτέρους; ἢ κἀκεῖνοι βελτίους ποιοῦσιν ἅπαντες; Κἀκεῖνοι. Πάντες ἄρα, ὡς ἔοικεν, Ἀθηναῖοι καλοὺς κἀγαθοὺς
ποιοῦσι πλὴν ἐμοῦ, ἐγὼ δὲ μόνος διαφθείρω. οὕτω λέγεις;
Πάνυ σφόδρα ταῦτα λέγω. Πολλήν γ' ἐμοῦ κατέγνωκας
δυστυχίαν. καί μοι ἀπόκριναι· ἢ καὶ περὶ ἵππους οὕτω 330
B σοι δοκεῖ ἔχειν; οἱ μὲν βελτίους ποιοῦντες αὐτοὺς πάντες
ἄνθρωποι εἶναι, εἷς δέ τις ὁ διαφθείρων; ἢ τοὐναντίον
τούτου πᾶν εἷς μέν τις ὁ βελτίους οἷός τ' ὢν ποιεῖν ἢ
πάνυ ὀλίγοι, οἱ ἱππικοί· οἱ δὲ πολλοὶ ἐάνπερ ξυνῶσι καὶ
χρῶνται ἵπποις, διαφθείρουσιν; οὐχ οὕτως ἔχει, ὦ Μέ- 335
λητε, καὶ περὶ ἵππων καὶ τῶν ἄλλων ἁπάντων ζῴων;
πάντως δήπου, ἐάν τε σὺ καὶ Ἄνυτος οὐ φῆτε ἐάν τε
φῆτε· πολλὴ γὰρ ἄν τις εὐδαιμονία εἴη περὶ τοὺς νέους,
εἰ εἷς μὲν μόνος αὐτοὺς διαφθείρει, οἱ δ' ἄλλοι ὠφελοῦ-
C σιν. ἀλλὰ γάρ, ὦ Μέλητε, ἱκανῶς ἐπιδείκνυσαι ὅτι οὐδε- 340
πώποτε ἐφρόντισας τῶν νέων, καὶ σαφῶς ἀποφαίνεις τὴν
σαυτοῦ ἀμέλειαν, ὅτι οὐδέν σοι μεμέληκε περὶ ὧν ἐμὲ
εἰσάγεις.

Ἔτι δὲ ἡμῖν εἰπέ, ὦ πρὸς Διὸς Μέλητε, πότερον
ἔστιν οἰκεῖν ἄμεινον ἐν πολίταις χρηστοῖς ἢ πονηροῖς; 345
ὦ 'τᾶν, ἀπόκριναι· οὐδὲν γάρ τοι χαλεπὸν ἐρωτῶ. οὐχ
οἱ μὲν πονηροὶ κακόν τι ἐργάζονται τοὺς ἀεὶ ἐγγυτάτω

ἑαυτῶν ὄντας, οἱ δ' ἀγαθοὶ ἀγαθόν τι; Πάνυ γε. Ἔστιν
οὖν ὅστις βούλεται ὑπὸ τῶν ξυνόντων βλάπτεσθαι μᾶλ- D
350 λον ἢ ὠφελεῖσθαι; ἀπόκριναι, ὦ 'γαθέ· καὶ γὰρ ὁ νόμος
κελεύει ἀποκρίνεσθαι. ἔσθ' ὅστις βούλεται βλάπτεσθαι;
Οὐ δῆτα. Φέρε δή, πότερον ἐμὲ εἰσάγεις δεῦρο ὡς
διαφθείροντα τοὺς νεωτέρους καὶ πονηροτέρους ποιοῦντα ἑκόντα ἢ ἄκοντα; Ἑκόντα ἔγωγε. Τί δῆτα, ὦ
355 Μέλητε; τοσοῦτον σὺ ἐμοῦ σοφώτερος εἶ τηλικούτου ὄντος τηλικόσδε ὤν, ὥστε σὺ μὲν ἔγνωκας ὅτι οἱ μὲν κακοὶ
κακόν τι ἐργάζονται ἀεὶ τοὺς μάλιστα πλησίον ἑαυτῶν, E
οἱ δὲ ἀγαθοὶ ἀγαθόν· ἐγὼ δὲ δὴ εἰς τοσοῦτον ἀμαθίας
ἥκω, ὥστε καὶ τοῦτ' ἀγνοῶ, ὅτι, ἐάν τινα μοχθηρὸν ποι-
360 ήσω τῶν ξυνόντων, κινδυνεύσω κακόν τι λαβεῖν ὑπ' αὐτοῦ,
ὥστε τοῦτο τὸ τοσοῦτον κακὸν ἑκὼν ποιῶ, ὡς φῂς σύ;
ταῦτα ἐγώ σοι οὐ πείθομαι, ὦ Μέλητε, οἶμαι δὲ οὐδὲ ἄλλον
ἀνθρώπων οὐδένα· ἀλλ' ἢ οὐ διαφθείρω ἤ, εἰ διαφθείρω,
ἄκων, ὥστε σύ γε κατ' ἀμφότερα ψεύδει. εἰ δὲ ἄκων 26
365 διαφθείρω, τῶν τοιούτων [καὶ ἀκουσίων] ἁμαρτημάτων οὐ
δεῦρο νόμος εἰσάγειν ἐστίν, ἀλλ' ἰδίᾳ λαβόντα διδάσκειν
καὶ νουθετεῖν· δῆλον γὰρ ὅτι, ἐὰν μάθω, παύσομαι ὅ γε
ἄκων ποιῶ. σὺ δὲ ξυγγενέσθαι μέν μοι καὶ διδάξαι ἔφυ-
γες καὶ οὐκ ἠθέλησας, δεῦρο δὲ εἰσάγεις, οἷ νόμος ἐστὶν
370 εἰσάγειν τοὺς κολάσεως δεομένους, ἀλλ' οὐ μαθήσεως.

Ἀλλὰ γάρ, ὦ ἄνδρες Ἀθηναῖοι, τοῦτο μὲν δῆλον
ἤδη ἐστίν, ὃ ἐγὼ ἔλεγον, ὅτι Μελήτῳ τούτων οὔτε μέγα B
οὔτε σμικρὸν πώποτε ἐμέλησεν. ὅμως δὲ δὴ λέγε ἡμῖν,
πῶς με φῂς διαφθείρειν, ὦ Μέλητε, τοὺς νεωτέρους; ἢ
375 δῆλον δὴ ὅτι κατὰ τὴν γραφήν, ἣν ἐγράψω, θεοὺς διδά-
σκοντα μὴ νομίζειν οὓς ἡ πόλις νομίζει, ἕτερα δὲ δαιμόνια καινά; οὐ ταῦτα λέγεις ὅτι διδάσκων διαφθείρω;
Πάνυ μὲν οὖν σφόδρα ταῦτα λέγω. Πρὸς αὐτῶν τοίνυν,

ὦ Μέλητε, τούτων τῶν θεῶν, ὧν νῦν ὁ λόγος ἐστίν, εἰπὲ
ἔτι σαφέστερον καὶ ἐμοὶ καὶ τοῖς ἀνδράσι τουτοισί. ἐγὼ 380
C γὰρ οὐ δύναμαι μαθεῖν, πότερον λέγεις διδάσκειν με νομίζειν εἶναί τινας θεούς, καὶ αὐτὸς ἄρα νομίζω εἶναι θεοὺς
καὶ οὐκ εἰμὶ τὸ παράπαν ἄθεος οὐδὲ ταύτῃ ἀδικῶ, οὐ
μέντοι οὕσπερ γε ἡ πόλις, ἀλλ' ἑτέρους, καὶ τοῦτ' ἔστιν
ὅ μοι ἐγκαλεῖς, ὅτι ἑτέρους· ἢ παντάπασί με φῂς οὔτε 385
αὐτὸν νομίζειν θεοὺς τούς τε ἄλλους ταῦτα διδάσκειν.
Ταῦτα λέγω, ὡς τὸ παράπαν οὐ νομίζεις θεούς. Ὦ θαυ-
D μάσιε Μέλητε, ἵνα τί ταῦτα λέγεις ; οὐδὲ ἥλιον οὐδὲ σελήνην ἄρα νομίζω θεοὺς εἶναι, ὥσπερ οἱ ἄλλοι ἄνθρωποι ;
Μὰ Δί', ὦ ἄνδρες δικασταί, ἐπεὶ τὸν μὲν ἥλιον λίθον φη- 390
σὶν εἶναι, τὴν δὲ σελήνην γῆν. Ἀναξαγόρου οἴει κατηγορεῖν, ὦ φίλε Μέλητε, καὶ οὕτω καταφρονεῖς τῶνδε καὶ οἴει
αὐτοὺς ἀπείρους γραμμάτων εἶναι, ὥστε οὐκ εἰδέναι ὅτι
τὰ Ἀναξαγόρου βιβλία τοῦ Κλαζομενίου γέμει τούτων τῶν
λόγων ; καὶ δὴ καὶ οἱ νέοι ταῦτα παρ' ἐμοῦ μανθάνουσιν, 395
E ἃ ἔξεστιν ἐνίοτε, εἰ πάνυ πολλοῦ, δραχμῆς ἐκ τῆς ὀρχή-
στρας πριαμένοις Σωκράτους καταγελᾶν, ἐὰν προσποιῆται
ἑαυτοῦ εἶναι, ἄλλως τε καὶ οὕτως ἄτοπα ὄντα. ἀλλ' ὦ
πρὸς Διός, οὑτωσί σοι δοκῶ οὐδένα νομίζειν θεὸν εἶναι ;
Οὐ μέντοι μὰ Δί', οὐδ' ὁπωστιοῦν. Ἄπιστός γ' εἶ, ὦ 400
Μέλητε, καὶ ταῦτα μέντοι, ὡς ἐμοὶ δοκεῖς, σαυτῷ. ἐμοὶ μὲν
γὰρ δοκεῖ οὑτοσί, ὦ ἄνδρες Ἀθηναῖοι, πάνυ εἶναι ὑβριστὴς καὶ ἀκόλαστος, καὶ ἀτεχνῶς τὴν γραφὴν ταύτην
ὕβρει τινὶ καὶ ἀκολασίᾳ καὶ νεότητι γράψασθαι. ἔοικε
27 γὰρ ὥσπερ αἴνιγμα ξυντιθέντι διαπειρωμένῳ, Ἆρα γνώ- 405
σεται Σωκράτης ὁ σοφὸς δὴ ἐμοῦ χαριεντιζομένου καὶ
ἐναντί' ἐμαυτῷ λέγοντος, ἢ ἐξαπατήσω αὐτὸν καὶ τοὺς
ἄλλους τοὺς ἀκούοντας ; οὗτος γὰρ ἐμοὶ φαίνεται τὰ ἐναντία λέγειν αὐτὸς ἑαυτῷ ἐν τῇ γραφῇ, ὥσπερ ἂν εἰ εἴποι

410 Ἀδικεῖ Σωκράτης θεοὺς οὐ νομίζων, ἀλλὰ θεοὺς νομίζων.
καί τοι τοῦτό ἐστι παίζοντος.

Ξυνεπισκέψασθε δή, ὦ ἄνδρες, ᾗ μοι φαίνεται ταῦτα
λέγειν· σὺ δὲ ἡμῖν ἀπόκριναι, ὦ Μέλητε. ὑμεῖς δέ, ὅπερ
κατ' ἀρχὰς ὑμᾶς παρῃτησάμην, μέμνησθέ μοι μὴ θορυβεῖν, B
415 ἐὰν ἐν τῷ εἰωθότι τρόπῳ τοὺς λόγους ποιῶμαι.

Ἔστιν ὅστις ἀνθρώπων, ὦ Μέλητε, ἀνθρώπεια μὲν
νομίζει πράγματ' εἶναι, ἀνθρώπους δὲ οὐ νομίζει; ἀπο-
κρινέσθω, ὦ ἄνδρες, καὶ μὴ ἄλλα καὶ ἄλλα θορυβείτω·
ἔσθ' ὅστις ἵππους μὲν οὐ νομίζει, ἱππικὰ δὲ πράγματα;
420 ἢ αὐλητὰς μὲν οὐ νομίζει εἶναι, αὐλητικὰ δὲ πράγματα;
οὐκ ἔστιν, ὦ ἄριστε ἀνδρῶν. εἰ μὴ σὺ βούλει ἀποκρίνασθαι, ἐγὼ σοὶ λέγω καὶ τοῖς ἄλλοις τουτοισί. ἀλλὰ τὸ
ἐπὶ τούτῳ γε ἀπόκριναι. ἔσθ' ὅστις δαιμόνια μὲν νομίζει C
πράγματ' εἶναι, δαίμονας δὲ οὐ νομίζει; Οὐκ ἔστιν. Ὡς
425 ὤνησας, ὅτι μόγις ἀπεκρίνω ὑπὸ τουτωνὶ ἀναγκαζόμενος.
οὐκοῦν δαιμόνια μὲν φῄς με καὶ νομίζειν καὶ διδάσκειν,
εἴτ' οὖν καινὰ εἴτε παλαιά· ἀλλ' οὖν δαιμόνιά γε νομίζω
κατὰ τὸν σὸν λόγον, καὶ ταῦτα καὶ διωμόσω ἐν τῇ ἀντι-
γραφῇ. εἰ δὲ δαιμόνια νομίζω, καὶ δαίμονας δήπου πολλὴ
430 ἀνάγκη νομίζειν μέ ἐστιν. οὐχ οὕτως ἔχει; ἔχει δή· τίθημι
γάρ σε ὁμολογοῦντα, ἐπειδὴ οὐκ ἀποκρίνει. τοὺς δὲ δαίμονας οὐχὶ ἤτοι θεούς γε ἡγούμεθα ἢ θεῶν παῖδας; D
φῂς ἢ οὔ; Πάνυ γε. Οὐκοῦν εἴπερ δαίμονας ἡγοῦμαι,
ὡς σὺ φῄς, εἰ μὲν θεοί τινές εἰσιν οἱ δαίμονες, τοῦτ'
435 ἂν εἴη ὃ ἐγώ φημί σε αἰνίττεσθαι καὶ χαριεντίζεσθαι,
θεοὺς οὐχ ἡγούμενον φάναι ἐμὲ θεοὺς αὖ ἡγεῖσθαι πάλιν,
ἐπειδήπερ γε δαίμονας ἡγοῦμαι· εἰ δ' αὖ οἱ δαίμονες
θεῶν παῖδές εἰσι νόθοι τινὲς ἢ ἐκ νυμφῶν ἢ ἔκ τινων
ἄλλων, ὧν δὴ καὶ λέγονται, τίς ἂν ἀνθρώπων θεῶν
440 μὲν παῖδας ἡγοῖτο εἶναι, θεοὺς δὲ μή; ὁμοίως γὰρ ἂν

E ἄτοπον εἴη, ὥσπερ ἂν εἴ τις ἵππων μὲν παῖδας ἡγοῖτο
ἢ καὶ ὄνων [τοὺς ἡμιόνους], ἵππους δὲ καὶ ὄνους μὴ
ἡγοῖτο εἶναι. ἀλλ', ὦ Μέλητε, οὐκ ἔστιν ὅπως σὺ ταῦτα
οὐχὶ ἀποπειρώμενος ἡμῶν ἐγράψω [τὴν γραφὴν ταύτην],
ἢ ἀπορῶν ὅ τι ἐγκαλοῖς ἐμοὶ ἀληθὲς ἀδίκημα· ὅπως δὲ σύ 445
τινα πείθοις ἂν καὶ σμικρὸν νοῦν ἔχοντα ἀνθρώπων, ὡς
οὐ τοῦ αὐτοῦ ἐστὶ καὶ δαιμόνια καὶ θεῖα ἡγεῖσθαι, καὶ
28 αὖ τοῦ αὐτοῦ μήτε δαίμονας μήτε θεοὺς μήτε ἥρωας,
οὐδεμία μηχανή ἐστιν.

   'Αλλὰ γάρ, ὦ ἄνδρες 'Αθηναῖοι, ὡς μὲν ἐγὼ οὐκ 450
ἀδικῶ κατὰ τὴν Μελήτου γραφήν, οὐ πολλῆς μοι δοκεῖ
εἶναι ἀπολογίας, ἀλλ' ἱκανὰ καὶ ταῦτα· ὃ δὲ καὶ ἐν τοῖς
ἔμπροσθεν ἔλεγον, ὅτι πολλή μοι ἀπέχθεια γέγονε καὶ
πρὸς πολλούς, εὖ ἴστε ὅτι ἀληθές ἐστι. καὶ τοῦτ' ἔστιν ὃ
ἐμὲ αἱρήσει, ἐάνπερ αἱρῇ, οὐ Μέλητος οὐδὲ 'Άνυτος, ἀλλ' 455
ἡ τῶν πολλῶν διαβολή τε καὶ φθόνος. ἃ δὴ πολλοὺς καὶ
ἄλλους καὶ ἀγαθοὺς ἄνδρας ᾕρηκεν, οἶμαι δὲ καὶ αἱρήσειν·
B οὐδὲν δὲ δεινόν, μὴ ἐν ἐμοὶ στῇ.

   ῎Ισως δ' ἂν οὖν εἴποι τις, Εἶτ' οὐκ αἰσχύνει, ὦ Σώκρατες, τοιοῦτον ἐπιτήδευμα ἐπιτηδεύσας, ἐξ οὗ κινδυ- 460
νεύεις νυνὶ ἀποθανεῖν; 'Εγὼ δὲ τούτῳ ἂν δίκαιον λόγον
ἀντείποιμι, ὅτι Οὐ καλῶς λέγεις, ὦ ἄνθρωπε, εἰ οἴει
δεῖν κίνδυνον ὑπολογίζεσθαι τοῦ ζῆν ἢ τεθνάναι ἄνδρα
ὅτου τι καὶ σμικρὸν ὄφελός ἐστιν, ἀλλ' οὐκ ἐκεῖνο μόνον
σκοπεῖν, ὅταν πράττῃ, πότερα δίκαια ἢ ἄδικα πράττει, 465
καὶ ἀνδρὸς ἀγαθοῦ ἔργα ἢ κακοῦ. φαῦλοι γὰρ ἂν τῷ
C γε σῷ λόγῳ εἶεν τῶν ἡμιθέων ὅσοι ἐν Τροίᾳ τετελευτή-
κασιν, οἵ τε ἄλλοι καὶ ὁ τῆς Θέτιδος υἱός, ὃς τοσοῦτον
τοῦ κινδύνου κατεφρόνησε παρὰ τὸ αἰσχρόν τι ὑπομεῖναι,
ὥστε ἐπειδὴ εἶπεν ἡ μήτηρ αὐτῷ προθυμουμένῳ ῞Εκτορα 470
ἀποκτεῖναι, θεὸς οὖσα, οὑτωσί πως, ὡς ἐγᾦμαι, ῏Ω παῖ,

εἰ τιμωρήσεις Πατρόκλῳ τῷ ἑταίρῳ τὸν φόνον καὶ Ἕκτορα ἀποκτενεῖς, αὐτὸς ἀποθανεῖ· αὐτίκα γάρ τοι,
φησί, μεθ᾽ Ἕκτορα πότμος ἑτοῖμος· ὁ δὲ ταῦτ᾽
475 ἀκούσας τοῦ μὲν θανάτου καὶ τοῦ κινδύνου ὠλιγώρησε,
πολὺ δὲ μᾶλλον δείσας τὸ ζῆν κακὸς ὢν καὶ τοῖς φίλοις D
μὴ τιμωρεῖν, Αὐτίκα, φησί, τεθναίην δίκην ἐπιθεὶς
τῷ ἀδικοῦντι, ἵνα μὴ ἐνθάδε μένω καταγέλαστος παρὰ
νηυσὶ κορωνίσιν, ἄχθος ἀρούρης. μὴ αὐτὸν οἴει
480 φροντίσαι θανάτου καὶ κινδύνου; οὕτω γὰρ ἔχει, ὦ
ἄνδρες Ἀθηναῖοι, τῇ ἀληθείᾳ· οὗ ἄν τις ἑαυτὸν τάξῃ
[ἢ] ἡγησάμενος βέλτιστον εἶναι ἢ ὑπ᾽ ἄρχοντος ταχθῇ,
ἐνταῦθα δεῖ, ὡς ἐμοὶ δοκεῖ, μένοντα κινδυνεύειν, μηδὲν
ὑπολογιζόμενον μήτε θάνατον μήτε ἄλλο μηδὲν πρὸ τοῦ
485 αἰσχροῦ.

Ἐγὼ οὖν δεινὰ ἂν εἴην εἰργασμένος, ὦ ἄνδρες Ἀθηναῖοι, εἰ, ὅτε μέν με οἱ ἄρχοντες ἔταττον, οὓς ὑμεῖς E
εἵλεσθε ἄρχειν μου, καὶ ἐν Ποτιδαίᾳ καὶ ἐν Ἀμφιπόλει
καὶ ἐπὶ Δηλίῳ, τότε μὲν οὗ ἐκεῖνοι ἔταττον ἔμενον
490 ὥσπερ καὶ ἄλλος τις καὶ ἐκινδύνευον ἀποθανεῖν, τοῦ δὲ
θεοῦ τάττοντος, ὡς ἐγὼ ᾠήθην τε καὶ ὑπέλαβον, φιλο-
σοφοῦντά με δεῖν ζῆν καὶ ἐξετάζοντα ἐμαυτὸν καὶ τοὺς
ἄλλους, ἐνταῦθα δὲ φοβηθεὶς ἢ θάνατον ἢ ἄλλο ὁτιοῦν 29
πρᾶγμα λίποιμι τὴν τάξιν. δεινὸν μέντ᾽ ἂν εἴη, καὶ ὡς
495 ἀληθῶς τότ᾽ ἄν με δικαίως εἰσάγοι τις εἰς δικαστήριον,
ὅτι οὐ νομίζω θεοὺς εἶναι ἀπειθῶν τῇ μαντείᾳ καὶ δεδιὼς θάνατον καὶ οἰόμενος σοφὸς εἶναι οὐκ ὤν. τὸ γάρ
τοι θάνατον δεδιέναι, ὦ ἄνδρες, οὐδὲν ἄλλο ἐστὶν ἢ
δοκεῖν σοφὸν εἶναι μὴ ὄντα· δοκεῖν γὰρ εἰδέναι ἐστὶν ἃ
500 οὐκ οἶδεν· οἶδε μὲν γὰρ οὐδεὶς τὸν θάνατον οὐδ᾽ εἰ τυγχάνει τῷ ἀνθρώπῳ πάντων μέγιστον ὂν τῶν ἀγαθῶν,
δεδίασι δ᾽ ὡς εὖ εἰδότες ὅτι μέγιστον τῶν κακῶν ἐστί.

Β καὶ τοῦτο πῶς οὐκ ἀμαθία ἐστὶν αὕτη ἡ ἐπονείδιστος, ἡ
τοῦ οἴεσθαι εἰδέναι ἃ οὐκ οἶδεν ; ἐγὼ δέ, ὦ ἄνδρες, τούτῳ
καὶ ἐνταῦθα ἴσως διαφέρω τῶν πολλῶν ἀνθρώπων, καὶ 505
εἰ δή τῳ σοφώτερός του φαίην εἶναι, τούτῳ ἄν, ὅτι
οὐκ εἰδὼς ἱκανῶς περὶ τῶν ἐν Ἅιδου οὕτω καὶ οἴομαι
οὐκ εἰδέναι, τὸ δὲ ἀδικεῖν καὶ ἀπειθεῖν τῷ βελτίονι, καὶ
θεῷ καὶ ἀνθρώπῳ, ὅτι κακὸν καὶ αἰσχρόν ἐστιν οἶδα.
πρὸ οὖν τῶν κακῶν, ὧν οἶδα ὅτι κακά ἐστιν, ἃ μὴ οἶδα 510
εἰ ἀγαθὰ ὄντα τυγχάνει, οὐδέποτε φοβήσομαι οὐδὲ φεύ-
C ξομαι. ὥστε οὐδ᾽ εἴ με νῦν ὑμεῖς ἀφίετε ᾿Ανύτῳ ἀπιστή-
σαντες, ὃς ἔφη ἢ τὴν ἀρχὴν οὐ δεῖν ἐμὲ δεῦρο εἰσελθεῖν
ἤ, ἐπειδὴ εἰσῆλθον, οὐχ οἷόν τε εἶναι τὸ μὴ ἀποκτεῖναί
με, λέγων πρὸς ὑμᾶς ὡς, εἰ διαφευξοίμην, ἤδη ἂν ὑμῶν 515
οἱ υἱεῖς ἐπιτηδεύοντες ἃ Σωκράτης διδάσκει πάντες παντάπασι διαφθαρήσονται,—εἴ μοι πρὸς ταῦτα εἴποιτε
Ὦ Σώκρατες, νῦν μὲν ᾿Ανύτῳ οὐ πεισόμεθα, ἀλλ᾽ ἀφίεμέν
σε, ἐπὶ τούτῳ μέντοι, ἐφ᾽ ᾧτε μηκέτι ἐν ταύτῃ τῇ ζητήσει διατρίβειν μηδὲ φιλοσοφεῖν· ἐὰν δὲ ἁλῷς ἔτι τοῦτο 520
D πράττων, ἀποθανεῖ· εἰ οὖν με, ὅπερ εἶπον, ἐπὶ τούτοις
ἀφίοιτε, εἴποιμ᾽ ἂν ὑμῖν ὅτι ᾿Εγὼ ὑμᾶς, ἄνδρες ᾿Αθη-
ναῖοι, ἀσπάζομαι μὲν καὶ φιλῶ, πείσομαι δὲ μᾶλλον τῷ
θεῷ ἢ ὑμῖν, καὶ ἕωσπερ ἂν ἐμπνέω καὶ οἷός τε ὦ, οὐ
μὴ παύσωμαι φιλοσοφῶν καὶ ὑμῖν παρακελευόμενός τε καὶ 525
ἐνδεικνύμενος ὅτῳ ἂν ἀεὶ ἐντυγχάνω ὑμῶν, λέγων οἷάπερ
εἴωθα, ὅτι Ὦ ἄριστε ἀνδρῶν, ᾿Αθηναῖος ὤν, πόλεως τῆς
μεγίστης καὶ εὐδοκιμωτάτης εἰς σοφίαν καὶ ἰσχύν, χρημάτων μὲν οὐκ αἰσχύνει ἐπιμελούμενος, ὅπως σοι ἔσται ὡς
E πλεῖστα, καὶ δόξης καὶ τιμῆς, φρονήσεως δὲ καὶ ἀληθείας 530
καὶ τῆς ψυχῆς, ὅπως ὡς βελτίστη ἔσται, οὐκ ἐπιμελεῖ οὐδὲ
φροντίζεις ; καὶ ἐάν τις ὑμῶν ἀμφισβητῇ καὶ φῇ ἐπιμελεῖσθαι, οὐκ εὐθὺς ἀφήσω αὐτὸν οὐδ᾽ ἄπειμι, ἀλλ᾽ ἐρή-

σομαι αὐτὸν καὶ ἐξετάσω καὶ ἐλέγξω, καὶ ἐάν μοι μὴ δοκῇ
535 κεκτῆσθαι ἀρετήν, φάναι δέ, ὀνειδιῶ ὅτι τὰ πλείστου ἄξια
περὶ ἐλαχίστου ποιεῖται, τὰ δὲ φαυλότερα περὶ πλείονος. 30
ταῦτα καὶ νεωτέρῳ καὶ πρεσβυτέρῳ, ὅτῳ ἂν ἐντυγχάνω,
ποιήσω, καὶ ξένῳ καὶ ἀστῷ, μᾶλλον δὲ τοῖς ἀστοῖς, ὅσῳ
μου ἐγγυτέρω ἐστὲ γένει. ταῦτα γὰρ κελεύει ὁ θεός, εὖ
540 ἴστε. καὶ ἐγὼ οἴομαι οὐδέν πω ὑμῖν μεῖζον ἀγαθὸν γενέσθαι ἐν τῇ πόλει ἢ τὴν ἐμὴν τῷ θεῷ ὑπηρεσίαν. οὐδὲν
γὰρ ἄλλο πράττων ἐγὼ περιέρχομαι ἢ πείθων ὑμῶν καὶ
νεωτέρους καὶ πρεσβυτέρους μήτε σωμάτων ἐπιμελεῖσθαι
μήτε χρημάτων πρότερον μηδὲ οὕτω σφόδρα ὡς τῆς ψυ- B
545 χῆς, ὅπως ὡς ἀρίστη ἔσται, λέγων ὅτι οὐκ ἐκ χρημάτων
ἀρετὴ γίγνεται, ἀλλ᾽ ἐξ ἀρετῆς χρήματα καὶ τἆλλα ἀγαθὰ
τοῖς ἀνθρώποις ἅπαντα καὶ ἰδίᾳ καὶ δημοσίᾳ. εἰ μὲν οὖν
ταῦτα λέγων διαφθείρω τοὺς νέους, ταῦτ᾽ ἂν εἴη βλαβερά.
εἰ δέ τίς μέ φησιν ἄλλα λέγειν ἢ ταῦτα, οὐδὲν λέγει. πρὸς
550 ταῦτα, φαίην ἄν, ὦ Ἀθηναῖοι, ἢ πείθεσθε Ἀνύτῳ ἢ μή,
καὶ ἢ ἀφίετε ἢ μὴ ἀφίετε, ὡς ἐμοῦ οὐκ ἂν ποιήσοντος
ἄλλα, οὐδ᾽ εἰ μέλλω πολλάκις τεθνάναι. C

Μὴ θορυβεῖτε, ἄνδρες Ἀθηναῖοι, ἀλλ᾽ ἐμμείνατέ μοι
οἷς ἐδεήθην ὑμῶν, μὴ θορυβεῖν ἐφ᾽ οἷς ἂν λέγω, ἀλλ᾽
555 ἀκούειν· καὶ γάρ, ὡς ἐγὼ οἶμαι, ὀνήσεσθε ἀκούοντες·
μέλλω γὰρ οὖν ἄττα ὑμῖν ἐρεῖν καὶ ἄλλα, ἐφ᾽ οἷς ἴσως
βοήσεσθε. ἀλλὰ μηδαμῶς ποιεῖτε τοῦτο. Εὖ γὰρ ἴστε,
ἐὰν ἐμὲ ἀποκτείνητε τοιοῦτον ὄντα, οἷον ἐγὼ λέγω, οὐκ
ἐμὲ μείζω βλάψετε ἢ ὑμᾶς αὐτούς. ἐμὲ μὲν γὰρ οὐδὲν
560 ἂν βλάψειεν οὔτε Μέλητος οὔτε Ἄνυτος. οὐδὲ γὰρ ἂν
δύναιτο· οὐ γὰρ οἴομαι θεμιτὸν εἶναι ἀμείνονι ἀνδρὶ ὑπὸ D
χείρονος βλάπτεσθαι. ἀποκτείνειε μέντ᾽ ἂν ἴσως ἢ ἐξ-
ελάσειεν ἢ ἀτιμώσειεν. ἀλλὰ ταῦτα οὗτος ἴσως οἴεται
καὶ ἄλλος τίς που μεγάλα κακά, ἐγὼ δ᾽ οὐκ οἴομαι,

ἀλλὰ πολὺ μᾶλλον ποιεῖν ἃ οὗτος νυνὶ ποιεῖ, ἄνδρα 565
ἀδίκως ἐπιχειρεῖν ἀποκτιννύναι. νῦν οὖν, ὦ ἄνδρες Ἀθηναῖοι, πολλοῦ δέω ἐγὼ ὑπὲρ ἐμαυτοῦ ἀπολογεῖσθαι, ὥς
τις ἂν οἴοιτο, ἀλλ᾽ ὑπὲρ ὑμῶν, μή τι ἐξαμάρτητε περὶ
τὴν τοῦ θεοῦ δόσιν ὑμῖν ἐμοῦ καταψηφισάμενοι. ἐὰν γὰρ
Ε ἐμὲ ἀποκτείνητε, οὐ ῥᾳδίως ἄλλον τοιοῦτον εὑρήσετε, 570
ἀτεχνῶς, εἰ καὶ γελοιότερον εἰπεῖν, προσκείμενον τῇ πόλει
ὑπὸ τοῦ θεοῦ, ὥσπερ ἵππῳ μεγάλῳ μὲν καὶ γενναίῳ, ὑπὸ
μεγέθους δὲ νωθεστέρῳ καὶ δεομένῳ ἐγείρεσθαι ὑπὸ μύω-
πός τινος· οἷον δή μοι δοκεῖ ὁ θεὸς ἐμὲ τῇ πόλει προσ-
τεθεικέναι τοιοῦτόν τινα, ὃς ὑμᾶς ἐγείρων καὶ πείθων 575
31 καὶ ὀνειδίζων ἕνα ἕκαστον οὐδὲν παύομαι τὴν ἡμέραν
ὅλην πανταχοῦ προσκαθίζων· τοιοῦτος οὖν ἄλλος οὐ ῥᾳδίως ὑμῖν γενήσεται, ὦ ἄνδρες, ἀλλ᾽ ἐὰν ἐμοὶ πείθησθε,
φείσεσθέ μου. ὑμεῖς δ᾽ ἴσως τάχ᾽ ἂν ἀχθόμενοι, ὥσπερ
οἱ νυστάζοντες ἐγειρόμενοι, κρούσαντες ἄν με, πειθόμενοι 580
Ἀνύτῳ, ῥᾳδίως ἂν ἀποκτείναιτε, εἶτα τὸν λοιπὸν βίον
καθεύδοντες διατελοῖτ᾽ ἄν, εἰ μή τινα ἄλλον ὁ θεὸς ὑμῖν
ἐπιπέμψειε κηδόμενος ὑμῶν. ὅτι δ᾽ ἐγὼ τυγχάνω ὢν τοιοῦτος, οἷος ὑπὸ τοῦ θεοῦ τῇ πόλει δεδόσθαι, ἐνθένδε
Β ἂν κατανοήσαιτε· οὐ γὰρ ἀνθρωπίνῳ ἔοικε τὸ ἐμὲ τῶν 585
μὲν ἐμαυτοῦ ἁπάντων ἠμεληκέναι καὶ ἀνέχεσθαι τῶν οἰκείων ἀμελουμένων τοσαῦτα ἤδη ἔτη, τὸ δὲ ὑμέτερον
πράττειν ἀεί, ἰδίᾳ ἑκάστῳ προσιόντα, ὥσπερ πατέρα ἢ
ἀδελφὸν πρεσβύτερον, πείθοντα ἐπιμελεῖσθαι ἀρετῆς. καὶ
εἰ μέν[τοι] τι ἀπὸ τούτων ἀπέλαυον καὶ μισθὸν λαμ- 590
βάνων ταῦτα παρεκελευόμην, εἶχον ἄν τινα λόγον· νῦν δὲ
ὁρᾶτε δὴ καὶ αὐτοί, ὅτι οἱ κατήγοροι τἆλλα πάντα ἀναισ-
χύντως οὕτω κατηγοροῦντες τοῦτό γε οὐχ οἷοί τε ἐγέ-
C νοντο ἀπαναισχυντῆσαι, παρασχόμενοι μάρτυρα, ὡς ἐγώ
ποτέ τινα ἢ ἐπραξάμην μισθὸν ἢ ᾔτησα· ἱκανὸν γάρ, 595

οἶμαι, ἐγὼ παρέχομαι τὸν μάρτυρα, ἀληθῆ ὡς λέγω, τὴν πενίαν.

Ἴσως ἂν οὖν δόξειεν ἄτοπον εἶναι, ὅτι δὴ ἐγὼ ἰδίᾳ μὲν ταῦτα ξυμβουλεύω περιιὼν καὶ πολυπραγμονῶν, 600 δημοσίᾳ δὲ οὐ τολμῶ ἀναβαίνων εἰς τὸ πλῆθος τὸ ὑμέτερον ξυμβουλεύειν τῇ πόλει. Τούτου δὲ αἴτιόν ἐστιν ὃ ὑμεῖς ἐμοῦ πολλάκις ἀκηκόατε πολλαχοῦ λέγοντος, ὅτι μοι θεῖόν τι καὶ δαιμόνιον γίγνεται [φωνή], ὃ δὴ καὶ D ἐν τῇ γραφῇ ἐπικωμῳδῶν Μέλητος ἐγράψατο. ἐμοὶ δὲ 605 τοῦτ᾽ ἐστὶν ἐκ παιδὸς ἀρξάμενον, φωνή τις γιγνομένη, ἣ ὅταν γένηται, ἀεὶ ἀποτρέπει με τούτου, ὃ ἂν μέλλω πράττειν, προτρέπει δὲ οὔποτε· τοῦτ᾽ ἔστιν ὅ μοι ἐναντιοῦται τὰ πολιτικὰ πράττειν. καὶ παγκάλως γέ μοι δοκεῖ ἐναντιοῦσθαι· εὖ γὰρ ἴστε, ὦ ἄνδρες Ἀθηναῖοι, εἰ ἐγὼ 610 [πάλαι] ἐπεχείρησα πράττειν τὰ πολιτικὰ πράγματα, πάλαι ἂν ἀπολώλη καὶ οὔτ᾽ ἂν ὑμᾶς ὠφελήκη οὐδὲν οὔτ᾽ ἂν E ἐμαυτόν. καί μοι μὴ ἄχθεσθε λέγοντι τἀληθῆ· οὐ γὰρ ἔστιν ὅστις ἀνθρώπων σωθήσεται οὔτε ὑμῖν οὔτε ἄλλῳ πλήθει οὐδενὶ γνησίως ἐναντιούμενος καὶ διακωλύων πολλὰ ἄδικα καὶ 615 παράνομα ἐν τῇ πόλει γίγνεσθαι, ἀλλ᾽ ἀναγκαῖόν ἐστι τὸν 32 τῷ ὄντι μαχούμενον ὑπὲρ τοῦ δικαίου, καὶ εἰ μέλλει ὀλίγον χρόνον σωθήσεσθαι, ἰδιωτεύειν ἀλλὰ μὴ δημοσιεύειν.

Μεγάλα δ᾽ ἔγωγε ὑμῖν τεκμήρια παρέξομαι τούτων, οὐ λόγους, ἀλλ᾽ ὃ ὑμεῖς τιμᾶτε, ἔργα. ἀκούσατε δή 620 μου τὰ ἐμοὶ ξυμβεβηκότα, ἵν᾽ εἰδῆτε ὅτι οὐδ᾽ ἂν ἑνὶ ὑπεικάθοιμι παρὰ τὸ δίκαιον δείσας θάνατον, μὴ ὑπείκων δὲ ἅμα καὶ ἅμ᾽ ἂν ἀπολοίμην. ἐρῶ δὲ ὑμῖν φορτικὰ μὲν καὶ δικανικά, ἀληθῆ δέ. Ἐγὼ γάρ, ὦ Ἀθηναῖοι, ἄλλην μὲν ἀρχὴν οὐδεμίαν πώποτε ἦρξα ἐν τῇ πόλει, ἐβούλευσα B 625 δέ· καὶ ἔτυχεν ἡμῶν ἡ φυλὴ [Ἀντιοχὶς] πρυτανεύουσα, ὅτε ὑμεῖς τοὺς δέκα στρατηγοὺς τοὺς οὐκ ἀνελομένους τοὺς

ἐκ τῆς ναυμαχίας ἐβούλεσθε ἀθρόους κρίνειν, παρανόμως,
ὡς ἐν τῷ ὑστέρῳ χρόνῳ πᾶσιν ὑμῖν ἔδοξε. τότ᾽ ἐγὼ μόνος
τῶν πρυτάνεων ἠναντιώθην [ὑμῖν] μηδὲν ποιεῖν παρὰ τοὺς
νόμους [, καὶ ἐναντία ἐψηφισάμην]· καὶ ἑτοίμων ὄντων 630
ἐνδεικνύναι με καὶ ἀπάγειν τῶν ῥητόρων, καὶ ὑμῶν κε-
C λευόντων καὶ βοώντων, μετὰ τοῦ νόμου καὶ τοῦ δικαίου
ᾤμην μᾶλλόν με δεῖν διακινδυνεύειν ἢ μεθ᾽ ὑμῶν γενέσθαι μὴ δίκαια βουλευομένων, φοβηθέντα δεσμὸν ἢ θάνατον. καὶ ταῦτα μὲν ἦν ἔτι δημοκρατουμένης τῆς πόλεως. 635
Ἐπειδὴ δὲ ὀλιγαρχία ἐγένετο, οἱ τριάκοντα αὖ μεταπεμ-
ψάμενοί με πέμπτον αὐτὸν εἰς τὴν θόλον προσέταξαν
ἀγαγεῖν ἐκ Σαλαμῖνος Λέοντα τὸν Σαλαμίνιον, ἵν᾽ ἀπο-
θάνοι· οἷα δὴ καὶ ἄλλοις ἐκεῖνοι πολλοῖς πολλὰ προσέταττον, βουλόμενοι ὡς πλείστους ἀναπλῆσαι αἰτιῶν· τότε 640
D μέντοι ἐγὼ οὐ λόγῳ ἀλλ᾽ ἔργῳ αὖ ἐνεδειξάμην, ὅτι ἐμοὶ
θανάτου μὲν μέλει, εἰ μὴ ἀγροικότερον ἦν εἰπεῖν, οὐδ᾽
ὁτιοῦν, τοῦ δὲ μηδὲν ἄδικον μηδ᾽ ἀνόσιον ἐργάζεσθαι,
τούτου δὲ τὸ πᾶν μέλει. ἐμὲ γὰρ ἐκείνη ἡ ἀρχὴ οὐκ ἐξέ-
πληξεν οὕτως ἰσχυρὰ οὖσα, ὥστε ἄδικόν τι ἐργάσασθαι, 645
ἀλλ᾽ ἐπειδὴ ἐκ τῆς θόλου ἐξήλθομεν, οἱ μὲν τέτταρες
ᾤχοντο εἰς Σαλαμῖνα καὶ ἤγαγον Λέοντα, ἐγὼ δὲ ᾠχόμην
ἀπιὼν οἴκαδε. καὶ ἴσως ἂν διὰ ταῦτ᾽ ἀπέθανον, εἰ μὴ ἡ
E ἀρχὴ διὰ ταχέων κατελύθη· καὶ τούτων ὑμῖν ἔσονται
πολλοὶ μάρτυρες. 650

Ἆρ᾽ οὖν ἄν με οἴεσθε τοσάδε ἔτη διαγενέσθαι, εἰ
ἔπραττον τὰ δημόσια, καὶ πράττων ἀξίως ἀνδρὸς ἀγαθοῦ ἐβοήθουν τοῖς δικαίοις καί, ὥσπερ χρή, τοῦτο περὶ
πλείστου ἐποιούμην; πολλοῦ γε δεῖ, ὦ ἄνδρες Ἀθηναῖοι.
33 οὐδὲ γὰρ ἂν ἄλλος ἀνθρώπων οὐδείς. ἀλλ᾽ ἐγὼ διὰ 655
παντὸς τοῦ βίου δημοσίᾳ τε εἴ πού τι ἔπραξα, τοιοῦτος
φανοῦμαι, καὶ ἰδίᾳ ὁ αὐτὸς οὗτος, οὐδενὶ πώποτε ξυγ-

χωρήσας οὐδὲν παρὰ τὸ δίκαιον οὔτε ἄλλῳ οὔτε τούτων
οὐδενί, οὓς οἱ διαβάλλοντές μέ φασιν ἐμοὺς μαθητὰς
660 εἶναι. ἐγὼ δὲ διδάσκαλος μὲν οὐδενὸς πώποτ' ἐγενόμην·
εἰ δέ τίς μου λέγοντος καὶ τὰ ἐμαυτοῦ πράττοντος ἐπι-
θυμεῖ ἀκούειν, εἴτε νεώτερος εἴτε πρεσβύτερος, οὐδενὶ
πώποτε ἐφθόνησα. οὐδὲ χρήματα μὲν λαμβάνων διαλέ-
γομαι, μὴ λαμβάνων δ' οὔ, ἀλλ' ὁμοίως καὶ πλουσίῳ B
665 καὶ πένητι παρέχω ἐμαυτὸν ἐρωτᾶν, καὶ ἐάν τις βούληται
ἀποκρινόμενος ἀκούειν ὧν ἂν λέγω. καὶ τούτων ἐγώ, εἴτε
τις χρηστὸς γίγνεται εἴτε μή, οὐκ ἂν δικαίως τὴν αἰτίαν
ὑπέχοιμι, ὧν μήτε ὑπεσχόμην μηδενὶ μηδὲν πώποτε μάθημα μήτε ἐδίδαξα. εἰ δέ τίς φησι παρ' ἐμοῦ πώποτέ τι
670 μαθεῖν ἢ ἀκοῦσαι ἰδίᾳ ὅ τι μὴ καὶ οἱ ἄλλοι πάντες, εὖ
ἴστε ὅτι οὐκ ἀληθῆ λέγει.

Ἀλλὰ διὰ τί δή ποτε μετ' ἐμοῦ χαίρουσί τινες πολὺν
χρόνον διατρίβοντες; Ἀκηκόατε, ὦ ἄνδρες Ἀθηναῖοι· C
πᾶσαν ὑμῖν τὴν ἀλήθειαν ἐγὼ εἶπον, ὅτι ἀκούοντες
675 χαίρουσιν ἐξεταζομένοις τοῖς οἰομένοις μὲν εἶναι σοφοῖς,
οὖσι δ' οὔ· ἔστι γὰρ οὐκ ἀηδές. ἐμοὶ δὲ τοῦτο, ὡς
ἐγώ φημι, προστέτακται ὑπὸ τοῦ θεοῦ πράττειν καὶ ἐκ
μαντείων καὶ ἐξ ἐνυπνίων καὶ παντὶ τρόπῳ, ᾧπερ τίς
ποτε καὶ ἄλλη θεία μοῖρα ἀνθρώπῳ καὶ ὁτιοῦν προσ-
680 έταξε πράττειν. Ταῦτα, ὦ Ἀθηναῖοι, καὶ ἀληθῆ ἐστι
καὶ εὐέλεγκτα. εἰ γὰρ δὴ ἔγωγε τῶν νέων τοὺς μὲν διαφθείρω, τοὺς δὲ διέφθαρκα, χρῆν δήπου, εἴτε τινὲς D
αὐτῶν πρεσβύτεροι γενόμενοι ἔγνωσαν ὅτι νέοις οὖσιν
αὐτοῖς ἐγὼ κακὸν πώποτέ τι ξυνεβούλευσα, νυνὶ αὐτοὺς
685 ἀναβαίνοντας ἐμοῦ κατηγορεῖν καὶ τιμωρεῖσθαι· εἰ δὲ
μὴ αὐτοὶ ἤθελον, τῶν οἰκείων τινὰς τῶν ἐκείνων, πα-
τέρας καὶ ἀδελφοὺς καὶ ἄλλους τοὺς προσήκοντας, εἴπερ
ὑπ' ἐμοῦ τι κακὸν ἐπεπόνθεσαν αὐτῶν οἱ οἰκεῖοι, νῦν

μεμνῆσθαι [καὶ τιμωρεῖσθαι]. πάντως δὲ πάρεισιν αὐτῶν
πολλοὶ ἐνταυθοῖ, οὓς ἐγὼ ὁρῶ, πρῶτον μὲν Κρίτων 690
E οὑτοσί, ἐμὸς ἡλικιώτης καὶ δημότης, Κριτοβούλου τοῦδε
πατήρ· ἔπειτα Λυσανίας ὁ Σφήττιος, Αἰσχίνου τοῦδε
πατήρ· ἔτι Ἀντιφῶν ὁ Κηφισιεὺς οὑτοσί, Ἐπιγένους πατήρ.
ἄλλοι τοίνυν οὗτοι, ὧν οἱ ἀδελφοὶ ἐν ταύτῃ τῇ διατριβῇ
γεγόνασι, Νικόστρατος, ὁ Θεοζοτίδου, ἀδελφὸς Θεοδότου 695
— καὶ ὁ μὲν Θεόδοτος τετελεύτηκεν, ὥστε οὐκ ἂν ἐκεῖνός
γε αὐτοῦ καταδεηθείη —, καὶ Πάραλος ὅδε, ὁ Δημοδόκου,
34 οὗ ἦν Θεάγης ἀδελφός· ὅδε δὲ Ἀδείμαντος, ὁ Ἀρίστωνος,
οὗ ἀδελφὸς οὑτοσὶ Πλάτων, καὶ Αἰαντόδωρος, οὗ Ἀπολλόδωρος ὅδε ἀδελφός. καὶ ἄλλους πολλοὺς ἐγὼ ἔχω ὑμῖν 700
εἰπεῖν, ὧν τινὰ ἐχρῆν μάλιστα μὲν ἐν τῷ ἑαυτοῦ λόγῳ
παρασχέσθαι Μέλητον μάρτυρα· εἰ δὲ τότε ἐπελάθετο,
νῦν παρασχέσθω, ἐγὼ παραχωρῶ, καὶ λεγέτω, εἴ τι ἔχει
τοιοῦτον. ἀλλὰ τούτου πᾶν τοὐναντίον εὑρήσετε, ὦ ἄνδρες, πάντας ἐμοὶ βοηθεῖν ἑτοίμους τῷ διαφθείροντι, τῷ 705
κακὰ ἐργαζομένῳ τοὺς οἰκείους αὐτῶν, ὥς φασι Μέλητος
B καὶ Ἄνυτος. αὐτοὶ μὲν γὰρ οἱ διεφθαρμένοι τάχ᾽ ἂν λόγον
ἔχοιεν βοηθοῦντες· οἱ δὲ ἀδιάφθαρτοι, πρεσβύτεροι ἤδη
ἄνδρες, οἱ τούτων προσήκοντες, τίνα ἄλλον ἔχουσι λόγον
βοηθοῦντες ἐμοὶ ἀλλ᾽ ἢ τὸν ὀρθόν τε καὶ δίκαιον, ὅτι ξυνί- 710
σασι Μελήτῳ μὲν ψευδομένῳ, ἐμοὶ δὲ ἀληθεύοντι;

Εἶεν δή, ὦ ἄνδρες· ἃ μὲν ἐγὼ ἔχοιμ᾽ ἂν ἀπολογεῖσθαι,
σχεδόν ἐστι ταῦτα καὶ ἄλλα ἴσως τοιαῦτα. Τάχα δ᾽
C ἄν τις ὑμῶν ἀγανακτήσειεν ἀναμνησθεὶς ἑαυτοῦ, εἰ ὁ
μὲν καὶ ἐλάττω τουτουὶ τοῦ ἀγῶνος ἀγῶνα ἀγωνιζό- 715
μενος ἐδεήθη τε καὶ ἱκέτευσε τοὺς δικαστὰς μετὰ πολλῶν δακρύων, παιδία τε αὑτοῦ ἀναβιβασάμενος, ἵνα ὅ
τι μάλιστα ἐλεηθείη, καὶ ἄλλους τῶν οἰκείων καὶ φίλων
πολλούς, ἐγὼ δὲ οὐδὲν ἄρα τούτων ποιήσω, καὶ ταῦτα

720 κινδυνεύων, ὡς ἂν δόξαιμι, τὸν ἔσχατον κίνδυνον. τάχ'
οὖν τις ταῦτα ἐννοήσας αὐθαδέστερον ἂν πρός με σχοίη,
καὶ ὀργισθεὶς αὐτοῖς τούτοις θεῖτο ἂν μετ' ὀργῆς τὴν
ψῆφον. εἰ δή τις ὑμῶν οὕτως ἔχει, — οὐκ ἀξιῶ μὲν γὰρ D
ἔγωγε· εἰ δ' οὖν, ἐπιεικῆ ἄν μοι δοκῶ πρὸς τοῦτον λέ-
725 γειν λέγων, ὅτι 'Εμοί, ὦ ἄριστε, εἰσὶ μέν πού τινες καὶ
οἰκεῖοι. καὶ γὰρ τοῦτο αὐτὸ τὸ τοῦ 'Ομήρου, οὐδ' ἐγὼ
ἀπὸ δρυὸς οὐδ' ἀπὸ πέτρης πέφυκα, ἀλλ' ἐξ ἀνθρώπων,
ὥστε καὶ οἰκεῖοί μοί εἰσι καὶ υἱεῖς, ὦ ἄνδρες 'Αθηναῖοι,
τρεῖς, εἷς μὲν μειράκιον ἤδη, δύο δὲ παιδία. ἀλλ' ὅμως
730 οὐδέν' αὐτῶν δεῦρο ἀναβιβασάμενος δεήσομαι ὑμῶν ἀπο-
ψηφίσασθαι. Τί δὴ οὖν οὐδὲν τούτων ποιήσω; Οὐκ αὐ-
θαδιζόμενος, ὦ ἄνδρες 'Αθηναῖοι, οὐδ' ὑμᾶς ἀτιμάζων, ἀλλ' E
εἰ μὲν θαρραλέως ἐγὼ ἔχω πρὸς θάνατον ἢ μή, ἄλλος
λόγος, πρὸς δ' οὖν δόξαν καὶ ἐμοὶ καὶ ὑμῖν καὶ ὅλῃ τῇ
735 πόλει οὔ μοι δοκεῖ καλὸν εἶναι ἐμὲ τούτων οὐδὲν ποιεῖν
καὶ τηλικόνδε ὄντα καὶ τοῦτο τοὔνομα ἔχοντα, εἴτ' οὖν
ἀληθὲς εἴτ' οὖν ψεῦδος· ἀλλ' οὖν δεδογμένον γέ ἐστι τὸ
Σωκράτη διαφέρειν τινὶ τῶν πολλῶν ἀνθρώπων· εἰ οὖν 35
ὑμῶν οἱ δοκοῦντες διαφέρειν εἴτε σοφίᾳ εἴτε ἀνδρείᾳ εἴτε
740 ἄλλῃ ἡτινιοῦν ἀρετῇ τοιοῦτοι ἔσονται, αἰσχρὸν ἂν εἴη·
οἷούσπερ ἐγὼ πολλάκις ἑώρακά τινας, ὅταν κρίνωνται,
δοκοῦντας μέν τι εἶναι, θαυμάσια δὲ ἐργαζομένους, ὡς
δεινόν τι οἰομένους πείσεσθαι εἰ ἀποθανοῦνται, ὥσπερ
ἀθανάτων ἐσομένων, ἂν ὑμεῖς αὐτοὺς μὴ ἀποκτείνητε·
745 οἳ ἐμοὶ δοκοῦσιν αἰσχύνην τῇ πόλει περιάπτειν, ὥστ'
ἄν τινα καὶ τῶν ξένων ὑπολαβεῖν ὅτι οἱ διαφέροντες
'Αθηναίων εἰς ἀρετήν, οὓς αὐτοὶ ἑαυτῶν ἔν τε ταῖς ἀρ- B
χαῖς καὶ ταῖς ἄλλαις τιμαῖς προκρίνουσιν, οὗτοι γυναικῶν
οὐδὲν διαφέρουσι. ταῦτα γάρ, ὦ ἄνδρες 'Αθηναῖοι, οὔτε
750 ἡμᾶς χρὴ ποιεῖν τοὺς δοκοῦντας καὶ ὁτιοῦν εἶναι, οὔτ',

ἂν ἡμεῖς ποιῶμεν, ὑμᾶς ἐπιτρέπειν, ἀλλὰ τοῦτο αὐτὸ
ἐνδείκνυσθαι, ὅτι πολὺ μᾶλλον καταψηφιεῖσθε τοῦ τὰ
ἐλεεινὰ ταῦτα δράματα εἰσάγοντος καὶ καταγέλαστον τὴν
πόλιν ποιοῦντος ἢ τοῦ ἡσυχίαν ἄγοντος.

Χωρὶς δὲ τῆς δόξης, ὦ ἄνδρες, οὐδὲ δίκαιόν μοι 755
C δοκεῖ εἶναι δεῖσθαι τοῦ δικαστοῦ οὐδὲ δεόμενον ἀπο-
φεύγειν, ἀλλὰ διδάσκειν καὶ πείθειν. οὐ γὰρ ἐπὶ τούτῳ
κάθηται ὁ δικαστής, ἐπὶ τῷ καταχαρίζεσθαι τὰ δίκαια,
ἀλλ' ἐπὶ τῷ κρίνειν ταῦτα· καὶ ὀμώμοκεν οὐ χαριεῖσθαι
οἷς ἂν δοκῇ αὐτῷ, ἀλλὰ δικάσειν κατὰ τοὺς νόμους. 760
οὔκουν χρὴ οὔτε ἡμᾶς ἐθίζειν ὑμᾶς ἐπιορκεῖν, οὔθ' ὑμᾶς
ἐθίζεσθαι· οὐδέτεροι γὰρ ἂν ἡμῶν εὐσεβοῖεν. μὴ οὖν
ἀξιοῦτέ με, ὦ ἄνδρες Ἀθηναῖοι, τοιαῦτα δεῖν πρὸς ὑμᾶς
πράττειν, ἃ μήτε ἡγοῦμαι καλὰ εἶναι μήτε δίκαια μήτε
D ὅσια, ἄλλως τε μέντοι νὴ Δία πάντως καὶ ἀσεβείας φεύ- 765
γοντα ὑπὸ Μελήτου τουτουί. σαφῶς γὰρ ἄν, εἰ πείθοιμι
ὑμᾶς καὶ τῷ δεῖσθαι βιαζοίμην ὀμωμοκότας, θεοὺς ἂν
διδάσκοιμι μὴ ἡγεῖσθαι ὑμᾶς εἶναι, καὶ ἀτεχνῶς ἀπολο-
γούμενος κατηγοροίην ἂν ἐμαυτοῦ ὡς θεοὺς οὐ νομίζω.
ἀλλὰ πολλοῦ δεῖ οὕτως ἔχειν· νομίζω τε γάρ, ὦ ἄνδρες 770
Ἀθηναῖοι, ὡς οὐδεὶς τῶν ἐμῶν κατηγόρων, καὶ ὑμῖν
ἐπιτρέπω καὶ τῷ θεῷ κρῖναι περὶ ἐμοῦ ὅπῃ μέλλει ἐμοί
τε ἄριστα εἶναι καὶ ὑμῖν.

E   Τὸ μὲν μὴ ἀγανακτεῖν, ὦ ἄνδρες Ἀθηναῖοι, ἐπὶ τούτῳ
36 τῷ γεγονότι, ὅτι μου κατεψηφίσασθε, ἄλλα τέ μοι 775
πολλὰ ξυμβάλλεται, καὶ οὐκ ἀνέλπιστόν μοι γέγονε τὸ
γεγονὸς τοῦτο, ἀλλὰ πολὺ μᾶλλον θαυμάζω ἑκατέρων
τῶν ψήφων τὸν γεγονότα ἀριθμόν. οὐ γὰρ ᾠόμην ἔγωγε
οὕτω παρ' ὀλίγον ἔσεσθαι, ἀλλὰ παρὰ πολύ· νῦν δέ, ὡς
ἔοικεν, εἰ τριάκοντα μόναι μετέπεσον τῶν ψήφων, ἀπο- 780

πεφεύγη ἄν. Μέλητον μὲν οὖν, ὡς ἐμοὶ δοκῶ, καὶ νῦν
ἀποπέφευγα, καὶ οὐ μόνον ἀποπέφευγα, ἀλλὰ παντὶ δῆλον τοῦτό γε, ὅτι, εἰ μὴ ἀνέβησαν Ἄνυτος καὶ Λύκων
κατηγορήσοντες ἐμοῦ, κἂν ὦφλε χιλίας δραχμάς, οὐ B
785 μεταλαβὼν τὸ πέμπτον μέρος τῶν ψήφων.

Τιμᾶται δ' οὖν μοι ὁ ἀνὴρ θανάτου. Εἶεν· ἐγὼ δὲ
δὴ τίνος ὑμῖν ἀντιτιμήσωμαι, ὦ ἄνδρες Ἀθηναῖοι; ἢ
δῆλον ὅτι τῆς ἀξίας; τί οὖν; τί ἄξιός εἰμι παθεῖν ἢ
ἀποτῖσαι, ὅ τι μαθὼν ἐν τῷ βίῳ οὐχ ἡσυχίαν ἦγον, ἀλλ'
790 ἀμελήσας ὧνπερ οἱ πολλοί, χρηματισμοῦ τε καὶ οἰκονομίας καὶ στρατηγιῶν καὶ δημηγοριῶν καὶ τῶν ἄλλων
ἀρχῶν καὶ ξυνωμοσιῶν καὶ στάσεων τῶν ἐν τῇ πόλει
γιγνομένων, ἡγησάμενος ἐμαυτὸν τῷ ὄντι ἐπιεικέστερον
εἶναι ἢ ὥστε εἰς ταῦτ' ἰόντα σώζεσθαι, ἐνταῦθα μὲν οὐκ C
795 ᾖα, οἷ ἐλθὼν μήτε ὑμῖν μήτε ἐμαυτῷ ἔμελλον μηδὲν
ὄφελος εἶναι, ἐπὶ δὲ τὸ ἰδίᾳ ἕκαστον ἰὼν εὐεργετεῖν τὴν
μεγίστην εὐεργεσίαν, ὡς ἐγώ φημι, [ἐνταῦθα ᾖα,] ἐπιχειρῶν ἕκαστον ὑμῶν πείθειν μὴ πρότερον μήτε τῶν ἑαυτοῦ
μηδενὸς ἐπιμελεῖσθαι, πρὶν ἑαυτοῦ ἐπιμεληθείη, ὅπως
800 ὡς βέλτιστος καὶ φρονιμώτατος ἔσοιτο, μήτε τῶν τῆς
πόλεως, πρὶν αὐτῆς τῆς πόλεως· τῶν τε ἄλλων οὕτω
κατὰ τὸν αὐτὸν τρόπον ἐπιμελεῖσθαι. τί οὖν εἰμὶ ἄξιος
παθεῖν τοιοῦτος ὤν; ἀγαθόν τι, ὦ ἄνδρες Ἀθηναῖοι, D
εἰ δεῖ γε κατὰ τὴν ἀξίαν τῇ ἀληθείᾳ τιμᾶσθαι· καὶ ταῦτά
805 γε ἀγαθὸν τοιοῦτον, ὅ τι ἂν πρέποι ἐμοί. τί οὖν πρέπει
ἀνδρὶ πένητι εὐεργέτῃ, δεομένῳ ἄγειν σχολὴν ἐπὶ τῇ
ὑμετέρᾳ παρακελεύσει; οὐκ ἔσθ' ὅ τι μᾶλλον, ὦ ἄνδρες
Ἀθηναῖοι, πρέπει οὕτως, ὡς τὸν τοιοῦτον ἄνδρα ἐν πρυτανείῳ σιτεῖσθαι, πολύ γε μᾶλλον ἢ εἴ τις ὑμῶν ἵππῳ ἢ
810 ξυνωρίδι ἢ ζεύγει νενίκηκεν Ὀλυμπίασιν. ὁ μὲν γὰρ ὑμᾶς
ποιεῖ εὐδαίμονας δοκεῖν [εἶναι], ἐγὼ δὲ εἶναι· καὶ ὁ μὲν

E τροφῆς οὐδὲν δεῖται, ἐγὼ δὲ δέομαι. εἰ οὖν δεῖ με κατὰ
37 τὸ δίκαιον τῆς ἀξίας τιμᾶσθαι, τούτου τιμῶμαι, ἐν
πρυτανείῳ σιτήσεως.

Ἴσως οὖν ὑμῖν καὶ ταυτὶ λέγων παραπλησίως δοκῶ 815
λέγειν ὥσπερ περὶ τοῦ οἴκτου καὶ τῆς ἀντιβολήσεως,
ἀπαυθαδιζόμενος· τὸ δὲ οὐκ ἔστιν, ὦ Ἀθηναῖοι, τοιοῦτον,
ἀλλὰ τοιόνδε μᾶλλον. πέπεισμαι ἐγὼ ἑκὼν εἶναι μηδένα
ἀδικεῖν ἀνθρώπων, ἀλλὰ ὑμᾶς τοῦτο οὐ πείθω· ὀλίγον
γὰρ χρόνον ἀλλήλοις διειλέγμεθα· ἐπεί, ὡς ἐγῷμαι, εἰ 820
ἦν ὑμῖν νόμος, ὥσπερ καὶ ἄλλοις ἀνθρώποις, περὶ θανά-
B του μὴ μίαν ἡμέραν μόνον κρίνειν, ἀλλὰ πολλάς, ἐπεί-
σθητε ἄν· νῦν δ᾽ οὐ ῥᾴδιον ἐν χρόνῳ ὀλίγῳ μεγάλας
διαβολὰς ἀπολύεσθαι. πεπεισμένος δὴ ἐγὼ μηδένα
ἀδικεῖν πολλοῦ δέω ἐμαυτόν γε ἀδικήσειν καὶ κατ᾽ 825
ἐμαυτοῦ ἐρεῖν αὐτός, ὡς ἄξιός εἰμί του κακοῦ καὶ τιμή-
σεσθαι τοιούτου τινὸς ἐμαυτῷ. τί δείσας; ἢ μὴ πάθω
τοῦτο, οὗ Μέλητός μοι τιμᾶται, ὅ φημι οὐκ εἰδέναι οὔτ᾽
εἰ ἀγαθὸν οὔτ᾽ εἰ κακόν ἐστιν; ἀντὶ τούτου δὴ ἕλωμαι
ὧν εὖ οἶδ᾽ ὅτι κακῶν ὄντων, τούτου τιμησάμενος ; 830
C πότερον δεσμοῦ; καὶ τί με δεῖ ζῆν ἐν δεσμωτηρίῳ,
δουλεύοντα τῇ ἀεὶ καθισταμένῃ ἀρχῇ [, τοῖς ἕνδεκα];
ἀλλὰ χρημάτων, καὶ δεδέσθαι ἕως ἂν ἐκτίσω; ἀλλὰ
ταὐτόν μοί ἐστιν, ὅπερ νῦν δὴ ἔλεγον· οὐ γὰρ ἔστι μοι
χρήματα, ὁπόθεν ἐκτίσω. Ἀλλὰ δὴ φυγῆς τιμήσωμαι ; 835
ἴσως γὰρ ἄν μοι τούτου τιμήσαιτε. πολλὴ μέντ᾽ ἄν με
φιλοψυχία ἔχοι, εἰ οὕτως ἀλόγιστος εἴην, ὥστε μὴ
δύνασθαι λογίζεσθαι, ὅτι ὑμεῖς μὲν ὄντες πολῖταί μου
D οὐχ οἷοί τε ἐγένεσθε ἐνεγκεῖν τὰς ἐμὰς διατριβὰς καὶ
τοὺς λόγους, ἀλλ᾽ ὑμῖν βαρύτεραι γεγόνασι καὶ ἐπι- 840
φθονώτεραι, ὥστε ζητεῖτε αὐτῶν νυνὶ ἀπαλλαγῆναι,
ἄλλοι δὲ ἄρα αὐτὰς οἴσουσι ῥᾳδίως. πολλοῦ γε δεῖ, ὦ

'Αθηναῖοι. καλὸς οὖν ἄν μοι ὁ βίος εἴη ἐξελθόντι τηλικῷδε ἀνθρώπῳ ἄλλην ἐξ ἄλλης πόλιν πόλεως ἀμει-
845 βομένῳ καὶ ἐξελαυνομένῳ ζῆν. εὖ γὰρ οἶδ' ὅτι, ὅποι ἂν ἔλθω, λέγοντος ἐμοῦ ἀκροάσονται οἱ νέοι ὥσπερ ἐνθάδε· κἂν μὲν τούτους ἀπελαύνω, οὗτοι ἐμὲ αὐτοὶ ἐξελῶσι, πείθοντες τοὺς πρεσβυτέρους· ἐὰν δὲ μὴ ἀπελαύνω, οἱ E τούτων πατέρες τε καὶ οἰκεῖοι δι' αὐτοὺς τούτους.

850 Ἴσως οὖν ἄν τις εἴποι, Σιγῶν δὲ καὶ ἡσυχίαν ἄγων, ὦ Σώκρατες, οὐχ οἷός τ' ἔσει ἡμῖν ἐξελθὼν ζῆν; Τουτὶ δή ἐστι πάντων χαλεπώτατον πεῖσαί τινας ὑμῶν. ἐάν τε γὰρ λέγω ὅτι τῷ θεῷ ἀπειθεῖν τοῦτ' ἐστὶ καὶ διὰ τοῦτ' ἀδύνατον ἡσυχίαν ἄγειν, οὐ πείσεσθέ μοι ὡς εἰρω-
855 νευομένῳ· ἐάν τ' αὖ λέγω ὅτι καὶ τυγχάνει μέγιστον 38 ἀγαθὸν ὂν ἀνθρώπῳ τοῦτο, ἑκάστης ἡμέρας περὶ ἀρετῆς τοὺς λόγους ποιεῖσθαι καὶ τῶν ἄλλων, περὶ ὧν ὑμεῖς ἐμοῦ ἀκούετε διαλεγομένου καὶ ἐμαυτὸν καὶ ἄλλους ἐξετάζοντος, ὁ δὲ ἀνεξέταστος βίος οὐ βιωτὸς ἀνθρώπῳ,
860 ταῦτα δ' ἔτι ἧττον πείσεσθέ μοι λέγοντι. τὰ δὲ ἔχει μὲν οὕτως, ὡς ἐγώ φημι, ὦ ἄνδρες, πείθειν δὲ οὐ ῥᾴδιον. Καὶ ἐγὼ ἅμ' οὐκ εἴθισμαι ἐμαυτὸν ἀξιοῦν κακοῦ οὐδενός. εἰ μὲν γὰρ ἦν μοι χρήματα, ἐτιμησάμην ἂν χρημάτων ὅσα B ἔμελλον ἐκτίσειν· οὐδὲν γὰρ ἂν ἐβλάβην· νῦν δέ—οὐ
865 γὰρ ἔστιν, εἰ μὴ ἄρα ὅσον ἂν ἐγὼ δυναίμην ἐκτῖσαι, τοσούτου βούλεσθέ μοι τιμῆσαι. ἴσως δ' ἂν δυναίμην ἐκτῖσαι ὑμῖν μνᾶν ἀργυρίου· τοσούτου οὖν τιμῶμαι. Πλάτων δὲ ὅδε, ὦ ἄνδρες Ἀθηναῖοι, καὶ Κρίτων καὶ Κριτόβουλος καὶ Ἀπολλόδωρος κελεύουσί με τριάκοντα
870 μνῶν τιμήσασθαι, αὐτοὶ δ' ἐγγυᾶσθαι· τιμῶμαι οὖν τοσούτου. ἐγγυηταὶ δ' ὑμῖν ἔσονται τοῦ ἀργυρίου οὗτοι ἀξιόχρεῳ.

C Οὐ πολλοῦ γ᾽ ἕνεκα χρόνου, ὦ ἄνδρες Ἀθηναῖοι,
ὄνομα ἕξετε καὶ αἰτίαν ὑπὸ τῶν βουλομένων τὴν πόλιν
λοιδορεῖν, ὡς Σωκράτη ἀπεκτόνατε, ἄνδρα σοφόν. φή- 875
σουσι γὰρ δή με σοφὸν εἶναι, εἰ καὶ μὴ εἰμί, οἱ βουλόμενοι ὑμῖν ὀνειδίζειν. εἰ οὖν περιεμείνατε ὀλίγον
χρόνον, ἀπὸ τοῦ αὐτομάτου ἂν ὑμῖν τοῦτο ἐγένετο· ὁρᾶτε
γὰρ δὴ τὴν ἡλικίαν, ὅτι πόρρω ἤδη ἐστὶ τοῦ βίου,
θανάτου δὲ ἐγγύς. λέγω δὲ τοῦτο οὐ πρὸς πάντας ὑμᾶς, 880
D ἀλλὰ πρὸς τοὺς ἐμοῦ καταψηφισαμένους θάνατον. λέγω
δὲ καὶ τόδε πρὸς τοὺς αὐτοὺς τούτους. Ἴσως με οἴεσθε,
ὦ ἄνδρες, ἀπορίᾳ λόγων ἑαλωκέναι τοιούτων, οἷς ἂν ὑμᾶς
ἔπεισα, εἰ ᾤμην δεῖν ἅπαντα ποιεῖν καὶ λέγειν, ὥστε
ἀποφυγεῖν τὴν δίκην. πολλοῦ γε δεῖ. ἀλλ᾽ ἀπορίᾳ μὲν 885
ἑάλωκα, οὐ μέντοι λόγων, ἀλλὰ τόλμης καὶ ἀναισχυντίας
καὶ τοῦ ἐθέλειν λέγειν πρὸς ὑμᾶς τοιαῦτα, οἷ᾽ ἂν ὑμῖν
ἥδιστ᾽ ἦν ἀκούειν, θρηνοῦντός τέ μου καὶ ὀδυρομένου καὶ
E ἄλλα ποιοῦντος καὶ λέγοντος πολλὰ καὶ ἀνάξια ἐμοῦ, ὡς
ἐγώ φημι· οἷα δὴ καὶ εἴθισθε ὑμεῖς τῶν ἄλλων ἀκούειν. 890
ἀλλ᾽ οὔτε τότε ᾠήθην δεῖν ἕνεκα τοῦ κινδύνου πρᾶξαι
οὐδὲν ἀνελεύθερον, οὔτε νῦν μοι μεταμέλει οὕτως ἀπο-
λογησαμένῳ, ἀλλὰ πολὺ μᾶλλον αἱροῦμαι ὧδε ἀπο-
λογησάμενος τεθνάναι ἢ ἐκείνως ζῆν· οὔτε γὰρ ἐν δίκῃ
οὔτ᾽ ἐν πολέμῳ οὔτ᾽ ἐμὲ οὔτ᾽ ἄλλον οὐδένα δεῖ τοῦτο 895
39 μηχανᾶσθαι, ὅπως ἀποφεύξεται πᾶν ποιῶν θάνατον. καὶ
γὰρ ἐν ταῖς μάχαις πολλάκις δῆλον γίγνεται ὅτι τό γε
ἀποθανεῖν ἄν τις ἐκφύγοι καὶ ὅπλα ἀφεὶς καὶ ἐφ᾽
ἱκετείαν τραπόμενος τῶν διωκόντων· καὶ ἄλλαι μηχαναὶ
πολλαί εἰσιν ἐν ἑκάστοις τοῖς κινδύνοις, ὥστε διαφεύγειν 900
B θάνατον, ἐάν τις τολμᾷ πᾶν ποιεῖν καὶ λέγειν. ἀλλὰ μὴ
οὐ τοῦτ᾽ ᾖ χαλεπόν, ὦ ἄνδρες Ἀθηναῖοι, θάνατον
ἐκφυγεῖν, ἀλλὰ πολὺ χαλεπώτερον πονηρίαν· θᾶττον γὰρ

θανάτου θεῖ. καὶ νῦν ἐγὼ μὲν ἅτε βραδὺς ὢν καὶ
905 πρεσβύτης ὑπὸ τοῦ βραδυτέρου ἑάλων, οἱ δ' ἐμοὶ κατήγοροι ἅτε δεινοὶ καὶ ὀξεῖς ὄντες ὑπὸ τοῦ θάττονος, τῆς
κακίας. καὶ νῦν ἐγὼ μὲν ἄπειμι ὑφ' ὑμῶν θανάτου δίκην
ὄφλων, οὗτοι δ' ὑπὸ τῆς ἀληθείας ὠφληκότες μοχθηρίαν
καὶ ἀδικίαν. καὶ ἐγώ τε τῷ τιμήματι ἐμμένω καὶ οὗτοι.
910 Ταῦτα μὲν που ἴσως οὕτω καὶ ἔδει σχεῖν, καὶ οἶμαι αὐτὰ
μετρίως ἔχειν.

Τὸ δὲ δὴ μετὰ τοῦτο ἐπιθυμῶ ὑμῖν χρησμῳδῆσαι, ὦ C
καταψηφισάμενοί μου· καὶ γάρ εἰμι ἤδη ἐνταῦθα, ἐν ᾧ
μάλιστ' ἄνθρωποι χρησμῳδοῦσιν, ὅταν μέλλωσιν ἀπο-
915 θανεῖσθαι. φημὶ γάρ, ὦ ἄνδρες, οἳ ἐμὲ ἀπεκτόνατε,
τιμωρίαν ὑμῖν ἥξειν εὐθὺς μετὰ τὸν ἐμὸν θάνατον πολὺ
χαλεπωτέραν νὴ Δί' ἢ οἵαν ἐμὲ ἀπεκτόνατε· νῦν γὰρ
τοῦτο εἰργάσασθε οἰόμενοι ἀπαλλάξεσθαι τοῦ διδόναι
ἔλεγχον τοῦ βίου. τὸ δὲ ὑμῖν πολὺ ἐναντίον ἀπο-
920 βήσεται, ὡς ἐγώ φημι. πλείους ἔσονται ὑμᾶς οἱ ἐλέγ-
χοντες, οὓς νῦν ἐγὼ κατεῖχον, ὑμεῖς δὲ οὐκ ᾐσθάνεσθε. D
καὶ χαλεπώτεροι ἔσονται ὅσῳ νεώτεροί εἰσι, καὶ ὑμεῖς
μᾶλλον ἀγανακτήσετε. εἰ γὰρ οἴεσθε ἀποκτείνοντες
ἀνθρώπους ἐπισχήσειν τοῦ ὀνειδίζειν τινὰ ὑμῖν ὅτι οὐκ
925 ὀρθῶς ζῆτε, οὐκ ὀρθῶς διανοεῖσθε· οὐ γὰρ ἔσθ' αὕτη ἡ
ἀπαλλαγὴ οὔτε πάνυ δυνατὴ οὔτε καλή, ἀλλ' ἐκείνη καὶ
καλλίστη καὶ ῥᾴστη, μὴ τοὺς ἄλλους κολούειν, ἀλλ'
ἑαυτὸν παρασκευάζειν, ὅπως ἔσται ὡς βέλτιστος. Ταῦτα
μὲν οὖν ὑμῖν τοῖς καταψηφισαμένοις μαντευσάμενος
930 ἀπαλλάττομαι.

Τοῖς δὲ ἀποψηφισαμένοις ἡδέως ἂν διαλεχθείην ὑπὲρ E
τοῦ γεγονότος τουτουὶ πράγματος, ἐν ᾧ οἱ ἄρχοντες
ἀσχολίαν ἄγουσι καὶ οὔπω ἔρχομαι οἷ ἐλθόντα με δεῖ
τεθνάναι. ἀλλά μοι, ὦ ἄνδρες, παραμείνατε τοσοῦτον

χρόνον· οὐδὲν γὰρ κωλύει διαμυθολογῆσαι πρὸς ἀλλή- 935
40 λους, ἕως ἔξεστιν. ὑμῖν γὰρ ὡς φίλοις οὖσιν ἐπιδεῖξαι
ἐθέλω τὸ νυνί μοι ξυμβεβηκὸς τί ποτε νοεῖ. Ἐμοὶ γάρ,
ὦ ἄνδρες δικασταί—ὑμᾶς γὰρ δικαστὰς καλῶν ὀρθῶς ἂν
καλοίην—θαυμάσιόν τι γέγονεν. ἡ γὰρ εἰωθυῖά μοι
μαντικὴ ἡ τοῦ δαιμονίου ἐν μὲν τῷ πρόσθεν χρόνῳ παντὶ 940
πάνυ πυκνὴ ἀεὶ ἦν καὶ πάνυ ἐπὶ σμικροῖς ἐναντιουμένη,
εἴ τι μέλλοιμι μὴ ὀρθῶς πράξειν· νυνὶ δὲ ξυμβέβηκέ μοι,
ἅπερ ὁρᾶτε καὶ αὐτοί, ταυτί, ἅ γε δὴ οἰηθείη ἄν τις καὶ
νομίζεται ἔσχατα κακῶν εἶναι. ἐμοὶ δὲ οὔτε ἐξιόντι
B ἕωθεν οἴκοθεν ἠναντιώθη τὸ τοῦ θεοῦ σημεῖον, οὔτε ἡνίκα 945
ἀνέβαινον ἐνταυθοῖ [ἐπὶ τὸ δικαστήριον], οὔτ' ἐν τῷ
λόγῳ οὐδαμοῦ μέλλοντί τι ἐρεῖν· καίτοι ἐν ἄλλοις λόγοις
πολλαχοῦ δή με ἐπέσχε λέγοντα μεταξύ. νυνὶ δὲ
οὐδαμοῦ περὶ ταύτην τὴν πρᾶξιν οὔτ' ἐν ἔργῳ οὐδενὶ οὔτ'
ἐν λόγῳ ἠναντίωταί μοι. τί οὖν αἴτιον εἶναι ὑπο- 950
λαμβάνω; ἐγὼ ὑμῖν ἐρῶ· κινδυνεύει γάρ μοι τὸ ξυμβεβηκὸς τοῦτο ἀγαθὸν γεγονέναι, καὶ οὐκ ἔσθ' ὅπως
C ἡμεῖς ὀρθῶς ὑπολαμβάνομεν, ὅσοι οἰόμεθα κακὸν εἶναι τὸ
τεθνάναι. μέγα μοι τεκμήριον τούτου γέγονεν· οὐ γὰρ
ἔσθ' ὅπως οὐκ ἠναντιώθη ἄν μοι τὸ εἰωθὸς σημεῖον, εἰ 955
μή τι ἔμελλον ἐγὼ ἀγαθὸν πράξειν.

Ἐννοήσωμεν δὲ καὶ τῇδε, ὡς πολλὴ ἐλπίς ἐστιν
ἀγαθὸν αὐτὸ εἶναι. Δυοῖν γὰρ θάτερόν ἐστι τὸ τεθνάναι·
ἢ γὰρ οἷον μηδὲν εἶναι μηδ' αἴσθησιν μηδεμίαν μηδενὸς
ἔχειν τὸν τεθνεῶτα, ἢ κατὰ τὰ λεγόμενα μεταβολή τις 960
τυγχάνει οὖσα καὶ μετοίκησις τῇ ψυχῇ τοῦ τόπου τοῦ
ἐνθένδε εἰς ἄλλον τόπον. καὶ εἴτε μηδεμία αἴσθησίς
D ἐστιν, ἀλλ' οἷον ὕπνος, ἐπειδάν τις καθεύδων μηδ' ὄναρ
μηδὲν ὁρᾷ, θαυμάσιον κέρδος ἂν εἴη ὁ θάνατος. ἐγὼ γὰρ
ἂν οἶμαι, εἴ τινα ἐκλεξάμενον δέοι ταύτην τὴν νύκτα, ἐν 965

ἢ οὕτω κατέδαρθεν, ὥστε μηδ' ὄναρ ἰδεῖν, καὶ τὰς ἄλλας
νύκτας τε καὶ ἡμέρας τὰς τοῦ βίου τοῦ ἑαυτοῦ ἀντι-
παραθέντα ταύτῃ τῇ νυκτὶ δέοι σκεψάμενον εἰπεῖν,
πόσας ἄμεινον καὶ ἥδιον ἡμέρας καὶ νύκτας ταύτης τῆς
970 νυκτὸς βεβίωκεν ἐν τῷ ἑαυτοῦ βίῳ, οἶμαι ἂν μὴ ὅτι
ἰδιώτην τινά, ἀλλὰ τὸν μέγαν βασιλέα εὐαριθμήτους ἂν Ε
εὑρεῖν αὐτὸν ταύτας πρὸς τὰς ἄλλας ἡμέρας καὶ νύκτας.
εἰ οὖν τοιοῦτον ὁ θάνατός ἐστι, κέρδος ἔγωγε λέγω· καὶ
γὰρ οὐδὲν πλείων ὁ πᾶς χρόνος φαίνεται οὕτω δὴ εἶναι ἢ
975 μία νύξ. εἰ δ' αὖ οἷον ἀποδημῆσαί ἐστιν ὁ θάνατος
ἐνθένδε εἰς ἄλλον τόπον, καὶ ἀληθῆ ἐστι τὰ λεγόμενα,
ὡς ἄρα ἐκεῖ εἰσὶν ἅπαντες οἱ τεθνεῶτες, τί μεῖζον ἀγαθὸν
τούτου εἴη ἄν, ὦ ἄνδρες δικασταί; εἰ γάρ τις ἀφικόμενος
εἰς Ἅιδου, ἀπαλλαγεὶς τούτων τῶν φασκόντων δικαστῶν 41
980 εἶναι, εὑρήσει τοὺς ἀληθῶς δικαστάς, οἵπερ καὶ λέγονται
ἐκεῖ δικάζειν, Μίνως τε καὶ Ῥαδάμανθυς καὶ Αἰακὸς καὶ
Τριπτόλεμος, καὶ ἄλλοι, ὅσοι τῶν ἡμιθέων δίκαιοι
ἐγένοντο ἐν τῷ ἑαυτῶν βίῳ, ἆρα φαύλη ἂν εἴη ἡ ἀποδημία; ἢ αὖ Ὀρφεῖ ξυγγενέσθαι καὶ Μουσαίῳ καὶ
985 Ἡσιόδῳ καὶ Ὁμήρῳ ἐπὶ πόσῳ ἄν τις δέξαιτ' ἂν ὑμῶν;
ἐγὼ μὲν γὰρ πολλάκις ἐθέλω τεθνάναι, εἰ ταῦτ' ἐστὶν
ἀληθῆ· ἐπεὶ ἔμοιγε καὶ αὐτῷ θαυμαστὴ ἂν εἴη ἡ δια-
τριβὴ αὐτόθι, ὁπότε ἐντύχοιμι Παλαμήδει καὶ Αἴαντι τῷ Β
Τελαμῶνος, καὶ εἴ τις ἄλλος τῶν παλαιῶν διὰ κρίσιν
990 ἄδικον τέθνηκεν, ἀντιπαραβάλλοντι τὰ ἐμαυτοῦ πάθη
πρὸς τὰ ἐκείνων, ὡς ἐγὼ οἶμαι, οὐκ ἂν ἀηδὲς εἴη. καὶ δὴ
τὸ μέγιστον, τοὺς ἐκεῖ ἐξετάζοντα καὶ ἐρευνῶντα ὥσπερ
τοὺς ἐνταῦθα διάγειν, τίς αὐτῶν σοφός ἐστι καὶ τίς
οἴεται μέν, ἔστι δ' οὔ. ἐπὶ πόσῳ δ' ἄν τις, ὦ ἄνδρες
995 δικασταί, δέξαιτο ἐξετάσαι τὸν ἐπὶ Τροίαν ἀγαγόντα τὴν
πολλὴν στρατιὰν ἢ Ὀδυσσέα ἢ Σίσυφον, ἢ ἄλλους C

μυρίους ἄν τις εἴποι καὶ ἄνδρας καὶ γυναῖκας; οἷς ἐκεῖ
διαλέγεσθαι καὶ ξυνεῖναι καὶ ἐξετάζειν ἀμήχανον ἂν εἴη
εὐδαιμονίας. πάντως οὐ δήπου τούτου γε ἕνεκα οἱ ἐκεῖ
ἀποκτείνουσι· τά τε γὰρ ἄλλα εὐδαιμονέστεροί εἰσιν οἱ 1000
ἐκεῖ τῶν ἐνθάδε, καὶ ἤδη τὸν λοιπὸν χρόνον ἀθάνατοί
εἰσιν, εἴπερ γε τὰ λεγόμενα ἀληθῆ ἐστίν.

Ἀλλὰ καὶ ὑμᾶς χρή, ὦ ἄνδρες δικασταί, εὐέλπιδας
εἶναι πρὸς τὸν θάνατον, καὶ ἕν τι τοῦτο διανοεῖσθαι
D ἀληθές, ὅτι οὐκ ἔστιν ἀνδρὶ ἀγαθῷ κακὸν οὐδὲν οὔτε 1005
ζῶντι οὔτε τελευτήσαντι, οὐδὲ ἀμελεῖται ὑπὸ θεῶν τὰ
τούτου πράγματα, οὐδὲ τὰ ἐμὰ νῦν ἀπὸ τοῦ αὐτομάτου
γέγονεν, ἀλλά μοι δῆλόν ἐστι τοῦτο, ὅτι ἤδη τεθνάναι
καὶ ἀπηλλάχθαι πραγμάτων βέλτιον ἦν μοι. διὰ τοῦτο
καὶ ἐμὲ οὐδαμοῦ ἀπέτρεψε τὸ σημεῖον, καὶ ἔγωγε τοῖς 1010
κιταψηφισαμένοις μου καὶ τοῖς κατηγόροις οὐ πάνυ
χαλεπαίνω. καίτοι οὐ ταύτῃ τῇ διανοίᾳ κατεψηφίζοντό
μου καὶ κατηγόρουν, ἀλλ᾽ οἰόμενοι βλάπτειν· τοῦτο
αὐτοῖς ἄξιον μέμφεσθαι.

E   Τοσόνδε μέντοι αὐτῶν δέομαι· τοὺς υἱεῖς μου, ἐπειδὰν 1015
ἡβήσωσι, τιμωρήσασθε, ὦ ἄνδρες, ταὐτὰ ταῦτα λυ-
ποῦντες, ἅπερ ἐγὼ ὑμᾶς ἐλύπουν, ἐὰν ὑμῖν δοκῶσιν ἢ
χρημάτων ἢ ἄλλου του πρότερον ἐπιμελεῖσθαι ἢ ἀρετῆς,
καὶ ἐὰν δοκῶσί τι εἶναι μηδὲν ὄντες, ὀνειδίζετε αὐτοῖς,
ὥσπερ ἐγὼ ὑμῖν, ὅτι οὐκ ἐπιμελοῦνται ὧν δεῖ, καὶ 1020
οἴονταί τι εἶναι ὄντες οὐδενὸς ἄξιοι. καὶ ἐὰν ταῦτα
42 ποιῆτε, δίκαια πεπονθὼς ἐγὼ ἔσομαι ὑφ᾽ ὑμῶν αὐτός
τε καὶ οἱ υἱεῖς.

Ἀλλὰ γὰρ ἤδη ὥρα ἀπιέναι, ἐμοὶ μὲν ἀποθανουμένῳ,
ὑμῖν δὲ βιωσομένοις. ὁπότεροι δὲ ἡμῶν ἔρχονται ἐπὶ 1025
ἄμεινον πρᾶγμα, ἄδηλον παντὶ πλὴν ἢ τῷ θεῷ.

CRITO.

*Socrates will not listen to Crito, who offers him the means
of escape.*

(SOCRATES. CRITO).

Τί τηνικάδε ἀφῖξαι, ὦ Κρίτων ; ἢ οὐ πρῷ ἔτι ἐστίν ; 43

ΚΡ. Πάνυ μὲν οὖν.

ΣΩ. Πηνίκα μάλιστα ;

ΚΡ. Ὄρθρος βαθύς.

5   ΣΩ. Θαυμάζω, ὅπως ἠθέλησέ σοι ὁ τοῦ δεσμωτηρίου
φύλαξ ὑπακοῦσαι.

ΚΡ. Ξυνήθης ἤδη μοί ἐστιν, ὦ Σώκρατες, διὰ τὸ
πολλάκις δεῦρο φοιτᾶν, καί τι καὶ εὐεργέτηται ὑπ' ἐμοῦ.

ΣΩ. Ἄρτι δὲ ἥκεις ἢ πάλαι ;

10   ΚΡ. Ἐπιεικῶς πάλαι.

ΣΩ. Εἶτα πῶς οὐκ εὐθὺς ἐπήγειράς με, ἀλλὰ σιγῇ B
παρακάθησαι ;

ΚΡ. Οὐ μὰ τὸν Δί', ὦ Σώκρατες, οὐδ' ἂν αὐτὸς
ἤθελον ἐν τοσαύτῃ τε ἀγρυπνίᾳ καὶ λύπῃ εἶναι. ἀλλὰ καὶ
15 σοῦ πάλαι θαυμάζω αἰσθανόμενος, ὡς ἡδέως καθεύδεις·
καὶ ἐπίτηδές σε οὐκ ἤγειρον, ἵνα ὡς ἥδιστα διάγοις. καὶ
πολλάκις μὲν δή σε καὶ πρότερον ἐν παντὶ τῷ βίῳ
εὐδαιμόνισα τοῦ τρόπου, πολὺ δὲ μάλιστα ἐν τῇ νῦν παρ-
εστώσῃ ξυμφορᾷ, ὡς ῥᾳδίως αὐτὴν καὶ πράως φέρεις.

20   ΣΩ. Καὶ γὰρ ἄν, ὦ Κρίτων, πλημμελὲς εἴη ἀγανακτεῖν τηλικοῦτον ὄντα, εἰ δεῖ ἤδη τελευτᾶν.

ΚΡ. Καὶ ἄλλοι, ὦ Σώκρατες, τηλικοῦτοι ἐν τοιαύταις C
ξυμφοραῖς ἁλίσκονται, ἀλλ' οὐδὲν αὐτοὺς ἐπιλύεται ἡ
ἡλικία τὸ μὴ οὐχὶ ἀγανακτεῖν τῇ παρούσῃ τύχῃ.

ΣΩ. Ἔστι ταῦτα. ἀλλὰ τί δὴ οὕτω πρῷ ἀφῖξαι ;   25

ΚΡ. Ἀγγελίαν, ὦ Σώκρατες, φέρων χαλεπήν, οὐ σοί, ὡς ἐμοὶ φαίνεται, ἀλλ᾽ ἐμοὶ καὶ τοῖς σοῖς ἐπιτηδείοις πᾶσι καὶ χαλεπὴν καὶ βαρεῖαν, ἣν ἐγώ, ὡς ἐμοὶ δοκῶ, ἐν τοῖς βαρύτατ᾽ ἂν ἐνέγκαιμι.

ΣΩ. Τίνα ταύτην ; ἢ τὸ πλοῖον ἀφῖκται ἐκ Δήλου, 30 D οὗ δεῖ ἀφικομένου τεθνάναι με ;

ΚΡ. Οὔ τοι δὴ ἀφῖκται, ἀλλὰ δοκεῖ μέν μοι ἥξειν τήμερον ἐξ ὧν ἀπαγγέλλουσιν ἥκοντές τινες ἀπὸ Σουνίου καὶ καταλιπόντες ἐκεῖ αὐτό. δῆλον οὖν ἐκ τούτων [τῶν ἀγγέλων], ὅτι ἥξει τήμερον, καὶ ἀνάγκη δὴ εἰς αὔριον 35 ἔσται, ὦ Σώκρατες, τὸν βίον σε τελευτᾶν.

ΣΩ. Ἀλλ᾽, ὦ Κρίτων, τύχῃ ἀγαθῇ. εἰ ταύτῃ τοῖς θεοῖς φίλον, ταύτῃ ἔστω. οὐ μέντοι οἶμαι ἥξειν αὐτὸ τήμερον.

44   ΚΡ. Πόθεν τοῦτο τεκμαίρει ;

ΣΩ. Ἐγώ σοι ἐρῶ. τῇ γάρ που ὑστεραίᾳ δεῖ με ἀπο- 40 θνήσκειν ἢ ᾗ ἂν ἔλθῃ τὸ πλοῖον.

ΚΡ. Φασί γέ τοι δὴ οἱ τούτων κύριοι.

ΣΩ. Οὐ τοίνυν τῆς ἐπιούσης ἡμέρας οἶμαι αὐτὸ ἥξειν, ἀλλὰ τῆς ἑτέρας. τεκμαίρομαι δὲ ἔκ τινος ἐνυπνίου, ὃ ἑώρακα ὀλίγον πρότερον ταύτης τῆς νυκτός· καὶ κινδυ- 45 νεύεις ἐν καιρῷ τινὶ οὐκ ἐγεῖραί με.

ΚΡ. Ἦν δὲ δὴ τί τὸ ἐνύπνιον ;

ΣΩ. Ἐδόκει τίς μοι γυνὴ προσελθοῦσα καλὴ καὶ B εὐειδής, λευκὰ ἱμάτια ἔχουσα, καλέσαι με καὶ εἰπεῖν, Ὦ Σώκρατες, Ἤματί κεν τριτάτῳ Φθίην ἐρίβωλον ἵκοιο.   50

ΚΡ. Ὡς ἄτοπον τὸ ἐνύπνιον, ὦ Σώκρατες.

ΣΩ. Ἐναργὲς μὲν οὖν, ὥς γέ μοι δοκεῖ, ὦ Κρίτων.

ΚΡ. Λίαν γε, ὡς ἔοικεν. ἀλλ᾽, ὦ δαιμόνιε Σώκρατες, ἔτι καὶ νῦν ἐμοὶ πείθου καὶ σώθητι· ὡς ἐμοί, ἐὰν σὺ ἀποθάνῃς, οὐ μία ξυμφορά ἐστιν, ἀλλὰ χωρὶς μὲν τοῦ 55

ἐστερῆσθαι τοιούτου ἐπιτηδείου, οἷον ἐγὼ οὐδένα μή ποτε
εὑρήσω, ἔτι δὲ καὶ πολλοῖς δόξω, οἳ ἐμὲ καὶ σὲ μὴ
σαφῶς ἴσασιν, ὡς οἷός τ' ὢν σε σώζειν, εἰ ἤθελον C
ἀναλίσκειν χρήματα, ἀμελῆσαι. καίτοι τίς ἂν αἰσχίων
60 εἴη ταύτης δόξα ἢ δοκεῖν χρήματα περὶ πλείονος ποιεῖσθαι ἢ φίλους; οὐ γὰρ πείσονται οἱ πολλοί, ὡς σὺ
αὐτὸς οὐκ ἠθέλησας ἀπιέναι ἐνθένδε ἡμῶν προθυμουμένων.

ΣΩ. Ἀλλὰ τί ἡμῖν, ὦ μακάριε Κρίτων, οὕτω τῆς τῶν
πολλῶν δόξης μέλει; οἱ γὰρ ἐπιεικέστατοι, ὧν μᾶλλον
65 ἄξιον φροντίζειν, ἡγήσονται αὐτὰ οὕτω πεπρᾶχθαι, ὥσπερ
ἂν πραχθῇ.

ΚΡ. Ἀλλ' ὁρᾷς δὴ ὅτι ἀνάγκη, ὦ Σώκρατες, καὶ τῆς D
τῶν πολλῶν δόξης μέλειν, αὐτὰ δὲ δῆλα τὰ παρόντα νυνί,
ὅτι οἷοί τ' εἰσὶν οἱ πολλοὶ οὐ τὰ σμικρότατα τῶν κακῶν
70 ἐξεργάζεσθαι, ἀλλὰ τὰ μέγιστα σχεδόν, ἐάν τις ἐν αὐτοῖς
διαβεβλημένος ᾖ.

ΣΩ. Εἰ γὰρ ὤφελον, ὦ Κρίτων, οἷοί τε εἶναι οἱ
πολλοὶ τὰ μέγιστα κακὰ ἐξεργάζεσθαι, ἵνα οἷοί τε ἦσαν
[αὖ] καὶ ἀγαθὰ τὰ μέγιστα, καὶ καλῶς ἂν εἶχε. νῦν δὲ
75 οὐδέτερα οἷοί τε· οὔτε γὰρ φρόνιμον οὔτε ἄφρονα δυνατοὶ
ποιῆσαι, ποιοῦσι δὲ τοῦτο ὅ τι ἂν τύχωσιν.

ΚΡ. Ταῦτα μὲν δὴ οὕτως ἐχέτω· τάδε δέ, ὦ Σώκρατες, E
εἰπέ μοι. ἆρά γε μὴ ἐμοῦ προμηθεῖ καὶ τῶν ἄλλων
ἐπιτηδείων, μή, ἐὰν σὺ ἐνθένδε ἐξέλθῃς, οἱ συκοφάνται
80 ἡμῖν πράγματα παρέχωσιν ὡς σὲ ἐνθένδε ἐκκλέψασι, καὶ
ἀναγκασθῶμεν ἢ καὶ πᾶσαν τὴν οὐσίαν ἀποβαλεῖν ἢ
συχνὰ χρήματα, ἢ καὶ ἄλλο τι πρὸς τούτοις παθεῖν; εἰ
γάρ τι τοιοῦτον φοβεῖ, ἔασον αὐτὸ χαίρειν· ἡμεῖς γάρ
που δίκαιοί ἐσμεν σώσαντές σε κινδυνεύειν τοῦτον τὸν 45
85 κίνδυνον καί, ἐὰν δέῃ, ἔτι τούτου μείζω. ἀλλ' ἐμοὶ
πείθου καὶ μὴ ἄλλως ποίει.

ΣΩ. Καὶ ταῦτα προμηθοῦμαι, ὦ Κρίτων, καὶ ἄλλα πολλά.

ΚΡ. Μήτε τοίνυν ταῦτα φοβοῦ· καὶ γὰρ οὐδὲ πολὺ τἀργύριόν ἐστιν, ὃ θέλουσι λαβόντες τινὲς σῶσαί σε καὶ 90 ἐξαγαγεῖν ἐνθένδε. ἔπειτα οὐχ ὁρᾷς τούτους τοὺς συκο- φάντας ὡς εὐτελεῖς, καὶ οὐδὲν ἂν δέοι ἐπ᾽ αὐτοὺς πολλοῦ B ἀργυρίου; σοὶ δὲ ὑπάρχει μὲν τὰ ἐμὰ χρήματα, ὡς ἐγὼ οἶμαι, ἱκανά· ἔπειτα καὶ εἴ τι ἐμοῦ κηδόμενος οὐκ οἴει δεῖν ἀναλίσκειν τἀμά, ξένοι οὗτοι ἐνθάδε ἔτοιμοι ἀνα- 95 λίσκειν· εἷς δὲ καὶ κεκόμικεν ἐπ᾽ αὐτὸ τοῦτο ἀργύριον ἱκανόν, Σιμμίας ὁ Θηβαῖος· ἔτοιμος δὲ καὶ Κέβης καὶ ἄλλοι πολλοὶ πάνυ. ὥστε, ὅπερ λέγω, μήτε ταῦτα φοβούμενος ἀποκάμῃς σαυτὸν σῶσαι, μήτε ὃ ἔλεγες ἐν τῷ δικαστηρίῳ, δυσχερές σοι γενέσθω, ὅτι οὐκ ἂν ἔχοις 100 ἐξελθὼν ὅ τι χρῷο σαυτῷ· πολλαχοῦ μὲν γὰρ καὶ C ἄλλοσε ὅποι ἂν ἀφίκῃ ἀγαπήσουσί σε· ἐὰν δὲ βούλῃ εἰς Θετταλίαν ἰέναι, εἰσὶν ἐμοὶ ἐκεῖ ξένοι, οἵ σε περὶ πολλοῦ ποιήσονται καὶ ἀσφάλειάν σοι παρέξονται, ὥστε σε μηδένα λυπεῖν τῶν κατὰ Θετταλίαν. 105

Ἔτι δέ, ὦ Σώκρατες, οὐδὲ δίκαιόν μοι δοκεῖς ἐπι- χειρεῖν πρᾶγμα, σαυτὸν προδοῦναι, ἐξὸν σωθῆναι· καὶ τοιαῦτα σπεύδεις περὶ σαυτὸν γενέσθαι, ἅπερ ἂν καὶ οἱ ἐχθροί σου σπεύσαιέν τε καὶ ἔσπευσαν σὲ διαφθεῖραι βουλόμενοι. πρὸς δὲ τούτοις καὶ τοὺς υἱεῖς τοὺς σαυτοῦ 110 D ἔμοιγε δοκεῖς προδιδόναι, οὕς σοι ἐξὸν καὶ ἐκθρέψαι καὶ ἐκπαιδεῦσαι οἰχήσει καταλιπών, καὶ τὸ σὸν μέρος, ὅ τι ἂν τύχωσι, τοῦτο πράξουσι· τεύξονται δέ, ὡς τὸ εἰκός, τοιούτων οἷάπερ εἴωθε γίγνεσθαι ἐν ταῖς ὀρφανίαις περὶ τοὺς ὀρφανούς. ἢ γὰρ οὐ χρὴ ποιεῖσθαι παῖδας, ἢ 115 ξυνδιαταλαιπωρεῖν καὶ τρέφοντα καὶ παιδεύοντα· σὺ δέ μοι δοκεῖς τὰ ῥᾳθυμότατα αἱρεῖσθαι· χρὴ δέ, ἅπερ ἂν

ἀνὴρ ἀγαθὸς καὶ ἀνδρεῖος ἕλοιτο, ταῦτα αἱρεῖσθαι, φάσκοντά γε δὴ ἀρετῆς διὰ παντὸς τοῦ βίου ἐπιμελεῖσθαι·
120 ὡς ἔγωγε καὶ ὑπὲρ σοῦ καὶ ὑπὲρ ἡμῶν τῶν σῶν ἐπι- E
τηδείων αἰσχύνομαι, μὴ δόξῃ ἅπαν τὸ πρᾶγμα τὸ περὶ σὲ
ἀνανδρίᾳ τινὶ τῇ ἡμετέρᾳ πεπρᾶχθαι, καὶ ἡ εἴσοδος τῆς
δίκης εἰς τὸ δικαστήριον ὡς εἰσῆλθες ἐξὸν μὴ εἰσελθεῖν,
καὶ αὐτὸς ὁ ἀγὼν τῆς δίκης ὡς ἐγένετο, καὶ τὸ τελευταῖον
125 δὴ τουτί, ὥσπερ κατάγελως τῆς πράξεως, κακίᾳ τινὶ καὶ
ἀνανδρίᾳ τῇ ἡμετέρᾳ διαπεφευγέναι ἡμᾶς δοκεῖν, οἵτινές 46
σε οὐχὶ ἐσώσαμεν οὐδὲ σὺ σαυτόν, οἷόν τε ὂν καὶ
δυνατόν, εἴ τι καὶ σμικρὸν ἡμῶν ὄφελος ἦν. ταῦτ' οὖν,
ὦ Σώκρατες, ὅρα μὴ ἅμα τῷ κακῷ καὶ αἰσχρὰ ᾖ σοί τε
130 καὶ ἡμῖν. ἀλλὰ βουλεύου, μᾶλλον δὲ οὐδὲ βουλεύεσθαι
ἔτι ὥρα, ἀλλὰ βεβουλεῦσθαι, μία δὲ βουλή· τῆς γὰρ
ἐπιούσης νυκτὸς πάντα ταῦτα δεῖ πεπρᾶχθαι. εἰ δ' ἔτι
περιμενοῦμεν, ἀδύνατον καὶ οὐκέτι οἷόν τε. ἀλλὰ παντὶ
τρόπῳ, ὦ Σώκρατες, πείθου μοι καὶ μηδαμῶς ἄλλως
135 ποίει.

ΣΩ. Ὦ φίλε Κρίτων, ἡ προθυμία σου πολλοῦ ἀξία, B
εἰ μετά τινος ὀρθότητος εἴη· εἰ δὲ μή, ὅσῳ μείζων,
τοσούτῳ χαλεπωτέρα. σκοπεῖσθαι οὖν χρὴ ἡμᾶς, εἴτε
ταῦτα πρακτέον εἴτε μή· ὡς ἐγὼ οὐ μόνον νῦν ἀλλὰ
140 καὶ ἀεὶ τοιοῦτος, οἷος τῶν ἐμῶν μηδενὶ ἄλλῳ πείθεσθαι
ἢ τῷ λόγῳ, ὃς ἄν μοι λογιζομένῳ βέλτιστος φαίνηται.
τοὺς δὲ λόγους, οὓς ἐν τῷ ἔμπροσθεν ἔλεγον, οὐ δύναμαι
νῦν ἐκβαλεῖν, ἐπειδή μοι ἥδε ἡ τύχη γέγονεν, ἀλλὰ
σχεδόν τι ὅμοιοι φαίνονταί μοι, καὶ τοὺς αὐτοὺς πρεσ-
145 βεύω καὶ τιμῶ οὕσπερ καὶ πρότερον· ὧν ἐὰν μὴ βελτίω C
ἔχωμεν λέγειν ἐν τῷ παρόντι, εὖ ἴσθι ὅτι οὐ μή σοι
ξυγχωρήσω, οὐδ' ἂν πλείω τῶν νῦν παρόντων· ἢ τῶν
πολλῶν δύναμις ὥσπερ παῖδας ἡμᾶς μορμολύττηται,

δεσμοὺς καὶ θανάτους ἐπιπέμπουσα καὶ χρημάτων ἀφαι-
ρέσεις. Πῶς οὖν ἂν μετριώτατα σκοποίμεθα αὐτά ; Εἰ 150
πρῶτον μὲν τοῦτον τὸν λόγον ἀναλάβοιμεν, ὃν σὺ λέγεις
περὶ τῶν δοξῶν, πότερον καλῶς ἐλέγετο ἑκάστοτε ἢ οὔ,
D ὅτι ταῖς μὲν δεῖ τῶν δοξῶν προσέχειν τὸν νοῦν, ταῖς δὲ
οὔ· ἢ πρὶν μὲν ἐμὲ δεῖν ἀποθνήσκειν καλῶς ἐλέγετο, νῦν
δὲ κατάδηλος ἄρα ἐγένετο, ὅτι ἄλλως ἕνεκα λόγου ἐλέ- 155
γετο, ἦν δὲ παιδιὰ καὶ φλυαρία ὡς ἀληθῶς ; ἐπιθυμῶ δ'
ἔγωγε ἐπισκέψασθαι, ὦ Κρίτων, κοινῇ μετὰ σοῦ, εἴ τί
μοι ἀλλοιότερος φανεῖται, ἐπειδὴ ὧδε ἔχω, ἢ ὁ αὐτός, καὶ
ἐάσομεν χαίρειν ἢ πεισόμεθα αὐτῷ. ἐλέγετο δέ πως, ὡς
ἐγῷμαι, ἑκάστοτε ὧδε ὑπὸ τῶν οἰομένων τι λέγειν, ὥσπερ 160
νῦν δὴ ἐγὼ ἔλεγον, ὅτι τῶν δοξῶν, ἃς οἱ ἄνθρωποι
E δοξάζουσι, δέοι τὰς μὲν περὶ πολλοῦ ποιεῖσθαι, τὰς δὲ
μή. τοῦτο πρὸς θεῶν, ὦ Κρίτων, οὐ δοκεῖ καλῶς σοι
λέγεσθαι ; σὺ γάρ, ὅσα γε τἀνθρώπεια, ἐκτὸς εἶ τοῦ
47 μέλλειν ἀποθνήσκειν αὔριον, καὶ οὐκ ἂν σε παρακρούοι ἡ 165
παροῦσα ξυμφορά· σκόπει δή· οὐχὶ καλῶς δοκεῖ σοι
λέγεσθαι, ὅτι οὐ πάσας χρὴ τὰς δόξας τῶν ἀνθρώπων
τιμᾶν, ἀλλὰ τὰς μέν, τὰς δ' οὔ ; οὐδὲ πάντων, ἀλλὰ τῶν
μέν, τῶν δ' οὔ ; τί φῄς ; ταῦτα οὐχὶ καλῶς λέγεται ;

KP. Καλῶς. 170

ΣΩ. Οὐκοῦν τὰς μὲν χρηστὰς τιμᾶν, τὰς δὲ πονηρὰς μή ;

KP. Ναί.

ΣΩ. Χρησταὶ δὲ οὐχ αἱ τῶν φρονίμων, πονηραὶ δὲ αἱ
τῶν ἀφρόνων ;

KP. Πῶς δ' οὔ ; 175

ΣΩ. Φέρε δή, πῶς αὖ τὰ τοιαῦτα ἐλέγετο ; γυμναζό-
B μενος ἀνὴρ καὶ τοῦτο πράττων πότερον παντὸς ἀνδρὸς
ἐπαίνῳ καὶ ψόγῳ καὶ δόξῃ τὸν νοῦν προσέχει, ἢ ἑνὸς
μόνου ἐκείνου, ὃς ἂν τυγχάνῃ ἰατρὸς ἢ παιδοτρίβης ὤν ;

180 ΚΡ. Ἑνὸς μόνου.

ΣΩ. Οὐκοῦν φοβεῖσθαι χρὴ τοὺς ψόγους καὶ ἀσπά ζεσθαι τοὺς ἐπαίνους τοὺς τοῦ ἑνὸς ἐκείνου, ἀλλὰ μὴ τοὺς τῶν πολλῶν.

ΚΡ. Δῆλα δή.

185 ΣΩ. Ταύτῃ ἄρα αὐτῷ πρακτέον καὶ γυμναστέον καὶ ἐδεστέον γε καὶ ποτέον, ᾗ ἂν τῷ ἑνὶ δοκῇ τῷ ἐπιστάτῃ καὶ ἐπαΐοντι, μᾶλλον ἢ ᾗ ξύμπασι τοῖς ἄλλοις.

ΚΡ. Ἔστι ταῦτα.

ΣΩ. Εἶεν. ἀπειθήσας δὲ τῷ ἑνὶ καὶ ἀτιμάσας αὐτοῦ C 190 τὴν δόξαν καὶ τοὺς ἐπαίνους, τιμήσας δὲ τοὺς τῶν πολλῶν λόγους καὶ μηδὲν ἐπαϊόντων, ἆρα οὐδὲν κακὸν πείσεται ;

ΚΡ. Πῶς γὰρ οὔ ;

ΣΩ. Τί δ' ἔστι τὸ κακὸν τοῦτο ; καὶ ποῖ τείνει, καὶ 195 εἰς τί τῶν τοῦ ἀπειθοῦντος ;

ΚΡ. Δῆλον ὅτι εἰς τὸ σῶμα· τοῦτο γὰρ διόλλυσιν.

ΣΩ. Καλῶς λέγεις. οὐκοῦν καὶ τἆλλα, ὦ Κρίτων, οὕτως, ἵνα μὴ πάντα διΐωμεν, καὶ δὴ καὶ περὶ τῶν δικαίων καὶ ἀδίκων καὶ αἰσχρῶν καὶ καλῶν καὶ ἀγαθῶν 200 καὶ κακῶν, περὶ ὧν νῦν ἡ βουλὴ ἡμῖν ἐστί, πότερον τῇ τῶν πολλῶν δόξῃ δεῖ ἡμᾶς ἕπεσθαι καὶ φοβεῖσθαι αὐτήν, D ἢ τῇ τοῦ ἑνός, εἴ τίς ἐστιν ἐπαίων, ὃν δεῖ καὶ αἰ- σχύνεσθαι καὶ φοβεῖσθαι μᾶλλον ἢ ξύμπαντας τοὺς ἄλλους ; ᾧ εἰ μὴ ἀκολουθήσομεν, διαφθεροῦμεν ἐκεῖνο 205 καὶ λωβησόμεθα, ὃ τῷ μὲν δικαίῳ βέλτιον ἐγίγνετο, τῷ δὲ ἀδίκῳ ἀπώλλυτο. ἢ οὐδέν ἐστι τοῦτο ;

ΚΡ. Οἶμαι ἔγωγε, ὦ Σώκρατες.

ΣΩ. Φέρε δή, ἐὰν τὸ ὑπὸ τοῦ ὑγιεινοῦ μὲν βέλτιον γιγνόμενον, ὑπὸ τοῦ νοσώδους δὲ διαφθειρόμενον, διο- 210 λέσωμεν πειθόμενοι μὴ τῇ τῶν ἐπαϊόντων δόξῃ, ἆρα

E βιωτὸν ἡμῖν ἐστι διεφθαρμένου αὐτοῦ; ἔστι δέ που τοῦτο τὸ σῶμα· ἢ οὐχί;

ΚΡ. Ναί.

ΣΩ. Ἆρ' οὖν βιωτὸν ἡμῖν ἐστι μετὰ μοχθηροῦ καὶ διεφθαρμένου σώματος; 215

ΚΡ. Οὐδαμῶς.

ΣΩ. Ἀλλὰ μετ' ἐκείνου ἄρα ἡμῖν βιωτὸν διεφθαρμέ- νου, ᾧ τὸ ἄδικον μὲν λωβᾶται, τὸ δὲ δίκαιον ὀνίνησιν; ἢ φαυλότερον ἡγούμεθα εἶναι τοῦ σώματος ἐκεῖνο, ὅ τί 48 ποτ' ἐστὶ τῶν ἡμετέρων, περὶ ὃ ἥ τε ἀδικία καὶ ἡ δι- 220 καιοσύνη ἐστίν;

ΚΡ. Οὐδαμῶς.

ΣΩ. Ἀλλὰ τιμιώτερον;

ΚΡ. Πολύ γε.

ΣΩ. Οὐκ ἄρα, ὦ βέλτιστε, πάνυ ἡμῖν οὕτω φρον- 225 τιστέον, τί ἐροῦσιν οἱ πολλοὶ ἡμᾶς, ἀλλ' ὅ τι ὁ ἐπαΐων περὶ τῶν δικαίων καὶ ἀδίκων, ὁ εἷς, καὶ αὐτὴ ἡ ἀλήθεια. ὥστε πρῶτον μὲν ταύτῃ οὐκ ὀρθῶς εἰσηγεῖ, εἰσηγούμενος τῆς τῶν πολλῶν δόξης δεῖν ἡμᾶς φροντίζειν περὶ τῶν δικαίων καὶ καλῶν καὶ ἀγαθῶν καὶ τῶν ἐναντίων. ἀλλὰ 230 μὲν δή, φαίη γ' ἄν τις, οἷοί τ' εἰσὶν ἡμᾶς οἱ πολλοὶ ἀπο- κτιννύναι;

Β ΚΡ. Δῆλα δὴ καὶ ταῦτα· φαίη γὰρ ἄν, ὦ Σώκρατες.

ΣΩ. Ἀληθῆ λέγεις. ἀλλ', ὦ θαυμάσιε, οὗτός τε ὁ λόγος, ὃν διεληλύθαμεν, ἔμοιγε δοκεῖ ὅμοιος εἶναι τῷ 235 καὶ πρότερον· καὶ τόνδε αὖ σκόπει, εἰ ἔτι μένει ἡμῖν ἢ οὔ, ὅτι οὐ τὸ ζῆν περὶ πλείστου ποιητέον, ἀλλὰ τὸ εὖ ζῆν.

ΚΡ. Ἀλλὰ μένει.

ΣΩ. Τὸ δὲ εὖ καὶ καλῶς καὶ δικαίως ὅτι ταὐτόν ἐστι, 240 μένει ἢ οὐ μένει;

ΚΡ. Μένει.

ΣΩ. Οὐκοῦν ἐκ τῶν ὁμολογουμένων τοῦτο σκεπτέον,
πότερον δίκαιον ἐμὲ ἐνθένδε πειρᾶσθαι ἐξιέναι μὴ ἀφι-
245 έντων Ἀθηναίων, ἢ οὐ δίκαιον· καὶ ἐὰν μὲν φαίνηται C
δίκαιον, πειρώμεθα, εἰ δὲ μή, ἐῶμεν. ἃς δὲ σὺ λέγεις
τὰς σκέψεις περί τε ἀναλώσεως χρημάτων καὶ δόξης
καὶ παίδων τροφῆς, μὴ ὡς ἀληθῶς ταῦτα, ὦ Κρίτων,
σκέμματα ᾖ τῶν ῥᾳδίως ἀποκτιννύντων καὶ ἀναβιωσκο-
250 μένων γ’ ἄν, εἰ οἷοί τε ἦσαν, οὐδενὶ ξὺν νῷ, τούτων
τῶν πολλῶν. ἡμῖν δ’, ἐπειδὴ ὁ λόγος οὕτως αἱρεῖ, μὴ
οὐδὲν ἄλλο σκεπτέον ᾖ ἢ ὅπερ νῦν δὴ ἐλέγομεν, πότερον
δίκαια πράξομεν καὶ χρήματα τελοῦντες τούτοις τοῖς ἐμὲ
ἐνθένδε ἐξάξουσι καὶ χάριτας, καὶ αὐτοὶ ἐξάγοντές τε D
255 καὶ ἐξαγόμενοι, ἢ τῇ ἀληθείᾳ ἀδικήσομεν πάντα ταῦτα
ποιοῦντες· κἂν φαινώμεθα ἄδικα αὐτὰ ἐργαζόμενοι, μὴ
οὐ δέῃ ὑπολογίζεσθαι οὔτ’ εἰ ἀποθνῄσκειν δεῖ παραμέ-
νοντας καὶ ἡσυχίαν ἄγοντας, οὔτε ἄλλο ὁτιοῦν πάσχειν
πρὸ τοῦ ἀδικεῖν.

260 ΚΡ. Καλῶς μέν μοι δοκεῖς λέγειν, ὦ Σώκρατες, ὅρα
δὲ τί δρῶμεν.

ΣΩ. Σκοπῶμεν, ὦ ’γαθέ, κοινῇ, καὶ εἴ πῃ ἔχεις
ἀντιλέγειν ἐμοῦ λέγοντος, ἀντίλεγε, καί σοι πείσομαι· εἰ
δὲ μή, παῦσαι ἤδη, ὦ μακάριε, πολλάκις μοι λέγων τὸν E
265 αὐτὸν λόγον, ὡς χρὴ ἐνθένδε ἀκόντων Ἀθηναίων ἐμὲ
ἀπιέναι· ὡς ἐγὼ περὶ πολλοῦ ποιοῦμαι πείσας σε ταῦτα
πράττειν, ἀλλὰ μὴ ἄκοντος. ὅρα δὲ δὴ τῆς σκέψεως τὴν
ἀρχήν, ἐάν σοι ἱκανῶς λέγηται, καὶ πειρῶ ἀποκρίνεσθαι
τὸ ἐρωτώμενον, ᾗ ἂν μάλιστα οἴῃ.

270 ΚΡ. Ἀλλὰ πειράσομαι. 49

ΣΩ. Οὐδενὶ τρόπῳ φαμὲν ἑκόντας ἀδικητέον εἶναι,
ἢ τινὶ μὲν ἀδικητέον τρόπῳ, τινὶ δὲ οὔ; ἢ οὐδαμῶς

τό γε ἀδικεῖν οὔτε ἀγαθὸν οὔτε καλόν, ὡς πολλάκις ἡμῖν
καὶ ἐν τῷ ἔμπροσθεν χρόνῳ ὡμολογήθη ; [ὅπερ καὶ ἄρτι
ἐλέγετο.] ἢ πᾶσαι ἡμῖν ἐκεῖναι αἱ πρόσθεν ὁμολογίαι ἐν 275
ταῖσδε ταῖς ὀλίγαις ἡμέραις ἐκκεχυμέναι εἰσί, καὶ πάλαι,
ὦ Κρίτων, ἆρα τηλικοίδε [γέροντες] ἄνδρες πρὸς ἀλλή-
B λους σπουδῇ διαλεγόμενοι ἐλάθομεν ἡμᾶς αὐτοὺς παίδων
οὐδὲν διαφέροντες ; ἢ παντὸς μᾶλλον οὕτως ἔχει, ὥσπερ
τότε ἐλέγετο ἡμῖν, εἴτε φασὶν οἱ πολλοὶ εἴτε μή ; καὶ 280
εἴτε δεῖ ἡμᾶς ἔτι τῶνδε χαλεπώτερα πάσχειν εἴτε καὶ
πραότερα, ὅμως τό γε ἀδικεῖν τῷ ἀδικοῦντι καὶ κακὸν καὶ
αἰσχρὸν τυγχάνει ὂν παντὶ τρόπῳ ; φαμὲν ἢ οὔ ;

ΚΡ. Φαμέν.

ΣΩ. Οὐδαμῶς ἄρα δεῖ ἀδικεῖν. 285

ΚΡ. Οὐ δῆτα.

ΣΩ. Οὐδὲ ἀδικούμενον ἄρα ἀνταδικεῖν, ὡς οἱ πολλοὶ
οἴονται, ἐπειδή γε οὐδαμῶς δεῖ ἀδικεῖν.

C ΚΡ. Οὐ φαίνεται.

ΣΩ. Τί δὲ δή, κακουργεῖν δεῖ, ὦ Κρίτων, ἢ οὔ ; 290

ΚΡ. Οὐ δεῖ δή που, ὦ Σώκρατες.

ΣΩ. Τί δέ ; ἀντικακουργεῖν κακῶς πάσχοντα, ὡς οἱ
πολλοί φασι, δίκαιον ἢ οὐ δίκαιον ;

ΚΡ. Οὐδαμῶς.

ΣΩ. Τὸ γάρ που κακῶς ποιεῖν ἀνθρώπους τοῦ ἀδικεῖν 295
οὐδὲν διαφέρει.

ΚΡ. Ἀληθῆ λέγεις.

ΣΩ. Οὔτε ἄρα ἀνταδικεῖν δεῖ οὔτε κακῶς ποιεῖν οὐδένα ἀνθρώπων, οὐδ' ἂν ὁτιοῦν πάσχῃ ὑπ' αὐτῶν. καὶ
D ὅρα, ὦ Κρίτων, ταῦτα καθομολογῶν, ὅπως μὴ παρὰ δόξαν 300
ὁμολογῇς. οἶδα γὰρ ὅτι ὀλίγοις τισὶ ταῦτα καὶ δοκεῖ
καὶ δόξει. οἷς οὖν οὕτω δέδοκται καὶ οἷς μή, τούτοις οὐκ
ἔστι κοινὴ βουλή, ἀλλ' ἀνάγκη τούτους ἀλλήλων κατα-

φρονεῖν, ὁρῶντας τὰ ἀλλήλων βουλεύματα. σκόπει δὴ
305 οὖν καὶ σὺ εὖ μάλα, πότερον κοινωνεῖς καὶ ξυνδοκεῖ σοι
καὶ ἀρχώμεθα ἐντεῦθεν βουλευόμενοι, ὡς οὐδέποτε ὀρθῶς
ἔχοντος οὔτε τοῦ ἀδικεῖν οὔτε τοῦ ἀνταδικεῖν οὔτε κακῶς
πάσχοντα ἀμύνεσθαι ἀντιδρῶντα κακῶς· ἢ ἀφίστασαι
καὶ οὐ κοινωνεῖς τῆς ἀρχῆς; ἐμοὶ μὲν γὰρ καὶ πάλαι E
310 οὕτω καὶ νῦν ἔτι δοκεῖ, σοὶ δ' εἴ πη ἄλλη δέδοκται, λέγε
καὶ δίδασκε. εἰ δὲ ἐμμένεις τοῖς πρόσθεν, τὸ μετὰ
τοῦτο ἄκουε.

ΚΡ. Ἀλλ' ἐμμένω τε καὶ ξυνδοκεῖ μοι· ἀλλὰ λέγε.

ΣΩ. Λέγω δὴ αὖ τὸ μετὰ τοῦτο, μᾶλλον δ' ἐρωτῶ·
315 πότερον ἃ ἄν τις ὁμολογήσῃ τῳ δίκαια ὄντα ποιητέον ἢ
ἐξαπατητέον;

ΚΡ. Ποιητέον.

ΣΩ. Ἐκ τούτων δὴ ἄθρει, ἀπιόντες ἐνθένδε ἡμεῖς μὴ
πείσαντες τὴν πόλιν πότερον κακῶς τινὰς ποιοῦμεν, καὶ 50
320 ταῦτα οὓς ἥκιστα δεῖ, ἢ οὔ; καὶ ἐμμένομεν οἷς ὡμολογή-
σαμεν δικαίοις οὖσιν ἢ οὔ;

ΚΡ. ·Οὐκ ἔχω, ὦ Σώκρατες, ἀποκρίνασθαι πρὸς ὃ
ἐρωτᾷς· οὐ γὰρ ἐννοῶ.

ΣΩ. Ἀλλ' ὧδε σκόπει. εἰ μέλλουσιν ἡμῖν ἐνθένδε
325 εἴτε ἀποδιδράσκειν, εἴθ' ὅπως δεῖ ὀνομάσαι τοῦτο, ἐλθόντες οἱ νόμοι καὶ τὸ κοινὸν τῆς πόλεως ἐπιστάντες ἔροιντο,
Εἰπέ μοι, ὦ Σώκρατες, τί ἐν νῷ ἔχεις ποιεῖν; ἄλλο τι
ἢ τούτῳ τῷ ἔργῳ, ᾧ ἐπιχειρεῖς, διανοεῖ τούς τε νόμους
ἡμᾶς ἀπολέσαι καὶ ξύμπασαν τὴν πόλιν τὸ σὸν μέρος; B
330 ἢ δοκεῖ σοι οἷόν τε ἔτι ἐκείνην τὴν πόλιν εἶναι καὶ μὴ
ἀνατετράφθαι, ἐν ᾗ ἂν αἱ γενόμεναι δίκαι μηδὲν ἰσχύω-
σιν, ἀλλ' ὑπὸ ἰδιωτῶν ἄκυροί τε γίγνωνται καὶ διαφθεί-
ρωνται; Τί ἐροῦμεν, ὦ Κρίτων, πρὸς ταῦτα καὶ ἄλλα
τοιαῦτα; πολλὰ γὰρ ἄν τις ἔχοι, ἄλλως τε καὶ ῥήτωρ,

εἰπεῖν ὑπὲρ τούτου τοῦ νόμου ἀπολλυμένου, ὃς τὰς δίκας 335
τὰς δικασθείσας προστάττει κυρίας εἶναι. ἢ ἐροῦμεν πρὸς

C αὐτοὺς ὅτι Ἠδίκει γὰρ ἡμᾶς ἡ πόλις καὶ οὐκ ὀρθῶς τὴν
δίκην ἔκρινε ; Ταῦτα ἢ τί ἐροῦμεν ;

ΚΡ. Ταῦτα νὴ Δί', ὦ Σώκρατες.

ΣΩ. Τί οὖν, ἂν εἴπωσιν οἱ νόμοι, Ὦ Σώκρατες, ἢ 340
καὶ ταῦτα ὡμολόγητο ἡμῖν τε καὶ σοί, ἢ ἐμμένειν ταῖς
δίκαις αἷς ἂν ἡ πόλις δικάζῃ ; εἰ οὖν αὐτῶν θαυμάζοιμεν
λεγόντων, ἴσως ἂν εἴποιεν ὅτι Ὦ Σώκρατες, μὴ θαύμαζε
τὰ λεγόμενα, ἀλλ' ἀποκρίνου, ἐπειδὴ καὶ εἴωθας χρῆσθαι
τῷ ἐρωτᾶν τε καὶ ἀποκρίνεσθαι. φέρε γάρ, τί ἐγκαλῶν 345

D ἡμῖν καὶ τῇ πόλει ἐπιχειρεῖς ἡμᾶς ἀπολλύναι ; οὐ πρῶτον μέν σε ἐγεννήσαμεν ἡμεῖς, καὶ δι' ἡμῶν ἐλάμβανε
τὴν μητέρα σου ὁ πατὴρ καὶ ἐφύτευσέ σε ; φράσον οὖν,
τούτοις ἡμῶν, [τοῖς νόμοις] τοῖς περὶ τοὺς γάμους, μέμ-
φει τι ὡς οὐ καλῶς ἔχουσιν ; Οὐ μέμφομαι, φαίην ἄν. 350
Ἀλλὰ τοῖς περὶ τὴν τοῦ γενομένου τροφήν τε καὶ παιδείαν, ἐν ᾗ καὶ σὺ ἐπαιδεύθης ; ἢ οὐ καλῶς προσέταττον
ἡμῶν οἱ ἐπὶ τούτοις τεταγμένοι [νόμοι], παραγγέλλοντες
τῷ πατρὶ τῷ σῷ σε ἐν μουσικῇ καὶ γυμναστικῇ παι-

E δεύειν ; Καλῶς, φαίην ἄν. Εἶεν. ἐπειδὴ δὲ ἐγένου τε 355
καὶ ἐξετράφης καὶ ἐπαιδεύθης, ἔχοις ἂν εἰπεῖν πρῶτον
μὲν ὡς οὐχὶ ἡμέτερος ἦσθα καὶ ἔκγονος καὶ δοῦλος,
αὐτός τε καὶ οἱ σοὶ πρόγονοι ; καὶ εἰ τοῦθ' οὕτως
ἔχει, ἆρ' ἐξ ἴσου οἴει εἶναι σοὶ τὸ δίκαιον καὶ ἡμῖν,
καὶ ἅττ' ἂν ἡμεῖς σε ἐπιχειρῶμεν ποιεῖν, καὶ σοὶ 360
ταῦτα ἀντιποιεῖν οἴει δίκαιον εἶναι ; ἢ πρὸς μὲν ἄρα
σοι τὸν πατέρα οὐκ ἐξ ἴσου ἦν τὸ δίκαιον καὶ πρὸς
τὸν δεσπότην, εἴ σοι ὢν ἐτύγχανεν, ὥστε, ἅπερ πά-
σχοις, ταῦτα καὶ ἀντιποιεῖν, οὔτε κακῶς ἀκούοντα

51 ἀντιλέγειν οὔτε τυπτόμενον ἀντιτύπτειν οὔτε ἄλλα 365

τοιαῦτα πολλά· πρὸς δὲ τὴν πατρίδα ἄρα καὶ τοὺς
νόμους ἐξέσται σοι, ὥστε, ἐάν σε ἐπιχειρῶμεν ἡμεῖς
ἀπολλύναι δίκαιον ἡγούμενοι εἶναι, καὶ σὺ δὲ ἡμᾶς
τοὺς νόμους καὶ τὴν πατρίδα καθ᾽ ὅσον δύνασαι ἐπι-
370 χειρήσεις ἀνταπολλύναι, καὶ φήσεις ταῦτα ποιῶν
δίκαια πράττειν, ὁ τῇ ἀληθείᾳ τῆς ἀρετῆς ἐπιμελό-
μενος; ἢ οὕτως εἶ σοφός, ὥστε λέληθέ σε ὅτι μητρός
τε καὶ πατρὸς καὶ τῶν ἄλλων προγόνων ἁπάντων τιμιώ-
τερόν ἐστιν ἡ πατρὶς καὶ σεμνότερον καὶ ἁγιώτερον καὶ
375 ἐν μείζονι μοίρᾳ καὶ παρὰ θεοῖς καὶ παρ᾽ ἀνθρώποις τοῖς B
νοῦν ἔχουσι, καὶ σέβεσθαι δεῖ καὶ μᾶλλον ὑπείκειν καὶ
θωπεύειν πατρίδα χαλεπαίνουσαν ἢ πατέρα, καὶ ἢ πείθειν
ἢ ποιεῖν ἃ ἂν κελεύῃ, καὶ πάσχειν, ἐάν τι προστάττῃ
παθεῖν, ἡσυχίαν ἄγοντα, ἐάν τε τύπτεσθαι ἐάν τε δεῖσθαι,
380 ἐάν τε εἰς πόλεμον ἄγῃ τρωθησόμενον ἢ ἀποθανούμενον,
ποιητέον ταῦτα, καὶ τὸ δίκαιον οὕτως ἔχει, καὶ οὐχὶ
ὑπεικτέον οὐδὲ ἀναχωρητέον οὐδὲ λειπτέον τὴν τάξιν,
ἀλλὰ καὶ ἐν πολέμῳ καὶ ἐν δικαστηρίῳ καὶ πανταχοῦ
ποιητέον ἃ ἂν κελεύῃ ἡ πόλις καὶ ἡ πατρίς, ἢ πείθειν C
385 αὐτὴν ᾗ τὸ δίκαιον πέφυκε, βιάζεσθαι δ᾽ οὐχ ὅσιον οὔτε
μητέρα οὔτε πατέρα, πολὺ δὲ τούτων ἔτι ἧττον τὴν
πατρίδα; Τί φήσομεν πρὸς ταῦτα, ὦ Κρίτων; ἀληθῆ
λέγειν τοὺς νόμους, ἢ οὔ;

ΚΡ. Ἔμοιγε δοκεῖ.

390 ΣΩ. Σκόπει τοίνυν, ὦ Σώκρατες, φαῖεν ἂν ἴσως οἱ
νόμοι, εἰ ἡμεῖς ταῦτα ἀληθῆ λέγομεν, ὅτι οὐ δίκαια ἡμᾶς
ἐπιχειρεῖς δρᾶν ἃ νῦν ἐπιχειρεῖς. ἡμεῖς γάρ σε γεννή-
σαντες, ἐκθρέψαντες, παιδεύσαντες, μεταδόντες ἁπάντων
ὧν οἷοί τ᾽ ἦμεν καλῶν σοὶ καὶ τοῖς ἄλλοις πᾶσι πολίταις, D
395 ὅμως προαγορεύομεν τῷ ἐξουσίαν πεποιηκέναι Ἀθηναίων
τῷ βουλομένῳ, ἐπειδὰν δοκιμασθῇ καὶ ἴδῃ τὰ ἐν τῇ

πόλει πράγματα καὶ ἡμᾶς τοὺς νόμους, ᾧ ἂν μὴ ἀρέ-
σκωμεν ἡμεῖς, ἐξεῖναι λαβόντα τὰ αὑτοῦ ἀπιέναι ὅποι
ἂν βούληται.   καὶ οὐδεὶς ἡμῶν [τῶν νόμων] ἐμποδών
ἐστιν οὐδ' ἀπαγορεύει, ἐάν τέ τις βούληται ὑμῶν εἰς 400
ἀποικίαν ἰέναι, εἰ μὴ ἀρέσκοιμεν ἡμεῖς τε καὶ ἡ πόλις,
ἐάν τε μετοικεῖν ἄλλοσέ ποι ἐλθών, ἰέναι ἐκεῖσε ὅποι ἂν
Ε βούληται, ἔχοντα τὰ αὑτοῦ. ὃς δ' ἂν ὑμῶν παραμείνῃ,
ὁρῶν ὃν τρόπον ἡμεῖς τάς τε δίκας δικάζομεν καὶ τᾶλλα
τὴν πόλιν διοικοῦμεν, ἤδη φαμὲν τοῦτον ὡμολογηκέναι 405
ἔργῳ ἡμῖν ἃ ἂν ἡμεῖς κελεύωμεν ποιήσειν ταῦτα, καὶ τὸν
μὴ πειθόμενον τριχῇ φαμὲν ἀδικεῖν, ὅτι τε γεννηταῖς
οὖσιν ἡμῖν οὐ πείθεται, καὶ ὅτι τροφεῦσι, καὶ ὅτι ὁμολογήσας ἡμῖν πείθεσθαι οὔτε πείθεται οὔτε πείθει ἡμᾶς, εἰ
52 μὴ καλῶς τι ποιοῦμεν, προτιθέντων ἡμῶν καὶ οὐκ ἀγρίως 410
ἐπιταττόντων ποιεῖν ἃ ἂν κελεύωμεν, ἀλλὰ ἐφιέντων δυοῖν
θάτερα, ἢ πείθειν ἡμᾶς ἢ ποιεῖν, τούτων οὐδέτερα ποιεῖ.

Ταύταις δή φαμεν καὶ σέ, ὦ Σώκρατες, ταῖς αἰτίαις
ἐνέξεσθαι, εἴπερ ποιήσεις ἃ ἐπινοεῖς, καὶ οὐχ ἥκιστα
Ἀθηναίων σέ, ἀλλ' ἐν τοῖς μάλιστα.   Εἰ οὖν ἐγὼ εἴποιμι, 415
διὰ τί δή; ἴσως ἄν μου δικαίως καθάπτοιντο, λέγοντες
ὅτι ἐν τοῖς μάλιστα Ἀθηναίων ἐγὼ αὐτοῖς ὡμολογηκὼς
τυγχάνω ταύτην τὴν ὁμολογίαν. φαῖεν γὰρ ἂν ὅτι Ὦ
Β Σώκρατες, μεγάλα ἡμῖν τούτων τεκμήριά ἐστιν, ὅτι σοι
καὶ ἡμεῖς ἠρέσκομεν καὶ ἡ πόλις· οὐ γὰρ ἄν ποτε τῶν 420
ἄλλων Ἀθηναίων ἁπάντων διαφερόντως ἐν αὐτῇ ἐπε-
δήμεις, εἰ μή σοι διαφερόντως ἤρεσκε, καὶ οὔτ' ἐπὶ
θεωρίαν πώποτε ἐκ τῆς πόλεως ἐξῆλθες, [ὅτι μὴ ἅπαξ
εἰς Ἰσθμόν,] οὔτε ἄλλοσε οὐδαμόσε, εἰ μή ποι στρατευ-
σόμενος, οὔτε ἄλλην ἀποδημίαν ἐποιήσω πώποτε, ὥσπερ 425
οἱ ἄλλοι ἄνθρωποι, οὐδ' ἐπιθυμία σε ἄλλης πόλεως οὐδ'
ἄλλων νόμων ἔλαβεν εἰδέναι, ἀλλὰ ἡμεῖς σοι ἱκανοὶ

ἦμεν καὶ ἡ ἡμετέρα πόλις· οὕτω σφόδρα ἡμᾶς ᾑροῦ, καὶ C
ὡμολόγεις καθ' ἡμᾶς πολιτεύεσθαι, τά τε ἄλλα καὶ παῖ-
430 δας ἐν αὐτῇ ἐποιήσω, ὡς ἀρεσκούσης σοι τῆς πόλεως.
ἔτι τοίνυν ἐν αὐτῇ τῇ δίκῃ ἐξῆν σοι φυγῆς τιμήσασθαι,
εἰ ἐβούλου, καὶ ὅπερ νῦν ἀκούσης τῆς πόλεως ἐπιχειρεῖς,
τότε ἑκούσης ποιῆσαι. σὺ δὲ τότε μὲν ἐκαλλωπίζου ὡς
οὐκ ἀγανακτῶν, εἰ δέοι τεθνάναι σε, ἀλλ' ᾑροῦ, ὡς
435 ἔφησθα, πρὸ τῆς φυγῆς θάνατον· νῦν δὲ οὔτ' ἐκείνους
τοὺς λόγους αἰσχύνει, οὔτε ἡμῶν τῶν νόμων ἐντρέπει,
ἐπιχειρῶν διαφθεῖραι, πράττεις τε ἅπερ ἂν δοῦλος φαυ- D
λότατος πράξειεν, ἀποδιδράσκειν ἐπιχειρῶν παρὰ τὰς
ξυνθήκας τε καὶ τὰς ὁμολογίας, καθ' ἃς ἡμῖν ξυνέθου
440 πολιτεύεσθαι. πρῶτον [μὲν] οὖν ἡμῖν τοῦτ' αὐτὸ ἀπόκριναι, εἰ ἀληθῆ λέγομεν φάσκοντές σε ὡμολογηκέναι
πολιτεύεσθαι καθ' ἡμᾶς ἔργῳ, ἀλλ' οὐ λόγῳ, ἢ οὐκ
ἀληθῆ. Τί φῶμεν πρὸς ταῦτα, ὦ Κρίτων ; ἄλλο τι
ἢ ὁμολογῶμεν ;

445   ΚΡ. Ἀνάγκη, ὦ Σώκρατες.

ΣΩ. Ἄλλο τι οὖν, ἂν φαῖεν, ἢ ξυνθήκας τὰς πρὸς
ἡμᾶς αὐτοὺς καὶ ὁμολογίας παραβαίνεις, οὐχ ὑπ' ἀνάγκης E
ὁμολογήσας οὐδὲ ἀπατηθεὶς οὐδὲ ἐν ὀλίγῳ χρόνῳ ἀναγ-
κασθεὶς βουλεύσασθαι, ἀλλ' ἐν ἔτεσιν ἑβδομήκοντα, ἐν
450 οἷς ἐξῆν σοι ἀπιέναι, εἰ μὴ ἠρέσκομεν ἡμεῖς μηδὲ δίκαιαι
ἐφαίνοντό σοι αἱ ὁμολογίαι εἶναι. σὺ δὲ οὔτε Λακεδαίμονα προῃροῦ οὔτε Κρήτην, ἃς δὴ ἑκάστοτε φῂς εὐνο-
μεῖσθαι, οὔτε ἄλλην οὐδεμίαν τῶν Ἑλληνίδων πόλεων
οὐδὲ τῶν βαρβαρικῶν, ἀλλ' ἐλάττω ἐξ αὐτῆς ἀπεδήμησας 53
455 ἢ οἱ χωλοί τε καὶ τυφλοὶ καὶ οἱ ἄλλοι ἀνάπηροι· οὕτω
σοι διαφερόντως τῶν ἄλλων Ἀθηναίων ἤρεσκεν ἡ πόλις
τε καὶ ἡμεῖς οἱ νόμοι δῆλον ὅτι· τίνι γὰρ ἂν πόλις
ἀρέσκοι ἄνευ νόμων ; νῦν δὲ δὴ οὐκ ἐμμενεῖς τοῖς ὡμο-

λογημένοις; ἐὰν ἡμῖν γε πείθῃ, ὦ Σώκρατες· καὶ οὐ
καταγέλαστός γε ἔσει ἐκ τῆς πόλεως ἐξελθών.   460

Σκόπει γὰρ δή, ταῦτα παραβὰς καὶ ἐξαμαρτάνων τι
τούτων τί ἀγαθὸν ἐργάσει σαυτὸν ἢ τοὺς ἐπιτηδείους
B τοὺς σαυτοῦ. ὅτι μὲν γὰρ κινδυνεύσουσί γέ σου οἱ ἐπιτήδειοι καὶ αὐτοὶ φεύγειν καὶ στερηθῆναι τῆς πόλεως ἢ
τὴν οὐσίαν ἀπολέσαι, σχεδόν τι δῆλον· αὐτὸς δὲ πρῶτον 465
μὲν ἐὰν εἰς τῶν ἐγγύτατά τινα πόλεων ἔλθῃς, ἢ Θήβαζε
ἢ Μέγαράδε—εὐνομοῦνται γὰρ ἀμφότεραι—, πολέμιος
ἥξεις, ὦ Σώκρατες, τῇ τούτων πολιτείᾳ, καὶ ὅσοιπερ
κήδονται τῶν αὐτῶν πόλεων, ὑποβλέψονταί σε διαφθορέα
ἡγούμενοι τῶν νόμων, καὶ βεβαιώσεις τοῖς δικασταῖς 470
C τὴν δόξαν, ὥστε δοκεῖν ὀρθῶς τὴν δίκην δικάσαι· ὅστις
γὰρ νόμων διαφθορεύς ἐστι, σφόδρα που δόξειεν ἂν νέων
γε καὶ ἀνοήτων ἀνθρώπων διαφθορεὺς εἶναι. πότερον
οὖν φεύξει τάς τε εὐνομουμένας πόλεις καὶ τῶν ἀνδρῶν
τοὺς κοσμιωτάτους; καὶ τοῦτο ποιοῦντι ἆρα ἄξιόν σοι 475
ζῆν ἔσται; ἢ πλησιάσεις τούτοις καὶ ἀναισχυντήσεις
διαλεγόμενος—τίνας λόγους, ὦ Σώκρατες; ἢ οὕσπερ
ἐνθάδε, ὡς ἡ ἀρετὴ καὶ ἡ δικαιοσύνη πλείστου ἄξιον
τοῖς ἀνθρώποις καὶ τὰ νόμιμα καὶ οἱ νόμοι; καὶ οὐκ οἴει
D ἄσχημον φανεῖσθαι τὸ τοῦ Σωκράτους πρᾶγμα; οἴεσθαί 480
γε χρή. Ἀλλ᾽ ἐκ μὲν τούτων τῶν τόπων ἀπαρεῖς, ἥξεις
δὲ εἰς Θετταλίαν παρὰ τοὺς ξένους τοὺς Κρίτωνος. ἐκεῖ
γὰρ δὴ πλείστη ἀταξία καὶ ἀκολασία, καὶ ἴσως ἂν ἡδέως
σου ἀκούοιεν ὡς γελοίως ἐκ τοῦ δεσμωτηρίου ἀπεδί-
δρασκες σκευήν τέ τινα περιθέμενος, ἢ διφθέραν λαβὼν ἢ 485
ἄλλα οἷα δὴ εἰώθασιν ἐνσκευάζεσθαι οἱ ἀποδιδράσκοντες,
καὶ τὸ σχῆμα τὸ σαυτοῦ μεταλλάξας. ὅτι δὲ γέρων ἀνὴρ
E σμικροῦ χρόνου τῷ βίῳ λοιποῦ ὄντος, ὡς τὸ εἰκός, ἐτόλ-
μησας οὕτω γλίσχρως ἐπιθυμεῖν ζῆν, νόμους τοὺς μεγί-

490 στους παραβάς, οὐδεὶς ὃς ἐρεῖ; ἴσως, ἂν μή τινα λυπῇς·
εἰ δὲ μή, ἀκούσει, ὦ Σώκρατες, πολλὰ καὶ ἀνάξια σαυτοῦ.
ὑπερχόμενος δὴ βιώσει πάντας ἀνθρώπους καὶ δουλεύων·
τί ποιῶν ἢ εὐωχούμενος ἐν Θετταλίᾳ, ὥσπερ ἐπὶ δεῖπνον
ἀποδεδημηκὼς εἰς Θετταλίαν; λόγοι δὲ ἐκεῖνοι οἱ περὶ
495 δικαιοσύνης τε καὶ τῆς ἄλλης ἀρετῆς ποῦ ἡμῖν ἔσονται; 54
Ἀλλὰ δὴ τῶν παίδων ἕνεκα βούλει ζῆν, ἵνα αὐτοὺς
ἐκθρέψῃς καὶ παιδεύσῃς; τί δέ; εἰς Θετταλίαν αὐτοὺς
ἀγαγὼν θρέψεις τε καὶ παιδεύσεις, ξένους ποιήσας, ἵνα
καὶ τοῦτό σου ἀπολαύσωσιν; ἢ τοῦτο μὲν οὔ, αὐτοῦ δὲ
500 τρεφόμενοι σοῦ ζῶντος βέλτιον θρέψονται καὶ παιδεύ-
σονται, μὴ ξυνόντος σοῦ αὐτοῖς; οἱ γὰρ ἐπιτήδειοι οἱ
σοὶ ἐπιμελήσονται αὐτῶν. πότερον ἐὰν εἰς Θετταλίαν
ἀποδημήσῃς, ἐπιμελήσονται, ἐὰν δὲ εἰς Ἅιδου ἀποδημήσῃς, οὐχὶ ἐπιμελήσονται; εἴπερ γέ τι ὄφελος αὐτῶν ἐστὶ
505 τῶν σοι φασκόντων ἐπιτηδείων εἶναι, οἴεσθαί γε χρή.   B
Ἀλλ', ὦ Σώκρατες, πειθόμενος ἡμῖν τοῖς σοῖς τροφεῦσι μήτε παῖδας περὶ πλείονος ποιοῦ μήτε τὸ ζῆν μήτε
ἄλλο μηδὲν πρὸ τοῦ δικαίου, ἵνα εἰς Ἅιδου ἐλθὼν ἔχῃς
πάντα ταῦτα ἀπολογήσασθαι τοῖς ἐκεῖ ἄρχουσιν· οὔτε
510 γὰρ ἐνθάδε σοι φαίνεται ταῦτα πράττοντι ἄμεινον εἶναι
οὐδὲ δικαιότερον οὐδὲ ὁσιώτερον, οὐδὲ ἄλλῳ τῶν σῶν
οὐδενί, οὔτε ἐκεῖσε ἀφικομένῳ ἄμεινον ἔσται. ἀλλὰ νῦν
μὲν ἠδικημένος ἄπει, ἐὰν ἀπίῃς, οὐχ ὑφ' ἡμῶν τῶν νόμων
ἀλλ' ὑπ' ἀνθρώπων· ἐὰν δὲ ἐξέλθῃς οὕτως αἰσχρῶς C
515 ἀνταδικήσας τε καὶ ἀντικακουργήσας, τὰς σαυτοῦ ὁμολογίας τε καὶ ξυνθήκας τὰς πρὸς ἡμᾶς παραβὰς καὶ κακὰ
ἐργασάμενος τούτους οὓς ἥκιστα ἔδει, σαυτόν τε καὶ
φίλους καὶ πατρίδα καὶ ἡμᾶς, ἡμεῖς τέ σοι χαλεπανοῦ-
μεν ζῶντι, καὶ ἐκεῖ οἱ ἡμέτεροι ἀδελφοὶ οἱ ἐν Ἅιδου
520 νόμοι οὐκ εὐμενῶς σε ὑποδέξονται, εἰδότες ὅτι καὶ ἡμᾶς

ἐπεχείρησας ἀπολέσαι τὸ σὸν μέρος. ἀλλὰ μή σε πείσῃ
D Κρίτων ποιεῖν ἃ λέγει μᾶλλον ἢ ἡμεῖς.

Ταῦτα, ὦ φίλε ἑταῖρε Κρίτων, εὖ ἴσθι ὅτι ἐγὼ δοκῶ
ἀκούειν, ὥσπερ οἱ κορυβαντιῶντες τῶν αὐλῶν δοκοῦσιν
ἀκούειν, καὶ ἐν ἐμοὶ αὕτη ἡ ἠχὴ τούτων τῶν λόγων 525
βομβεῖ καὶ ποιεῖ μὴ δύνασθαι τῶν ἄλλων ἀκούειν·
ἀλλὰ ἴσθι, ὅσα γε τὰ νῦν ἐμοὶ δοκοῦντα, ἐὰν λέγῃς
παρὰ ταῦτα, μάτην ἐρεῖς. ὅμως μέντοι εἴ τι οἴει πλέον
ποιήσειν, λέγε.

ΚΡ. Ἀλλ᾽, ὦ Σώκρατες, οὐκ ἔχω λέγειν.   530

Ε ΣΩ. Ἔα τοίνυν, ὦ Κρίτων, καὶ πράττωμεν ταύτῃ,
ἐπειδὴ ταύτῃ ὁ θεὸς ὑφηγεῖται.

PHAEDO.

Socrates about to die.

(ECHECRATES. PHAEDO.)

57   Αὐτός, ὦ Φαίδων, παρεγένου Σωκράτει ἐκείνῃ τῇ
ἡμέρᾳ, ᾗ τὸ φάρμακον ἔπιεν ἐν τῷ δεσμωτηρίῳ, ἢ ἄλλου
του ἤκουσας ;

ΦΑΙΔ. Αὐτός, ὦ Ἐχέκρατες.

ΕΧ. Τί οὖν δή ἐστιν ἄττα εἶπεν ὁ ἀνὴρ πρὸ τοῦ 5
θανάτου ; καὶ πῶς ἐτελεύτα ; ἡδέως γὰρ ἂν ἐγὼ ἀκού-
σαιμι. καὶ γὰρ οὔτε τῶν πολιτῶν Φλιασίων οὐδεὶς πάνυ
τι ἐπιχωριάζει τὰ νῦν Ἀθήναζε, οὔτε τις ξένος ἀφῖκται
Β χρόνου συχνοῦ ἐκεῖθεν, ὅστις ἂν ἡμῖν σαφές τι ἀγγεῖλαι
οἷός τ᾽ ἦν περὶ τούτων, πλήν γε δὴ ὅτι φάρμακον πιὼν 10
ἀποθάνοι· τῶν δὲ ἄλλων οὐδὲν εἶχε φράζειν.

58   ΦΑΙΔ. Οὐδὲ τὰ περὶ τῆς δίκης ἄρα ἐπύθεσθε ὃν
τρόπον ἐγένετο ;

ΕΧ. Ναί, ταῦτα μὲν ἡμῖν ἤγγειλέ τις, καὶ ἐθαυμά-
ζομέν γε ὅτι πάλαι γενομένης αὐτῆς πολλῷ ὕστερον
15 φαίνεται ἀποθανών. τί οὖν ἦν τοῦτο, ὦ Φαίδων ;

ΦΑΙΔ. Τύχη τις αὐτῷ, ὦ Ἐχέκρατες, συνέβη. ἔτυχε
γὰρ τῇ προτεραίᾳ τῆς δίκης ἡ πρύμνα ἐστεμμένη τοῦ
πλοίου ὃ εἰς Δῆλον Ἀθηναῖοι πέμπουσιν.

ΕΧ. Τοῦτο δὲ δὴ τί ἐστιν ;

20 ΦΑΙΔ. Τοῦτό ἐστι τὸ πλοῖον, ὥς φασιν Ἀθηναῖοι,
ἐν ᾧ Θησεύς ποτε εἰς Κρήτην τοὺς δὶς ἑπτὰ ἐκείνους
ᾤχετο ἄγων καὶ ἔσωσέ τε καὶ αὐτὸς ἐσώθη. τῷ οὖν Β
Ἀπόλλωνι εὔξαντο, ὡς λέγεται, τότε, εἰ σωθεῖεν, ἑκάστου
ἔτους θεωρίαν ἀπάξειν εἰς Δῆλον· ἣν δὴ ἀεὶ καὶ νῦν ἔτι
25 ἐξ ἐκείνου κατ' ἐνιαυτὸν τῷ θεῷ πέμπουσιν. ἐπειδὰν οὖν
ἄρξωνται τῆς θεωρίας, νόμος ἐστὶν αὐτοῖς ἐν τῷ χρόνῳ
τούτῳ καθαρεύειν τὴν πόλιν καὶ δημοσίᾳ μηδένα ἀποκτιννύναι, πρὶν ἂν εἰς Δῆλόν τε ἀφίκηται τὸ πλοῖον καὶ
πάλιν δεῦρο· τοῦτο δ' ἐνίοτε ἐν πολλῷ χρόνῳ γίγνεται,
30 ὅταν τύχωσιν ἄνεμοι ἀπολαβόντες αὐτούς· ἀρχὴ δ' ἐστὶ C
τῆς θεωρίας, ἐπειδὰν ὁ ἱερεὺς τοῦ Ἀπόλλωνος στέψῃ τὴν
πρύμναν τοῦ πλοίου· τοῦτο δ' ἔτυχεν, ὥσπερ λέγω, τῇ
προτεραίᾳ τῆς δίκης γεγονός. διὰ ταῦτα καὶ πολὺς χρόνος
ἐγένετο τῷ Σωκράτει ἐν τῷ δεσμωτηρίῳ ὁ μεταξὺ τῆς
35 δίκης τε καὶ τοῦ θανάτου.

ΕΧ. Τί δὲ δὴ τὰ περὶ αὐτὸν τὸν θάνατον, ὦ Φαίδων ;
τί ἦν τὰ λεχθέντα καὶ πραχθέντα, καὶ τίνες οἱ παραγενόμενοι τῶν ἐπιτηδείων τῷ ἀνδρί ; ἢ οὐκ εἴων οἱ
ἄρχοντες παρεῖναι, ἀλλ' ἔρημος ἐτελεύτα φίλων ;

40 ΦΑΙΔ. Οὐδαμῶς, ἀλλὰ παρῆσάν τινες, καὶ πολλοί γε. D

ΕΧ. Ταῦτα δὴ πάντα προθυμήθητι ὡς σαφέστατα
ἡμῖν ἀπαγγεῖλαι, εἰ μή τίς σοι ἀσχολία τυγχάνει οὖσα.

ΦΑΙΔ. Ἀλλὰ σχολάζω γε, καὶ πειράσομαι ὑμῖν

διηγήσασθαι· καὶ γὰρ τὸ μεμνῆσθαι Σωκράτους καὶ αὐτὸν
λέγοντα καὶ ἄλλου ἀκούοντα ἔμοιγε ἀεὶ πάντων ἥδιστον. 45

ΕΧ. Ἀλλὰ μήν, ὦ Φαίδων, καὶ τοὺς ἀκουσομένους
γε τοιούτους ἑτέρους ἔχεις. ἀλλὰ πειρῶ ὡς ἂν δύνῃ ἀκριβέστατα διελθεῖν πάντα.

Ε ΦΑΙΔ. Καὶ μὴν ἔγωγε θαυμάσια ἔπαθον παραγενόμενος. οὔτε γὰρ ὡς θανάτῳ παρόντα με ἀνδρὸς ἐπιτηδείου 50
ἔλεος εἰσῄει. εὐδαίμων γάρ μοι ἀνὴρ ἐφαίνετο, ὦ Ἐχέκρατες, καὶ τοῦ τρόπου καὶ τῶν λόγων, ὡς ἀδεῶς καὶ
γενναίως ἐτελεύτα, ὥστε μοι ἐκεῖνον παρίστασθαι μηδ᾽
εἰς Ἅιδου ἰόντα ἄνευ θείας μοίρας ἰέναι, ἀλλὰ κἀκεῖσε
59 ἀφικόμενον εὖ πράξειν, εἴπερ τις πώποτε καὶ ἄλλος. διὰ 55
δὴ ταῦτα οὐδὲν πάνυ μοι ἐλεεινὸν εἰσῄει, ὡς εἰκὸς ἂν
δόξειεν εἶναι παρόντι πένθει· οὔτε αὖ ἡδονὴ ὡς ἐν
φιλοσοφίᾳ ἡμῶν ὄντων, ὥσπερ εἰώθειμεν· καὶ γὰρ οἱ
λόγοι τοιοῦτοί τινες ἦσαν· ἀλλ᾽ ἀτεχνῶς ἄτοπόν τί μοι
πάθος παρῆν καί τις ἀήθης κρᾶσις ἀπό τε τῆς ἡδονῆς 60
συγκεκραμένη ὁμοῦ καὶ ἀπὸ τῆς λύπης, ἐνθυμουμένῳ ὅτι
αὐτίκα ἐκεῖνος ἔμελλε τελευτᾶν. καὶ πάντες οἱ παρόντες
σχεδόν τι οὕτω διεκείμεθα, ὁτὲ μὲν γελῶντες, ἐνίοτε δὲ
δακρύοντες, εἷς δὲ ἡμῶν καὶ διαφερόντως, Ἀπολλόδωρος·
Β οἶσθα γάρ που τὸν ἄνδρα καὶ τὸν τρόπον αὐτοῦ. 65

ΕΧ. Πῶς γὰρ οὔ;

ΦΑΙΔ. Ἐκεῖνός τε τοίνυν παντάπασιν οὕτως εἶχε,
καὶ αὐτὸς ἔγωγε ἐτεταράγμην καὶ οἱ ἄλλοι.

ΕΧ. Ἔτυχον δέ, ὦ Φαίδων, τίνες παραγενόμενοι;

ΦΑΙΔ. Οὗτός τε δὴ ὁ Ἀπολλόδωρος τῶν ἐπιχωρίων 70
παρῆν καὶ Κριτόβουλος καὶ ὁ πατὴρ αὐτοῦ Κρίτων, καὶ
ἔτι Ἑρμογένης καὶ Ἐπιγένης καὶ Αἰσχίνης καὶ Ἀντι-
σθένης. ἦν δὲ καὶ Κτήσιππος ὁ Παιανιεὺς καὶ Μενέξενος καὶ
ἄλλοι τινὲς τῶν ἐπιχωρίων· Πλάτων δέ, οἶμαι, ἠσθένει.

75 ΕΧ. Ξένοι δέ τινες παρῆσαν;   C

ΦΑΙΔ. Ναί, Σιμμίας τέ γε ὁ Θηβαῖος καὶ Κέβης καὶ
Φαιδώνδης, καὶ Μεγαρόθεν Εὐκλείδης τε καὶ Τερψίων.

ΕΧ. Τί δέ; 'Αρίστιππος καὶ Κλεόμβροτος παρεγένοντο;

80 ΦΑΙΔ. Οὐ δῆτα· ἐν Αἰγίνῃ γὰρ ἐλέγοντο εἶναι.

ΕΧ. "Αλλος δέ τις παρῆν;

ΦΑΙΔ. Σχεδόν τι οἶμαι τούτους παραγενέσθαι.

ΕΧ. Τί οὖν δή; τίνες, φής, ἦσαν οἱ λόγοι;

ΦΑΙΔ. 'Εγώ σοι ἐξ ἀρχῆς πάντα πειράσομαι διηγή-
85 σασθαι. ἀεὶ γὰρ δὴ καὶ τὰς πρόσθεν ἡμέρας εἰώθειμεν D
φοιτᾶν καὶ ἐγὼ καὶ οἱ ἄλλοι παρὰ τὸν Σωκράτη, συλ-
λεγόμενοι ἕωθεν εἰς τὸ δικαστήριον, ἐν ᾧ καὶ ἡ δίκη
ἐγένετο· πλησίον γὰρ ἦν τοῦ δεσμωτηρίου. περιεμένομεν
οὖν ἑκάστοτε, ἕως ἀνοιχθείη τὸ δεσμωτήριον, διατρίβοντες
90 μετ' ἀλλήλων· ἀνεῴγετο γὰρ οὐ πρῴ· ἐπειδὴ δὲ ἀνοιχθείη, εἰσῇμεν παρὰ τὸν Σωκράτη καὶ τὰ πολλὰ διημερεύο-
μεν μετ' αὐτοῦ. καὶ δὴ καὶ τότε πρωϊαίτερον ξυνελέγημεν.
τῇ γὰρ προτεραίᾳ ἡμέρᾳ ἐπειδὴ ἐξήλθομεν ἐκ τοῦ
δεσμωτηρίου ἑσπέρας, ἐπυθόμεθα ὅτι τὸ πλοῖον ἐκ Δήλου E
95 ἀφιγμένον εἴη. παρηγγείλαμεν οὖν ἀλλήλοις ἥκειν ὡς
πρωϊαίτατα εἰς τὸ εἰωθός. καὶ ἥκομεν, καὶ ἡμῖν ἐξελθὼν
ὁ θυρωρός, ὅσπερ εἰώθει ὑπακούειν, εἶπε περιμένειν καὶ
μὴ πρότερον παριέναι, ἕως ἂν αὐτὸς κελεύσῃ· Λύουσι
γάρ, ἔφη, οἱ ἕνδεκα Σωκράτη καὶ παραγγέλλουσιν, ὅπως
100 ἂν τῇδε τῇ ἡμέρᾳ τελευτήσῃ. οὐ πολὺν δ' οὖν χρόνον
ἐπισχὼν ἧκε καὶ ἐκέλευσεν ἡμᾶς εἰσιέναι. εἰσελθόντες
οὖν κατελαμβάνομεν τὸν μὲν Σωκράτη ἄρτι λελυμένον, 60
τὴν δὲ Ξανθίππην, γιγνώσκεις γάρ, ἔχουσάν τε τὸ
παιδίον αὐτοῦ καὶ παρακαθημένην· ὡς οὖν εἶδεν ἡμᾶς
105 ἡ Ξανθίππη, ἀνευφήμησέ τε καὶ τοιαῦτ' ἄττα εἶπεν, οἷα

δὴ εἰώθασιν αἱ γυναῖκες, ὅτι Ὦ Σώκρατες, ὕστατον δή
σε προσεροῦσι νῦν οἱ ἐπιτήδειοι καὶ σὺ τούτους. Καὶ ὁ
Σωκράτης βλέψας εἰς τὸν Κρίτωνα, Ὦ Κρίτων, ἔφη,
ἀπαγέτω τις ταύτην οἴκαδε. Καὶ ἐκείνην μὲν ἀπῆγόν
B τινες τῶν τοῦ Κρίτωνος βοῶσάν τε καὶ κοπτομένην· ὁ δὲ 110
Σωκράτης ἀνακαθιζόμενος ἐπὶ τὴν κλίνην συνέκαμψέ τε
τὸ σκέλος καὶ ἐξέτριψε τῇ χειρί, καὶ τρίβων ἅμα Ὡς
ἄτοπον, ἔφη, ὦ ἄνδρες, ἔοικέ τι εἶναι τοῦτο, ὃ καλοῦσιν
οἱ ἄνθρωποι ἡδύ· ὡς θαυμασίως πέφυκε πρὸς τὸ δοκοῦν
ἐναντίον εἶναι, τὸ λυπηρόν, τῷ ἅμα μὲν αὐτὼ μὴ ἐθέλειν 115
παραγίγνεσθαι τῷ ἀνθρώπῳ, ἐὰν δέ τις διώκῃ τὸ ἕτερον
καὶ λαμβάνῃ, σχεδόν τι ἀναγκάζεσθαι λαμβάνειν καὶ τὸ
ἕτερον, ὥσπερ ἐκ μιᾶς κορυφῆς συνημμένω δύ' ὄντε. καί
C μοι δοκεῖ, ἔφη, εἰ ἐνενόησεν αὐτὰ Αἴσωπος, μῦθον ἂν
συνθεῖναι, ὡς ὁ θεὸς βουλόμενος αὐτὰ διαλλάξαι πολε- 120
μοῦντα, ἐπειδὴ οὐκ ἠδύνατο, ξυνῆψεν εἰς ταὐτὸν αὐτοῖς
τὰς κορυφάς, καὶ διὰ ταῦτα ᾧ ἂν τὸ ἕτερον παραγένηται
ἐπακολουθεῖ ὕστερον καὶ τὸ ἕτερον. ὥσπερ οὖν καὶ αὐτῷ
μοι ἔοικεν, ἐπειδὴ ὑπὸ τοῦ δεσμοῦ ἦν ἐν τῷ σκέλει
πρότερον τὸ ἀλγεινόν, ἥκειν δὴ φαίνεται ἐπακολουθοῦν 125
τὸ ἡδύ.
Ὁ οὖν Κέβης ὑπολαβὼν Νὴ τὸν Δία, ὦ Σώκρατες,
D ἔφη, εὖ γ' ἐποίησας ἀναμνήσας με. περὶ γάρ τοι τῶν
ποιημάτων ὧν πεποίηκας ἐντείνας τοὺς τοῦ Αἰσώπου
λόγους καὶ τὸ εἰς τὸν Ἀπόλλω προοίμιον καὶ ἄλλοι τινές 130
με ἤδη ἤροντο, ἀτὰρ καὶ Εὔηνος πρώην, ὅ τί ποτε δια-
νοηθείς, ἐπειδὴ δεῦρο ἦλθες, ἐποίησας αὐτά, πρότερον
οὐδὲν πώποτε ποιήσας. εἰ οὖν τί σοι μέλει τοῦ ἔχειν ἐμὲ
Εὐήνῳ ἀποκρίνασθαι, ὅταν με αὖθις ἔρηται, εὖ οἶδα γὰρ
ὅτι ἐρήσεται, εἰπέ, τί χρή με λέγειν. Λέγε τοίνυν, ἔφη, 135
αὐτῷ, ὦ Κέβης, τἀληθῆ, ὅτι οὐκ ἐκείνῳ βουλόμενος οὐδὲ

τοῖς ποιήμασιν αὐτοῦ ἀντίτεχνος εἶναι ἐποίησα ταῦτα·
ᾔδειν γὰρ ὡς οὐ ῥᾴδιον εἴη· ἀλλ' ἐνυπνίων τινῶν ἀπο- E
πειρώμενος τί λέγει, καὶ ἀφοσιούμενος εἰ ἄρα πολλάκις
140 ταύτην τὴν μουσικήν μοι ἐπιτάττοι ποιεῖν. ἦν γὰρ δὴ ἄττα
τοιάδε· πολλάκις μοι φοιτῶν τὸ αὐτὸ ἐνύπνιον ἐν τῷ
παρελθόντι βίῳ, ἄλλοτ' ἐν ἄλλῃ ὄψει φαινόμενον, τὰ
αὐτὰ δὲ λέγον, Ὦ Σώκρατες, ἔφη, μουσικὴν ποίει καὶ
ἐργάζου. καὶ ἐγὼ ἔν γε τῷ πρόσθεν χρόνῳ, ὅπερ ἔπρατ-
145 τον, τοῦτο ὑπελάμβανον αὐτό μοι παρακελεύεσθαί τε καὶ 61.
ἐπικελεύειν, ὥσπερ οἱ τοῖς θέουσι διακελευόμενοι, καὶ
ἐμοὶ οὕτω τὸ ἐνύπνιον, ὅπερ ἔπραττον, τοῦτο ἐπικελεύειν,
μουσικὴν ποιεῖν, ὡς φιλοσοφίας μὲν οὔσης μεγίστης
μουσικῆς, ἐμοῦ δὲ τοῦτο πράττοντος. νῦν δ' ἐπειδὴ ἥ τε
150 δίκη ἐγένετο καὶ ἡ τοῦ θεοῦ ἑορτὴ διεκώλυέ με ἀποθνήσκειν, ἔδοξε χρῆναι, εἰ ἄρα πολλάκις μοι προστάττοι τὸ
ἐνύπνιον ταύτην τὴν δημώδη μουσικὴν ποιεῖν, μὴ ἀπειθῆ-
σαι αὐτῷ, ἀλλὰ ποιεῖν. ἀσφαλέστερον γὰρ εἶναι μὴ
ἀπιέναι πρὶν ἀφοσιώσασθαι ποιήσαντα ποιήματα, πειθό- B
155 μενον τῷ ἐνυπνίῳ. οὕτω δὴ πρῶτον μὲν εἰς τὸν θεὸν
ἐποίησα, οὗ ἦν ἡ παροῦσα θυσία· μετὰ δὲ τὸν θεόν,
ἐννοήσας ὅτι τὸν ποιητὴν δέοι, εἴπερ μέλλοι ποιητὴς
εἶναι, ποιεῖν μύθους, ἀλλ' οὐ λόγους, καὶ αὐτὸς οὐκ ἦ
μυθολογικός, διὰ ταῦτα δὴ οὓς προχείρους εἶχον καὶ
160 ἠπιστάμην μύθους τοὺς Αἰσώπου, τούτους ἐποίησα, οἷς
πρώτοις ἐνέτυχον.

Ταῦτα οὖν, ὦ Κέβης, Εὐήνῳ φράζε, καὶ ἐρρῶσθαι καί,
ἂν σωφρονῇ, ἐμὲ διώκειν ὡς τάχιστα. ἄπειμι δέ, ὡς
ἔοικε, τήμερον· κελεύουσι γὰρ Ἀθηναῖοι. Καὶ ὁ Σιμμίας, C
165 Οἷον παρακελεύει, ἔφη, τοῦτο, ὦ Σώκρατες, Εὐήνῳ;
πολλὰ γὰρ ἤδη ἐντετύχηκα τῷ ἀνδρί· σχεδὸν οὖν ἐξ ὧν
ἐγὼ ᾔσθημαι, οὐδ' ὁπωστιοῦν σοι ἑκὼν εἶναι πείσεται.

Τί δαί ; ἦ δ' ὅς· οὐ φιλόσοφος Εὔηνος ; Ἔμοιγε δοκεῖ, ἔφη ὁ Σιμμίας. Ἐθελήσει τοίνυν, ἔφη, καὶ Εὔηνος καὶ πᾶς ὅτῳ ἀξίως τούτου τοῦ πράγματος μέτεστιν. οὐ μέντοι 170 γ' ἴσως βιάσεται αὐτόν· οὐ γάρ φασι θεμιτὸν εἶναι. Καὶ ἅμα λέγων ταῦτα καθῆκε τὰ σκέλη ἀπὸ τῆς κλίνης D ἐπὶ τὴν γῆν, καὶ καθεζόμενος οὕτως ἤδη τὰ λοιπὰ διελέγετο.

Ἤρετο οὖν αὐτὸν ὁ Κέβης, Πῶς τοῦτο λέγεις, ὦ 175 Σώκρατες, τὸ μὴ θεμιτὸν εἶναι ἑαυτὸν βιάζεσθαι, ἐθέλειν δ' ἂν τῷ ἀποθνήσκοντι τὸν φιλόσοφον ἕπεσθαι ; Τί δαί, ὦ Κέβης ; οὐκ ἀκηκόατε σύ τε καὶ Σιμμίας περὶ τῶν τοιούτων Φιλολάῳ συγγεγονότες ; Οὐδέν γε σαφές, ὦ Σώκρατες. Ἀλλὰ μὴν κἀγὼ ἐξ ἀκοῆς περὶ αὐτῶν λέγω· 180 ἃ μὲν οὖν τυγχάνω ἀκηκοώς, φθόνος οὐδεὶς λέγειν. καὶ E γὰρ ἴσως καὶ μάλιστα πρέπει μέλλοντα ἐκεῖσε ἀποδημεῖν διασκοπεῖν τε καὶ μυθολογεῖν περὶ τῆς ἀποδημίας τῆς ἐκεῖ, ποίαν τινὰ αὐτὴν οἰόμεθα εἶναι· τί γὰρ ἄν τις καὶ ποιοῖ ἄλλο ἐν τῷ μέχρι ἡλίου δυσμῶν χρόνῳ ;   185

Κατὰ τί οὖν δή ποτε οὔ φασι θεμιτὸν εἶναι αὐτὸν ἑαυτὸν ἀποκτιννύναι, ὦ Σώκρατες ; ἤδη γὰρ ἔγωγε, ὅπερ νῦν δὴ σὺ ἤρου, καὶ Φιλολάου ἤκουσα, ὅτε παρ' ἡμῖν διῃτᾶτο, ἤδη δὲ καὶ ἄλλων τινῶν, ὡς οὐ δέοι τοῦτο ποιεῖν· σαφὲς δὲ περὶ αὐτῶν οὐδενὸς πώποτε οὐδὲν 190 62 ἀκήκοα. Ἀλλὰ προθυμεῖσθαι χρή, ἔφη· τάχα γὰρ ἂν καὶ ἀκούσαις. ἴσως μέντοι θαυμαστόν σοι φανεῖται, εἰ τοῦτο μόνον τῶν ἄλλων ἁπάντων ἁπλοῦν ἐστὶ καὶ οὐδέποτε τυγχάνει τῷ ἀνθρώπῳ, ὥσπερ καὶ τἆλλα, ἔστιν ὅτε καὶ οἷς βέλτιον τεθνάναι ἢ ζῆν. οἷς δὲ βέλτιον τεθνάναι, 195 θαυμαστὸν ἴσως σοι φαίνεται, εἰ τούτοις τοῖς ἀνθρώποις μὴ ὅσιόν ἐστιν αὐτοὺς ἑαυτοὺς εὖ ποιεῖν, ἀλλ' ἄλλον δεῖ περιμένειν εὐεργέτην. Καὶ ὁ Κέβης ἠρέμα ἐπιγελάσας,

Ἴττω Ζεύς, ἔφη, τῇ αὑτοῦ φωνῇ εἰπών. Καὶ γὰρ ἂν
200 δόξειεν, ἔφη ὁ Σωκράτης, οὕτω γ᾽ εἶναι ἄλογον· οὐ μέντοι B
ἀλλ᾽ ἴσως ἔχει τινὰ λόγον. ὁ μὲν οὖν ἐν ἀπορρήτοις
λεγόμενος περὶ αὐτῶν λόγος, ὡς ἔν τινι φρουρᾷ ἐσμὲν
οἱ ἄνθρωποι καὶ οὐ δεῖ δὴ ἑαυτὸν ἐκ ταύτης λύειν οὐδ᾽
ἀποδιδράσκειν, μέγας τέ τίς μοι φαίνεται καὶ οὐ ῥᾴδιος
205 διιδεῖν· οὐ μέντοι ἀλλὰ τόδε γέ μοι δοκεῖ, ὦ Κέβης, εὖ
λέγεσθαι, τὸ θεοὺς εἶναι ἡμῶν τοὺς ἐπιμελουμένους καὶ
ἡμᾶς τοὺς ἀνθρώπους ἐν τῶν κτημάτων τοῖς θεοῖς εἶναι·
ἢ σοὶ οὐ δοκεῖ οὕτως ; Ἔμοιγε, ἔφη ὁ Κέβης. Οὐκοῦν,
ἦ δ᾽ ὅς, καὶ σὺ ἂν τῶν σαυτοῦ κτημάτων εἴ τι αὐτὸ ἑαυτὸ C
210 ἀποκτιννύοι, μὴ σημήναντός σου ὅτι βούλει αὐτὸ τεθνάναι, χαλεπαίνοις ἂν αὐτῷ, καὶ εἴ τινα ἔχοις τιμωρίαν,
τιμωροῖο ἄν ; Πάνυ γ᾽, ἔφη. Ἴσως τοίνυν ταύτῃ οὐκ
ἄλογον μὴ πρότερον αὐτὸν ἀποκτιννύναι δεῖν, πρὶν ἂν
ἀνάγκην τινὰ ὁ θεὸς ἐπιπέμψῃ, ὥσπερ καὶ τὴν νῦν
215 παροῦσαν ἡμῖν.

’Αλλ᾽ εἰκός, ἔφη ὁ Κέβης, τοῦτό γε φαίνεται. ὁ μέντοι
νῦν δὴ ἔλεγες, τὸ τοὺς φιλοσόφους ῥᾳδίως ἂν ἐθέλειν
ἀποθνήσκειν, ἔοικε τοῦτο, ὦ Σώκρατες, ἀτόπῳ, εἴπερ ὃ D
νῦν δὴ ἐλέγομεν εὐλόγως ἔχει, τὸ θεόν τε εἶναι τὸν
220 ἐπιμελούμενον ἡμῶν καὶ ἡμᾶς ἐκείνου κτήματα εἶναι.
τὸ γὰρ μὴ ἀγανακτεῖν τοὺς φρονιμωτάτους ἐκ ταύτης
τῆς θεραπείας ἀπιόντας, ἐν ᾗ ἐπιστατοῦσιν αὐτῶν οἵπερ
ἄριστοί εἰσι τῶν ὄντων ἐπιστάται, θεοί, οὐκ ἔχει λόγον.
οὐ γάρ που αὐτός γε αὑτοῦ οἴεται ἄμεινον ἐπιμελήσεσθαι
225 ἐλεύθερος γενόμενος· ἀλλ᾽ ἀνόητος μὲν ἄνθρωπος τάχ᾽
ἂν οἰηθείη ταῦτα, φευκτέον εἶναι ἀπὸ τοῦ δεσπότου, καὶ
οὐκ ἂν λογίζοιτο ὅτι οὐ δεῖ ἀπό γε τοῦ ἀγαθοῦ φεύγειν, E
ἀλλ᾽ ὅ τι μάλιστα παραμένειν, διὸ ἀλογίστως ἂν φεύγοι·
ὁ δὲ νοῦν ἔχων ἐπιθυμοῖ που ἂν ἀεὶ εἶναι παρὰ τῷ αὑτοῦ

βελτίονι. καίτοι οὕτως, ὦ Σώκρατες, τοὐναντίον εἶναι 230
εἰκὸς ἢ ὃ νῦν δὴ ἐλέγετο· τοὺς μὲν γὰρ φρονίμους
ἀγανακτεῖν ἀποθνήσκοντας πρέπει, τοὺς δ' ἄφρονας χαίρειν. Ἀκούσας οὖν ὁ Σωκράτης ἡσθῆναί τέ μοι ἔδοξε τῇ
63 τοῦ Κέβητος πραγματείᾳ, καὶ ἐπιβλέψας εἰς ἡμᾶς Ἀεί
τοι, ἔφη, ὁ Κέβης λόγους τινὰς ἀνερευνᾷ, καὶ οὐ πάνυ 235
εὐθέως ἐθέλει πείθεσθαι ὅ τι ἄν τις εἴπῃ. Καὶ ὁ Σιμμίας
Ἀλλὰ μήν, ἔφη, ὦ Σώκρατες, νῦν γε δοκεῖ τί μοι καὶ
αὐτῷ λέγειν Κέβης· τί γὰρ ἂν βουλόμενοι ἄνδρες σοφοὶ
ὡς ἀληθῶς δεσπότας ἀμείνους αὑτῶν φεύγοιεν καὶ ῥᾳδίως
ἀπαλλάττοιντο αὐτῶν; καί μοι δοκεῖ Κέβης εἰς σὲ τείνειν 240
τὸν λόγον, ὅτι οὕτω ῥᾳδίως φέρεις καὶ ἡμᾶς ἀπολείπων
B καὶ ἄρχοντας ἀγαθούς, ὡς αὐτὸς ὁμολογεῖς, θεούς. Δίκαια,
ἔφη, λέγετε. οἶμαι γὰρ ὑμᾶς λέγειν ὅτι χρή με πρὸς
ταῦτα ἀπολογήσασθαι ὥσπερ ἐν δικαστηρίῳ. Πάνυ μὲν
οὖν, ἔφη ὁ Σιμμίας. 245

Φέρε δή, ᾗ δ' ὅς, πειραθῶ πρὸς ὑμᾶς πιθανώτερον
ἀπολογήσασθαι ἢ πρὸς τοὺς δικαστάς. ἐγὼ γάρ, ἔφη, ὦ
Σιμμία τε καὶ Κέβης, εἰ μὲν μὴ ᾤμην ἥξειν πρῶτον μὲν
παρὰ θεοὺς ἄλλους σοφούς τε καὶ ἀγαθούς, ἔπειτα καὶ
παρ' ἀνθρώπους τετελευτηκότας ἀμείνους τῶν ἐνθάδε, 250
ἠδίκουν ἂν οὐκ ἀγανακτῶν τῷ θανάτῳ· νῦν δὲ εὖ ἴστε
C ὅτι παρ' ἄνδρας τε ἐλπίζω ἀφίξεσθαι ἀγαθούς· καὶ τοῦτο
μὲν οὐκ ἂν πάνυ διισχυρισαίμην· ὅτι μέντοι παρὰ θεοὺς
δεσπότας πάνυ ἀγαθοὺς ἥξειν, εὖ ἴστε ὅτι, εἴπερ τι ἄλλο
τῶν τοιούτων, διισχυρισαίμην ἂν καὶ τοῦτο. ὥστε διὰ 255
ταῦτα οὐχ ὁμοίως ἀγανακτῶ, ἀλλ' εὔελπίς εἰμι εἶναί τι
τοῖς τετελευτηκόσι καί, ὥσπερ γε καὶ πάλαι λέγεται,
πολὺ ἄμεινον τοῖς ἀγαθοῖς ἢ τοῖς κακοῖς. Τί οὖν, ἔφη ὁ
Σιμμίας, ὦ Σώκρατες; πότερον αὐτὸς ἔχων τὴν διάνοιαν
D ταύτην ἐν νῷ ἔχεις ἀπιέναι, ἢ κἂν ἡμῖν μεταδοίης; κοινὸν 260

γὰρ δὴ ἔμοιγε δοκεῖ καὶ ἡμῖν εἶναι ἀγαθὸν τοῦτο. καὶ
ἅμα σοι ἡ ἀπολογία ἔσται, ἐὰν ἅπερ λέγεις ἡμᾶς πείσῃς.
Ἀλλὰ πειράσομαί γε, ἔφη. πρῶτον δὲ Κρίτωνα τόνδε
σκεψώμεθα, τί ἐστιν ὃ βούλεσθαί μοι δοκεῖ πάλαι εἰπεῖν.
265 Τί δέ, ὦ Σώκρατες, ἔφη ὁ Κρίτων, ἄλλο γε ἢ πάλαι μοι
λέγει ὁ μέλλων σοι δώσειν τὸ φάρμακον, ὅτι χρή σοι
φράζειν ὡς ἐλάχιστα διαλέγεσθαι; φησὶ γὰρ θερμαί-
νεσθαι μᾶλλον τοὺς διαλεγομένους, δεῖν δὲ οὐδὲν τοιοῦτον
προσφέρειν τῷ φαρμάκῳ· εἰ δὲ μή, ἐνίοτε ἀναγκάζεσθαι E
270 καὶ δὶς καὶ τρὶς πίνειν τούς τι τοιοῦτον ποιοῦντας. Καὶ
ὁ Σωκράτης, Ἔα, ἔφη, χαίρειν αὐτόν· ἀλλὰ μόνον τὸ
ἑαυτοῦ παρασκευαζέτω ὡς καὶ δὶς δώσων, ἐὰν δὲ δέῃ, καὶ
τρίς. Ἀλλὰ σχεδὸν μέν τι ἤδη, ἔφη ὁ Κρίτων· ἀλλά
μοι πάλαι πράγματα παρέχει. Ἔα αὐτόν, ἔφη.
275   Ἀλλ' ὑμῖν δὴ τοῖς δικασταῖς βούλομαι ἤδη τὸν λόγον
ἀποδοῦναι, ὥς μοι φαίνεται εἰκότως ἀνὴρ τῷ ὄντι ἐν
φιλοσοφίᾳ διατρίψας τὸν βίον θαρρεῖν μέλλων ἀποθανεῖ- 64
σθαι καὶ εὔελπις εἶναι ἐκεῖ μέγιστα οἴσεσθαι ἀγαθά,
ἐπειδὰν τελευτήσῃ· πῶς ἂν οὖν δὴ τοῦθ' οὕτως ἔχοι, ὦ
280 Σιμμία τε καὶ Κέβης, ἐγὼ πειράσομαι φράσαι.

Κινδυνεύουσι γὰρ ὅσοι τυγχάνουσιν ὀρθῶς ἁπτόμενοι
φιλοσοφίας λεληθέναι τοὺς ἄλλους, ὅτι οὐδὲν ἄλλο αὐτοὶ
ἐπιτηδεύουσιν ἢ ἀποθνήσκειν τε καὶ τεθνάναι. εἰ οὖν
τοῦτο ἀληθές, ἄτοπον δήπου ἂν εἴη προθυμεῖσθαι μὲν ἐν
285 παντὶ τῷ βίῳ μηδὲν ἄλλο ἢ τοῦτο, ἥκοντος δὲ δὴ αὐτοῦ
ἀγανακτεῖν, ὃ πάλαι προεθυμοῦντό τε καὶ ἐπετήδευον.
Καὶ ὁ Σιμμίας γελάσας Νὴ τὸν Δία, ἔφη, ὦ Σώκρατες, B
οὐ πάνυ γέ με νῦν δὴ γελασείοντα ἐποίησας γελάσαι.
οἶμαι γὰρ ἂν δὴ τοὺς πολλοὺς αὐτὸ τοῦτο ἀκούσαντας
290 δοκεῖν εὖ πάνυ εἰρῆσθαι εἰς τοὺς φιλοσοφοῦντας καὶ
ξυμφάναι ἂν τοὺς μὲν παρ' ἡμῖν ἀνθρώπους καὶ πάνυ,

ὅτι τῷ ὄντι οἱ φιλοσοφοῦντες θανατῶσι καὶ σφᾶς γε οὐ
λελήθασιν, ὅτι ἄξιοί εἰσι τοῦτο πάσχειν. Καὶ ἀληθῆ
γ᾽ ἂν λέγοιεν, ὦ Σιμμία, πλήν γε τοῦ σφᾶς μὴ λεληθέναι. λέληθε γὰρ αὐτοὺς ᾗ τε θανατῶσι καὶ ᾗ ἄξιοί 295
εἰσι θανάτου καὶ οἵου θανάτου οἱ ὡς ἀληθῶς φιλόσοφοι.
C εἴπωμεν γάρ, ἔφη, πρὸς ἡμᾶς αὐτούς, χαίρειν εἰπόντες
ἐκείνοις· ἡγούμεθά τι τὸν θάνατον εἶναι; Πάνυ γε, ἔφη
ὑπολαβὼν ὁ Σιμμίας. Ἆρα μὴ ἄλλο τι ἢ τὴν τῆς ψυχῆς
ἀπὸ τοῦ σώματος ἀπαλλαγήν; καὶ εἶναι τοῦτο τὸ τεθ- 300
νάναι, χωρὶς μὲν ἀπὸ τῆς ψυχῆς ἀπαλλαγὲν αὐτὸ καθ᾽
αὑτὸ τὸ σῶμα γεγονέναι, χωρὶς δὲ τὴν ψυχὴν ἀπὸ τοῦ
σώματος ἀπαλλαγεῖσαν αὐτὴν καθ᾽ αὑτὴν εἶναι; ἆρα μὴ
ἄλλο τι ὁ θάνατος ἢ τοῦτο; Οὔκ, ἀλλὰ τοῦτο, ἔφη.
Σκέψαι δή, ὦ ᾽γαθέ, ἐὰν ἄρα καὶ σοὶ ξυνδοκῇ ἅπερ καὶ 305
D ἐμοί. ἐκ γὰρ τούτων μᾶλλον οἶμαι ἡμᾶς εἴσεσθαι περὶ
ὧν σκοποῦμεν. φαίνεταί σοι φιλοσόφου ἀνδρὸς εἶναι
ἐσπουδακέναι περὶ τὰς ἡδονὰς καλουμένας τὰς τοιάσδε,
οἷον σιτίων τε καὶ ποτῶν; Ἥκιστά γε, ὦ Σώκρατες, ἔφη
ὁ Σιμμίας. Τί δέ; τὰς τῶν ἀφροδισίων; Οὐδαμῶς. 310
Τί δέ; τὰς ἄλλας τὰς περὶ τὸ σῶμα θεραπείας δοκεῖ σοι
ἐντίμους ἡγεῖσθαι ὁ τοιοῦτος; οἷον ἱματίων διαφερόντων
κτήσεις καὶ ὑποδημάτων καὶ τοὺς ἄλλους καλλωπισμοὺς
τοὺς περὶ τὸ σῶμα πότερον τιμᾶν σοι δοκεῖ ἢ ἀτιμάζειν,
E καθ᾽ ὅσον μὴ πολλὴ ἀνάγκη μετέχειν αὐτῶν; Ἀτιμάζειν 315
ἔμοιγε δοκεῖ, ἔφη, ὅ γε ὡς ἀληθῶς φιλόσοφος. Οὐκοῦν
ὅλως δοκεῖ σοι, ἔφη, ἡ τοῦ τοιούτου πραγματεία οὐ περὶ
τὸ σῶμα εἶναι, ἀλλὰ καθ᾽ ὅσον δύναται ἀφεστάναι αὐτοῦ,
πρὸς δὲ τὴν ψυχὴν τετράφθαι; Ἔμοιγε. Ἆρ᾽ οὖν πρῶτον μὲν ἐν τοῖς τοιούτοις δῆλός ἐστιν ὁ φιλόσοφος 320
65 ἀπολύων ὅ τι μάλιστα τὴν ψυχὴν ἀπὸ τῆς τοῦ σώματος
κοινωνίας διαφερόντως τῶν ἄλλων ἀνθρώπων; Φαίνεται.

Καὶ δοκεῖ γέ που, ὦ Σιμμία, τοῖς πολλοῖς ἀνθρώποις, ᾧ μηδὲν ἡδὺ τῶν τοιούτων μηδὲ μετέχει αὐτῶν, οὐκ ἄξιον 325 εἶναι ζῆν, ἀλλ' ἐγγύς τι τείνειν τοῦ τεθνάναι ὁ μηδὲν φροντίζων τῶν ἡδονῶν αἳ διὰ τοῦ σώματός εἰσιν. Πάνυ μὲν οὖν ἀληθῆ λέγεις.

Τί δὲ δὴ περὶ αὐτὴν τὴν τῆς φρονήσεως κτῆσιν; πότερον ἐμπόδιον τὸ σῶμα ἢ οὔ, ἐάν τις αὐτὸ ἐν τῇ 330 ζητήσει κοινωνὸν συμπαραλαμβάνῃ; οἷον τὸ τοιόνδε λέγω· ἆρα ἔχει ἀλήθειάν τινα ὄψις τε καὶ ἀκοὴ τοῖς B ἀνθρώποις, ἢ τά γε τοιαῦτα καὶ οἱ ποιηταὶ ἡμῖν ἀεὶ θρυλοῦσιν, ὅτι οὔτ' ἀκούομεν ἀκριβὲς οὐδὲν οὔτε ὁρῶμεν; καίτοι εἰ αὗται τῶν περὶ τὸ σῶμα αἰσθήσεων μὴ 335 ἀκριβεῖς εἰσι μηδὲ σαφεῖς, σχολῇ αἵ γε ἄλλαι· πᾶσαι γάρ που τούτων φαυλότεραί εἰσιν. ἤ σοι οὐ δοκοῦσιν; Πάνυ μὲν οὖν, ἔφη. Πότε οὖν, ἦ δ' ὅς, ἡ ψυχὴ τῆς ἀληθείας ἅπτεται; ὅταν μὲν γὰρ μετὰ τοῦ σώματος ἐπιχειρῇ τι σκοπεῖν, δῆλον ὅτι τότε ἐξαπατᾶται ὑπ' 340 αὐτοῦ. Ἀληθῆ λέγεις. Ἆρ' οὖν οὐκ ἐν τῷ λογίζεσθαι, C εἴπερ που ἄλλοθι, κατάδηλον αὐτῇ γίγνεταί τι τῶν ὄντων; Ναί. Λογίζεται δέ γέ που τότε κάλλιστα, ὅταν μηδὲν τούτων αὐτὴν παραλυπῇ, μήτε ἀκοὴ μήτε ὄψις μήτε ἀλγηδὼν μήτε τις ἡδονή, ἀλλ' ὅ τι μάλιστα 345 αὐτὴ καθ' αὑτὴν γίγνηται ἐῶσα χαίρειν τὸ σῶμα, καὶ καθ' ὅσον δύναται μὴ κοινωνοῦσα αὐτῷ μηδ' ἁπτομένη ὀρέγηται τοῦ ὄντος. Ἔστι ταῦτα. Οὐκοῦν καὶ ἐνταῦθα ἡ τοῦ φιλοσόφου ψυχὴ μάλιστα ἀτιμάζει τὸ σῶμα καὶ D φεύγει ἀπ' αὐτοῦ, ζητεῖ δὲ αὐτὴ καθ' αὑτὴν γίγνεσθαι; 350 Φαίνεται. Τί δὲ δὴ τὰ τοιάδε, ὦ Σιμμία; φαμέν τι εἶναι δίκαιον αὐτὸ ἢ οὐδέν; Φαμὲν μέντοι νὴ Δία. Καὶ αὖ καλόν γέ τι καὶ ἀγαθόν; Πῶς δ' οὔ; Ἤδη οὖν πώποτέ τι τῶν τοιούτων τοῖς ὀφθαλμοῖς εἶδες; Οὐδαμῶς, ἦ δ' ὅς. Ἀλλ' ἄλλῃ τινὶ αἰσθήσει τῶν διὰ τοῦ σώματος ἐφήψω αὐτῶν; λέγω δὲ περὶ πάντων, οἷον 355 μεγέθους πέρι, ὑγιείας, ἰσχύος, καὶ τῶν ἄλλων ἑνὶ λόγῳ E ἁπάντων τῆς οὐσίας, ὃ τυγχάνει ἕκαστον ὄν· ἆρα διὰ τοῦ σώματος αὐτῶν τἀληθέστατον θεωρεῖται, ἢ ὧδ' ἔχει· ὃς ἂν μάλιστα ἡμῶν καὶ ἀκριβέστατα παρασκευάσηται αὐτὸ ἕκαστον διανοηθῆναι περὶ οὗ σκοπεῖ, οὗτος ἂν 360 ἐγγύτατα ἴοι τοῦ γνῶναι ἕκαστον; Πάνυ μὲν οὖν. Ἆρ' οὖν ἐκεῖνος ἂν τοῦτο ποιήσειε καθαρώτατα, ὅστις ὅ τι μάλιστα αὐτῇ τῇ διανοίᾳ ἴοι ἐφ' ἕκαστον, μήτε τὴν ὄψιν παρατιθέμενος ἐν τῷ διανοεῖσθαι μήτε τινὰ ἄλλην αἴ- 66 σθησιν ἐφέλκων μηδεμίαν μετὰ τοῦ λογισμοῦ, ἀλλ' αὐτῇ 365 καθ' αὑτὴν εἰλικρινεῖ τῇ διανοίᾳ χρώμενος αὐτὸ καθ' αὑτὸ εἰλικρινὲς ἕκαστον ἐπιχειροῖ θηρεύειν τῶν ὄντων, ἀπαλλαγεὶς ὅ τι μάλιστα ὀφθαλμῶν τε καὶ ὤτων καί, ὡς ἔπος εἰπεῖν, ξύμπαντος τοῦ σώματος, ὡς ταράττοντος καὶ οὐκ ἐῶντος τὴν ψυχὴν κτήσασθαι ἀλήθειάν τε καὶ 370 φρόνησιν, ὅταν κοινωνῇ, ἆρ' οὐχ οὗτός ἐστιν, ὦ Σιμμία, εἴπερ τις καὶ ἄλλος, ὁ τευξόμενος τοῦ ὄντος; Ὑπερφυῶς, ἔφη, ὁ Σιμμίας, ὡς ἀληθῆ λέγεις, ὦ Σώκρατες.

B Οὐκοῦν ἀνάγκη, ἔφη, ἐκ πάντων τούτων παρίστασθαι δόξαν τοιάνδε τινὰ τοῖς γνησίως φιλοσόφοις, ὥστε καὶ 375 πρὸς ἀλλήλους τοιαῦτ' ἄττα λέγειν, ὅτι Κινδυνεύει τοι ὥσπερ ἀτραπός τις ἡμᾶς ἐκφέρειν μετὰ τοῦ λόγου ἐν τῇ σκέψει, ὅτι, ἕως ἂν τὸ σῶμα ἔχωμεν καὶ ξυμπεφυρμένη ᾖ ἡμῶν ἡ ψυχὴ μετὰ τοῦ τοιούτου κακοῦ, οὐ μή ποτε κτησώμεθα ἱκανῶς οὗ ἐπιθυμοῦμεν· φαμὲν δὲ τοῦτο εἶναι 380 τὸ ἀληθές. μυρίας μὲν γὰρ ἡμῖν ἀσχολίας παρέχει τὸ C σῶμα διὰ τὴν ἀναγκαίαν τροφήν· ἔτι δέ, ἄν τινες νόσοι προσπέσωσιν, ἐμποδίζουσιν ἡμῶν τὴν τοῦ ὄντος θήραν. ἐρώτων δὲ καὶ ἐπιθυμιῶν καὶ φόβων καὶ εἰδώλων παντο-

385 δαπῶν καὶ φλυαρίας ἐμπίπλησιν ἡμᾶς πολλῆς, ὥστε τὸ
λεγόμενον ὡς ἀληθῶς τῷ ὄντι ὑπ' αὐτοῦ οὐδὲ φρονῆσαι
ἡμῖν ἐγγίγνεται οὐδέποτε οὐδέν. καὶ γὰρ πολέμους καὶ
στάσεις καὶ μάχας οὐδὲν ἄλλο παρέχει ἢ τὸ σῶμα καὶ αἱ
τούτου ἐπιθυμίαι. διὰ γὰρ τὴν τῶν χρημάτων κτῆσιν
390 πάντες οἱ πόλεμοι ἡμῖν γίγνονται, τὰ δὲ χρήματα ἀναγ-
καζόμεθα κτᾶσθαι διὰ τὸ σῶμα, δουλεύοντες τῇ τούτου D
θεραπείᾳ· καὶ ἐκ τούτου ἀσχολίαν ἄγομεν φιλοσοφίας
πέρι διὰ πάντα ταῦτα. τὸ δ' ἔσχατον πάντων, ὅτι, ἐάν
τις ἡμῖν καὶ σχολὴ γένηται ἀπ' αὐτοῦ καὶ τραπώμεθα
395 πρὸς τὸ σκοπεῖν τι, ἐν ταῖς ζητήσεσιν αὖ πανταχοῦ
παραπῖπτον θόρυβον παρέχει καὶ ταραχὴν καὶ ἐκπλήττει,
ὥστε μὴ δύνασθαι ὑπ' αὐτοῦ καθορᾶν τἀληθές, ἀλλὰ
τῷ ὄντι ἡμῖν δέδεικται ὅτι, εἰ μέλλομέν ποτε καθαρῶς
τι εἴσεσθαι, ἀπαλλακτέον αὐτοῦ καὶ αὐτῇ τῇ ψυχῇ
400 θεατέον αὐτὰ τὰ πράγματα· καὶ τότε, ὡς ἔοικεν, ἡμῖν E
ἔσται οὗ ἐπιθυμοῦμέν τε καὶ φαμεν ἐρασταὶ εἶναι, φρονήσεως, ἐπειδὰν τελευτήσωμεν, ὡς ὁ λόγος σημαίνει, ζῶσι
δὲ οὔ. εἰ γὰρ μὴ οἷόν τε μετὰ τοῦ σώματος μηδὲν
καθαρῶς γνῶναι, δυοῖν θάτερον, ἢ οὐδαμοῦ ἔστι κτή-
405 σασθαι τὸ εἰδέναι ἢ τελευτήσασι· τότε γὰρ αὐτὴ καθ'
αὑτὴν ἔσται ἡ ψυχὴ χωρὶς τοῦ σώματος, πρότερον δ' οὔ. 67
καὶ ἐν ᾧ ἂν ζῶμεν, οὕτως, ὡς ἔοικεν, ἐγγυτάτω ἐσόμεθα
τοῦ εἰδέναι, ἐὰν ὅ τι μάλιστα μηδὲν ὁμιλῶμεν τῷ σώματι
μηδὲ κοινωνῶμεν, ὅ τι μὴ πᾶσα ἀνάγκη, μηδὲ ἀνα-
410 πιμπλώμεθα τῆς τούτου φύσεως, ἀλλὰ καθαρεύωμεν ἀπ'
αὐτοῦ, ἕως ἂν ὁ θεὸς αὐτὸς ἀπολύσῃ ἡμᾶς. καὶ οὕτω μὲν
καθαροὶ ἀπαλλαττόμενοι τῆς τοῦ σώματος ἀφροσύνης, ὡς
τὸ εἰκός, μετὰ τοιούτων τε ἐσόμεθα καὶ γνωσόμεθα δι'
ἡμῶν αὐτῶν πᾶν τὸ εἰλικρινές· τοῦτο δ' ἐστὶν ἴσως τὸ B
415 ἀληθές. μὴ καθαρῷ γὰρ καθαροῦ ἐφάπτεσθαι μὴ οὐ

θεμιτὸν ᾖ. Τοιαῦτα οἶμαι, ὦ Σιμμία, ἀναγκαῖον εἶναι
πρὸς ἀλλήλους λέγειν τε καὶ δοξάζειν πάντας τοὺς ὀρθῶς
φιλομαθεῖς. ἢ οὐ δοκεῖ σοι οὕτως ; Πάντος γε μᾶλλον,
ὦ Σώκρατες.

Οὐκοῦν, ἔφη ὁ Σωκράτης, εἰ ταῦτ' ἀληθῆ, ὦ ἑταῖρε, 420
πολλὴ ἐλπὶς ἀφικομένῳ οἷ ἐγὼ πορεύομαι, ἐκεῖ ἱκανῶς,
εἴπερ που ἄλλοθι, κτήσασθαι τοῦτο οὗ ἕνεκα ἡ πολλὴ
πραγματεία ἡμῖν ἐν τῷ παρελθόντι βίῳ γέγονεν, ὥστε
C ἥ γε ἀποδημία ἡ νῦν ἐμοὶ προστεταγμένη μετὰ ἀγαθῆς
ἐλπίδος γίγνεται καὶ ἄλλῳ ἀνδρί, ὃς ἡγεῖταί οἱ παρε- 425
σκευάσθαι τὴν διάνοιαν ὥσπερ κεκαθαρμένην. Πάνυ
μὲν οὖν, ἔφη ὁ Σιμμίας. Κάθαρσις δὲ εἶναι ἆρα οὐ
τοῦτο ξυμβαίνει, ὅπερ πάλαι ἐν τῷ λόγῳ λέγεται, τὸ
χωρίζειν ὅ τι μάλιστα ἀπὸ τοῦ σώματος τὴν ψυχὴν
καὶ ἐθίσαι αὐτὴν καθ' αὑτὴν πανταχόθεν ἐκ τοῦ σώματος 430
συναγείρεσθαί τε καὶ ἀθροίζεσθαι, καὶ οἰκεῖν κατὰ τὸ
δυνατὸν καὶ ἐν τῷ νῦν παρόντι καὶ ἐν τῷ ἔπειτα μόνην
D καθ' αὑτήν, ἐκλυομένην ὥσπερ ἐκ δεσμῶν ἐκ τοῦ σώματος ; Πάνυ μὲν οὖν, ἔφη. Οὐκοῦν τοῦτό γε θάνατος
ὀνομάζεται, λύσις καὶ χωρισμὸς ψυχῆς ἀπὸ σώματος ; 435
Παντάπασί γ', ἦ δ' ὅς. Λύειν δέ γε αὐτήν, ὥς φαμεν,
προθυμοῦνται ἀεὶ μάλιστα καὶ μόνοι οἱ φιλοσοφοῦντες
ὀρθῶς, καὶ τὸ μελέτημα αὐτὸ τοῦτό ἐστι τῶν φιλοσόφων,
λύσις καὶ χωρισμὸς ψυχῆς ἀπὸ σώματος, ἢ οὔ ; Φαίνεται.
Οὐκοῦν, ὅπερ ἐν ἀρχῇ ἔλεγον, γελοῖον ἂν εἴη ἄνδρα 440
παρασκευάζονθ' ἑαυτὸν ἐν τῷ βίῳ ὅ τι ἐγγυτάτω ὄντα
E τοῦ τεθνάναι οὕτω ζῆν, κἄπειθ' ἥκοντος αὐτῷ τούτου
ἀγανακτεῖν ; οὐ γελοῖον ; Πῶς δ' οὔ ; Τῷ ὄντι ἄρα, ἔφη,
ὦ Σιμμία, οἱ ὀρθῶς φιλοσοφοῦντες ἀποθνήσκειν μελε-
τῶσι, καὶ τὸ τεθνάναι ἥκιστ' αὐτοῖς ἀνθρώπων φοβερόν. 445
ἐκ τῶνδε δὲ σκόπει. εἰ γὰρ διαβέβληνται μὲν πανταχῇ

τῷ σώματι, αὐτὴν δὲ καθ᾽ αὑτὴν ἐπιθυμοῦσι τὴν ψυχὴν
ἔχειν, τούτου δὲ γιγνομένου εἰ φοβοῖντο καὶ ἀγανακτοῖεν,
οὐ πολλὴ ἂν ἀλογία εἴη, εἰ μὴ ἄσμενοι ἐκεῖσε ἴοιεν, οἷ
450 ἀφικομένοις ἐλπίς ἐστιν οὗ διὰ βίου ἤρων τυχεῖν· ἤρων 68.
δὲ φρονήσεως· ᾧ τε διεβέβληντο, τούτου ἀπηλλάχθαι
ξυνόντος αὐτοῖς; ἢ ἀνθρωπίνων μὲν παιδικῶν καὶ γυναικῶν καὶ υἱέων ἀποθανόντων πολλοὶ δὴ ἑκόντες ἠθέλησαν
εἰς Ἅιδου ἐλθεῖν, ὑπὸ ταύτης ἀγόμενοι τῆς ἐλπίδος, τῆς
455 τοῦ ὄψεσθαί τε ἐκεῖ ὧν ἐπεθύμουν καὶ ξυνέσεσθαι·
φρονήσεως δὲ ἄρα τις τῷ ὄντι ἐρῶν, καὶ λαβὼν σφόδρα
τὴν αὐτὴν ταύτην ἐλπίδα, μηδαμοῦ ἄλλοθι ἐντεύξεσθαι
αὐτῇ ἀξίως λόγου ἢ ἐν Ἅιδου, ἀγανακτήσει τε ἀποθνή- B.
σκων καὶ οὐκ ἄσμενος εἶσιν αὐτόσε; οἴεσθαί γε χρή,
460 ἐὰν τῷ ὄντι γ᾽ ᾖ, ὦ ἑταῖρε, φιλόσοφος· σφόδρα γὰρ
αὐτῷ ταῦτα δόξει, μηδαμοῦ ἄλλοθι καθαρῶς ἐντεύξεσθαι
φρονήσει ἀλλ᾽ ἢ ἐκεῖ. εἰ δὲ τοῦτο οὕτως ἔχει, ὅπερ ἄρτι
ἔλεγον, οὐ πολλὴ ἂν ἀλογία εἴη, εἰ φοβοῖτο τὸν θάνατον
ὁ τοιοῦτος; Πολλὴ μέντοι νὴ Δία, ἦ δ᾽ ὅς.
465 Οὐκοῦν ἱκανόν σοι τεκμήριον, ἔφη, τοῦτο ἀνδρὸς ὃν ἂν
ἴδῃς ἀγανακτοῦντα μέλλοντα ἀποθανεῖσθαι, ὅτι οὐκ ἄρ᾽
ἦν φιλόσοφος ἀλλά τις φιλοσώματος; ὁ αὐτὸς δέ που C.
οὗτος τυγχάνει ὢν καὶ φιλοχρήματος καὶ φιλότιμος,
ἤτοι τὰ ἕτερα τούτων ἢ ἀμφότερα. Πάνυ γ᾽, ἔφη, ἔχει
470 οὕτως ὡς λέγεις. Ἆρ᾽ οὖν, ἔφη, ὦ Σιμμία, οὐ καὶ ἡ
ὀνομαζομένη ἀνδρία τοῖς οὕτω διακειμένοις μάλιστα
προσήκει; Πάντως δήπου, ἔφη. Οὐκοῦν καὶ ἡ σωφροσύνη, ἣν καὶ οἱ πολλοὶ ὀνομάζουσι σωφροσύνην, τὸ περὶ
τὰς ἐπιθυμίας μὴ ἐπτοῆσθαι ἀλλ᾽ ὀλιγώρως ἔχειν καὶ
475 κοσμίως, ἆρ᾽ οὐ τούτοις μόνοις προσήκει, τοῖς μάλιστα
τοῦ σώματος ὀλιγωροῦσί τε καὶ ἐν φιλοσοφίᾳ ζῶσιν; D.
Ἀνάγκη, ἔφη. Εἰ γὰρ ἐθελήσεις, ἦ δ᾽ ὅς, ἐννοῆσαι τὴν

γε τῶν ἄλλων ἀνδρίαν τε καὶ σωφροσύνην, δόξει σοι
εἶναι ἄτοπος. Πῶς δή, ὦ Σώκρατες; Οἶσθα, ἦ δ' ὅς,
ὅτι τὸν θάνατον ἡγοῦνται πάντες οἱ ἄλλοι τῶν μεγάλων 480
κακῶν εἶναι; Καὶ μάλα, ἔφη. Οὐκοῦν φόβῳ μειζόνων
κακῶν ὑπομένουσιν αὐτῶν οἱ ἀνδρεῖοι τὸν θάνατον, ὅταν
ὑπομένωσιν; Ἔστι ταῦτα. Τῷ δεδιέναι ἄρα καὶ δέει
ἀνδρεῖοί εἰσι πάντες πλὴν οἱ φιλόσοφοι. καίτοι ἄτοπόν
Ε γε δέει τινὰ καὶ δειλίᾳ ἀνδρεῖον εἶναι. Πάνυ μὲν οὖν. 485
Τί δέ; οἱ κόσμιοι αὐτῶν οὐ ταὐτὸν τοῦτο πεπόνθασιν;
ἀκολασίᾳ τινὶ σώφρονές εἰσι; καίτοι φαμέν γέ που
ἀδύνατον εἶναι, ἀλλ' ὅμως αὐτοῖς συμβαίνει τούτῳ ὅμοιον
εἶναι τὸ πάθος τὸ περὶ ταύτην τὴν εὐήθη σωφροσύνην.
φοβούμενοι γὰρ ἑτέρων ἡδονῶν στερηθῆναι καὶ ἐπι- 490
θυμοῦντες ἐκείνων, ἄλλων ἀπέχονται ὑπ' ἄλλων κρατού-
69 μενοι. καίτοι καλοῦσί γε ἀκολασίαν τὸ ὑπὸ τῶν ἡδονῶν
ἄρχεσθαι· ἀλλ' ὅμως ξυμβαίνει αὐτοῖς κρατουμένοις ὑφ'
ἡδονῶν κρατεῖν ἄλλων ἡδονῶν. τοῦτο δ' ὅμοιόν ἐστιν
ᾧ νῦν δὴ ἐλέγετο, τῷ τρόπον τινὰ δι' ἀκολασίαν αὐτοὺς 495
σεσωφρονίσθαι. Ἔοικε γάρ. Ὦ μακάριε Σιμμία, μὴ
γὰρ οὐχ αὕτη ᾖ ἡ ὀρθὴ πρὸς ἀρετὴν ἀλλαγή, ἡδονὰς πρὸς
ἡδονὰς καὶ λύπας πρὸς λύπας καὶ φόβον πρὸς φόβον
καταλλάττεσθαι, καὶ μείζω πρὸς ἐλάττω, ὥσπερ νομίσματα, ἀλλ' ᾖ ἐκεῖνο μόνον τὸ νόμισμα ὀρθόν, ἀνθ' 500
Β οὗ δεῖ ἅπαντα ταῦτα καταλλάττεσθαι, φρόνησις, καὶ
τούτου μὲν πάντα καὶ μετὰ τούτου ὠνούμενά τε καὶ
πιπρασκόμενα τῷ ὄντι ᾖ, καὶ ἀνδρία καὶ σωφροσύνη καὶ
δικαιοσύνη, καὶ ξυλλήβδην ἀληθὴς ἀρετὴ ᾖ μετὰ φρονήσεως, καὶ προσγιγνομένων καὶ ἀπογιγνομένων καὶ ἡδονῶν 505
καὶ φόβων καὶ τῶν ἄλλων πάντων τῶν τοιούτων· χωρι-
ζόμενα δὲ φρονήσεως καὶ ἀλλαττόμενα ἀντὶ ἀλλήλων,
μὴ σκιαγραφία τις ᾖ ἡ τοιαύτη ἀρετὴ καὶ τῷ ὄντι

ἀνδραποδώδης τε καὶ οὐδὲν ὑγιὲς οὐδ' ἀληθὲς ἔχουσα,
510 τὸ δ' ἀληθὲς τῷ ὄντι ἦ κάθαρσίς τις τῶν τοιούτων C
πάντων, καὶ ἡ σωφροσύνη καὶ ἡ δικαιοσύνη καὶ ἡ
ἀνδρία καὶ αὐτὴ ἡ φρόνησις μὴ καθαρμός τις ᾖ. καὶ
κινδυνεύουσι καὶ οἱ τὰς τελετὰς ἡμῖν οὗτοι καταστήσαντες οὐ φαῦλοί τινες εἶναι, ἀλλὰ τῷ ὄντι πάλαι
515 αἰνίττεσθαι ὅτι ὃς ἂν ἀμύητος καὶ ἀτέλεστος εἰς Ἅιδου
ἀφίκηται, ἐν βορβόρῳ κείσεται, ὁ δὲ κεκαθαρμένος τε
καὶ τετελεσμένος ἐκεῖσε ἀφικόμενος μετὰ θεῶν οἰκήσει.
εἰσὶ γὰρ δή, φασὶν οἱ περὶ τὰς τελετάς, ναρθηκοφόροι
μὲν πολλοί, βάκχοι δέ τε παῦροι· οὗτοι δ' εἰσὶ κατὰ τὴν D
520 ἐμὴν δόξαν οὐκ ἄλλοι ἢ οἱ πεφιλοσοφηκότες ὀρθῶς.
ὧν δὴ καὶ ἐγὼ κατά γε τὸ δυνατὸν οὐδὲν ἀπέλιπον ἐν
τῷ βίῳ ἀλλὰ παντὶ τρόπῳ προὐθυμήθην γενέσθαι. εἰ
δὲ ὀρθῶς προὐθυμήθην καί τι ἠνυσάμην, ἐκεῖσε ἐλθόντες
τὸ σαφὲς εἰσόμεθα, ἐὰν θεὸς ἐθέλῃ, ὀλίγον ὕστερον, ὡς
525 ἐμοὶ δοκεῖ.

Ταῦτ' οὖν ἐγώ, ἔφη, ὦ Σιμμία τε καὶ Κέβης, ἀπο-
λογοῦμαι, ὡς εἰκότως ὑμᾶς τε ἀπολείπων καὶ τοὺς ἐνθάδε
δεσπότας οὐ χαλεπῶς φέρω οὐδ' ἀγανακτῶ, ἡγούμενος
κἀκεῖ οὐδὲν ἧττον ἢ ἐνθάδε δεσπόταις τε ἀγαθοῖς ἐντεύ- E
530 ξεσθαι καὶ ἑταίροις· τοῖς δὲ πολλοῖς ἀπιστίαν παρέχει·
εἴ τι οὖν ὑμῖν πιθανώτερός εἰμι ἐν τῇ ἀπολογίᾳ ἢ τοῖς
Ἀθηναίων δικασταῖς, εὖ ἂν ἔχοι.

The Death of Socrates.

(114 D to end).

Τὸ μὲν οὖν ταῦτα διισχυρίσασθαι οὕτως ἔχειν, ὡς ἐγὼ D
διελήλυθα, οὐ πρέπει νοῦν ἔχοντι ἀνδρί· ὅτι μέντοι ἢ

ταῦτ' ἐστὶν ἢ τοιαῦτ' ἄττα περὶ τὰς ψυχὰς ἡμῶν καὶ
τὰς οἰκήσεις, ἐπείπερ ἀθάνατόν γε ἡ ψυχὴ φαίνεται 5
οὖσα, τοῦτο καὶ πρέπειν μοι δοκεῖ καὶ ἄξιον κινδυνεῦσαι
οἰομένῳ οὕτως ἔχειν· καλὸς γὰρ ὁ κίνδυνος, καὶ χρὴ τὰ
τοιαῦτα ὥσπερ ἐπᾴδειν ἑαυτῷ, διὸ δὴ ἔγωγε καὶ πάλαι
μηκύνω τὸν μῦθον. ἀλλὰ τούτων δὴ ἕνεκα θαρρεῖν χρὴ
περὶ τῇ ἑαυτοῦ ψυχῇ ἄνδρα, ὅστις ἐν τῷ βίῳ τὰς μὲν 10
E ἄλλας ἡδονὰς τὰς περὶ τὸ σῶμα καὶ τοὺς κόσμους εἴασε
χαίρειν, ὡς ἀλλοτρίους τε ὄντας καὶ πλέον θάτερον
ἡγησάμενος ἀπεργάζεσθαι, τὰς δὲ περὶ τὸ μανθάνειν
ἐσπούδασέ τε καὶ κοσμήσας τὴν ψυχὴν οὐκ ἀλλοτρίῳ
ἀλλὰ τῷ αὐτῆς κόσμῳ, σωφροσύνῃ τε καὶ δικαιοσύνῃ 15
115 καὶ ἀνδρίᾳ καὶ ἐλευθερίᾳ καὶ ἀληθείᾳ, οὕτω περιμένει
τὴν εἰς Ἅιδου πορείαν, ὡς πορευσόμενος ὅταν ἡ εἱμαρ-
μένη καλῇ. ὑμεῖς μὲν οὖν, ἔφη, ὦ Σιμμία τε καὶ Κέβης
καὶ οἱ ἄλλοι, εἰσαῦθις ἔν τινι χρόνῳ ἕκαστοι πορεύσεσθε·
ἐμὲ δὲ νῦν ἤδη καλεῖ, φαίη ἂν ἀνὴρ τραγικός, ἡ εἱμαρ- 20
μένη, καὶ σχεδόν τί μοι ὥρα τραπέσθαι πρὸς τὸ λουτρόν·
δοκεῖ γὰρ δὴ βέλτιον εἶναι λουσάμενον πιεῖν τὸ φάρμακον καὶ μὴ πράγματα ταῖς γυναιξὶ παρέχειν νεκρὸν
λούειν.

B   Ταῦτα δὴ εἰπόντος αὐτοῦ ὁ Κρίτων, Εἶεν, ἔφη, ὦ Σώ- 25
κρατες· τί δὲ τούτοις ἢ ἐμοὶ ἐπιστέλλεις ἢ περὶ τῶν παίδων ἢ περὶ ἄλλου του, ὅ τι ἄν σοι ποιοῦντες ἡμεῖς ἐν
χάριτι μάλιστα ποιοῖμεν; Ἅπερ ἀεὶ λέγω, ἔφη, ὦ Κρίτων,
οὐδὲν καινότερον· ὅτι ὑμῶν αὐτῶν ἐπιμελούμενοι ὑμεῖς
καὶ ἐμοὶ καὶ τοῖς ἐμοῖς καὶ ὑμῖν αὐτοῖς ἐν χάριτι ποιήσετε 30
ἅττ' ἂν ποιῆτε, κἂν μὴ νῦν ὁμολογήσητε· ἐὰν δὲ ὑμῶν
μὲν αὐτῶν ἀμελῆτε, καὶ μὴ θέλητε ὥσπερ κατ' ἴχνη κατὰ
τὰ νῦν τε εἰρημένα καὶ τὰ ἐν τῷ ἔμπροσθεν χρόνῳ ζῆν,
C οὐδ' ἐὰν πολλὰ ὁμολογήσητε ἐν τῷ παρόντι καὶ σφόδρα,

35 οὐδὲν πλέον ποιήσετε. Ταῦτα μὲν τοίνυν προθυμηθησό-
μεθα, ἔφη, οὕτω ποιεῖν· θάπτωμεν δέ σε τίνα τρόπον;
Ὅπως ἄν, ἔφη, βούλησθε, ἐάνπερ γε λάβητέ με καὶ μὴ
ἐκφύγω ὑμᾶς. Γελάσας δὲ ἅμα ἡσυχῇ καὶ πρὸς ἡμᾶς
ἀποβλέψας εἶπεν, Οὐ πείθω, ἔφη, ὦ ἄνδρες, Κρίτωνα,
40 ὡς ἐγώ εἰμι οὗτος ὁ Σωκράτης, ὁ νυνὶ διαλεγόμενος
καὶ διατάττων ἕκαστον τῶν λεγομένων, ἀλλ᾽ οἴεταί με ·
ἐκεῖνον εἶναι, ὃν ὄψεται ὀλίγον ὕστερον νεκρόν, καὶ
ἐρωτᾷ δή, πῶς με θάπτῃ. ὅτι δὲ ἐγὼ πάλαι πολὺν λόγον D
πεποίημαι, ὡς, ἐπειδὰν πίω τὸ φάρμακον, οὐκέτι ὑμῖν
45 παραμενῶ, ἀλλ᾽ οἰχήσομαι ἀπιὼν εἰς μακάρων δή τινας
εὐδαιμονίας, ταῦτά μοι δοκῶ αὐτῷ ἄλλως λέγειν, παρα-
μυθούμενος ἅμα μὲν ὑμᾶς, ἅμα δ᾽ ἐμαυτόν. ἐγγυήσασθε
οὖν με πρὸς Κρίτωνα, ἔφη, τὴν ἐναντίαν ἐγγύην ἢ ἣν
οὗτος πρὸς τοὺς δικαστὰς ἠγγυᾶτο. οὗτος μὲν γὰρ ἦ μὴν
50 παραμενεῖν· ὑμεῖς δὲ ἦ μὴν μὴ παραμενεῖν ἐγγυήσασθε,
ἐπειδὰν ἀποθάνω, ἀλλὰ οἰχήσεσθαι ἀπιόντα, ἵνα Κρίτων E
ῥᾷον φέρῃ, καὶ μὴ ὁρῶν μου τὸ σῶμα ἢ καιόμενον ἢ
κατορυττόμενον ἀγανακτῇ ὑπὲρ ἐμοῦ, ὡς δεινὰ πάσχοντος,
μηδὲ λέγῃ ἐν τῇ ταφῇ, ὡς ἢ προτίθεται Σωκράτη ἢ
55 ἐκφέρει ἢ κατορύττει. εὖ γὰρ ἴσθι, ἦ δ᾽ ὅς, ὦ ἄριστε
Κρίτων, τὸ μὴ καλῶς λέγειν οὐ μόνον εἰς αὐτὸ τοῦτο
πλημμελές, ἀλλὰ καὶ κακόν τι ἐμποιεῖ ταῖς ψυχαῖς.
ἀλλὰ θαρρεῖν τε χρὴ καὶ φάναι τοὐμὸν σῶμα θάπτειν,
καὶ θάπτειν οὕτως, ὅπως ἄν σοι φίλον ᾖ καὶ μάλιστα 116
60 ἡγῇ νόμιμον εἶναι.

Ταῦτ᾽ εἰπὼν ἐκεῖνος μὲν ἀνίστατο εἰς οἴκημά τι ὡς
λουσόμενος, καὶ ὁ Κρίτων εἵπετο αὐτῷ, ἡμᾶς δ᾽ ἐκέλευε
περιμένειν. περιεμένομεν οὖν πρὸς ἡμᾶς αὐτοὺς διαλεγόμενοι περὶ τῶν εἰρημένων καὶ ἀνασκοποῦντες, τοτὲ δ᾽
65 αὖ περὶ τῆς ξυμφορᾶς διεξιόντες, ὅση ἡμῖν γεγονυῖα εἴη,

ἀτεχνῶς ἡγούμενοι ὥσπερ πατρὸς στερηθέντες διάξειν
Β ὀρφανοὶ τὸν ἔπειτα βίον. ἐπειδὴ δὲ ἐλούσατο καὶ
ἠνέχθη παρ' αὐτὸν τὰ παιδία—δύο γὰρ αὐτῷ υἱεῖς σμικροὶ ἦσαν, εἷς δὲ μέγας—καὶ αἱ οἰκεῖαι γυναῖκες ἀφίκοντο,
ἐκείναις ἐναντίον τοῦ Κρίτωνος διαλεχθείς τε καὶ ἐπι- 70
στείλας ἄττα ἐβούλετο, τὰς μὲν γυναῖκας καὶ τὰ παιδία
ἀπιέναι ἐκέλευσεν, αὐτὸς δὲ ἦκε παρ' ἡμᾶς. καὶ ἦν ἤδη
ἐγγὺς ἡλίου δυσμῶν· χρόνον γὰρ πολὺν διέτριψεν ἔνδον.
ἐλθὼν δ' ἐκαθέζετο λελουμένος, καὶ οὐ πόλλ' ἄττα μετὰ
ταῦτα διελέχθη, καὶ ἦκεν ὁ τῶν ἔνδεκα ὑπηρέτης καὶ 75
C στὰς παρ' αὐτόν, Ὦ Σώκρατες, ἔφη, οὐ καταγνώσομαί
γε σοῦ ὅπερ τῶν ἄλλων καταγιγνώσκω, ὅτι μοι χαλε-
παίνουσι καὶ καταρῶνται, ἐπειδὰν αὐτοῖς παραγγέλλω
πίνειν τὸ φάρμακον ἀναγκαζόντων τῶν ἀρχόντων. σὲ δ'
ἐγὼ καὶ ἄλλως ἔγνωκα ἐν τούτῳ τῷ χρόνῳ γενναιότατον 80
καὶ πραότατον καὶ ἄριστον ἄνδρα ὄντα τῶν πώποτε δεῦρο
ἀφικομένων, καὶ δὴ καὶ νῦν εὖ οἶδ' ὅτι οὐκ ἐμοὶ χαλε-
παίνεις, γιγνώσκεις γὰρ τοὺς αἰτίους, ἀλλ' ἐκείνοις. νῦν
οὖν, οἶσθα γὰρ ἃ ἦλθον ἀγγέλλων, χαῖρέ τε καὶ πειρῶ
D ὡς ῥᾷστα φέρειν τὰ ἀναγκαῖα. Καὶ ἅμα δακρύσας μετα- 85
στρεφόμενος ἀπήει. Καὶ ὁ Σωκράτης ἀναβλέψας πρὸς
αὐτόν, Καὶ σύ, ἔφη, χαῖρε, καὶ ἡμεῖς ταῦτα ποιήσομεν.
Καὶ ἅμα πρὸς ἡμᾶς, Ὡς ἀστεῖος, ἔφη, ὁ ἄνθρωπος· καὶ
παρὰ πάντα μοι τὸν χρόνον προσῄει καὶ διελέγετο ἐνίοτε
καὶ ἦν ἀνδρῶν λῷστος, καὶ νῦν ὡς γενναίως με ἀποδα- 90
κρύει. ἀλλ' ἄγε δή, ὦ Κρίτων, πειθώμεθα αὐτῷ, καὶ
ἐνεγκάτω τις τὸ φάρμακον, εἰ τέτριπται· εἰ δὲ μή, τρι-
E ψάτω ὁ ἄνθρωπος. Καὶ ὁ Κρίτων, Ἀλλ' οἶμαι, ἔφη,
ἔγωγε, ὦ Σώκρατες, ἔτι ἥλιον εἶναι ἐπὶ τοῖς ὄρεσι καὶ
οὔπω δεδυκέναι. καὶ ἅμα ἐγὼ οἶδα καὶ ἄλλους πάνυ ὀψὲ 95
πίνοντας, ἐπειδὰν παραγγελθῇ αὐτοῖς, δειπνήσαντάς τε

καὶ πιόντας εὖ μάλα, καὶ ξυγγενομένους γ᾽ ἐνίους ὧν ἂν
τύχωσιν ἐπιθυμοῦντες. ἀλλὰ μηδὲν ἐπείγου· ἔτι γὰρ
ἐγχωρεῖ. Καὶ ὁ Σωκράτης, Εἰκότως γ᾽, ἔφη, ὦ Κρίτων,
100 ἐκεῖνοί τε ταῦτα ποιοῦσιν, οὓς σὺ λέγεις, οἴονται γὰρ
κερδανεῖν ταῦτα ποιήσαντες, καὶ ἔγωγε ταῦτα εἰκότως οὐ
ποιήσω· οὐδὲν γὰρ οἶμαι κερδανεῖν ὀλίγον ὕστερον πιὼν 117
ἄλλο γε ἢ γέλωτα ὀφλήσειν παρ᾽ ἐμαυτῷ, γλιχόμενος
τοῦ ζῆν καὶ φειδόμενος οὐδενὸς ἔτι ἐνόντος. ἀλλ᾽ ἴθι,
105 ἔφη, πείθου καὶ μὴ ἄλλως ποίει.

Καὶ ὁ Κρίτων ἀκούσας ἔνευσε τῷ παιδὶ πλησίον
ἑστῶτι. καὶ ὁ παῖς ἐξελθὼν καὶ συχνὸν χρόνον διατρίψας ἧκεν ἄγων τὸν μέλλοντα διδόναι τὸ φάρμακον,
ἐν κύλικι φέροντα τετριμμένον. ἰδὼν δὲ ὁ Σωκράτης τὸν
110 ἄνθρωπον, Εἶεν, ἔφη, ὦ βέλτιστε, σὺ γὰρ τούτων ἐπιστήμων, τί χρὴ ποιεῖν; Οὐδὲν ἄλλο, ἔφη, ἢ πιόντα
περιιέναι, ἕως ἄν σου βάρος ἐν τοῖς σκέλεσι γένηται,
ἔπειτα κατακεῖσθαι· καὶ οὕτως αὐτὸ ποιήσει. Καὶ ἅμα B
ὤρεξε τὴν κύλικα τῷ Σωκράτει. καὶ ὃς λαβὼν καὶ μάλα
115 ἵλεως, ὦ Ἐχέκρατες, οὐδὲν τρέσας οὐδὲ διαφθείρας οὔτε
τοῦ χρώματος οὔτε τοῦ προσώπου, ἀλλ᾽, ὥσπερ εἰώθει,
ταυρηδὸν ὑποβλέψας πρὸς τὸν ἄνθρωπον, Τί λέγεις,
ἔφη, περὶ τοῦδε τοῦ πόματος πρὸς τὸ ἀποσπεῖσαί τινι;
ἔξεστιν, ἢ οὔ; Τοσοῦτον, ἔφη, ὦ Σώκρατες, τρίβομεν,
120 ὅσον οἰόμεθα μέτριον εἶναι πιεῖν. Μανθάνω, ἦ δ᾽ ὅς·
ἀλλ᾽ εὔχεσθαί γέ που τοῖς θεοῖς ἔξεστί τε καὶ χρή, τὴν C
μετοίκησιν τὴν ἐνθένδε ἐκεῖσε εὐτυχῆ γενέσθαι· ἃ δὴ
καὶ ἐγὼ εὔχομαί τε καὶ γένοιτο ταύτῃ. Καὶ ἅμα εἰπὼν
ταῦτα ἐπισχόμενος καὶ μάλα εὐχερῶς καὶ εὐκόλως ἐξέπιε.
125 καὶ ἡμῶν οἱ πολλοὶ τέως μὲν ἐπιεικῶς οἷοί τε ἦσαν
κατέχειν τὸ μὴ δακρύειν, ὡς δὲ εἴδομεν πίνοντά τε καὶ
πεπωκότα, οὐκέτι, ἀλλ᾽ ἐμοῦ γε βίᾳ καὶ αὐτοῦ ἀστακτὶ

ἐχώρει τὰ δάκρυα, ὥστε ἐγκαλυψάμενος ἀπέκλαιον ἐμαυτόν· οὐ γὰρ δὴ ἐκεῖνόν γε, ἀλλὰ τὴν ἐμαυτοῦ τύχην,
D οἵου ἀνδρὸς ἑταίρου ἐστερημένος εἴην. ὁ δὲ Κρίτων ἔτι 130
πρότερος ἐμοῦ, ἐπειδὴ οὐχ οἷός τ᾽ ἦν κατέχειν τὰ δάκρυα,
ἐξανέστη. ᾽Απολλόδωρος δὲ καὶ ἐν τῷ ἔμπροσθεν
χρόνῳ οὐδὲν ἐπαύετο δακρύων, καὶ δὴ καὶ τότε ἀναβρυχησάμενος, κλαίων καὶ ἀγανακτῶν οὐδένα ὄντινα
οὐ κατέκλασε τῶν παρόντων, πλήν γε αὐτοῦ Σωκρά- 135
τους. ἐκεῖνος δέ, Οἷα, ἔφη, ποιεῖτε, ὦ θαυμάσιοι. ἐγὼ
μέντοι οὐχ ἥκιστα τούτου ἕνεκα τὰς γυναῖκας ἀπέπεμψα,
ἵνα μὴ τοιαῦτα πλημμελοῖεν· καὶ γὰρ ἀκήκοα, ὅτι ἐν
E εὐφημίᾳ χρὴ τελευτᾶν. ἀλλ᾽ ἡσυχίαν τε ἄγετε καὶ
καρτερεῖτε. Καὶ ἡμεῖς ἀκούσαντες ᾐσχύνθημέν τε καὶ 140
ἐπέσχομεν τοῦ δακρύειν. ὁ δὲ περιελθών, ἐπειδή οἱ
βαρύνεσθαι ἔφη τὰ σκέλη, κατεκλίθη ὕπτιος· οὕτω γὰρ
ἐκέλευεν ὁ ἄνθρωπος. καὶ ἅμα ἐφαπτόμενος αὐτοῦ οὗτος ὁ
δοὺς τὸ φάρμακον, διαλιπὼν χρόνον ἐπεσκόπει τοὺς πόδας
καὶ τὰ σκέλη, κἄπειτα σφόδρα πιέσας αὐτοῦ τὸν πόδα ἤ- 145
ρετο, εἰ αἰσθάνοιτο· ὁ δ᾽ οὐκ ἔφη. καὶ μετὰ τοῦτο αὖθις
118 τὰς κνήμας· καὶ ἐπανιὼν οὕτως ἡμῖν ἐπεδείκνυτο, ὅτι
ψύχοιτό τε καὶ πήγνυτο. καὶ αὐτὸς ἥπτετο καὶ εἶπεν ὅτι,
ἐπειδὰν πρὸς τῇ καρδίᾳ γένηται αὐτῷ, τότε οἰχήσεται.
ἤδη οὖν σχεδόν τι αὐτοῦ ἦν τὰ περὶ τὸ ἦτρον ψυχόμενα, 150
καὶ ἐκκαλυψάμενος, ἐνεκεκάλυπτο γάρ, εἶπεν, ὃ δὴ τελευταῖον ἐφθέγξατο, ῏Ω Κρίτων, ἔφη, τῷ ᾽Ασκληπιῷ ὀφείλομεν ἀλεκτρυόνα. ἀλλ᾽ ἀπόδοτε καὶ μὴ ἀμελήσητε. ᾽Αλλὰ
ταῦτα, ἔφη, ἔσται, ὁ Κρίτων· ἀλλ᾽ ὅρα, εἴ τι ἄλλο λέγεις.
Ταῦτα ἐρομένου αὐτοῦ οὐδὲν ἔτι ἀπεκρίνατο, ἀλλ᾽ ὀλίγον 155
χρόνον διαλιπὼν ἐκινήθη τε καὶ ὁ ἄνθρωπος ἐξεκάλυψεν
αὐτόν, καὶ ὃς τὰ ὄμματα ἔστησεν· ἰδὼν δὲ ὁ Κρίτων
ξυνέλαβε τὸ στόμα τε καὶ τοὺς ὀφθαλμούς.

Ἥδε ἡ τελευτή, ὦ Ἐχέκρατες, τοῦ ἑταίρου ἡμῖν ἐγέ-
160 νετο, ἀνδρός, ὡς ἡμεῖς φαῖμεν ἄν, τῶν τότε ὧν ἐπει-
ράθημεν ἀρίστου καὶ ἄλλως φρονιμωτάτου καὶ δικαιο-
τάτου.

SYMPOSIUM.

The Praise of Socrates by Alcibiades.
(215 A—216 C).

Σωκράτη δ' ἐγὼ ἐπαινεῖν, ὦ ἄνδρες, οὕτως ἐπιχειρήσω,
δι' εἰκόνων. οὗτος μὲν οὖν ἴσως οἰήσεται ἐπὶ τὰ
γελοιότερα, ἔσται δ' ἡ εἰκὼν τοῦ ἀληθοῦς ἕνεκα, οὐ
τοῦ γελοίου. φημὶ γὰρ δὴ ὁμοιότατον αὐτὸν εἶναι τοῖς
5 Σειληνοῖς τούτοις τοῖς ἐν τοῖς ἑρμογλυφείοις καθημένοις,
οὕς τινας ἐργάζονται οἱ δημιουργοὶ σύριγγας ἢ αὐλοὺς B
ἔχοντας, οἳ διχάδε διοιχθέντες φαίνονται ἔνδοθεν ἀγάλματα ἔχοντες θεῶν. καὶ φημὶ αὖ ἐοικέναι αὐτὸν τῷ
Σατύρῳ τῷ Μαρσύᾳ. ὅτι μὲν οὖν τό γε εἶδος ὅμοιος
10 εἶ τούτοις, ὦ Σώκρατες, οὐδ' αὐτὸς ἄν που ἀμφι-
σβητήσαις· ὡς δὲ καὶ τἆλλα ἔοικας, μετὰ τοῦτο ἄκουε.
ὑβριστὴς εἶ· ἢ οὔ ; ἐὰν γὰρ μὴ ὁμολογῇς, μάρτυρας παρέξομαι. ἀλλ' οὐκ αὐλητής ; πολύ γε θαυμασιώτερος
ἐκείνου· ὁ μέν γε δι' ὀργάνων ἐκήλει τοὺς ἀνθρώπους C
15 τῇ ἀπὸ τοῦ στόματος δυνάμει, καὶ ἔτι νυνὶ ὃς ἂν τὰ
ἐκείνου αὐλῇ. ἃ γὰρ Ὄλυμπος ηὔλει, Μαρσύου λέγω
τούτου διδάξαντος. τὰ οὖν ἐκείνου ἐάν τε ἀγαθὸς αὐλη-
τὴς αὐλῇ ἐάν τε φαύλη αὐλητρίς, μόνα κατέχεσθαι ποιεῖ
καὶ δηλοῖ τοὺς τῶν θεῶν τε καὶ τελετῶν δεομένους διὰ τὸ
20 θεῖα εἶναι. σὺ δ' ἐκείνου τοσοῦτον μόνον διαφέρεις, ὅτι
ἄνευ ὀργάνων ψιλοῖς λόγοις ταὐτὸν τοῦτο ποιεῖς· ἡμεῖς
γοῦν ὅταν μέν του ἄλλου ἀκούωμεν λέγοντος καὶ πάνυ D

ἀγαθοῦ ῥήτορος ἄλλους λόγους, οὐδὲν μέλει, ὡς ἔπος
εἰπεῖν, οὐδενί· ἐπειδὰν δὲ σοῦ τις ἀκούῃ ἢ τῶν σῶν
λόγων, ἄλλου λέγοντος, κἂν πάνυ φαῦλος ᾖ ὁ λέγων, 25
ἐάν τε γυνὴ ἀκούῃ ἐάν τε ἀνὴρ ἐάν τε μειράκιον, ἐκπε-
πληγμένοι ἐσμὲν καὶ κατεχόμεθα. ἐγὼ γοῦν, ὦ ἄνδρες,
εἰ μὴ ἔμελλον κομιδῇ δόξειν μεθύειν, εἶπον ὁμόσας ἂν
ὑμῖν οἷα δὴ πέπονθα αὐτὸς ὑπὸ τῶν τούτου λόγων καὶ
E πάσχω ἔτι καὶ νυνί. ὅταν γὰρ ἀκούω, πολύ μοι μᾶλλον 30
ἢ τῶν κορυβαντιώντων ἥ τε καρδία πηδᾷ καὶ δάκρυα
ἐκχεῖται ὑπὸ τῶν λόγων τῶν τούτου. ὁρῶ δὲ καὶ ἄλλους
παμπόλλους τὰ αὐτὰ πάσχοντας. Περικλέους δὲ ἀκούων
καὶ ἄλλων ἀγαθῶν ῥητόρων εὖ μὲν ἡγούμην λέγειν,
τοιοῦτον δ' οὐδὲν ἔπασχον, οὐδὲ τεθορύβητό μου ἡ 35
ψυχὴ οὐδ' ἠγανάκτει ὡς ἀνδραποδωδῶς διακειμένου.
ἀλλ' ὑπὸ τουτουὶ τοῦ Μαρσύου πολλάκις δὴ οὕτω διε-
216 τέθην, ὥστε μοι δόξαι μὴ βιωτὸν εἶναι ἔχοντι ὡς ἔχω.
καὶ ταῦτα, Σώκρατες, οὐκ ἐρεῖς ὡς οὐκ ἀληθῆ. καὶ ἔτι
γε νῦν ξύνοιδ' ἐμαυτῷ ὅτι εἰ ἐθέλοιμι παρέχειν τὰ ὦτα, 40
οὐκ ἂν καρτερήσαιμι, ἀλλὰ ταὐτὰ ἂν πάσχοιμι. ἀναγ-
κάζει γάρ με ὁμολογεῖν ὅτι πολλοῦ ἐνδεὴς ὢν αὐτὸς ἔτι
ἐμαυτοῦ μὲν ἀμελῶ, τὰ δ' Ἀθηναίων πράττω. βίᾳ οὖν
ὥσπερ ἀπὸ τῶν Σειρήνων ἐπισχόμενος τὰ ὦτα οἴχομαι
B φεύγων, ἵνα μὴ αὐτοῦ καθήμενος παρὰ τούτῳ καταγη- 45
ράσω. πέπονθα δὲ πρὸς τοῦτον μόνον ἀνθρώπων, ὃ οὐκ
ἄν τις οἴοιτο ἐν ἐμοὶ ἐνεῖναι, τὸ αἰσχύνεσθαι ὁντινοῦν·
ἐγὼ δὲ τοῦτον μόνον αἰσχύνομαι. ξύνοιδα γὰρ ἐμαυτῷ
ἀντιλέγειν μὲν οὐ δυναμένῳ ὡς οὐ δεῖ ποιεῖν ἃ οὗτος
κελεύει, ἐπειδὰν δὲ ἀπέλθω, ἡττημένῳ τῆς τιμῆς τῆς 50
ὑπὸ τῶν πολλῶν. δραπετεύω οὖν αὐτὸν καὶ φεύγω, καὶ
C ὅταν ἴδω, αἰσχύνομαι τὰ ὡμολογημένα. καὶ πολλάκις
μὲν ἡδέως ἂν ἴδοιμι αὐτὸν μὴ ὄντα ἐν ἀνθρώποις· εἰ δ'

αὖ τοῦτο γένοιτο, εὖ οἶδα ὅτι πολὺ μεῖζον ἂν ἀχθοίμην,
55 ὥστε οὐκ ἔχω ὅ τι χρήσομαι τούτῳ τῷ ἀνθρώπῳ.

The same continued.   Socrates in the Field.
220 C—222 A.

Καὶ ταῦτα μὲν δὴ ταῦτα·   C
          οἷον δ' αὖ τόδ' ἔρεξε καὶ ἔτλη καρτερὸς ἀνὴρ
ἐκεῖ ποτὲ ἐπὶ στρατείας, ἄξιον ἀκοῦσαι. ξυννοήσας γὰρ
αὐτόθι ἕωθέν τι εἱστήκει σκοπῶν, καὶ ἐπειδὴ οὐ προὔ-
60 χώρει αὐτῷ, οὐκ ἀνίει ἀλλὰ εἱστήκει ζητῶν. καὶ ἤδη ἦν
μεσημβρία, καὶ ἄνθρωποι ᾐσθάνοντο, καὶ θαυμάζοντες
ἄλλος ἄλλῳ ἔλεγεν ὅτι Σωκράτης ἐξ ἑωθινοῦ φροντίζων
τι ἔστηκε. τελευτῶντες δέ τινες τῶν Ἰώνων, ἐπειδὴ ἑσπέ-
ρα ἦν, δειπνήσαντες, καὶ γὰρ θέρος τότε γ' ἦν, χαμεύ-
65 νια ἐξενεγκάμενοι ἅμα μὲν ἐν τῷ ψύχει καθηῦδον, ἅμα D
δὲ ἐφύλαττον αὐτὸν εἰ καὶ τὴν νύκτα ἑστήξοι. ὁ δὲ
εἱστήκει μέχρι ἕως ἐγένετο καὶ ἥλιος ἀνέσχεν. ἔπειτα
ᾤχετ' ἀπιὼν προσευξάμενος τῷ ἡλίῳ. Εἰ δὲ βούλεσθε ἐν
ταῖς μάχαις· τοῦτο γὰρ δὴ δίκαιόν γε αὐτῷ ἀποδοῦναι.
70 ὅτε γὰρ ἡ μάχη ἦν ἐξ ἧς ἐμοὶ καὶ τἀριστεῖα ἔδοσαν οἱ
στρατηγοί, οὐδεὶς ἄλλος ἐμὲ ἔσωσεν ἀνθρώπων ἢ οὗτος,
τετρωμένον οὐκ ἐθέλων ἀπολιπεῖν, ἀλλὰ συνδιέσωσε καὶ
τὰ ὅπλα καὶ αὐτὸν ἐμέ. καὶ ἐγὼ μέν, ὦ Σώκρατες, καὶ Ε
τότε ἐκέλευον σοὶ διδόναι τἀριστεῖα τοὺς στρατηγούς, καὶ
75 τοῦτό γέ μοι οὔτε μέμψει οὔτε ἐρεῖς ὅτι ψεύδομαι· ἀλλὰ
γὰρ τῶν στρατηγῶν πρὸς τὸ ἐμὸν ἀξίωμα ἀποβλεπόντων
καὶ βουλομένων ἐμοὶ διδόναι τἀριστεῖα, αὐτὸς προθυμό-
τερος ἐγένου τῶν στρατηγῶν ἐμὲ λαβεῖν ἢ σαυτόν.
Ἔτι τοίνυν, ὦ ἄνδρες, ἄξιον ἦν θεάσασθαι Σωκράτη,
80 ὅτε ἀπὸ Δηλίου φυγῇ ἀνεχώρει τὸ στρατόπεδον· ἔτυχον 221

γὰρ παραγενόμενος ἵππον ἔχων, οὗτος δὲ ὅπλα. ἀνεχώρει οὖν ἐσκεδασμένων ἤδη τῶν ἀνθρώπων οὗτός τε
ἅμα καὶ Λάχης· καὶ ἐγὼ περιτυγχάνω, καὶ ἰδὼν εὐθὺς
παρακελεύομαί τε αὐτοῖν θαρρεῖν καὶ ἔλεγον ὅτι οὐκ
ἀπολείψω αὐτώ. ἐνταῦθα δὴ καὶ κάλλιον ἐθεασάμην 85
Σωκράτη ἢ ἐν Ποτιδαίᾳ. αὐτὸς γὰρ ἧττον ἐν φόβῳ ἢ
διὰ τὸ ἐφ' ἵππου εἶναι· πρῶτον μὲν ὅσον περιῆν Λά-
B χητος τῷ ἔμφρων εἶναι· ἔπειτα ἔμοιγε ἐδόκει, ὦ 'Αρισ-
τόφανες, τὸ σὸν δὴ τοῦτο, καὶ ἐκεῖ διαπορεύεσθαι ὥσπερ
καὶ ἐνθάδε, βρενθυόμενος καὶ τὠφθαλμὼ παραβάλλων, 90
ἠρέμα περισκοπῶν καὶ τοὺς φιλίους καὶ τοὺς πολεμίους,
δῆλος ὢν παντὶ καὶ πάνυ πόρρωθεν ὅτι εἴ τις ἅψεται
τούτου τοῦ ἀνδρός, μάλα ἐρρωμένως ἀμυνεῖται. διὸ καὶ
ἀσφαλῶς ἀπῄει καὶ οὗτος καὶ ὁ ἕτερος· σχεδὸν γάρ τι
τῶν οὕτω διακειμένων ἐν τῷ πολέμῳ οὐδὲ ἅπτονται, ἀλλὰ 95
C τοὺς προτροπάδην φεύγοντας διώκουσι. ⌊Πολλὰ μὲν οὖν
ἄν τις καὶ ἄλλα ἔχοι Σωκράτη ἐπαινέσαι καὶ θαυμάσια·
ἀλλὰ τῶν μὲν ἄλλων ἐπιτηδευμάτων τάχ' ἄν τις καὶ περὶ
ἄλλου τοιαῦτα εἴποι, τὸ δὲ μηδενὶ ἀνθρώπων ὅμοιον
εἶναι, μήτε τῶν παλαιῶν μήτε τῶν νῦν ὄντων, τοῦτο 100
ἄξιον παντὸς θαύματος. οἷος γὰρ 'Αχιλλεὺς ἐγένετο,
ἀπεικάσειεν ἄν τις καὶ Βρασίδαν καὶ ἄλλους, καὶ οἷος
D αὖ Περικλῆς, καὶ Νέστορα καὶ 'Αντήνορα, εἰσὶ δὲ καὶ
ἕτεροι· καὶ τοὺς ἄλλους κατὰ ταῦτ' ἄν τις ἀπεικάζοι.
οἷος δὲ οὑτοσὶ γέγονε τὴν ἀτοπίαν ἄνθρωπος, καὶ αὐτὸς 105
καὶ οἱ λόγοι αὐτοῦ, οὐδ' ἐγγὺς ἂν εὕροι τις ζητῶν, [οὔτε
τῶν νῦν οὔτε τῶν παλαιῶν,] εἰ μὴ ἄρα εἰ οἷς ἐγὼ λέγω
ἀπεικάζοι τις αὐτόν, ἀνθρώπων μὲν μηδενί, τοῖς δὲ
Σειληνοῖς καὶ Σατύροις, αὐτὸν καὶ τοὺς λόγους. καὶ γὰρ
οὖν καὶ τοῦτο ἐν τοῖς πρώτοις παρέλιπον, ὅτι καὶ οἱ 110
λόγοι αὐτοῦ ὁμοιότατοί εἰσι τοῖς Σειληνοῖς τοῖς διοιγο-

μένοις. εἰ γὰρ ἐθέλει τις τῶν Σωκράτους ἀκούειν λόγων, E
φανεῖεν ἂν [πάνυ] γελοῖοι τὸ πρῶτον· τοιαῦτα καὶ ὀνόματα καὶ ῥήματα ἔξωθεν περιαμπέχονται, Σατύρου δή
115 τινα ὑβριστοῦ δοράν. ὄνους γὰρ κανθηλίους λέγει καὶ
χαλκέας τινὰς καὶ σκυτοτόμους καὶ βυρσοδέψας, καὶ ἀεὶ
διὰ τῶν αὐτῶν ταὐτὰ φαίνεται λέγειν, ὥστε ἄπειρος καὶ
ἀνόητος ἄνθρωπος πᾶς ἂν τῶν λόγων καταγελάσειε
διοιγομένους δὲ ἰδὼν αὖ τις καὶ ἐντὸς αὐτῶν γιγνόμενος 222
120 πρῶτον μὲν νοῦν ἔχοντας ἔνδον μόνους εὑρήσει τῶν
λόγων, ἔπειτα θειοτάτους καὶ πλεῖστ' ἀγάλματ' ἀρετῆς
ἐν αὑτοῖς ἔχοντας καὶ ἐπὶ πλεῖστον τείνοντας, μᾶλλον δὲ
ἐπὶ πᾶν ὅσον προσήκει σκοπεῖν τῷ μέλλοντι καλῷ κἀγαθῷ
ἔσεσθαι.

PHAEDRUS.

A walk by the Ilissus.

(SOCRATES. PHAEDRUS.)

228 A—230 E.

ΣΩ. Ὦ Φαῖδρε, εἰ ἐγὼ Φαῖδρον ἀγνοῶ, καὶ ἐμαυτοῦ
ἐπιλέλησμαι. ἀλλὰ γὰρ οὐδέτερά ἐστι τούτων. εὖ οἶδα
ὅτι Λυσίου λόγον ἀκούων ἐκεῖνος οὐ μόνον ἅπαξ ἤκουσεν,
ἀλλὰ πολλάκις ἐπαναλαμβάνων ἐκέλευέν οἱ λέγειν· ὁ δὲ
5 ἐπείθετο προθύμως. τῷ δὲ οὐδὲ ταῦτα ἦν ἱκανά, ἀλλὰ B
τελευτῶν παραλαβὼν τὸ βιβλίον, ἃ μάλιστα ἐπεθύμει
ἐπεσκόπει. καὶ τοῦτο δρῶν, ἐξ ἑωθινοῦ καθήμενος, ἀπει-
πὼν εἰς περίπατον ᾔει, ὡς μὲν ἐγὼ οἶμαι, νὴ τὸν κύνα,
ἐξεπιστάμενος τὸν λόγον, εἰ μὴ πάνυ τις ἦν μακρός.
10 ἐπορεύετο δ' ἐκτὸς τείχους, ἵνα μελετῴη. ἀπαντήσας δὲ
τῷ νοσοῦντι περὶ λόγων ἀκοήν, ἰδὼν μὲν ἰδὼν ἥσθη ὅτι
ἕξοι τὸν συγκορυβαντιῶντα, καὶ προάγειν ἐκέλευε· δεο- C

μένου δὲ λέγειν τοῦ τῶν λόγων ἐραστοῦ, ἐθρύπτετο ὡς
δὴ οὐκ ἐπιθυμῶν λέγειν· τελευτῶν δὲ ἔμελλε, καὶ εἰ μή
τις ἑκὼν ἀκούοι, βίᾳ ἐρεῖν. σὺ οὖν, ὦ Φαῖδρε, αὐτοῦ 15·
δεήθητι, ὅπερ τάχα πάντως ποιήσει, νῦν ἤδη ποιεῖν.

ΦΑΙ. Ἐμοὶ ὡς ἀληθῶς πολὺ κράτιστόν ἐστιν οὕτως
ὅπως δύναμαι λέγειν· ὥς μοι δοκεῖς σὺ οὐδαμῶς με
ἀφήσειν πρὶν ἂν εἴπω ἁμῶς γέ πως.

ΣΩ. Πάνυ γάρ σοι ἀληθῆ δοκῶ. 20

D ΦΑΙ. Οὑτωσὶ τοίνυν ποιήσω. τῷ ὄντι γάρ, ὦ Σώκρατες, παντὸς μᾶλλον τά γε ῥήματα οὐκ ἐξέμαθον· τὴν
μέντοι διάνοιαν σχεδὸν ἁπάντων, οἷς ἔφη διαφέρειν τὰ
τοῦ ἐρῶντος ἢ τὰ τοῦ μή, ἐν κεφαλαίοις ἐφεξῆς δίειμι,
ἀρξάμενος ἀπὸ τοῦ πρώτου. 25

ΣΩ. Δείξας γε πρῶτον, ὦ φιλότης, τί ἄρα ἐν τῇ
ἀριστερᾷ ἔχεις ὑπὸ τῷ ἱματίῳ. τοπάζω γάρ σε ἔχειν τὸν
λόγον αὐτόν. εἰ δὲ τοῦτό ἐστιν, οὑτωσὶ διανοοῦ περὶ
E ἐμοῦ, ὡς ἐγώ σε πάνυ μὲν φιλῶ, παρόντος δὲ καὶ Λυσίου
ἐμαυτόν σοι ἐμμελετᾶν παρέχειν οὐ πάνυ δέδοκται. ἀλλ' 30
ἴθι, δείκνυε.

ΦΑΙ. Παῦε. ἐκκέκρουκάς με ἐλπίδος, ὦ Σώκρατες,
ἣν εἶχον ἐν σοὶ ὡς ἐγγυμνασόμενος. ἀλλὰ ποῦ δὴ βούλει
καθιζόμενοι ἀναγνῶμεν;

229 ΣΩ. Δεῦρ' ἐκτραπόμενοι κατὰ τὸν Ἰλισσὸν ἴωμεν, 35
εἶτα ὅπου ἂν δόξῃ ἐν ἡσυχίᾳ καθιζησόμεθα.

ΦΑΙ. Εἰς καιρόν, ὡς ἔοικεν, ἀνυπόδητος ὢν ἔτυχον·
σὺ μὲν γὰρ δὴ ἀεί. ῥᾷστον οὖν ἡμῖν κατὰ τὸ ὑδάτιον
βρέχουσι τοὺς πόδας ἰέναι, καὶ οὐκ ἀηδές, ἄλλως τε καὶ
τήνδε τὴν ὥραν τοῦ ἔτους τε καὶ τῆς ἡμέρας. 40

ΣΩ. Πρόαγε δή, καὶ σκόπει ἅμα ὅπου καθιζησόμεθα.

ΦΑΙ. Ὁρᾷς οὖν ἐκείνην τὴν ὑψηλοτάτην πλάτανον;
ΣΩ. Τί μήν;

ΦΑΙ. Ἐκεῖ σκιά τ' ἐστὶ καὶ πνεῦμα μέτριον, καὶ πόα B
45 καθίζεσθαι ἤ, ἂν βουλώμεθα, κατακλιθῆναι.

ΣΩ. Προάγοις ἄν.

ΦΑΙ. Εἰπέ μοι, ὦ Σώκρατες, οὐκ ἐνθένδε μέντοι
ποθὲν ἀπὸ τοῦ Ἰλισσοῦ λέγεται ὁ Βορέας τὴν Ὠρείθυιαν
ἁρπάσαι;

50 ΣΩ. Λέγεται γάρ.

ΦΑΙ. Ἆρ' οὖν ἐνθένδε; χαρίεντα γοῦν καὶ καθαρὰ
καὶ διαφανῆ τὰ ὑδάτια φαίνεται, καὶ ἐπιτήδεια κόραις
παίζειν παρ' αὐτά.

ΣΩ. Οὔκ, ἀλλὰ κάτωθεν ὅσον δύ' ἢ τρία στάδια, ᾗ C
55 πρὸς τὸ τῆς Ἄγρας διαβαίνομεν· καὶ πού τίς ἐστι βωμὸς
αὐτόθι Βορέου.

ΦΑΙ. Οὐ πάνυ νενόηκα· ἀλλ' εἰπὲ πρὸς Διός, ὦ
Σώκρατες· σὺ τοῦτο τὸ μυθολόγημα πείθει ἀληθὲς
εἶναι;

60 ΣΩ. Ἀλλ' εἰ ἀπιστοίην, ὥσπερ οἱ σοφοί, οὐκ ἂν
ἄτοπος εἴην· εἶτα σοφιζόμενος φαίην αὐτὴν πνεῦμα
Βορέου κατὰ τῶν πλησίον πετρῶν σὺν Φαρμακείᾳ παί-
ζουσαν ὦσαι, καὶ οὕτω δὴ τελευτήσασαν λεχθῆναι ὑπὸ
τοῦ Βορέου ἀνάρπαστον γεγονέναι. ἢ ἐξ Ἀρείου πάγου· D
65 λέγεται γὰρ αὖ καὶ οὗτος ὁ λόγος, ὡς ἐκεῖθεν ἀλλ' οὐκ
ἐνθένδε ἡρπάσθη. ἐγὼ δέ, ὦ Φαῖδρε, ἄλλως μὲν τὰ
τοιαῦτα χαρίεντα ἡγοῦμαι, λίαν δὲ δεινοῦ καὶ ἐπιπόνου
καὶ οὐ πάνυ εὐτυχοῦς ἀνδρός, κατ' ἄλλο μὲν οὐδέν, ὅτι δ'
αὐτῷ ἀνάγκη μετὰ τοῦτο τὸ τῶν Ἱπποκενταύρων εἶδος
70 ἐπανορθοῦσθαι, καὶ αὖθις τὸ τῆς Χιμαίρας. καὶ ἐπιρρεῖ
δὲ ὄχλος τοιούτων Γοργόνων καὶ Πηγάσων, καὶ ἄλλων
ἀμηχάνων πλήθη τε καὶ ἀτοπίαι τερατολόγων τινῶν E
φύσεων· αἷς εἴ τις ἀπιστῶν προσβιβᾷ κατὰ τὸ εἰκὸς
ἕκαστον, ἅτε ἀγροίκῳ τινὶ σοφίᾳ χρώμενος, πολλῆς

αὐτῷ σχολῆς δεήσει. ἐμοὶ δὲ πρὸς αὐτὰ οὐδαμῶς ἐστὶ 75
σχολή. τὸ δὲ αἴτιον, ὦ φίλε, τούτου τόδε. οὐ δύναμαί
πω κατὰ τὸ Δελφικὸν γράμμα γνῶναι ἐμαυτόν· γελοῖον
230 δή μοι φαίνεται τοῦτο ἔτι ἀγνοοῦντα τὰ ἀλλότρια σκοπεῖν. ὅθεν δὴ χαίρειν ἐάσας ταῦτα, πειθόμενος δὲ τῷ
νομιζομένῳ περὶ αὐτῶν, ὃ νῦν δὴ ἔλεγον, σκοπῶ οὐ 80
ταῦτα ἀλλὰ ἐμαυτόν, εἴτε τι θηρίον τυγχάνω Τυφῶνος
πολυπλοκώτερον καὶ μᾶλλον ἐπιτεθυμμένον, εἴτε ἡμερώ-
τερόν τε καὶ ἁπλούστερον ζῷον, θείας τινὸς καὶ ἀτύφου
μοίρας φύσει μετέχον. Ἀτάρ, ὦ ἑταῖρε, μεταξὺ τῶν
λόγων, ἆρ᾽ οὐ τόδε ἦν τὸ δένδρον ἐφ᾽ ὅπερ ἦγες ἡμᾶς;   85
B   ΦΑΙ. Τοῦτο μὲν οὖν αὐτό.

ΣΩ. Νὴ τὴν Ἥραν, καλή γε ἡ καταγωγή. ἥ τε γὰρ
πλάτανος αὕτη μάλ᾽ ἀμφιλαφής τε καὶ ὑψηλή, τοῦ τε
ἄγνου τὸ ὕψος καὶ τὸ σύσκιον πάγκαλον, καὶ ὡς ἀκμὴν
ἔχει τῆς ἄνθης, ὡς ἂν εὐωδέστατον παρέχοι τὸν τόπον. 90
ἥ τε αὖ πηγὴ χαριεστάτη ὑπὸ τῆς πλατάνου ῥεῖ μάλα
ψυχροῦ ὕδατος, ὥστε γε τῷ ποδὶ τεκμήρασθαι· Νυμφῶν
τέ τινων καὶ Ἀχελῴου ἱερὸν ἀπὸ τῶν κορῶν τε καὶ
C ἀγαλμάτων ἔοικεν εἶναι. εἰ δ᾽ αὖ βούλει, τὸ εὔπνουν τοῦ
τόπου ὡς ἀγαπητὸν καὶ σφόδρα ἡδύ· θερινόν τε καὶ 95
λιγυρὸν ὑπηχεῖ τῷ τῶν τεττίγων χορῷ. πάντων δὲ
κομψότατον τὸ τῆς πόας, ὅτι ἐν ἠρέμα προσάντει ἱκανὴ
πέφυκε κατακλινέντι τὴν κεφαλὴν παγκάλως ἔχειν. ὥστε
ἄριστά σοι ἐξενάγηται, ὦ φίλε Φαῖδρε.

ΦΑΙ. Σὺ δέ γε, ὦ θαυμάσιε, ἀτοπώτατός τις φαίνει. 100
ἀτεχνῶς γάρ, ὃ λέγεις, ξεναγουμένῳ τινὶ καὶ οὐκ ἐπιχω-
D ρίῳ ἔοικας· οὕτως ἐκ τοῦ ἄστεος οὔτ᾽ εἰς τὴν ὑπερορίαν
ἀποδημεῖς, οὔτ᾽ ἔξω τείχους ἔμοιγε δοκεῖς τὸ παράπαν
ἐξιέναι.

ΣΩ. Συγγίγνωσκέ μοι, ὦ ἄριστε. φιλομαθὴς γάρ 105

εἰμι. τὰ μὲν οὖν χωρία καὶ τὰ δένδρα οὐδέν μ' ἐθέλει
διδάσκειν, οἱ δ' ἐν τῷ ἄστει ἄνθρωποι. σὺ μέντοι δοκεῖς μοι τῆς ἐξόδου τὸ φάρμακον εὑρηκέναι. ὥσπερ γὰρ
οἱ τὰ πεινῶντα θρέμματα θαλλὸν ἤ τινα καρπὸν προ-
110 σείοντες ἄγουσι, σὺ ἐμοὶ λόγους οὕτω προτείνων ἐν
βιβλίοις τήν τε Ἀττικὴν φαίνει περιάξειν ἅπασαν καὶ E
ὅποι ἂν ἄλλοσε βούλῃ. νῦν οὖν ἐν τῷ παρόντι δεῦρ'
ἀφικόμενος ἐγὼ μέν μοι δοκῶ κατακεῖσθαι, σὺ δ' ἐν
ὁποίῳ σχήματι οἴει ῥᾷστα ἀναγνώσεσθαι, τοῦθ' ἑλόμενος
115 ἀναγίγνωσκε.

The Figure of the Soul.   The Procession of the Gods.

(SOCRATES.)

245 C—249 D.

Ψυχὴ πᾶσα ἀθάνατος. τὸ γὰρ ἀεικίνητον ἀθάνατον·
τὸ δ' ἄλλο κινοῦν καὶ ὑπ' ἄλλου κινούμενον, παῦλαν ἔχον
κινήσεως, παῦλαν ἔχει ζωῆς. μόνον δὴ τὸ αὐτὸ κινοῦν,
ἅτε οὐκ ἀπολεῖπον ἑαυτό, οὔ ποτε λήγει κινούμενον, ἀλλὰ
120 καὶ τοῖς ἄλλοις ὅσα κινεῖται τοῦτο πηγὴ καὶ ἀρχὴ κινή- D
σεως. ἀρχὴ δὲ ἀγένητον. ἐξ ἀρχῆς γὰρ ἀνάγκη πᾶν τὸ
γιγνόμενον γίγνεσθαι, αὐτὴν δὲ μηδ' ἐξ ἑνός· εἰ γὰρ ἔκ
του ἀρχὴ γίγνοιτο, οὐκ ἂν ἐξ ἀρχῆς γίγνοιτο. ἐπειδὴ δὲ
ἀγένητόν ἐστι, καὶ ἀδιάφθορον αὐτὸ ἀνάγκη εἶναι. ἀρχῆς
125 γὰρ δὴ ἀπολομένης οὔτε αὐτή ποτε ἔκ του οὔτε ἄλλο ἐξ
ἐκείνης γενήσεται, εἴπερ ἐξ ἀρχῆς δεῖ τὰ πάντα γίγνεσθαι.
οὕτω δὴ κινήσεως μὲν ἀρχὴ τὸ αὐτὸ αὐτὸ κινοῦν. τοῦτο
δὲ οὔτ' ἀπόλλυσθαι οὔτε γίγνεσθαι δυνατόν, ἢ πάντα τε
οὐρανὸν πᾶσάν τε γένεσιν συμπεσοῦσαν στῆναι καὶ E
130 μήποτε αὖθις ἔχειν ὅθεν κινηθέντα γενήσεται. ἀθανάτου
δὲ πεφασμένου τοῦ ὑφ' ἑαυτοῦ κινουμένου, ψυχῆς οὐσίαν

τε καὶ λόγον τοῦτον αὐτόν τις λέγων οὐκ αἰσχυνεῖται. πᾶν γὰρ σῶμα ᾧ μὲν ἔξωθεν τὸ κινεῖσθαι, ἄψυχον, ᾧ δὲ ἔνδοθεν αὐτῷ ἐξ αὐτοῦ, ἔμψυχον, ὡς ταύτης οὔσης φύσεως ψυχῆς. εἰ δ' ἔστι τοῦτο οὕτως ἔχον, μὴ ἄλλο τι 135 246 εἶναι τὸ αὐτὸ ἑαυτὸ κινοῦν ἢ ψυχήν, ἐξ ἀνάγκης ἀγένητόν τε καὶ ἀθάνατον ψυχὴ ἂν εἴη. Περὶ μὲν οὖν ἀθανασίας αὐτῆς ἱκανῶς.

Περὶ δὲ τῆς ἰδέας αὐτῆς ὧδε λεκτέον· οἷον μέν ἐστι, πάντη πάντως θείας εἶναι καὶ μακρᾶς διηγήσεως, ᾧ δὲ 140 ἔοικεν, ἀνθρωπίνης τε καὶ ἐλάττονος. ταύτη οὖν λέγωμεν. Ἐοικέτω δὴ ξυμφύτῳ δυνάμει ὑποπτέρου ζεύγους τε καὶ ἡνιόχου. θεῶν μὲν οὖν ἵπποι τε καὶ ἡνίοχοι πάντες αὐτοί τε ἀγαθοὶ καὶ ἐξ ἀγαθῶν, τὸ δὲ τῶν ἄλλων B μέμικται. καὶ πρῶτον μὲν ἡμῶν ὁ ἄρχων ξυνωρίδος 145 ἡνιοχεῖ, εἶτα τῶν ἵππων ὁ μὲν αὐτῷ καλός τε καὶ ἀγαθὸς καὶ ἐκ τοιούτων, ὁ δὲ ἐξ ἐναντίων τε καὶ ἐναντίος. χαλεπὴ δὴ καὶ δύσκολος ἐξ ἀνάγκης ἡ περὶ ἡμᾶς ἡνιόχησις. Πῆ δὴ οὖν θνητόν τε καὶ ἀθάνατον ζῷον ἐκλήθη, πειρατέον εἰπεῖν. πᾶσα ἡ ψυχὴ παντὸς ἐπιμελεῖται τοῦ 150 ἀψύχου, πάντα δὲ οὐρανὸν περιπολεῖ, ἄλλοτ' ἐν ἄλλοις C εἴδεσι γιγνομένη. τελέα μὲν οὖν οὖσα καὶ ἐπτερωμένη μετεωροπορεῖ τε καὶ πάντα τὸν κόσμον διοικεῖ· ἡ δὲ πτερορρυήσασα φέρεται, ἕως ἂν στερεοῦ τινὸς ἀντιλάβηται, οὗ κατοικισθεῖσα, σῶμα γήϊνον λαβοῦσα, αὐτὸ 155 αὐτὸ δοκοῦν κινεῖν διὰ τὴν ἐκείνης δύναμιν, ζῷον τὸ ξύμπαν ἐκλήθη, ψυχὴ καὶ σῶμα παγέν, θνητόν τ' ἔσχεν ἐπωνυμίαν· ἀθάνατον δὲ οὐδ' ἐξ ἑνὸς λόγου λελογισμένου, ἀλλὰ πλάττομεν οὔτε ἰδόντες οὔτε ἱκανῶς νοήD σαντες θεόν, ἀθάνατόν τι ζῷον, ἔχον μὲν ψυχήν, ἔχον δὲ 160 σῶμα, τὸν ἀεὶ δὲ χρόνον ταῦτα ξυμπεφυκότα. Ἀλλὰ ταῦτα μὲν δή, ὅπῃ τῷ θεῷ φίλον, ταύτῃ ἐχέτω τε καὶ

λεγέσθω. τὴν δ' αἰτίαν τῆς τῶν πτερῶν ἀποβολῆς, δι'
ἣν ψυχῆς ἀπορρεῖ, λάβωμεν. ἔστι δέ τις τοιάδε.

165 Πέφυκεν ἡ πτεροῦ δύναμις τὸ ἐμβριθὲς ἄγειν ἄνω
μετεωρίζουσα, ᾗ τὸ τῶν θεῶν γένος οἰκεῖ. κεκοινώνηκε
δέ πη μάλιστα τῶν περὶ τὸ σῶμα τοῦ θείου. τὸ δὲ θεῖον
καλόν, σοφόν, ἀγαθὸν καὶ πᾶν ὅ τι τοιοῦτον. τούτοις E
δὴ τρέφεταί τε καὶ αὔξεται μάλιστά γε τὸ τῆς ψυχῆς
170 πτέρωμα, αἰσχρῷ δὲ καὶ κακῷ καὶ τοῖς ἐναντίοις φθίνει
τε καὶ διόλλυται. ὁ μὲν δὴ μέγας ἡγεμὼν ἐν οὐρανῷ
Ζεύς, ἐλαύνων πτηνὸν ἅρμα, πρῶτος πορεύεται, διακο-
σμῶν πάντα καὶ ἐπιμελούμενος· τῷ δ' ἕπεται στρατιὰ
θεῶν τε καὶ δαιμόνων, κατὰ ἔνδεκα μέρη κεκοσμημένη. 247
175 μένει γὰρ Ἑστία ἐν θεῶν οἴκῳ μόνη· τῶν δὲ ἄλλων ὅσοι
ἐν τῷ τῶν δώδεκα ἀριθμῷ τεταγμένοι θεοὶ ἄρχοντες,
ἡγοῦνται κατὰ τάξιν ἣν ἕκαστος ἐτάχθη. πολλαὶ μὲν οὖν
καὶ μακάριαι θέαι τε καὶ διέξοδοι ἐντὸς οὐρανοῦ, ἃς
θεῶν γένος εὐδαιμόνων ἐπιστρέφεται, πράττων ἕκαστος
180 αὐτῶν τὸ αὑτοῦ. ἕπεται δὲ ὁ ἀεὶ ἐθέλων τε καὶ δυνά-
μενος. φθόνος γὰρ ἔξω θείου χοροῦ ἵσταται. ὅταν δὲ δὴ
πρὸς δαῖτα καὶ ἐπὶ θοίνην ἴωσιν, ἄκραν ὑπὸ τὴν ὑπου- B
ράνιον ἀψῖδα πορεύονται πρὸς ἄναντες ἤδη. τὰ μὲν
θεῶν ὀχήματα ἰσορρόπως εὐήνια ὄντα ῥᾳδίως πορεύεται,
185 τὰ δὲ ἄλλα μόγις· βρίθει γὰρ ὁ τῆς κάκης ἵππος μετέ-
χων, ἐπὶ τὴν γῆν ῥέπων τε καὶ βαρύνων, ᾧ μὴ καλῶς
ᾖ τεθραμμένος τῶν ἡνιόχων. ἔνθα δὴ πόνος τε καὶ
ἀγὼν ἔσχατος ψυχῇ πρόκειται. αἱ μὲν γὰρ ἀθάνατοι
καλούμεναι, ἡνίκ' ἂν πρὸς ἄκρῳ γένωνται, ἔξω πορευ- C
190 θεῖσαι ἔστησαν ἐπὶ τῷ τοῦ οὐρανοῦ νώτῳ, στάσας δὲ
αὐτὰς περιάγει ἡ περιφορά, αἱ δὲ θεωροῦσι τὰ ἔξω τοῦ
οὐρανοῦ· τὸν δὲ ὑπερουράνιον τόπον οὔ τέ τις ὕμνησέ
πω τῶν τῇδε ποιητὴς οὔ τέ ποθ' ὑμνήσει κατ' ἀξίαν.

ἔχει δὲ ὧδε. τολμητέον γὰρ οὖν τό γε ἀληθὲς εἰπεῖν,
ἄλλως τε καὶ περὶ ἀληθείας λέγοντα. ἡ γὰρ ἀχρώματός 195
τε καὶ ἀσχημάτιστος καὶ ἀναφὴς οὐσία ὄντως ψυχῆς
οὖσα κυβερνήτῃ μόνῳ θεατὴ νῷ· περὶ ἣν τὸ τῆς ἀλη-
D θοῦς ἐπιστήμης γένος τοῦτον ἔχει τὸν τόπον. ἅτ' οὖν
θεοῦ διάνοια νῷ τε καὶ ἐπιστήμῃ ἀκηράτῳ τρεφομένη,
καὶ ἀπάσης ψυχῆς, ὅση ἂν μέλλῃ τὸ προσῆκον δέξεσθαι, 200
ἰδοῦσα διὰ χρόνου τὸ ὂν ἀγαπᾷ τε καὶ θεωροῦσα τἀληθῆ
τρέφεται καὶ εὐπαθεῖ, ἕως ἂν κύκλῳ ἡ περιφορὰ εἰς
ταὐτὸν περιενέγκῃ. ἐν δὲ τῇ περιόδῳ καθορᾷ μὲν αὐτὴν
δικαιοσύνην, καθορᾷ δὲ σωφροσύνην, καθορᾷ δὲ ἐπιστήμην, οὐχ ᾗ γένεσις πρόσεστιν, οὐδ' ἥ ἐστί που ἑτέρα 205
E ἐν ἑτέρῳ οὖσα ὧν ἡμεῖς νῦν ὄντων καλοῦμεν, ἀλλὰ τὴν
ἐν τῷ ὅ ἐστιν ὂν ὄντως ἐπιστήμην οὖσαν· καὶ τἆλλα
ὡσαύτως τὰ ὄντα ὄντως θεασαμένη καὶ ἑστιαθεῖσα, δῦσα
πάλιν εἰς τὸ εἴσω τοῦ οὐρανοῦ, οἴκαδε ἦλθεν. ἐλθούσης
δὲ αὐτῆς ὁ ἡνίοχος πρὸς τὴν φάτνην τοὺς ἵππους στήσας 210
παρέβαλεν ἀμβροσίαν τε καὶ ἐπ' αὐτῇ νέκταρ ἐπότισε.
248 καὶ οὗτος μὲν θεῶν βίος. αἱ δὲ ἄλλαι ψυχαί, ἡ μὲν ἄριστα θεῷ ἑπομένη καὶ εἰκασμένη ὑπερῆρεν εἰς τὸν ἔξω
τόπον τὴν τοῦ ἡνιόχου κεφαλήν, καὶ συμπεριηνέχθη τὴν
περιφοράν, θορυβουμένη ὑπὸ τῶν ἵππων καὶ μόγις κα- 215
θορῶσα τὰ ὄντα· ἡ δὲ τοτὲ μὲν ἦρε, τοτὲ δὲ ἔδυ, βια-
ζομένων δὲ τῶν ἵππων τὰ μὲν εἶδε, τὰ δ' οὔ. αἱ δὲ δὴ
ἄλλαι γλιχόμεναι μὲν ἅπασαι τοῦ ἄνω ἕπονται, ἀδυνα-
τοῦσαι δὲ ὑποβρύχιαι ξυμπεριφέρονται, πατοῦσαι ἀλλήλας
B καὶ ἐπιβάλλουσαι, ἑτέρα πρὸ τῆς ἑτέρας πειρωμένη γενέ- 220
σθαι. θόρυβος οὖν καὶ ἄμιλλα καὶ ἱδρὼς ἔσχατος γίγνεται.
οὗ δὴ κακίᾳ ἡνιόχων πολλαὶ μὲν χωλεύονται, πολλαὶ δὲ
πολλὰ πτερὰ θραύονται· πᾶσαι δέ, πολὺν ἔχουσαι πόνον,
ἀτελεῖς τῆς τοῦ ὄντος θέας ἀπέρχονται, καὶ ἀπελθοῦσαι

225 τροφῇ δοξαστῇ χρῶνται. οὗ δ' ἕνεχ' ἡ πολλὴ σπουδὴ τὸ
ἀληθείας ἰδεῖν πεδίον οὗ ἐστίν, ἥ τε δὴ προσήκουσα
ψυχῆς τῷ ἀρίστῳ νομὴ ἐκ τοῦ ἐκεῖ λειμῶνος τυγχάνει
οὖσα, ἥ τε τοῦ πτεροῦ φύσις, ᾧ ψυχὴ κουφίζεται, τούτῳ C
τρέφεται. θεσμός τε Ἀδραστείας ὅδε, ἥτις ἂν ψυχὴ θεῷ
230 ξυνοπαδὸς γενομένη κατίδῃ τι τῶν ἀληθῶν, μέχρι τε
τῆς ἑτέρας περιόδου εἶναι ἀπήμονα, κἂν ἀεὶ τοῦτο δύνηται ποιεῖν, ἀεὶ ἀβλαβῆ εἶναι· ὅταν δὲ ἀδυνατήσασα ἐπι-
σπέσθαι μὴ ἴδῃ, καί τινι συντυχίᾳ χρησαμένη λήθης τε
καὶ κακίας πλησθεῖσα βαρυνθῇ, βαρυνθεῖσα δὲ πτερορ-
235 ρυήσῃ τε καὶ ἐπὶ τὴν γῆν πέσῃ, τότε νόμος ταύτην μὴ
φυτεῦσαι εἰς μηδεμίαν θηρείαν φύσιν ἐν τῇ πρώτῃ γενέ- D
σει, ἀλλὰ τὴν μὲν πλεῖστα ἰδοῦσαν εἰς γονὴν ἀνδρὸς γε-
νησομένου φιλοσόφου ἢ φιλοκάλου ἢ μουσικοῦ τινὸς καὶ
ἐρωτικοῦ, τὴν δὲ δευτέραν εἰς βασιλέως ἐννόμου ἢ πολε-
240 μικοῦ καὶ ἀρχικοῦ, τρίτην εἰς πολιτικοῦ ἤ τινος οἰκονο-
μικοῦ ἢ χρηματιστικοῦ, τετάρτην εἰς φιλοπόνου γυμνα-
στικοῦ ἢ περὶ σώματος ἴασίν τινα ἐσομένου, πέμπτην
μαντικὸν βίον ἤ τινα τελεστικὸν ἕξουσαν· ἕκτῃ ποιητικὸς E
ἢ τῶν περὶ μίμησίν τις ἄλλος ἁρμόσει, ἑβδόμῃ δημι-
245 ουργικὸς ἢ γεωργικός, ὀγδόῃ σοφιστικὸς ἢ δημοτικός,
ἐννάτῃ τυραννικός· ἐν δὴ τούτοις ἅπασιν ὃς μὲν ἂν δικαίως διαγάγῃ, ἀμείνονος μοίρας μεταλαμβάνει, ὃς δ' ἂν
ἀδίκως, χείρονος. εἰς μὲν γὰρ τὸ αὐτὸ ὅθεν ἥκει ἡ
ψυχὴ ἑκάστη, οὐκ ἀφικνεῖται ἐτῶν μυρίων· οὐ γὰρ πτε-
250 ροῦται πρὸ τοσούτου χρόνου, πλὴν ἡ τοῦ φιλοσοφήσαν- 249
τος ἀδόλως ἢ ἐρασθέντος μετὰ φιλοσοφίας. αὗται δὲ
τρίτῃ περιόδῳ τῇ χιλιετεῖ, ἐὰν ἕλωνται τρὶς ἐφεξῆς
τὸν βίον τοῦτον, οὕτω πτερωθεῖσαι τρισχιλιοστῷ ἔτει
ἀπέρχονται. αἱ δὲ ἄλλαι, ὅταν τὸν πρῶτον βίον τελευτή-
255 σωσι, κρίσεως ἔτυχον. κριθεῖσαι δέ, αἱ μὲν εἰς τὰ ὑπὸ

γῆς δικαιωτήρια ἐλθοῦσαι δίκην ἐκτίνουσιν, αἱ δ᾽ εἰς τοὐ-
ρανοῦ τινὰ τόπον ὑπὸ τῆς δίκης κουφισθεῖσαι διάγουσιν
B ἀξίως οὗ ἐν ἀνθρώπου εἴδει ἐβίωσαν βίου. τῷ δὲ χιλιο-
στῷ ἀμφότεραι ἀφικνούμεναι ἐπὶ κλήρωσίν τε καὶ αἵρεσιν
τοῦ δευτέρου βίου, αἱροῦνται ὃν ἂν ἐθέλῃ ἑκάστη. ἔνθα 260
καὶ εἰς θηρίου βίον ἀνθρωπίνη ψυχὴ ἀφικνεῖται, καὶ ἐκ
θηρίου, ὅς ποτε ἄνθρωπος ἦν, πάλιν εἰς ἄνθρωπον. οὐ
γὰρ ἥ γε μή ποτε ἰδοῦσα τὴν ἀλήθειαν εἰς τόδε ἥξει τὸ
σχῆμα. δεῖ γὰρ ἄνθρωπον ξυνιέναι κατ᾽ εἶδος λεγόμενον,
ἐκ πολλῶν ἰὸν αἰσθήσεων εἰς ἓν λογισμῷ ξυναιρούμενον. 265
C τοῦτο δέ ἐστιν ἀνάμνησις ἐκείνων, ἅ ποτ᾽ εἶδεν ἡμῶν ἡ
ψυχὴ συμπορευθεῖσα θεῷ καὶ ὑπεριδοῦσα ἃ νῦν εἶναί
φαμεν, καὶ ἀνακύψασα εἰς τὸ ὂν ὄντως. διὸ δὴ δικαίως
μόνη πτεροῦται ἡ τοῦ φιλοσόφου διάνοια· πρὸς γὰρ ἐκείνοις ἀεί ἐστι μνήμῃ κατὰ δύναμιν, πρὸς οἷσπερ θεὸς 270
ὢν θεῖός ἐστι. τοῖς δὲ δὴ τοιούτοις ἀνὴρ ὑπομνήμασιν
ὀρθῶς χρώμενος, τελέους ἀεὶ τελετὰς τελούμενος, τέλεος
D ὄντως μόνος γίγνεται. ἐξιστάμενος δὲ τῶν ἀνθρωπίνων
σπουδασμάτων, καὶ πρὸς τῷ θείῳ γιγνόμενος, νουθετεῖ-
ται μὲν ὑπὸ τῶν πολλῶν ὡς παρακινῶν, ἐνθουσιάζων δὲ 275
λέληθε τοὺς πολλούς.

The Cicadae.

(SOCRATES, PHAEDRUS.)

258 D—259 D.

ΦΑΙ. Δῆλον δή.

ΣΩ. Τίς οὖν ὁ τρόπος τοῦ καλῶς τε καὶ μὴ γράφειν;
δεόμεθά τι, ὦ Φαῖδρε, Λυσίαν τε περὶ τούτων ἐξετάσαι
καὶ ἄλλον ὅστις πώποτέ τι γέγραφεν ἢ γράψει, εἴτε 280
πολιτικὸν σύγγραμμα εἴτε ἰδιωτικόν, ἐν μέτρῳ ὡς ποιητής, ἢ ἄνευ μέτρου ὡς ἰδιώτης;

ΦΑΙ. Ἐρωτᾷς εἰ δεόμεθα; τίνος μὲν οὖν ἕνεκα κἄν E
τις ὡς εἰπεῖν ζῴη, ἀλλ' ἢ τῶν τοιούτων ἡδονῶν ἕνεκα;
285 οὐ γάρ που ἐκείνων γε ὧν προλυπηθῆναι δεῖ ἢ μηδὲ
ἡσθῆναι, ὃ δὴ ὀλίγου πᾶσαι αἱ περὶ τὸ σῶμα ἡδοναὶ
ἔχουσι· διὸ καὶ δικαίως ἀνδραποδώδεις κέκληνται.

ΣΩ. Σχολὴ μὲν δή, ὡς ἔοικε. καὶ ἅμα μοι δοκοῦσιν
ὡς ἐν τῷ πνίγει ὑπὲρ κεφαλῆς ἡμῶν οἱ τέττιγες ᾄδοντες
290 καὶ ἀλλήλοις διαλεγόμενοι καθορᾶν. εἰ οὖν ἴδοιεν καὶ 259
νῷ καθάπερ τοὺς πολλοὺς ἐν μεσημβρίᾳ μὴ διαλεγομένους ἀλλὰ νυστάζοντας καὶ κηλουμένους ὑφ' αὑτῶν
δι' ἀργίαν τῆς διανοίας, δικαίως ἂν καταγελῷεν, ἡγούμενοι ἀνδράποδα ἄττα σφίσιν ἐλθόντα εἰς τὸ καταγώγιον
295 ὥσπερ προβάτια μεσημβριάζοντα περὶ τὴν κρήνην εὕδειν·
ἐὰν δὲ ὁρῶσι διαλεγομένους καὶ παραπλέοντάς σφας
ὥσπερ Σειρῆνας ἀκηλήτους, ὃ γέρας παρὰ θεῶν ἔχου- B
σιν ἀνθρώποις διδόναι, τάχ' ἂν δοῖεν ἀγασθέντες.

ΦΑΙ. Ἔχουσι δὲ δὴ τί τοῦτο; ἀνήκοος γάρ, ὡς
300 ἔοικε, τυγχάνω ὤν.

ΣΩ. Οὐ μὲν δὴ πρέπει γε φιλόμουσον ἄνδρα τῶν
τοιούτων ἀνήκοον εἶναι. λέγεται δ' ὥς ποτ' ἦσαν οὗτοι
ἄνθρωποι τῶν πρὶν Μούσας γεγονέναι. γενομένων δὲ
Μουσῶν καὶ φανείσης ᾠδῆς, οὕτως ἄρα τινὲς τῶν τότε
305 ἐξεπλάγησαν ὑφ' ἡδονῆς, ὥστε ᾄδοντες ἠμέλησαν σίτων C
τε καὶ ποτῶν, καὶ ἔλαθον τελευτήσαντες αὑτούς. ἐξ ὧν
τὸ τεττίγων γένος μετ' ἐκεῖνο φύεται, γέρας τοῦτο παρὰ
Μουσῶν λαβόν, μηδὲν τροφῆς δεῖσθαι γενόμενόν, ἀλλ'
ἄσιτόν τε καὶ ἄποτον εὐθὺς ᾄδειν, ἕως ἂν τελευτήσῃ, καὶ
310 μετὰ ταῦτα ἐλθὸν παρὰ Μούσας ἀπαγγέλλειν τίς τίνα
αὐτῶν τιμᾷ τῶν ἐνθάδε. Τερψιχόρᾳ μὲν οὖν τοὺς ἐν
τοῖς χοροῖς τετιμηκότας αὐτὴν ἀπαγγέλλοντες ποιοῦσι
προσφιλεστέρους, τῇ δὲ Ἐρατοῖ τοὺς ἐν τοῖς ἐρωτικοῖς, D

καὶ ταῖς ἄλλαις οὕτω, κατὰ τὸ εἶδος ἑκάστης τιμῆς. τῇ δὲ
πρεσβυτάτῃ Καλλιόπῃ καὶ τῇ μετ' αὐτὴν Οὐρανίᾳ τοὺς 315
ἐν φιλοσοφίᾳ διάγοντάς τε καὶ τιμῶντας τὴν ἐκείνων
μουσικὴν ἀγγέλλουσιν, αἳ δὴ μάλιστα τῶν Μουσῶν περί
τε οὐρανὸν καὶ λόγους οὖσαι θείους τε καὶ ἀνθρωπίνους
ἰᾶσι καλλίστην φωνήν. πολλῶν δὴ οὖν ἕνεκεν λεκτέον τι
καὶ οὐ καθευδητέον ἐν τῇ μεσημβρίᾳ.   320

Theuth.

(SOCRATES, PHAEDRUS.)

274 B—275 B.

ΣΩ. Οἶσθ' οὖν ὅπῃ μάλιστα θεῷ χαριεῖ λόγων πέρι
πράττων ἢ λέγων;

ΦΑΙ. Οὐδαμῶς. σὺ δέ;

C ΣΩ. Ἀκοήν γ' ἔχω λέγειν τῶν προτέρων, τὸ δ' ἀληθὲς αὐτοὶ ἴσασιν. εἰ δὲ τοῦτο εὕροιμεν αὐτοί, ἆρά γ' 325
ἂν ἔθ' ἡμῖν μέλοι τι τῶν ἀνθρωπίνων δοξασμάτων;

ΦΑΙ. Γελοῖον ἤρου. ἀλλ' ἃ φῂς ἀκηκοέναι, λέγε.

ΣΩ. Ἤκουσα τοίνυν περὶ Ναύκρατιν τῆς Αἰγύπτου
γενέσθαι τῶν ἐκεῖ παλαιῶν τινὰ θεῶν, οὗ καὶ τὸ ὄρνεον
τὸ ἱερόν, ὃ δὴ καλοῦσιν Ἶβιν· αὐτῷ δὲ ὄνομα τῷ δαί- 330
μονι εἶναι Θεύθ. τοῦτον δὲ πρῶτον ἀριθμόν τε καὶ λο-
D γισμὸν εὑρεῖν καὶ γεωμετρίαν καὶ ἀστρονομίαν, ἔτι δὲ
πεττείας τε καὶ κυβείας, καὶ δὴ καὶ γράμματα. βασιλέως
δ' αὖ τότε ὄντος Αἰγύπτου ὅλης Θαμοῦ περὶ τὴν μεγάλην πόλιν τοῦ ἄνω τόπου, ἣν οἱ Ἕλληνες Αἰγυπτίας Θή- 335
βας καλοῦσι, καὶ τὸν θεὸν Ἄμμωνα, παρὰ τοῦτον ἐλθὼν
ὁ Θεὺθ τὰς τέχνας ἀπέδειξε, καὶ ἔφη δεῖν διαδοθῆναι
τοῖς ἄλλοις Αἰγυπτίοις. ὁ δὲ ἤρετο ἥντινα ἑκάστη ἔχοι
ὠφέλειαν. διεξιόντος δέ, ὅ τι καλῶς ἢ μὴ καλῶς δοκοῖ

340 λέγειν, τὸ μὲν ἔψεγε, τὸ δ' ἐπήνει. πολλὰ μὲν δὴ περὶ Ε
ἑκάστης τῆς τέχνης ἐπ' ἀμφότερα Θαμοῦν τῷ Θεὺθ λέγεται ἀποφήνασθαι, ἃ λόγος πολὺς ἂν εἴη διελθεῖν.
ἐπειδὴ δὲ ἐπὶ τοῖς γράμμασιν ἦν, Τοῦτο δέ, ὦ βασιλεῦ,
τὸ μάθημα, ἔφη ὁ Θεύθ, σοφωτέρους Αἰγυπτίους καὶ
345 μνημονικωτέρους παρέξει· μνήμης τε γὰρ καὶ σοφίας
φάρμακον εὑρέθη. ὁ δ' εἶπεν Ὦ τεχνικώτατε Θεύθ, ἄλλος μὲν τεκεῖν δυνατὸς τὰ τῆς τέχνης, ἄλλος δὲ κρῖναι
τίν' ἔχει μοῖραν βλάβης τε καὶ ὠφελείας τοῖς μέλλουσι
χρῆσθαι. καὶ νῦν σύ, πατὴρ ὢν γραμμάτων, δι' εὔνοιαν 275
350 τοὐναντίον εἶπες ἢ δύναται. τοῦτο γὰρ τῶν μαθόντων
λήθην μὲν ἐν ψυχαῖς παρέξει, μνήμης ἀμελετησίᾳ, ἅτε
διὰ πίστιν γραφῆς ἔξωθεν ὑπ' ἀλλοτρίων τύπων, οὐκ
ἔνδον αὐτοὺς ὑφ' αὑτῶν ἀναμιμνησκομένους. οὔκουν
μνήμης ἀλλ' ὑπομνήσεως φάρμακον εὗρες. σοφίας δὲ
355 τοῖς μαθηταῖς δόξαν, οὐκ ἀλήθειαν πορίζεις· πολυήκοοι
γάρ σοι γενόμενοι ἄνευ διδαχῆς, πολυγνώμονες εἶναι
δόξουσιν, ἀγνώμονες ὡς ἐπὶ τὸ πλῆθος ὄντες καὶ χαλεποὶ Β
ξυνεῖναι, δοξόσοφοι γεγονότες ἀντὶ σοφῶν.

ΦΑΙ. Ὦ Σώκρατες, ῥᾳδίως σὺ Αἰγυπτίους καὶ ὁπο-
360 δαποὺς ἂν ἐθέλῃς λόγους ποιεῖς.

CRATYLUS.

The Imitative Power of Letters.

(SOCRATES, HERMOGENES, CRATYLUS.)

425 B—428 D.

ΣΩ. Τί οὖν; σὺ πιστεύεις σαυτῷ οἷός τ' ἂν εἶναι
ταῦτα οὕτω διελέσθαι; ἐγὼ μὲν γὰρ οὔ.

ΕΡΜ. Πολλοῦ ἄρα δέω ἔγωγε.

ΣΩ. Ἐάσομεν οὖν, ἢ βούλει οὕτως, ὅπως ἂν δυνώ-
μεθα, καὶ ἂν σμικρόν τι αὐτῶν οἷοί τ' ὦμεν κατιδεῖν, ἐπι- 5
C χειρῶμεν, προειπόντες, ὥσπερ ὀλίγον πρότερον τοῖς
θεοῖς, ὅτι οὐδὲν εἰδότες τῆς ἀληθείας τὰ τῶν ἀνθρώπων
δόγματα περὶ αὐτῶν εἰκάζομεν, οὕτω δὲ καὶ νῦν αὖ εἰπόντες ἡμῖν αὐτοῖς ἴωμεν, ὅτι εἰ μέν τι χρηστὸν ἔδει
αὐτὰ διελέσθαι εἴτε ἄλλον ὁντινοῦν εἴτε ἡμᾶς, οὕτως ἔδει 10
αὐτὰ διαιρεῖσθαι, νῦν δέ, τὸ λεγόμενον, κατὰ δύναμιν
δεήσει ἡμᾶς περὶ αὐτῶν πραγματεύεσθαι; δοκεῖ ταῦτα;
ἢ πῶς λέγεις;

ΕΡΜ.   Πάνυ μὲν οὖν σφόδρα ἔμοιγε δοκεῖ.

D ΣΩ. Γελοῖα μὲν οἶμαι φανεῖσθαι, ὦ Ἑρμόγενες, 15
γράμμασι καὶ συλλαβαῖς τὰ πράγματα μεμιμημένα κατάδηλα γιγνόμενα· ὅμως δὲ ἀνάγκη. οὐ γὰρ ἔχομεν τούτου
βέλτιον, εἰς ὅ τι ἐπανενέγκωμεν περὶ ἀληθείας τῶν πρώτων ὀνομάτων, εἰ μὴ ἄρα δή, ὥσπερ οἱ τραγῳδοποιοί,
ἐπειδάν τι ἀπορῶσιν, ἐπὶ τὰς μηχανὰς καταφεύγουσι 20
θεοὺς αἴροντες, καὶ ἡμεῖς οὕτως εἰπόντες ἀπαλλαγῶμεν,
ὅτι τὰ πρῶτα ὀνόματα οἱ θεοὶ ἔθεσαν καὶ διὰ ταῦτα
E ὀρθῶς ἔχει. ἆρα καὶ ἡμῖν κράτιστος οὗτος τῶν λόγων;
ἢ ἐκεῖνος, ὅτι παρὰ βαρβάρων τινῶν αὐτὰ παρειλήφαμεν,
εἰσὶ δὲ ἡμῶν ἀρχαιότεροι βάρβαροι; ἢ ὅτι ὑπὸ παλαιό- 25
426 τητος ἀδύνατον αὐτὰ ἐπισκέψασθαι, ὥσπερ καὶ τὰ βαρ-
βαρικά; αὗται γὰρ ἂν πᾶσαι ἐκδύσεις εἶεν καὶ μάλα
κομψαὶ τῷ μὴ ἐθέλοντι λόγον διδόναι περὶ τῶν πρώτων
ὀνομάτων, ὡς ὀρθῶς κεῖται. καίτοι ὅτῳ τις τρόπῳ τῶν
πρώτων ὀνομάτων τὴν ὀρθότητα μὴ οἶδεν, ἀδύνατόν που 30
τῶν γε ὑστέρων εἰδέναι, ἃ ἐξ ἐκείνων ἀνάγκη δηλοῦσθαι,
ὧν τις πέρι μηδὲν οἶδεν· ἀλλὰ δῆλον ὅτι τὸν φάσκοντα
περὶ αὐτῶν τεχνικὸν εἶναι περὶ τῶν πρώτων ὀνομάτων
B μάλιστά τε καὶ καθαρώτατα δεῖ ἔχειν ἀποδεῖξαι, ἢ εὖ

35 εἰδέναι ὅτι τά γε ὕστερα ἤδη φλυαρήσει. ἢ σοὶ ἄλλως
δοκεῖ;

ΕΡΜ. Οὐδ᾽ ὁπωστιοῦν, ὦ Σώκρατες, ἄλλως.

ΣΩ. Ἃ μὲν τοίνυν ἐγὼ ᾔσθημαι περὶ τῶν πρώτων
ὀνομάτων, πάνυ μοι δοκεῖ ὑβριστικὰ εἶναι καὶ γελοῖα.
40 τούτων οὖν σοι μεταδώσω, ἂν βούλῃ· σὺ δ᾽ ἄν τι ἔχῃς
βέλτιόν ποθεν λαβεῖν, πειρᾶσθαι καὶ ἐμοὶ μεταδιδόναι.

ΕΡΜ. Ποιήσω ταῦτα. ἀλλὰ θαρρῶν λέγε.

ΣΩ. Πρῶτον μὲν τοίνυν τὸ ῥῶ ἔμοιγε φαίνεται ὥσπερ C
ὄργανον εἶναι πάσης τῆς κινήσεως, ἣν οὐδ᾽ εἴπομεν δι᾽ ὅ
45 τι ἔχει τοῦτο τοὔνομα· ἀλλὰ γὰρ δῆλον ὅτι ἵεσις βούλεται εἶναι· οὐ γὰρ ἦτα ἐχρώμεθα ἀλλὰ εἶ τὸ παλαιόν.
ἡ δὲ ἀρχὴ ἀπὸ τοῦ κίειν· ξενικὸν δὲ τοὔνομα· τοῦτο δ᾽
ἐστὶν ἰέναι. εἰ οὖν τις τὸ παλαιὸν αὐτῆς εὕροι ὄνομα
εἰς τὴν ἡμετέραν φωνὴν συμβαῖνον, ἵεσις ἂν ὀρθῶς
50 καλοῖτο· νῦν δὲ ἀπό τε τοῦ ξενικοῦ τοῦ κίειν καὶ ἀπὸ τῆς
τοῦ ἦτα μεταβολῆς καὶ τῆς τοῦ νῦ ἐνθέσεως κίνησις
κέκληται, ἔδει δὲ κιείνησιν καλεῖσθαι ἢ εἶσιν. ἡ δὲ D
στάσις ἀπόφασις τοῦ ἰέναι βούλεται εἶναι, διὰ δὲ τὸν
καλλωπισμὸν στάσις ὠνόμασται. Τὸ δ᾽ οὖν ῥῶ τὸ
55 στοιχεῖον, ὥσπερ λέγω, καλὸν ἔδοξεν ὄργανον εἶναι τῆς
κινήσεως τῷ τὰ ὀνόματα τιθεμένῳ πρὸς τὸ ἀφομοιοῦν τῇ
φορᾷ· πολλαχοῦ γοῦν χρῆται αὐτῷ εἰς αὐτήν· πρῶτον
μὲν ἐν αὐτῷ τῷ ῥεῖν καὶ ῥοῇ διὰ τούτου τοῦ γράμματος
τὴν φορὰν μιμεῖται, εἶτα ἐν τῷ τρόμῳ, εἶτα ἐν τῷ τραχεῖ, E
60 ἔτι δὲ ἐν τοῖς τοιοῖσδε ῥήμασιν, οἷον κρούειν, θραύειν,
ἐρείκειν, θρύπτειν, κερματίζειν, ῥυμβεῖν· πάντα ταῦτα τὸ
πολὺ ἀπεικάζει διὰ τοῦ ῥῶ· ἑώρα γάρ, οἶμαι, τὴν γλῶτταν
ἐν τούτῳ ἥκιστα μένουσαν, μάλιστα δὲ σειομένην· διὸ
φαίνεταί μοι τούτῳ πρὸς ταῦτα κατακεχρῆσθαι. τῷ δ᾽ αὖ
65 ἰῶτα πρὸς τὰ λεπτὰ πάντα, ἃ δὴ μάλιστα διὰ πάντων ἴοι

427 ἄν. διὰ ταῦτα τὸ ἰέναι καὶ τὸ ἵεσθαι διὰ τοῦ ἰῶτα ἀπομι-
μεῖται, ὥσπερ γε διὰ τοῦ φῖ καὶ τοῦ ψῖ καὶ τοῦ σῖγμα καὶ
τοῦ ζῆτα, ὅτι πνευματώδη τὰ γράμματα, πάντα τὰ τοιαῦτα
μεμίμηται αὐτοῖς ὀνομάζων, οἷον τὸ ψυχρὸν καὶ τὸ ζέον
καὶ τὸ σείεσθαι καὶ ὅλως σεισμόν.   καὶ ὅταν που τὸ φυ- 70
σῶδες μιμῆται, πανταχοῦ ἐνταῦθα ὡς τὸ πολὺ τὰ τοιαῦτα γράμματα ἐπιφέρειν φαίνεται ὁ τὰ ὀνόματα τιθέμενος.
τῆς δ' αὖ τοῦ δέλτα συμπιέσεως καὶ τοῦ ταῦ καὶ ἀπερεί-
Β σεως τῆς γλώττης τὴν δύναμιν χρήσιμον φαίνεται ἡγή-
σασθαι πρὸς τὴν μίμησιν τοῦ δεσμοῦ καὶ τῆς στάσεως. 75
ὅτι δὲ ὀλισθάνει μάλιστα ἐν τῷ λάβδα ἡ γλῶττα κατιδών,
ἀφομοιῶν ὠνόμασε τά τε λεῖα καὶ αὐτὸ τὸ ὀλισθάνειν
καὶ τὸ λιπαρὸν καὶ τὸ κολλῶδες καὶ τἆλλα πάντα τὰ τοιαῦτα.   ᾗ δὲ ὀλισθανούσης τῆς γλώττης ἀντιλαμβάνεται
ἡ τοῦ γάμμα δύναμις, τὸ γλίσχρον ἀπεμιμήσατο καὶ 80
C γλυκὺ καὶ γλοιῶδες.   τοῦ δ' αὖ νῦ τὸ εἴσω αἰσθόμενος
τῆς φωνῆς, τὸ ἔνδον καὶ τὰ ἐντὸς ὠνόμασεν, ὡς ἀφομοιῶν
τοῖς γράμμασι τὰ ἔργα.   τὸ δ' αὖ ἄλφα τῷ μεγάλῳ
ἀπέδωκε, καὶ τῷ μήκει τὸ ἦτα, ὅτι μεγάλα τὰ γράμματα.
εἰς δὲ τὸ γογγύλον τοῦ οὖ δεόμενος σημείου, τοῦτο 85
πλεῖστον αὐτῷ εἰς τὸ ὄνομα ἐνεκέρασε.   καὶ τἆλλα οὕτω
φαίνεται προσβιβάζειν καὶ κατὰ γράμματα καὶ κατὰ
συλλαβὰς ἑκάστῳ τῶν ὄντων σημεῖόν τε καὶ ὄνομα ποιῶν
ὁ νομοθέτης, ἐκ δὲ τούτων τὰ λοιπὰ ἤδη αὐτοῖς τούτοις
συντιθέναι ἀπομιμούμενος. Αὕτη μοι φαίνεται, ὦ Ἑρμό- 90
D γενες, βούλεσθαι εἶναι ἡ τῶν ὀνομάτων ὀρθότης, εἰ μή τι
ἄλλο Κρατύλος ὅδε λέγει.

ΕΡΜ.   Καὶ μήν, ὦ Σώκρατες, πολλά γέ μοι πολλάκις
πράγματα παρέχει Κρατύλος, ὥσπερ κατ' ἀρχὰς ἔλεγον,
φάσκων μὲν εἶναι ὀρθότητα ὀνομάτων, ἥτις δ' ἐστὶν 95
οὐδὲν σαφὲς λέγων, ὥστε με μὴ δύνασθαι εἰδέναι,

πότερον ἑκὼν ἢ ἄκων οὕτως ἀσαφῶς ἑκάστοτε περὶ αὐτῶν
λέγει. Νῦν οὖν μοι, ὦ Κρατύλε, ἐναντίον Σωκράτους
εἰπέ, πότερον ἀρέσκει σοι ᾗ λέγει Σωκράτης περὶ ὀνομά- E
των, ἢ ἔχεις πῃ ἄλλῃ κάλλιον λέγειν; καὶ εἰ ἔχεις,
λέγε, ἵνα ἤτοι μάθῃς παρὰ Σωκράτους ἢ διδάξῃς ἡμᾶς
ἀμφοτέρους.

ΚΡ. Τί δαί, ὦ Ἑρμόγενες; δοκεῖ σοι ῥᾴδιον εἶναι
οὕτω ταχὺ μαθεῖν τε καὶ διδάξαι ὁτιοῦν πρᾶγμα, μὴ ὅτι
τοσοῦτον, ὃ δὴ δοκεῖ ἐν τοῖς μέγιστον εἶναι;

ΕΡΜ. Μὰ Δί' οὐκ ἔμοιγε. ἀλλὰ τὸ τοῦ Ἡσιόδου 428
καλῶς μοι φαίνεται ἔχειν, τὸ εἰ καί τις σμικρὸν ἐπὶ σμικρῷ καταθείη, προὔργου εἶναι. εἰ οὖν καὶ σμικρόν τι
οἷός τ' εἶ πλέον ποιῆσαι, μὴ ἀπόκαμνε, ἀλλ' εὐεργέτει
καὶ Σωκράτη τόνδε, δίκαιος δ' εἶ, καὶ ἐμέ.

ΣΩ. Καὶ μὲν δὴ ἔγωγε καὶ αὐτός, ὦ Κρατύλε, οὐδὲν
ἂν ἰσχυρισαίμην ὧν εἴρηκα, ᾗ δέ μοι ἐφαίνετο, μεθ' Ἑρ-
μογένους ἐπεσκεψάμην, ὥστε τούτου γε ἕνεκα θαρρῶν
λέγε, εἴ τι ἔχεις βέλτιον, ὡς ἐμοῦ ἐνδεξομένου. εἰ μέντοι B
ἔχεις τι σὺ κάλλιον τούτων λέγειν, οὐκ ἂν θαυμάζοιμι·
δοκεῖς γάρ μοι αὐτός τε ἐσκέφθαι τὰ τοιαῦτα καὶ παρ'
ἄλλων μεμαθηκέναι. ἐὰν οὖν λέγῃς τι κάλλιον, ἕνα τῶν
μαθητῶν περὶ ὀρθότητος ὀνομάτων καὶ ἐμὲ γράφου.

ΚΡ. Ἀλλὰ μὲν δή, ὦ Σώκρατες, ὥσπερ σὺ λέγεις,
μεμέληκέ τέ μοι περὶ αὐτῶν καὶ ἴσως ἄν σε ποιησαίμην
μαθητήν. φοβοῦμαι μέντοι, μὴ τούτου πᾶν τοὐναντίον
ᾖ, ὅτι μοί πως ἐπέρχεται λέγειν πρὸς σὲ τὸ τοῦ Ἀχιλλέως, C
ὃ ἐκεῖνος ἐν Λιταῖς πρὸς τὸν Αἴαντα λέγει. φησὶ δὲ

Αἶαν Διογενὲς Τελαμώνιε, κοίρανε λαῶν,
    πάντα τί μοι κατὰ θυμὸν ἐείσω μυθήσασθαι.

καὶ ἐμοὶ σύ, ὦ Σώκρατες, ἐπιεικῶς φαίνει κατὰ
νοῦν χρησμῳδεῖν, εἴτε παρ' Εὐθύφρονος ἐπίπνους γενό-

μενος, εἴτε καὶ ἄλλη τις Μοῦσα πάλαι σε ἐνοῦσα ἐλελήθει.

D ΣΩ. Ὦ 'γαθὲ Κρατύλε, θαυμάζω καὶ αὐτὸς πάλαι 130
τὴν ἐμαυτοῦ σοφίαν, καὶ ἀπιστῶ. δοκεῖ οὖν μοι χρῆναι
ἐπανασκέψασθαι τί καὶ λέγω. τὸ γὰρ ἐξαπατᾶσθαι αὐτὸν
ὑφ' αὑτοῦ πάντων χαλεπώτατον· ὅταν γὰρ μηδὲ σμικρὸν
ἀποστατῇ ἀλλ' ἀεὶ παρῇ ὁ ἐξαπατήσων, πῶς οὐ δεινόν;
δεῖ δή, ὡς ἔοικε, θαμὰ μεταστρέφεσθαι ἐπὶ τὰ προειρη- 135
μένα, καὶ πειρᾶσθαι, τὸ ἐκείνου τοῦ ποιητοῦ, βλέπειν
ἅμα πρόσσω καὶ ὀπίσσω.

GORGIAS.

The Pilot.

(SOCRATES. CALLICLES.)

511 C—512 B.

ΣΩ. Τί δέ, ὦ βέλτιστε; ἦ καὶ ἡ τοῦ νεῖν ἐπιστήμη
σεμνή τίς σοι δοκεῖ εἶναι;

ΚΑΛ. Μὰ Δί' οὐκ ἔμοιγε.

ΣΩ. Καὶ μὴν σώζει γε καὶ αὕτη ἐκ θανάτου τοὺς
ἀνθρώπους, ὅταν εἰς τοιοῦτον ἐμπέσωσιν οὗ δεῖ ταύτης 5
τῆς ἐπιστήμης. εἰ δ' αὕτη σοι δοκεῖ σμικρὰ εἶναι, ἐγὼ
D σοι μείζονα ταύτης ἐρῶ, τὴν κυβερνητικήν, ἣ οὐ μόνον
τὰς ψυχὰς σώζει ἀλλὰ καὶ τὰ σώματα καὶ τὰ χρήματα
ἐκ τῶν ἐσχάτων κινδύνων, ὥσπερ ἡ ῥητορική. καὶ αὕτη
μὲν προσεσταλμένη ἐστὶ καὶ κοσμία, καὶ οὐ σεμνύνεται 10
ἐσχηματισμένη ὡς ὑπερήφανόν τι διαπραττομένη, ἀλλὰ
ταὐτὰ διαπραξαμένη τῇ δικανικῇ, ἐὰν μὲν ἐξ Αἰγίνης
δεῦρο σώσῃ, οἶμαι δύ' ὀβολοὺς ἐπράξατο, ἐὰν δὲ ἐξ

Αἰγύπτου ἢ ἐκ τοῦ Πόντου, ἐὰν πάμπολυ ταύτης τῆς
15 μεγάλης εὐεργεσίας, σώσασ' ἃ νῦν δὴ ἔλεγον, καὶ αὐτὸν E
καὶ παῖδας καὶ χρήματα καὶ γυναῖκας, ἀποβιβάσασ' εἰς
τὸν λιμένα δύο δραχμὰς ἐπράξατο, καὶ αὐτὸς ὁ ἔχων τὴν
τέχνην καὶ ταῦτα διαπραξάμενος ἐκβὰς παρὰ τὴν θάλατταν καὶ τὴν ναῦν περιπατεῖ ἐν μετρίῳ σχήματι.
20 λογίζεσθαι γάρ, οἶμαι, ἐπίσταται ὅτι ἄδηλόν ἐστιν οὕ-
στινάς τε ὠφέληκε τῶν συμπλεόντων οὐκ ἐάσας κατα-
ποντωθῆναι καὶ οὕστινας ἔβλαψεν, εἰδὼς ὅτι οὐδὲν
αὐτοὺς βελτίους ἐξεβίβασεν ἢ οἷοι ἐνέβησαν, οὔτε τὰ 512
σώματα οὔτε τὰς ψυχάς. λογίζεται οὖν ὅτι οὐκ, εἰ μέν
25 τις μεγάλοις καὶ ἀνιάτοις νοσήμασι κατὰ τὸ σῶμα συνε-
χόμενος μὴ ἀπεπνίγη, οὗτος μὲν ἄθλιός ἐστιν ὅτι οὐκ
ἀπέθανε, καὶ οὐδὲν ὑπ' αὐτοῦ ὠφέληται· εἰ δέ τις ἄρα ἐν
τῷ τοῦ σώματος τιμιωτέρῳ, τῇ ψυχῇ, πολλὰ νοσήματα
ἔχει καὶ ἀνίατα, τούτῳ δὲ βιωτέον ἐστὶ καὶ τοῦτον
30 ὀνήσειεν, ἄν τε ἐκ θαλάττης ἄν τε ἐκ δικαστηρίου
ἄν τε ἄλλοθεν ὁποθενοῦν σώσῃ, ἀλλ' οἶδεν ὅτι οὐκ B
ἄμεινόν ἐστι ζῆν τῷ μοχθηρῷ ἀνθρώπῳ· κακῶς γὰρ
ἀνάγκη ἐστὶ ζῆν.

The Judgement of the Dead.

(SOCRATES. CALLICLES.)

521 C—end.

ΚΑΛ. Ὥς μοι δοκεῖς, ὦ Σώκρατες, πιστεύειν μηδ' ἂν
35 ἕν τούτων παθεῖν, ὡς οἰκῶν ἐκποδὼν καὶ οὐκ ἂν εἰσαχ-
θεὶς εἰς δικαστήριον ὑπὸ πάνυ ἴσως μοχθηροῦ ἀνθρώπου
καὶ φαύλου !

ΣΩ. Ἀνόητος ἄρα εἰμί, ὦ Καλλίκλεις, ὡς ἀληθῶς, εἰ
μὴ οἴομαι ἐν τῇδε τῇ πόλει ὀντινοῦν ἄν, ὅ τι τύχοι,

τοῦτο παθεῖν. τόδε μέντοι εὖ οἶδ᾽ ὅτι, ἐάνπερ εἰσίω εἰς 40
δικαστήριον περὶ τούτων τινὸς κινδυνεύων ὧν σὺ λέγεις,
D πονηρός τίς με ἔσται ὁ εἰσάγων· οὐδεὶς γὰρ ἂν χρηστὸς
μὴ ἀδικοῦντ᾽ ἄνθρωπον εἰσαγάγοι. καὶ οὐδέν γε ἄτοπον
εἰ ἀποθάνοιμι. βούλει σοι εἴπω δι᾽ ὅ τι ταῦτα προσδοκῶ;
    ΚΑΛ.   Πάνυ γε.   45
    ΣΩ.   Οἶμαι μετ᾽ ὀλίγων ᾽Αθηναίων, ἵνα μὴ εἴπω μό-
νος, ἐπιχειρεῖν τῇ ὡς ἀληθῶς πολιτικῇ τέχνῃ καὶ πράττειν
τὰ πολιτικὰ μόνος τῶν νῦν. ἅτε οὖν οὐ πρὸς χάριν λέγων
τοὺς λόγους οὓς λέγω ἑκάστοτε, ἀλλὰ πρὸς τὸ βέλτιστον,
E οὐ πρὸς τὸ ἥδιστον, καὶ οὐκ ἐθέλων ποιεῖν ἃ σὺ παραι- 50
νεῖς, τὰ κομψὰ ταῦτα, οὐχ ἕξω ὅ τι λέγω ἐν τῷ δικαστηρίῳ. ὁ αὐτὸς δέ μοι ἥκει λόγος ὅνπερ πρὸς Πῶλον
ἔλεγον· κρινοῦμαι γὰρ ὡς ἐν παιδίοις ἰατρὸς ἂν κρίνοιτο
κατηγοροῦντος ὀψοποιοῦ. σκόπει γάρ, τί ἂν ἀπολογοῖτο
ὁ τοιοῦτος ἄνθρωπος ἐν τούτοις ληφθείς, εἰ αὐτοῦ κατη- 55
γοροῖ τις λέγων ὅτι ᾽Ω παῖδες, πολλὰ ὑμᾶς καὶ κακὰ ὅδε
εἴργασται ἀνὴρ καὶ αὐτούς, καὶ τοὺς νεωτάτους ὑμῶν
522 διαφθείρει τέμνων τε καὶ κάων, καὶ ἰσχναίνων καὶ πνίγων
ἀπορεῖν ποιεῖ, πικρότατα πόματα διδοὺς καὶ πεινῆν καὶ
διψῆν ἀναγκάζων, οὐχ ὥσπερ ἐγὼ πολλὰ καὶ ἡδέα καὶ 60
παντοδαπὰ εὐώχουν ὑμᾶς. τί ἂν οἴει ἐν τούτῳ τῷ κακῷ
ἀποληφθέντα ἰατρὸν ἔχειν εἰπεῖν; ἢ εἰ εἴποι τὴν ἀλήθειαν, ὅτι Ταῦτα πάντα ἐγὼ ἐποίουν, ὦ παῖδες, ὑγιεινῶς, ὁπόσον οἴει ἂν ἀναβοῆσαι τοὺς τοιούτους δικαστάς;
οὐ μέγα;   65
    ΚΑΛ.   ῞Ισως· οἴεσθαί γε χρή.
    ΣΩ.   Οὐκοῦν οἴει ἐν πάσῃ ἀπορίᾳ ἂν αὐτὸν ἔχεσθαι
B ὅ τι χρὴ εἰπεῖν;
    ΚΑΛ.   Πάνυ γε.
    ΣΩ.   Τοιοῦτον μέντοι καὶ ἐγὼ οἶδα ὅτι πάθος 70

πάθοιμι ἂν εἰσελθὼν εἰς δικαστήριον. οὔτε γὰρ ἡδονὰς ἃς ἐκπεπόρικα ἔξω αὐτοῖς λέγειν, ἃς οὗτοι εὐεργεσίας καὶ ὠφελείας νομίζουσιν, ἐγὼ δὲ οὔτε τοὺς πορίζον-
τας ζηλῶ οὔτε οἷς πορίζεται· ἐάν τέ τίς με ἢ νεωτέρους
75 φῇ διαφθείρειν ἀπορεῖν ποιοῦντα, ἢ τοὺς πρεσβυτέρους
κακηγορεῖν λέγοντα πικροὺς λόγους ἢ ἰδίᾳ ἢ δημοσίᾳ, οὔτε
τὸ ἀληθὲς ἔξω εἰπεῖν, ὅτι Δικαίως πάντα ταῦτα ἐγὼ C
λέγω, καὶ πράττω τὸ ὑμέτερον δὴ τοῦτο, ὦ ἄνδρες δικασταί, οὔτε ἄλλο οὐδέν. ὥστε ἴσως, ὅ τι ἂν τύχω, τοῦτο
80 πείσομαι.

    ΚΑΛ. Δοκεῖ οὖν σοι, ὦ Σώκρατες, καλῶς ἔχειν ἄν-
θρωπος ἐν πόλει οὕτω διακείμενος καὶ ἀδύνατος ὢν
ἑαυτῷ βοηθεῖν;

    ΣΩ. Εἰ ἐκεῖνό γε ἐν αὐτῷ ὑπάρχοι, ὦ Καλλίκλεις,
85 ὃ σὺ πολλάκις ὡμολόγησας· εἰ βεβοηθηκὼς εἴη αὐτῷ,
μήτε περὶ ἀνθρώπους μήτε περὶ θεοὺς ἄδικον μηδὲν μήτε D
εἰρηκὼς μήτε εἰργασμένος. αὕτη γάρ τις βοήθεια ἑαυτῷ
πολλάκις ἡμῖν ὡμολόγηται κρατίστη εἶναι. εἰ μὲν οὖν
ἐμέ τις ἐξελέγχοι ταύτην τὴν βοήθειαν ἀδύνατον ὄντα
90 ἐμαυτῷ καὶ ἄλλῳ βοηθεῖν, αἰσχυνοίμην ἂν καὶ ἐν πολλοῖς
καὶ ἐν ὀλίγοις ἐξελεγχόμενος καὶ μόνος ὑπὸ μόνου, καὶ εἰ
διὰ ταύτην τὴν ἀδυναμίαν ἀποθνήσκοιμι, ἀγανακτοίην
ἄν. εἰ δὲ κολακικῆς ῥητορικῆς ἐνδείᾳ τελευτῴην ἔγωγε,
εὖ οἶδα ὅτι ῥᾳδίως ἴδοις ἄν με φέροντα τὸν θάνατον. E
95 αὐτὸ μὲν γὰρ τὸ ἀποθνήσκειν οὐδεὶς φοβεῖται, ὅστις μὴ
παντάπασιν ἀλόγιστός τε καὶ ἄνανδρός ἐστι, τὸ δὲ ἀδικεῖν
φοβεῖται· πολλῶν γὰρ ἀδικημάτων γέμοντα τὴν ψυχὴν εἰς
Ἅιδου ἀφικέσθαι πάντων ἔσχατον κακῶν ἐστίν. εἰ δὲ
βούλει, σοί ἐγώ, ὡς τοῦτο οὕτως ἔχει, ἐθέλω λόγον λέξαι.
100 ΚΑΛ. Ἀλλ' ἐπείπερ γε καὶ τἆλλα ἐπέρανας, καὶ
τοῦτο πέρανον.

523 ΣΩ. Ἄκουε δή, φασί, μάλα καλοῦ λόγου, ὃν σὺ μὲν
ἡγήσει μῦθον, ὡς ἐγὼ οἶμαι, ἐγὼ δὲ λόγον· ὡς ἀληθῆ
γὰρ ὄντα σοι λέξω ἃ μέλλω λέγειν. Ὥσπερ γὰρ Ὅμηρος
λέγει, διενείμαντο τὴν ἀρχὴν ὁ Ζεὺς καὶ ὁ Ποσειδῶν 105
καὶ ὁ Πλούτων, ἐπειδὴ παρὰ τοῦ πατρὸς παρέλαβον. ἦν
οὖν νόμος ὅδε περὶ ἀνθρώπων ἐπὶ Κρόνου, καὶ ἀεὶ καὶ
νῦν ἔτι ἔστιν ἐν θεοῖς, τῶν ἀνθρώπων τὸν μὲν δικαίως
B τὸν βίον διελθόντα καὶ ὁσίως, ἐπειδὰν τελευτήσῃ, εἰς
μακάρων νήσους ἀπιόντα οἰκεῖν ἐν πάσῃ εὐδαιμονίᾳ 110
ἐκτὸς κακῶν, τὸν δὲ ἀδίκως καὶ ἀθέως εἰς τὸ τῆς τί-
σεώς τε καὶ δίκης δεσμωτήριον, ὃ δὴ τάρταρον καλοῦσιν,
ἰέναι. τούτων δὲ δικασταὶ ἐπὶ Κρόνου καὶ ἔτι νεωστὶ
τοῦ Διὸς τὴν ἀρχὴν ἔχοντος ζῶντες ἦσαν ζώντων, ἐκείνῃ
τῇ ἡμέρᾳ δικάζοντες ᾗ μέλλοιεν τελευτᾶν. κακῶς οὖν αἱ 115
δίκαι ἐκρίνοντο. ὅ τε οὖν Πλούτων καὶ οἱ ἐπιμεληταὶ οἱ
ἐκ μακάρων νήσων ἰόντες ἔλεγον πρὸς τὸν Δία ὅτι
C φοιτῷέν σφιν ἄνθρωποι ἑκατέρωσε ἀνάξιοι. εἶπεν οὖν
ὁ Ζεύς, Ἀλλ’ ἐγώ, ἔφη, παύσω τοῦτο γιγνόμενον. νῦν
μὲν γὰρ κακῶς αἱ δίκαι δικάζονται. ἀμπεχόμενοι γάρ, 120
ἔφη, οἱ κρινόμενοι κρίνονται· ζῶντες γὰρ κρίνονται. πολλοὶ οὖν, ἦ δ’ ὅς, ψυχὰς πονηρὰς ἔχοντες ἠμφιεσμένοι
εἰσὶ σώματά τε καλὰ καὶ γένη καὶ πλούτους, καί, ἐπειδὰν
ἡ κρίσις ᾖ, ἔρχονται αὐτοῖς πολλοὶ μάρτυρες, μαρτυρή-
σοντες ὡς δικαίως βεβιώκασιν. οἱ οὖν δικασταὶ ὑπό τε 125
D τούτων ἐκπλήττονται, καὶ ἅμα καὶ αὐτοὶ ἀμπεχόμενοι
δικάζουσι, πρὸ τῆς ψυχῆς τῆς αὑτῶν ὀφθαλμοὺς καὶ ὦτα
καὶ ὅλον τὸ σῶμα προκεκαλυμμένοι. ταῦτα δὴ αὐτοῖς
πάντα ἐπίπροσθεν γίγνεται, καὶ τὰ αὐτῶν ἀμφιέσματα
καὶ τὰ τῶν κρινομένων. πρῶτον μὲν οὖν, ἔφη, παυστέον 130
ἐστὶ προειδότας αὐτοὺς τὸν θάνατον· νῦν γὰρ προΐσασι.
τοῦτο μὲν οὖν καὶ δὴ εἴρηται τῷ Προμηθεῖ ὅπως ἂν

παύσῃ αὐτῶν. ἔπειτα γυμνοὺς κριτέον ἁπάντων τούτων· Ε
τεθνεῶτας γὰρ δεῖ κρίνεσθαι. καὶ τὸν κριτὴν δεῖ γυμνὸν
135 εἶναι, τεθνεῶτα, αὐτῇ τῇ ψυχῇ αὐτὴν τὴν ψυχὴν θεω-
ροῦντα ἐξαίφνης ἀποθανόντος ἑκάστου, ἔρημον πάντων
τῶν συγγενῶν καὶ καταλιπόντα ἐπὶ τῆς γῆς πάντα ἐκεῖνον
τὸν κόσμον, ἵνα δικαία ἡ κρίσις ᾖ. ἐγὼ μὲν οὖν ταῦτα
ἐγνωκὼς πρότερος ἢ ὑμεῖς ἐποιησάμην δικαστὰς υἱεῖς
140 ἐμαυτοῦ, δύο μὲν ἐκ τῆς Ἀσίας, Μίνω τε καὶ Ῥαδάμανθυν, ἕνα δὲ ἐκ τῆς Εὐρώπης, Αἰακόν· οὗτοι οὖν 524
ἐπειδὰν τελευτήσωσι, δικάσουσιν ἐν τῷ λειμῶνι, ἐν τῇ
τριόδῳ ἐξ ἧς φέρετον τὼ ὁδώ, ἡ μὲν εἰς μακάρων νήσους,
ἡ δ᾽ εἰς τάρταρον. καὶ τοὺς μὲν ἐκ τῆς Ἀσίας Ῥαδάμαν-
145 θυς κρινεῖ, τοὺς δὲ ἐκ τῆς Εὐρώπης Αἰακός· Μίνῳ δὲ
πρεσβεῖα δώσω, ἐπιδιακρίνειν, ἐὰν ἀπορῆτόν τι τὼ ἑτέρω,
ἵνα ὡς δικαιοτάτη ἡ κρίσις ᾖ περὶ τῆς πορείας τοῖς
ἀνθρώποις.

Ταῦτ᾽ ἔστιν, ὦ Καλλίκλεις, ἃ ἐγὼ ἀκηκοὼς πιστεύω
150 ἀληθῆ εἶναι· καὶ ἐκ τούτων τῶν λόγων τοιόνδε τι λογί- Β
ζομαι συμβαίνειν. Ὁ θάνατος τυγχάνει ὤν, ὡς ἐμοὶ
δοκεῖ, οὐδὲν ἄλλο ἢ δυοῖν πραγμάτοιν διάλυσις, τῆς ψυχῆς
καὶ τοῦ σώματος, ἀπ᾽ ἀλλήλοιν. ἐπειδὰν δὲ διαλυθῆτον
ἄρα ἀπ᾽ ἀλλήλοιν, οὐ πολὺ ἧττον ἑκάτερον αὐτοῖν ἔχει
155 τὴν ἕξιν τὴν αὑτοῦ ἥνπερ καὶ ὅτε ἔζη ὁ ἄνθρωπος, τό
τε σῶμα τὴν φύσιν τὴν αὑτοῦ καὶ τὰ θεραπεύματα καὶ τὰ
παθήματα, ἔνδηλα πάντα. οἷον εἴ τινος μέγα ἦν τὸ
σῶμα φύσει ἢ τροφῇ ἢ ἀμφότερα ζῶντος, τούτου καὶ C
ἐπειδὰν ἀποθάνῃ ὁ νεκρὸς μέγας· καὶ εἰ παχύς, παχὺς
160 καὶ ἀποθανόντος, καὶ τἆλλα οὕτως. καὶ εἰ αὖ ἐπετήδευε
κομᾶν, κομήτης τούτου καὶ ὁ νεκρός. μαστιγίας αὖ εἴ
τις ἦν καὶ ἴχνη εἶχε τῶν πληγῶν οὐλὰς ἐν τῷ σώματι ἢ
ὑπὸ μαστίγων ἢ ἄλλων τραυμάτων ζῶν, καὶ τεθνεῶτος

τὸ σῶμα ἔστιν ἰδεῖν ταῦτα ἔχον. κατεαγότα τε εἴ του ἦν
μέλη ἢ διεστραμμένα ζῶντος, καὶ τεθνεῶτος ταὐτὰ ταῦτα 165
D ἔνδηλα. ἐνὶ δὲ λόγῳ, οἷος εἶναι παρεσκεύαστο τὸ σῶμα
ζῶν, ἔνδηλα ταῦτα καὶ τελευτήσαντος ἢ πάντα ἢ τὰ
πολλὰ ἐπί τινα χρόνον. ταὐτὸν δή μοι δοκεῖ τοῦτ᾽ ἄρα
καὶ περὶ τὴν ψυχὴν εἶναι, ὦ Καλλίκλεις· ἔνδηλα πάντα
ἐστὶν ἐν τῇ ψυχῇ, ἐπειδὰν γυμνωθῇ τοῦ σώματος, τά τε 170
τῆς φύσεως καὶ τὰ παθήματα ἃ διὰ τὴν ἐπιτήδευσιν
ἑκάστου πράγματος ἔσχεν ἐν τῇ ψυχῇ ὁ ἄνθρωπος.
Ἐπειδὰν οὖν ἀφίκωνται παρὰ τὸν δικαστήν, οἱ μὲν ἐκ
E τῆς Ἀσίας παρὰ τὸν Ῥαδάμανθυν, ὁ Ῥαδάμανθυς ἐκείνους ἐπιστήσας θεᾶται ἑκάστου τὴν ψυχήν, οὐκ εἰδὼς 175
ὅτου ἐστίν, ἀλλὰ πολλάκις τοῦ μεγάλου βασιλέως ἐπιλαβόμενος ἢ ἄλλου ὁτουοῦν βασιλέως ἢ δυνάστου κατεῖδεν οὐδὲν ὑγιὲς ὂν τῆς ψυχῆς, ἀλλὰ διαμεμαστιγω-
μένην καὶ οὐλῶν μεστὴν ὑπὸ ἐπιορκιῶν καὶ ἀδικίας, ἃ
525 ἑκάστῳ ἡ πρᾶξις αὐτοῦ ἐξωμόρξατο εἰς τὴν ψυχήν, καὶ 180
πάντα σκολιὰ ὑπὸ ψεύδους καὶ ἀλαζονείας καὶ οὐδὲν
εὐθὺ διὰ τὸ ἄνευ ἀληθείας τεθράφθαι· καὶ ὑπὸ ἐξουσίας
καὶ τρυφῆς καὶ ὕβρεως καὶ ἀκρατίας τῶν πράξεων ἀσυμ-
μετρίας τε καὶ αἰσχρότητος γέμουσαν τὴν ψυχὴν εἶδεν.
ἰδὼν δὲ ἀτίμως ταύτην ἀπέπεμψεν εὐθὺ τῆς φρουρᾶς, οἷ 185
μέλλει ἐλθοῦσα ἀνατλῆναι τὰ προσήκοντα πάθη.

B Προσήκει δὲ παντὶ τῷ ἐν τιμωρίᾳ ὄντι, ὑπ᾽ ἄλλου
ὀρθῶς τιμωρουμένῳ, ἢ βελτίονι γίγνεσθαι καὶ ὀνίνασθαι
ἢ παραδείγματι τοῖς ἄλλοις γίγνεσθαι, ἵνα ἄλλοι ὁρῶντες
πάσχοντα ἃ ἂν πάσχῃ φοβούμενοι βελτίους γίγνωνται. 190
εἰσὶ δὲ οἱ μὲν ὠφελούμενοί τε καὶ δίκην διδόντες ὑπὸ
θεῶν τε καὶ ἀνθρώπων οὗτοι οἳ ἂν ἰάσιμα ἁμαρτήματα
ἁμάρτωσιν· ὅμως δὲ δι᾽ ἀλγηδόνων καὶ ὀδυνῶν γίγνεται
αὐτοῖς ἡ ὠφέλεια καὶ ἐνθάδε καὶ ἐν Ἅιδου· οὐ γὰρ οἷόν

195 τε ἄλλως ἀδικίας ἀπαλλάττεσθαι. οἳ δ' ἂν τὰ ἔσχατα C
ἀδικήσωσι καὶ διὰ τοιαῦτα ἀδικήματα ἀνίατοι γένωνται,
ἐκ τούτων τὰ παραδείγματα γίγνεται, καὶ οὗτοι αὐτοὶ
μὲν οὐκέτι ὀνίνανται οὐδέν, ἅτε ἀνίατοι ὄντες, ἄλλοι δὲ
ὀνίνανται οἱ τούτους ὁρῶντες διὰ τὰς ἁμαρτίας τὰ μέ-
200 γιστα καὶ ὀδυνηρότατα καὶ φοβερώτατα πάθη πάσχοντας
τὸν ἀεὶ χρόνον, ἀτεχνῶς παραδείγματα ἀνηρτημένους
ἐκεῖ ἐν Ἅιδου ἐν τῷ δεσμωτηρίῳ, τοῖς ἀεὶ τῶν ἀδίκων
ἀφικνουμένοις θεάματα καὶ νουθετήματα. ὧν ἐγώ φημι D
ἕνα καὶ Ἀρχέλαον ἔσεσθαι, εἰ ἀληθῆ λέγει Πῶλος, καὶ
205 ἄλλον ὅστις ἂν τοιοῦτος τύραννος ᾖ. οἶμαι δὲ καὶ τοὺς
πολλοὺς εἶναι τούτων τῶν παραδειγμάτων ἐκ τυράννων
καὶ βασιλέων καὶ δυναστῶν καὶ τὰ τῶν πόλεων πραξάντων γεγονότας· οὗτοι γὰρ διὰ τὴν ἐξουσίαν μέγιστα καὶ
ἀνοσιώτατα ἁμαρτήματα ἁμαρτάνουσι. μαρτυρεῖ δὲ τού-
210 τοις καὶ Ὅμηρος· βασιλέας γὰρ καὶ δυνάστας ἐκεῖνος
πεποίηκε τοὺς ἐν Ἅιδου τὸν ἀεὶ χρόνον τιμωρουμένους, E
Τάνταλον καὶ Σίσυφον καὶ Τιτυόν. Θερσίτην δέ, καὶ
εἴ τις ἄλλος πονηρὸς ἦν ἰδιώτης, οὐδεὶς πεποίηκε μεγά-
λαις τιμωρίαις συνεχόμενον ὡς ἀνίατον· οὐ γάρ, οἶμαι,
215 ἐξῆν αὐτῷ· διὸ καὶ εὐδαιμονέστερος ἦν ἢ οἷς ἐξῆν.
ἀλλὰ γάρ, ὦ Καλλίκλεις, ἐκ τῶν δυναμένων εἰσὶ καὶ οἱ
σφόδρα πονηροὶ γιγνόμενοι ἄνθρωποι· οὐδὲν μὴν κωλύει 526
καὶ ἐν τούτοις ἀγαθοὺς ἄνδρας ἐγγίγνεσθαι, καὶ σφόδρα
γε ἄξιον ἄγασθαι τῶν γιγνομένων· χαλεπὸν γάρ, ὦ
220 Καλλίκλεις, καὶ πολλοῦ ἐπαίνου ἄξιον ἐν μεγάλῃ ἐξου-
σίᾳ τοῦ ἀδικεῖν γενόμενον δικαίως διαβιῶναι. ὀλίγοι
δὲ γίγνονται οἱ τοιοῦτοι· ἐπεὶ καὶ ἐνθάδε καὶ ἄλλοθι
γεγόνασιν, οἶμαι δὲ καὶ ἔσονται καλοὶ κἀγαθοὶ ταύτην
τὴν ἀρετὴν τὴν τοῦ δικαίως διαχειρίζειν ἃ ἄν τις ἐπι- B
225 τρέπῃ· εἷς δὲ καὶ πάνυ ἐλλόγιμος γέγονε καὶ εἰς τοὺς

ἄλλους Ἕλληνας, Ἀριστείδης ὁ Λυσιμάχου. οἱ δὲ πολλοί, ὦ ἄριστε, κακοὶ γίγνονται τῶν δυναστῶν.

Ὅπερ οὖν ἔλεγον, ἐπειδὰν ὁ Ῥαδάμανθυς ἐκεῖνος
τοιοῦτόν τινα λάβῃ, ἄλλο μὲν περὶ αὐτοῦ οὐκ οἶδεν
οὐδέν, οὔθ' ὅστις οὔθ' ὧντινων, ὅτι δὲ πονηρός τις· 230
καὶ τοῦτο κατιδὼν ἀπέπεμψεν εἰς τάρταρον, ἐπισημηνά-
μενος, ἐάν τε ἰάσιμος ἐάν τε ἀνίατος δοκῇ εἶναι· ὁ δὲ
C ἐκεῖσε ἀφικόμενος τὰ προσήκοντα πάσχει· ἐνίοτε δ'
ἄλλην εἰσιδὼν ὁσίως βεβιωκυῖαν καὶ μετ' ἀληθείας,
ἀνδρὸς ἰδιώτου ἢ ἄλλου τινός, μάλιστα μέν, ἔγωγέ φημι, 235
ὦ Καλλίκλεις, φιλοσόφου τὰ αὑτοῦ πράξαντος καὶ οὐ
πολυπραγμονήσαντος ἐν τῷ βίῳ, ἠγάσθη τε καὶ ἐς μακάρων νήσους ἀπέπεμψε. ταὐτὰ ταῦτα καὶ ὁ Αἰακός.
ἑκάτερος δὲ τούτων ῥάβδον ἔχων δικάζει. ὁ δὲ Μίνως
ἐπισκοπῶν κάθηται μόνος ἔχων χρυσοῦν σκῆπτρον, ὥς 240
D φησιν Ὀδυσσεὺς ὁ Ὁμήρου ἰδεῖν αὐτὸν

χρύσεον σκῆπτρον ἔχοντα, θεμιστεύοντα νέκυσσιν.

Ἐγὼ μὲν οὖν, ὦ Καλλίκλεις, ὑπὸ τούτων τῶν λόγων
πέπεισμαι, καὶ σκοπῶ ὅπως ἀποφανοῦμαι τῷ κριτῇ ὡς
ὑγιεστάτην τὴν ψυχήν. χαίρειν οὖν ἐάσας τὰς τιμὰς 245
τὰς τῶν πολλῶν ἀνθρώπων, τὴν ἀλήθειαν σκοπῶν πειράσομαι τῷ ὄντι ὡς ἂν δύνωμαι βέλτιστος ὢν καὶ ζῆν καὶ
E ἐπειδὰν ἀποθνήσκω ἀποθνήσκειν. παρακαλῶ δὲ καὶ τοὺς
ἄλλους πάντας ἀνθρώπους, καθ' ὅσον δύναμαι, καὶ δὴ
καὶ σὲ ἀντιπαρακαλῶ ἐπὶ τοῦτον τὸν βίον καὶ τὸν ἀγῶνα 250
τοῦτον, ὃν ἐγώ φημι ἀντὶ πάντων τῶν ἐνθάδε ἀγώνων
εἶναι, καὶ ὀνειδίζω σοι ὅτι οὐχ οἷός τ' ἔσει σαυτῷ βοηθῆσαι, ὅταν ἡ δίκη σοι ᾖ καὶ ἡ κρίσις ἣν νῦν δὴ ἐγὼ
ἔλεγον, ἀλλὰ ἐλθὼν παρὰ τὸν δικαστὴν τὸν τῆς Αἰγίνης
527 υἱόν, ἐπειδάν σου ἐπιλαβόμενος ἄγῃ, χασμήσει καὶ 255
ἰλιγγιάσεις οὐδὲν ἧττον ἢ ἐγὼ ἐνθάδε σὺ ἐκεῖ, καί σε

ἴσως τυπτήσει τις καὶ ἐπὶ κόρρης ἀτίμως καὶ πάντως
προπηλακιεῖ.

Τάχα δ᾽ οὖν ταῦτα μῦθός σοι δοκεῖ λέγεσθαι, ὥσπερ
260 γραός, καὶ καταφρονεῖς αὐτῶν. καὶ οὐδέν γ᾽ ἂν ἦν θαυμαστὸν καταφρονεῖν τούτων, εἴ πῃ ζητοῦντες εἴχομεν
αὐτῶν βελτίω καὶ ἀληθέστερα εὑρεῖν· νῦν δὲ ὁρᾷς ὅτι
τρεῖς ὄντες ὑμεῖς, οἵπερ σοφώτατοί ἐστε τῶν νῦν Ἑλλήνων, σύ τε καὶ Πῶλος καὶ Γοργίας, οὐκ ἔχετε ἀπο- B
265 δεῖξαι ὡς δεῖ ἄλλον τινὰ βίον ζῆν ἢ τοῦτον ὅσπερ καὶ
ἐκεῖσε φαίνεται συμφέρων, ἀλλ᾽ ἐν τοσούτοις λόγοις
τῶν ἄλλων ἐλεγχομένων μόνος οὗτος ἠρεμεῖ ὁ λόγος, ὡς
εὐλαβητέον ἐστὶ τὸ ἀδικεῖν μᾶλλον ἢ τὸ ἀδικεῖσθαι, καὶ
παντὸς μᾶλλον ἀνδρὶ μελετητέον οὐ τὸ δοκεῖν εἶναι
270 ἀγαθὸν ἀλλὰ τὸ εἶναι, καὶ ἰδίᾳ καὶ δημοσίᾳ· ἐὰν δέ τις
κατά τι κακὸς γίγνηται, κολαστέος ἐστί, καὶ τοῦτο δεύτερον ἀγαθὸν μετὰ τὸ εἶναι δίκαιον, τὸ γίγνεσθαι καὶ C
κολαζόμενον διδόναι δίκην· καὶ πᾶσαν κολακείαν καὶ
τὴν περὶ ἑαυτὸν καὶ τὴν περὶ τοὺς ἄλλους, καὶ περὶ
275 ὀλίγους καὶ περὶ πολλούς, φευκτέον· καὶ τῇ ῥητορικῇ
οὕτω χρηστέον, ἐπὶ τὸ δίκαιον ἀεί, καὶ τῇ ἄλλῃ πάσῃ
πράξει.

Ἐμοὶ οὖν πειθόμενος ἀκολούθησον ἐνταῦθα, οἷ ἀφικόμενος εὐδαιμονήσεις καὶ ζῶν καὶ τελευτήσας, ὡς ὁ λόγος
280 σημαίνει. καὶ ἔασόν τινά σου καταφρονῆσαι ὡς ἀνοήτου
καὶ προπηλακίσαι, ἐὰν βούληται, καὶ ναὶ μὰ Δία σύ γε D
θαρρῶν πατάξαι τὴν ἄτιμον ταύτην πληγήν· οὐδὲν γὰρ
δεινὸν πείσει, ἐὰν τῷ ὄντι ᾖς καλὸς κἀγαθός, ἀσκῶν
ἀρετήν. κἄπειτα οὕτω κοινῇ ἀσκήσαντες, τότε ἤδη, ἐὰν
285 δοκῇ χρῆναι, ἐπιθησόμεθα τοῖς πολιτικοῖς, ἢ ὁποῖον ἂν
τι ἡμῖν δοκῇ, τότε βουλευσόμεθα, βελτίους ὄντες βουλεύεσθαι ἢ νῦν. αἰσχρὸν γὰρ ἔχοντάς γε ὡς νῦν φαινό-

μεθα ἔχειν, ἔπειτα νεανιεύεσθαι ὥς τι ὄντας, οἷς οὐδέποτε
ταὐτὰ δοκεῖ περὶ τῶν αὐτῶν, καὶ ταῦτα περὶ τῶν μεγί-
Ε στων· εἰς τοσοῦτον ἥκομεν ἀπαιδευσίας· ὥσπερ οὖν 290
ἡγεμόνι τῷ λόγῳ χρησώμεθα τῷ νῦν παραφανέντι, ὃς
ἡμῖν σημαίνει ὅτι οὗτος ὁ τρόπος ἄριστος τοῦ βίου, καὶ
τὴν δικαιοσύνην καὶ τὴν ἄλλην ἀρετὴν ἀσκοῦντας καὶ ζῆν
καὶ τεθνάναι. τούτῳ οὖν ἐπώμεθα, καὶ τοὺς ἄλλους
παρακαλῶμεν, μὴ ἐκείνῳ ᾧ σὺ πιστεύων ἐμὲ παρακαλεῖς· 295
ἔστι γὰρ οὐδενὸς ἄξιος, ὦ Καλλίκλεις.

FIRST ALCIBIADES.

*Who is Alcibiades, compared with the Kings of Sparta, or
with the Great King?*

(SOCRATES. ALCIBIADES.)
120 E—124 B.

ΣΩ. Σκεψώμεθα δή, τοῖς ἐκείνων τὰ ἡμέτερα ἀντιτι-
θέντες, πρῶτον μὲν εἰ δοκοῦσι φαυλοτέρων γενῶν εἶναι
οἱ Λακεδαιμονίων καὶ Περσῶν βασιλεῖς. ἢ οὐκ ἴσμεν
ὡς οἱ μὲν Ἡρακλέους, οἱ δὲ Ἀχαιμένους ἔκγονοι, τὸ δ᾽
Ἡρακλέους τε γένος καὶ τὸ Ἀχαιμένους εἰς Περσέα τὸν 5
Διὸς ἀναφέρεται ;

121 ΑΛ. Καὶ γὰρ τὸ ἡμέτερον, ὦ Σώκρατες, εἰς Εὐρυσάκη,
τὸ δ᾽ Εὐρυσάκους εἰς Δία.

ΣΩ. Καὶ γὰρ τὸ ἡμέτερον, ὦ γενναῖε Ἀλκιβιάδη, εἰς
Δαίδαλον, ὁ δὲ Δαίδαλος εἰς Ἥφαιστον τὸν Διός. ἀλλὰ 10
τὰ μὲν τούτων ἀπ᾽ αὐτῶν ἀρξάμενα βασιλεῖς εἰσιν ἐκ
βασιλέων μέχρι Διός, οἱ μὲν Ἄργους τε καὶ Λακεδαί-
μονος, οἱ δὲ τῆς Περσίδος τὸ ἀεί, πολλάκις δὲ καὶ τῆς
Ἀσίας, ὥσπερ καὶ νῦν· ἡμεῖς δὲ αὐτοί τε ἰδιῶται καὶ

15 οἱ πατέρες. εἰ δὲ καὶ τοὺς προγόνους σε δέοι καὶ τὴν Β
πατρίδα Εὐρυσάκους ἐπιδεῖξαι Σαλαμῖνα ἢ τὴν Αἰακοῦ
τοῦ ἔτι προτέρου Αἴγιναν Ἀρτοξέρξῃ τῷ Ξέρξου, πόσον
ἂν οἴει γέλωτα ὀφλεῖν; ἀλλ᾽ ὅρα μὴ τῷ τε γένους ὄγκῳ
ἐλαττώμεθα τῶν ἀνδρῶν καὶ τῇ ἄλλῃ τροφῇ. ἢ οὐκ
20 ᾔσθησαι τοῖς τε Λακεδαιμονίων βασιλεῦσιν ὡς μεγάλα
τὰ ὑπάρχοντα, ὧν αἱ γυναῖκες δημοσίᾳ φυλάττονται ὑπὸ
τῶν ἐφόρων, ὅπως εἰς δύναμιν μὴ λάθῃ ἐξ ἄλλου γενόμενος ὁ βασιλεὺς ἢ ἐξ Ἡρακλειδῶν; ὁ δὲ Περσῶν C
τοσοῦτον ὑπερβάλλει, ὥστε οὐδεὶς ὑποψίαν ἔχει ὡς ἐξ
25 ἄλλου ἂν βασιλεὺς γένοιτο ἢ ἐξ αὐτοῦ· διὸ οὐ φρου-
ρεῖται ἡ βασιλέως γυνὴ ἀλλ᾽ ἢ ὑπὸ φόβου. ἐπειδὰν δὲ
γένηται ὁ παῖς ὁ πρεσβύτατος, οὗπερ ἡ ἀρχή, πρῶτον
μὲν ἑορτάζουσι πάντες οἱ ἐν τῇ βασιλέως, ὧν ἂν ἄρχῃ,
εἶτα εἰς τὸν ἄλλον χρόνον ταύτῃ τῇ ἡμέρᾳ βασιλέως
30 γενέσια ἅπασα θύει καὶ ἑορτάζει ἡ Ἀσία· ἡμῶν δὲ γενομένων, τὸ τοῦ κωμῳδοποιοῦ, οὐδ᾽ οἱ γείτονες σφόδρα D
αἰσθάνονται, ὦ Ἀλκιβιάδη. μετὰ τοῦτο τρέφεται ὁ παῖς
οὐχ ὑπὸ γυναικὸς τροφοῦ ὀλίγου ἀξίας, ἀλλ᾽ ὑπ᾽ εὐνούχων
οἳ ἂν δοκῶσι τῶν περὶ βασιλέα ἄριστοι εἶναι· οἷς τά τε
35 ἄλλα πρυστέτακται ἐπιμέλεσθαι τοῦ γενομένου, καὶ ὅπως
ὅ τι κάλλιστος ἔσται μηχανᾶσθαι, ἀναπλάττοντας τὰ
μέλη τοῦ παιδὸς καὶ κατορθοῦντας· καὶ ταῦτα δρῶντες
ἐν μεγάλῃ τιμῇ εἰσίν. ἐπειδὰν δὲ ἑπτέτεις γένωνται οἱ E
παῖδες, ἐπὶ τοὺς ἵππους καὶ ἐπὶ τοὺς τούτων διδασκάλους
40 φοιτῶσι, καὶ ἐπὶ τὰς θήρας ἄρχονται ἰέναι. δὶς ἑπτὰ δὲ
γενόμενον ἐτῶν τὸν παῖδα παραλαμβάνουσιν οὓς ἐκεῖνοι
βασιλείους παιδαγωγοὺς ὀνομάζουσιν· εἰσὶ δὲ ἐξειλεγ-
μένοι Περσῶν οἱ ἄριστοι δόξαντες ἐν ἡλικίᾳ τέτταρες, ὅ
τε σοφώτατος καὶ ὁ δικαιότατος καὶ ὁ σωφρονέστατος
45 καὶ ὁ ἀνδρειότατος. ὧν ὁ μὲν μαγείαν τε διδάσκει τὴν 122

Ζωροάστρου τοῦ Ὡρομάζου—ἔστι δὲ τοῦτο θεῶν θεραπεία—, διδάσκει δὲ καὶ τὰ βασιλικά· ὁ δὲ δικαιότατος
ἀληθεύειν διὰ παντὸς τοῦ βίου· ὁ δὲ σωφρονέστατος μηδ'
ὑπὸ μιᾶς ἄρχεσθαι τῶν ἡδονῶν, ἵνα ἐλεύθερος εἶναι ἐθί-
ζηται καὶ ὄντως βασιλεύς, ἄρχων πρῶτον τῶν ἐν αὑτῷ, 50
ἀλλὰ μὴ δουλεύων· ὁ δὲ ἀνδρειότατος ἄφοβον καὶ ἀδεᾶ
παρασκευάζων, ὡς ὅταν δείσῃ δοῦλον ὄντα. σοὶ δ', ὦ
B Ἀλκιβιάδη, Περικλῆς ἐπέστησε παιδαγωγὸν τῶν οἰκετῶν τὸν ἀχρειότατον ὑπὸ γήρως, Ζώπυρον τὸν Θρᾷκα.
διῆλθον δὲ καὶ τὴν ἄλλην ἄν σοι τῶν ἀνταγωνιστῶν 55
τροφήν τε καὶ παιδείαν, εἰ μὴ πολὺ ἔργον ἦν· καὶ ἅμα
ταῦτα ἱκανὰ δηλῶσαι καὶ τἆλλα ὅσα τούτοις ἀκόλουθα.
τῆς δὲ σῆς γενέσεως, ὦ Ἀλκιβιάδη, καὶ τροφῆς καὶ
παιδείας, ἢ ἄλλου ὁτουοῦν Ἀθηναίων, ὡς ἔπος εἰπεῖν,
οὐδενὶ μέλει, εἰ μὴ εἴ τις φίλος σου τυγχάνει ὤν. εἰ δ' 60
C αὖ ἐθέλεις εἰς πλούτους ἀποβλέψαι καὶ τρυφὰς καὶ ἐσθῆ-
τας ἱματίων θ' ἕλξεις καὶ μύρων ἀλοιφὰς καὶ θεραπόντων
πλήθους ἀκολουθίας τήν τε ἄλλην ἁβρότητα τὴν Περσῶν, αἰσχυνθείης ἂν ἐπὶ σεαυτῷ, αἰσθόμενος ὅσον
αὐτῶν ἐλλείπεις. 65

Εἰ δ' αὖ ἐθελήσεις εἰς σωφροσύνην τε καὶ κοσμιότητα
ἀποβλέψαι καὶ εὐχέρειαν καὶ εὐκολίαν καὶ μεγαλοφροσύ-
νην καὶ εὐταξίαν καὶ ἀνδρίαν καὶ καρτερίαν καὶ φιλο-
πονίαν καὶ φιλονικίαν καὶ φιλοτιμίας τὰς Λακεδαιμονίων,
D παῖδα ἂν ἡγήσαιο σαυτὸν πᾶσι τοῖς τοιούτοις. εἰ δ' αὖ 70
τι καὶ πλούτῳ προσέχεις καὶ κατὰ τοῦτο οἴει τι εἶναι,
μηδὲ τοῦτο ἡμῖν ἄρρητον ἔστω, ἐάν πως αἴσθῃ οὗ εἶ.
τοῦτο μὲν γὰρ εἰ ἐθέλεις εἰς τοὺς Λακεδαιμονίων πλούτους ἰδεῖν, γνώσει ὅτι πολὺ τἀνθάδε τῶν ἐκεῖ ἐλλείπει.
γῆν μὲν γὰρ ὅσην ἔχουσι τῆς θ' ἑαυτῶν καὶ Μεσσήνης, 75
οὐδ' ἂν εἷς ἀμφισβητήσειε τῶν τῇδε πλήθει οὐδὲ ἀρετῇ,

οὐδ' αὖ ἀνδραπόδων κτήσει, τῶν τε ἄλλων καὶ τῶν
Εἰλωτικῶν, οὐδὲ μὴν ἵππων γε, οὐδ' ὅσ' ἄλλα βοσκήματα
κατὰ Μεσσήνην νέμεται. ἀλλὰ ταῦτα μὲν πάντα ἐῶ E
80 χαίρειν, χρυσίον δὲ καὶ ἀργύριον οὐκ ἔστιν ἐν πᾶσιν
Ἕλλησιν ὅσον ἐν Λακεδαίμονι ἰδίᾳ· πολλὰς γὰρ ἤδη
γενεὰς εἰσέρχεται μὲν αὐτόσε ἐξ ἁπάντων τῶν Ἑλλήνων,
πολλάκις δὲ καὶ ἐκ τῶν βαρβάρων, ἐξέρχεται δὲ οὐδαμόσε, ἀλλ' ἀτεχνῶς κατὰ τὸν Αἰσώπου μῦθον ὃν ἡ 123
85 ἀλώπηξ πρὸς τὸν λέοντα εἶπε, καὶ τοῦ εἰς Λακεδαίμονα
νομίσματος εἰσιόντος μὲν τὰ ἴχνη τὰ ἐκεῖσε τετραμμένα
δῆλα, ἐξιόντος δὲ οὐδαμῇ ἄν τις ἴδοι, ὥστε εὖ χρὴ
εἰδέναι ὅτι καὶ χρυσῷ καὶ ἀργύρῳ οἱ ἐκεῖ πλουσιώτατοί
εἰσι τῶν Ἑλλήνων, καὶ αὐτῶν ἐκείνων ὁ βασιλεύς· ἔκ τε
90 γὰρ τῶν τοιούτων μέγισται λήψεις καὶ πλεῖσταί εἰσι τοῖς
βασιλεῦσιν. ἔτι δὲ καὶ ὁ βασιλικὸς φόρος οὐκ ὀλίγος
γίγνεται, ὃν τελοῦσιν οἱ Λακεδαιμόνιοι τοῖς βασιλεῦσι.
καὶ τὰ μὲν Λακεδαιμονίων ὡς πρὸς Ἑλληνικοὺς μὲν B
πλούτους μεγάλα, ὡς δὲ πρὸς τοὺς Περσικοὺς καὶ τοῦ
95 ἐκείνων βασιλέως οὐδέν· ἐπεί ποτ' ἐγὼ ἤκουσα ἀνδρὸς
ἀξιοπίστου τῶν ἀναβεβηκότων παρὰ βασιλέα, ὃς ἔφη
παρελθεῖν χώραν πάνυ πολλὴν καὶ ἀγαθήν, ἐγγὺς ἡμερησίαν ὁδόν, ἣν καλεῖν τοὺς ἐπιχωρίους ζώνην τῆς βασιλέως
γυναικός· εἶναι δὲ καὶ ἄλλην ἣν αὖ καλεῖσθαι καλύπτραν,
100 καὶ ἄλλους πολλοὺς τόπους καλοὺς καὶ ἀγαθοὺς εἰς τὸν C
κόσμον ἐξῃρημένους τὸν τῆς γυναικός, καὶ ὀνόματα ἔχειν
ἐκάστους τῶν τόπων ἀπὸ ἐκάστου τῶν κόσμων. ὥστε οἶμαι ἐγώ, εἴ τις εἴποι τῇ βασιλέως μητρί, Ξέρξου δὲ γυ-
ναικί, Ἀμήστριδι, ὅτι Ἐν νῷ ἔχει σοῦ τῷ υἱεῖ ἀντιτάττε-
105 σθαι ὁ Δεινομάχης υἱός, ᾗ ἔστι κόσμος ἴσως ἄξιος μνῶν
πεντήκοντα, εἰ πάνυ πολλοῦ, τῷ δ' υἱεῖ αὐτῆς γῆς πλέθρα Ἐρχίασιν οὐδὲ τριακόσια, θαυμάσαι ἂν ὅτῳ ποτὲ

D πιστεύων ἐν νῷ ἔχει οὗτος ὁ Ἀλκιβιάδης τῷ Ἀρτοξέρξῃ
διαγωνίζεσθαι, καὶ οἶμαι ἂν αὐτὴν εἰπεῖν ὅτι Οὐκ ἔσθ᾽
ὅτῳ ἄλλῳ πιστεύων οὗτος ὁ ἀνὴρ ἐπιχειρεῖ πλὴν ἐπιμε- 110
λείᾳ τε καὶ σοφίᾳ· ταῦτα γὰρ μόνα ἄξια λόγου ἐν Ἕλλησιν. ἐπεὶ εἴ γε πύθοιτο ὅτι ὁ Ἀλκιβιάδης οὗτος νῦν ἐπιχειρεῖ πρῶτον μὲν ἔτη οὐδέπω γεγονὼς σφόδρα εἴκοσιν,
ἔπειτα παντάπασιν ἀπαίδευτος, πρὸς δὲ τούτοις, τοῦ
φίλου αὐτῷ λέγοντος ὅτι χρὴ πρῶτον μαθόντα καὶ ἐπι- 115
E μεληθέντα αὐτοῦ καὶ ἀσκήσαντα οὕτως ἰέναι διαγωνιού-
μενον βασιλεῖ, οὐκ ἐθέλει, ἀλλά φησιν ἐξαρκεῖν καὶ ὡς
ἔχει, οἶμαι ἂν αὐτὴν θαυμάσαι τε καὶ ἐρέσθαι Τί οὖν
ποτ᾽ ἔστιν ὅτῳ πιστεύει τὸ μειράκιον; εἰ οὖν λέγοιμεν
ὅτι κάλλει τε καὶ μεγέθει καὶ γένει καὶ πλούτῳ καὶ 120
φύσει τῆς ψυχῆς, ἡγήσαιτ᾽ ἂν ἡμᾶς, ὦ Ἀλκιβιάδη, μαί-
νεσθαι πρὸς τὰ παρὰ σφίσιν ἀποβλέψασα πάντα τὰ
τοιαῦτα. οἶμαι δὲ κἂν Λαμπιδώ, τὴν Λεωτυχίδου μὲν
124 θυγατέρα, Ἀρχιδάμου δὲ γυναῖκα, Ἄγιδος δὲ μητέρα, οἳ
πάντες βασιλεῖς γεγόνασι, θαυμάσαι ἂν καὶ ταύτην εἰς 125
τὰ παρὰ σφίσιν ὑπάρχοντα ἀποβλέψασαν, εἰ σὺ ἐν νῷ
ἔχεις τῷ υἱεῖ αὐτῆς διαγωνίζεσθαι οὕτω κακῶς ἠγμένος.
καίτοι οὐκ αἰσχρὸν δοκεῖ εἶναι, εἰ αἱ τῶν πολεμίων
γυναῖκες βέλτιον περὶ ἡμῶν διανοοῦνται, οἵους χρὴ ὄντας
σφίσιν ἐπιχειρεῖν, ἢ ἡμεῖς περὶ ἡμῶν αὐτῶν; ἀλλ᾽, ὦ 130
μακάριε, πειθόμενος ἐμοί τε καὶ τῷ ἐν Δελφοῖς γράμματι,
B Γνῶθι σαυτόν, ὅτι οὗτοι ἡμῖν εἰσὶν ἀντίπαλοι, ἀλλ᾽
οὐχ οὓς σὺ οἴει· ὧν ἄλλῳ μὲν οὐδ᾽ ἂν ἑνὶ περιγενοίμεθα,
εἰ μὴ ἐπιμελείᾳ τε ἂν καὶ τέχνῃ. ὧν σὺ εἰ ἀπολειφθήσει,
καὶ τοῦ ὀνομαστὸς γενέσθαι ἀπολειφθήσει ἐν Ἕλλησί 135
τε καὶ βαρβάροις, οὗ μοι δοκεῖς ἐρᾶν ὡς οὐδεὶς ἄλλος
ἄλλου.

REPUBLIC.

Book I.

A Calm Old Age.

(Socrates and others. Cephalus.)

[Beginning—331 D.]

Κατέβην χθὲς εἰς Πειραιᾶ μετὰ Γλαύκωνος τοῦ Ἀρί- 327
στωνος προσευξόμενός τε τῇ θεῷ καὶ ἅμα τὴν ἑορτὴν
βουλόμενος θεάσασθαι τίνα τρόπον ποιήσουσιν ἅτε νῦν
πρῶτον ἄγοντες. καλὴ μὲν οὖν μοι καὶ ἡ τῶν ἐπιχωρίων
5 πομπὴ ἔδοξεν εἶναι, οὐ μέντοι ἧττον ἐφαίνετο πρέπειν
ἣν οἱ Θρᾷκες ἔπεμπον. προσευξάμενοι δὲ καὶ θεωρήσαντες
ἀπῇμεν πρὸς τὸ ἄστυ. κατιδὼν οὖν πόρρωθεν ἡμᾶς οἴ-B
καδε ὡρμημένους Πολέμαρχος ὁ Κεφάλου ἐκέλευσε δρα-
μόντα τὸν παῖδα περιμεῖναί ἑ κελεῦσαι. καί μου ὄπι-
10 σθεν ὁ παῖς λαβόμενος τοῦ ἱματίου, Κελεύει ὑμᾶς, ἔφη, ·
Πολέμαρχος περιμεῖναι. Καὶ ἐγὼ μετεστράφην τε καὶ
ἠρόμην ὅπου αὐτὸς εἴη. Οὗτος, ἔφη, ὄπισθεν προσέρχε-
ται· ἀλλὰ περιμένετε. Ἀλλὰ περιμενοῦμεν, ἦ δ' ὃς ὁ
Γλαύκων. Καὶ ὀλίγῳ ὕστερον ὅ τε Πολέμαρχος ἧκε καὶ C
15 Ἀδείμαντος ὁ τοῦ Γλαύκωνος ἀδελφὸς καὶ Νικήρατος
ὁ Νικίου καὶ ἄλλοι τινές, ὡς ἀπὸ τῆς πομπῆς. ὁ οὖν
Πολέμαρχος ἔφη Ὦ Σώκρατες, δοκεῖτέ μοι πρὸς ἄστυ
ὡρμῆσθαι ὡς ἀπιόντες. Οὐ γὰρ κακῶς δοξάζεις, ἦν δ'
ἐγώ. Ὁρᾷς οὖν ἡμᾶς, ἔφη, ὅσοι ἐσμέν; Πῶς γὰρ οὔ;
20 Ἢ τοίνυν τούτων, ἔφη, κρείττους γένεσθε ἢ μένετ' αὐτοῦ. Οὐκοῦν, ἦν δ' ἐγώ, ἔτι ἓν λείπεται, τὸ ἢν πείσω-
μεν ὑμᾶς ὡς χρὴ ἡμᾶς ἀφεῖναι. Ἢ καὶ δύναισθ' ἄν,
ἦ δ' ὅς, πεῖσαι μὴ ἀκούοντας; Οὐδαμῶς, ἔφη ὁ Γλαύκων. Ὡς τοίνυν μὴ ἀκουσομένων, οὕτω διανοεῖσθε.

K 2

328 Καὶ ὁ Ἀδείμαντος, Ἀρά γε, ἦ δ' ὅς, οὐδ' ἴστε ὅτι λαμ- 25
πὰς ἔσται πρὸς ἑσπέραν ἀφ' ἵππων τῇ θεῷ; Ἀφ' ἵππων;
ἦν δ' ἐγώ· καινόν γε τοῦτο. λαμπάδια ἔχοντες διαδώσου-
σιν ἀλλήλοις ἁμιλλώμενοι τοῖς ἵπποις; ἢ πῶς λέγεις;
Οὕτως, ἔφη ὁ Πολέμαρχος· καὶ πρός γε παννυχίδα ποιήσουσιν, ἣν ἄξιον θεάσασθαι· ἐξαναστησόμεθα γὰρ μετὰ 30
τὸ δεῖπνον καὶ τὴν παννυχίδα θεασόμεθα, καὶ ξυνεσόμεθά
τε πολλοῖς τῶν νέων αὐτόθι καὶ διαλεξόμεθα· ἀλλὰ μέ-
B νετε καὶ μὴ ἄλλως ποιεῖτε.　Καὶ ὁ Γλαύκων, Ἔοικεν,
ἔφη, μενετέον εἶναι.　Ἀλλ' εἰ δοκεῖ, ἦν δ' ἐγώ, οὕτω
χρὴ ποιεῖν.　35

Ἦιμεν οὖν οἴκαδε εἰς τοῦ Πολεμάρχου, καὶ Λυσίαν
τε αὐτόθι κατελάβομεν καὶ Εὐθύδημον, τοὺς τοῦ Πολεμάρχου ἀδελφούς, καὶ δὴ καὶ Θρασύμαχον τὸν Χαλκηδό-
νιον καὶ Χαρμαντίδην τὸν Παιανιέα καὶ Κλειτοφῶντα τὸν
Ἀριστωνύμου· ἦν δ' ἔνδον καὶ ὁ πατὴρ ὁ τοῦ Πολεμάρ- 40
χου Κέφαλος· καὶ μάλα πρεσβύτης μοι ἔδοξεν εἶναι· διὰ
C χρόνου γὰρ καὶ ἑωράκη αὐτόν· καθῆστο δὲ ἐστεφανω-
μένος ἐπί τινος προσκεφαλαίου τε καὶ δίφρου· τεθυκὼς
γὰρ ἐτύγχανεν ἐν τῇ αὐλῇ· ἐκαθεζόμεθα οὖν παρ' αὐτόν.
ἔκειντο γὰρ δίφροι τινὲς αὐτόθι κύκλῳ. εὐθὺς οὖν με 45
ἰδὼν ὁ Κέφαλος ἠσπάζετό τε καὶ εἶπεν Ὦ Σώκρατες,
οὐ δὲ θαμίζεις ἡμῖν καταβαίνων εἰς τὸν Πειραιᾶ· χρῆν
μέντοι. εἰ μὲν γὰρ ἐγὼ ἔτι ἐν δυνάμει ἦ τοῦ ῥᾳδίως
πορεύεσθαι πρὸς τὸ ἄστυ, οὐδὲν ἄν σε ἔδει δεῦρο ἰέναι,
D ἀλλ' ἡμεῖς ἂν παρὰ σὲ ἦμεν· νῦν δέ σε χρὴ πυκνότερον 50
δεῦρο ἰέναι· ὡς εὖ ἴσθι ὅτι ἔμοιγε ὅσον αἱ ἄλλαι αἱ κατὰ
τὸ σῶμα ἡδοναὶ ἀπομαραίνονται, τοσοῦτον αὔξονται αἱ
περὶ τοὺς λόγους ἐπιθυμίαι τε καὶ ἡδοναί. μὴ οὖν ἄλλως
ποίει, ἀλλὰ τοῖσδέ τε τοῖς νεανίαις ξύνισθι καὶ δεῦρο
παρ' ἡμᾶς φοίτα ὡς παρὰ φίλους τε καὶ πάνυ οἰκείους. 55

Καὶ μήν, ἦν δ' ἐγώ, ὦ Κέφαλε, χαίρω [γε] διαλεγόμενος
τοῖς σφόδρα πρεσβύταις. δοκεῖ γάρ μοι χρῆναι παρ' Ε
αὐτῶν πυνθάνεσθαι, ὥσπερ τινὰ ὁδὸν προεληλυθότων, ἣν
καὶ ἡμᾶς ἴσως δεήσει πορεύεσθαι, ποία τίς ἐστι, τραχεῖα
60 καὶ χαλεπή, ἢ ῥᾳδία καὶ εὔπορος. καὶ δὴ καὶ σοῦ ἡδέως
ἂν πυθοίμην ὅ τί σοι φαίνεται τοῦτο, ἐπειδὴ ἐνταῦθα
ἤδη εἶ τῆς ἡλικίας, ὃ δὴ ἐπὶ γήραος οὐδῷ φασὶν εἶναι
οἱ ποιηταί, πότερον χαλεπὸν τοῦ βίου, ἢ πῶς σὺ αὐτὸ
ἐξαγγέλλεις.

65 Ἐγώ σοι, ἔφη, νὴ τὸν Δία ἐρῶ, ὦ Σώκρατες, οἷόν γέ 329
μοι φαίνεται. πολλάκις γὰρ συνερχόμεθά τινες εἰς ταὐτὸ
παραπλησίαν ἡλικίαν ἔχοντες, διασώζοντες τὴν παλαιὰν
παροιμίαν. οἱ οὖν πλεῖστοι ἡμῶν ὀλοφύρονται ξυνιόντες,
τὰς ἐν τῇ νεότητι ἡδονὰς ποθοῦντες καὶ ἀναμιμνησκό-
70 μενοι περί τε τἀφροδίσια καὶ περὶ πότους καὶ εὐωχίας
καὶ ἄλλ' ἄττα ἃ τῶν τοιούτων ἔχεται, καὶ ἀγανακτοῦσιν
ὡς μεγάλων τινῶν ἀπεστερημένοι καὶ τότε μὲν εὖ ζῶντες,
νῦν δὲ οὐδὲ ζῶντες. ἔνιοι δὲ καὶ τὰς τῶν οἰκείων προπη- Β
λακίσεις τοῦ γήρως ὀδύρονται, καὶ ἐπὶ τούτῳ δὴ τὸ γῆρας
75 ὑμνοῦσιν ὅσων κακῶν σφίσιν αἴτιον. ἐμοὶ δὲ δοκοῦσιν,
ὦ Σώκρατες, οὗτοι οὐ τὸ αἴτιον αἰτιᾶσθαι. εἰ γὰρ ἦν
τοῦτ' αἴτιον, κἂν ἐγὼ τὰ αὐτὰ ταῦτα ἐπεπόνθη ἕνεκά γε
γήρως καὶ οἱ ἄλλοι πάντες ὅσοι ἐνταῦθα ἦλθον ἡλικίας·
νῦν δ' ἔγωγε ἤδη ἐντετύχηκα οὐχ οὕτως ἔχουσι καὶ ἄλλοις,
80 καὶ δὴ καὶ Σοφοκλεῖ ποτὲ τῷ ποιητῇ παρεγενόμην ἐρωτω-
μένῳ ὑπό τινος Πῶς, ἔφη, ὦ Σοφόκλεις, ἔχεις πρὸς C
τἀφροδίσια; Καὶ ὅς, Εὐφήμει, ἔφη, ὦ ἄνθρωπε· ἀσμενέστατα μέντοι αὐτὸ ἀπέφυγον, ὥσπερ λυττῶντά τινα καὶ
ἄγριον δεσπότην ἀποφυγών. Εὖ οὖν μοι καὶ τότε ἔδοξεν
85 ἐκεῖνος εἰπεῖν, καὶ νῦν οὐχ ἧττον. παντάπασι γὰρ τῶν
γε τοιούτων ἐν τῷ γήρᾳ πολλὴ εἰρήνη γίγνεται καὶ

ἐλευθερία, ἐπειδὰν αἱ ἐπιθυμίαι παύσωνται κατατείνουσαι
καὶ χαλάσωσι, παντάπασι τὸ τοῦ Σοφοκλέους γίγνεται,
D δεσποτῶν πάνυ πολλῶν [ἔστι] καὶ μαινομένων ἀπηλλάχθαι. ἀλλὰ καὶ τούτων πέρι καὶ τῶν γε πρὸς τοὺς 90
οἰκείους μία τις αἰτία ἐστίν, οὐ τὸ γῆρας, ὦ Σώκρατες,
ἀλλ᾽ ὁ τρόπος τῶν ἀνθρώπων. ἂν μὲν γὰρ κόσμιοι καὶ
εὔκολοι ὦσι, καὶ τὸ γῆρας μετρίως ἐστὶν ἐπίπονον· εἰ δὲ
μή, καὶ γῆρας, ὦ Σώκρατες, καὶ νεότης χαλεπὴ τῷ
τοιούτῳ ξυμβαίνει.   95

Καὶ ἐγὼ ἀγασθεὶς αὐτοῦ εἰπόντος ταῦτα βουλόμενος
E ἔτι λέγειν αὐτὸν ἐκίνουν καὶ εἶπον Ὦ Κέφαλε, οἶμαί σου
τοὺς πολλούς, ὅταν ταῦτα λέγῃς, οὐκ ἀποδέχεσθαι, ἀλλ᾽
ἡγεῖσθαί σε ῥᾳδίως τὸ γῆρας φέρειν οὐ διὰ τὸν τρόπον
ἀλλὰ διὰ τὸ πολλὴν οὐσίαν κεκτῆσθαι· τοῖς γὰρ πλου- 100
σίοις πολλὰ παραμύθιά φασιν εἶναι. Ἀληθῆ, ἔφη, λέγεις·
οὐ γὰρ ἀποδέχονται. καὶ λέγουσι μέν τι, οὐ μέντοι γε
ὅσον οἴονται, ἀλλὰ τὸ τοῦ Θεμιστοκλέους εὖ ἔχει, ὃς τῷ
330 Σεριφίῳ λοιδορουμένῳ καὶ λέγοντι, ὅτι οὐ δι᾽ αὑτὸν ἀλλὰ
διὰ τὴν πόλιν εὐδοκιμοῖ, ἀπεκρίνατο ὅτι οὔτ᾽ ἂν αὐτὸς 105
Σερίφιος ὢν ὀνομαστὸς ἐγένετο οὔτ᾽ ἐκεῖνος Ἀθηναῖος.
καὶ τοῖς δὴ μὴ πλουσίοις, χαλεπῶς δὲ τὸ γῆρας φέρουσιν
εὖ ἔχει ὁ αὐτὸς λόγος, ὅτι οὔτ᾽ ἂν ὁ ἐπιεικὴς πάνυ τι
ῥᾳδίως γῆρας μετὰ πενίας ἐνέγκοι οὔθ᾽ ὁ μὴ ἐπιεικὴς
πλουτήσας εὔκολός ποτ᾽ ἂν ἑαυτῷ γένοιτο. Πότερον δέ, 110
ἦν δ᾽ ἐγώ, ὦ Κέφαλε, ὧν κέκτησαι τὰ πλέω παρέλαβες
B ἢ ἐπεκτήσω; Ποῖ᾽ ἐπεκτησάμην, ἔφη, ὦ Σώκρατες; μέσος
τις γέγονα χρηματιστὴς τοῦ τε πάππου καὶ τοῦ πατρός.
ὁ μὲν γὰρ πάππος τε καὶ ὁμώνυμος ἐμοὶ σχεδόν τι ὅσην
ἐγὼ νῦν οὐσίαν κέκτημαι παραλαβὼν πολλάκις τοσαύτην 115
ἐποίησε, Λυσανίας δὲ ὁ πατὴρ ἔτι ἐλάττω αὐτὴν ἐποίησε
τῆς νῦν οὔσης· ἐγὼ δὲ ἀγαπῶ, ἐὰν μὴ ἐλάττω καταλίπω

τούτοισιν, ἀλλὰ βραχεῖ γέ τινι πλείω ἢ παρέλαβον. Οὔ
τοι ἔνεκα ἠρόμην, ἦν δ' ἐγώ, ὅτι μοι ἔδοξας οὐ σφόδρα
120 ἀγαπᾶν τὰ χρήματα. τοῦτο δὲ ποιοῦσιν ὡς τὸ πολὺ οἳ C
ἂν μὴ αὐτοὶ κτήσωνται· οἱ δὲ κτησάμενοι διπλῇ ἢ οἱ ἄλλοι ἀσπάζονται αὐτά. ὥσπερ γὰρ οἱ ποιηταὶ τὰ αὐτῶν
ποιήματα καὶ οἱ πατέρες τοὺς παῖδας ἀγαπῶσι, ταύτῃ
τε δὴ καὶ οἱ χρηματισάμενοι περὶ τὰ χρήματα σπουδά-
125 ζουσιν ὡς ἔργον ἑαυτῶν, καὶ κατὰ τὴν χρείαν, ᾗπερ οἱ
ἄλλοι. χαλεποὶ οὖν καὶ ξυγγενέσθαι εἰσίν, οὐδὲν ἐθέ-
λοντες ἐπαινεῖν ἀλλ' ἢ τὸν πλοῦτον. Ἀληθῆ, ἔφη,
λέγεις.

Πάνυ μὲν οὖν, ἦν δ' ἐγώ. ἀλλά μοι ἔτι τοσόνδε εἰπέ· D
130 τί μέγιστον οἴει ἀγαθὸν ἀπολελαυκέναι τοῦ πολλὴν
οὐσίαν κεκτῆσθαι; Ὅ, ἦ δ' ὅς, ἴσως οὐκ ἂν πολλοὺς
πείσαιμι λέγων. εὖ γὰρ ἴσθι, ἔφη, ὦ Σώκρατες, ὅτι,
ἐπειδάν τις ἐγγὺς ᾖ τοῦ οἴεσθαι τελευτήσειν, εἰσέρχεται
αὐτῷ δέος καὶ φροντὶς περὶ ὧν ἔμπροσθεν οὐκ εἰσῄει. οἵ
135 τε γὰρ λεγόμενοι μῦθοι περὶ τῶν ἐν Ἅιδου, ὡς τὸν
ἐνθάδε ἀδικήσαντα δεῖ ἐκεῖ διδόναι δίκην, καταγελώμενοι
τέως, τότε δὴ στρέφουσιν αὐτοῦ τὴν ψυχὴν μὴ ἀληθεῖς E
ὦσι· καὶ αὐτὸς ἤτοι ὑπὸ τῆς τοῦ γήρως ἀσθενείας ἢ καὶ
ὥσπερ ἤδη ἐγγυτέρω ὢν τῶν ἐκεῖ μᾶλλόν τι καθορᾷ αὐτά·
140 ὑποψίας δ' οὖν καὶ δείματος μεστὸς γίγνεται καὶ ἀνα-
λογίζεται ἤδη καὶ σκοπεῖ, εἴ τινά τι ἠδίκηκεν. ὁ μὲν οὖν
εὑρίσκων ἑαυτοῦ ἐν τῷ βίῳ πολλὰ ἀδικήματα καὶ ἐκ τῶν
ὕπνων, ὥσπερ οἱ παῖδες, θαμὰ ἐγειρόμενος δειμαίνει καὶ
ζῇ μετὰ κακῆς ἐλπίδος· τῷ δὲ μηδὲν ἑαυτῷ ἄδικον ξυν- 331
145 ειδότι ἡδεῖα ἐλπὶς ἀεὶ πάρεστι καὶ ἀγαθὴ γηροτρόφος,
ὡς καὶ Πίνδαρος λέγει. χαριέντως γάρ τοι, ὦ Σώκρατες, τοῦτ' ἐκεῖνος εἶπεν, ὅτι ὃς ἂν δικαίως καὶ ὁσίως
τὸν βίον διαγάγῃ, γλυκεῖά οἱ καρδίαν ἀτάλλοισα

γηροτρόφος συναορεῖ ἐλπίς, ἃ μάλιστα θνατῶν
πολύστροφον γνώμαν κυβερνᾷ. εὖ οὖν λέγει θαυ- 150
μαστῶς ὡς σφόδρα.Χ πρὸς δὴ τοῦτ᾽ ἔγωγε τίθημι τὴν τῶν
B χρημάτων κτῆσιν πλείστου ἀξίαν εἶναι, οὔ τι παντὶ ἀνδρὶ
ἀλλὰ τῷ ἐπιεικεῖ. τὸ γὰρ μηδὲ ἄκοντά τινα ἐξαπατῆσαι
ἢ ψεύσασθαι, μηδ᾽ αὖ ὀφείλοντα ἢ θεῷ θυσίας τινὰς ἢ
ἀνθρώπῳ χρήματα ἔπειτα ἐκεῖσε ἀπιέναι δεδιότα, μέγα 155
μέρος εἰς τοῦτο ἡ τῶν χρημάτων κτῆσις συμβάλλεται·
ἔχει δὲ καὶ ἄλλας χρείας πολλάς· ἀλλά γε ἓν ἀνθ᾽ ἑνὸς
οὐκ ἐλάχιστον ἔγωγε θείην ἂν εἰς τοῦτο ἀνδρὶ νοῦν
ἔχοντι, ὦ Σώκρατες, πλοῦτον χρησιμώτατον εἶναι. Χ
C Παγκάλως, ἦν δ᾽ ἐγώ, λέγεις, ὦ Κέφαλε. τοῦτο δ᾽ 160
αὐτό, τὴν δικαιοσύνην, πότερα τὴν ἀλήθειαν αὐτὸ φήσομεν εἶναι ἁπλῶς οὕτως καὶ τὸ ἀποδιδόναι, ἄν τίς τι
παρά του λάβῃ, ἢ καὶ αὐτὰ ταῦτα ἔστιν ἐνίοτε μὲν δικαίως, ἐνίοτε δὲ ἀδίκως ποιεῖν ; οἷον τοιόνδε λέγω· πᾶς
ἄν που εἴποι, εἴ τις λάβοι παρὰ φίλου ἀνδρὸς σωφρονοῦν- 165
τος ὅπλα, εἰ μανεὶς ἀπαιτοῖ, ὅτι οὔτε χρὴ τὰ τοιαῦτα
ἀποδιδόναι, οὔτε δίκαιος ἂν εἴη ὁ ἀποδιδούς, οὐδ᾽ αὖ
πρὸς τὸν οὕτως ἔχοντα πάντα ἐθέλων τἀληθῆ λέγειν.
D Ὀρθῶς, ἔφη, λέγεις. Οὐκ ἄρα οὗτος ὅρος ἐστὶ δικαιοσύνης, ἀληθῆ τε λέγειν καὶ ἃ ἂν λάβῃ τις ἀποδιδόναι.   170
Πάνυ μὲν οὖν, ἔφη, ὦ Σώκρατες, ὑπολαβὼν ὁ Πολέμαρχος, εἴπερ γέ τι χρὴ Σιμωνίδῃ πείθεσθαι. Καὶ
μέντοι, ἔφη ὁ Κέφαλος, καὶ παραδίδωμι ὑμῖν τὸν λόγον.
δεῖ γάρ με ἤδη τῶν ἱερῶν ἐπιμεληθῆναι. Οὐκοῦν, ἔφην
ἐγώ, ὁ Πολέμαρχος τῶν γε σῶν κληρονόμος ; Πάνυ γε, 175
ἦ δ᾽ ὃς γελάσας, καὶ ἅμα ᾔει πρὸς τὰ ἱερά.

Book II.

The Tales of the Poets about the Gods not to be endured in the new State.

(Socrates. Adeimantus.)

[376 E—End.]

Τίς οὖν ἡ παιδεία ; ἢ χαλεπὸν εὑρεῖν βελτίω τῆς ὑπὸ τοῦ πολλοῦ χρόνου εὑρημένης ; ἔστι δέ που ἡ μὲν ἐπὶ σώμασι γυμναστική, ἡ δ' ἐπὶ ψυχῇ μουσική. Ἔστι γάρ. Ἀρ' οὖν οὐ μουσικῇ πρότερον ἀρξόμεθα παιδεύοντες ἢ
5 γυμναστικῇ ; Πῶς δ' οὔ ; Μουσικῆς δ', εἶπον, τίθης λόγους, ἢ οὔ ; Ἔγωγε. Λόγων δὲ διττὸν εἶδος, τὸ μὲν ἀληθές, ψεῦδος δ' ἕτερον ; Ναί. Παιδευτέον δ' ἐν ἀμφο-377 τέροις, πρότερον δ' ἐν τοῖς ψευδέσιν ; Οὐ μανθάνω, ἔφη, πῶς λέγεις. Οὐ μανθάνεις, ἦν δ' ἐγώ, ὅτι πρῶτον τοῖς
10 παιδίοις μύθους λέγομεν ; τοῦτο δέ που, ὡς τὸ ὅλον εἰπεῖν ψεῦδος, ἔνι δὲ καὶ ἀληθῆ. πρότερον δὲ μύθοις πρὸς τὰ παιδία ἢ γυμνασίοις χρώμεθα. Ἔστι ταῦτα. Τοῦτο δὴ ἔλεγον, ὅτι μουσικῆς πρότερον ἁπτέον ἢ γυμναστικῆς. Ὀρθῶς, ἔφη. Οὐκοῦν οἶσθ' ὅτι ἀρχὴ παντὸς
15 ἔργου μέγιστον, ἄλλως τε καὶ νέῳ καὶ ἀπαλῷ ὁτῳοῦν ; B μάλιστα γὰρ δὴ τότε πλάττεται καὶ ἐνδύεται τύπος, ὃν ἄν τις βούληται ἐνσημήνασθαι ἑκάστῳ. Κομιδῇ μὲν οὖν. Ἀρ' οὖν ῥᾳδίως οὕτω παρήσομεν τοὺς ἐπιτυχόντας ὑπὸ τῶν ἐπιτυχόντων μύθους πλασθέντας ἀκούειν τοὺς
20 παῖδας καὶ λαμβάνειν ἐν ταῖς ψυχαῖς ὡς ἐπὶ τὸ πολὺ ἐναντίας δόξας ἐκείναις, ἅς, ἐπειδὰν τελεωθῶσιν, ἔχειν οἰησόμεθα δεῖν αὐτούς ; Οὐδ' ὁπωστιοῦν παρήσομεν. Πρῶτον δὴ ἡμῖν, ὡς ἔοικεν, ἐπιστατητέον τοῖς μυθοποιοῖς, καὶ ὃν μὲν ἂν καλὸν ποιήσωσιν, ἐγκριτέον, ὃν δ' C
25 ἂν μή, ἀποκριτέον. τοὺς δ' ἐγκριθέντας πείσομεν τὰς

τροφούς τε καὶ μητέρας λέγειν τοῖς παισί, καὶ πλάττειν
τὰς ψυχὰς αὐτῶν τοῖς μύθοις πολὺ μᾶλλον ἢ τὰ σώματα
ταῖς χερσίν· ὧν δὲ νῦν λέγουσι τοὺς πολλοὺς ἐκβλητέον.
Ποίους δή; ἔφη. Ἐν τοῖς μείζοσιν, ἦν δ' ἐγώ, μύθοις
D ὀψόμεθα καὶ τοὺς ἐλάττους. δεῖ γὰρ δὴ τὸν αὐτὸν τύπον 30
εἶναι καὶ ταὐτὸν δύνασθαι τούς τε μείζους καὶ τοὺς
ἐλάττους. ἢ οὐκ οἴει; Ἔγωγ', ἔφη· ἀλλ' οὐκ ἐννοῶ
οὐδὲ τοὺς μείζους τίνας λέγεις. Οὓς Ἡσίοδός τε, εἶπον,
καὶ Ὅμηρος ἡμῖν ἐλεγέτην καὶ οἱ ἄλλοι ποιηταί. οὗτοι
γάρ που μύθους τοῖς ἀνθρώποις ψευδεῖς συντιθέντες 35
ἔλεγόν τε καὶ λέγουσιν. Ποίους δή, ἦ δ' ὅς, καὶ τί
αὐτῶν μεμφόμενος λέγεις; Ὅπερ, ἦν δ' ἐγώ, χρὴ καὶ
πρῶτον καὶ μάλιστα μέμφεσθαι, ἄλλως τε καὶ ἐάν τις μὴ
E καλῶς ψεύδηται. Τί τοῦτο; Ὅταν εἰκάζῃ τις κακῶς τῷ
λόγῳ περὶ θεῶν τε καὶ ἡρώων οἷοί εἰσιν, ὥσπερ γραφεὺς 40
μηδὲν ἐοικότα γράφων οἷς ἂν ὅμοια βουληθῇ γράψαι.
Καὶ γάρ, ἔφη, ὀρθῶς ἔχει τά γε τοιαῦτα μέμφεσθαι.
ἀλλὰ πῶς δὴ λέγομεν καὶ ποῖα; Πρῶτον μέν, ἦν δ' ἐγώ,
τὸ μέγιστον καὶ περὶ τῶν μεγίστων ψεῦδος ὁ εἰπὼν οὐ
καλῶς ἐψεύσατο, ὡς Οὐρανός τε εἰργάσατο ἅ φησι 45
δρᾶσαι αὐτὸν Ἡσίοδος, ὅ τε αὖ Κρόνος ὡς ἐτιμωρήσατο
378 αὐτόν. τὰ δὲ δὴ τοῦ Κρόνου ἔργα καὶ πάθη ὑπὸ τοῦ
υἱέος, οὐδ' ἂν εἰ ἦν ἀληθῆ, ᾤμην δεῖν ῥᾳδίως οὕτω
λέγεσθαι πρὸς ἄφρονάς τε καὶ νέους, ἀλλὰ μάλιστα μὲν
σιγᾶσθαι, εἰ δὲ ἀνάγκη τις ἦν λέγειν, δι' ἀπορρήτων 50
ἀκούειν ὡς ὀλιγίστους, θυσαμένους οὐ χοῖρον ἀλλά τι
μέγα καὶ ἄπορον θῦμα, ὅπως ὅ τι ἐλαχίστοις συνέβη
ἀκοῦσαι. Καὶ γάρ, ἦ δ' ὅς, οὗτοί γε οἱ λόγοι χαλεποί.

κολάζων παντὶ τρόπῳ, ἀλλὰ δρῴη ἂν ὅπερ θεῶν οἱ
πρῶτοί τε καὶ μέγιστοι. Οὐ μὰ τὸν Δία, ἦ δ' ὅς, οὐδὲ
αὐτῷ μοι δοκεῖ ἐπιτήδεια εἶναι λέγειν. Οὐδέ γε, ἦν δ'
60 ἐγώ, τὸ παράπαν ὡς θεοὶ θεοῖς πολεμοῦσί τε καὶ ἐπι-
βουλεύουσι καὶ μάχονται—οὐδὲ γὰρ ἀληθῆ—, εἴ γε δεῖ C
ἡμῖν τοὺς μέλλοντας τὴν πόλιν φυλάξειν αἴσχιστον
νομίζειν τὸ ῥᾳδίως ἀλλήλοις ἀπεχθάνεσθαι· πολλοῦ δεῖ
γιγαντομαχίας τε μυθολογητέον αὐτοῖς καὶ ποικιλτέον,
65 καὶ ἄλλας ἔχθρας πολλὰς καὶ παντοδαπὰς θεῶν τε καὶ
ἡρώων πρὸς συγγενεῖς τε καὶ οἰκείους αὐτῶν· ἀλλ' εἴ πως
μέλλομεν πείσειν, ὡς οὐδεὶς πώποτε πολίτης ἕτερος ἑτέρῳ
ἀπήχθετο οὐδ' ἔστι τοῦτο ὅσιον, τοιαῦτα [λεκτέα] μᾶλλον
πρὸς τὰ παιδία εὐθὺς καὶ γέρουσι καὶ γραυσὶ καὶ D
70 πρεσβυτέροις γιγνομένοις, καὶ τοὺς ποιητὰς ἐγγὺς τούτων
ἀναγκαστέον λογοποιεῖν. Ἥρας δὲ δεσμοὺς ὑπὸ υἱέος
καὶ Ἡφαίστου ῥίψεις ὑπὸ πατρός, μέλλοντος τῇ μητρὶ
τυπτομένῃ ἀμύνειν, καὶ θεομαχίας ὅσας Ὅμηρος πεποίηκεν οὐ παραδεκτέον εἰς τὴν πόλιν, οὔτ' ἐν ὑπονοίαις
75 πεποιημένας οὔτε ἄνευ ὑπονοιῶν. ὁ γὰρ νέος οὐχ οἷός τε
κρίνειν ὅ τί τε ὑπόνοια καὶ ὃ μή, ἀλλ' ἃ ἂν τηλικοῦτος
ὢν λάβῃ ἐν ταῖς δόξαις δυσέκνιπτά τε καὶ ἀμετάστατα E
φιλεῖ γίγνεσθαι. ὧν δὴ ἴσως ἕνεκα περὶ παντὸς ποιητέον ἃ πρῶτα ἀκούουσιν ὅ τι κάλλιστα μεμυθολογημένα
80 πρὸς ἀρετὴν ἀκούειν. Ἔχει γάρ, ἔφη, λόγον. ἀλλ' εἴ
τις αὖ καὶ ταῦτα ἐρωτῴη ἡμᾶς, ταῦτα ἄττα ἐστὶ καὶ τίνες
οἱ μῦθοι, τίνας ἂν φαῖμεν; Καὶ ἐγὼ εἶπον Ὦ Ἀδείμαντε,
οὐκ ἐσμὲν ποιηταὶ ἐγώ τε καὶ σὺ ἐν τῷ παρόντι, ἀλλ' 379
οἰκισταὶ πόλεως. οἰκισταῖς δὲ τοὺς μὲν τύπους προσήκει
85 εἰδέναι ἐν οἷς δεῖ μυθολογεῖν τοὺς ποιητάς, παρ' οὓς ἐὰν
ποιῶσιν οὐκ ἐπιτρεπτέον, οὐ μὴν αὐτοῖς γε ποιητέον μύθους. Ὀρθῶς, ἔφη· ἀλλ' αὐτὸ δὴ τοῦτο, οἱ τύποι περὶ

θεολογίας τίνες ἂν εἶεν ; Τοιοίδε πού τινες, ἦν δ' ἐγώ·
οἷος τυγχάνει ὁ θεὸς ὤν, ἀεὶ δήπου ἀποδοτέον, ἐάν τέ
τις αὐτὸν ἐν ἔπεσι ποιῇ [ἐάν τε ἐν μέλεσιν] ἐάν τε ἐν 90
τραγῳδίᾳ. Δεῖ γάρ. Οὐκοῦν ἀγαθὸς ὅ γε θεὸς τῷ ὄντι
B τε καὶ λεκτέον οὕτως ; Τί μήν ; Ἀλλὰ μὴν οὐδέν γε τῶν
ἀγαθῶν βλαβερόν· ἦ γάρ ; Οὔ μοι δοκεῖ. Ἆρ' οὖν ὃ μὴ
βλαβερὸν βλάπτει ; Οὐδαμῶς. Ὁ δὲ μὴ βλάπτει κακόν
τι ποιεῖ ; Οὐδὲ τοῦτο. Ὁ δέ γε μηδὲν κακὸν ποιεῖ οὐδ' 95
ἂν τινος εἴη κακοῦ αἴτιον ; Πῶς γάρ ; Τί δέ ; ὠφέλιμον
τὸ ἀγαθόν ; Ναί. Αἴτιον ἄρα εὐπραγίας ; Ναί. Οὐκ
ἄρα πάντων γε αἴτιον τὸ ἀγαθόν, ἀλλὰ τῶν μὲν εὖ
C ἐχόντων αἴτιον, τῶν δὲ κακῶν ἀναίτιον. Παντελῶς γ',
ἔφη. Οὐδ' ἄρα, ἦν δ' ἐγώ, ὁ θεός, ἐπειδὴ ἀγαθός, πάν- 100
των ἂν εἴη αἴτιος, ὡς οἱ πολλοὶ λέγουσιν, ἀλλὰ ὀλίγων
μὲν τοῖς ἀνθρώποις αἴτιος, πολλῶν δὲ ἀναίτιος· πολὺ
γὰρ ἐλάττω τἀγαθὰ τῶν κακῶν ἡμῖν. καὶ τῶν μὲν
ἀγαθῶν οὐδένα ἄλλον αἰτιατέον, τῶν δὲ κακῶν ἄλλ'
ἄττα δεῖ ζητεῖν τὰ αἴτια, ἀλλ' οὐ τὸν θεόν. Ἀληθέστατα, 105
ἔφη, δοκεῖς μοι λέγειν. Οὐκ ἄρα, ἦν δ' ἐγώ, ἀποδεκτέον
D οὔτε Ὁμήρου οὔτ' ἄλλου ποιητοῦ ταύτην τὴν ἁμαρτίαν
περὶ τοὺς θεοὺς ἀνοήτως ἁμαρτάνοντος καὶ λέγοντος, ὡς
δοιοὶ πίθοι

κατακείαται ἐν Διὸς οὔδει 110
κηρῶν ἔμπλειοι, ὁ μὲν ἐσθλῶν, αὐτὰρ ὁ δειλῶν·
καὶ ᾧ μὲν ἂν μίξας ὁ Ζεὺς δῷ ἀμφοτέρων,
ἄλλοτε μέν τε κακῷ ὅ γε κύρεται, ἄλλοτε δ' ἐσθλῷ·
ᾧ δ' ἂν μή, ἀλλ' ἄκρατα τὰ ἕτερα, τὸν δὲ
κακὴ βούβρωστις ἐπὶ χθόνα δῖαν ἐλαύνει· 115

E οὐδ' ὡς ταμίας ἡμῖν Ζεὺς

ἀγαθῶν τε κακῶν τε τέτυκται.

Τὴν δὲ τῶν ὅρκων καὶ σπονδῶν σύγχυσιν, ἣν ὁ Πάν-

δαρος συνέχεεν, ἐάν τις φῇ δι' Ἀθηνᾶς τε καὶ Διὸς γεγο-
120 νέναι, οὐκ ἐπαινεσόμεθα· οὐδὲ θεῶν ἔριν τε καὶ κρίσιν
διὰ Θέμιτός τε καὶ Διός· οὐδ' αὖ, ὡς Αἰσχύλος λέγει, 380
ἐατέον ἀκούειν τοὺς νέους, ὅτι

θεὸς μὲν αἰτίαν φύει βροτοῖς,
ὅταν κακῶσαι δῶμα παμπήδην θέλῃ.

125 ἀλλ' ἐάν τις ποιῇ ἐν οἷς ταῦτα τὰ ἰαμβεῖα ἔνεστι, τὰ τῆς
Νιόβης πάθη ἢ τὰ Πελοπιδῶν ἢ τὰ Τρωϊκὰ ἤ τι ἄλλο
τῶν τοιούτων, ἢ οὐ θεοῦ ἔργα ἐατέον αὐτὰ λέγειν, ἢ εἰ
θεοῦ, ἐξευρετέον αὐτοῖς σχεδὸν ὃν νῦν ἡμεῖς λόγον ζητοῦ-
μεν, καὶ λεκτέον, ὡς ὁ μὲν θεὸς δίκαιά τε καὶ ἀγαθὰ
130 εἰργάζετο, οἱ δὲ ὠνίναντο κολαζόμενοι· ὡς δὲ ἄθλιοι μὲν B
οἱ δίκην διδόντες, ἦν δὲ δὴ ὁ δρῶν ταῦτα θεός, οὐκ
ἐατέον λέγειν τὸν ποιητήν. ἀλλ', εἰ μὲν ὅτι ἐδεήθησαν
κολάσεως λέγοιεν, ὡς ἄθλιοι οἱ κακοί, διδόντες δὲ δίκην
ὠφελοῦντο ὑπὸ τοῦ θεοῦ, ἐατέον· κακῶν δὲ αἴτιον φάναι
135 θεόν τινι γίγνεσθαι ἀγαθὸν ὄντα, διαμαχετέον παντὶ
τρόπῳ μήτε τινὰ λέγειν ταῦτα ἐν τῇ αὑτοῦ πόλει, εἰ
μέλλει εὐνομήσεσθαι, μήτε τινὰ ἀκούειν, μήτε νεώτερον
μήτε πρεσβύτερον, μήτε ἐν μέτρῳ μήτε ἄνευ μέτρου μυ- C
θολογοῦντα, ὡς οὔτε ὅσια ἂν λεγόμενα, εἰ λέγοιτο, οὔτε
140 ξύμφορα ἡμῖν οὔτε σύμφωνα αὐτὰ αὑτοῖς. Σύμψηφός
σοί εἰμι, ἔφη, τούτου τοῦ νόμου, καί μοι ἀρέσκει. Οὗτος
μὲν τοίνυν, ἦν δ' ἐγώ, εἷς ἂν εἴη τῶν περὶ θεοὺς νόμων
τε καὶ τύπων, ἐν ᾧ δεήσει τοὺς λέγοντας λέγειν καὶ τοὺς
ποιοῦντας ποιεῖν, μὴ πάντων αἴτιον τὸν θεὸν ἀλλὰ τῶν
145 ἀγαθῶν. Καὶ μάλ', ἔφη, ἀπόχρη.

Τί δὲ δὴ ὁ δεύτερος ὅδε; ἆρα γόητα τὸν θεὸν οἴει D
εἶναι καὶ οἷον ἐξ ἐπιβουλῆς φαντάζεσθαι ἄλλοτε ἐν ἄλλαις ἰδέαις, τοτὲ μὲν αὐτὸν γιγνόμενον καὶ ἀλλάττοντα τὸ
αὑτοῦ εἶδος εἰς πολλὰς μορφάς, τοτὲ δὲ ἡμᾶς ἀπατῶντα

καὶ ποιοῦντα περὶ αὐτοῦ τοιαῦτα δοκεῖν, ἢ ἁπλοῦν τε 150
εἶναι καὶ πάντων ἥκιστα τῆς ἑαυτοῦ ἰδέας ἐκβαίνειν ;
Οὐκ ἔχω, ἔφη, νῦν γε οὕτως εἰπεῖν. Τί δὲ τόδε ; οὐκ
ἀνάγκη, εἴπερ τι ἐξίσταιτο τῆς αὐτοῦ ἰδέας, ἢ αὐτὸ ὑφ᾽
E ἑαυτοῦ μεθίστασθαι ἢ ὑπ᾽ ἄλλου ; Ἀνάγκη. Οὐκοῦν ὑπὸ
μὲν ἄλλου τὰ ἄριστα ἔχοντα ἥκιστα ἀλλοιοῦταί τε καὶ 155
κινεῖται ; οἷον σῶμα ὑπὸ σιτίων τε καὶ ποτῶν καὶ πόνων,
καὶ πᾶν φυτὸν ὑπὸ εἰλήσεών τε καὶ ἀνέμων καὶ τῶν τοιούτων παθημάτων, οὐ τὸ ὑγιέστατον καὶ ἰσχυρότατον
381 ἥκιστα ἀλλοιοῦται ; Πῶς δ᾽ οὔ ; Ψυχὴν δὲ οὐ τὴν ἀνδρειο-
τάτην καὶ φρονιμωτάτην ἥκιστ᾽ ἄν τι ἔξωθεν πάθος ταρά- 160
ξειέ τε καὶ ἀλλοιώσειεν ; Ναί. Καὶ μήν που καὶ τά γε
ξύνθετα πάντα σκεύη τε καὶ οἰκοδομήματα [καὶ ἀμφιέ-
σματα] κατὰ τὸν αὐτὸν λόγον τὰ εὖ εἰργασμένα καὶ εὖ
ἔχοντα ὑπὸ χρόνου τε καὶ τῶν ἄλλων παθημάτων ἥκιστα
ἀλλοιοῦται. Ἔστι δὴ ταῦτα. Πᾶν δὴ τὸ καλῶς ἔχον ἢ 165
B φύσει ἢ τέχνῃ ἢ ἀμφοτέροις ἐλαχίστην μεταβολὴν ὑπ᾽
ἄλλου ἐνδέχεται. Ἔοικεν. Ἀλλὰ μὴν ὁ θεός γε καὶ
τὰ τοῦ θεοῦ πάντῃ ἄριστα ἔχει. Πῶς δ᾽ οὔ ; Ταύτῃ
μὲν δὴ ἥκιστα ἂν πολλὰς μορφὰς ἴσχοι ὁ θεός. Ἥκιστα
δῆτα.
                                                         170
Ἀλλ᾽ ἆρα αὐτὸς αὑτὸν μεταβάλλοι ἂν καὶ ἀλλοιοῖ ;
Δῆλον, ἔφη, ὅτι, εἴπερ ἀλλοιοῦται. Πότερον οὖν ἐπὶ τὸ
βέλτιόν τε καὶ κάλλιον μεταβάλλει ἑαυτὸν ἢ ἐπὶ τὸ χεῖρον καὶ τὸ αἴσχιον ἑαυτοῦ ; Ἀνάγκη, ἔφη, ἐπὶ τὸ χεῖρον,
C εἴπερ ἀλλοιοῦται· οὐ γάρ που ἐνδεᾶ γε φήσομεν τὸν θεὸν 175
κάλλους ἢ ἀρετῆς εἶναι. Ὀρθότατα, ἦν δ᾽ ἐγώ, λέγεις,
καὶ οὕτως ἔχοντος δοκεῖ ἂν τίς σοι, ὦ Ἀδείμαντε, ἑκὼν
αὑτὸν χείρω ποιεῖν ὁπῃοῦν ἢ θεῶν ἢ ἀνθρώπων ; Ἀδύνατον, ἔφη. Ἀδύνατον ἄρα, ἔφην, καὶ θεῷ ἐθέλειν αὑτὸν
ἀλλοιοῦν, ἀλλ᾽, ὡς ἔοικε, κάλλιστος καὶ ἄριστος ὢν εἰς 180

τὸ δυνατὸν ἕκαστος αὐτῶν μένει ἀεὶ ἁπλῶς ἐν τῇ αὐτοῦ
μορφῇ. Ἅπασα, ἔφη, ἀνάγκη ἔμοιγε δοκεῖ. Μηδεὶς ἄρα,
ἦν δ' ἐγώ, ὦ ἄριστε, λεγέτω ἡμῖν τῶν ποιητῶν, ὡς   D

   θεοὶ ξείνοισιν ἐοικότες ἀλλοδαποῖσι,
185 παντοῖοι τελέθοντες, ἐπιστρωφῶσι πόληας·

μηδὲ Πρωτέως καὶ Θέτιδος καταψευδέσθω μηδείς, μηδ'
ἐν τραγῳδίαις μηδ' ἐν τοῖς ἄλλοις ποιήμασιν εἰσαγέτω
Ἥραν ἠλλοιωμένην ὡς ἱέρειαν ἀγείρουσαν

   Ἰνάχου Ἀργείου ποταμοῦ παισὶν βιοδώροις·

190 καὶ ἄλλα τοιαῦτα πολλὰ μὴ ἡμῖν ψευδέσθωσαν. μηδ' αὖ E
ὑπὸ τούτων ἀναπειθόμεναι αἱ μητέρες τὰ παιδία ἐκδει-
ματούντων, λέγουσαι τοὺς μύθους κακῶς, ὡς ἄρα θεοί
τινες περιέρχονται νύκτωρ πολλοῖς ξένοις καὶ παντοδαποῖς ἰνδαλλόμενοι, ἵνα μὴ ἅμα μὲν εἰς θεοὺς βλασφη-
195 μῶσιν, ἅμα δὲ τοὺς παῖδας ἀπεργάζωνται δειλοτέρους.
Μὴ γάρ, ἔφη. Ἀλλ' ἄρα, ἦν δ' ἐγώ, αὐτοὶ μὲν οἱ θεοί
εἰσιν οἷοι μὴ μεταβάλλειν, ἡμῖν δὲ ποιοῦσι δοκεῖν σφᾶς
παντοδαποὺς φαίνεσθαι, ἐξαπατῶντες καὶ γοητεύοντες;
Ἴσως, ἔφη. Τί δέ; ἦν δ' ἐγώ· ψεύδεσθαι θεὸς ἐθέλοι 382
200 ἂν ἢ λόγῳ ἢ ἔργῳ φάντασμα προτείνων; Οὐκ οἶδα, ἦ δ'
ὅς. Οὐκ οἶσθα, ἦν δ' ἐγώ, ὅτι τό γε ὡς ἀληθῶς ψεῦδος,
εἰ οἷόν τε τοῦτο εἰπεῖν, πάντες θεοί τε καὶ ἄνθρωποι
μισοῦσιν; Πῶς, ἔφη, λέγεις; Οὕτως, ἦν δ' ἐγώ, ὅτι τῷ
κυριωτάτῳ που ἑαυτῶν ψεύδεσθαι καὶ περὶ τὰ κυριώτατα
205 οὐδεὶς ἑκὼν ἐθέλει, ἀλλὰ πάντων μάλιστα φοβεῖται ἐκεῖ
αὐτὸ κεκτῆσθαι. Οὐδὲ νῦν πω, ἦ δ' ὅς, μανθάνω. Οἴει
γάρ τί με, ἔφην, σεμνὸν λέγειν. ἐγὼ δὲ λέγω ὅτι τῇ B
ψυχῇ περὶ τὰ ὄντα ψεύδεσθαί τε καὶ ἐψεῦσθαι καὶ ἀμαθῆ
εἶναι καὶ ἐνταῦθα ἔχειν τε καὶ κεκτῆσθαι τὸ ψεῦδος
210 πάντες ἥκιστα ἂν δέξαιντο καὶ μισοῦσι μάλιστα αὐτὸ ἐν
τῷ τοιούτῳ. Πολύ γε, ἔφη. Ἀλλὰ μὴν ὀρθότατά γ' ἄν,

ὃ νῦν δὴ ἔλεγον, τοῦτο ὡς ἀληθῶς ψεῦδος καλοῖτο, ἡ ἐν
τῇ ψυχῇ ἄγνοια ἡ τοῦ ἐψευσμένου· ἐπεὶ τό γε ἐν τοῖς
λόγοις μίμημά τι τοῦ ἐν τῇ ψυχῇ ἐστὶ παθήματος καὶ
C ὕστερον γεγονὸς εἴδωλον, οὐ πάνυ ἄκρατον ψεῦδος. ἢ οὐχ 215
οὕτω ; Πάνυ μὲν οὖν. Τὸ μὲν δὴ τῷ ὄντι ψεῦδος οὐ
μόνον ὑπὸ θεῶν ἀλλὰ καὶ ὑπ᾽ ἀνθρώπων μισεῖται. Δοκεῖ
μοι. Τί δὲ δή ; τὸ ἐν τοῖς λόγοις ψεῦδος πότε καὶ τῷ
χρήσιμον, ὥστε μὴ ἄξιον εἶναι μίσους ; ἆρ᾽ οὐ πρός τε
τοὺς πολεμίους καὶ τῶν καλουμένων φίλων ὅταν διὰ 220
μανίαν ἤ τινα ἄνοιαν κακόν τι ἐπιχειρῶσι πράττειν, τότε
ἀποτροπῆς ἕνεκα ὡς φάρμακον χρήσιμον γίγνεται ; καὶ
D ἐν αἷς νῦν δὴ ἐλέγομεν ταῖς μυθολογίαις διὰ τὸ μὴ εἰδέναι ὅπῃ τἀληθὲς ἔχει περὶ τῶν παλαιῶν ἀφομοιοῦντες τῷ
ἀληθεῖ τὸ ψεῦδος ὅ τι μάλιστα, οὕτω χρήσιμον ποιοῦμεν ; 225
Καὶ μάλα, ἦ δ᾽ ὅς, οὕτως ἔχει. Κατὰ τί δὴ οὖν τούτων
τῷ θεῷ τὸ ψεῦδος χρήσιμον ; πότερον διὰ τὸ μὴ εἰδέναι
τὰ παλαιὰ ἀφομοιῶν ἂν ψεύδοιτο ; Γελοῖον μέντ᾽ ἂν εἴη,
ἔφη. Ποιητὴς μὲν ἄρα ψευδὴς ἐν θεῷ οὐκ ἔνι. Οὔ μοι
E δοκεῖ. Ἀλλὰ δεδιὼς τοὺς ἐχθροὺς ψεύδοιτο ; Πολλοῦ γε 230
δεῖ. Ἀλλὰ δι᾽ οἰκείων ἄνοιαν ἢ μανίαν ; Ἀλλ᾽ οὐδείς,
ἔφη, τῶν ἀνοήτων καὶ μαινομένων θεοφιλής. Οὐκ ἄρα
ἔστιν οὗ ἕνεκα ἂν θεὸς ψεύδοιτο. Οὐκ ἔστιν. Πάντῃ
ἄρα ἀψευδὲς τὸ δαιμόνιόν τε καὶ τὸ θεῖον. Παντάπασι
μὲν οὖν, ἔφη. Κομιδῇ ἄρα ὁ θεὸς ἁπλοῦν καὶ ἀληθὲς ἔν 235
τε ἔργῳ καὶ ἐν λόγῳ, καὶ οὔτε αὐτὸς μεθίσταται οὔτε
ἄλλους ἐξαπατᾷ, [οὔτε κατὰ φαντασίας] οὔτε κατὰ
λόγους οὔτε κατὰ σημείων πομπάς, οὔθ᾽ ὕπαρ οὔτ᾽ ὄναρ.
383 Οὕτως, ἔφη, ἔμοιγε καὶ αὐτῷ φαίνεται σοῦ λέγοντος.
Συγχωρεῖς ἄρα, ἔφην, τοῦτον δεύτερον τύπον εἶναι, ἐν ᾧ 240
δεῖ περὶ θεῶν καὶ λέγειν καὶ ποιεῖν, ὡς μήτε αὐτοὺς
γόητας ὄντας τῷ μεταβάλλειν ἑαυτοὺς μήτε ἡμᾶς ψεύδεσι

παράγειν ἐν λόγῳ ἢ ἐν ἔργῳ; Συγχωρῶ. Πολλὰ ἄρα
Ὁμήρου ἐπαινοῦντες ἄλλα τοῦτο οὐκ ἐπαινεσόμεθα, τὴν
245 τοῦ ἐνυπνίου πομπὴν ὑπὸ Διὸς τῷ Ἀγαμέμνονι· οὐδὲ
Αἰσχύλου, ὅταν φῇ ἡ Θέτις τὸν Ἀπόλλω ἐν τοῖς αὑτῆς
γάμοις ᾄδοντα ἐνδατεῖσθαι τὰς ἑὰς εὐπαιδίας

     νόσων τ᾽ ἀπείρους καὶ μακραίωνας βίους.
     ξύμπαντά τ᾽ εἰπὼν θεοφιλεῖς ἐμὰς τύχας
250   παιῶν᾽ ἐπευφήμησεν, εὐθυμῶν ἐμέ.
     κἀγὼ τὸ Φοίβου θεῖον ἀψευδὲς στόμα
     ἤλπιζον εἶναι, μαντικῇ βρύον τέχνῃ,
     ὁ δ᾽, αὐτὸς ὑμνῶν, αὐτὸς ἐν θοίνῃ παρών,
     αὐτὸς τάδ᾽ εἰπών, αὐτός ἐστιν ὁ κτανὼν
255   τὸν παῖδα τὸν ἐμόν.

ὅταν τις τοιαῦτα λέγῃ περὶ θεῶν, χαλεπανοῦμέν τε καὶ
χορὸν οὐ δώσομεν, οὐδὲ τοὺς διδασκάλους ἐάσομεν ἐπὶ
παιδείᾳ χρῆσθαι τῶν νέων, εἰ μέλλουσιν ἡμῖν οἱ φύλακες
θεοσεβεῖς τε καὶ θεῖοι γίγνεσθαι, καθ᾽ ὅσον ἀνθρώπῳ
260 ἐπὶ πλεῖστον οἷόν τε. Παντάπασιν, ἔφη, ἔγωγε τοὺς
τύπους τούτους συγχωρῶ, καὶ ὡς νόμοις ἂν χρῴμην.

Book III.

Physic and Surgery to be Heroic.

(SOCRATES, GLAUCON.)

405 C— 408 C.

Τὸ δὲ ἰατρικῆς, ἦν δ᾽ ἐγώ, δεῖσθαι ὅ τι μὴ τραυμάτων
ἕνεκα ἤ τινων ἐπετείων νοσημάτων ἐπιπεσόντων, ἀλλὰ δι᾽
ἀργίαν τε καὶ δίαιταν οἵαν διήλθομεν, ῥευμάτων τε καὶ
πνευμάτων ὥσπερ λίμνας ἐμπιπλαμένους φύσας τε καὶ
5 κατάρρους νοσήμασιν ὀνόματα τίθεσθαι ἀναγκάζειν τοὺς
κομψοὺς Ἀσκληπιάδας, οὐκ αἰσχρὸν δοκεῖ; Καὶ μάλ᾽, ἔφη,
ὡς ἀληθῶς καινὰ ταῦτα καὶ ἄτοπα νοσημάτων ὀνόματα.
Οἷα, ἦν δ᾽ ἐγώ, ὡς οἶμαι, οὐκ ἦν ἐπ᾽ Ἀσκληπιοῦ. τεκ-

Ἐμαίρομαι δέ, ὅτι αὐτοῦ οἱ υἱεῖς ἐν Τροίᾳ Εὐρυπύλῳ τε-
τρωμένῳ ἐπ᾽ οἶνον Πράμνειον ἄλφιτα πολλὰ ἐπιπασθέντα 10
406 καὶ τυρὸν ἐπιξυσθέντα, ἃ δὴ δοκεῖ φλεγματώδη εἶναι,
οὐκ ἐμέμψαντο τῇ δούσῃ πιεῖν, οὐδὲ Πατρόκλῳ τῷ ἰω-
μένῳ ἐπετίμησαν. Καὶ μὲν δή, ἔφη, ἄτοπόν γε τὸ πῶμα
οὕτως ἔχοντι. Οὔκ, εἴ γ᾽ ἐννοεῖς, εἶπον, ὅτι τῇ παιδα-
γωγικῇ τῶν νοσημάτων ταύτῃ τῇ νῦν ἰατρικῇ πρὸ τοῦ 15
Ἀσκληπιάδαι οὐκ ἐχρῶντο, ὥς φασι, πρὶν Ἡρόδικον γενέ-
σθαι· Ἡρόδικος δὲ παιδοτρίβης ὢν καὶ νοσώδης γενόμενος, μίξας γυμναστικὴν ἰατρικῇ, ἀπέκναισε πρῶτον μὲν
B καὶ μάλιστα ἑαυτόν, ἔπειτ᾽ ἄλλους ὕστερον πολλούς. Πῇ
δή ; ἔφη. Μακρόν, ἦν δ᾽ ἐγώ, τὸν θάνατον αὐτῷ ποιή- 20
σας. παρακολουθῶν γὰρ τῷ νοσήματι θανασίμῳ ὄντι οὔτε
ἰάσασθαι, οἶμαι, οἷός τ᾽ ἦν ἑαυτόν, ἐν ἀσχολίᾳ τε πάντων ἰατρευόμενος διὰ βίου ἔζη ἀποκναιόμενος, εἴ τι τῆς
εἰωθυίας διαίτης ἐκβαίη, δυσθανατῶν δὲ ὑπὸ σοφίας εἰς
γῆρας ἀφίκετο. Καλὸν ἄρα τὸ γέρας, ἔφη, τῆς τέχνης 25
C ἠνέγκατο. Οἷον εἰκός, ἦν δ᾽ ἐγώ, τὸν μὴ εἰδότα ὅτι
Ἀσκληπιὸς οὐκ ἀγνοίᾳ οὐδὲ ἀπειρίᾳ τούτου τοῦ εἴδους τῆς
ἰατρικῆς τοῖς ἐκγόνοις οὐ κατέδειξεν αὐτό, ἀλλ᾽ εἰδὼς ὅτι
πᾶσι τοῖς εὐνομουμένοις ἔργον τι ἑκάστῳ ἐν τῇ πόλει προστέτακται, ὃ ἀναγκαῖον ἐργάζεσθαι, καὶ οὐδενὶ σχολὴ διὰ 30
βίου κάμνειν ἰατρευομένῳ. ὃ ἡμεῖς γελοίως ἐπὶ μὲν τῶν
δημιουργῶν αἰσθανόμεθα, ἐπὶ δὲ τῶν πλουσίων τε καὶ
εὐδαιμόνων δοκούντων εἶναι οὐκ αἰσθανόμεθα. Πῶς ; ἔφη.
D Τέκτων μέν, ἦν δ᾽ ἐγώ, κάμνων ἀξιοῖ παρὰ τοῦ ἰατροῦ
φάρμακον πιὼν ἐξεμέσαι τὸ νόσημα ἢ κάτω καθαρθεὶς 35
ἢ καύσει ἢ τομῇ χρησάμενος ἀπηλλάχθαι· ἐὰν δέ τις αὐτῷ μικρὰν δίαιταν προστάττῃ, πιλίδιά τε περὶ τὴν κεφαλὴν περιτιθεὶς καὶ τὰ τούτοις ἑπόμενα, ταχὺ εἶπεν ὅτι
οὐ σχολὴ κάμνειν οὐδὲ λυσιτελεῖ οὕτω ζῆν, νοσήματι τὸν

40 νοῦν προσέχοντα, τῆς δὲ προκειμένης ἐργασίας ἀμελοῦντα·
καὶ μετὰ ταῦτα χαίρειν εἰπὼν τῷ τοιούτῳ ἰατρῷ, εἰς τὴν Ε
εἰωθυῖαν δίαιταν ἐμβάς, ὑγιὴς γενόμενος ζῇ τὰ ἑαυτοῦ
πράττων· ἐὰν δὲ μὴ ἱκανὸν ᾖ τὸ σῶμα ὑπενεγκεῖν, τελευτήσας πραγμάτων ἀπηλλάγη. Καὶ τῷ τοιούτῳ μέν γ’,
45 ἔφη, δοκεῖ πρέπειν οὕτω ἰατρικῇ χρῆσθαι. Ἆρα, ἦν δ’
ἐγώ, ὅτι ἦν τι αὐτῷ ἔργον, ὃ εἰ μὴ πράττοι, οὐκ ἐλυσι- 407
τέλει ζῆν ; Δῆλον, ἔφη. Ὁ δὲ δὴ πλούσιος, ὥς φαμεν,
οὐδὲν ἔχει τοιοῦτον ἔργον προκείμενον, οὗ ἀναγκαζομένῳ
ἀπέχεσθαι ἀβίωτον. Οὔκουν δὴ λέγεταί γε. Φωκυλίδου
50 γάρ, ἦν δ’ ἐγώ, οὐκ ἀκούεις πῶς φησὶ δεῖν, ὅταν τῳ
ἤδη βίος ᾖ, ἀρετὴν ἀσκεῖν. Οἶμαι δέ γε, ἔφη, καὶ πρότερον. Μηδέν, εἶπον, περὶ τούτου αὐτῷ μαχώμεθα, ἀλλ
ἡμᾶς αὐτοὺς διδάξωμεν, πότερον μελετητέον τοῦτο τῷ
πλουσίῳ καὶ ἀβίωτον τῷ μὴ μελετῶντι, ἢ νοσοτροφία τε- Β
55 κτονικῇ μὲν καὶ ταῖς ἄλλαις τέχναις ἐμπόδιον τῇ προσέξει
τοῦ νοῦ, τὸ δὲ Φωκυλίδου παρακέλευμα οὐδὲν ἐμποδίζει.
Ναὶ μὰ τὸν Δία, ἦ δ’ ὅς, σχεδόν γέ τι πάντων μάλιστα
ἥ γε περαιτέρω γυμναστικῆς ἡ περιττὴ αὕτη ἐπιμέλεια
τοῦ σώματος· καὶ γὰρ πρὸς οἰκονομίας καὶ πρὸς στρα-
60 τείας καὶ πρὸς ἑδραίους ἐν πόλει ἀρχὰς δύσκολος. Τὸ δὲ
δὴ μέγιστον, ὅτι καὶ πρὸς μαθήσεις ἀστινασοῦν καὶ ἐν-
νοήσεις τε καὶ μελέτας πρὸς ἑαυτὸν χαλεπή, κεφαλῆς τινὰς C
ἀεὶ διατάσεις καὶ ἰλίγγους ὑποπτεύουσα καὶ αἰτιωμένη ἐκ
φιλοσοφίας ἐγγίγνεσθαι, ὥστε, ὅπῃ ταύτῃ ἀρετὴ ἀσκεῖται
65 καὶ δοκιμάζεται, πάντῃ ἐμπόδιος· κάμνειν γὰρ οἴεσθαι
ποιεῖ ἀεὶ καὶ ὠδίνοντα μήποτε λήγειν περὶ τοῦ σώματος.
Εἰκός γε, ἔφη. Οὔκουν ταῦτα γιγνώσκοντα φῶμεν καὶ
Ἀσκληπιὸν τοὺς μὲν φύσει τε καὶ διαίτῃ ὑγιεινῶς ἔχοντας
τὰ σώματα, νόσημα δέ τι ἀποκεκριμένον ἴσχοντας ἐν αὐ- D
70 τοῖς, τούτοις μὲν καὶ ταύτῃ τῇ ἕξει καταδεῖξαι ἰατρικήν,

φαρμάκοις τε καὶ τομαῖς τὰ νοσήματα ἐκβάλλοντα αὐτῶν
τὴν εἰωθυῖαν προστάττειν δίαιταν, ἵνα μὴ τὰ πολιτικὰ
βλάπτοι, τὰ δ᾽ εἴσω διὰ παντὸς νενοσηκότα σώματα οὐκ
ἐπιχειρεῖν διαίταις κατὰ σμικρὸν ἀπαντλοῦντα καὶ ἐπιχέοντα μακρὸν καὶ κακὸν βίον ἀνθρώπῳ ποιεῖν, καὶ ἔκγονα 75
αὐτῶν, ὡς τὸ εἰκός, ἕτερα τοιαῦτα φυτεύειν, ἀλλὰ τὸν
E μὴ δυνάμενον ἐν τῇ καθεστηκυίᾳ περιόδῳ ζῆν μὴ οἴεσθαι
δεῖν θεραπεύειν, ὡς οὔτε αὐτῷ οὔτε πόλει λυσιτελῆ; Πο-
λιτικόν, ἔφη, λέγεις Ἀσκληπιόν.‖ Δῆλον, ἦν δ᾽ ἐγώ· καὶ
οἱ παῖδες αὐτοῦ, ὅτι τοιοῦτος ἦν, οὐχ ὁρᾷς ὡς καὶ ἐν 80
408 Τροίᾳ ἀγαθοὶ πρὸς τὸν πόλεμον ἐφάνησαν, καὶ τῇ ἰατρικῇ, ὡς ἐγὼ λέγω, ἐχρῶντο; ἢ οὐ μέμνησαι ὅτι καὶ τῷ
Μενέλεῳ ἐκ τοῦ τραύματος οὗ ὁ Πάνδαρος ἔβαλεν
          αἷμ᾽ ἐκμυζήσαντ᾽ ἐπί τ᾽ ἤπια φάρμακ᾽ ἔπασσον,
ὅ τι δ᾽ ἐχρῆν μετὰ τοῦτο ἢ πιεῖν ἢ φαγεῖν οὐδὲν μᾶλλον 85
ἢ τῷ Εὐρυπύλῳ προσέταττον, ὡς ἱκανῶν ὄντων τῶν φαρ-
μάκων ἰάσασθαι ἄνδρας πρὸ τῶν τραυμάτων ὑγιεινούς τε
B καὶ κοσμίους ἐν διαίτῃ, κἂν εἰ τύχοιεν ἐν τῷ παραχρῆμα
κυκεῶνα πιόντες, νοσώδη δὲ φύσει τε καὶ ἀκόλαστον οὔτε
αὐτοῖς οὔτε τοῖς ἄλλοις ᾤοντο λυσιτελεῖν ζῆν, οὐδ᾽ ἐπὶ 90
τούτοις τὴν τέχνην δεῖν εἶναι, οὐδὲ θεραπευτέον αὐτούς,
οὐδ᾽ εἰ Μίδου πλουσιώτεροι εἶεν.   Πάνυ κομψούς, ἔφη,
.λέγεις Ἀσκληπιοῦ παῖδας. Πρέπει, ἦν δ᾽ ἐγώ. καίτοι ἀπει-
θοῦντές γε ἡμῖν οἱ τραγῳδοποιοί τε καὶ Πίνδαρος Ἀπόλλωνος μέν φασιν Ἀσκληπιὸν εἶναι, ὑπὸ δὲ χρυσοῦ πεισθῆ- 95
C ναι πλούσιον ἄνδρα θανάσιμον ἤδη ὄντα ἰάσασθαι, ὅθεν
δὴ καὶ κεραυνωθῆναι αὐτόν. ἡμεῖς δὲ κατὰ τὰ προειρη-
μένα οὐ πειθόμεθα αὐτοῖς ἀμφότερα, ἀλλ᾽ εἰ μὲν θεοῦ ἦν,
οὐκ ἦν, φήσομεν, αἰσχροκερδής· εἰ δ᾽ αἰσχροκερδής, οὐκ
ἦν θεοῦ. 100

The 'Noble Lie.'

(SOCRATES, GLAUCON.)
414 B—end.

Τίς ἂν οὖν ἡμῖν, ἦν δ' ἐγώ, μηχανὴ γένοιτο τῶν ψευ-
δῶν τῶν ἐν δέοντι γιγνομένων, ὧν δὴ νῦν ἐλέγομεν, γενναῖόν τι ἐν ψευδομένους πεῖσαι μάλιστα μὲν καὶ αὐτοὺς C
τοὺς ἄρχοντας, εἰ δὲ μή, τὴν ἄλλην πόλιν; Ποῖόν τι;
105 ἔφη. Μηδὲν καινόν, ἦν δ' ἐγώ, ἀλλὰ Φοινικικόν τι,
πρότερον μὲν ἤδη πολλαχοῦ γεγονός, ὥς φασιν οἱ ποιηταὶ καὶ πεπείκασιν, ἐφ' ἡμῶν δὲ οὐ γεγονὸς οὐδ' οἶδα
εἰ γενόμενον ἄν, πεῖσαι δὲ συχνῆς πειθοῦς. Ὡς ἔοικας,
ἔφη, ὀκνοῦντι λέγειν. Δόξω δέ σοι, ἦν δ' ἐγώ, καὶ μάλ'
110 εἰκότως ὀκνεῖν, ἐπειδὰν εἴπω. Λέγ', ἔφη, καὶ μὴ φοβοῦ.
Λέγω δή· καίτοι οὐκ οἶδα ὁποίᾳ τόλμῃ ἢ ποίοις λόγοις D
χρώμενος ἐρῶ· καὶ ἐπιχειρήσω πρῶτον μὲν αὐτοὺς τοὺς
ἄρχοντας πείθειν καὶ τοὺς στρατιώτας, ἔπειτα δὲ καὶ τὴν
ἄλλην πόλιν, ὡς ἄρ' ἃ ἡμεῖς αὐτοὺς ἐτρέφομέν τε καὶ
115 ἐπαιδεύομεν, ὥσπερ ὀνείρατα ἐδόκουν ταῦτα πάντα πάσχειν τε καὶ γίγνεσθαι περὶ αὐτούς, ἦσαν δὲ τότε τῇ
ἀληθείᾳ ὑπὸ γῆς ἐντὸς πλαττόμενοι καὶ τρεφόμενοι καὶ
αὐτοὶ καὶ τὰ ὅπλα αὐτῶν καὶ ἡ ἄλλη σκευὴ δημιουργουμένη, ἐπειδὴ δὲ παντελῶς ἐξειργασμένοι ἦσαν, καὶ ἡ γῆ E
120 αὐτοὺς μήτηρ οὖσα ἀνῆκε, καὶ νῦν δεῖ ὡς περὶ μητρὸς
καὶ τροφοῦ τῆς χώρας ἐν ᾗ εἰσὶ βουλεύεσθαί τε καὶ ἀμύνειν αὐτούς, ἐάν τις ἐπ' αὐτὴν ἴῃ, καὶ ὑπὲρ τῶν ἄλλων
πολιτῶν ὡς ἀδελφῶν ὄντων καὶ γηγενῶν διανοεῖσθαι.
Οὐκ ἐτός, ἔφη, πάλαι ᾐσχύνου τὸ ψεῦδος λέγειν. Πάνυ,
125 ἦν δ' ἐγώ, εἰκότως· ἀλλ' ὅμως ἄκουε καὶ τὸ λοιπὸν τοῦ 415
μύθου. ἐστὲ μὲν γὰρ δὴ πάντες οἱ ἐν τῇ πόλει ἀδελφοί,
ὡς φήσομεν πρὸς αὐτοὺς μυθολογοῦντες, ἀλλ' ὁ θεὸς

πλάττων, ὅσοι μὲν ὑμῶν ἱκανοὶ ἄρχειν, χρυσὸν ἐν τῇ
γενέσει ξυνέμιξεν αὐτοῖς, διὸ τιμιώτατοί εἰσιν· ὅσοι δ᾽
ἐπίκουροι, ἄργυρον· σίδηρον δὲ καὶ χαλκὸν τοῖς τε γεωργοῖς 130
καὶ τοῖς ἄλλοις δημιουργοῖς. ἅτε οὖν ξυγγενεῖς ὄντες πάντες τὸ μὲν πολὺ ὁμοίους ἂν ὑμῖν αὐτοῖς γεννῷτε, ἔστι
δ᾽ ὅτε ἐκ χρυσοῦ γεννηθείη ἂν ἀργυροῦν καὶ ἐξ ἀργυροῦ
χρυσοῦν ἔκγονον καὶ τἆλλα πάντα οὕτως ἐξ ἀλλήλων. τοῖς
οὖν ἄρχουσι καὶ πρῶτον καὶ μάλιστα παραγγέλλει ὁ θεός, 135
ὅπως μηδενὸς οὕτω φύλακες ἀγαθοὶ ἔσονται μηδ᾽ οὕτω
σφόδρα φυλάξουσι μηδὲν ὡς τοὺς ἐκγόνους, ὅ τι αὐτοῖς
τούτων ἐν ταῖς ψυχαῖς παραμέμικται, καὶ ἐάν τε σφέτε-
ρος ἔκγονος ὑπόχαλκος ἢ ὑποσίδηρος γένηται, μηδενὶ
C τρόπῳ κατελεήσουσιν, ἀλλὰ τὴν τῇ φύσει προσήκουσαν 140
τιμὴν ἀποδόντες ὤσουσιν εἰς δημιουργοὺς ἢ εἰς γεωργούς,
καὶ ἂν αὖ ἐκ τούτων τις ὑπόχρυσος ἢ ὑπάργυρος φυῇ,
τιμήσαντες ἀνάξουσι τοὺς μὲν εἰς φυλακήν, τοὺς δὲ εἰς
ἐπικουρίαν, ὡς χρησμοῦ ὄντος τότε τὴν πόλιν διαφθα-
ρῆναι, ὅταν αὐτὴν ὁ σίδηρος ἢ ὁ χαλκὸς φυλάξῃ. τοῦτον 145
οὖν τὸν μῦθον ὅπως ἂν πεισθεῖεν, ἔχεις τινὰ μηχανήν ;
D Οὐδαμῶς, ἔφη, ὅπως γ᾽ ἂν αὐτοὶ οὗτοι· ὅπως μέντ᾽ ἂν
οἱ τούτων υἱεῖς καὶ οἱ ἔπειτα οἵ τ᾽ ἄλλοι ἄνθρωποι οἱ
ὕστερον. Ἀλλὰ καὶ τοῦτο, ἦν δ᾽ ἐγώ, εὖ ἂν ἔχοι πρὸς
τὸ μᾶλλον αὐτοὺς τῆς πόλεώς τε καὶ ἀλλήλων κήδεσθαι· 150
σχεδὸν γάρ τι μανθάνω ὃ λέγεις. καὶ τοῦτο μὲν δὴ ἕξει
ὅπῃ ἂν αὐτὸ ἡ φήμη ἀγάγῃ· ἡμεῖς δὲ τούτους τοὺς γη-
γενεῖς ὁπλίσαντες προάγωμεν ἡγουμένων τῶν ἀρχόντων.
ἐλθόντες δὲ θεασάσθων τῆς πόλεως ὅπου κάλλιστον στρα-
E τοπεδεύσασθαι, ὅθεν τούς τε ἔνδον μάλιστ᾽ ἂν κατέχοιεν, 155
εἴ τις μὴ ἐθέλοι τοῖς νόμοις πείθεσθαι, τούς τε ἔξωθεν
ἀπαμύνοιεν, εἰ πολέμιος ὥσπερ λύκος ἐπὶ ποίμνην τις ἴοι·
στρατοπεδευσάμενοι δέ, θύσαντες οἷς χρή, εὐνὰς ποιησά-

σθων. ἢ πῶς ; Οὕτως, ἔφη. Οὐκοῦν τοιαύτας, οἷας χει-
160 μῶνός τε στέγειν καὶ θέρους ἱκανὰς εἶναι ; Πῶς γὰρ οὐχί ;
οἰκήσεις γάρ, ἔφη, δοκεῖς μοι λέγειν. Ναί, ἦν δ᾽ ἐγώ,
στρατιωτικάς γε, ἀλλ᾽ οὐ χρηματιστικάς. Πῶς, ἔφη, αὖ 416
τοῦτο λέγεις διαφέρειν ἐκείνου ; Ἐγώ σοι, ἦν δ᾽ ἐγώ,
πειράσομαι εἰπεῖν. δεινότατον γάρ που πάντων καὶ
165 αἴσχιστον ποιμέσι τοιούτους γε καὶ οὕτω τρέφειν κύνας
ἐπικούρους ποιμνίων, ὥστε ὑπὸ ἀκολασίας ἢ λιμοῦ ἤ
τινος ἄλλου κακοῦ ἔθους αὐτοὺς τοὺς κύνας ἐπιχειρῆσαι τοῖς προβάτοις κακουργεῖν καὶ ἀντὶ κυνῶν λύκοις
ὁμοιωθῆναι. Δεινόν, ἦ δ᾽ ὅς· πῶς δ᾽ οὔ ; Οὐκοῦν
170 φυλακτέον παντὶ τρόπῳ μὴ τοιοῦτον ἡμῖν οἱ ἐπίκουροι B
ποιήσωσι πρὸς τοὺς πολίτας, ἐπειδὴ αὐτῶν κρείττους
εἰσίν, ἀντὶ ξυμμάχων εὐμενῶν δεσπόταις ἀγρίοις ἀφο-
μοιωθῶσιν ; Φυλακτέον, ἔφη. Οὐκοῦν τὴν μεγίστην τῆς
εὐλαβείας παρεσκευασμένοι ἂν εἶεν, εἰ τῷ ὄντι καλῶς
175 πεπαιδευμένοι εἰσίν ; Ἀλλὰ μὴν εἰσί γ᾽, ἔφη. Καὶ
ἔγωγ᾽ εἶπον, Τοῦτο μὲν οὐκ ἄξιον διισχυρίζεσθαι, ὦ
φίλε Γλαύκων· ὃ μέντοι ἄρτι ἐλέγομεν, ἄξιον, ὅτι δεῖ
αὐτοὺς τῆς ὀρθῆς τυχεῖν παιδείας, ἥτις ποτέ ἐστιν, εἰ C
μέλλουσι τὸ μέγιστον ἔχειν πρὸς τὸ ἥμεροι εἶναι αὐτοῖς
180 τε καὶ τοῖς φυλαττομένοις ὑπ᾽ αὐτῶν. Καὶ ὀρθῶς γε, ἦ
δ᾽ ὅς. Πρὸς τοίνυν τῇ παιδείᾳ ταύτῃ φαίη ἄν τις νοῦν
ἔχων δεῖν καὶ τὰς οἰκήσεις καὶ τὴν ἄλλην οὐσίαν τοιαύτην αὐτοῖς παρεσκευάσθαι, ἥτις μήτε τοὺς φύλακας ὡς
ἀρίστους εἶναι παύσοι αὐτούς, κακουργεῖν τε μὴ ἐπαροῖ
185 περὶ τοὺς ἄλλους πολίτας. Καὶ ἀληθῶς γε φήσει. Ὅρα D
δή, εἶπον ἐγώ, εἰ τοιόνδε τινὰ τρόπον δεῖ αὐτοὺς ζῆν τε
καὶ οἰκεῖν, εἰ μέλλουσι τοιοῦτοι ἔσεσθαι· πρῶτον μὲν
οὐσίαν κεκτημένον μηδεμίαν μηδένα ἰδίαν, ἂν μὴ πᾶσα
ἀνάγκη· ἔπειτα οἴκησιν καὶ ταμιεῖον μηδενὶ εἶναι μηδὲν

τοιοῦτον, εἰς ὃ οὐ πᾶς ὁ βουλόμενος εἴσεισι· τὰ δ' ἐπι- 190
τήδεια, ὅσων δέονται ἄνδρες ἀθληταὶ πολέμου σώφρονές
Ε τε καὶ ἀνδρεῖοι, ταξαμένους παρὰ τῶν ἄλλων πολιτῶν
δέχεσθαι μισθὸν τῆς φυλακῆς τοσοῦτον, ὅσον μήτε περι-
εῖναι αὐτοῖς εἰς τὸν ἐνιαυτὸν μήτε ἐνδεῖν· φοιτῶντας δὲ
εἰς ξυσσίτια, ὥσπερ ἐστρατοπεδευμένους, κοινῇ ζῆν· 195
χρυσίον δὲ καὶ ἀργύριον εἰπεῖν αὐτοῖς ὅτι θεῖον παρὰ
θεῶν ἀεὶ ἐν τῇ ψυχῇ ἔχουσι καὶ οὐδὲν προσδέονται τοῦ
ἀνθρωπείου, οὐδὲ ὅσια τὴν ἐκείνου κτῆσιν τῇ τοῦ θνητοῦ
χρυσοῦ κτήσει ξυμμιγνύντας μιαίνειν, διότι πολλὰ καὶ
417 ἀνόσια περὶ τὸ τῶν πολλῶν νόμισμα γέγονε, τὸ παρ' 200
ἐκείνοις δὲ ἀκήρατον· ἀλλὰ μόνοις αὐτοῖς τῶν ἐν τῇ
πόλει μεταχειρίζεσθαι καὶ ἅπτεσθαι χρυσοῦ καὶ ἀργύρου
οὐ θέμις, οὐδ' ὑπὸ τὸν αὐτὸν ὄροφον ἰέναι οὐδὲ περιά-
ψασθαι οὐδὲ πίνειν ἐξ ἀργύρου ἢ χρυσοῦ. καὶ οὕτω μὲν
σώζοιντό τ' ἂν καὶ σώζοιεν τὴν πόλιν· ὁπότε δ' αὐτοὶ 205
γῆν τε ἰδίαν καὶ οἰκίας καὶ νομίσματα κτήσονται, οἰκο-
νόμοι μὲν καὶ γεωργοὶ ἀντὶ φυλάκων ἔσονται, δεσπόται δ'
Β ἐχθροὶ ἀντὶ ξυμμάχων τῶν ἄλλων πολιτῶν γενήσονται,
μισοῦντες δὲ δὴ καὶ μισούμενοι καὶ ἐπιβουλεύοντες καὶ
ἐπιβουλευόμενοι διάξουσι πάντα τὸν βίον, πολὺ πλείω 210
καὶ μᾶλλον δεδιότες τοὺς ἔνδον ἢ τοὺς ἔξωθεν πολεμίους,
θέοντες ἤδη τότε ἐγγύτατα ὀλέθρου αὐτοί τε καὶ ἡ ἄλλη
πόλις. τούτων οὖν πάντων ἕνεκα, ἦν δ' ἐγώ, φῶμεν οὕτω
δεῖν κατεσκευάσθαι τοὺς φύλακας οἰκήσεώς τε πέρι καὶ
τῶν ἄλλων, καὶ ταῦτα νομοθετήσωμεν, ἢ μή; Πάνυ γε, 215
ἦ δ' ὃς ὁ Γλαύκων.

Book V.

The Philosopher must be King, or the King Philosopher.

(Socrates, Glaucon.)

472 B—474 B.

Οὐκοῦν, ἦν δ' ἐγώ, πρῶτον μὲν τόδε χρὴ ἀναμνη-
σθῆναι, ὅτι ἡμεῖς ζητοῦντες δικαιοσύνην οἷόν ἐστι καὶ
ἀδικίαν δεῦρο ἥκομεν. Χρή· ἀλλὰ τί τοῦτό γ'; ἔφη.
Οὐδέν· ἀλλ' ἐὰν εὕρωμεν οἷόν ἐστι δικαιοσύνη, ἆρα καὶ
5 ἄνδρα τὸν δίκαιον ἀξιώσομεν μηδὲν δεῖν αὐτῆς ἐκείνης
διαφέρειν, ἀλλὰ πανταχῇ τοιοῦτον εἶναι οἷον δικαιοσύνη C
ἐστίν; ἢ ἀγαπήσομεν, ἐὰν ὅ τι ἐγγύτατα αὐτῆς ᾖ καὶ
πλεῖστα τῶν ἄλλων ἐκείνης μετέχῃ; Οὕτως, ἔφη· ἀγαπήσομεν. Παραδείγματος ἄρα ἕνεκα, ἦν δ' ἐγώ, ἐζητοῦ-
10 μεν αὐτό τε δικαιοσύνην οἷόν ἐστι, καὶ ἄνδρα τὸν τελέως
δίκαιον, εἰ γένοιτο, οἷος ἂν εἴη γενόμενος, καὶ ἀδικίαν αὖ
καὶ τὸν ἀδικώτατον, ἵνα εἰς ἐκείνους ἀποβλέποντες, οἷοι
ἂν ἡμῖν φαίνωνται εὐδαιμονίας τε πέρι καὶ τοῦ ἐναντίου,
ἀναγκαζώμεθα καὶ περὶ ἡμῶν αὐτῶν ὁμολογεῖν, ὃς ἂν
15 ἐκείνοις ὅ τι ὁμοιότατος ᾖ, τὴν ἐκείνοις μοῖραν ὁμοιοτά- D
την ἕξειν, ἀλλ' οὐ τούτου ἕνεκα, ἵν' ἀποδείξωμεν ὡς
δυνατὰ ταῦτα γίγνεσθαι. Τοῦτο μέν, ἔφη, ἀληθὲς λέγεις.
Οἴει ἂν οὖν ἧττόν τι ἀγαθὸν ζωγράφον εἶναι ὃς ἂν γρά-
ψας παράδειγμα οἷον ἂν εἴη ὁ κάλλιστος ἄνθρωπος καὶ
20 πάντα εἰς τὸ γράμμα ἱκανῶς ἀποδοὺς μὴ ἔχῃ ἀποδεῖξαι
ὡς καὶ δυνατὸν γενέσθαι τοιοῦτον ἄνδρα; Μὰ Δί' οὐκ
ἔγωγ', ἔφη. Τί οὖν; οὐ καὶ ἡμεῖς, φαμέν, παράδειγμα
ἐποιοῦμεν λόγῳ ἀγαθῆς πόλεως; Πάνυ γε. Ἧττόν τι E
οὖν οἴει ἡμᾶς εὖ λέγειν τούτου ἕνεκα, ἐὰν μὴ ἔχωμεν
25 ἀποδεῖξαι ὡς δυνατὸν οὕτω πόλιν οἰκῆσαι ὡς ἐλέγετο;
Οὐ δῆτα, ἔφη. Τὸ μὲν τοίνυν ἀληθές, ἦν δ' ἐγώ, οὕ-

τως· εἰ δὲ δὴ καὶ τοῦτο προθυμηθῆναι δεῖ σὴν χάριν, ἀποδεῖξαι πῇ μάλιστα καὶ κατὰ τί δυνατώτατ' ἂν εἴη, πάλιν μοι πρὸς τὴν τοιαύτην ἀπόδειξιν τὰ αὐτὰ διομο-
473 λόγησαι. Τὰ ποῖα; Ἆρ' οἷόν τέ τι πραχθῆναι ὡς λέγε- 30 ται, ἢ φύσιν ἔχει πρᾶξιν λέξεως ἧττον ἀληθείας ἐφάπτε- σθαι, κἂν εἰ μή τῳ δοκεῖ; ἀλλὰ σὺ πότερον ὁμολογεῖς οὕτως ἢ οὔ; Ὁμολογῶ, ἔφη. Τοῦτο μὲν δὴ μὴ ἀνάγκαζέ με, οἷα τῷ λόγῳ διήλθομεν, τοιαῦτα παντάπασι καὶ τῷ ἔργῳ δεῖν γιγνόμενα ἀποφαίνειν· ἀλλ', ἐὰν οἷοί τε γενώ- 35 μεθα εὑρεῖν ὡς ἂν ἐγγύτατα τῶν εἰρημένων πόλις οἰκή- σειεν, φάναι ἡμᾶς ἐξευρηκέναι ὡς δυνατὰ ταῦτα γίγνεσθαι

B ἃ σὺ ἐπιτάττεις. ἢ οὐκ ἀγαπήσεις τούτων τυγχάνων; ἐγὼ μὲν γὰρ ἂν ἀγαπῴην. Καὶ γὰρ ἐγώ, ἔφη. Τὸ δὲ δὴ μετὰ τοῦτο, ὡς ἔοικε, πειρώμεθα ζητεῖν τε καὶ ἀποδει- 40 κνύναι, τί ποτε νῦν κακῶς ἐν ταῖς πόλεσι πράττεται δι' ὃ οὐχ οὕτως οἰκοῦνται, καὶ τίνος ἂν σμικροτάτου μετα- βαλόντος ἔλθοι εἰς τοῦτον τὸν τρόπον τῆς πολιτείας πόλις, μάλιστα μὲν ἑνός, εἰ δὲ μή, δυοῖν, εἰ δὲ μή, ὅ τι ὀλιγίστων τὸν ἀριθμὸν καὶ σμικροτάτων τὴν δύναμιν. 45

C Παντάπασι μὲν οὖν, ἔφη. Ἑνὸς μὲν τοίνυν, ἦν δ' ἐγώ, μεταβαλόντος δοκοῦμέν μοι ἔχειν δεῖξαι ὅτι μεταπέσοι ἄν, οὐ μέντοι σμικροῦ γε οὐδὲ ῥᾳδίου, δυνατοῦ δέ. Τίνος; ἔφη. Ἐπ' αὐτὸ δή, ἦν δ' ἐγώ, εἶμι ὃ τῷ μεγίστῳ προσει- κάζομεν κύματι. εἰρήσεται δ' οὖν, εἰ καὶ μέλλει γέλωτί 50 τε ἀτεχνῶς ὥσπερ κῦμα ἐκγελῶν καὶ ἀδοξίᾳ κατακλύσειν. σκόπει δὲ ὃ μέλλω λέγειν. Λέγε, ἔφη. Ἐὰν μή, ἦν δ'

D ἐγώ, ἢ οἱ φιλόσοφοι βασιλεύσωσιν ἐν ταῖς πόλεσιν ἢ οἱ βασιλῆς τε νῦν λεγόμενοι καὶ δυνάσται φιλοσοφήσωσι γνησίως τε καὶ ἱκανῶς, καὶ τοῦτο εἰς ταὐτὸν ξυμπέσῃ, 55 δύναμίς τε πολιτικὴ καὶ φιλοσοφία, τῶν δὲ νῦν πορευο- μένων χωρὶς ἐφ' ἑκάτερον αἱ πολλαὶ φύσεις ἐξ ἀνάγκης

ἀποκλεισθῶσιν, οὐκ ἔστι κακῶν παῦλα, ὦ φίλε Γλαύκων,
ταῖς πόλεσι, δοκῶ δ' οὐδὲ τῷ ἀνθρωπίνῳ γένει, οὐδὲ αὕτη
60 ἡ πολιτεία μή ποτε πρότερον φυῇ τε εἰς τὸ δυνατὸν καὶ E
φῶς ἡλίου ἴδῃ, ἣν νῦν λόγῳ διεληλύθαμεν. || ἀλλὰ τοῦτό
ἐστιν, ὃ ἐμοὶ πάλαι ὄκνον ἐντίθησι λέγειν, ὁρῶντι ὡς
πολὺ παρὰ δόξαν ῥηθήσεται· χαλεπὸν γὰρ ἰδεῖν, ὅτι
οὐκ ἂν ἄλλη τις εὐδαιμονήσειεν οὔτε ἰδίᾳ οὔτε δημοσίᾳ.
65 Καὶ ὅς, Ὦ Σώκρατες, ἔφη, τοιοῦτον ἐκβέβληκας ῥῆμά τε
καὶ λόγον, ὃν εἰπὼν ἡγοῦ ἐπὶ σὲ πάνυ πολλούς τε καὶ οὐ
φαύλους νῦν οὕτως, οἷον ῥίψαντας τὰ ἱμάτια, γυμνοὺς 474
λαβόντας ὅ τι ἑκάστῳ παρέτυχεν ὅπλον, θεῖν διατεταμέ-
νους ὡς θαυμάσια ἐργασομένους· οὓς εἰ μὴ ἀμυνεῖ τῷ
70 λόγῳ καὶ ἐκφεύξει, τῷ ὄντι τωθαζόμενος δώσεις δίκην.
Οὐκοῦν σύ μοι, ἦν δ' ἐγώ, τούτων αἴτιος ; Καλῶς γ', ἔφη,
ἐγὼ ποιῶν. ἀλλά τοί σε οὐ προδώσω, ἀλλ' ἀμυνῶ οἷς
δύναμαι· δύναμαι δὲ εὐνοίᾳ τε καὶ τῷ παρακελεύεσθαι,
καὶ ἴσως ἂν ἄλλου του ἐμμελέστερόν σοι ἀποκρινοίμην. B
75 ἀλλ' ὡς ἔχων τοιοῦτον βοηθὸν πειρῶ τοῖς ἀπιστοῦσιν
ἐνδείξασθαι ὅτι ἔχει ᾗ σὺ λέγεις.

Book VI.

The Apologue of the Pilot.

(SOCRATES, ADEIMANTUS.)

487 A—489 C.

Καὶ ὁ Ἀδείμαντος, Ὦ Σώκρατες, ἔφη, πρὸς μὲν ταῦτά B
σοι οὐδεὶς ἂν οἷός τ' εἴη ἀντειπεῖν· ἀλλὰ γὰρ τοιόνδε τι
πάσχουσιν οἱ ἀκούοντες ἑκάστοτε ἃ νῦν λέγεις· ἡγοῦνται
δι' ἀπειρίαν τοῦ ἐρωτᾶν καὶ ἀποκρίνεσθαι ὑπὸ τοῦ λόγου
5 παρ' ἕκαστον τὸ ἐρώτημα σμικρὸν παραγόμενοι, ἀθροι-
σθέντων τῶν σμικρῶν ἐπὶ τελευτῆς τῶν λόγων μέγα τὸ
σφάλμα καὶ ἐναντίον τοῖς πρώτοις ἀναφαίνεσθαι, καὶ

C ὥσπερ ὑπὸ τῶν πεττεύειν δεινῶν οἱ μὴ τελευτῶντες ἀπο-
κλείονται καὶ οὐκ ἔχουσιν ὅ τι φέρωσιν, οὕτω καὶ σφεῖς
τελευτῶντες ἀποκλείεσθαι, καὶ οὐκ ἔχειν ὅ τι λέγωσιν 10
ὑπὸ πεττείας αὖ ταύτης τινὸς ἑτέρας, οὐκ ἐν ψήφοις ἀλλ᾽
ἐν λόγοις· ἐπεὶ τό γε ἀληθὲς οὐδέν τι μᾶλλον ταύτῃ
ἔχειν. λέγω δ᾽ εἰς τὸ παρὸν ἀποβλέψας. νῦν γὰρ φαίη
ἄν τίς σοι λόγῳ μὲν οὐκ ἔχειν καθ᾽ ἕκαστον τὸ ἐρωτώμενον ἐναντιοῦσθαι, ἔργῳ δὲ ὁρᾶν, ὅσοι ἂν ἐπὶ φιλο- 15
D σοφίαν ὁρμήσαντες μὴ τοῦ πεπαιδεῦσθαι ἕνεκα ἁψάμενοι
νέοι ὄντες ἀπαλλάττωνται, ἀλλὰ μακρότερον ἐνδιατρί-
ψωσι, τοὺς μὲν πλείστους καὶ πάνυ ἀλλοκότους γιγνομένους, ἵνα μὴ παμπονήρους εἴπωμεν, τοὺς δ᾽ ἐπιεικε-
στάτους δοκοῦντας ὅμως τοῦτό γε ὑπὸ τοῦ ἐπιτηδεύματος 20
οὗ σὺ ἐπαινεῖς πάσχοντας, ἀχρήστους ταῖς πόλεσι
γιγνομένους. Καὶ ἐγὼ ἀκούσας, Οἴει οὖν, εἶπον, τοὺς
ταῦτα λέγοντας ψεύδεσθαι ; Οὐκ οἶδα, ἦ δ᾽ ὅς, ἀλλὰ τὸ
E σοὶ δοκοῦν ἡδέως ἂν ἀκούοιμι. Ἀκούοις ἄν, ὅτι ἔμοιγε
φαίνονται τἀληθῆ λέγειν. Πῶς οὖν, ἔφη, εὖ ἔχει λέγειν, 25
ὅτι οὐ πρότερον κακῶν παύσονται αἱ πόλεις, πρὶν ἂν ἐν
αὐταῖς οἱ φιλόσοφοι ἄρξωσιν, οὓς ἀχρήστους ὁμολογοῦ-
μεν αὐταῖς εἶναι ; Ἐρωτᾷς, ἦν δ᾽ ἐγώ, ἐρώτημα δεόμενον
ἀποκρίσεως δι᾽ εἰκόνος λεγομένης. Σὺ δέ γε, ἔφη,
οἶμαι, οὐκ εἴωθας δι᾽ εἰκόνων λέγειν. 30

Εἶεν, εἶπον· σκώπτεις ἐμβεβληκώς με εἰς λόγον οὕτω
488 δυσαπόδεικτον ; ἄκουε δ᾽ οὖν τῆς εἰκόνος, ἵν᾽ ἔτι μᾶλλον
ἴδῃς ὡς γλίσχρως εἰκάζω. οὕτω γὰρ χαλεπὸν τὸ πάθος
τῶν ἐπιεικεστάτων, ὃ πρὸς τὰς πόλεις πεπόνθασιν, ὥστε
οὐδ᾽ ἔστιν ἐν οὐδὲν ἄλλο τοιοῦτον πεπονθός, ἀλλὰ δεῖ ἐκ 35
πολλῶν αὐτὸ ξυναγαγεῖν εἰκάζοντα καὶ ἀπολογούμενον
ὑπὲρ αὐτῶν οἷον οἱ γραφῆς τραγελάφους καὶ τὰ τοιαῦτα
μιγνύντες γράφουσι. νόησον γὰρ τοιουτονὶ γενόμενον εἴτε

πολλῶν νεῶν πέρι εἴτε μιᾶς· ναύκληρον μεγέθει μὲν καὶ
40 ῥώμῃ ὑπὲρ τοὺς ἐν τῇ νηὶ πάντας, ὑπόκωφον δὲ καὶ B
ὁρῶντα ὡσαύτως βραχύ τι καὶ γιγνώσκοντα περὶ ναυτι-
κῶν ἕτερα τοιαῦτα, τοὺς δὲ ναύτας στασιάζοντας πρὸς
ἀλλήλους περὶ τῆς κυβερνήσεως, ἕκαστον οἰόμενον δεῖν
κυβερνᾶν, μήτε μαθόντα πώποτε τὴν τέχνην μήτε ἔχοντα
45 ἀποδεῖξαι διδάσκαλον ἑαυτοῦ μηδὲ χρόνον ἐν ᾧ ἐμάνθανε,
πρὸς δὲ τούτοις φάσκοντας μηδὲ διδακτὸν εἶναι, ἀλλὰ
καὶ τὸν λέγοντα ὡς διδακτὸν ἑτοίμους κατατέμνειν, C
αὐτοὺς δὲ αὐτῷ ἀεὶ τῷ ναυκλήρῳ περικεχύσθαι δεομένους
καὶ πάντα ποιοῦντας ὅπως ἂν σφίσι τὸ πηδάλιον ἐπι-
50 τρέψῃ, ἐνίοτε δ' ἂν μὴ πείθωσιν ἀλλὰ ἄλλοι μᾶλλον,
τοὺς μὲν ἄλλους ἢ ἀποκτιννύντας ἢ ἐκβάλλοντας ἐκ τῆς
νεώς, τὸν δὲ γενναῖον ναύκληρον μανδραγόρᾳ ἢ μέθῃ ἤ
τινι ἄλλῳ ξυμποδίσαντας τῆς νεὼς ἄρχειν χρωμένους
τοῖς ἐνοῦσι, καὶ πίνοντάς τε καὶ εὐωχουμένους πλεῖν ὡς
55 τὸ εἰκὸς τοὺς τοιούτους, πρὸς δὲ τούτοις ἐπαινοῦντας
ναυτικὸν μὲν καλοῦντας καὶ κυβερνητικὸν καὶ ἐπιστά- D
μενον τὰ κατὰ ναῦν, ὃς ἂν ξυλλαμβάνειν δεινὸς ᾖ, ὅπως
ἄρξουσιν ἢ πείθοντες ἢ βιαζόμενοι τὸν ναύκληρον, τὸν
δὲ μὴ τοιοῦτον ψέγοντας ὡς ἄχρηστον, τοῦ δὲ ἀληθινοῦ
60 κυβερνήτου πέρι μηδ' ἐπαΐοντες, ὅτι ἀνάγκη αὐτῷ τὴν
ἐπιμέλειαν ποιεῖσθαι ἐνιαυτοῦ καὶ ὡρῶν καὶ οὐρανοῦ καὶ
ἄστρων καὶ πνευμάτων καὶ πάντων τῶν τῇ τέχνῃ προση-
κόντων, εἰ μέλλει τῷ ὄντι νεὼς ἀρχικὸς ἔσεσθαι, ὅπως
δὲ κυβερνήσει ἐάν τέ τινες βούλωνται ἐάν τε μή, μήτε E
65 τέχνην τούτου μήτε μελέτην οἰόμενοι δυνατὸν εἶναι
λαβεῖν ἅμα καὶ τὴν κυβερνητικήν. τοιούτων δὲ περὶ τὰς
ναῦς γιγνομένων τὸν ὡς ἀληθῶς κυβερνητικὸν οὐχ ἡγεῖ
ἂν τῷ ὄντι μετεωροσκόπον τε καὶ ἀδολέσχην καὶ ἄχρη-
στόν σφισι καλεῖσθαι ὑπὸ τῶν ἐν ταῖς οὕτω κατεσκευ- 489

ἀσμέναις ναυσὶ πλωτήρων; Καὶ μάλα, ἔφη ὁ ᾿Αδείμαντος. 70
Οὐ δή, ἦν δ᾽ ἐγώ, οἶμαι δεῖσθαί σε ἐξεταζομένην τὴν
εἰκόνα ἰδεῖν, ὅτι ταῖς πόλεσι πρὸς τοὺς ἀληθινοὺς φιλοσόφους τὴν διάθεσιν ἔοικεν, ἀλλὰ μανθάνειν ὃ λέγω.
Καὶ μάλα, ἔφη. Πρῶτον μὲν τοίνυν ἐκεῖνον τὸν θαυ-
μάζοντα, ὅτι οἱ φιλόσοφοι οὐ τιμῶνται ἐν ταῖς πόλεσι, 75
B δίδασκέ τε τὴν εἰκόνα καὶ πειρῶ πείθειν, ὅτι πολὺ ἂν θαυ-
μαστότερον ἦν, εἰ ἐτιμῶντο. ᾿Αλλὰ διδάξω, ἔφη. Καὶ
ὅτι τοίνυν τἀληθῆ λέγει, ὡς ἄχρηστοι τοῖς πολλοῖς οἱ
ἐπιεικέστατοι τῶν ἐν φιλοσοφίᾳ· τῆς μέντοι ἀχρηστίας
τοὺς μὴ χρωμένους κέλευε αἰτιᾶσθαι ἀλλὰ μὴ τοὺς 80
ἐπιεικεῖς. οὐ γὰρ ἔχει φύσιν κυβερνήτην ναυτῶν δεῖσθαι
ἄρχεσθαι ὑφ᾽ αὑτοῦ οὐδὲ τοὺς σοφοὺς ἐπὶ τὰς τῶν
C πλουσίων θύρας ἰέναι, ἀλλ᾽ ὁ τοῦτο κομψευσάμενος
ἐψεύσατο, τὸ δὲ ἀληθὲς πέφυκεν, ἐάν τε πλούσιος ἐάν τε
πένης κάμνῃ, ἀναγκαῖον εἶναι ἐπὶ ἰατρῶν θύρας ἰέναι καὶ 85
πάντα τὸν ἄρχεσθαι δεόμενον ἐπὶ τὰς τοῦ ἄρχειν δυναμένου, οὐ τὸν ἄρχοντα δεῖσθαι τῶν ἀρχομένων ἄρχεσθαι,
οὗ ἂν τῇ ἀληθείᾳ τι ὄφελος ᾖ. ἀλλὰ τοὺς νῦν πολιτικοὺς
ἄρχοντας ἀπεικάζων οἷς ἄρτι ἐλέγομεν ναύταις οὐχ ἁμαρτήσει, καὶ τοὺς ὑπὸ τούτων ἀχρήστους λεγομένους καὶ 90
μετεωρολέσχας τοῖς ὡς ἀληθῶς κυβερνήταις. ᾿Ορθότατα,
ἔφη.

<h1 style="text-align:center">Book VII.</h1>

The Simile of the Cave.

(Socrates, Glaucon.)

Beginning—520 E.

514   Μετὰ ταῦτα δή, εἶπον, ἀπείκασον τοιούτῳ πάθει τὴν
ἡμετέραν φύσιν παιδείας τε πέρι καὶ ἀπαιδευσίας· ἰδὲ γὰρ
ἀνθρώπους οἷον ἐν καταγείῳ οἰκήσει σπηλαιώδει, ἀναπε-
πταμένην πρὸς τὸ φῶς τὴν εἴσοδον ἐχούσῃ μακρὰν παρ᾽

5 ἅπαν τὸ σπήλαιον, ἐν ταύτῃ ἐκ παίδων ὄντας ἐν δεσμοῖς
καὶ τὰ σκέλη καὶ τοὺς αὐχένας, ὥστε μένειν τε αὐτοῦ
εἴς τε τὸ πρόσθεν μόνον ὁρᾶν, κύκλῳ δὲ τὰς κεφαλὰς B
ὑπὸ τοῦ δεσμοῦ ἀδυνάτους περιάγειν, φῶς δὲ αὐτοῖς πυρὸς ἄνωθεν καὶ πόρρωθεν καομένου ὄπισθεν αὐτῶν, με-
10 ταξὺ δὲ τοῦ πυρὸς καὶ τῶν δεσμωτῶν ἐπάνω ὁδόν, παρ'
ἣν ἰδὲ τειχίον παρῳκοδομημένον, ὥσπερ τοῖς θαυματο-
ποιοῖς πρὸ τῶν ἀνθρώπων πρόκειται τὰ παραφράγματα,
ὑπὲρ ὧν τὰ θαύματα δεικνύασιν. Ὁρῶ, ἔφη. Ὅρα τοίνυν παρὰ τοῦτο τὸ τειχίον φέροντας ἀνθρώπους σκεύη τε
15 παντοδαπὰ ὑπερέχοντα τοῦ τειχίου καὶ ἀνδριάντας καὶ 515
ἄλλα ζῷα λίθινά τε καὶ ξύλινα καὶ παντοῖα εἰργασμένα,
οἷον εἰκός, τοὺς μὲν φθεγγομένους, τοὺς δὲ σιγῶντας
τῶν παραφερόντων. Ἄτοπον, ἔφη, λέγεις εἰκόνα καὶ
δεσμώτας ἀτόπους. Ὁμοίους ἡμῖν, ἦν δ' ἐγώ· τοὺς γὰρ
20 τοιούτους πρῶτον μὲν ἑαυτῶν τε καὶ ἀλλήλων οἴει ἄν τι
ἑωρακέναι ἄλλο πλὴν τὰς σκιὰς τὰς ὑπὸ τοῦ πυρὸς εἰς τὸ
καταντικρὺ αὐτῶν τοῦ σπηλαίου προσπιπτούσας; Πῶς
γάρ, ἔφη, εἰ ἀκινήτους γε τὰς κεφαλὰς ἔχειν ἠναγκα-
σμένοι εἶεν διὰ βίου; Τί δὲ τῶν παραφερομένων, οὐ B
25 ταὐτὸν τοῦτο; Τί μήν; Εἰ οὖν διαλέγεσθαι οἷοί τ' εἶεν
πρὸς ἀλλήλους, οὐ ταὐτὰ ἡγεῖ ἂν τὰ παριόντα αὐτοὺς
νομίζειν ὀνομάζειν ἅπερ ὁρῶεν; Ἀνάγκη. Τί δ'; εἰ
καὶ ἠχὼ τὸ δεσμωτήριον ἐκ τοῦ καταντικρὺ ἔχοι, ὁπότε
τις τῶν παριόντων φθέγξαιτο, οἴει ἂν ἄλλο τι αὐτοὺς
30 ἡγεῖσθαι τὸ φθεγγόμενον ἢ τὴν παριοῦσαν σκιάν; Μὰ
Δί' οὐκ ἔγωγ', ἔφη. Παντάπασι δή, ἦν δ' ἐγώ, οἱ
τοιοῦτοι οὐκ ἂν ἄλλο τι νομίζοιεν τὸ ἀληθὲς ἢ τὰς τῶν C
σκευαστῶν σκιάς. Πολλὴ ἀνάγκη, ἔφη. Σκόπει δή, ἦν
δ' ἐγώ, αὐτῶν λύσιν τε καὶ ἴασιν τῶν δεσμῶν καὶ τῆς
35 ἀφροσύνης, οἵα τις ἂν εἴη, εἰ φύσει τοιάδε ξυμβαίνοι

αὐτοῖς· ὁπότε τις λυθείη καὶ ἀναγκάζοιτο ἐξαίφνης
ἀνίστασθαί τε καὶ περιάγειν τὸν αὐχένα καὶ βαδίζειν καὶ
πρὸς τὸ φῶς ἀναβλέπειν, πάντα δὲ ταῦτα ποιῶν ἀλγοῖ
τε καὶ διὰ τὰς μαρμαρυγὰς ἀδυνατοῖ καθορᾶν ἐκεῖνα ὧν
D τότε τὰς σκιὰς ἑώρα, τί ἂν οἴει αὐτὸν εἰπεῖν, εἴ τις αὐτῷ 40
λέγοι ὅτι τότε μὲν ἑώρα φλυαρίας, νῦν δὲ μᾶλλόν τι
ἐγγυτέρω τοῦ ὄντος καὶ πρὸς μᾶλλον ὄντα τετραμμένος
ὀρθότερα βλέποι, καὶ δὴ καὶ ἕκαστον τῶν παριόντων
δεικνὺς αὐτῷ ἀναγκάζοι ἐρωτῶν ἀποκρίνεσθαι ὅ τι ἔστιν ;
οὐκ οἴει αὐτὸν ἀπορεῖν τε ἂν καὶ ἡγεῖσθαι τὰ τότε ὁρώ- 45
μενα ἀληθέστερα ἢ τὰ νῦν δεικνύμενα ; Πολύ γ᾽, ἔφη.
E Οὐκοῦν κἂν εἰ πρὸς αὐτὸ τὸ φῶς ἀναγκάζοι αὐτὸν
βλέπειν, ἀλγεῖν τε ἂν τὰ ὄμματα καὶ φεύγειν ἀπο-
στρεφόμενον πρὸς ἐκεῖνα ἃ δύναται καθορᾶν, καὶ νομίζειν ταῦτα τῷ ὄντι σαφέστερα τῶν δεικνυμένων ; Οὕτως, 50
ἔφη. Εἰ δέ, ἦν δ᾽ ἐγώ, ἐντεῦθεν ἕλκοι τις αὐτὸν βίᾳ διὰ
τραχείας τῆς ἀναβάσεως καὶ ἀνάντους, καὶ μὴ ἀνείη πρὶν
ἐξελκύσειεν εἰς τὸ τοῦ ἡλίου φῶς, ἆρα οὐχὶ ὀδυνᾶσθαί
τε ἂν καὶ ἀγανακτεῖν ἑλκόμενον, καὶ ἐπειδὴ πρὸς τὸ φῶς
516 ἔλθοι, αὐγῆς ἂν ἔχοντα τὰ ὄμματα μεστὰ ὁρᾶν οὐδ᾽ ἂν 55
ἓν δύνασθαι τῶν νῦν λεγομένων ἀληθῶν ; Οὐ γὰρ ἄν,
ἔφη, ἐξαίφνης γε. Συνηθείας δή, οἶμαι, δέοιτ᾽ ἄν, εἰ
μέλλοι τὰ ἄνω ὄψεσθαι· καὶ πρῶτον μὲν τὰς σκιὰς ἂν
ῥᾷστα καθορῷ, καὶ μετὰ τοῦτο ἐν τοῖς ὕδασι τά τε τῶν
ἀνθρώπων καὶ τὰ τῶν ἄλλων εἴδωλα, ὕστερον δὲ αὐτά· 60
ἐκ δὲ τούτων τὰ ἐν τῷ οὐρανῷ καὶ αὐτὸν τὸν οὐρανὸν
νύκτωρ ἂν ῥᾷον θεάσαιτο, προσβλέπων τὸ τῶν ἄστρων
B τε καὶ σελήνης φῶς, ἢ μεθ᾽ ἡμέραν τὸν ἥλιόν τε καὶ τὸ
τοῦ ἡλίου. Πῶς δ᾽ οὔ ; Τελευταῖον δή, οἶμαι, τὸν ἥλιον,
οὐκ ἐν ὕδασιν οὐδ᾽ ἐν ἀλλοτρίᾳ ἕδρᾳ φαντάσματα αὐτοῦ, 65
ἀλλ᾽ αὐτὸν καθ᾽ αὑτὸν ἐν τῇ αὑτοῦ χώρᾳ δύναιτ᾽ ἂν

κατιδεῖν καὶ θεάσασθαι οἷός ἐστιν. Ἀναγκαῖον, ἔφη.
Καὶ μετὰ ταῦτ᾽ ἂν ἤδη συλλογίζοιτο περὶ αὐτοῦ, ὅτι αὐτὸς
ὁ τάς τε ὥρας παρέχων καὶ ἐνιαυτοὺς καὶ πάντα ἐπιτρο-
70 πεύων τὰ ἐν τῷ ὁρωμένῳ τόπῳ, καὶ ἐκείνων ὧν σφεῖς C
ἑώρων τρόπον τινὰ πάντων αἴτιος. Δῆλον, ἔφη, ὅτι ἐπὶ
ταῦτα ἂν μετ᾽ ἐκεῖνα ἔλθοι. Τί οὖν ; ἀναμιμνησκόμενον ·
αὐτὸν τῆς πρώτης οἰκήσεως καὶ τῆς ἐκεῖ σοφίας καὶ τῶν
τότε ξυνδεσμωτῶν οὐκ ἂν οἴει αὐτὸν μὲν εὐδαιμονίζειν
75 τῆς μεταβολῆς, τοὺς δὲ ἐλεεῖν ; Καὶ μάλα. Τιμαὶ δὲ καὶ
ἔπαινοι εἴ τινες αὐτοῖς ἦσαν τότε παρ᾽ ἀλλήλων καὶ γέρα
τῷ ὀξύτατα καθορῶντι τὰ παριόντα, καὶ μνημονεύοντι
μάλιστα ὅσα τε πρότερα αὐτῶν καὶ ὕστερα εἰώθει καὶ D
ἅμα πορεύεσθαι, καὶ ἐκ τούτων δὴ δυνατώτατα ἀπομαν-
80 τευομένῳ τὸ μέλλον ἥξειν, δοκεῖς ἂν αὐτὸν ἐπιθυμητικῶς
αὐτῶν ἔχειν καὶ ζηλοῦν τοὺς παρ᾽ ἐκείνοις τιμωμένους τε
καὶ ἐνδυναστεύοντας, ἢ τὸ τοῦ Ὁμήρου ἂν πεπονθέναι
καὶ σφόδρα βούλεσθαι ἐπάρουρον ἐόντα θητευέμεν
ἄλλῳ ἀνδρὶ παρ᾽ ἀκλήρῳ καὶ ὁτιοῦν ἂν πεπονθέναι
85 μᾶλλον ἢ ᾽κεῖνά τε δοξάζειν καὶ ἐκείνως ζῆν ; Οὕτως,
ἔφη, ἔγωγε οἶμαι, πᾶν μᾶλλον πεπονθέναι ἂν δέξασθαι E
ἢ ζῆν ἐκείνως. Καὶ τόδε δὴ ἐννόησον, ἦν δ᾽ ἐγώ. εἰ πάλιν ὁ τοιοῦτος καταβὰς εἰς τὸν αὐτὸν θᾶκον καθίζοιτο, ἆρ᾽
οὐ σκότους ἂν ἀνάπλεως σχοίη τοὺς ὀφθαλμούς, ἐξαίφνης
90 ἥκων ἐκ τοῦ ἡλίου ; Καὶ μάλα γ᾽, ἔφη. Τὰς δὲ δὴ σκιὰς
ἐκείνας πάλιν εἰ δέοι αὐτὸν γνωματεύοντα διαμιλλᾶσθαι
τοῖς ἀεὶ δεσμώταις ἐκείνοις, ἐν ᾧ ἀμβλυώττει, πρὶν κατα- 517
στῆναι τὰ ὄμματα, οὗτος δ᾽ ὁ χρόνος μὴ πάνυ ὀλίγος
εἴη τῆς συνηθείας, ἆρ᾽ οὐ γέλωτ᾽ ἂν παράσχοι, καὶ λέγοιτο
95 ἂν περὶ αὐτοῦ, ὡς ἀναβὰς ἄνω διεφθαρμένος ἥκει τὰ
ὄμματα, καὶ ὅτι οὐκ ἄξιον οὐδὲ πειρᾶσθαι ἄνω ἰέναι ;
καὶ τὸν ἐπιχειροῦντα λύειν τε καὶ ἀνάγειν, εἴ πως ἐν

M

ταῖς χερσὶ δύναιντο λαβεῖν, καὶ ἀποκτείνειαν ἄν ; Σφόδρα γ', ἔφη. Ταύτην τοίνυν, ἦν δ' ἐγώ, τὴν εἰκόνα, ὦ
φίλε Γλαύκων, προσαπτέον ἅπασαν τοῖς ἔμπροσθεν 100
B λεγομένοις, τὴν μὲν δι' ὄψεως φαινομένην ἕδραν τῇ τοῦ
δεσμωτηρίου οἰκήσει ἀφομοιοῦντα, τὸ δὲ τοῦ πυρὸς ἐν
αὐτῇ φῶς τῇ τοῦ ἡλίου δυνάμει· τὴν δὲ ἄνω ἀνάβασιν
καὶ θέαν τῶν ἄνω τὴν εἰς τὸν νοητὸν τόπον τῆς ψυχῆς
ἄνοδον τιθεὶς οὐχ ἁμαρτήσει τῆς γ' ἐμῆς ἐλπίδος, ἐπειδὴ 105
ταύτης ἐπιθυμεῖς ἀκούειν. θεὸς δέ που οἶδεν, εἰ ἀληθὴς
οὖσα τυγχάνει. τὰ δ' οὖν ἐμοὶ φαινόμενα οὕτω φαίνεται,
ἐν τῷ γνωστῷ τελευταία ἡ τοῦ ἀγαθοῦ ἰδέα καὶ μόγις
C ὁρᾶσθαι, ὀφθεῖσα δὲ συλλογιστέα εἶναι ὡς ἄρα πᾶσι πάντων αὕτη ὀρθῶν τε καὶ καλῶν αἰτία, ἔν τε ὁρατῷ φῶς 110
καὶ τὸν τούτου κύριον τεκοῦσα, ἔν τε νοητῷ αὐτὴ κυρία
ἀλήθειαν καὶ νοῦν παρασχομένη, καὶ ὅτι δεῖ ταύτην ἰδεῖν
τὸν μέλλοντα ἐμφρόνως πράξειν ἢ ἰδίᾳ ἢ δημοσίᾳ. Ξυν-
οίομαι, ἔφη, καὶ ἐγώ, ὅν γε δὴ τρόπον δύναμαι. Ἴθι
τοίνυν, ἦν δ' ἐγώ, καὶ τόδε ξυννοιήθητι καὶ μὴ θαυμάσῃς, 115
ὅτι οἱ ἐνταῦθα ἐλθόντες οὐκ ἐθέλουσι τὰ τῶν ἀνθρώπων
D πράττειν, ἀλλ' ἄνω ἀεὶ ἐπείγονται αὐτῶν αἱ ψυχαὶ
διατρίβειν. εἰκὸς γάρ που οὕτως, εἴπερ αὖ κατὰ τὴν προ-
ειρημένην εἰκόνα τοῦτ' ἔχει. Εἰκὸς μέντοι, ἔφη. Τί δέ ;
τόδε οἴει τι θαυμαστόν, εἰ ἀπὸ θείων, ἦν δ' ἐγώ, θεω- 120
ριῶν ἐπὶ τὰ ἀνθρώπειά τις ἐλθὼν κακὰ ἀσχημονεῖ τε καὶ
φαίνεται σφόδρα γελοῖος ἔτι ἀμβλυώττων καὶ πρὶν ἱκανῶς
συνήθης γενέσθαι τῷ παρόντι σκότῳ ἀναγκαζόμενος ἐν
δικαστηρίοις ἢ ἄλλοθί που ἀγωνίζεσθαι περὶ τῶν τοῦ
δικαίου σκιῶν ἢ ἀγαλμάτων ὧν αἱ σκιαί, καὶ διαμιλλᾶ- 125
E σθαι περὶ τούτου, ὅπῃ ποτὲ ὑπολαμβάνεται ταῦτα ὑπὸ
τῶν αὐτὴν δικαιοσύνην μὴ πώποτε ἰδόντων ; Οὐδ' ὁπωσ-
518 τιοῦν θαυμαστόν, ἔφη. Ἀλλ' εἰ νοῦν γε ἔχοι τις, ἦν δ'

ἐγώ, μεμνῇτ' ἄν, ὅτι διτταὶ καὶ ἀπὸ διττῶν γίγνονται
130 ἐπιταράξεις ὄμμασιν, ἔκ τε φωτὸς εἰς σκότος μεθισταμέ-
νων καὶ ἐκ σκότους εἰς φῶς. ταὐτὰ δὲ ταῦτα νομίσας
γίγνεσθαι καὶ περὶ ψυχήν, ὁπότε ἴδοι θορυβουμένην τινὰ
καὶ ἀδυνατοῦσάν τι καθορᾶν, οὐκ ἂν ἀλογίστως γελῷ,
ἀλλ' ἐπισκοποῖ ἄν, πότερον ἐκ φανοτέρου βίου ἥκουσα
135 ὑπὸ ἀηθείας ἐσκότωται ἢ ἐξ ἀμαθίας πλείονος εἰς φανότερον ἰοῦσα ὑπὸ λαμπροτέρου μαρμαρυγῆς ἐμπέπλησται, B
καὶ οὕτω δὴ τὴν μὲν εὐδαιμονίσειεν ἂν τοῦ πάθους τε
καὶ βίου, τὴν δὲ ἐλεήσειεν, καὶ εἰ γελᾶν ἐπ' αὐτῇ βού-
λοιτο, ἧττον ἂν καταγέλαστος ὁ γέλως αὐτῷ εἴη ἢ
140 ὁ ἐπὶ τῇ ἄνωθεν ἐκ φωτὸς ἡκούσῃ. Καὶ μάλα, ἔφη,
μετρίως λέγεις. Δεῖ δή, εἶπον, ἡμᾶς τοιόνδε νομίσαι
περὶ αὐτῶν, εἰ ταῦτ' ἀληθῆ, τὴν παιδείαν οὐχ οἵαν τινὲς
ἐπαγγελλόμενοί φασιν εἶναι τοιαύτην καὶ εἶναι. φασὶ δέ
που οὐκ ἐνούσης ἐν τῇ ψυχῇ ἐπιστήμης σφεῖς ἐντιθέναι, C
145 οἷον τυφλοῖς ὀφθαλμοῖς ὄψιν ἐντιθέντες. Φασὶ γὰρ οὖν,
ἔφη. Ὁ δέ γε νῦν λόγος, ἦν δ' ἐγώ, σημαίνει ταύτην τὴν
ἐνοῦσαν ἑκάστου δύναμιν ἐν τῇ ψυχῇ καὶ τὸ ὄργανον ᾧ
καταμανθάνει ἕκαστος, οἷον εἰ ὄμμα μὴ δυνατὸν ἦν ἄλλως
ἢ ξὺν ὅλῳ τῷ σώματι στρέφειν πρὸς τὸ φανὸν ἐκ τοῦ
150 σκοτώδους, οὕτω ξὺν ὅλῃ τῇ ψυχῇ ἐκ τοῦ γιγνομένου
περιακτέον εἶναι, ἕως ἂν εἰς τὸ ὂν καὶ τοῦ ὄντος τὸ φα-
νότατον δυνατὴ γένηται ἀνασχέσθαι θεωμένη. τοῦτο δ'
εἶναί φαμεν τἀγαθόν. ἦ γάρ; Ναί. Τούτου τοίνυν, ἦν D
δ' ἐγώ, αὐτοῦ τέχνη ἂν εἴη, τῆς περιαγωγῆς, τίνα τρό-
155 πον ὡς ῥᾷστά τε καὶ ἀνυσιμώτατα μεταστραφήσεται, οὐ
τοῦ ἐμποιῆσαι αὐτῷ τὸ ὁρᾶν, ἀλλ' ὡς ἔχοντι μὲν αὐτό,
οὐκ ὀρθῶς δὲ τετραμμένῳ οὐδὲ βλέποντι οἷ ἔδει, τοῦτο
διαμηχανήσασθαι. Ἔοικε γάρ, ἔφη. Αἱ μὲν τοίνυν ἄλλαι
ἀρεταὶ καλούμεναι ψυχῆς κινδυνεύουσιν ἐγγύς τι εἶναι

τῶν τοῦ σώματος· τῷ ὄντι γὰρ οὐκ ἐνοῦσαι πρότερον ὕστε- 160
E ρον ἐμποιεῖσθαι ἔθεσι καὶ ἀσκήσεσιν· ἡ δὲ τοῦ φρονῆσαι
παντὸς μᾶλλον θειοτέρου τινὸς τυγχάνει, ὡς ἔοικεν, οὖσα,
ὃ τὴν μὲν δύναμιν οὐδέποτε ἀπόλλυσιν, ὑπὸ δὲ τῆς περι-
519 αγωγῆς χρήσιμον καὶ ὠφέλιμον καὶ ἄχρηστον αὖ καὶ
βλαβερὸν γίγνεται. ἢ οὔπω ἐννενόηκας, τῶν λεγομένων 165
πονηρῶν μέν, σοφῶν δέ, ὡς δριμὺ μὲν βλέπει τὸ ψυχάριον καὶ ὀξέως διορᾷ ταῦτα ἐφ᾽ ἃ τέτραπται, ὡς οὐ φαύλην ἔχον τὴν ὄψιν, κακίᾳ δ᾽ ἠναγκασμένον ὑπηρετεῖν,
ὥστε ὅσῳ ἂν ὀξύτερον βλέπῃ, τοσούτῳ πλείω κακὰ ἐργα-
ζόμενον ; Πάνυ μὲν οὖν, ἔφη. Τοῦτο μέντοι, ἦν δ᾽ ἐγώ, 170
τὸ τῆς τοιαύτης φύσεως εἰ ἐκ παιδὸς εὐθὺς κοπτόμενον
περιεκόπη τὰς τῆς γενέσεως ξυγγενεῖς ὥσπερ μολυβδίδας,
B αἳ δὴ ἐδωδαῖς τε καὶ τοιούτων ἡδοναῖς τε καὶ λιχνείαις
προσφυεῖς γιγνόμεναι [περὶ τὰ] κάτω στρέφουσι τὴν τῆς
ψυχῆς ὄψιν· ὧν εἰ ἀπαλλαγὲν περιεστρέφετο εἰς τἀληθῆ, 175
καὶ ἐκεῖνα ἂν τὸ αὐτὸ τοῦτο τῶν αὐτῶν ἀνθρώπων ὀξύτατα
ἑώρα, ὥσπερ καὶ ἐφ᾽ ἃ νῦν τέτραπται. Εἰκός γε, ἔφη.
Τί δέ ; τόδε οὐκ εἰκός, ἦν δ᾽ ἐγώ, καὶ ἀνάγκη ἐκ τῶν
προειρημένων, μήτε τοὺς ἀπαιδεύτους καὶ ἀληθείας ἀπεί-
C ρους ἱκανῶς ἄν ποτε πόλιν ἐπιτροπεῦσαι, μήτε τοὺς ἐν 180
παιδείᾳ ἐωμένους διατρίβειν διὰ τέλους, τοὺς μὲν ὅτι
σκοπὸν ἐν τῷ βίῳ οὐκ ἔχουσιν ἕνα, οὗ στοχαζομένους δεῖ
ἅπαντα πράττειν ἃ ἂν πράττωσιν ἰδίᾳ τε καὶ δημοσίᾳ,
τοὺς δὲ ὅτι ἑκόντες εἶναι οὐ πράξουσιν ἡγούμενοι ἐν
μακάρων νήσοις ζῶντες ἔτι ἀπῳκίσθαι ; Ἀληθῆ, ἔφη. 185
Ἡμέτερον δὴ ἔργον, ἦν δ᾽ ἐγώ, τῶν οἰκιστῶν τάς τε
βελτίστας φύσεις ἀναγκάσαι ἀφικέσθαι πρὸς τὸ μάθημα
ὃ ἐν τῷ πρόσθεν ἔφαμεν εἶναι μέγιστον, ἰδεῖν τε τὸ
D ἀγαθὸν καὶ ἀναβῆναι ἐκείνην τὴν ἀνάβασιν, καὶ ἐπειδὰν
ἀναβάντες ἱκανῶς ἴδωσι, μὴ ἐπιτρέπειν αὐτοῖς ὃ νῦν ἐπι- 190

τρέπεται. Τὸ ποῖον δή; Τὸ αὑτοῦ, ἦν δ' ἐγώ, καταμένειν
καὶ μὴ ἐθέλειν πάλιν καταβαίνειν παρ' ἐκείνους τοὺς
δεσμώτας μηδὲ μετέχειν τῶν παρ' ἐκείνοις πόνων τε καὶ
τιμῶν, εἴτε φαυλότεραι εἴτε σπουδαιότεραι. Ἔπειτ', ἔφη,
195 ἀδικήσομεν αὐτούς, καὶ ποιήσομεν χεῖρον ζῆν, δυνατὸν
αὐτοῖς ὂν ἄμεινον; Ἐπελάθου, ἦν δ' ἐγώ, πάλιν, ὦ φίλε, Ε
ὅτι νόμῳ οὐ τοῦτο μέλει, ὅπως ἕν τι γένος ἐν πόλει διαφερόντως εὖ πράξει, ἀλλ' ἐν ὅλῃ τῇ πόλει τοῦτο μη-
χανᾶται ἐγγενέσθαι, ξυναρμόττων τοὺς πολίτας πειθοῖ τε
200 καὶ ἀνάγκῃ, ποιῶν μεταδιδόναι ἀλλήλοις τῆς ὠφελείας
ἣν ἂν ἕκαστοι τὸ κοινὸν δυνατοὶ ὦσιν ὠφελεῖν, καὶ αὐτὸς 520
ἐμποιῶν τοιούτους ἄνδρας ἐν τῇ πόλει, οὐχ ἵνα ἀφίῃ
τρέπεσθαι ὅπῃ ἕκαστος βούλεται, ἀλλ' ἵνα καταχρῆται
αὐτὸς αὐτοῖς ἐπὶ τὸν ξύνδεσμον τῆς πόλεως. Ἀληθῆ,
205 ἔφη· ἐπελαθόμην γάρ. Σκέψαι τοίνυν, εἶπον, ὦ Γλαύκων, ὅτι οὐδ' ἀδικήσομεν τοὺς παρ' ἡμῖν φιλοσόφους
γιγνομένους, ἀλλὰ δίκαια πρὸς αὐτοὺς ἐροῦμεν, προσ-
αναγκάζοντες τῶν ἄλλων ἐπιμελεῖσθαί τε καὶ φυλάττειν.
ἐροῦμεν γὰρ ὅτι οἱ μὲν ἐν ταῖς ἄλλαις πόλεσι τοιοῦτοι Β
210 γιγνόμενοι εἰκότως οὐ μετέχουσι τῶν ἐν αὐταῖς πόνων·
αὐτόματοι γὰρ ἐμφύονται ἀκούσης τῆς ἐν ἑκάστῃ πολιτείας, δίκην δ' ἔχει τό γε αὐτοφυὲς μηδενὶ τροφὴν
ὀφεῖλον μηδ' ἐκτίνειν τῷ προθυμεῖσθαι τὰ τροφεῖα· ὑμᾶς
δ' ἡμεῖς ὑμῖν τε αὐτοῖς τῇ τε ἄλλῃ πόλει ὥσπερ ἐν
215 σμήνεσιν ἡγεμόνας τε καὶ βασιλέας ἐγεννήσαμεν, ἄμεινόν τε καὶ τελεώτερον ἐκείνων πεπαιδευμένους καὶ C
μᾶλλον δυνατοὺς ἀμφοτέρων μετέχειν. καταβατέον οὖν
ἐν μέρει ἑκάστῳ εἰς τὴν τῶν ἄλλων ξυνοίκησιν καὶ
ξυνεθιστέον τὰ σκοτεινὰ θεάσασθαι· ξυνεθιζόμενοι γὰρ
220 μυρίῳ βέλτιον ὄψεσθε τῶν ἐκεῖ καὶ γνώσεσθε ἕκαστα
τὰ εἴδωλα ἄττα ἐστὶ καὶ ὧν, διὰ τὸ τἀληθῆ ἑωρακέναι

καλῶν τε καὶ δικαίων καὶ ἀγαθῶν πέρι. καὶ οὕτω ὕπαρ
ἡμῖν καὶ ὑμῖν ἡ πόλις οἰκήσεται, ἀλλ' οὐκ ὄναρ, ὡς νῦν
αἱ πολλαὶ ὑπὸ σκιαμαχούντων τε πρὸς ἀλλήλους καὶ
D στασιαζόντων περὶ τοῦ ἄρχειν οἰκοῦνται, ὡς μεγάλου 225
τινὸς ἀγαθοῦ ὄντος. τὸ δέ που ἀληθὲς ὧδε ἔχει· ἐν
πόλει ᾗ ἥκιστα πρόθυμοι ἄρχειν οἱ μέλλοντες ἄρξειν,
ταύτην ἄριστα καὶ ἀστασιαστότατα ἀνάγκη οἰκεῖσθαι, τὴν
δ' ἐναντίους ἄρχοντας σχοῦσαν ἐναντίως. Πάνυ μὲν οὖν,
ἔφη. Ἀπειθήσουσιν οὖν ἡμῖν, οἴει, οἱ τρόφιμοι ταῦτ' 230
ἀκούοντες, καὶ οὐκ ἐθελήσουσι ξυμπονεῖν ἐν τῇ πόλει
ἕκαστοι ἐν μέρει, τὸν δὲ πολὺν χρόνον μετ' ἀλλήλων
E οἰκεῖν ἐν τῷ καθαρῷ; Ἀδύνατον, ἔφη· δίκαια γὰρ δὴ
δικαίοις ἐπιτάξομεν· παντὸς μὴν μᾶλλον ὡς ἐπ' ἀναγκαῖον αὐτῶν ἕκαστος εἶσι τὸ ἄρχειν, τοὐναντίον τῶν νῦν 235
ἐν ἑκάστῃ πόλει ἀρχόντων.

Book VIII.

Democracy.

(SOCRATES, ADEIMANTUS.)

557 A—558 C.

557 Δημοκρατία δή, οἶμαι, γίγνεται, ὅταν οἱ πένητες νικήσαντες τοὺς μὲν ἀποκτείνωσι τῶν ἑτέρων, τοὺς δὲ ἐκ-
βάλωσι, τοῖς δὲ λοιποῖς ἐξ ἴσου μεταδῶσι πολιτείας τε
καὶ ἀρχῶν [καὶ ὡς τὸ πολὺ ἀπὸ κλήρων αἱ ἀρχαὶ ἐν αὐτῇ
γίγνονται]. Ἔστι γάρ, ἔφη, αὕτη ἡ κατάστασις δημο- 5
κρατίας, ἐάν τε καὶ δι' ὅπλων γένηται ἐάν τε καὶ διὰ φόβον
ὑπεξελθόντων τῶν ἑτέρων.

Τίνα δὴ οὖν, ἦν δ' ἐγώ, οὗτοι τρόπον οἰκοῦσι ; καὶ
B ποία τις ἡ τοιαύτη αὖ πολιτεία ; δῆλον γὰρ ὅτι ὁ τοιοῦ-
τος ἀνὴρ δημοκρατικός τις ἀναφανήσεται. Δῆλον, ἔφη. 10
Οὐκοῦν πρῶτον μὲν δὴ ἐλεύθεροι, καὶ ἐλευθερίας ἡ πόλις

μεστὴ καὶ παρρησίας γίγνεται, καὶ ἐξουσία ἐν αὐτῇ ποιεῖν
ὅ τί τις βούλεται; Λέγεταί γε δή, ἔφη. Ὅπου δέ γε
ἐξουσία, δῆλον ὅτι ἰδίαν ἕκαστος ἂν κατασκευὴν τοῦ αὐτοῦ βίου κατασκευάζοιτο ἐν αὐτῇ, ἥτις ἕκαστον ἀρέσκοι.
Δῆλον. Παντοδαποὶ δὴ ἂν, οἶμαι, ἐν ταύτῃ τῇ πολι-C
τείᾳ μάλιστ' ἐγγίγνοιντο ἄνθρωποι. Πῶς γὰρ οὔ; Κινδυνεύει, ἦν δ' ἐγώ, καλλίστη αὕτη τῶν πολιτειῶν εἶναι·
ὥσπερ ἱμάτιον ποικίλον πᾶσιν ἄνθεσι πεποικιλμένον, οὕτω
καὶ αὕτη πᾶσιν ἤθεσι πεποικιλμένη καλλίστη ἂν φαί-
νοιτο· καὶ ἴσως μέν, ἦν δ' ἐγώ, καὶ ταύτην, ὥσπερ οἱ
παῖδές τε καὶ αἱ γυναῖκες τὰ ποικίλα θεώμενοι, καλλίστην ἂν πολλοὶ κρίνειαν. Καὶ μάλ', ἔφη. Καὶ ἔστι γε,
ὦ μακάριε, ἦν δ' ἐγώ, ἐπιτήδειον ζητεῖν ἐν αὐτῇ πολι-D
τείαν. Τί δή; Ὅτι πάντα γένη πολιτειῶν ἔχει διὰ τὴν
ἐξουσίαν, καὶ κινδυνεύει τῷ βουλομένῳ πόλιν κατασκευά-
ζειν, ὃ νῦν δὴ ἡμεῖς ἐποιοῦμεν, ἀναγκαῖον εἶναι εἰς δη-
μοκρατουμένην ἐλθόντι πόλιν, ὃς ἂν αὐτὸν ἀρέσκῃ τρόπος, τοῦτον ἐκλέξασθαι, ὥσπερ εἰς παντοπώλιον ἀφικομένῳ πολιτειῶν, καὶ ἐκλεξαμένῳ οὕτω κατοικίζειν. Ἴσως
γοῦν, ἔφη, οὐκ ἂν ἀποροῖ παραδειγμάτων. Τὸ δὲ μηδε-E
μίαν ἀνάγκην, εἶπον, εἶναι ἄρχειν ἐν ταύτῃ τῇ πόλει,
μηδ' ἂν ᾖς ἱκανὸς ἄρχειν, μηδὲ αὖ ἄρχεσθαι, ἐὰν μὴ
βούλῃ, μηδὲ πολεμεῖν πολεμούντων, μηδὲ εἰρήνην ἄγειν
τῶν ἄλλων ἀγόντων, ἐὰν μὴ ἐπιθυμῇς εἰρήνης, μηδὲ αὖ,
ἐάν τις ἄρχειν νόμος σε διακωλύῃ ἢ δικάζειν, μηδὲν
ἧττον καὶ ἄρχειν καὶ δικάζειν, ἐὰν αὐτῷ σοι ἐπίῃ, ἆρ'558
οὐ θεσπεσία καὶ ἡδεῖα ἡ τοιαύτη διαγωγὴ ἐν τῷ παραυτίκα; Ἴσως, ἔφη, ἔν γε τούτῳ. Τί δέ; ἡ πραότης ἐνίων
τῶν δικασθέντων οὐ κομψή; ἢ οὔπω εἶδες ἐν τοιαύτῃ
πολιτείᾳ, ἀνθρώπων καταψηφισθέντος θανάτου ἢ φυγῆς,
οὐδὲν ἧττον αὐτῶν μενόντων τε καὶ ἀναστρεφομένων ἐν

μέσῳ, καὶ ὡς οὔτε φροντίζοντος οὔτε ὁρῶντος οὐδενὸς
περινοστεῖ ὥσπερ ἥρως ; Καὶ πολλούς γ’, ἔφη. Ἡ δὲ
B συγγνώμη καὶ οὐδ’ ὁπωστιοῦν σμικρολογία αὐτῆς, ἀλλὰ 45
καταφρόνησις ὧν ἡμεῖς ἐλέγομεν σεμνύνοντες, ὅτε τὴν
πόλιν ᾠκίζομεν, ὡς εἰ μή τις ὑπερβεβλημένην φύσιν ἔχοι,
οὔποτ’ ἂν γένοιτο ἀνὴρ ἀγαθός, εἰ μὴ παῖς ὢν εὐθὺς
παίζοι ἐν καλοῖς καὶ ἐπιτηδεύοι τὰ τοιαῦτα πάντα, ὡς μεγαλοπρεπῶς καταπατήσασ’ ἅπαντα ταῦτα οὐδὲν φροντίζει, 50
ἐξ ὁποίων ἄν τις ἐπιτηδευμάτων ἐπὶ τὰ πολιτικὰ ἰὼν
C πράττῃ, ἀλλὰ τιμᾷ, ἐὰν φῇ μόνον εὔνους εἶναι τῷ πλήθει. Πάνυ γ’, ἔφη, γενναία. Ταῦτά τε δή, ἔφην, ἔχοι
ἂν καὶ τούτων ἄλλα ἀδελφὰ δημοκρατία, καὶ εἴη, ὡς
ἔοικεν, ἡδεῖα πολιτεία καὶ ἄναρχος καὶ ποικίλη, ἰσότητά 55
τινα ὁμοίως ἴσοις τε καὶ ἀνίσοις διανέμουσα. Καὶ μάλ’,
ἔφη, γνώριμα λέγεις.

Democracy becomes Anarchy.

(SOCRATES, ADEIMANTUS.)

562 A—563 E.

Ἡ καλλίστη δή, ἦν δ’ ἐγώ, πολιτεία τε καὶ ὁ κάλλιστος ἀνὴρ λοιπὰ ἂν ἡμῖν εἴη διελθεῖν, τυραννίς τε καὶ
τύραννος. Κομιδῇ γ’, ἔφη. Φέρε δή, τίς τρόπος τυραννίδος, ὦ φίλε ἑταῖρε, γίγνεται ; ὅτι μὲν γὰρ ἐκ δημοκρατίας μεταβάλλει σχεδὸν δῆλον. Δῆλον. Ἆρ’ οὖν τρόπον 5
τινὰ τὸν αὐτὸν ἔκ τε ὀλιγαρχίας δημοκρατία γίγνεται καὶ
B ἐκ δημοκρατίας τυραννίς ; Πῶς ; Ὁ προὔθεντο, ἦν δ’ ἐγώ,
ἀγαθόν, καὶ δι’ οὗ ἡ ὀλιγαρχία καθίστατο—τοῦτο δ’ ἦν
ὑπέρπλουτος· ἦ γάρ ; Ναί. Ἡ πλούτου τοίνυν ἀπληστία καὶ ἡ τῶν ἄλλων ἀμέλεια διὰ χρηματισμὸν αὐτὴν 10
ἀπώλλυ. Ἀληθῆ, ἔφη. Ἆρ’ οὖν καὶ ὁ δημοκρατία ὁρίζεται ἀγαθόν, ἡ τούτου ἀπληστία καὶ ταύτην καταλύει ;

Λέγεις δ' αὐτὴν τί ὁρίζεσθαι ; Τὴν ἐλευθερίαν, εἶπον.
τοῦτο γάρ που ἐν δημοκρατουμένῃ πόλει ἀκούσαις ἂν ὡς C
15 ἔχει τε κάλλιστον καὶ διὰ ταῦτα ἐν μόνῃ ταύτῃ ἄξιον
οἰκεῖν ὅστις φύσει ἐλεύθερος. Λέγεται γὰρ δή, ἔφη, καὶ
πολὺ τοῦτο τὸ ῥῆμα. Ἆρ' οὖν, ἦν δ' ἐγώ, ὅπερ ᾖα
νῦν δὴ ἐρῶν, ἡ τοῦ τοιούτου ἀπληστία καὶ ἡ τῶν ἄλλων
ἀμέλεια καὶ ταύτην τὴν πολιτείαν μεθίστησί τε καὶ πα-
20 ρασκευάζει τυραννίδος δεηθῆναι ; Πῶς ; ἔφη. Ὅταν,
οἶμαι, δημοκρατουμένη πόλις ἐλευθερίας διψήσασα κακῶν
οἰνοχόων προστατούντων τύχῃ, καὶ πορρωτέρω τοῦ δέον- D
τος ἀκράτου αὐτῆς μεθυσθῇ, τοὺς ἄρχοντας δή, ἂν μὴ
πάνυ πρᾶοι ὦσι καὶ πολλὴν παρέχωσι τὴν ἐλευθερίαν,
25 κολάζει αἰτιωμένη ὡς μιαρούς τε καὶ ὀλιγαρχικούς. Δρῶσι
γάρ, ἔφη, τοῦτο. Τοὺς δέ γε, εἶπον, τῶν ἀρχόντων
κατηκόους προπηλακίζει ὡς ἐθελοδούλους τε καὶ οὐδὲν
ὄντας, τοὺς δὲ ἄρχοντας μὲν ἀρχομένοις, ἀρχομένους δὲ
ἄρχουσιν ὁμοίους ἰδίᾳ τε καὶ δημοσίᾳ ἐπαινεῖ τε καὶ
30 τιμᾷ. ἆρ' οὐκ ἀνάγκη ἐν τοιαύτῃ πόλει ἐπὶ πᾶν τὸ τῆς E
ἐλευθερίας ἰέναι ; Πῶς γὰρ οὔ ; Καὶ καταδύεσθαί γε,
ἦν δ' ἐγώ, ὦ φίλε, εἴς τε τὰς ἰδίας οἰκίας καὶ τελευτᾶν
μέχρι τῶν θηρίων τὴν ἀναρχίαν ἐμφυομένην. Πῶς, ἦ δ'
ὅς, τὸ τοιοῦτον λέγομεν ; Οἷον, ἔφην, πατέρα μὲν ἐθί-
35 ζεσθαι παιδὶ ὅμοιον γίγνεσθαι καὶ φοβεῖσθαι τοὺς υἱεῖς,
υἱὸν δὲ πατρί, καὶ μήτε αἰσχύνεσθαι μήτε δεδιέναι τοὺς
γονέας, ἵνα δὴ ἐλεύθερος ᾖ· μέτοικον δὲ ἀστῷ καὶ ἀστὸν 563
μετοίκῳ ἐξισοῦσθαι, καὶ ξένον ὡσαύτως. Γίγνεται γὰρ
οὕτως, ἔφη. Ταῦτά τε, ἦν δ' ἐγώ, καὶ σμικρὰ τοιάδε
40 ἄλλα γίγνεται· διδάσκαλός τε ἐν τῷ τοιούτῳ φοιτητὰς
φοβεῖται καὶ θωπεύει, φοιτηταί τε διδασκάλων ὀλιγω-
ροῦσιν, οὕτω δὲ καὶ παιδαγωγῶν· καὶ ὅλως οἱ μὲν νέοι
πρεσβυτέροις ἀπεικάζονται καὶ διαμιλλῶνται καὶ ἐν λό-

γοις καὶ ἐν ἔργοις, οἱ δὲ γέροντες ξυγκαθιέντες τοῖς νέοις
B εὐτραπελίας τε καὶ χαριεντισμοῦ ἐμπίπλανται, μιμούμενοι 45
τοὺς νέους, ἵνα δὴ μὴ δοκῶσιν ἀηδεῖς εἶναι μηδὲ δεσπο-
τικοί. Πάνυ μὲν οὖν, ἔφη. Τὸ δέ γε, ἦν δ' ἐγώ, ἔσχατον, ὦ φίλε, τῆς ἐλευθερίας τοῦ πλήθους, ὅσον γίγνεται
ἐν τῇ τοιαύτῃ πόλει, ὅταν δὴ οἱ ἐωνημένοι καὶ αἱ ἐωνη-
μέναι μηδὲν ἧττον ἐλεύθεροι ὦσι τῶν πριαμένων. ἐν γυ- 50
ναιξὶ δὲ πρὸς ἄνδρας καὶ ἀνδράσι πρὸς γυναῖκας ὅση ἡ
ἰσονομία καὶ ἐλευθερία γίγνεται, ὀλίγου ἐπελαθόμεθ'
C εἰπεῖν. Οὐκοῦν κατ' Αἰσχύλον, ἔφη, ἐροῦμεν ὅ τι νῦν ἦλθ'
ἐπὶ στόμα; Πάνυ γε, εἶπον· καὶ ἔγωγε οὕτω λέγω· τὸ μὲν
γὰρ τῶν θηρίων τῶν ὑπὸ τοῖς ἀνθρώποις ὅσῳ ἐλευθερώ- 55
τερά ἐστιν ἐνταῦθα ἢ ἐν ἄλλῃ, οὐκ ἄν τις πείθοιτο ἄπειρος. ἀτεχνῶς γὰρ αἵ τε κύνες κατὰ τὴν παροιμίαν οἷαί-
περ αἱ δέσποιναι, γίγνονταί τε δὴ καὶ ἵπποι καὶ ὄνοι,
πάνυ ἐλευθέρως καὶ σεμνῶς εἰθισμένοι πορεύεσθαι, κατὰ
τὰς ὁδοὺς ἐμβάλλοντες τῷ ἀεὶ ἀπαντῶντι, ἐὰν μὴ ἐξίστη- 60
D ται· καὶ τἆλλα πάντα οὕτω μεστὰ ἐλευθερίας γίγνεται.
Τὸ ἐμόν γ', ἔφη, ἐμοὶ λέγεις ὄναρ· αὐτὸς γὰρ εἰς ἀγρὸν
πορευόμενος θαμὰ αὐτὸ πάσχω. Τὸ δὲ δὴ κεφάλαιον,
ἦν δ' ἐγώ, πάντων τούτων ξυννηθροισμένων ἐννοεῖς, ὡς
ἀπαλὴν τὴν ψυχὴν τῶν πολιτῶν ποιεῖ, ὥστε κἂν ὁτιοῦν 65
δουλείας τις προσφέρηται, ἀγανακτεῖν καὶ μὴ ἀνέχεσθαι ;
τελευτῶντες γάρ που οἶσθ' ὅτι οὐδὲ τῶν νόμων φροντί-
ζουσι γεγραμμένων ἢ ἀγράφων, ἵνα δὴ μηδαμῇ μηδεὶς
E αὐτοῖς ᾖ δεσπότης. Καὶ μάλ', ἔφη, οἶδα. Αὕτη μὲν
τοίνυν, ἦν δ' ἐγώ, ὦ φίλε, ἡ ἀρχὴ οὑτωσὶ καλὴ καὶ νεα- 70
νική, ὅθεν τυραννὶς φύεται, ὡς ἐμοὶ δοκεῖ.

Book IX.

The Soul compared to a multiform Creature. The Duty of the Just Man. The Eternal Pattern of our City.

(Socrates, Glaucon.)

588 A—end.

Εἶεν δή, εἶπον· ἐπειδὴ ἐνταῦθα λόγου γεγόναμεν, B ἀναλάβωμεν τὰ πρῶτα λεχθέντα, δι' ἃ δεῦρ' ἥκομεν. ἦν δέ που λεγόμενον λυσιτελεῖν ἀδικεῖν τῷ τελέως μὲν ἀδίκῳ, δοξαζομένῳ δὲ δικαίῳ· ἢ οὐχ οὕτως ἐλέχθη ; Οὕτω μὲν 5 οὖν. Νῦν δή, ἔφην, αὐτῷ διαλεγώμεθα, ἐπειδὴ διωμολογησάμεθα τό τε ἀδικεῖν καὶ τὸ δίκαια πράττειν ἣν ἑκάτερον ἔχει δύναμιν. Πῶς ; ἔφη. Εἰκόνα πλάσαντες τῆς ψυχῆς λόγῳ, ἵνα εἰδῇ ὁ ἐκεῖνα λέγων οἷα ἔλεγεν. Ποίαν τινά ; ἦ δ' ὅς. Τῶν τοιούτων τινά, ἦν δ' ἐγώ, οἷαι C 10 μυθολογοῦνται παλαιαὶ γενέσθαι φύσεις, ἥ τε Χιμαίρας καὶ ἡ Σκύλλης καὶ Κερβέρου, καὶ ἄλλαι τινὲς συχναὶ λέγονται ξυμπεφυκυῖαι ἰδέαι πολλαὶ εἰς ἓν γενέσθαι. Λέγονται γάρ, ἔφη. Πλάττε τοίνυν μίαν μὲν ἰδέαν θηρίου ποικίλου καὶ πολυκεφάλου, ἡμέρων δὲ θηρίων ἔχοντος κεφα- 15 λὰς κύκλῳ καὶ ἀγρίων, καὶ δυνατοῦ μεταβάλλειν καὶ φύειν ἐξ αὐτοῦ πάντα ταῦτα. Δεινοῦ πλάστου, ἔφη, τὸ ἔργον· ὅμως δέ, ἐπειδὴ εὐπλαστότερον κηροῦ καὶ τῶν τοι- D ούτων λόγος, πεπλάσθω. Μίαν δὴ τοίνυν ἄλλην ἰδέαν λέοντος, μίαν δὲ ἀνθρώπου· πολὺ δὲ μέγιστον ἔστω τὸ 20 πρῶτον καὶ δεύτερον τὸ δεύτερον. Ταῦτα, ἔφη, ῥᾷω· καὶ πέπλασται. Σύναπτε τοίνυν αὐτὰ εἰς ἓν τρία ὄντα, ὥστε πῃ ξυμπεφυκέναι ἀλλήλοις. Συνῆπται, ἔφη. Περίπλασον δὴ αὐτοῖς ἔξωθεν ἑνὸς εἰκόνα, τὴν τοῦ ἀνθρώπου, ὥστε τῷ μὴ δυναμένῳ τὰ ἐντὸς ὁρᾶν, ἀλλὰ τὸ ἔξω E

μόνον ἔλυτρον ὁρῶντι ἓν ζῷον φαίνεσθαι, ἄνθρωπον. Πε- 25
ριπέπλασται, ἔφη. Λέγωμεν δὴ τῷ λέγοντι, ὡς λυσιτελεῖ
τούτῳ ἀδικεῖν τῷ ἀνθρώπῳ, δίκαια δὲ πράττειν οὐ ξυμ-
φέρει, ὅτι οὐδὲν ἄλλο φησὶν ἢ λυσιτελεῖν αὐτῷ τὸ παν-
τοδαπὸν θηρίον εὐωχοῦντι ποιεῖν ἰσχυρὸν καὶ τὸν λέοντα
καὶ τὰ περὶ τὸν λέοντα, τὸν δὲ ἄνθρωπον λιμοκτονεῖν 30
589 καὶ ποιεῖν ἀσθενῆ, ὥστε ἕλκεσθαι ὅπῃ ἂν ἐκείνων ὁπότε-
ρον ἄγῃ, καὶ μηδὲν ἕτερον ἑτέρῳ ξυνεθίζειν μηδὲ φίλον
ποιεῖν, ἀλλ' ἐᾶν αὐτὰ ἐν αὑτοῖς δάκνεσθαί τε καὶ μα-
χόμενα ἐσθίειν ἄλληλα. Παντάπασι γάρ, ἔφη, ταῦτ' ἂν
λέγοι ὁ τὸ ἀδικεῖν ἐπαινῶν. Οὐκοῦν αὖ ὁ τὰ δίκαια 35
λέγων λυσιτελεῖν φαίη ἂν δεῖν ταῦτα πράττειν καὶ ταῦτα
λέγειν, ὅθεν τοῦ ἀνθρώπου ὁ ἐντὸς ἄνθρωπος ἔσται ἐγκρα-
B τέστατος, καὶ τοῦ πολυκεφάλου θρέμματος ἐπιμελήσεται
ὥσπερ γεωργός, τὰ μὲν ἥμερα τρέφων καὶ τιθασεύων,
τὰ δὲ ἄγρια ἀποκωλύων φύεσθαι, ξύμμαχον ποιησάμενος 46
τὴν τοῦ λέοντος φύσιν, καὶ κοινῇ πάντων κηδόμενος,
φίλα ποιησάμενος ἀλλήλοις τε καὶ αὑτῷ, οὕτω θρέψει;
Κομιδῇ γὰρ αὖ λέγει ταῦτα ὁ τὸ δίκαιον ἐπαινῶν. Κατὰ
πάντα τρόπον δὴ ὁ μὲν τὰ δίκαια ἐγκωμιάζων ἀληθῆ ἂν
C λέγοι, ὁ δὲ τὰ ἄδικα ψεύδοιτο. πρός τε γὰρ ἡδονὴν καὶ 45
πρὸς εὐδοξίαν καὶ ὠφελίαν σκοπουμένῳ ὁ μὲν ἐπαινέτης
τοῦ δικαίου ἀληθεύει, ὁ δὲ ψέκτης οὐδὲν ὑγιὲς οὐδ' εἰδὼς
ψέγει ὅ τι ψέγει. Οὔ μοι δοκεῖ, ἦ δ' ὅς, οὐδαμῇ γε.
Πείθωμεν τοίνυν αὐτὸν πράως, οὐ γὰρ ἑκὼν ἁμαρτάνει,
ἐρωτῶντες Ὦ μακάριε, οὐ καὶ τὰ καλὰ καὶ αἰσχρὰ νό- 50
μιμα διὰ τὰ τοιαῦτ' ἂν φαῖμεν γεγονέναι; τὰ μὲν καλὰ
D τὰ ὑπὸ τῷ ἀνθρώπῳ, μᾶλλον δὲ ἴσως τὰ ὑπὸ τῷ θείῳ
τὰ θηριώδη ποιοῦντα τῆς φύσεως, αἰσχρὰ δὲ τὰ ὑπὸ τῷ
ἀγρίῳ τὸ ἥμερον δουλούμενα; ξυμφήσει; ἢ πῶς; Ἐὰν
ἐμοί, ἔφη, πείθηται. Ἔστιν οὖν, εἶπον, ὅτῳ λυσιτελεῖ 55

ἐκ τούτου τοῦ λόγου χρυσίον λαμβάνειν ἀδίκως, εἴπερ
τοιόνδε τι γίγνεται, λαμβάνων τὸ χρυσίον ἅμα καταδου-
λοῦται τὸ βέλτιστον ἑαυτοῦ τῷ μοχθηροτάτῳ ; ἢ εἰ μὲν
λαβὼν χρυσίον υἱὸν ἢ θυγατέρα ἐδουλοῦτο, καὶ ταῦτ' εἰς E
60 ἀγρίων τε καὶ κακῶν ἀνδρῶν, οὐκ ἂν αὐτῷ ἐλυσιτέλει
οὐδ' ἂν πάμπολυ ἐπὶ τούτῳ λαμβάνειν, εἰ δὲ τὸ ἑαυτοῦ
θειότατον ὑπὸ τῷ ἀθεωτάτῳ τε καὶ μιαρωτάτῳ δουλοῦται
καὶ μηδὲν ἐλεεῖ, οὐκ ἄρα ἄθλιός ἐστι καὶ πολὺ ἐπὶ δει-590
νοτέρῳ ὀλέθρῳ χρυσὸν δωροδοκεῖ ἢ Ἐριφύλη ἐπὶ τῇ τοῦ
65 ἀνδρὸς ψυχῇ τὸν ὅρμον δεξαμένη ; Πολὺ μέντοι, ἦ δ' ὃς
ὁ Γλαύκων· ἐγὼ γάρ σοι ὑπὲρ ἐκείνου ἀποκρινοῦμαι.
Οὐκοῦν καὶ τὸ ἀκολασταίνειν οἴει διὰ τοιαῦτα πάλαι ψέ-
γεσθαι, ὅτι ἀνίεται ἐν τῷ τοιούτῳ τὸ δεινὸν τὸ μέγα
ἐκεῖνο καὶ πολυειδὲς θρέμμα πέρα τοῦ δέοντος ; Δῆλον,
70 ἔφη. Ἡ δ' αὐθάδεια καὶ δυσκολία ψέγεται οὐχ ὅταν τὸ
λεοντῶδές τε καὶ ὀφεῶδες αὔξηται καὶ συντείνηται ἀναρ-B
μόστως ; Πάνυ μὲν οὖν. Τρυφὴ δὲ καὶ μαλθακία οὐκ ἐπὶ
τῇ αὐτοῦ τούτου χαλάσει τε καὶ ἀνέσει ψέγεται, ὅταν ἐν
αὐτῷ δειλίαν ἐμποιῇ ; Τί μήν ; Κολακεία δὲ καὶ ἀνελευ-
75 θερία οὐχ ὅταν τις τὸ αὐτὸ τοῦτο, τὸ θυμοειδές, ὑπὸ
τῷ ὀχλώδει θηρίῳ ποιῇ καὶ ἕνεκα χρημάτων καὶ τῆς
ἐκείνου ἀπληστίας προπηλακιζόμενον ἐθίζῃ ἐκ νέου ἀντὶ
λέοντος πίθηκον γίγνεσθαι ; Καὶ μάλα, ἔφη. Βαναυσία C
δὲ καὶ χειροτεχνία διὰ τί, οἴει, ὄνειδος φέρει ; ἢ δι' ἄλλο
80 τι φήσομεν ἢ ὅταν τις ἀσθενὲς φύσει ἔχῃ τὸ τοῦ βελτίστου
εἶδος, ὥστε μὴ ἂν δύνασθαι ἄρχειν τῶν ἐν αὐτῷ θρεμ-
μάτων, ἀλλὰ θεραπεύειν ἐκεῖνα, καὶ τὰ θωπεύματα αὐτῶν μόνον δύνηται μανθάνειν ; Ἔοικεν, ἔφη. Οὐκοῦν
ἵνα καὶ ὁ τοιοῦτος ὑπὸ ὁμοίου ἄρχηται οἷόυπερ ὁ βέλτι-
85 στος, δοῦλον αὐτόν φαμεν δεῖν εἶναι ἐκείνου τοῦ βελτί- D
στου, ἔχοντος ἐν αὑτῷ τὸ θεῖον ἄρχον, οὐκ ἐπὶ βλάβῃ τῇ

τοῦ δούλου οἰόμενοι δεῖν ἄρχεσθαι αὐτόν, ὥσπερ Θρασύ-
μαχος ᾤετο τοὺς ἀρχομένους, ἀλλ᾽ ὡς ἄμεινον ὂν παντὶ
ὑπὸ θείου καὶ φρονίμου ἄρχεσθαι, μάλιστα μὲν οἰκεῖον
ἔχοντος ἐν αὑτῷ, εἰ δὲ μή, ἔξωθεν ἐφεστῶτος, ἵνα εἰς 90
δύναμιν πάντες ὅμοιοι ὦμεν καὶ φίλοι τῷ αὐτῷ κυβερνώ-
μενοι ; Καὶ ὀρθῶς γ᾽, ἔφη. Δηλοῖ δέ γε, ἦν δ᾽ ἐγώ, καὶ
E ὁ νόμος ὅτι τοιοῦτον βουλεύεται πᾶσι τοῖς ἐν τῇ πόλει
ξύμμαχος ὤν· καὶ ἡ τῶν παίδων ἀρχή, τὸ μὴ ἐᾶν ἐλευθέρους εἶναι, ἕως ἂν ἐν αὐτοῖς ὥσπερ ἐν πόλει πολιτείαν 95
591 καταστήσωμεν, καὶ τὸ βέλτιστον θεραπεύσαντες τῷ παρ᾽
ἡμῖν τοιούτῳ ἀντικαταστήσωμεν φύλακα ὅμοιον καὶ ἄρχοντα ἐν αὐτῷ, καὶ τότε δὴ ἐλεύθερον ἀφίεμεν. Δηλοῖ
γάρ, ἦ δ᾽ ὅς. Πῇ δὴ οὖν φήσομεν, ὦ Γλαύκων, καὶ
κατὰ τίνα λόγον λυσιτελεῖν ἀδικεῖν, ἢ ἀκολασταίνειν ἤ τι 100
αἰσχρὸν ποιεῖν, ἐξ ὧν πονηρότερος μὲν ἔσται, πλείω δὲ
χρήματα ἢ ἄλλην τινὰ δύναμιν κεκτήσεται ; Οὐδαμῇ, ἦ
δ᾽ ὅς. Πῇ δ᾽ ἀδικοῦντα λανθάνειν καὶ μὴ διδόναι δίκην
B λυσιτελεῖν ; ἢ οὐχὶ ὁ μὲν λανθάνων ἔτι πονηρότερος γίγνεται, τοῦ δὲ μὴ λανθάνοντος καὶ κολαζομένου τὸ μὲν θη- 105
ριῶδες κοιμίζεται καὶ ἡμεροῦται, τὸ δὲ ἥμερον ἐλευθε-
ροῦται, καὶ ὅλη ἡ ψυχὴ εἰς τὴν βελτίστην φύσιν καθι-
σταμένη τιμιωτέραν ἕξιν λαμβάνει, σωφροσύνην τε καὶ
δικαιοσύνην μετὰ φρονήσεως κτωμένη, ἢ σῶμα ἰσχύν τε
καὶ κάλλος μετὰ ὑγιείας λαμβάνον, τοσούτῳ ὅσῳπερ ψυχὴ 110
σώματος τιμιωτέρα ; Παντάπασι μὲν οὖν, ἔφη. Οὐκοῦν
C ὅ γε νοῦν ἔχων πάντα τὰ αὑτοῦ εἰς τοῦτο ξυντείνας βιώ-
σεται, πρῶτον μὲν τὰ μαθήματα τιμῶν, ἃ τοιαύτην αὑτοῦ τὴν ψυχὴν ἀπεργάσεται, τὰ δὲ ἄλλ᾽ ἀτιμάζων ; Δῆλον, ἔφη. Ἔπειτά γ᾽, εἶπον, τὴν τοῦ σώματος ἕξιν καὶ 115
τροφὴν οὐχ ὅπως τῇ θηριώδει καὶ ἀλόγῳ ἡδονῇ ἐπιτρέ-
ψας ἐνταῦθα τετραμμένος ζήσει, ἀλλ᾽ οὐδὲ πρὸς ὑγίειαν

βλέπων, οὐδὲ τοῦτο πρεσβεύων, ὅπως ἰσχυρὸς ἢ ὑγιὴς ἢ
καλὸς ἔσται, ἐὰν μὴ καὶ σωφρονήσειν μέλλῃ ἀπ' αὐτῶν,
120 ἀλλ' ἀεὶ τὴν ἐν τῷ σώματι ἁρμονίαν τῆς ἐν τῇ ψυχῇ D
ἕνεκα ξυμφωνίας ἁρμοττόμενος [φαίνηται]. Παντάπασι
μὲν οὖν, ἔφη, ἐάνπερ μέλλῃ τῇ ἀληθείᾳ μουσικὸς εἶναι.
Οὐκοῦν, εἶπον, καὶ τὴν ἐν τῇ τῶν χρημάτων κτήσει
ξύνταξίν τε καὶ ξυμφωνίαν; καὶ τὸν ὄγκον τοῦ πλήθους
125 οὐκ ἐκπληττόμενος ὑπὸ τοῦ τῶν πολλῶν μακαρισμοῦ
ἄπειρον αὐξήσει, ἀπέραντα κακὰ ἔχων; Οὐκ οἴομαι,
ἔφη. Ἀλλ' ἀποβλέπων γε, εἶπον, πρὸς τὴν ἐν αὐτῷ E
πολιτείαν, καὶ φυλάττων, μή τι παρακινῇ αὐτοῦ τῶν
ἐκεῖ διὰ πλῆθος οὐσίας ἢ δι' ὀλιγότητα, οὕτως κυβερνῶν
130 προσθήσει καὶ ἀναλώσει τῆς οὐσίας καθ' ὅσον ἂν οἷός τ'
ᾖ. Κομιδῇ μὲν οὖν, ἔφη. Ἀλλὰ μὴν καὶ τιμάς γε, εἰς
ταὐτὸν ἀποβλέπων, τῶν μὲν μεθέξει καὶ γεύσεται ἑκών, 592
ἃς ἂν ἡγῆται ἀμείνω αὐτὸν ποιήσειν, ἃς δ' ἂν λύσειν
τὴν ὑπάρχουσαν ἕξιν, φεύξεται ἰδίᾳ καὶ δημοσίᾳ. Οὐκ
135 ἄρα, ἔφη, τά γε πολιτικὰ ἐθελήσει πράττειν, ἐάνπερ τούτου κήδηται. Νὴ τὸν κύνα, ἦν δ' ἐγώ, ἔν γε τῇ ἑαυτοῦ
πόλει καὶ μάλα, οὐ μέντοι ἴσως ἔν γε τῇ πατρίδι, ἐὰν
μὴ θεία τις ξυμβῇ τύχη. Μανθάνω, ἔφη· ἐν ᾗ νῦν
διήλθομεν οἰκίζοντες πόλει λέγεις, τῇ ἐν λόγοις κειμένῃ,
140 ἐπεὶ γῆς γε οὐδαμοῦ οἶμαι αὐτὴν εἶναι. Ἀλλ', ἦν δ' ἐγώ, B
ἐν οὐρανῷ ἴσως παράδειγμα ἀνάκειται τῷ βουλομένῳ
ὁρᾶν καὶ ὁρῶντι ἑαυτὸν κατοικίζειν. διαφέρει δὲ οὐδὲν
εἴτε που ἔστιν εἴτε ἔσται· τὸ γὰρ ταύτης μόνης ἂν πράξειεν, ἄλλης δὲ οὐδεμιᾶς. Εἰκός γ', ἔφη.

Book X.

The Tale of Er, the Son of Armenius.

(SOCRATES.)

613 E—end.

ἃ μὲν τοίνυν, ἦν δ' ἐγώ, ζῶντι τῷ δικαίῳ παρὰ θεῶν
614 τε καὶ ἀνθρώπων ἆθλά τε καὶ μισθοὶ καὶ δῶρα γίγνεται
πρὸς ἐκείνοις τοῖς ἀγαθοῖς οἷς αὐτὴ παρείχετο ἡ δικαιοσύνη, τοιαῦτ' ἂν εἴη. Καὶ μάλ', ἔφη, καλά τε καὶ βέ-
βαια. Ταῦτα τοίνυν, ἦν δ' ἐγώ, οὐδέν ἐστι πλήθει οὐδὲ 5
μεγέθει πρὸς ἐκεῖνα, ἃ τελευτήσαντα ἑκάτερον περιμένει·
χρὴ δ' αὐτὰ ἀκοῦσαι, ἵνα τελέως ἑκάτερος αὐτῶν ἀπειλήφῃ τὰ ὑπὸ τοῦ λόγου ὀφειλόμενα ἀκοῦσαι. Λέγοις ἄν,
B ἔφη, ὡς οὐ πολλὰ ἀλλ' ἥδιον ἀκούοντι. Ἀλλ' οὐ μέντοι
σοι, ἦν δ' ἐγώ, Ἀλκίνου γε ἀπόλογον ἐρῶ, ἀλλ' ἀλκίμου 10
μὲν ἀνδρός, Ἠρὸς τοῦ Ἀρμενίου, τὸ γένος Παμφύλου·
ὅς ποτε ἐν πολέμῳ τελευτήσας, ἀναιρεθέντων δεκαταίων
τῶν νεκρῶν ἤδη διεφθαρμένων, ὑγιὴς μὲν ἀνῃρέθη, κο-
μισθεὶς δ' οἴκαδε μέλλων θάπτεσθαι, δωδεκαταῖος ἐπὶ
τῇ πυρᾷ κείμενος ἀνεβίω, ἀναβιοὺς δ' ἔλεγεν ἃ ἐκεῖ ἴδοι. 15
ἔφη δέ, ἐπειδή οὐ ἐκβῆναι τὴν ψυχήν, πορεύεσθαι μετὰ
C πολλῶν, καὶ ἀφικνεῖσθαι σφᾶς εἰς τόπον τινὰ δαιμόνιον,
ἐν ᾧ τῆς τε γῆς δύ' εἶναι χάσματα ἐχομένω ἀλλήλοιν καὶ
τοῦ οὐρανοῦ αὖ ἐν τῷ ἄνω ἄλλα καταντικρύ. δικαστὰς
δὲ μεταξὺ τούτων καθῆσθαι, οὕς, ἐπειδὴ διαδικάσειαν, 20
τοὺς μὲν δικαίους κελεύειν πορεύεσθαι τὴν εἰς δεξιάν τε
καὶ ἄνω διὰ τοῦ οὐρανοῦ, σημεῖα περιάψαντας τῶν δεδι-
κασμένων ἐν τῷ πρόσθεν, τοὺς δὲ ἀδίκους τὴν εἰς ἀρι-
στεράν τε καὶ κάτω, ἔχοντας καὶ τούτους ἐν τῷ ὄπισθεν
D σημεῖα πάντων ὧν ἔπραξαν. ἑαυτοῦ δὲ προσελθόντος 25

εἰπεῖν ὅτι δέοι αὐτὸν ἄγγελον ἀνθρώποις γενέσθαι τῶν
ἐκεῖ καὶ διακελεύοιντό οἱ ἀκούειν τε καὶ θεᾶσθαι πάντα
τὰ ἐν τῷ τόπῳ. ὁρᾶν δὴ ταύτῃ μὲν καθ᾽ ἑκάτερον τὸ
χάσμα τοῦ οὐρανοῦ τε καὶ τῆς γῆς ἀπιούσας τὰς ψυχάς,
30 ἐπειδὴ αὐταῖς δικασθείη, κατὰ δὲ τὼ ἑτέρω ἐκ μὲν τοῦ
ἀνιέναι ἐκ τῆς γῆς μεστὰς αὐχμοῦ τε καὶ κόνεως, ἐκ δὲ τοῦ
ἑτέρου καταβαίνειν ἑτέρας ἐκ τοῦ οὐρανοῦ καθαράς. καὶ
τὰς ἀεὶ ἀφικνουμένας ὥσπερ ἐκ πολλῆς πορείας φαίνε- E
σθαι ἥκειν, καὶ ἀσμένας εἰς τὸν λειμῶνα ἀπιούσας οἷον
35 ἐν πανηγύρει κατασκηνᾶσθαι, καὶ ἀσπάζεσθαί τε ἀλλήλας
ὅσαι γνώριμαι, καὶ πυνθάνεσθαι τάς τε ἐκ τῆς γῆς ἡκού-
σας παρὰ τῶν ἑτέρων τὰ ἐκεῖ καὶ τὰς ἐκ τοῦ οὐρανοῦ
τὰ παρ᾽ ἐκείναις. διηγεῖσθαι δὲ ἀλλήλαις τὰς μὲν ὀδυ-
ρομένας τε καὶ κλαούσας, ἀναμιμνησκομένας ὅσα τε καὶ 615
40 οἷα πάθοιεν καὶ ἴδοιεν ἐν τῇ ὑπὸ γῆς πορείᾳ—εἶναι δὲ
τὴν πορείαν χιλιέτη—τὰς δ᾽ αὖ ἐκ τοῦ οὐρανοῦ εὐπα-
θείας διηγεῖσθαι καὶ θέας ἀμηχάνους τὸ κάλλος. τὰ μὲν
οὖν πολλά, ὦ Γλαύκων, πολλοῦ χρόνου διηγήσασθαι· τὸ
δ᾽ οὖν κεφάλαιον ἔφη τόδε εἶναι, ὅσα πώποτέ τινα ἠδί-
45 κησαν καὶ ὅσους ἕκαστοι, ὑπὲρ ἁπάντων δίκην δεδωκέναι
ἐν μέρει, ὑπὲρ ἑκάστου δεκάκις—τοῦτο δ᾽ εἶναι κατὰ
ἑκατονταετηρίδα ἑκάστην, ὡς βίου ὄντος τοσούτου τοῦ B
ἀνθρωπίνου—, ἵνα δεκαπλάσιον τὸ ἔκτισμα τοῦ ἀδική-
ματος ἐκτίνοιεν. καὶ οἷον εἴ τινες πολλῶν θανάτων ἦσαν
50 αἴτιοι, ἢ πόλεις προδόντες ἢ στρατόπεδα καὶ εἰς δουλείας
ἐμβεβληκότες, ἤ τινος ἄλλης κακουχίας μεταίτιοι, πάντων
τούτων δεκαπλασίας ἀλγηδόνας ὑπὲρ ἑκάστου κομίσαιντο,
καὶ αὖ εἴ τινας εὐεργεσίας εὐεργετηκότες καὶ δίκαιοι καὶ
ὅσιοι γεγονότες εἶεν, κατὰ ταὐτὰ τὴν ἀξίαν κομίζοιντο.
55 τῶν δὲ εὐθὺς γενομένων καὶ ὀλίγον χρόνον βιούντων πέρι C
ἄλλα ἔλεγεν οὐκ ἄξια μνήμης. εἰς δὲ θεοὺς ἀσεβείας τε

καὶ εὐσεβείας καὶ γονέας καὶ αὐτόχειρος φόνου μείζους
ἔτι τοὺς μισθοὺς διηγεῖτο. ἔφη γὰρ δὴ παραγενέσθαι ἐρω-
τωμένῳ ἑτέρῳ ὑπὸ ἑτέρου, ὅπου εἴη Ἀρδιαῖος ὁ μέγας.
ὁ δὲ Ἀρδιαῖος οὗτος τῆς Παμφυλίας ἔν τινι πόλει τύραν- 60
νος ἐγεγόνει, ἤδη χιλιοστὸν ἔτος εἰς ἐκεῖνον τὸν χρόνον,
D γέροντά τε πατέρα ἀποκτείνας καὶ πρεσβύτερον ἀδελφόν,
καὶ ἄλλα δὴ πολλά τε καὶ ἀνόσια εἰργασμένος, ὡς ἐλέγετο. ἔφη οὖν τὸν ἐρωτώμενον εἰπεῖν, Οὐχ ἥκει, φάναι,
οὐδ' ἂν ἥξει δεῦρο. ἐθεασάμεθα γὰρ οὖν δὴ καὶ τοῦτο 65
τῶν δεινῶν θεαμάτων· ἐπειδὴ ἐγγὺς τοῦ στομίου ἦμεν
μέλλοντες ἀνιέναι καὶ τἆλλα πάντα πεπονθότες, ἐκεῖνόν
τε κατείδομεν ἐξαίφνης καὶ ἄλλους σχεδόν τι αὐτῶν τοὺς
πλείστους τυράννους· ἦσαν δὲ καὶ ἰδιῶταί τινες τῶν με-
E γάλα ἡμαρτηκότων· οὓς οἰομένους ἤδη ἀναβήσεσθαι οὐκ 70
ἐδέχετο τὸ στόμιον ἀλλ' ἐμυκᾶτο, ὁπότε τις τῶν οὕτως
ἀνιάτως ἐχόντων εἰς πονηρίαν ἢ μὴ ἱκανῶς δεδωκὼς δίκην
ἐπιχειροῖ ἀνιέναι. ἐνταῦθα δὴ ἄνδρες, ἔφη, ἄγριοι, διά-
πυροι ἰδεῖν, παρεστῶτες καὶ καταμανθάνοντες τὸ φθέγμα,
τοὺς μὲν διαλαβόντες ἦγον, τὸν δὲ Ἀρδιαῖον καὶ ἄλλους 75
616 συμποδίσαντες χεῖράς τε καὶ πόδας καὶ κεφαλήν, κατα-
βαλόντες καὶ ἐκδείραντες, εἷλκον παρὰ τὴν ὁδὸν ἐκτὸς
ἐπ' ἀσπαλάθων κνάπτοντες, καὶ τοῖς ἀεὶ παριοῦσι σημαίνοντες, ὧν ἕνεκά τε καὶ εἰς ὅ τι [τὸν Τάρταρον]
ἐμπεσούμενοι ἄγοιντο. ἔνθα δὴ φόβων, ἔφη, πολλῶν 80
καὶ παντοδαπῶν σφίσι γεγονότων τοῦτον ὑπερβάλλειν
[τὸν φόβον], μὴ γένοιτο ἑκάστῳ τὸ φθέγμα, ὅτε ἀνα-
βαίνοι, καὶ ἀσμενέστατα ἕκαστον σιγήσαντος ἀναβῆναι.
B καὶ τὰς μὲν δὴ δίκας τε καὶ τιμωρίας τοιαύτας τινὰς
εἶναι, καὶ αὖ τὰς εὐεργεσίας ταύταις ἀντιστρόφους· ἐπειδὴ 85
δὲ τοῖς ἐν τῷ λειμῶνι ἑκάστοις ἑπτὰ ἡμέραι γένοιντο,
ἀναστάντας ἐντεῦθεν δεῖν τῇ ὀγδόῃ πορεύεσθαι, καὶ

ἀφικνεῖσθαι τεταρταίους ὅθεν καθορᾶν ἄνωθεν διὰ παντὸς τοῦ οὐρανοῦ καὶ γῆς τεταμένον φῶς εὐθύ, οἷον κίονα,
90 μάλιστα τῇ ἴριδι προσφερῆ, λαμπρότερον δὲ καὶ καθαρώ-
τερον. εἰς ὃ ἀφικέσθαι προελθόντας ἡμερησίαν ὁδόν, καὶ
ἰδεῖν αὐτόθι κατὰ μέσον τὸ φῶς ἐκ τοῦ οὐρανοῦ τὰ ἄκρα C
αὐτοῦ τῶν δεσμῶν τεταμένα· εἶναι γὰρ τοῦτο τὸ φῶς
ξύνδεσμον τοῦ οὐρανοῦ, οἷον τὰ ὑποζώματα τῶν τριή-
95 ρων, οὕτω πᾶσαν ξυνέχον τὴν περιφοράν· ἐκ δὲ τῶν
ἄκρων τεταμένον Ἀνάγκης ἄτρακτον, δι’ οὗ πάσας ἐπι-
στρέφεσθαι τὰς περιφοράς· οὗ τὴν μὲν ἠλακάτην τε καὶ
τὸ ἄγκιστρον εἶναι ἐξ ἀδάμαντος, τὸν δὲ σφόνδυλον μι-
κτὸν ἔκ τε τούτου καὶ ἄλλων γενῶν. τὴν δὲ τοῦ σφον-
100 δύλου φύσιν εἶναι τοιάνδε· τὸ μὲν σχῆμα οἷαπερ ἡ τοῦ D
ἐνθάδε· νοῆσαι δὲ δεῖ ἐξ ὧν ἔλεγε τοιόνδε αὐτὸν εἶναι,
ὥσπερ ἂν εἰ ἐν ἑνὶ μεγάλῳ σφονδύλῳ κοίλῳ καὶ ἐξεγλυμ-
μένῳ διαμπερὲς ἄλλος τοιοῦτος ἐλάττων ἐγκέοιτο ἁρμότ-
των, καθάπερ οἱ κάδοι οἱ εἰς ἀλλήλους ἁρμόττοντες· καὶ
105 οὕτω δὴ τρίτον ἄλλον καὶ τέταρτον καὶ ἄλλους τέτταρας.
ὀκτὼ γὰρ εἶναι τοὺς ξύμπαντας σφονδύλους, ἐν ἀλλήλοις
ἐγκειμένους, κύκλους ἄνωθεν τὰ χείλη φαίνοντας, νῶτον E
συνεχὲς ἑνὸς σφονδύλου ἀπεργαζομένους περὶ τὴν ἠλα-
κάτην· ἐκείνην δὲ διὰ μέσου τοῦ ὀγδόου διαμπερὲς ἐλη-
110 λάσθαι. τὸν μὲν οὖν πρῶτόν τε καὶ ἐξωτάτω σφόνδυλον
πλατύτατον τὸν τοῦ χείλους κύκλον ἔχειν, τὸν δὲ τοῦ
ἕκτου δεύτερον, τρίτον δὲ τὸν τοῦ τετάρτου, τέταρτον δὲ
τὸν τοῦ ὀγδόου, πέμπτον δὲ τὸν τοῦ ἑβδόμου, ἕκτον δὲ
τὸν τοῦ πέμπτου, ἕβδομον δὲ τὸν τοῦ τρίτου, ὄγδοον δὲ
115 τὸν τοῦ δευτέρου. καὶ τὸν μὲν τοῦ μεγίστου ποικίλον,
τὸν δὲ τοῦ ἑβδόμου λαμπρότατον, τὸν δὲ τοῦ ὀγδόου τὸ
χρῶμα ἀπὸ τοῦ ἑβδόμου ἔχειν προσλάμποντος, τὸν δὲ τοῦ 617
δευτέρου καὶ πέμπτου παραπλήσια ἀλλήλοις, ξανθότερα

ἐκείνων, τρίτον δὲ λευκότατον χρῶμα ἔχειν, τέταρτον δὲ
ὑπέρυθρον, δεύτερον δὲ λευκότητι τὸν ἕκτον. κυκλεῖσθαι 120
δὲ δὴ στρεφόμενον τὸν ἄτρακτον ὅλον μὲν τὴν αὐτὴν φο-
ράν, ἐν δὲ τῷ ὅλῳ περιφερομένῳ τοὺς μὲν ἐντὸς ἑπτὰ
κύκλους τὴν ἐναντίαν τῷ ὅλῳ ἠρέμα περιφέρεσθαι, αὐτῶν
B δὲ τούτων τάχιστα μὲν ἰέναι τὸν ὄγδοον, δευτέρους δὲ
καὶ ἅμα ἀλλήλοις τόν τε ἕβδομον καὶ ἕκτον καὶ πέμπτον· 125
τὸν τρίτον δὲ φορᾷ ἰέναι, ὡς σφίσι φαίνεσθαι, ἐπανακυκλούμενον τὸν τέταρτον· τέταρτον δὲ τὸν τρίτον καὶ ʼ
πέμπτον τὸν δεύτερον. στρέφεσθαι δὲ αὐτὸν ἐν τοῖς τῆς
Ἀνάγκης γόνασιν. ἐπὶ δὲ τῶν κύκλων αὐτοῦ ἄνωθεν ἐφ᾽
ἑκάστου βεβηκέναι Σειρῆνα συμπεριφερομένην, φωνὴν 130
μίαν ἱεῖσαν ἀνὰ τόνον· ἐκ πασῶν δὲ ὀκτὼ οὐσῶν μίαν
ἁρμονίαν ξυμφωνεῖν. ἄλλας δὲ καθημένας πέριξ δι᾽ ἴσου
C τρεῖς, ἐν θρόνῳ ἑκάστην, θυγατέρας τῆς Ἀνάγκης, Μοίρας, λευχειμονούσας, στέμματα ἐπὶ τῶν κεφαλῶν ἐχού-
σας, Λάχεσίν τε καὶ Κλωθὼ καὶ Ἄτροπον, ὑμνεῖν πρὸς 135
τὴν τῶν Σειρήνων ἁρμονίαν, Λάχεσιν μὲν τὰ γεγονότα,
Κλωθὼ δὲ τὰ ὄντα, Ἄτροπον δὲ τὰ μέλλοντα. καὶ τὴν
μὲν Κλωθὼ τῇ δεξιᾷ χειρὶ ἐφαπτομένην συνεπιστρέφειν
τοῦ ἀτράκτου τὴν ἔξω περιφοράν, διαλείπουσαν χρόνον,
τὴν δὲ Ἄτροπον τῇ ἀριστερᾷ τὰς ἐντὸς αὖ ὡσαύτως· τὴν 140
D δὲ Λάχεσιν ἐν μέρει ἑκατέρας ἑκατέρᾳ τῇ χειρὶ ἐφάπτεσθαι. σφᾶς οὖν, ἐπειδὴ ἀφικέσθαι, εὐθὺς δεῖν ἰέναι πρὸς
τὴν Λάχεσιν. προφήτην οὖν τινὰ σφᾶς πρῶτον μὲν ἐν
τάξει διαστῆσαι, ἔπειτα λαβόντα ἐκ τῶν τῆς Λαχέσεως
γονάτων κλήρους τε καὶ βίων παραδείγματα, ἀναβάντα 145
ἐπί τι βῆμα ὑψηλὸν εἰπεῖν· Ἀνάγκης θυγατρὸς κόρης
Λαχέσεως λόγος. Ψυχαὶ ἐφήμεροι, ἀρχὴ ἄλλης περιόδου
E θνητοῦ γένους θανατηφόρου. οὐχ ὑμᾶς δαίμων λήξεται,
ἀλλ᾽ ὑμεῖς δαίμονα αἱρήσεσθε. πρῶτος δ᾽ ὁ λαχὼν πρῶ-

150 τος αἱρείσθω βίον, ᾧ συνέσται ἐξ ἀνάγκης. ἀρετὴ δὲ
ἀδέσποτον, ἣν τιμῶν καὶ ἀτιμάζων πλέον καὶ ἔλαττον
αὐτῆς ἕκαστος ἕξει. αἰτία ἑλομένου· θεὸς ἀναίτιος. Ταῦτα
εἰπόντα ῥῖψαι ἐπὶ πάντας τοὺς κλήρους, τὸν δὲ παρ᾽ αὐτὸν πεσόντα ἕκαστον ἀναιρεῖσθαι, πλὴν οὗ· ἓ δὲ οὐκ ἐᾶν·
155 τῷ δὲ ἀνελομένῳ δῆλον εἶναι, ὁπόστος εἰλήχειν· μετὰ δὲ 618
τοῦτο αὖθις τὰ τῶν βίων παραδείγματα εἰς τὸ πρόσθεν
σφῶν θεῖναι ἐπὶ τὴν γῆν, πολὺ πλείω τῶν παρόντων.
εἶναι δὲ παντοδαπά· ζῴων τε γὰρ πάντων βίους καὶ δὴ
καὶ τοὺς ἀνθρωπίνους ἅπαντας. τυραννίδας τε γὰρ ἐν
160 αὐτοῖς εἶναι, τὰς μὲν διατελεῖς, τὰς δὲ καὶ μεταξὺ δια-
φθειρομένας καὶ εἰς πενίας τε καὶ φυγὰς καὶ εἰς πτωχείας
τελευτώσας· εἶναι δὲ καὶ δοκίμων ἀνδρῶν βίους, τοὺς μὲν
ἐπὶ εἴδεσι καὶ κατὰ κάλλη καὶ τὴν ἄλλην ἰσχύν τε καὶ B
ἀγωνίαν, τοὺς δ᾽ ἐπὶ γένεσι καὶ προγόνων ἀρεταῖς, καὶ
165 ἀδοκίμων κατὰ ταὐτά, ὡσαύτως δὲ καὶ γυναικῶν· ψυχῆς
δὲ τάξιν οὐκ ἐνεῖναι διὰ τὸ ἀναγκαίως ἔχειν ἄλλον ἑλο-
μένην βίον ἀλλοίαν γίγνεσθαι· τὰ δ᾽ ἄλλα ἀλλήλοις τε
καὶ πλούτοις καὶ πενίαις, τὰ δὲ νόσοις, τὰ δὲ ὑγιείαις
μεμῖχθαι, τὰ δὲ καὶ μεσοῦν τούτων. || ἔνθα δή, ὡς ἔοικεν,
170 ὦ φίλε Γλαύκων, ὁ πᾶς κίνδυνος ἀνθρώπῳ, καὶ διὰ
ταῦτα μάλιστα ἐπιμελητέον, ὅπως ἕκαστος ἡμῶν τῶν C
ἄλλων μαθημάτων ἀμελήσας τούτου τοῦ μαθήματος καὶ
ζητητὴς καὶ μαθητὴς ἔσται, ἐάν ποθεν οἷός τ᾽ ᾖ μαθεῖν
καὶ ἐξευρεῖν, τίς αὐτὸν ποιήσει δυνατὸν καὶ ἐπιστήμονα,
175 βίον καὶ χρηστὸν καὶ πονηρὸν διαγιγνώσκοντα, τὸν βελτίω
ἐκ τῶν δυνατῶν ἀεὶ πανταχοῦ αἱρεῖσθαι, ἀναλογιζόμενον
πάντα τὰ νῦν δὴ ῥηθέντα καὶ ξυντιθέμενα ἀλλήλοις καὶ
διαιρούμενα πρὸς ἀρετὴν βίου πῶς ἔχει, καὶ εἰδέναι, τί
κάλλος πενίᾳ ἢ πλούτῳ κραθὲν καὶ μετὰ ποίας τινὸς ψυ- D
180 χῆς ἕξεως κακὸν ἢ ἀγαθὸν ἐργάζεται, καὶ τί εὐγένειαι καὶ

δυσγένειαι καὶ ἰδιωτεῖαι καὶ ἀρχαὶ καὶ ἰσχύες καὶ ἀσθέ-
νειαι καὶ εὐμαθίαι καὶ δυσμαθίαι καὶ πάντα τὰ τοιαῦτα
τῶν φύσει περὶ ψυχὴν ὄντων καὶ τῶν ἐπικτήτων τί ξυγ-
κεραννύμενα πρὸς ἄλληλα ἐργάζεται, ὥστε ἐξ ἁπάντων
αὐτῶν δυνατὸν εἶναι συλλογισάμενον αἱρεῖσθαι, πρὸς τὴν 185
τῆς ψυχῆς φύσιν ἀποβλέποντα, τόν τε χείρω καὶ τὸν
Ε ἀμείνω βίον, χείρω μὲν καλοῦντα ὃς αὐτὴν ἐκεῖσε ἄξει,
εἰς τὸ ἀδικωτέραν, γίγνεσθαι, ἀμείνω δὲ ὅστις εἰς τὸ
δικαιοτέραν, τὰ δὲ ἄλλα πάντα, χαίρειν ἐάσει.‖ ἑωράκαμεν
γὰρ ὅτι ζῶντί τε καὶ τελευτήσαντι αὕτη κρατίστη αἵρεσις. 190
619 ἀδαμαντίνως δὴ δεῖ ταύτην τὴν δόξαν ἔχοντα εἰς Ἅιδου
ἰέναι, ὅπως ἂν ᾖ καὶ ἐκεῖ ἀνέκπληκτος ὑπὸ πλούτων τε
καὶ τῶν τοιούτων κακῶν, καὶ μὴ ἐμπεσὼν εἰς τυραννίδας
καὶ ἄλλας τοιαύτας πράξεις πολλὰ μὲν ἐργάσηται καὶ
ἀνήκεστα κακά, ἔτι δὲ αὐτὸς μείζω πάθῃ, ἀλλὰ γνῷ τὸν 195
μέσον ἀεὶ τῶν τοιούτων βίον αἱρεῖσθαι καὶ φεύγειν τὰ
ὑπερβάλλοντα ἑκατέρωσε καὶ ἐν τῷδε τῷ βίῳ κατὰ τὸ
δυνατὸν καὶ ἐν παντὶ τῷ ἔπειτα· οὕτω γὰρ εὐδαιμονέ-
Β στατος γίγνεται ἄνθρωπος. καὶ δὴ οὖν καὶ τότε ὁ ἐκεῖθεν
ἄγγελος ἤγγελλε τὸν μὲν προφήτην οὕτως εἰπεῖν· καὶ τε- 200
λευταίῳ ἐπιόντι, ξὺν νῷ ἑλομένῳ, συντόνως ζῶντι κεῖται
βίος ἀγαπητός, οὐ κακός. μήτε ὁ ἄρχων αἱρέσεως ἀμε-
λείτω μήτε ὁ τελευτῶν ἀθυμείτω. εἰπόντος δὲ ταῦτα τὸν
πρῶτον λαχόντα ἔφη εὐθὺς ἐπιόντα τὴν μεγίστην τυραν-
νίδα ἑλέσθαι, καὶ ὑπὸ ἀφροσύνης τε καὶ λαιμαργίας οὐ 205
C πάντα ἱκανῶς ἀνασκεψάμενον ἑλέσθαι, ἀλλ’ αὐτὸν λαθεῖν
ἐνοῦσαν εἱμαρμένην παίδων αὐτοῦ βρώσεις καὶ ἄλλα
κακά· ἐπειδὴ δὲ κατὰ σχολὴν σκέψασθαι, κόπτεσθαί τε
καὶ ὀδύρεσθαι τὴν αἵρεσιν, οὐκ ἐμμένοντα τοῖς προρρη-
θεῖσιν ὑπὸ τοῦ προφήτου· οὐ γὰρ ἑαυτὸν αἰτιᾶσθαι τῶν 210
κακῶν, ἀλλὰ τύχην τε καὶ δαίμονας καὶ πάντα μᾶλλον

ἀνθ' ἑαυτοῦ. εἶναι δὲ αὐτὸν τῶν ἐκ τοῦ οὐρανοῦ ἡκόντων,
ἐν τεταγμένῃ πολιτείᾳ ἐν τῷ προτέρῳ βίῳ βεβιωκότα,
ἔθει ἄνευ φιλοσοφίας ἀρετῆς μετειληφότα. ὡς δὲ καὶ D
215 εἰπεῖν, οὐκ ἐλάττους εἶναι ἐν τοῖς τοιούτοις ἁλισκομένους
τοὺς ἐκ τοῦ οὐρανοῦ ἥκοντας, ἅτε πόνων ἀγυμνάστους·
τῶν δ' ἐκ τῆς γῆς τοὺς πολλούς, ἅτε αὐτούς τε πεπονη-
κότας ἄλλους τε ἑωρακότας, οὐκ ἐξ ἐπιδρομῆς τὰς αἱρέσεις
ποιεῖσθαι. διὸ δὴ καὶ μεταβολὴν τῶν κακῶν καὶ τῶν ἀγα-
220 θῶν ταῖς πολλαῖς τῶν ψυχῶν γίγνεσθαι καὶ διὰ τὴν τοῦ
κλήρου τύχην· ἐπεὶ εἴ τις ἀεί, ὁπότε εἰς τὸν ἐνθάδε βίον
ἀφικνοῖτο, ὑγιῶς φιλοσοφοῖ καὶ ὁ κλῆρος αὐτῷ τῆς αἱρέ- E
σεως μὴ ἐν τελευταίοις πίπτοι, κινδυνεύει ἐκ τῶν ἐκεῖθεν
ἀπαγγελλομένων οὐ μόνον ἐνθάδε εὐδαιμονεῖν ἄν, ἀλλὰ
225 καὶ τὴν ἐνθένδε ἐκεῖσε καὶ δεῦρο πάλιν πορείαν οὐκ ἂν
χθονίαν καὶ τραχεῖαν πορεύεσθαι, ἀλλὰ λείαν τε καὶ οὐρα-
νίαν. ταύτην γὰρ δὴ ἔφη τὴν θέαν ἀξίαν εἶναι ἰδεῖν,
ὡς ἕκασται αἱ ψυχαὶ ᾑροῦντο τοὺς βίους· ἐλεεινήν τε 620
γὰρ ἰδεῖν εἶναι καὶ γελοίαν καὶ θαυμασίαν. κατὰ συνή-
230 θειαν γὰρ τοῦ προτέρου βίου τὰ πολλὰ αἱρεῖσθαι. ἰδεῖν
μὲν γὰρ ψυχὴν ἔφη τὴν ποτε Ὀρφέως γενομένην κύκνου
βίον αἱρουμένην, μίσει τοῦ γυναικείου γένους διὰ τὸν ὑπ'
ἐκείνων θάνατον οὐκ ἐθέλουσαν ἐν γυναικὶ γεννηθεῖσαν
γενέσθαι· ἰδεῖν δὲ τὴν Θαμύρου ἀηδόνος ἑλομένην· ἰδεῖν
235 δὲ καὶ κύκνον μεταβάλλοντα εἰς ἀνθρωπίνου βίον αἵρε- B
σιν, καὶ ἄλλα ζῷα μουσικὰ ὡσαύτως. εἰκοστὴν δὲ λαχοῦσαν ψυχὴν ἑλέσθαι λέοντος βίον· εἶναι δὲ τὴν Αἴαντος
τοῦ Τελαμωνίου, φεύγουσαν ἄνθρωπον γενέσθαι, μεμνη-
μένην τῆς τῶν ὅπλων κρίσεως. τὴν δ' ἐπὶ τούτῳ Ἀγα-
240 μέμνονος· ἔχθρᾳ δὲ καὶ ταύτην τοῦ ἀνθρωπίνου γένους
διὰ τὰ πάθη ἀετοῦ διαλλάξαι βίον. ἐν μέσοις δὲ λαχοῦσαν τὴν Ἀταλάντης ψυχήν, κατιδοῦσαν μεγάλας τιμὰς

ἀθλητοῦ ἀνδρός, οὐ δύνασθαι παρελθεῖν, ἀλλὰ λαβεῖν.

C μετὰ δὲ ταύτην ἰδεῖν τὴν Ἐπειοῦ τοῦ Πανοπέως εἰς τεχνικῆς γυναικὸς ἰοῦσαν φύσιν· πόρρω δ' ἐν ὑστάτοις 245 ἰδεῖν τὴν τοῦ γελωτοποιοῦ Θερσίτου πίθηκον ἐνδυομένην. κατὰ τύχην δὲ τὴν Ὀδυσσέως λαχοῦσαν πασῶν ὑστάτην αἱρησομένην ἰέναι, μνήμῃ δὲ τῶν προτέρων πόνων φιλοτιμίας λελωφηκυῖαν ζητεῖν περιιοῦσαν χρόνον πολὺν βίον ἀνδρὸς ἰδιώτου ἀπράγμονος, καὶ μόγις εὑρεῖν κείμενόν 250 που καὶ παρημελημένον ὑπὸ τῶν ἄλλων, καὶ εἰπεῖν

D ἰδοῦσαν ὅτι τὰ αὐτὰ ἂν ἔπραξε καὶ πρώτη λαχοῦσα, καὶ ἀσμένην ἑλέσθαι. καὶ ἐκ τῶν ἄλλων δὴ θηρίων ὡσαύτως εἰς ἀνθρώπους ἰέναι καὶ εἰς ἄλληλα, τὰ μὲν ἄδικα εἰς τὰ ἄγρια, τὰ δὲ δίκαια εἰς τὰ ἥμερα μεταβάλλοντα, καὶ 255 πάσας μίξεις μίγνυσθαι. ἐπειδὴ δ' οὖν πάσας τὰς ψυχὰς τοὺς βίους ᾑρῆσθαι, ὥσπερ ἔλαχον, ἐν τάξει προσιέναι πρὸς τὴν Λάχεσιν· ἐκείνην δ' ἑκάστῳ ὃν εἵλετο δαίμονα,

E τοῦτον φύλακα ξυμπέμπειν τοῦ βίου καὶ ἀποπληρωτὴν τῶν αἱρεθέντων. ὃν πρῶτον μὲν ἄγειν αὐτὴν πρὸς τὴν 260 Κλωθὼ ὑπὸ τὴν ἐκείνης χεῖρά τε καὶ ἐπιστροφὴν τῆς τοῦ ἀτράκτου δίνης, κυροῦντα ἣν λαχὼν εἵλετο μοῖραν· ταύτης δ' ἐφαψάμενον αὖθις ἐπὶ τὴν τῆς Ἀτρόπου ἄγειν νῆσιν, ἀμετάστροφα τὰ ἐπικλωσθέντα ποιοῦντα· ἐντεῦθεν

621 δὲ δὴ ἀμεταστρεπτὶ ὑπὸ τὸν τῆς Ἀνάγκης ἰέναι θρόνον, 265 καὶ δι' ἐκείνου διεξελθόντα, ἐπειδὴ καὶ οἱ ἄλλοι διῆλθον, πορεύεσθαι ἅπαντας εἰς τὸ τῆς Λήθης πεδίον διὰ καύματός τε καὶ πνίγους δεινοῦ· καὶ γὰρ εἶναι αὐτὸ κενὸν δένδρων τε καὶ ὅσα γῆ φύει. σκηνᾶσθαι οὖν σφᾶς ἤδη ἑσπέρας γιγνομένης παρὰ τὸν Ἀμέλητα ποταμόν, οὗ τὸ 270 ὕδωρ ἀγγεῖον οὐδὲν στέγειν. μέτρον μὲν οὖν τι τοῦ ὕδατος πᾶσιν ἀναγκαῖον εἶναι πιεῖν, τοὺς δὲ φρονήσει μὴ σωζομένους πλέον πίνειν τοῦ μέτρου· τὸν δὲ ἀεὶ πιόντα

πάντων ἐπιλανθάνεσθαι. ἐπειδὴ δὲ κοιμηθῆναι καὶ μέσας B
275 νύκτας γενέσθαι, βροντήν τε καὶ σεισμὸν γενέσθαι, καὶ
ἐντεῦθεν ἐξαπίνης ἄλλον ἄλλῃ φέρεσθαι ἄνω εἰς τὴν γένεσιν, ἄττοντας ὥσπερ ἀστέρας. αὐτὸς δὲ τοῦ μὲν ὕδατος
κωλυθῆναι πιεῖν· ὅπῃ μέντοι καὶ ὅπως εἰς τὸ σῶμα ἀφίκοιτο, οὐκ εἰδέναι, ἀλλ' ἐξαίφνης ἀναβλέψας ἰδεῖν ἕωθεν
280 αὐτὸν κείμενον ἐπὶ τῇ πυρᾷ.

Καὶ οὕτως, ὦ Γλαύκων, μῦθος ἐσώθη καὶ οὐκ ἀπώλετο, καὶ ἡμᾶς ἂν σώσειεν, ἂν πειθώμεθα αὐτῷ, καὶ τὸν C
τῆς Λήθης ποταμὸν εὖ διαβησόμεθα καὶ τὴν ψυχὴν οὐ
μιανθησόμεθα· ἀλλ' ἂν ἐμοὶ πειθώμεθα, νομίζοντες ἀθά-
285 νατον ψυχὴν καὶ δυνατὴν πάντα μὲν κακὰ ἀνέχεσθαι,
πάντα δὲ ἀγαθά, τῆς ἄνω ὁδοῦ ἀεὶ ἑξόμεθα καὶ δικαιοσύνην μετὰ φρονήσεως παντὶ τρόπῳ ἐπιτηδεύσομεν, ἵνα
καὶ ἡμῖν αὐτοῖς φίλοι ὦμεν καὶ τοῖς θεοῖς, αὐτοῦ τε
μένοντες ἐνθάδε, καὶ ἐπειδὰν τὰ ἆθλα αὐτῆς κομιζώμεθα, D
290 ὥσπερ οἱ νικηφόροι περιαγειρόμενοι, καὶ ἐνθάδε καὶ ἐν
τῇ χιλιέτει πορείᾳ, ἣν διεληλύθαμεν, εὖ πράττωμεν.

TIMAEUS.

The Tale of Atlantis.
(CRITIAS. SOCRATES.)
20 D—26 E.

ΚΡ. Ἄκουε δή, ὦ Σώκρατες, λόγου μάλα μὲν ἀτό-
που, παντάπασί γε μὴν ἀληθοῦς, ὡς ὁ τῶν ἑπτὰ σοφώτατος Σόλων ποτ' ἔφη. ἦν μὲν οὖν οἰκεῖος καὶ σφόδρα E
φίλος ἡμῖν Δρωπίδου τοῦ προπάππου, καθάπερ λέγει
5 πολλαχοῦ καὶ αὐτὸς ἐν τῇ ποιήσει· πρὸς δὲ Κριτίαν τὸν
ἡμέτερον πάππον εἶπεν, ὡς ἀπεμνημόνευεν αὖ πρὸς ἡμᾶς

ὁ γέρων, ὅτι μεγάλα καὶ θαυμαστὰ τῆσδ' εἴη παλαιὰ
ἔργα τῆς πόλεως ὑπὸ χρόνου καὶ φθορᾶς ἀνθρώπων
ἠφανισμένα, πάντων δὲ ἓν μέγιστον, οὗ νῦν ἐπιμνησθεῖσι
21 πρέπον ἂν ἡμῖν εἴη σοί τε ἀποδοῦναι χάριν καὶ τὴν 10
θεὸν ἅμα ἐν τῇ πανηγύρει δικαίως τε καὶ ἀληθῶς οἷόν-
περ ὑμνοῦντας ἐγκωμιάζειν.

ΣΩ. Εὖ λέγεις. ἀλλὰ δὴ ποῖον ἔργον τοῦτο Κριτίας
οὐ λεγόμενον μέν, ὡς δὲ πραχθὲν ὄντως ὑπὸ τῆσδε τῆς
πόλεως ἀρχαῖον διηγεῖτο κατὰ τὴν Σόλωνος ἀκοήν; 15

ΚΡ. Ἐγὼ φράσω παλαιὸν ἀκηκοὼς λόγον οὐ νέου
ἀνδρός. ἦν μὲν γὰρ δὴ τότε Κριτίας, ὡς ἔφη, σχεδὸν
B ἐγγὺς ἤδη τῶν ἐνενήκοντα ἐτῶν, ἐγὼ δέ πη μάλιστα δε-
κέτης· ἡ δὲ Κουρεῶτις ἡμῖν οὖσα ἐτύγχανεν Ἀπατουρίων.
τὸ δὴ τῆς ἑορτῆς σύνηθες ἑκάστοτε καὶ τότε ξυνέβη τοῖς 20
παισίν· ἆθλα γὰρ ἡμῖν οἱ πατέρες ἔθεσαν ῥαψῳδίας.
πολλῶν μὲν οὖν δὴ καὶ πολλὰ ἐλέχθη ποιητῶν ποιήματα,
ἅτε δὲ νέα κατ' ἐκεῖνον τὸν χρόνον ὄντα τὰ Σόλωνος
πολλοὶ τῶν παίδων ᾔσαμεν. εἶπεν οὖν δή τις τῶν φρατέ-
ρων, εἴτε δὴ δοκοῦν αὐτῷ τότε εἴτε καὶ χάριν τινὰ τῷ 25
C Κριτίᾳ φέρων, δοκεῖν οἱ τά τε ἄλλα σοφώτατον γεγονέναι
Σόλωνα καὶ κατὰ τὴν ποίησιν αὖ τῶν ποιητῶν πάντων
ἐλευθεριώτατον. ὁ δὴ γέρων, σφόδρα γὰρ οὖν μέμνημαι,
μάλα τε ἥσθη καὶ διαμειδιάσας εἶπεν· Εἴ γε, ὦ Ἀμύ-
νανδρε, μὴ παρέργῳ τῇ ποιήσει κατεχρήσατο, ἀλλ' ἐσπου- 30
δάκει καθάπερ ἄλλοι, τόν τε λόγον ὃν ἀπ' Αἰγύπτου
δεῦρο ἠνέγκατο ἀπετέλεσε, καὶ μὴ διὰ τὰς στάσεις ὑπὸ
κακῶν τε ἄλλων, ὅσα εὗρεν ἐνθάδε ἥκων, ἠναγκάσθη
D καταμελῆσαι, κατά γ' ἐμὴν δόξαν οὔτε Ἡσίοδος οὔτε
Ὅμηρος οὔτε ἄλλος οὐδεὶς ποιητὴς εὐδοκιμώτερος ἐγένετο 35
ἂν ποτε αὐτοῦ. Τίς δ' ἦν ὁ λόγος, ἦ δ' ὅς, ὦ Κριτία; Ἡ
περὶ μεγίστης, ἔφη, καὶ ὀνομαστοτάτης πασῶν δικαιότατ'

ἂν πράξεως οὔσης, ἣν ἥδε ἡ πόλις ἔπραξε μέν, διὰ δὲ
χρόνον καὶ φθορὰν τῶν ἐργασαμένων οὐ διήρκεσε δεῦρο
40 ὁ λόγος. Λέγε ἐξ ἀρχῆς, ἦ δ' ὅς, τί τε καὶ πῶς καὶ παρὰ
τίνων ὡς ἀληθῆ διακηκοὼς ἔλεγεν ὁ Σόλων. Ἔστι τις
κατ' Αἴγυπτον, ἦ δ' ὅς, ἐν τῷ Δέλτα, περὶ ὃ κατὰ κορυ- Ε
φὴν σχίζεται τὸ τοῦ Νείλου ῥεῦμα, Σαϊτικὸς ἐπικαλού-
μενος νομός, τούτου δὲ τοῦ νομοῦ μεγίστη πόλις Σάϊς,
45 ὅθεν δὴ καὶ Ἄμασις ἦν ὁ βασιλεύς· οἷς τῆς πόλεως θεὸς
ἀρχηγός τίς ἐστιν, Αἰγυπτιστὶ μὲν τοὔνομα Νηίθ, Ἑλλη-
νιστὶ δέ, ὡς ὁ ἐκείνων λόγος, Ἀθηνᾶ· μάλα δὲ φιλαθή-
ναιοι καί τινα τρόπον οἰκεῖοι τῶνδ' εἶναί φασιν. οἳ δὴ
Σόλων ἔφη πορευθεὶς σφόδρα τε γενέσθαι παρ' αὐτοῖς ἔν-
50 τιμος, καὶ δὴ καὶ τὰ παλαιὰ ἀνερωτῶν τοὺς μάλιστα περὶ 22
ταῦτα τῶν ἱερέων ἐμπείρους σχεδὸν οὔτε αὐτὸν οὔτε ἄλλον
Ἕλληνα οὐδένα οὐδέν, ὡς ἔπος εἰπεῖν, εἰδότα περὶ τῶν τοιούτων ἀνευρεῖν. καί ποτε προαγαγεῖν βουληθεὶς αὐτοὺς
περὶ τῶν ἀρχαίων εἰς λόγους, τῶν τῇδε τὰ ἀρχαιότατα
55 λέγειν ἐπιχειρεῖν, περὶ Φορωνέως τε τοῦ πρώτου λεχθέν-
τος καὶ Νιόβης, καὶ μετὰ τὸν κατακλυσμὸν αὖ περὶ Δευ-
καλίωνος καὶ Πύρρας ὡς διεγένοντο μυθολογεῖν, καὶ
τοὺς ἐξ αὐτῶν γενεαλογεῖν, καὶ τὰ τῶν ἐτῶν ὅσα ἦν οἷς Β
ἔλεγε πειρᾶσθαι διαμνημονεύων τοὺς χρόνους ἀριθμεῖν·
60 καί τινα εἰπεῖν τῶν ἱερέων εὖ μάλα παλαιόν· Ὦ Σόλων,
Σόλων, Ἕλληνες ἀεὶ παῖδές ἐστε, γέρων δὲ Ἕλλην οὐκ
ἔστιν. Ἀκούσας οὖν, Πῶς τί τοῦτο λέγεις ; φάναι. Νέοι
ἐστέ, εἰπεῖν, τὰς ψυχὰς πάντες· οὐδεμίαν γὰρ ἐν αὐταῖς
ἔχετε δι' ἀρχαίαν ἀκοὴν παλαιὰν δόξαν οὐδὲ μάθημα
65 χρόνῳ πολιὸν οὐδέν. τὸ δὲ τούτων αἴτιον τόδε. πολλαὶ Γ
καὶ κατὰ πολλὰ φθοραὶ γεγόνασιν ἀνθρώπων καὶ ἔσονται,
πυρὶ μὲν καὶ ὕδατι μέγισται, μυρίοις δὲ ἄλλοις ἕτεραι
βραχύτεραι. τὸ γὰρ οὖν καὶ παρ' ὑμῖν λεγόμενον, ὥς

ποτε Φαέθων Ἡλίου παῖς τὸ τοῦ πατρὸς ἅρμα ζεύξας
διὰ τὸ μὴ δυνατὸς εἶναι κατὰ τὴν τοῦ πατρὸς ὁδὸν ἐλαύ- 70
νειν τά τ᾽ ἐπὶ γῆς ξυνέκαυσε καὶ αὐτὸς κεραυνωθεὶς
διεφθάρη, τοῦτο μύθου μὲν σχῆμα ἔχον λέγεται, τὸ δ᾽
D ἀληθές ἐστι τῶν περὶ γῆν καὶ κατ᾽ οὐρανὸν ἰόντων παρ-
άλλαξις καὶ διὰ μακρῶν χρόνων γιγνομένη τῶν ἐπὶ γῆς
πυρὶ πολλῷ φθορά. τότε οὖν ὅσοι κατ᾽ ὄρη καὶ ἐν ὑψη- 75
λοῖς τόποις καὶ ἐν ξηροῖς οἰκοῦσι, μᾶλλον διόλλυνται τῶν
ποταμοῖς καὶ θαλάττῃ προσοικούντων· ἡμῖν δὲ ὁ Νεῖλος
εἴς τε τὰ ἄλλα σωτὴρ καὶ τότε ἐκ ταύτης τῆς ἀπορίας
σώζει λυόμενος. ὅταν δ᾽ αὖ οἱ θεοὶ τὴν γῆν ὕδασι καθαί-
ροντες κατακλύζωσιν, οἱ μὲν ἐν τοῖς ὄρεσι διασώζονται 80
E βουκόλοι νομεῖς τε, οἱ δ᾽ ἐν ταῖς παρ᾽ ὑμῖν πόλεσιν εἰς
τὴν θάλατταν ὑπὸ τῶν ποταμῶν φέρονται, κατὰ δὲ
τήνδε τὴν χώραν οὔτε τότε οὔτε ἄλλοτε ἄνωθεν ἐπὶ τὰς
ἀρούρας ὕδωρ ἐπιρρεῖ· τὸ δ᾽ ἐναντίον κάτωθεν ἐπανιέναι
πέφυκεν. ὅθεν καὶ δι᾽ ἃς αἰτίας τἀνθάδε σωζόμενα λέγε- 85
ται παλαιότατα. τὸ δὲ ἀληθές, ἐν πᾶσι τοῖς τόποις ὅπου
μὴ χειμὼν ἐξαίσιος ἢ καῦμα ἀπείργει, πλέον, τοτὲ δὲ
23 ἔλαττον ἀεὶ γένος ἐστὶν ἀνθρώπων· ὅσα δὲ ἢ παρ᾽ ὑμῖν
ἢ τῇδε ἢ καὶ κατ᾽ ἄλλον τόπον ὧν ἀκοῇ ἴσμεν, εἴ πού
τι καλὸν ἢ μέγα γέγονεν ἢ καί τινα διαφορὰν ἄλλην 90
ἔχον, πάντα γεγραμμένα ἐκ παλαιοῦ τῇδ᾽ ἐστὶν ἐν τοῖς
ἱεροῖς καὶ σεσωσμένα. τὰ δὲ παρ᾽ ὑμῖν καὶ τοῖς ἄλλοις
ἄρτι κατεσκευασμένα ἑκάστοτε τυγχάνει γράμμασι καὶ
ἅπασιν ὁπόσων πόλεις δέονται, καὶ πάλιν δι᾽ εἰωθότων
ἐτῶν ὥσπερ νόσημα ἥκει φερόμενον αὐτοῖς ῥεῦμα οὐρά- 95
B νιον καὶ τοὺς ἀγραμμάτους τε καὶ ἀμούσους ἔλιπεν ὑμῶν,
ὥστε πάλιν ἐξ ἀρχῆς οἷον νέοι γίγνεσθε, οὐδὲν εἰδότες
οὔτε τῶν τῇδε οὔτε τῶν παρ᾽ ὑμῖν, ὅσα ἦν ἐν τοῖς πα-
λαιοῖς χρόνοις. τὰ γοῦν νῦν δὴ γενεαλογηθέντα, ὦ

100 Σόλων, περὶ τῶν παρ' ὑμῖν ἃ διῆλθες, παίδων βραχύ
τι διαφέρει μύθων, οἳ πρῶτον μὲν ἕνα γῆς κατακλυσμὸν
μέμνησθε πολλῶν ἔμπροσθεν γεγονότων, ἔτι δὲ τὸ κάλλιστον καὶ ἄριστον γένος ἐπ' ἀνθρώπους ἐν τῇ χώρᾳ τῇ
παρ' ὑμῖν οὐκ ἴστε γεγονός, ἐξ ὧν σύ τε καὶ πᾶσα ἡ πό-
105 λις ἔστι τὰ νῦν ὑμῶν περιλειφθέντος ποτὲ σπέρματος C
βραχέος, ἀλλ' ὑμᾶς λέληθε διὰ τὸ τοὺς περιγενομένους
ἐπὶ πολλὰς γενεὰς γράμμασι τελευτᾶν ἀφώνους. ἦν γὰρ
δή ποτε, ὦ Σόλων, ὑπὲρ τὴν μεγίστην φθορὰν ὕδασιν ἡ
νῦν Ἀθηναίων οὖσα πόλις ἀρίστη πρός τε τὸν πόλεμον
110 καὶ κατὰ πάντα εὐνομωτάτη διαφερόντως· ᾗ κάλλιστα
ἔργα καὶ πολιτεῖαί γενέσθαι λέγονται κάλλισται πασῶν,
ὁπόσων νῦν ὑπὸ τὸν οὐρανὸν ἡμεῖς ἀκοὴν παρεδεξάμεθα.
Ἀκούσας οὖν ὁ Σόλων ἔφη θαυμάσαι καὶ πᾶσαν προθυ- D
μίαν σχεῖν δεόμενος τῶν ἱερέων πάντα δι' ἀκριβείας οἱ
115 τὰ περὶ τῶν πάλαι πολιτῶν ἐξῆς διελθεῖν. τὸν οὖν ἱερέα
φάναι· Φθόνος οὐδείς, ὦ Σόλων, ἀλλὰ σοῦ τε ἕνεκα ἐρῶ
καὶ τῆς πόλεως ὑμῶν, μάλιστα δὲ τῆς θεοῦ χάριν, ἣ τήν
τε ὑμετέραν καὶ τήνδ' ἔλαχε καὶ ἔθρεψε καὶ ἐπαίδευσε,
προτέραν μὲν τὴν παρ' ὑμῖν ἔτεσι χιλίοις, ἐκ Γῆς τε καὶ
120 Ἡφαίστου τὸ σπέρμα παραλαβοῦσα ὑμῶν, τήνδε δὲ ὑστέ- E
ραν. τῆς δὲ ἐνθάδε διακοσμήσεως παρ' ἡμῖν ἐν τοῖς ἱεροῖς γράμμασιν ὀκτακισχιλίων ἐτῶν ἀριθμὸς γέγραπται.
περὶ δὴ τῶν ἐνακισχίλια γεγονότων ἔτη πολιτῶν σοι δη-
λώσω διὰ βραχέων νόμους τε καὶ τῶν ἔργων αὐτοῖς ὃ
125 κάλλιστον ἐπράχθη· τὸ δ' ἀκριβὲς περὶ πάντων ἐφεξῆς 24
εἰσαῦθις κατὰ σχολήν, αὐτὰ τὰ γράμματα λαβόντες, διέ-
ξιμεν. τοὺς μὲν οὖν νόμους σκόπει πρὸς τοὺς τῇδε.
πολλὰ γὰρ παραδείγματα τῶν τότε παρ' ὑμῖν ὄντων ἐνθάδε νῦν ἀνευρήσεις, πρῶτον μὲν τὸ τῶν ἱερέων γένος
130 ἀπὸ τῶν ἄλλων χωρὶς ἀφωρισμένον, μετὰ δὲ τοῦτο τὸ

τῶν δημιουργῶν, ὅτι καθ᾽ αὑτὸ ἕκαστον ἄλλῳ δὲ οὐκ ἐπι-
μιγνύμενον δημιουργεῖ, τό τε τῶν νομέων καὶ τὸ τῶν
θηρευτῶν τό τε τῶν γεωργῶν. καὶ δὴ καὶ τὸ μάχιμον
B γένος ᾔσθησαί που τῇδε ἀπὸ πάντων τῶν γενῶν κεχωρι-
σμένον, οἷς οὐδὲν ἄλλο πλὴν τὰ περὶ τὸν πόλεμον ὑπὸ 135
τοῦ νόμου προσετάχθη μέλειν. ἔτι δὲ ἡ τῆς ὁπλίσεως αὑτῶν σχέσις ἀσπίδων καὶ δοράτων, οἷς ἡμεῖς πρῶτοι τῶν
περὶ τὴν Ἀσίαν ὡπλίσμεθα, τῆς θεοῦ, καθάπερ ἐν ἐκείνοις
τοῖς τόποις, παρ᾽ ὑμῖν πρώτοις ἐνδειξαμένης. τὸ δ᾽ αὖ
περὶ τῆς φρονήσεως, ὁρᾷς που τὸν νόμον τῇδε ὅσην ἐπι- 140
C μέλειαν ἐποιήσατο εὐθὺς κατ᾽ ἀρχὰς περί τε τὸν κόσμον
ἅπαντα, μέχρι μαντικῆς καὶ ἰατρικῆς πρὸς ὑγίειαν, ἐκ
τούτων θείων ὄντων εἰς τὰ ἀνθρώπινα ἀνευρών, ὅσα τε
ἄλλα τούτοις ἕπεται μαθήματα, πάντα κτησάμενος. ταύτην οὖν δὴ τότε ξύμπασαν τὴν διακόσμησιν καὶ σύνταξιν 145
ἡ θεὸς προτέρους ὑμᾶς διακοσμήσασα κατῴκισεν, ἐκλεξαμένη τὸν τόπον ἐν ᾧ γεγένησθε, τὴν εὐκρασίαν τῶν ὡρῶν
D ἐν αὐτῷ κατιδοῦσα, ὅτι φρονιμωτάτους ἄνδρας οἴσοι· ἅτ᾽
οὖν φιλοπόλεμός τε καὶ φιλόσοφος ἡ θεὸς οὖσα τὸν προσ-
φερεστάτους αὑτῇ μέλλοντα οἴσειν τόπον ἄνδρας, τοῦτον 150
ἐκλεξαμένη πρῶτον κατῴκισεν. ᾠκεῖτε δὴ οὖν νόμοις τε
τοιούτοις χρώμενοι καὶ ἔτι μᾶλλον εὐνομούμενοι πάσῃ τε
πάντας ἀνθρώπους ὑπερβεβηκότες ἀρετῇ, καθάπερ εἰκὸς
γεννήματα καὶ παιδεύματα θεῶν ὄντας. πολλὰ μὲν οὖν
ὑμῶν καὶ μεγάλα ἔργα τῆς πόλεως τῇδε γεγραμμένα θαυ- 155
E μάζεται, πάντων μὴν ἓν ὑπερέχει μεγέθει καὶ ἀρετῇ· λέγει γὰρ τὰ γεγραμμένα, ὅσην ἡ πόλις ὑμῶν ἔπαυσέ ποτε
δύναμιν ὕβρει πορευομένην ἅμα ἐπὶ πᾶσαν Εὐρώπην καὶ
Ἀσίαν, ἔξωθεν ὁρμηθεῖσαν ἐκ τοῦ Ἀτλαντικοῦ πελάγους·
τότε γὰρ πορεύσιμον ἦν τὸ ἐκεῖ πέλαγος· νῆσον γὰρ πρὸ 160
τοῦ στόματος εἶχεν, ὃ καλεῖτε, ὥς φατε ὑμεῖς, Ἡρακλέ-

ους στήλας· ἡ δὲ νῆσος ἅμα Λιβύης ἦν καὶ Ἀσίας μείζων, ἐξ ἧς ἐπιβατὸν ἐπὶ τὰς ἄλλας νήσους τοῖς τότ'
ἐγίγνετο πορευομένοις, ἐκ δὲ τῶν νήσων ἐπὶ τὴν καταντι-
165 κρὺ πᾶσαν ἤπειρον τὴν περὶ τὸν ἀληθινὸν ἐκεῖνον πόν- 25
τον. τάδε μὲν γάρ, ὅσα ἐντὸς τοῦ στόματος οὗ λέγομεν,
φαίνεται λιμὴν στενόν τινα ἔχων εἴσπλουν· ἐκεῖνο δὲ πέλαγος ὄντως ἥ τε περιέχουσα αὐτὸ γῆ παντελῶς ἀληθῶς
ὀρθότατ' ἂν λέγοιτο ἤπειρος. ἐν δὲ δὴ τῇ Ἀτλαντίδι νήσῳ
170 ταύτῃ μεγάλη συνέστη καὶ θαυμαστὴ δύναμις βασιλέων,
κρατοῦσα μὲν ἁπάσης τῆς νήσου, πολλῶν δὲ ἄλλων νήσων
καὶ μερῶν τῆς ἠπείρου· πρὸς δὲ τούτοις ἔτι τῶν ἐντὸς
τῇδε Λιβύης μὲν ἦρχον μέχρι πρὸς Αἴγυπτον, τῆς δὲ Εὐ- B
ρώπης μέχρι Τυρρηνίας. αὕτη δὴ πᾶσα ξυναθροισθεῖσα
175 εἰς ἓν ἡ δύναμις τόν τε παρ' ὑμῖν καὶ τὸν παρ' ἡμῖν καὶ
τὸν ἐντὸς τοῦ στόματος πάντα τόπον μιᾷ ποτ' ἐπεχείρη-
σεν ὁρμῇ δουλοῦσθαι. τότε οὖν ὑμῶν, ὦ Σόλων, τῆς πόλεως ἡ δύναμις εἰς ἅπαντας ἀνθρώπους διαφανὴς ἀρετῇ
τε καὶ ῥώμῃ ἐγένετο· πάντων γὰρ προστᾶσα εὐψυχίᾳ καὶ
180 τέχναις ὅσαι κατὰ πόλεμον, τὰ μὲν τῶν Ἑλλήνων ἡγου- C
μένη, τὰ δ' αὐτὴ μονωθεῖσα ἐξ ἀνάγκης τῶν ἄλλων ἀπο-
στάντων, ἐπὶ τοὺς ἐσχάτους ἀφικομένη κινδύνους, κρα-
τήσασα μὲν τῶν ἐπιόντων τρόπαια ἔστησε, τοὺς δὲ μήπω
δεδουλωμένους διεκώλυσε δουλωθῆναι, τοὺς δ' ἄλλους,
185 ὅσοι κατοικοῦμεν ἐντὸς ὅρων Ἡρακλείων, ἀφθόνως ἅπαντας ἠλευθέρωσεν. ὑστέρῳ δὲ χρόνῳ σεισμῶν ἐξαισίων καὶ
κατακλυσμῶν γενομένων, μιᾶς ἡμέρας καὶ νυκτὸς χαλεπῆς
ἐλθούσης, τό τε παρ' ὑμῶν μάχιμον πᾶν ἀθρόον ἔδυ D
κατὰ γῆς, ἥ τε Ἀτλαντὶς νῆσος ὡσαύτως κατὰ τῆς θα-
190 λάττης δῦσα ἠφανίσθη· διὸ καὶ νῦν ἄπορον καὶ ἀδιερεύ-
νητον γέγονε τὸ ἐκεῖ πέλαγος, πηλοῦ κάρτα βαθέος ἐμπο-
δὼν ὄντος, ὃν ἡ νῆσος ἱζομένη παρέσχετο.

Τὰ μὲν δὴ ῥηθέντα, ὦ Σώκρατες, ὑπὸ τοῦ παλαιοῦ
E Κριτίου κατ' ἀκοὴν τὴν Σόλωνος, ὡς συντόμως εἰπεῖν,
ἀκήκοας· λέγοντος δὲ δὴ χθὲς σοῦ περὶ πολιτείας καὶ τῶν 195
ἀνδρῶν οὓς ἔλεγες, ἐθαύμαζον ἀναμιμνησκόμενος αὐτὰ
ἃ νῦν λέγω, κατανοῶν ὡς δαιμονίως ἔκ τινος τύχης οὐκ
ἄπο σκοποῦ ξυνηνέχθης τὰ πολλὰ οἷς Σόλων εἶπεν. οὐ
26 μὴν ἐβουλήθην παραχρῆμα εἰπεῖν· διὰ χρόνου γὰρ οὐχ
ἱκανῶς ἐμεμνήμην. ἐνενόησα οὖν ὅτι χρεὼν εἴη με πρὸς 200
ἐμαυτὸν πρῶτον ἱκανῶς πάντα ἀναλαβόντα λέγειν οὕτως.
ὅθεν ταχὺ ξυνωμολόγησά σοι τἀπιταχθέντα χθές, ἡγούμενος, ὅπερ ἐν ἅπασι τοῖς τοιοῖσδε μέγιστον ἔργον, λόγου
τινὰ πρέποντα τοῖς βουλήμασιν ὑποθέσθαι, τούτου μετρίως ἡμᾶς εὐπορήσειν. οὕτω δή, καθάπερ ὅδ᾽ εἶπε, χθές 205
B τε εὐθὺς ἐνθένδε ἀπιὼν πρὸς τούσδε ἀνέφερον αὐτὰ ἀναμιμνησκόμενος, ἀπελθών τε σχεδόν τι πάντα ἐπισκοπῶν
τῆς νυκτὸς ἀνέλαβον. ὡς δή τοι, τὸ λεγόμενον, τὰ παίδων μαθήματα θαυμαστὸν ἔχει τι μνημεῖον· ἐγὼ γὰρ ἃ
μὲν χθὲς ἤκουσα, οὐκ ἂν οἶδα εἰ δυναίμην ἅπαντα ἐν 210
μνήμῃ πάλιν λαβεῖν· ταῦτα δὲ ἃ πάμπολυν χρόνον δια-
κήκοα, παντάπασι θαυμάσαιμ᾽ ἂν εἴ τί με αὐτῶν διαπέ-
φευγεν. ἦν μὲν οὖν μετὰ πολλῆς ἡδονῆς καὶ παιδικῆς
C τότε ἀκουόμενα, καὶ τοῦ πρεσβύτου προθύμως με διδά-
σκοντος, ἅτ᾽ ἐμοῦ πολλάκις ἐπανερωτῶντος, ὥστε οἷον 215
ἐγκαύματα ἀνεκπλύτου γραφῆς ἔμμονά μοι γέγονε. καὶ δὴ
καὶ τοῖσδε εὐθὺς ἔλεγον ἕωθεν αὐτὰ ταῦτα, ἵνα εὐποροῖεν
λόγων μετ᾽ ἐμοῦ. νῦν οὖν, οὗπερ ἕνεκα πάντα ταῦτα εἴρηται, λέγειν εἰμὶ ἕτοιμος, ὦ Σώκρατες, μὴ μόνον ἐν
κεφαλαίοις ἀλλ᾽ ὥσπερ ἤκουσα καθ᾽ ἕκαστον. τοὺς δὲ πο- 220
λίτας καὶ τὴν πόλιν ἣν χθὲς ἡμῖν ὡς ἐν μύθῳ διῄεισθα
D σύ, μετενεγκόντες ἐπὶ τἀληθὲς δεῦρο θήσομεν ὡς ἐκείνην
τήνδε οὖσαν, καὶ τοὺς πολίτας οὓς διενοοῦ φήσομεν ἐκεί-

225 νους τοὺς ἀληθινοὺς εἶναι προγόνους ἡμῶν οὓς ἔλεγεν ὁ
ἱερεύς· πάντως ἁρμόσουσι, καὶ οὐκ ἀπασόμεθα λέγοντες
αὐτοὺς εἶναι τοὺς ἐν τῷ τότε ὄντας χρόνῳ. κοινῇ δὲ δια-
λαμβάνοντες ἅπαντες πειρασόμεθα τὸ πρέπον εἰς δύναμιν
οἷς ἐπέταξας ἀποδοῦναι. σκοπεῖν οὖν δὴ χρή, ὦ Σώκρα-
230 τες, εἰ κατὰ νοῦν ὁ λόγος ἡμῖν οὗτος, ἤ τινα ἔτ' ἄλλον
ἀντ' αὐτοῦ ζητητέον.

PHILEBUS.

The Young Man 'bitten' by Logic.

(SOCRATES, PROTARCHUS.)

15 C—17 A.

ΣΩ. Εἶεν. πόθεν οὖν τις ταύτης ἄρξηται πολλῆς D
οὔσης καὶ παντοίας περὶ τὰ ἀμφισβητούμενα μάχης; ἆρ'
ἐνθένδε;

ΠΡΩ. Πόθεν;

5 ΣΩ. Φαμέν που ταὐτὸν ἓν καὶ πολλὰ ὑπὸ λόγων γιγνόμενα περιτρέχειν πάντη καθ' ἕκαστον τῶν λεγομένων
ἀεὶ καὶ πάλαι καὶ νῦν. καὶ τοῦτο οὔτε μὴ παύσηταί ποτε
οὔτε ἤρξατο νῦν, ἀλλ' ἔστι τὸ τοιοῦτον, ὡς ἐμοὶ φαίνεται, τῶν λόγων αὐτῶν ἀθάνατόν τι καὶ ἀγήρων πάθος
10 ἐν ἡμῖν. ὁ δὲ πρῶτον αὐτοῦ γευσάμενος ἑκάστοτε τῶν
νέων, ἡσθεὶς ὥς τινα σοφίας εὑρηκὼς θησαυρόν, ὑφ' E
ἡδονῆς ἐνθουσιᾷ τε καὶ πάντα κινεῖ λόγον ἄσμενος, τοτὲ
μὲν ἐπὶ θάτερα κυκλῶν καὶ συμφύρων εἰς ἕν, τοτὲ δὲ
πάλιν ἀνειλίττων καὶ διαμερίζων, εἰς ἀπορίαν αὐτὸν μὲν
15 πρῶτον καὶ μάλιστα καταβάλλων, δεύτερον δ' ἀεὶ τὸν
ἐχόμενον, ἄν τε νεώτερος ἄν τε πρεσβύτερος ἄν τε ἧλιξ

16 ὧν τυγχάνῃ, φειδόμενος οὔτε πατρὸς οὔτε μητρὸς οὔτε
ἄλλου τῶν ἀκουόντων οὐδενός, ὀλίγου δὲ καὶ τῶν ἄλλων
ζῴων, οὐ μόνον τῶν ἀνθρώπων, ἐπεὶ βαρβάρων γε οὐδενὸς ἂν φείσαιτο, εἴπερ μόνον ἑρμηνέα ποθὲν ἔχοι.   20

ΠΡΩ. Ἆρ᾽, ὦ Σώκρατες, οὐχ ὁρᾷς ἡμῶν τὸ πλῆθος,
ὅτι νέοι πάντες ἐσμέν ; καὶ οὐ φοβεῖ μή σοι μετὰ Φιλήβου ξυνεπιθώμεθα, ἐὰν ἡμᾶς λοιδορῇς ; ὅμως δέ, μανθάνομεν γὰρ ὃ λέγεις, εἴ τις τρόπος ἔστι καὶ μηχανὴ τὴν
μὲν τοιαύτην ταραχὴν ἡμῖν ἔξω τοῦ λόγου εὐμενῶς πως 25
B ἀπελθεῖν, ὁδὸν δέ τινα καλλίω ταύτης ἐπὶ τὸν λόγον
ἀνευρεῖν, σύ τε προθυμοῦ τοῦτο καὶ ἡμεῖς συνακολουθή-
σομεν εἰς δύναμιν· οὐ γὰρ σμικρὸς ὁ παρὼν λόγος, ὦ
Σώκρατες.

ΣΩ. Οὐ γὰρ οὖν, ὦ παῖδες, ὥς φησιν ὑμᾶς προσ- 30
αγορεύων Φίληβος. οὐ μὴν ἔστι καλλίων ὁδὸς οὐδ᾽ ἂν γένοιτο, ἧς ἐγὼ ἐραστὴς μέν εἰμι ἀεί, πολλάκις δέ με ἤδη
διαφυγοῦσα ἔρημον καὶ ἄπορον κατέστησεν.

ΠΡΩ. Τίς αὕτη ; λεγέσθω μόνον.

C ΣΩ. Ἣν δηλῶσαι μὲν οὐ πάνυ χαλεπόν, χρῆσθαι δὲ 35
παγχάλεπον. πάντα γὰρ ὅσα τέχνης ἐχόμενα ἀνευρέθη
πώποτε, διὰ ταύτης φανερὰ γέγονε. σκόπει δὲ ἣν λέγω.

ΠΡΩ. Λέγε μόνον.

ΣΩ. Θεῶν μὲν εἰς ἀνθρώπους δόσις, ὥς γε καταφαίνεται ἐμοί, ποθὲν ἐκ θεῶν ἐρρίφη διά τινος Προμηθέως 40
ἅμα φανοτάτῳ τινὶ πυρί. καὶ οἱ μὲν παλαιοί, κρείττονες
ἡμῶν καὶ ἐγγυτέρω θεῶν οἰκοῦντες, ταύτην φήμην παρέδοσαν, ὡς ἐξ ἑνὸς μὲν καὶ ἐκ πολλῶν ὄντων τῶν ἀεὶ
λεγομένων εἶναι, πέρας δὲ καὶ ἀπειρίαν ἐν αὑτοῖς ξύμφυ-
τον ἐχόντων. δεῖν οὖν ἡμᾶς τούτων οὕτω διακεκοσμημέ- 45
D νων ἀεὶ μίαν ἰδέαν περὶ παντὸς ἑκάστοτε θεμένους ζη-
τεῖν· εὑρήσειν γὰρ ἐνοῦσαν. ἐὰν οὖν μεταλάβωμεν, μετὰ

μίαν δύο, εἴ πως εἰσί, σκοπεῖν, εἰ δὲ μή, τρεῖς ἢ τινα
ἄλλον ἀριθμόν, καὶ τῶν ἐν ἐκείνων ἕκαστον πάλιν ὡσαύ-
50 τως, μέχριπερ ἂν τὸ κατ᾽ ἀρχὰς ἓν μὴ ὅτι ἓν καὶ πολλὰ
καὶ ἄπειρά ἐστι μόνον ἴδῃ τις, ἀλλὰ καὶ ὁπόσα. τὴν δὲ
τοῦ ἀπείρου ἰδέαν πρὸς τὸ πλῆθος μὴ προσφέρειν, πρὶν
ἄν τις τὸν ἀριθμὸν αὐτοῦ πάντα κατίδῃ τὸν μεταξὺ τοῦ
ἀπείρου τε καὶ τοῦ ἑνός· τότε δὴ δεῖ τὸ ἐν ἕκαστον τῶν Ε
55 πάντων εἰς τὸ ἄπειρον μεθέντα χαίρειν ἐᾶν. οἱ μὲν οὖν
θεοί, ὅπερ εἶπον, οὕτως ἡμῖν παρέδοσαν σκοπεῖν καὶ
μανθάνειν καὶ διδάσκειν ἀλλήλους· οἱ δὲ νῦν τῶν ἀνθρώπων σοφοὶ ἐν μέν, ὅπως ἂν τύχωσι, καὶ πολλὰ 17
θᾶττον καὶ βραδύτερον ποιοῦσι τοῦ δέοντος, μετὰ δὲ τὸ
60 ἐν ἄπειρα εὐθύς· τὰ δὲ μέσα αὐτοὺς ἐκφεύγει· οἷς διακεχώρισται τό τε διαλεκτικῶς πάλιν καὶ τὸ ἐριστικῶς ἡμᾶς
ποιεῖσθαι πρὸς ἀλλήλους τοὺς λόγους.

THEAETETUS.

The Philosopher and the Rhetorician.

(Socrates, Theodorus.)

172 C—177 C.

ΘΕΟ.   Οὐκοῦν σχολὴν ἄγομεν, ὦ Σώκρατες ;

ΣΩ.   Φαινόμεθα. καὶ πολλάκις μέν γε δή, ὦ δαιμόνιε, καὶ ἄλλοτε κατενόησα, ἀτὰρ καὶ νῦν, ὡς εἰκότως
οἱ ἐν ταῖς φιλοσοφίαις πολὺν χρόνον διατρίψαντες εἰς τὰ
5 δικαστήρια ἰόντες γελοῖοι φαίνονται ῥήτορες.

ΘΕΟ.   Πῶς δὴ οὖν λέγεις ;

ΣΩ.   Κινδυνεύουσιν οἱ ἐν δικαστηρίοις καὶ τοῖς τοιούτοις ἐκ νέων κυλινδούμενοι πρὸς τοὺς ἐν φιλοσοφίᾳ

D καὶ τῇ τοιᾷδε διατριβῇ τεθραμμένους ὡς οἰκέται πρὸς ἐλευθέρους τεθράφθαι. 10

ΘΕΟ. Πῇ δή;

ΣΩ. ῟Ηι τοῖς μέν, τοῦτο ὃ σὺ εἶπες, ἀεὶ πάρεστι σχολὴ καὶ τοὺς λόγους ἐν εἰρήνῃ ἐπὶ σχολῆς ποιοῦνται, ὥσπερ ἡμεῖς νυνὶ τρίτον ἤδη λόγον ἐκ λόγου μεταλαμβάνομεν, οὕτω κἀκεῖνοι, ἐὰν αὐτοὺς ὁ ἐπελθὼν τοῦ προ- 15 κειμένου μᾶλλον, καθάπερ ἡμᾶς, ἀρέσῃ· καὶ διὰ μακρῶν ἢ βραχέων μέλει οὐδὲν λέγειν, ἂν μόνον τύχωσι τοῦ ὄντος. οἱ δὲ ἐν ἀσχολίᾳ τε ἀεὶ λέγουσι· κατεπείγει γὰρ ὕδωρ

E ῥέον, καὶ οὐκ ἐγχωρεῖ περὶ οὗ ἂν ἐπιθυμήσωσι τοὺς λόγους ποιεῖσθαι, ἀλλ' ἀνάγκην ἔχων ὁ ἀντίδικος ἐφέ- 20 στηκε καὶ ὑπογραφὴν παραναγιγνωσκομένην, ὧν ἐκτὸς οὐ ῥητέον· (ἣν ἀντωμοσίαν καλοῦσιν·) οἱ δὲ λόγοι ἀεὶ περὶ ὁμοδούλου πρὸς δεσπότην καθήμενον, ἐν χειρὶ τὴν δίκην ἔχοντα, καὶ οἱ ἀγῶνες οὐδέποτε τὴν ἄλλως ἀλλ' ἀεὶ τὴν περὶ αὐτοῦ· πολλάκις δὲ καὶ περὶ ψυχῆς ὁ δρόμος· 25

173 ὥστ' ἐξ ἁπάντων τούτων ἔντονοι καὶ δριμεῖς γίγνονται, ἐπιστάμενοι τὸν δεσπότην λόγῳ τε θωπεῦσαι καὶ ἔργῳ χαρίσασθαι, σμικροὶ δὲ καὶ οὐκ ὀρθοὶ τὰς ψυχάς. τὴν γὰρ αὔξην καὶ τὸ εὐθύ τε καὶ τὸ ἐλεύθερον ἡ ἐκ νέων δουλεία ἀφῄρηται, ἀναγκάζουσα πράττειν σκολιά, μεγά- 30 λους κινδύνους καὶ φόβους ἔτι ἀπαλαῖς ψυχαῖς ἐπιβάλλουσα, οὓς οὐ δυνάμενοι μετὰ τοῦ δικαίου καὶ ἀληθοῦς ὑποφέρειν, εὐθὺς ἐπὶ τὸ ψεῦδός τε καὶ τὸ ἀλλήλους ἀνταδικεῖν τρεπόμενοι πολλὰ κάμπτονται καὶ

B συγκλῶνται, ὥσθ' ὑγιὲς οὐδὲν ἔχοντες τῆς διανοίας εἰς 35 ἄνδρας ἐκ μειρακίων τελευτῶσι, δεινοί τε καὶ σοφοὶ γεγονότες, ὡς οἴονται. Καὶ οὗτοι μὲν δὴ τοιοῦτοι, ὦ Θεόδωρε· τοὺς δὲ τοῦ ἡμετέρου χοροῦ πότερον βούλει διελθόντες ἢ ἐάσαντες πάλιν ἐπὶ τὸν λόγον τρεπώμεθα,

40 ἵνα μὴ καί, ὃ νῦν δὴ ἐλέγομεν, λίαν πολὺ τῇ ἐλευθερίᾳ
καὶ μεταλήψει τῶν λόγων καταχρώμεθα;

ΘΕΟ. Μηδαμῶς, ὦ Σώκρατες, ἀλλὰ διελθόντες.
πάνυ γὰρ εὖ τοῦτο εἴρηκας, ὅτι οὐχ ἡμεῖς οἱ ἐν τῷ C
τοιῷδε χορεύοντες τῶν λόγων ὑπηρέται, ἀλλ' οἱ λόγοι
45 οἱ ἡμέτεροι ὥσπερ οἰκέται, καὶ ἕκαστος αὐτῶν περιμένει
ἀποτελεσθῆναι ὅταν ἡμῖν δοκῇ· οὔτε γὰρ δικαστὴς οὔτε
θεατής, ὥσπερ ποιηταῖς, ἐπιτιμήσων τε καὶ ἄρξων ἐπι-
στατεῖ παρ' ἡμῖν.

ΣΩ. Λέγωμεν δή, ὡς ἔοικεν, ἐπεὶ σοί γε δοκεῖ, περὶ
50 τῶν κορυφαίων· τί γὰρ ἄν τις τούς γε φαύλως διατρί-
βοντας ἐν φιλοσοφίᾳ λέγοι; Οὗτοι δέ που ἐκ νέων πρῶτον μὲν εἰς ἀγορὰν οὐκ ἴσασι τὴν ὁδόν, οὐδὲ ὅπου δικα- D
στήριον ἢ βουλευτήριον ἤ τι κοινὸν ἄλλο τῆς πόλεως
συνέδριον· νόμους δὲ καὶ ψηφίσματα λεγόμενα ἢ γεγραμ-
55 μένα οὔτε ὁρῶσιν οὔτε ἀκούουσι. σπουδαὶ δὲ ἑταιρειῶν
ἐπ' ἀρχὰς καὶ σύνοδοι καὶ δεῖπνα καὶ σὺν αὐλητρίσι
κῶμοι, οὐδὲ ὄναρ πράττειν προσίσταται αὐτοῖς. εὖ δὲ ἢ
κακῶς τις γέγονεν ἐν πόλει, ἢ τί τῳ κακόν ἐστιν ἐκ προγόνων γεγονὸς ἢ πρὸς ἀνδρῶν ἢ γυναικῶν, μᾶλλον αὐτὸν
60 λέληθεν ἢ οἱ τῆς θαλάττης λεγόμενοι χόες. καὶ ταῦτα
πάντ' οὐδ' ὅτι οὐκ οἶδεν, οἶδεν· οὐδὲ γὰρ αὐτῶν ἀπέχεται E
τοῦ εὐδοκιμεῖν χάριν, ἀλλὰ τῷ ὄντι τὸ σῶμα μόνον ἐν τῇ
πόλει κεῖται αὐτοῦ καὶ ἐπιδημεῖ, ἡ δὲ διάνοια, ταῦτα
πάντα ἡγησαμένη σμικρὰ καὶ οὐδέν, ἀτιμάσασα πανταχῇ
65 φέρεται κατὰ Πίνδαρον, τά τε γᾶς ὑπένερθε καὶ τὰ ἐπίπεδα γεωμετροῦσα, οὐρανοῦ τε ὕπερ ἀστρονομοῦσα, καὶ
πᾶσαν πάντῃ φύσιν ἐρευνωμένη τῶν ὄντων ἑκάστου ὅλου, 174
εἰς τῶν ἐγγὺς οὐδὲν αὐτὴν συγκαθιεῖσα.

ΘΕΟ. Πῶς τοῦτο λέγεις, ὦ Σώκρατες;

70 ΣΩ. Ὥσπερ καὶ Θαλῆν ἀστρονομοῦντα, ὦ Θεόδωρε,

καὶ ἄνω βλέποντα, πεσόντα εἰς φρέαρ, Θρᾷττά τις ἐμμελὴς καὶ χαρίεσσα θεραπαινὶς ἀποσκῶψαι λέγεται, ὡς
τὰ μὲν ἐν οὐρανῷ προθυμοῖτο εἰδέναι, τὰ δ' ἔμπροσθεν
αὑτοῦ καὶ παρὰ πόδας λανθάνοι αὐτόν. ταὐτὸν δὲ ἀρκεῖ
B σκῶμμα ἐπὶ πάντας ὅσοι ἐν φιλοσοφίᾳ διάγουσι. τῷ γὰρ 75
ὄντι τὸν τοιοῦτον ὁ μὲν πλησίον καὶ ὁ γείτων λέληθεν,
οὐ μόνον ὅ τι πράττει, ἀλλ' ὀλίγου καὶ εἰ ἄνθρωπός
ἐστιν ἤ τι ἄλλο θρέμμα· τί δέ ποτ' ἐστὶν ἄνθρωπος καὶ
τί τῇ τοιαύτῃ φύσει προσήκει διάφορον τῶν ἄλλων ποιεῖν
ἢ πάσχειν, ζητεῖ τε καὶ πράγματ' ἔχει διερευνώμενος. 80
μανθάνεις γάρ που, ὦ Θεόδωρε. ἢ οὔ ;

ΘΕΟ. Ἔγωγε· καὶ ἀληθῆ λέγεις.

ΣΩ. Τοιγάρτοι, ὦ φίλε, ἰδίᾳ τε συγγιγνόμενος ὁ
C τοιοῦτος ἑκάστῳ καὶ δημοσίᾳ, ὅπερ ἀρχόμενος ἔλεγον,
ὅταν ἐν δικαστηρίῳ ἤ που ἄλλοθι ἀναγκασθῇ περὶ τῶν 85
παρὰ πόδας καὶ τῶν ἐν ὀφθαλμοῖς διαλέγεσθαι, γέλωτα
παρέχει οὐ μόνον Θρᾴτταις ἀλλὰ καὶ τῷ ἄλλῳ ὄχλῳ, εἰς
φρέατά τε καὶ πᾶσαν ἀπορίαν ἐμπίπτων ὑπὸ ἀπειρίας,
καὶ ἡ ἀσχημοσύνη δεινή, δόξαν ἀβελτερίας παρεχομένη.
ἔν τε γὰρ ταῖς λοιδορίαις ἴδιον ἔχει οὐδὲν οὐδένα λοιδο- 90
ρεῖν, ἅτ' οὐκ εἰδὼς κακὸν οὐδὲν οὐδενὸς ἐκ τοῦ μὴ με-
D μελετηκέναι· ἀπορῶν οὖν γελοῖος φαίνεται· ἔν τε τοῖς
ἐπαίνοις καὶ ταῖς τῶν ἄλλων μεγαλαυχίαις, οὐ προσποιή-
τως, ἀλλὰ τῷ ὄντι γελῶν ἔνδηλος γιγνόμενος ληρώδης
δοκεῖ εἶναι. τύραννόν τε γὰρ ἢ βασιλέα ἐγκωμιαζόμενον 95
ἕνα τῶν νομέων, οἷον συβώτην, ἢ ποιμένα, ἤ τινα βου-
κόλον ἡγεῖται ἀκούειν εὐδαιμονιζόμενον πολὺ βδάλλοντα·
δυσκολώτερον δὲ ἐκείνων ζῷον καὶ ἐπιβουλότερον ποιμαί-
νειν τε καὶ βδάλλειν νομίζει αὐτούς· ἄγροικον δὲ καὶ
ἀπαίδευτον ὑπὸ ἀσχολίας οὐδὲν ἧττον τῶν νομέων τὸν 100
E τοιοῦτον ἀναγκαῖον γίγνεσθαι, σηκὸν ἐν ὄρει τὸ τεῖχος

περιβεβλημένον. γῆς δὲ ὅταν μυρία πλέθρα ἢ ἔτι πλείω
ἀκούσῃ ὥς τις ἄρα κεκτημένος θαυμαστὰ πλήθει κέκτηται, πάνσμικρα δοκεῖ ἀκούειν εἰς ἅπασαν εἰωθὼς τὴν γῆν
105 βλέπειν. τὰ δὲ δὴ γένη ὑμνούντων, ὡς γενναῖός εἰς ἑπτὰ
πάππους πλουσίους ἔχων ἀποφῆναι, παντάπασιν ἀμβλὺ
καὶ ἐπὶ σμικρὸν ὁρώντων ἡγεῖται τὸν ἔπαινον, ὑπὸ ἀπαι- 175
δευσίας οὐ δυναμένων εἰς τὸ πᾶν ἀεὶ βλέπειν οὐδὲ λογίζεσθαι ὅτι πάππων καὶ προγόνων μυριάδες ἑκάστῳ γεγό-
110 νασιν ἀναρίθμητοι, ἐν αἷς πλούσιοι καὶ πτωχοὶ καὶ
βασιλεῖς καὶ δοῦλοι βάρβαροί τε καὶ Ἕλληνες πολλάκις
μύριοι γεγόνασιν ὁτῳοῦν, ἀλλ' ἐπὶ πέντε καὶ εἴκοσι
καταλόγῳ προγόνων σεμνυνομένων καὶ ἀναφερόντων εἰς
Ἡρακλέα τὸν Ἀμφιτρύωνος ἄτοπα αὐτῷ καταφαίνεται
115 τῆς σμικρολογίας, ὅτι δὲ ὁ ἀπ' Ἀμφιτρύωνος εἰς τὸ ἄνω Β
πεντεκαιεικοστὸς τοιοῦτος ἦν, οἷα συνέβαινεν αὐτῷ τύχῃ,
καὶ ὁ πεντηκοστὸς ἀπ' αὐτοῦ, γελᾷ οὐ δυναμένων λογί-
ζεσθαί τε καὶ χαυνότητα ἀνοήτου ψυχῆς ἀπαλλάττειν.
ἐν ἅπασι δὴ τούτοις ὁ τοιοῦτος ὑπὸ τῶν πολλῶν κατα-
120 γελᾶται, τὰ μὲν ὑπερηφάνως ἔχων, ὡς δοκεῖ, τὰ δ' ἐν
ποσὶν ἀγνοῶν τε καὶ ἐν ἑκάστοις ἀπορῶν.

ΘΕΟ. Παντάπασι τὰ γιγνόμενα λέγεις, ὦ Σώκρατες.

ΣΩ. Ὅταν δέ γέ τινα αὐτός, ὦ φίλε, ἑλκύσῃ ἄνω,
καὶ ἐθελήσῃ τις αὐτῷ ἐκβῆναι ἐκ τοῦ Τί ἐγὼ σὲ ἀδικῶ ἢ C
125 σὺ ἐμέ; εἰς σκέψιν αὐτῆς δικαιοσύνης τε καὶ ἀδικίας, τί
τε ἑκάτερον αὐτοῖν καὶ τί τῶν πάντων ἢ ἀλλήλων διαφέ-
ρετον; ἢ ἐκ τοῦ Εἰ βασιλεὺς εὐδαίμων κεκτημένος τ' αὖ
πολὺ χρυσίον, βασιλείας πέρι καὶ ἀνθρωπίνης ὅλως
εὐδαιμονίας καὶ ἀθλιότητος ἐπὶ σκέψιν, ποίω τέ τινε
130 ἐστὸν καὶ τίνα τρόπον ἀνθρώπου φύσει προσήκει τὸ μὲν
κτήσασθαι αὐτοῖν, τὸ δὲ ἀποφυγεῖν,—περὶ τούτων ἁπάντων ὅταν αὖ δέῃ λόγον διδόναι τὸν σμικρὸν ἐκεῖνον τὴν D

ψυχὴν καὶ δριμὺν καὶ δικανικόν, πάλιν αὖ τὰ ἀντίστροφα
ἀποδίδωσιν· ἰλιγγιῶν τε ἀφ’ ὑψηλοῦ κρεμασθεὶς καὶ
βλέπων μετέωρος ἄνωθεν ὑπὸ ἀηθείας ἀδημονῶν τε καὶ 135
ἀπορῶν καὶ βαρβαρίζων γέλωτα Θρᾴτταις μὲν οὐ παρέχει
οὐδ’ ἄλλῳ ἀπαιδεύτῳ οὐδενί, οὐ γὰρ αἰσθάνονται, τοῖς δ’
ἐναντίως ἢ ὡς ἀνδραπόδοις τραφεῖσιν ἅπασιν. Οὗτος
δὴ ἑκατέρου τρόπος, ὦ Θεόδωρε, ὁ μὲν τῷ ὄντι ἐν ἐλευθερίᾳ τε καὶ σχολῇ τεθραμμένου, ὃν δὴ φιλόσοφον καλεῖς, 140
ᾧ ἀνεμέσητον εὐήθει δοκεῖν καὶ οὐδενὶ εἶναι, ὅταν εἰς
δουλικὰ ἐμπέσῃ διακονήματα, οἷον στρωματόδεσμον μὴ
ἐπισταμένου συσκευάσασθαι μηδὲ ὄψον ἡδῦναι ἢ θῶπας
λόγους· ὁ δ’ αὖ τὰ μὲν τοιαῦτα πάντα δυναμένου τορῶς
τε καὶ ὀξέως διακονεῖν, ἀναβάλλεσθαι δὲ οὐκ ἐπιστα- 145
μένου ἐπιδέξια ἐλευθέρως οὐδέ γ’ ἁρμονίαν λόγων λα-
176 βόντος ὀρθῶς ὑμνῆσαι θεῶν τε καὶ ἀνδρῶν εὐδαιμόνων
βίον ἀληθῆ.

ΘΕΟ. Εἰ πάντας, ὦ Σώκρατες, πείθοις ἃ λέγεις
ὥσπερ ἐμέ, πλείων ἂν εἰρήνη καὶ κακὰ ἐλάττω κατ’ 150
ἀνθρώπους εἴη.

ΣΩ. ’Αλλ’ οὔτ’ ἀπολέσθαι τὰ κακὰ δυνατόν, ὦ Θεό-
δωρε· ὑπεναντίον γάρ τι τῷ ἀγαθῷ ἀεὶ εἶναι ἀνάγκη·
οὔτ’ ἐν θεοῖς αὐτὰ ἱδρύσθαι, τὴν δὲ θνητὴν φύσιν καὶ
τόνδε τὸν τόπον περιπολεῖ ἐξ ἀνάγκης. διὸ καὶ πειρᾶσθαι 155
χρὴ ἐνθένδε ἐκεῖσε φεύγειν ὅ τι τάχιστα. φυγὴ δὲ ὁμοίωσις θεῷ κατὰ τὸ δυνατόν· ὁμοίωσις δὲ δίκαιον καὶ ὅσιον
μετὰ φρονήσεως γενέσθαι. ἀλλὰ γάρ, ὦ ἄριστε, οὐ πάνυ
ῥᾴδιον πεῖσαι ὡς ἄρα οὐχ ὧν ἕνεκα οἱ πολλοί φασι δεῖν
πονηρίαν μὲν φεύγειν, ἀρετὴν δὲ διώκειν, τούτων χάριν 160
τὸ μὲν ἐπιτηδευτέον, τὸ δ’ οὔ, ἵνα δὴ μὴ κακὸς καὶ ἵνα
ἀγαθὸς δοκῇ εἶναι. ταῦτα γάρ ἐστιν ὁ λεγόμενος γραῶν
ὕθλος, ὡς ἐμοὶ φαίνεται. τὸ δὲ ἀληθὲς ὧδε λέγωμεν.

θεὸς οὐδαμῇ οὐδαμῶς ἄδικος, ἀλλ' ὡς οἷόν τε δικαιότατος, C
165 καὶ οὐκ ἔστιν αὐτῷ ὁμοιότερον οὐδὲν ἢ ὃς ἂν ἡμῶν αὖ
γένηται ὅ τι δικαιότατος. περὶ τούτου καὶ ἡ ὡς ἀληθῶς
δεινότης ἀνδρὸς καὶ οὐδενία τε καὶ ἀνανδρία. ἡ μὲν γὰρ
τούτου γνῶσις σοφία καὶ ἀρετὴ ἀληθινή, ἡ δὲ ἄγνοια
ἀμαθία καὶ κακία ἐναργής· αἱ δ' ἄλλαι δεινότητές τε
170 δοκοῦσαι καὶ σοφίαι ἐν μὲν πολιτικαῖς δυναστείαις
γιγνόμεναι φορτικαί, ἐν δὲ τέχναις βάναυσοι. τῷ οὖν
ἀδικοῦντι καὶ ἀνόσια λέγοντι ἢ πράττοντι μακρῷ ἄριστ' D
ἔχει τὸ μὴ συγχωρεῖν δεινῷ ὑπὸ πανουργίας εἶναι. ἀγάλ-
λονται γὰρ τῷ ὀνείδει, καὶ οἴονται ἀκούειν ὅτι οὐ λῆροί
175 εἰσι, γῆς ἄλλως ἄχθη, ἀλλ' ἄνδρες οἵους δεῖ ἐν πόλει
τοὺς σωθησομένους. λεκτέον οὖν τἀληθές, ὅτι τοσούτῳ
μᾶλλόν εἰσιν οἷοι οὐκ οἴονται, ὅτι οὐχὶ οἴονται· ἀγνοοῦσι
γὰρ ζημίαν ἀδικίας, ὃ δεῖ ἥκιστα ἀγνοεῖν. οὐ γάρ ἐστιν
ἣν δοκοῦσι, πληγαί τε καὶ θάνατοι, ὧν ἐνίοτε πάσχουσιν
180 οὐδὲν ἀδικοῦντες, ἀλλὰ ἣν ἀδύνατον ἐκφυγεῖν. E

ΘΕΟ. Τίνα δὴ λέγεις ;

ΣΩ. Παραδειγμάτων, ὦ φίλε, ἐν τῷ ὄντι ἑστώτων,
τοῦ μὲν θείου εὐδαιμονεστάτου, τοῦ δὲ ἀθέου ἀθλιωτά-
του, οὐχ ὁρῶντες ὅτι οὕτως ἔχει, ὑπὸ ἠλιθιότητός τε καὶ
185 τῆς ἐσχάτης ἀνοίας λανθάνουσι τῷ μὲν ὁμοιούμενοι διὰ
τὰς ἀδίκους πράξεις, τῷ δὲ ἀνομοιούμενοι. οὗ δὴ τί- 177
νουσι δίκην ζῶντες τὸν εἰκότα βίον ᾧ ὁμοιοῦνται. ἐὰν δ'
εἴπωμεν ὅτι, ἂν μὴ ἀπαλλαγῶσι τῆς δεινότητος, καὶ τε-
λευτήσαντας αὐτοὺς ἐκεῖνος μὲν ὁ τῶν κακῶν καθαρὸς
190 τόπος οὐ δέξεται, ἐνθάδε δὲ τὴν αὐτοῖς ὁμοιότητα τῆς
διαγωγῆς ἀεὶ ἕξουσι, κακοὶ κακοῖς συνόντες, ταῦτα δὴ
καὶ παντάπασιν ὡς δεινοὶ καὶ πανοῦργοι ἀνοήτων τινῶν
ἀκούσονται.

ΘΕΟ. Καὶ μάλα δή, ὦ Σώκρατες.

Β ΣΩ. Οἶδά τοι, ὦ ἑταῖρε. ἐν μέντοι τι αὐτοῖς συμ- 195
βέβηκεν, ὅτι ἂν ἰδίᾳ λόγον δέῃ δοῦναί τε καὶ δέξασθαι
περὶ ὧν ψέγουσι, καὶ ἐθελήσωσιν ἀνδρικῶς πολὺν χρόνον
ὑπομεῖναι καὶ μὴ ἀνάνδρως φεύγειν, τότε ἀτόπως, ὦ
δαιμόνιε, τελευτῶντες οὐκ ἀρέσκουσιν αὐτοὶ αὑτοῖς περὶ
ὧν λέγουσι, καὶ ἡ ῥητορικὴ ἐκείνη πως ἀπομαραίνεται, 200
ὥστε παίδων μηδὲν δοκεῖν διαφέρειν. Περὶ μὲν οὖν
τούτων, ἐπειδὴ καὶ πάρεργα τυγχάνει λεγόμενα, ἀπο-
C στῶμεν· εἰ δὲ μή, πλείω ἀεὶ ἐπιρρέοντα καταχώσει ἡμῶν
τὸν ἐξ ἀρχῆς λόγον· ἐπὶ δὲ τὰ ἔμπροσθεν ἴωμεν, εἰ καὶ
σοὶ δοκεῖ.

205

LAWS.

Βοοκ Ι.

We are but puppets of the Gods.

(The Athenian Stranger, Cleinias.)

644 D—645 C.

ΑΘ. Περὶ δὴ τούτων διανοηθῶμεν οὑτωσί. θαῦμα
μὲν ἕκαστον ἡμῶν ἡγησώμεθα τῶν ζῴων θεῖον, εἴτε ὡς
παίγνιον ἐκείνων εἴτε ὡς σπουδῇ τινὶ ξυνεστηκός· οὐ γὰρ
Ε δὴ τοῦτό γε γιγνώσκομεν· τόδε δὲ ἴσμεν, ὅτι ταῦτα τὰ
πάθη ἐν ἡμῖν οἷον νεῦρα ἢ μήρινθοί τινες ἐνοῦσαι σπῶσί 5
τε ἡμᾶς καὶ ἀλλήλαις ἀνθέλκουσιν ἐναντίαι οὖσαι ἐπ᾽
ἐναντίας πράξεις, οὗ δὴ διωρισμένη ἀρετὴ καὶ κακία κεῖ-
ται· μιᾷ γάρ φησιν ὁ λόγος δεῖν τῶν ἕλξεων ξυνεπόμενον
ἀεὶ καὶ μηδαμῇ ἀπολειπόμενον ἐκείνης ἀνθέλκειν τοῖς
645 ἄλλοις νεύροις ἕκαστον, ταύτην δ᾽ εἶναι τὴν τοῦ λογισμοῦ 10
ἀγωγὴν χρυσῆν καὶ ἱεράν, τῆς πόλεως κοινὸν νόμον ἐπι-

καλουμένην, ἄλλας δὲ σκληρὰς καὶ σιδηρᾶς, τὴν δὲ μα-
λακὴν ἅτε χρυσῆν οὖσαν, τὰς δὲ ἄλλας παντοδαποῖς εἴδε-
σιν ὁμοίας. δεῖν δὴ τῇ καλλίστῃ ἀγωγῇ τῇ τοῦ νόμου ἀεὶ
15 ξυλλαμβάνειν· ἅτε γὰρ τοῦ λογισμοῦ καλοῦ μὲν ὄντος,
πράου δὲ καὶ οὐ βιαίου, δεῖσθαι ὑπηρετῶν αὐτοῦ τὴν
ἀγωγήν, ὅπως ἂν ἡμῖν τὸ χρυσοῦν γένος νικᾷ τὰ ἄλλα
γένη. καὶ οὕτω δὴ περὶ θαυμάτων ὡς ὄντων ἡμῶν ὁ Β
μῦθος ἀρετῆς σεσωσμένος ἂν εἴη, καὶ τὸ κρείττω ἑαυ-
20 τοῦ καὶ ἥττω εἶναι τρόπον τινὰ φανερὸν ἂν γίγνοιτο μᾶλλον ὃ νοεῖ, καὶ ὅτι πόλιν καὶ ἰδιώτην, τὸν μὲν λόγον
ἀληθῆ λαβόντα ἐν ἑαυτῷ περὶ τῶν ἕλξεων τούτων τούτῳ
ἑπόμενον δεῖ ζῆν, πόλιν δὲ ἢ παρὰ θεῶν τινος ἢ παρὰ
τούτου τοῦ γνόντος ταῦτα λόγον παραλαβοῦσαν, νόμον
25 θεμένην, αὑτῇ τε ὁμιλεῖν καὶ ταῖς ἄλλαις πόλεσιν. οὕτω
καὶ κακία δὴ καὶ ἀρετὴ σαφέστερον ἡμῖν διηρθρωμένον C
ἂν εἴη. ἐναργεστέρου δ' αὐτοῦ γενομένου καὶ παιδεία καὶ
τἆλλα ἐπιτηδεύματα ἴσως ἔσται μᾶλλον καταφανῆ, καὶ
δὴ καὶ τὸ περὶ τῆς ἐν τοῖς οἴνοις διατριβῆς, ὃ δοξασθείη
30 μὲν ἂν εἶναι φαύλου πέρι μῆκος πολὺ λόγων περιττὸν
εἰρημένον.

ΚΛ. Φανείη δὲ τάχ' ἂν ἴσως τοῦ μήκους γ' αὐτῶν
οὐκ ἀπάξιον.

.

Book III.

*Periodical Catastrophes of the World. The Origin of
Society.*

(The Athenian, Cleinias, Megillus.)

Beginning—682 E.

Ταῦτα μὲν οὖν δὴ ταύτῃ· πολιτείας δ' ἀρχὴν τίνα 676

ποτὲ φῶμεν γεγονέναι; μῶν οὐκ ἐνθένδε τις ἂν αὐτὴν
ῥᾷστά τε καὶ κάλλιστα κατίδοι;

ΚΛ. Πόθεν;

ΑΘ. Ὅθεν περ καὶ τὴν τῶν πόλεων ἐπίδοσιν εἰς 5
ἀρετὴν μεταβαίνουσαν ἅμα καὶ κακίαν ἑκάστοτε θεατέον.

ΚΛ. Λέγεις δὲ πόθεν;

B ΑΘ. Οἶμαι μὲν ἀπὸ χρόνου μήκους τε καὶ ἀπειρίας
καὶ τῶν μεταβολῶν ἐν τῷ τοιούτῳ.

ΚΛ. Πῶς λέγεις; 10

ΑΘ. Φέρε, ἀφ' οὗ πόλεις τ' εἰσὶ καὶ ἄνθρωποι πολι-
τευόμενοι, δοκεῖς ἂν ποτε κατανοῆσαι χρόνου πλῆθος
ὅσον γέγονεν;

ΚΛ. Οὔκουν ῥᾴδιόν γε οὐδαμῶς.

ΑΘ. Τὸ δέ γε, ὡς ἄπλετόν τι καὶ ἀμήχανον ἂν εἴη. 15

ΚΛ. Πάνυ μὲν οὖν τοῦτό γε.

ΑΘ. Μῶν οὖν οὐ μυρίαι μὲν ἐπὶ μυρίαις ἡμῖν γεγόνασι πόλεις ἐν τούτῳ τῷ χρόνῳ, κατὰ τὸν αὐτὸν δὲ τοῦ
C πλήθους λόγον οὐκ ἐλάττους ἐφθαρμέναι; πεπολιτευ-
μέναι δ' αὖ πάσας πολιτείας πολλάκις ἑκασταχοῦ; καὶ 20
τοτὲ μὲν ἐξ ἐλαττόνων μείζους, τοτὲ δὲ ἐκ μειζόνων
ἐλάττους, καὶ χείρους ἐκ βελτιόνων γεγόνασι καὶ βελτίους
ἐκ χειρόνων;

ΚΛ. Ἀναγκαῖον.

ΑΘ. Ταύτης δὴ πέρι λάβωμεν, εἰ δυναίμεθα, τῆς 25
μεταβολῆς τὴν αἰτίαν· τάχα γὰρ ἂν ἴσως δείξειεν ἡμῖν
τὴν πρώτην τῶν πολιτειῶν γένεσιν καὶ μετάβασιν.

ΚΛ. Εὖ λέγεις, καὶ προθυμεῖσθαι δεῖ σὲ μὲν ὃ διανοεῖ
περὶ αὐτῶν ἀποφαινόμενον, ἡμᾶς δὲ ξυνεπομένους.

677 ΑΘ. Ἆρ' οὖν ὑμῖν οἱ παλαιοὶ λόγοι ἀλήθειαν ἔχειν 30
τινὰ δοκοῦσιν;

ΚΛ. Ποῖοι δή;

ΑΘ. Τὸ πολλὰς ἀνθρώπων φθορὰς γεγονέναι κατα-
κλυσμοῖς τε καὶ νόσοις καὶ ἄλλοις πολλοῖς, ἐν οἷς βραχύ
35 τι τῶν ἀνθρώπων λείπεσθαι γένος.

ΚΛ. Πάνυ μὲν οὖν πιθανὸν τὸ τοιοῦτον πᾶν παντί.

ΑΘ. Φέρε δή, νοήσωμεν μίαν τῶν πολλῶν ταύτην
τὴν τῷ κατακλυσμῷ ποτὲ γενομένην.

ΚΛ. Τὸ ποῖόν τι περὶ αὐτῆς διανοηθέντες ;

40 ΑΘ. ῾Ως οἱ τότε περιφυγόντες τὴν φθορὰν σχεδὸν B
ὄρειοί τινες ἂν εἶεν νομῆς, ἐν κορυφαῖς που σμικρὰ ζώ-
πυρα τοῦ τῶν ἀνθρώπων διασεσωσμένα γένους.

ΚΛ. Δῆλον.

ΑΘ. Καὶ δὴ τοὺς τοιούτους γε ἀνάγκη που τῶν ἄλ-
45 λων ἀπείρους εἶναι τεχνῶν καὶ τῶν ἐν τοῖς ἄστεσι πρὸς
ἀλλήλους μηχανῶν εἴς τε πλεονεξίας καὶ φιλονεικίας, καὶ
ὁπόσ᾽ ἄλλα κακουργήματα πρὸς ἀλλήλους ἐπινοοῦσιν.

ΚΛ. Εἰκὸς γοῦν.

ΑΘ. Θῶμεν δὴ τὰς ἐν τοῖς πεδίοις πόλεις καὶ πρὸς C
50 θαλάττῃ κατοικούσας ἄρδην ἐν τῷ τότε χρόνῳ διαφθεί-
ρεσθαι ;

ΚΛ. Θῶμεν.

ΑΘ. Οὐκοῦν ὄργανά τε πάντα ἀπόλλυσθαι, καὶ εἴ τι
τέχνης ἦν ἐχόμενον σπουδαίως εὑρημένον ἢ πολιτικῆς ἢ
55 καὶ σοφίας τινὸς ἑτέρας, πάντα ἔρρειν ταῦτα ἐν τῷ τότε
χρόνῳ φήσομεν ;

ΚΛ. Πῶς γὰρ ἄν, ὦ ἄριστε, εἴ γε ἔμενε τάδε οὕτω
τὸν πάντα χρόνον ὡς νῦν διακεκόσμηται, καινὸν ἀνευρί-
σκετό ποτε καὶ ὁτιοῦν ; οὔ τι μὲν γὰρ μυριάκις μύρια ἔτη D
60 διελάνθανεν ἄρα τοὺς τότε, χίλια δ᾽ ἀφ᾽ οὗ γέγονεν ἢ
δὶς τοσαῦτα ἔτη τὰ μὲν Δαιδάλῳ καταφανῆ, τὰ δὲ
᾽Ορφεῖ, τὰ δὲ Παλαμήδει, τὰ δὲ περὶ μουσικὴν Μαρσύᾳ καὶ ᾽Ολύμπῳ, περὶ λύραν δὲ ᾽Αμφίονι, τὰ δ᾽ ἄλλα

ἄλλοις πάμπολλα, ὡς ἔπος εἰπεῖν χθὲς καὶ πρώην γε-
γονότα.   65

ΑΘ.   Ἆρ' οἶσθ', ὦ Κλεινία, τὸν φίλον ὅτι παρέλιπες,
τὸν ἀτεχνῶς χθὲς γενόμενον ;

ΚΛ.   Μῶν φράζεις Ἐπιμενίδην ;

Ε   ΑΘ.   Ναὶ τοῦτον· πολὺ γὰρ ὑμῖν ὑπερεπήδησε τῷ
μηχανήματι τοὺς ξύμπαντας, ὦ φίλε, ὃ λόγῳ μὲν Ἡσί- 70
οδος ἐμαντεύετο πάλαι, τῷ δ' ἔργῳ ἐκεῖνος ἀπετέλεσεν,
ὡς ὑμεῖς φατέ.

ΚΛ.   Φαμὲν γὰρ οὖν.

ΑΘ.   Οὐκοῦν οὕτω δὴ λέγωμεν ἔχειν τότε, ὅτε ἐγένετο ἡ φθορά, τὰ περὶ τοὺς ἀνθρώπους πράγματα, μυ- 75
ρίαν μέν τινα φοβερὰν ἐρημίαν, γῆς δ' ἀφθόνου πλῆθος
πάμπολυ, ζῴων δὲ τῶν ἄλλων ἐρρόντων βουκόλι' ἄττα,
καὶ εἴ τί που αἰγῶν περιλειφθὲν ἐτύγχανε γένος, σπάνια
678 καὶ ταῦτα νέμουσιν εἶναι ζῆν τότε κατ' ἀρχάς.

ΚΛ.   Τί μήν ;   80

ΑΘ.   Πόλεως δὲ καὶ πολιτείας πέρι καὶ νομοθεσίας,
ὧν νῦν ὁ λόγος ἡμῖν παρέστηκεν, ἆρ' ὡς ἔπος εἰπεῖν
οἰόμεθα καὶ μνήμην εἶναι τὸ παράπαν ;

ΚΛ.   Οὐδαμῶς.

ΑΘ.   Οὐκοῦν ἐξ ἐκείνων τῶν διακειμένων οὕτω τὰ 85
νῦν γέγονεν ἡμῖν ξύμπαντα, πόλεις τε καὶ πολιτεῖαι
καὶ τέχναι καὶ νόμοι καὶ πολλὴ μὲν πονηρία, πολλὴ δὲ
καὶ ἀρετή ;

ΚΛ.   Πῶς λέγεις ;

Β   ΑΘ.   Ἆρ' οἰόμεθα, ὦ θαυμάσιε, τοὺς τότε ἀπείρους 90
ὄντας πολλῶν μὲν καλῶν τῶν κατὰ τὰ ἄστη, πολλῶν δὲ
καὶ τῶν ἐναντίων τελέους πρὸς ἀρετὴν ἢ καὶ πρὸς κακίαν
γεγονέναι ;

ΚΛ.   Καλῶς εἶπες, καὶ μανθάνομεν ὃ λέγεις.

95 ΑΘ. Οὐκοῦν προϊόντος μὲν τοῦ χρόνου, πληθύοντος
δ' ἡμῶν τοῦ γένους εἰς πάντα τὰ νῦν καθεστηκότα προε-
λήλυθε πάντα ;

ΚΛ. Ὀρθότατα.

ΑΘ. Οὐκ ἐξαίφνης γε, ὡς εἰκός, κατὰ σμικρὸν δὲ
100 ἐν παμπόλλῳ τινὶ χρόνῳ.

ΚΛ. Καὶ μάλα πρέπει τοῦθ' οὕτως.   C

ΑΘ. Ἐκ γὰρ τῶν ὑψηλῶν εἰς τὰ πεδία καταβαίνειν,
οἶμαι, πᾶσι φόβος ἔναυλος ἐγεγόνει.

ΚΛ. Πῶς δ' οὔ ;

105 ΑΘ. Ἆρ' οὐκ ἄσμενοι μὲν ἑαυτοὺς ἑώρων δι' ὀλιγότητα ἐν τοῖς περὶ ἐκεῖνον τὸν χρόνον, πορεῖα δέ, ὥστ'
ἐπ' ἀλλήλους τότε πορεύεσθαι κατὰ γῆν ἢ κατὰ θάλατταν,
σὺν ταῖς τέχναις ὡς ἔπος εἰπεῖν πάντα σχεδὸν ἀπολώλει ;
ξυμμίσγειν οὖν ἀλλήλοις οὐκ ἦν, οἶμαι, σφόδρα δυνατόν·
110 σίδηρος γὰρ καὶ χαλκὸς καὶ πάντα τὰ μεταλλεῖα συγκε- D
χυμένα ἠφάνιστο, ὥστε ἀπορία πᾶσα ἦν τοῦ ἀνακαθαί-
ρεσθαι τὰ τοιαῦτα, δρυοτομίας τε εἶχον σπάνιν. εἰ γὰρ
πού τι καὶ περιγεγονὸς ἦν ὄργανον ἐν ὄρεσι, ταῦτα μὲν
ταχὺ κατατριβέντα ἠφάνιστο, ἄλλα δ' οὐκ ἔμελλε γενή-
115 σεσθαι, πρὶν πάλιν ἢ τῶν μεταλλέων ἀφίκοιτο εἰς ἀνθρώπους τέχνη.

ΚΛ. Πῶς γὰρ ἄν ;

ΑΘ. Γενεαῖς δὴ πόσαις ὕστερον οἰόμεθα τοῦθ' οὕτω
γεγονέναι ;

120 ΚΛ. Δῆλον ὅτι παμπόλλαις τισίν.   E

ΑΘ. Οὐκοῦν καὶ τέχναι ὅσαιπερ σιδήρου δέονται καὶ χαλκοῦ καὶ τῶν τοιούτων ἀπάντων, τὸν αὐτὸν χρόνον καὶ ἔτι πλείονα ἠφανισμέναι ἂν εἶεν ἐν
τῷ τότε ;

125 ΚΛ. Τί μήν ;

ΑΘ. Καὶ τοίνυν στάσις ἅμα καὶ πόλεμος ἀπολώλει
κατὰ τὸν τότε χρόνον πολλαχῇ.

ΚΛ. Πῶς ;

ΑΘ. Πρῶτον μὲν ἠγάπων καὶ ἐφιλοφρονοῦντο ἀλλήλους δι᾽ ἐρημίαν, ἔπειτα οὐ περιμάχητος ἦν αὐτοῖς ἡ 130
679 τροφή. νομῆς γὰρ οὐκ ἦν σπάνις, εἰ μή τισι κατ᾽ ἀρχὰς
ἴσως, ᾗ δὴ τὸ πλεῖστον διέζων ἐν τῷ τότε χρόνῳ· γά-
λακτος γὰρ καὶ κρεῶν οὐδαμῶς ἐνδεεῖς ἦσαν, ἔτι δὲ θη-
ρεύοντες οὐ φαύλην οὐδ᾽ ὀλίγην τροφὴν παρείχοντο. καὶ
μὴν ἀμπεχόνης γε καὶ στρωμνῆς καὶ οἰκήσεων καὶ σκευῶν 135
ἐμπύρων τε καὶ ἀπύρων εὐπόρουν· αἱ πλαστικαὶ γὰρ καὶ
ὅσαι πλεκτικαὶ τῶν τεχνῶν οὐδὲ ἐν προσδέονται σιδήρου·
B ταῦτα δὲ πάντα τούτω τὼ τέχνα θεὸς ἔδωκε πορίζειν
τοῖς ἀνθρώποις, ἵν᾽ ὁπότε εἰς τὴν τοιαύτην ἀπορίαν ἔλ-
θοιεν, ἔχοι βλάστην καὶ ἐπίδοσιν τὸ τῶν ἀνθρώπων γέ- 140
νος. πένητες μὲν δὴ διὰ τὸ τοιοῦτον σφόδρα οὐκ ἦσαν,
οὐδ᾽ ὑπὸ πενίας ἀναγκαζόμενοι διάφοροι ἑαυτοῖς ἐγίγ-
νοντο· πλούσιοι δ᾽ οὐκ ἄν ποτ᾽ ἐγένοντο ἄχρυσοί τε καὶ
ἀνάργυροι ὄντες, ὃ τότε ἐν ἐκείνοις παρῆν. ᾗ δ᾽ ἄν ποτε
ξυνοικίᾳ μήτε πλοῦτος ξυνοικῇ μήτε πενία, σχεδὸν ἐν 145
C ταύτῃ γενναιότατα ἤθη γίγνοιτ᾽ ἄν· οὔτε γὰρ ὕβρις οὔτ᾽
ἀδικία, ζῆλοί τε αὖ καὶ φθόνοι οὐκ ἐγγίγνονται. ἀγαθοὶ
μὲν δὴ διὰ ταῦτά τε ἦσαν καὶ διὰ τὴν λεγομένην εὐή-
θειαν· ἃ γὰρ ἤκουον καλὰ καὶ αἰσχρά, εὐήθεις ὄντες
ἡγοῦντο ἀληθέστατα λέγεσθαι καὶ ἐπείθοντο. ψεῦδος γὰρ 150
ὑπονοεῖν οὐδεὶς ἠπίστατο διὰ σοφίαν, ὥσπερ τὰ νῦν,
ἀλλὰ περὶ θεῶν τε καὶ ἀνθρώπων τὰ λεγόμενα ἀληθῆ
νομίζοντες ἔζων κατὰ ταῦτα· διόπερ ἦσαν τοιοῦτοι παν-
D τάπασιν, οἵους αὐτοὺς ἡμεῖς ἄρτι διεληλύθαμεν.

ΚΛ. Ἐμοὶ γοῦν δὴ καὶ τῷδε οὕτω ταῦτα ξυνδοκεῖ. 155

ΑΘ. Οὐκοῦν εἴπωμεν ὅτι γενεαὶ διαβιοῦσαι πολλαὶ

τοῦτον τὸν τρόπον τῶν πρὸ κατακλυσμοῦ γεγονότων καὶ
τῶν νῦν ἀτεχνότεροι μὲν καὶ ἀμαθέστεροι πρός τε τὰς
ἄλλας μέλλουσιν εἶναι τέχνας καὶ πρὸς τὰς πολεμικάς,
160 ὅσαι τε πεζαὶ καὶ ὅσαι κατὰ θάλατταν γίγνονται τὰ νῦν,
καὶ ὅσαι δὴ κατὰ πόλιν μόνον αὐτοῦ δίκαι καὶ στάσεις
λεγόμεναι, λόγοις ἔργοις τε μεμηχανημέναι πάσας μηχα- Ε
νὰς εἰς τὸ κακουργεῖν τε ἀλλήλους καὶ ἀδικεῖν, εὐηθέστε-
ροι δὲ καὶ ἀνδρειότεροι καὶ ἅμα σωφρονέστεροι καὶ ξύμ-
165 παντα δικαιότεροι; τὸ δὲ τούτων αἴτιον ἤδη διεληλύθαμεν.

ΚΛ. Ὀρθῶς λέγεις.

ΑΘ. Λελέχθω δὴ ταῦτα ἡμῖν καὶ τὰ τούτοις ξυνε-
πόμενα ἔτι πάντα εἰρήσθω τοῦδ' ἕνεκα, ἵνα νοήσωμεν
170 τοῖς τότε νόμων τίς ποτ' ἦν χρεία καὶ τίς ἦν νομοθέτης 680
αὐτοῖς.

ΚΛ. Καὶ καλῶς γε εἴρηκας.

ΑΘ. Ἆρ' οὖν ἐκεῖνοι μὲν οὔτ' ἐδέοντο νομοθετῶν
οὔτε πω ἐφίλει κατὰ τούτους τοὺς χρόνους γίγνεσθαι τὸ
175 τοιοῦτον; οὐδὲ γὰρ γράμματα ἔστι πω τοῖς ἐν τούτῳ τῷ
μέρει τῆς περιόδου γεγονόσιν, ἀλλ' ἔθεσι καὶ τοῖς λεγομένοις πατρίοις νόμοις ἑπόμενοι ζῶσιν.

ΚΛ. Εἰκὸς γοῦν.

ΑΘ. Πολιτείας δέ γε ἤδη καὶ τρόπος ἐστί τις οὗτος.

180 ΚΛ. Τίς;

ΑΘ. Δοκοῦσί μοι πάντες τὴν ἐν τούτῳ τῷ χρόνῳ Β
πολιτείαν δυναστείαν καλεῖν, ἣ καὶ νῦν ἔτι πολλαχοῦ καὶ
ἐν Ἕλλησι καὶ κατὰ βαρβάρους ἐστί· λέγει δ' αὐτήν που
καὶ Ὅμηρος γεγονέναι περὶ τὴν τῶν Κυκλώπων οἴκησιν,
185 εἰπὼν

τοῖσιν δ' οὔτ' ἀγοραὶ βουληφόροι οὔτε θέμιστες,
ἀλλ' οἵ γ' ὑψηλῶν ὀρέων ναίουσι κάρηνα

P

ἐν σπέσσι γλαφυροῖσι, θεμιστεύει δὲ ἕκαστος
C   παίδων ἠδ' ἀλόχων, οὐδ' ἀλλήλων ἀλέγουσιν.

ΚΛ. Ἔοικέ γε ὁ ποιητὴς ὑμῖν οὗτος γεγονέναι χα- 190
ρίεις. καὶ γὰρ δὴ καὶ ἄλλα αὐτοῦ διεληλύθαμεν μάλ'
ἀστεῖα, οὐ μὴν πολλά γε· οὐ γὰρ σφόδρα χρώμεθα οἱ
Κρῆτες τοῖς ξενικοῖς ποιήμασιν.

ΜΕ. Ἡμεῖς δ' αὖ χρώμεθα μέν, καὶ ἔοικέ γε κρατεῖν
τῶν τοιούτων ποιητῶν, οὐ μέντοι Λακωνικόν γε ἀλλά 195
D τινα μᾶλλον Ἰωνικὸν βίον διεξέρχεται ἑκάστοτε. νῦν μὴν
εὖ τῷ σῷ λόγῳ ἔοικε μαρτυρεῖν, τὸ ἀρχαῖον αὐτῶν ἐπὶ
τὴν ἀγριότητα διὰ μυθολογίας ἐπανενεγκών.

ΑΘ. Ναί. ξυμμαρτυρεῖ γὰρ καὶ λάβωμέν γε αὐτὸν
μηνυτὴν ὅτι τοιαῦται πολιτεῖαι γίγνονταί ποτε.   200

ΚΛ. Καλῶς.

ΑΘ. Μῶν οὖν οὐκ ἐκ τούτων τῶν κατὰ μίαν οἴκησιν καὶ κατὰ γένος διεσπαρμένων ὑπὸ ἀπορίας τῆς ἐν
ταῖς φθοραῖς, ἐν οἷς τὸ πρεσβύτατον ἄρχει διὰ τὸ τὴν
E ἀρχὴν αὐτοῖς ἐκ πατρὸς καὶ μητρὸς γεγονέναι, οἷς ἐπό- 205
μενοι καθάπερ ὄρνιθες ἀγέλην μίαν ποιήσουσι, πατρονο-
μούμενοι καὶ βασιλείαν πασῶν δικαιοτάτην βασιλευό-
μενοι ;

ΚΛ. Πάνυ μὲν οὖν.

ΑΘ. Μετὰ δὲ ταῦτά γε εἰς τὸ κοινὸν μείζους ποιοῦν- 210
τες πόλεις πλείους συνέρχονται, καὶ ἐπὶ γεωργίας τὰς ἐν
681 ταῖς ὑπωρείαις τρέπονται πρώτας, περιβόλους τε αἱμασι-
ώδεις τινάς, τειχῶν ἐρύματα, τῶν θηρίων ἕνεκα ποιοῦνται, μίαν οἰκίαν αὖ κοινὴν καὶ μεγάλην ἀποτελοῦντες.

ΚΛ. Τὸ γοῦν εἰκὸς ταῦθ' οὕτω γίγνεσθαι.   215

ΑΘ. Τί δέ ; τόδε ἆρα οὐκ εἰκός ;

ΚΛ. Τὸ ποῖον ;

ΑΘ. Τῶν οἰκήσεων τούτων μειζόνων αὐξανομένων

ἐκ τῶν ἐλαττόνων καὶ πρώτων ἑκάστην τῶν σμικρῶν πα-
220 ρεῖναι κατὰ γένος ἔχουσαν τόν τε πρεσβύτατον ἄρχοντα
καὶ αὑτῆς ἔθη ἄττα ἴδια διὰ τὸ χωρὶς ἀλλήλων οἰκεῖν, B
ἕτερα ἀφ' ἑτέρων ὄντων τῶν γεννητόρων τε καὶ θρεψάν-
των, ἃ εἰθίσθησαν περὶ θεούς τε καὶ ἑαυτοὺς κοσμιωτέρων
μὲν κοσμιώτερα καὶ ἀνδρικῶν ἀνδρικώτερα· καὶ κατὰ
225 τρόπον οὕτως ἑκάστους τὰς αὑτῶν ἂν αἱρέσεις εἰς τοὺς
παῖδας ἀποτυπουμένους καὶ παίδων παῖδας, ὃ λέγομεν,
ἥκειν ἔχοντας ἰδίους νόμους εἰς τὴν μείζονα ξυνοικίαν.

ΚΛ. Πῶς γὰρ οὔ;

ΑΘ. Καὶ μὴν τούς γε αὑτῶν νόμους ἀρέσκειν ἑκά- C
230 στοις ἀναγκαῖόν που, τοὺς δὲ τῶν ἄλλων ὑστέρους.

ΚΛ. Οὕτως.

ΑΘ. Ἀρχῇ δὴ νομοθεσίας οἷον ἐμβάντες ἐλάθομεν,
ὡς ἔοικεν.

ΚΛ. Πάνυ μὲν οὖν.

235 ΑΘ. Τὸ γοῦν μετὰ ταῦτα ἀναγκαῖον αἱρεῖσθαι τοὺς
συνελθόντας τούτους κοινούς τινας ἑαυτῶν, οἳ δὴ τὰ πάντων ἰδόντες νόμιμα, τά σφισιν ἀρέσκοντα αὑτῶν μάλιστα
εἰς τὸ κοινὸν τοῖς ἡγεμόσι καὶ ἀγαγοῦσι τοὺς δήμους οἷον
βασιλεῦσι φανερὰ δείξαντες ἑλέσθαι τε δόντες, αὐτοὶ μὲν D
240 νομοθέται κληθήσονται, τοὺς δὲ ἄρχοντας καταστήσαντες,
ἀριστοκρατίαν τινὰ ἐκ τῶν δυναστειῶν ποιήσαντες ἢ καί
τινα βασιλείαν, ἐν ταύτῃ τῇ μεταβολῇ τῆς πολιτείας οἰ-
κήσουσιν.

ΚΛ. Ἐφεξῆς γοῦν ἂν οὕτω τε καὶ ταύτῃ γίγνοιτο.

245 ΑΘ. Τρίτον τοίνυν εἴπωμεν ἔτι πολιτείας σχῆμα
γιγνόμενον, ἐν ᾧ δὴ πάντα εἴδη καὶ παθήματα πολιτειῶν καὶ ἅμα πόλεων ξυμπίπτει γίγνεσθαι.

ΚΛ. Τὸ ποῖον δὴ τοῦτο;

ΑΘ. Ὁ μετὰ τὸ δεύτερον καὶ Ὅμηρος ἐπεσημήνατο, E

λέγων τὸ τρίτον οὕτω γεγονέναι· κτίσσε δὲ Δαρδανίην 250
γάρ πού φησιν,

ἐπεὶ οὔπω Ἴλιος ἱρή
ἐν πεδίῳ πεπόλιστο, πόλις μερόπων ἀνθρώπων,
ἀλλ᾽ ἔθ᾽ ὑπωρείας ᾤκουν πολυπιδάκου Ἴδης.

682 λέγει γὰρ δὴ ταῦτα τὰ ἔπη καὶ ἐκεῖνα ἃ περὶ τῶν Κυκλώ- 255
πων εἴρηκε κατὰ θεόν πως εἰρημένα καὶ κατὰ φύσιν·
θεῖον γὰρ οὖν δὴ καὶ τὸ ποιητικὸν [ἐνθεαστικὸν] ὂν γένος
ὑμνῳδοῦν πολλῶν τῶν κατ᾽ ἀλήθειαν γιγνομένων ξύν τισι
Χάρισι καὶ Μούσαις ἐφάπτεται ἑκάστοτε.

ΚΛ. Καὶ μάλα.   260

ΑΘ. Εἰς δὴ τὸ πρόσθεν προέλθωμεν ἔτι τοῦ νῦν
ἐπελθόντος ἡμῖν μύθου. τάχα γὰρ ἂν σημήνειέ τι τῆς
ἡμετέρας πέρι βουλήσεως. οὐκοῦν χρή ;

Β ΚΛ. Πάνυ μὲν οὖν.

ΑΘ. Κατῳκίσθη δή, φαμέν, ἐκ τῶν ὑψηλῶν εἰς 265
μέγα τε καὶ καλὸν πεδίον Ἴλιον, ἐπὶ λόφον τινὰ οὐχ
ὑψηλὸν καὶ ἔχοντα ποταμοὺς πολλοὺς ἄνωθεν ἐκ τῆς
Ἴδης ὡρμημένους.

ΚΛ. Φασὶ γοῦν.

ΑΘ. Ἆρ᾽ οὖν οὐκ ἐν πολλοῖς τισὶ χρόνοις τοῖς μετὰ 270
τὸν κατακλυσμὸν τοῦτο οἰόμεθα γεγονέναι ;

ΚΛ. Πῶς δ᾽ οὐκ ἐν πολλοῖς ;

ΑΘ. Δεινὴ γοῦν ἔοικεν αὐτοῖς λήθη τότε παρεῖναι
C τῆς νῦν λεγομένης φθορᾶς, ὅθ᾽ οὕτως ὑπὸ ποταμοὺς
πολλοὺς καὶ ἐκ τῶν ὑψηλῶν ῥέοντας πόλιν ὑπέθεσαν, 275
πιστεύσαντες οὐ σφόδρα ὑψηλοῖς τισὶ λόφοις.

ΚΛ. Δῆλον οὖν ὡς παντάπασί τινα μακρὸν ἀπεῖχον
χρόνον τοῦ τοιούτου πάθους.

ΑΘ. Καὶ ἄλλαι γε, οἶμαι, πόλεις τότε κατῴκουν ἤδη
πολλαὶ πληθυόντων τῶν ἀνθρώπων.   28c

ΚΛ. Τί μήν ;

ΑΘ. Αἴ γέ που καὶ ἐπεστρατεύσαντο αὐτῇ, καὶ κατὰ θάλατταν δὲ ἴσως, ἀφόβως ἤδη πάντων χρωμένων τῇ θαλάττῃ.

285 ΚΛ. Φαίνεται.   D

ΑΘ. Δέκα δ᾽ ἔτη που μείναντες Ἀχαιοὶ τὴν Τροίαν ἀνάστατον ἐποίησαν.

ΚΛ. Καὶ μάλα.

ΑΘ. Οὐκοῦν ἐν τούτῳ τῷ χρόνῳ, ὄντι δεκέτει, ὃν 290 τὸ Ἴλιον ἐπολιορκεῖτο, τὰ τῶν πολιορκούντων ἑκάστων οἴκοι κακὰ πολλὰ ξυνέβαινε γιγνόμενα περὶ τὰς στάσεις τῶν νέων, οἳ καὶ ἀφικομένους τοὺς στρατιώτας εἰς τὰς αὐτῶν πόλεις τε καὶ οἰκίας οὐ καλῶς οὐδ᾽ ἐν δίκῃ ὑπε- δέξαντο, ἀλλ᾽ ὥστε θανάτους τε καὶ σφαγὰς καὶ φυγὰς E 295 γενέσθαι παμπόλλας; οἳ πάλιν ἐκπεσόντες κατῆλθον με- ταβαλόντες ὄνομα, Δωριῆς ἀντ᾽ Ἀχαιῶν κληθέντες διὰ τὸ τὸν συλλέξαντα εἶναι τὰς τότε φυγὰς Δωριᾶ. καὶ δὴ ταῦτά γε ἤδη πάνθ᾽ ὑμεῖς, ὦ Λακεδαιμόνιοι, τἀντεῦθεν μυθολογεῖτέ τε καὶ διαπεραίνετε.

Book IV.

Our Laws to be not merely imperative, but persuasive.

(The Athenian, Cleinias.)

719 C—720 E.

ΑΘ. Τάδε. Παλαιὸς μῦθος, ὦ νομοθέτα, ὑπό τε C αὐτῶν ἡμῶν ἀεὶ λεγόμενός ἐστι καὶ τοῖς ἄλλοις πᾶσι ξυν- δεδογμένος, ὅτι ποιητής, ὁπόταν ἐν τῷ τρίποδι τῆς Μού- σης καθίζηται, τότε οὐκ ἔμφρων ἐστίν, οἷον δὲ κρήνη 5 τις τὸ ἐπιὸν ῥεῖν ἑτοίμως ἐᾷ, καὶ τῆς τέχνης οὔσης μιμή-

σεως ἀναγκάζεται ἐναντίως ἀλλήλοις ἀνθρώπους ποιῶν
διατιθεμένους ἐναντία λέγειν αὐτῷ πολλάκις, οἶδε δὲ οὔτ᾽
εἰ ταῦτα οὔτ᾽ εἰ θάτερα ἀληθῆ τῶν λεγομένων. τῷ δὲ
D νομοθέτῃ τοῦτο οὐκ ἔστι ποιεῖν ἐν τῷ νόμῳ, δύο περὶ
ἑνός, ἀλλὰ ἕνα περὶ ἑνὸς ἀεὶ δεῖ λόγον ἀποφαίνεσθαι. 10
σκέψαι δ᾽ ἐξ αὐτῶν τῶν ὑπὸ σοῦ νῦν δὴ λεχθέντων. οὔσης
γὰρ ταφῆς τῆς μὲν ὑπερβεβλημένης, τῆς δὲ ἐλλειπούσης,
τῆς δὲ μετρίας, τὴν μίαν ἑλόμενος σύ, τὴν μέσην, ταύτην προστάττεις καὶ ἐπῄνεσας ἁπλῶς. ἐγὼ δέ, εἰ μὲν
γυνή μοι διαφέρουσα εἴη πλούτῳ καὶ θάπτειν αὐτὴν δια- 15
κελεύοιτο ἐν τῷ ποιήματι, τὸν ὑπερβάλλοντα ἂν τάφον
E ἐπαινοίην, φειδωλὸς δ᾽ αὖ τις καὶ πένης ἀνὴρ τὸν κατα-
δεᾶ, μέτρον δὲ οὐσίας κεκτημένος καὶ μέτριος αὐτὸς ὢν
τὸν αὐτὸν ἂν ἐπαινέσοι. σοὶ δ᾽ οὐχ οὕτω ῥητέον ὡς νῦν
εἶπες μέτριον εἰπών, ἀλλὰ τί τὸ μέτριον καὶ ὁπόσον 20
ῥητέον, ἢ τὸν τοιοῦτον λόγον μήπω σοι διανοοῦ γίγνεσθαι
νόμον.

ΚΛ. Ἀληθέστατα λέγεις.

ΑΘ. Πότερον οὖν ἡμῖν ὁ τεταγμένος ἐπὶ τοῖς νόμοις
μηδὲν τοιοῦτον προαγορεύῃ ἐν ἀρχῇ τῶν νόμων, ἀλλ᾽ 25
εὐθὺς ὃ δεῖ ποιεῖν καὶ μὴ φράζῃ τε καὶ ἐπαπειλήσας τὴν
720 ζημίαν ἐπ᾽ ἄλλον τρέπηται νόμον, παραμυθίας δὲ καὶ
πειθοῦς τοῖς νομοθετουμένοις μηδὲ ἓν προσδιδῷ; καθάπερ
ἰατρὸς δέ τις ὁ μὲν οὕτως, ὁ δ᾽ ἐκείνως ἡμᾶς εἴωθεν
ἑκάστοτε θεραπεύειν,—ἀναμιμνησκώμεθα δὲ τὸν τρόπον 30
ἑκάτερον, ἵνα τοῦ νομοθέτου δεώμεθα, καθάπερ ἰατροῦ
δέοιντο ἂν παῖδες τὸν πρᾳότατον αὐτὸν θεραπεύειν τρόπον ἑαυτούς. οἷον δὴ τί λέγομεν; εἰσὶ πού τινες ἰατροί,
φαμέν, καί τινες ὑπηρέται τῶν ἰατρῶν, ἰατροὺς δὲ καλοῦμεν δή που καὶ τούτους. 35

B ΚΛ. Πάνυ μὲν οὖν.

ΑΘ. Ἐάν τέ γ' ἐλεύθεροι ὦσιν ἐάν τε δοῦλοι, κατ'
ἐπίταξιν δὲ τῶν δεσποτῶν καὶ θεωρίαν καὶ κατ' ἐμπειρίαν
τὴν τέχνην κτῶνται, κατὰ φύσιν δὲ μή, καθάπερ οἱ ἐλεύ-
40 θεροι αὐτοί τε μεμαθήκασιν οὕτω τούς τε αὑτῶν διδάσκουσι παῖδας. θείης ἂν ταῦτα δύο γένη τῶν καλουμένων
ἰατρῶν ;

ΚΛ. Πῶς γὰρ οὔ ;

ΑΘ. Ἆρ' οὖν καὶ ξυννοεῖς ὅτι δούλων καὶ ἐλευθέρων
45 ὄντων τῶν καμνόντων ἐν ταῖς πόλεσι τοὺς μὲν δούλους C
σχεδόν τι οἱ δοῦλοι τὰ πολλὰ ἰατρεύουσι περιτρέχοντες
καὶ ἐν τοῖς ἰατρείοις περιμένοντες, καὶ οὔτε τινὰ λόγον
ἑκάστου πέρι νοσήματος ἑκάστου τῶν οἰκετῶν οὐδεὶς τῶν
τοιούτων ἰατρῶν δίδωσιν οὐδ' ἀποδέχεται, προστάξας δ'
50 αὐτῷ τὰ δόξαντα ἐξ ἐμπειρίας ὡς ἀκριβῶς εἰδώς, καθάπερ τύραννος, αὐθαδῶς οἴχεται ἀποπηδήσας πρὸς ἄλλον
κάμνοντα οἰκέτην, καὶ ῥᾳστώνην οὕτω τῷ δεσπότῃ παρα-
σκευάζει τῶν καμνόντων τῆς ἐπιμελείας ; ὁ δὲ ἐλεύθερος D
ὡς ἐπὶ τὸ πλεῖστον τὰ τῶν ἐλευθέρων νοσήματα θερα-
55 πεύει τε καὶ ἐπισκοπεῖ, καὶ ταῦτα ἐξετάζων ἀπ' ἀρχῆς
καὶ κατὰ φύσιν, τῷ κάμνοντι κοινούμενος αὐτῷ τε καὶ
τοῖς φίλοις, ἅμα μὲν αὐτὸς μανθάνει τι παρὰ τῶν νο-
σούντων, ἅμα δέ, καθ' ὅσον οἷός τ' ἐστί, διδάσκει τὸν
ἀσθενοῦντα αὐτόν, καὶ οὐ πρότερον ἐπέταξε πρὶν ἄν πῃ
60 ξυμπείσῃ, τότε δὲ μετὰ πειθοῦς ἡμερούμενον ἀεὶ παρασκευάζων τὸν κάμνοντα, εἰς τὴν ὑγίειαν ἄγων, ἀποτελεῖν E
πειρᾶται. πότερον οὕτως ἢ ἐκείνως ἰατρός τε ἰώμενος
ἀμείνων καὶ γυμναστὴς γυμνάζων ; διχῇ τὴν μίαν ἀποτε-
λῶν δύναμιν, ἢ μοναχῇ καὶ κατὰ τὸ χεῖρον τοῖν δυοῖν καὶ
65 ἀγριώτερον ἀπεργαζόμενος ;

ΚΛ. Πολύ που διαφέρον, ὦ ξένε, τὸ διπλῇ.

Book VII.

*Comedy to be acted by slaves.   Tragedy to be referred to
our Magistrates.*

(The Athenian.)

816 D—817 D.

Τὰ μὲν οὖν τῶν καλῶν σωμάτων καὶ γενναίων ψυχῶν
εἰς τὰς χορείας, οἵας εἴρηται δεῖν αὐτὰς εἶναι, διαπεπέ-
ρανται· τὰ δὲ τῶν αἰσχρῶν σωμάτων καὶ διανοημάτων
καὶ τῶν ἐπὶ τὰ τοῦ γέλωτος κωμῳδήματα τετραμμένων,
κατὰ λέξιν τε καὶ ᾠδὴν καὶ κατὰ ὄρχησιν καὶ κατὰ τὰ 5
τούτων πάντων μιμήματα κεκωμῳδημένα, ἀνάγκη μὲν
θεάσασθαι καὶ γνωρίζειν· ἄνευ γὰρ γελοίων τὰ σπουδαῖα
E καὶ πάντων τῶν ἐναντίων τὰ ἐναντία μαθεῖν μὲν οὐ δυνατόν, εἰ μέλλει τις φρόνιμος ἔσεσθαι, ποιεῖν δὲ οὐκ ἂν
δυνατὸν ἀμφότερα, εἴ τις αὖ μέλλει καὶ σμικρὸν ἀρετῆς 10
μεθέξειν, ἀλλὰ αὐτῶν ἕνεκα τούτων καὶ μανθάνειν αὐτὰ
δεῖ, τοῦ μή ποτε δι’ ἄγνοιαν δρᾶν ἢ λέγειν ὅσα γελοῖα
μηδὲν δέον, δούλοις δὲ τὰ τοιαῦτα καὶ ξένοις ἐμμίσθοις
προστάττειν μιμεῖσθαι, σπουδὴν δὲ περὶ αὐτὰ εἶναι μηδέποτε μηδ’ ἡντινοῦν μηδέ τινα μανθάνοντα αὐτὰ γίγνε- 15
σθαι φανερὸν τῶν ἐλευθέρων, μήτε γυναῖκα μήτε ἄνδρα,
καινὸν δὲ ἀεί τι περὶ αὐτὰ φαίνεσθαι τῶν μιμημάτων.
ὅσα μὲν οὖν περὶ γέλωτά ἐστι παίγνια, ἃ δὴ κωμῳδίαν
817 πάντες λέγομεν, οὕτω τῷ νόμῳ καὶ λόγῳ κείσθω· τῶν δὲ
σπουδαίων, ὥς φασι, τῶν περὶ τραγῳδίαν ἡμῖν ποιητῶν, 20
ἐάν ποτέ τινες αὐτῶν ἡμᾶς ἐλθόντες ἐπανερωτήσωσιν
οὑτωσί πως, Ὦ ξένοι, πότερον φοιτῶμεν ὑμῖν εἰς τὴν
πόλιν τε καὶ χώραν ἢ μή, καὶ τὴν ποίησιν φέρωμέν τε
καὶ ἄγωμεν, ἢ πῶς ὑμῖν δέδοκται περὶ τὰ τοιαῦτα δρᾶν ;

25 τί οὖν ἂν πρὸς ταῦτα ὀρθῶς ἀποκριναίμεθα τοῖς θείοις
ἀνδράσιν ; ἐμοὶ μὲν γὰρ δοκεῖ τάδε, Ὦ ἄριστοι, φάναι, B
τῶν ξένων, ἡμεῖς ἐσμὲν τραγῳδίας αὐτοὶ ποιηταὶ κατὰ
δύναμιν ὅ τι καλλίστης ἅμα καὶ ἀρίστης· πᾶσα οὖν ἡμῖν
ἡ πολιτεία ξυνέστηκε μίμησις τοῦ καλλίστου καὶ ἀρίστου
30 βίου, ὃ δή φαμεν ἡμεῖς γε ὄντως εἶναι τραγῳδίαν τὴν
ἀληθεστάτην. ποιηταὶ μὲν οὖν ὑμεῖς, ποιηταὶ δὲ καὶ
ἡμεῖς ἐσμὲν τῶν αὐτῶν, ὑμῖν ἀντίτεχνοί τε καὶ ἀνταγω-
νισταὶ τοῦ καλλίστου δράματος, ὃ δὴ νόμος ἀληθὴς μόνος ἀποτελεῖν πέφυκεν, ὡς ἡ παρ᾽ ἡμῶν ἐστὶν ἐλπίς..
35 μὴ δὴ δόξητε ἡμᾶς ῥᾳδίως γε οὕτως ὑμᾶς ποτὲ παρ᾽ C
ἡμῖν ἐάσειν σκηνάς τε πήξαντας κατ᾽ ἀγορὰν καὶ καλλι-
φώνους ὑποκριτὰς εἰσαγαγομένους, μεῖζον φθεγγομένους
ἡμῶν, ἐπιτρέψειν ὑμῖν δημηγορεῖν πρὸς παῖδάς τε καὶ
γυναῖκας καὶ τὸν πάντα ὄχλον, τῶν αὐτῶν λέγοντας ἐπι-
40 τηδευμάτων πέρι μὴ τὰ αὐτὰ ἅπερ ἡμεῖς, ἀλλ᾽ ὡς τὸ
πολὺ καὶ ἐναντία τὰ πλεῖστα· σχεδὸν γάρ τοι κἂν μαι-
νοίμεθα τελέως ἡμεῖς τε καὶ ἅπασα ἡ πόλις, ἥτις οὖν D
ὑμῖν ἐπιτρέποι δρᾶν τὰ νῦν λεγόμενα, πρὶν κρῖναι τὰς
ἀρχὰς εἴτε ῥητὰ καὶ ἐπιτήδεια πεποιήκατε λέγειν εἰς τὸ
45 μέσον εἴτε μή. νῦν οὖν, ὦ παῖδες μαλακῶν Μουσῶν
ἔκγονοι, ἐπιδείξαντες τοῖς ἄρχουσι πρῶτον τὰς ὑμετέρας
παρὰ τὰς ἡμετέρας ᾠδάς, ἂν μὲν τὰ αὐτά γε ᾖ καὶ βελτίω τὰ παρ᾽ ὑμῶν φαίνηται λεγόμενα, δώσομεν ὑμῖν
χορόν, εἰ δὲ μή, ὦ φίλοι, οὐκ ἂν ποτε δυναίμεθα.

Book X.

*Atheism a disease of the young mind, to be cured by
persuasion and patience.*

(The Athenian, Cleinias.)

887 C—891 A.

ΑΘ. Εὐχήν μοι δοκεῖ παρακαλεῖν ὁ λεγόμενος ὑπὸ
σοῦ νῦν λόγος, ἐπειδὴ προθύμως συντείνεις· μέλλειν δὲ
οὐκέτι ἐγχωρεῖ λέγειν. φέρε δή, πῶς ἄν τις μὴ θυμῷ
λέγοι περὶ θεῶν ὡς εἰσίν; ἀνάγκη γὰρ δὴ χαλεπῶς φέρειν καὶ μισεῖν ἐκείνους οἱ τούτων ἡμῖν αἴτιοι τῶν λόγων 5
γεγένηνται καὶ γίγνονται νῦν, οὐ πειθόμενοι τοῖς μύθοις,
οὓς ἐκ νέων παίδων ἔτι ἐν γάλαξι τρεφόμενοι τροφῶν τε
ἤκουον καὶ μητέρων, οἷον ἐν ἐπῳδαῖς μετά τε παιδιᾶς
καὶ μετὰ σπουδῆς λεγομένων, καὶ μετὰ θυσιῶν ἐν εὐχαῖς
αὐτοὺς ἀκούοντές τε καὶ ὄψεις ὁρῶντες ἑπομένας αὐτοῖς 10
ἃς ἥδιστα ὅ γε νέος ὁρᾷ τε καὶ ἀκούει πραττομένας,
θυόντων ἐν σπουδῇ τῇ μεγίστῃ τοὺς αὑτῶν γονέας ὑπὲρ
αὑτῶν τε καὶ ἐκείνων ἐσπουδακότας, ὡς ὅ τι μάλιστα
Ε οὖσι θεοῖς εὐχαῖς προσδιαλεγομένους καὶ ἱκετείαις, ἀνα-
τέλλοντός τε ἡλίου καὶ σελήνης καὶ πρὸς δυσμὰς ἰόντων 15
προκυλίσεις ἅμα καὶ προσκυνήσεις ἀκούοντές τε καὶ ὁρῶντες Ἑλλήνων τε καὶ βαρβάρων πάντων ἐν συμφοραῖς
παντοίαις ἐχομένων καὶ ἐν εὐπραγίαις, οὐχ ὡς οὐκ ὄντων ἀλλ' ὡς ὅ τι μάλιστα ὄντων καὶ οὐδαμῇ ὑποψίαν
ἐνδιδόντων ὡς οὐκ εἰσὶ θεοί,—τούτων δὴ πάντων ὅσοι 20
καταφρονήσαντες οὐδὲ ἐξ ἑνὸς ἱκανοῦ λόγου, ὡς φαῖεν
ἂν ὅσοι καὶ σμικρὸν νοῦ κέκτηνται, νῦν ἀναγκάζουσιν
888 ἡμᾶς λέγειν ἃ λέγομεν, πῶς τούτους ἄν τις ἐν πραέσι
λόγοις δύναιτο νουθετῶν ἅμα διδάσκειν περὶ θεῶν πρῶ-

25 τον ὡς εἰσί; τολμητέον δέ· οὐ γὰρ ἅμα γε δεῖ μανῆναι
τοὺς μὲν ὑπὸ λαιμαργίας ἡδονῆς ἡμῶν τοὺς δ' ὑπὸ τοῦ
θυμοῦσθαι τοῖς τοιούτοις. ἴτω δὴ πρόρρησις τοιάδε τις
ἄθυμος τοῖς οὕτω τὴν διάνοιαν διεφθαρμένοις, καὶ λέγωμεν πράως, σβέσαντες τὸν θυμόν, ὡς ἑνὶ διαλεγόμενοι
30 τῶν τοιούτων, Ὦ παῖ, νέος εἶ· προϊὸν δέ σε ὁ χρόνος
ποιήσει πολλὰ ὧν νῦν δοξάζεις μεταβαλόντα ἐπὶ τἀναντία B
τίθεσθαι. περίμεινον οὖν εἰς τότε κριτὴς περὶ τῶν μεγίστων γίγνεσθαι. μέγιστον δὲ ὃ νῦν οὐδὲν ἡγεῖ σύ, τὸ
περὶ τοὺς θεοὺς ὀρθῶς διανοηθέντα ζῆν καλῶς ἢ μή.
35 πρῶτον δὲ περὶ αὐτῶν ἕν τι μέγα σοι μηνύων οὐκ ἄν
ποτε φανείην ψευδής, τὸ τοιόνδε. οὐ σὺ μόνος οὐδὲ οἱ
σοὶ φίλοι πρῶτοι καὶ πρῶτον ταύτην τὴν δόξαν περὶ θεῶν
ἔσχετε, γίγνονται δὲ ἀεὶ πλείους ἢ ἐλάττους ταύτην τὴν
νόσον ἔχοντες. τόδε τοίνυν σοι παραγεγονὼς αὐτῶν πολ-
40 λοῖσι φράζοιμ' ἄν, τὸ μηδένα πώποτε λαβόντα ἐκ νέου C
ταύτην τὴν δόξαν περὶ θεῶν, ὡς οὐκ εἰσί, διατελέσαι
πρὸς γῆρας μείναντα ἐν ταύτῃ τῇ διανοήσει· τὰ δύο
μέντοι πάθη περὶ θεοὺς μεῖναι, πολλοῖσι μὲν οὔ, μεῖναι
δὲ οὖν τισί, τὸ τοὺς θεοὺς εἶναι μέν, φροντίζειν δὲ οὐ-
45 δὲν τῶν ἀνθρωπίνων, καὶ τὸ μετὰ τοῦτο, ὡς φροντί-
ζουσι μέν, εὐπαραμύθητοι δ' εἰσὶ θύμασι καὶ εὐχαῖς. τὸ
δὴ σαφὲς ἂν γενόμενόν σοι περὶ αὐτῶν κατὰ δύναμιν
δόγμα, ἂν ἐμοὶ πείθῃ, περιμενεῖς ἀνασκοπῶν εἴτε οὕτως
εἴτε ἄλλως ἔχει, πυνθανόμενος παρά τε τῶν ἄλλων καὶ D
50 δὴ καὶ μάλιστα καὶ παρὰ τοῦ νομοθέτου. ἐν δὲ δὴ τούτῳ
τῷ χρόνῳ μὴ τολμήσῃς περὶ θεοὺς μηδὲν ἀσεβῆσαι. πειρατέον γὰρ τῷ τοὺς νόμους σοι τιθέντι νῦν καὶ εἰς αὖθις διδάσκειν περὶ αὐτῶν τούτων ὡς ἔχει.

ΚΛ. Κάλλισθ' ἡμῖν, ὦ ξένε, μέχρι γε τοῦ νῦν εἴρηται.

55 ΑΘ. Παντάπασι μὲν οὖν, ὦ Μέγιλλέ τε καὶ Κλει-

νία· λελήθαμεν δ' ἡμᾶς αὐτοὺς εἰς θαυμαστὸν λόγον ἐμ-
πεπτωκότες.

ΚΛ. Τὸν ποῖον δὴ λέγεις ;

Ε ΑΘ. Τὸν παρὰ πολλοῖς δοξαζόμενον εἶναι σοφώτατον
ἁπάντων λόγων. 60

ΚΛ. Φράζ' ἔτι σαφέστερον.

ΑΘ. Λέγουσί πού τινες ὡς πάντα ἐστὶ τὰ πράγματα
γιγνόμενα καὶ γενόμενα καὶ γενησόμενα τὰ μὲν φύσει, τὰ
δὲ τύχῃ, τὰ δὲ διὰ τέχνην.

ΚΛ. Οὐκοῦν καλῶς ; 65

ΑΘ. Εἰκός γέ τοί που σοφοὺς ἄνδρας ὀρθῶς λέγειν.
889 ἑπόμενοί γε μὴν αὐτοῖς σκεψώμεθα τοὺς ἐκεῖθεν, τί ποτε
καὶ τυγχάνουσι διανοούμενοι.

ΚΛ. Πάντως.

ΑΘ. Ἔοικε, φασί, τὰ μὲν μέγιστα αὐτῶν καὶ κάλ- 70
λιστα ἀπεργάζεσθαι φύσιν καὶ τύχην, τὰ δὲ σμικρότερα
τέχνην, ἣν δὴ παρὰ φύσεως λαμβάνουσαν τὴν τῶν μεγάλων καὶ πρώτων γένεσιν ἔργων πλάττειν καὶ τεκταίνε-
σθαι πάντα τὰ σμικρότερα, ἃ δὴ τεχνικὰ πάντες προσαγορεύομεν. 75

ΚΛ. Πῶς λέγεις ;

Β ΑΘ. Ὧδ' ἔτι σαφέστερον ἐρῶ. πῦρ καὶ ὕδωρ καὶ γῆν
καὶ ἀέρα φύσει πάντα εἶναι καὶ τύχῃ φασί, τέχνῃ δὲ
οὐδὲν τούτων. καὶ τὰ μετὰ ταῦτα αὖ σώματα, γῆς τε
καὶ ἡλίου καὶ σελήνης ἄστρων τε πέρι, διὰ τούτων γεγο- 80
νέναι παντελῶς ὄντων ἀψύχων· τύχῃ δὲ φερόμενα τῇ τῆς
δυνάμεως ἕκαστα ἑκάστων, ᾗ ξυμπέπτωκεν ἁρμόττοντα
οἰκείως πως, θερμὰ ψυχροῖς ἢ ξηρὰ πρὸς ὑγρὰ καὶ μα-
C λακὰ πρὸς σκληρά, καὶ πάντα ὁπόσα τῇ τῶν ἐναντίων
κράσει κατὰ τύχην ἐξ ἀνάγκης συνεκεράσθη, ταύτῃ καὶ 85
κατὰ ταῦτα οὕτω γεγεννηκέναι τόν τε οὐρανὸν ὅλον καὶ

πάντα ὁπόσα κατ' οὐρανόν, καὶ ζῷα αὖ καὶ φυτὰ ξύμπαντα, ὡρῶν πασῶν ἐκ τούτων γενομένων, οὐ διὰ νοῦν,
φασίν, οὐδὲ διά τινα θεὸν οὐδὲ διὰ τέχνην, ἀλλὰ ὃ λέ-
90 γομεν, φύσει καὶ τύχῃ. τέχνην δὲ ὕστερον ἐκ τούτων
ὑστέραν γενομένην, αὐτὴν θνητὴν ἐκ θνητῶν, ὕστερα γε- D
γεννηκέναι παιδιάς τινας ἀληθείας οὐ σφόδρα μετεχούσας,
ἀλλὰ εἴδωλ' ἄττα ξυγγενῆ ἑαυτῶν, οἷ' ἡ γραφικὴ γεννᾷ
καὶ μουσικὴ καὶ ὅσαι ταύταις εἰσὶ συνέριθοι τέχναι. αἱ
95 δέ τι καὶ σπουδαῖον ἄρα γεννῶσι τῶν τεχνῶν, εἶναι ταύτας ὁπόσαι τῇ φύσει ἐκοίνωσαν τὴν αὑτῶν δύναμιν, οἷον
αὖ ἰατρικὴ καὶ γεωργικὴ καὶ γυμναστική. καὶ δὴ καὶ τὴν
πολιτικὴν σμικρόν τι μέρος εἶναί φασι κοινωνοῦν φύσει,
τέχνῃ δὲ τὸ πολύ. οὕτω δὲ καὶ τὴν νομοθεσίαν πᾶσαν
100 οὐ φύσει, τέχνῃ δέ· ἧς οὐκ ἀληθεῖς εἶναι τὰς θέσεις.   E

ΚΛ.   Πῶς λέγεις ;

ΑΘ.   Θεούς, ὦ μακάριε, εἶναι πρῶτόν φασιν οὗτοι
τέχνῃ, οὐ φύσει, ἀλλά τισι νόμοις, καὶ τούτους ἄλλους
ἄλλῃ, ὅπῃ ἕκαστοι ἑαυτοῖσι συνωμολόγησαν νομοθετού-
105 μενοι· καὶ δὴ καὶ τὰ καλὰ φύσει μὲν ἄλλα εἶναι, νόμῳ
δὲ ἕτερα· τὰ δὲ [δὴ] δίκαια οὐδ' εἶναι τὸ παράπαν φύσει,
ἀλλ' ἀμφισβητοῦντας διατελεῖν ἀλλήλοις καὶ μετατιθεμέ-
νους ἀεὶ ταῦτα· ἃ δ' ἂν μετάθωνται καὶ ὅταν, τότε κύ-
ρια ἕκαστα εἶναι, γιγνόμενα τέχνῃ καὶ τοῖς νόμοις, ἀλλ' 890
110 οὐ δή τινι φύσει. ταῦτ' ἐστίν, ὦ φίλοι, ἃ ἀπαντᾷ ἀνδρῶν
σοφῶν πάρα νέοις ἀνθρώποις, ἰδιωτῶν τε καὶ ποιητῶν,
φασκόντων εἶναι τὸ δικαιότατον ὅ τί τις ἂν νικᾷ βια-
ζόμενος, ὅθεν ἀσέβειαί τε ἀνθρώποις ἐμπίπτουσι νέοις,
ὡς οὐκ ὄντων θεῶν οἵους ὁ νόμος προστάττει διανοεῖ-
115 σθαι δεῖν, στάσεις τε διὰ ταῦτα, ἑλκόντων πρὸς τὸν κατὰ
φύσιν ὀρθὸν βίον, ὅς ἐστι τῇ ἀληθείᾳ κρατοῦντα ζῆν
τῶν ἄλλων καὶ μὴ δουλεύοντα ἑτέροισι κατὰ νόμον.

B ΚΛ. Οἷον διελήλυθας, ὦ ξένε, λόγον καὶ ὅσην λώβην
ἀνθρώπων νέων δημοσίᾳ πόλεσί τε καὶ ἰδίοις οἴκοις !

ΑΘ. Ἀληθῆ μέντοι λέγεις, ὦ Κλεινία. τί οὖν οἴει 120
χρῆναι δρᾶν τὸν νομοθέτην οὕτω τούτων πάλαι παρε-
σκευασμένων ; ἢ μόνον ἀπειλεῖν στάντα ἐν τῇ πόλει ξύμπασι τοῖς ἀνθρώποις, ὡς εἰ μὴ φήσουσιν εἶναι θεοὺς
καὶ διανοηθήσονται δοξάζοντες τοιούτους οἵους φησὶν ὁ
νόμος·—καὶ περὶ καλῶν καὶ δικαίων καὶ περὶ ἁπάντων 125
C τῶν μεγίστων ὁ αὐτὸς λόγος, ὅσα τε πρὸς ἀρετὴν τείνει
καὶ κακίαν, ὡς δεῖ ταῦτα οὕτω πράττειν διανοουμένους
ὅπῃπερ ἂν ὁ νομοθέτης ὑφηγήσηται γράφων· ὃς δ᾽ ἂν
μὴ παρέχηται ἑαυτὸν τοῖς νόμοις εὐπειθῆ, τὸν μὲν δεῖν
τεθνάναι, τὸν δέ τινα πληγαῖς καὶ δεσμοῖς, τὸν δὲ ἀτι- 130
μίαις, ἄλλους δὲ πενίαις κολάζεσθαι καὶ φυγαῖς· πειθὼ
δὲ τοῖς ἀνθρώποις, ἅμα τιθέντα αὐτοῖς τοὺς νόμους,
μηδεμίαν ἔχειν τοῖς λόγοις προσάπτοντα εἰς δύναμιν
ἡμεροῦν ;

D ΚΛ. Μηδαμῶς, ὦ ξένε, ἀλλ᾽ εἴπερ τυγχάνει γε οὖσα 135
καὶ σμικρὰ πειθώ τις περὶ τὰ τοιαῦτα, δεῖ μηδαμῇ κάμνειν τόν γε ἄξιον καὶ σμικροῦ νομοθέτην, ἀλλὰ πᾶσαν,
τὸ λεγόμενον, φωνὴν ἱέντα τῷ παλαιῷ νόμῳ ἐπίκουρον
γίγνεσθαι λόγῳ, ὡς εἰσὶ θεοὶ καὶ ὅσα νῦν δὴ διῆλθες
σύ, καὶ δὴ καὶ νόμῳ αὐτῷ βοηθῆσαι καὶ τέχνῃ, ὡς ἐστὸν 140
φύσει ἢ φύσεως οὐχ ἥττονι, εἴπερ νοῦ γέ ἐστι γεννήματα
κατὰ λόγον ὀρθὸν ὃν σύ τε λέγειν μοι φαίνει καὶ ἐγώ
σοι πιστεύω τὰ νῦν.

E ΑΘ. Ὦ προθυμότατε Κλεινία, τί δ᾽ οὐ χαλεπά τέ
ἐστι ξυνακολουθεῖν λόγοις οὕτως εἰς πλήθη λεγόμενα, 145
μήκη τε αὖ κέκτηται διωλύγια ;

ΚΛ. Τί δαί, ὦ ξένε ; περὶ μέθης μὲν καὶ μουσικῆς
οὕτω μακρὰ λέγοντας ἡμᾶς αὐτοὺς περιεμείναμεν, περὶ

θεῶν δὲ καὶ τῶν τοιούτων οὐχ ὑπομενοῦμεν ; καὶ μὴν
150 καὶ νομοθεσίᾳ γέ ἐστί που τῇ μετὰ φρονήσεως μεγίστη
βοήθεια, διότι τὰ περὶ νόμους προστάγματα ἐν γράμμασι 891
τεθέντα, ὡς δώσοντα εἰς πάντα χρόνον ἔλεγχον, πάντως
ἠρεμεῖ, ὥστε οὔτ᾽ εἰ χαλεπὰ κατ᾽ ἀρχὰς ἀκούειν ἐστὶ φο-
βητέον, ἅ γ᾽ ἔσται καὶ τῷ δυσμαθεῖ πολλάκις ἐπανιόντι
155 σκοπεῖν, οὔτε εἰ μακρά, ὠφέλιμα δέ, διὰ ταῦτα λόγον
οὐδαμῇ ἔχει οὐδὲ ὅσιον ἔμοιγε εἶναι φαίνεται τὸ μὴ οὐ
βοηθεῖν τούτοις τοῖς λόγοις πάντα ἄνδρα κατὰ δύναμιν.

NOTES.

THE following notes are intended for those who possess some knowledge of the Greek language. A few remarks may be permitted upon
the plan which has been followed in their composition, and may excuse
the length of some of them. The getting up of classical texts ought
not to be allowed to become a matter of pure memory, but should
much rather be used to cultivate the faculties, and notably the habits of
precise observation and cool judgment. The first point with regard to
any difficulty is to know exactly what the facts are; the next, to apply
good sense to them. We cannot too severely condemn the 'scholiastic'
method of explanation, which gives two or three ways of taking a
passage, without thoroughly discussing the merits of each. Such a procedure is very likely to result in making the pupil think that one interpretation is as good as another, and that all he has to do is to remember a
string of incongruous renderings. Either one explanation is preferable, and
then a reason should be given; or it may be fairly doubted which of two
or more renderings is the best, and then the proof *pro tanto* on each side
should be adduced. The importance of such an intellectual exercise is
obvious. Accuracy and judgment are invaluable in all professions;
but we may take as an instance the case of the lawyer. No qualities
are more useful to him than the two we have mentioned; and both are
intellectual habits highly cultivable. The construing of a statute, or of
an obscurely-worded will, the tracing of a confused title, the sifting of
conflicting evidence, the disentanglement of complicated rights, are
things not very different in quality from the interpretation of a difficult
passage.

On the other hand, there are dangers to be guarded against. Two
may be specified. We must never over-refine. That is 'the scholar's
fault.' We must judge when distinctions are of importance, and when
they are not. The first and great thing is to see clearly the general
meaning and connection; after that we may proceed, step by step, to
make out the details. Again, our sole object should be to know pre-

cisely what our author means. We must have no foregone conclusions; we must never 'read ourselves into him.'

Thus far we have spoken of the method of interpretation. A new question arises; What is that exactly which we interpret? Where does our text come from? Even in a schoolbook attention should be paid to this point. The case of ancient writings is quite different from that of modern books, written since the invention of printing. We have here to inquire which of comparatively few *written* books best preserve the exact words of our author. We must entirely put aside the delusion that there is a certain *textus receptus*, as to which everybody is agreed, with the exception of occasional various readings; and also the notion that one text is pretty nearly as good as another, and that all we have to do is to master, or think we master, the words before us. There is always a right way and a wrong way; unless the evidence be only enough to let us decide *non liquet*; a perfectly legitimate conclusion. But we should always know the exact premises upon which we are proceeding. It may be said, Why not take a good, or even a tolerably good text, and confine yourself to explaining that? The answer is; Such a plan is proper in a quite elementary book; but whenever we begin really to discuss difficulties, we shall find that the reading and the interpretation are inextricably connected. In a small work like this, minute details would be out of place; but we may briefly indicate the principal sources of our text. All important variants will be discussed *ad locos.* The utility of discussing such variations is much the same as that of discussing interpretations.

We may distinguish three stages of the Platonic text. The first is that of the 'Vulgate,' of which Stephanus and his correctors are the representatives. This text derives principally from inferior and interpolated codices. We may remember that it was the only one Heindorf (1802) had before him; which will account for his frequent emendations. The second period is that of the collation of the better codices, dating from the edition of Bekker (1816 and subsequent years), and Gaisford's *Lectiones Platonicae* (1820), which latter contains the readings of the Clarkian manuscript. Upon these collations the subsequent editions have been mainly founded. Four recensions of the complete works have been constantly referred to for the following notes; those of the Zürich editors, Baiter, Orelli, and Winckelmann; of Stallbaum; of K. F. Hermann; and of the Didot edition of Hirschig and Schneider. These all repose mainly upon Bekker, with corrections and partial recollations. The third stage is that in which the text stands at present. The best codices are being very accurately recollated, a proceeding quite necessary; the filiation of MSS., *i.e.* their descent from one another, or from lost archetypes, is being made out; and emendations are being made upon something like system, *e. g.* according to the blunders of codices with regard to particular words or syllables. The names may be mentioned of Professors Wagner and Martin Schanz (see list of editions), the former much assisted by Mr. I. Bywater of Exeter College, Oxford. It is to be regretted that Herr Schanz has as yet only given us six dialogues, and the first half of the *Laws*.

The MSS. of Plato are numerous, but of very different value. One thing has gradually become apparent, the great superiority of two codices (A and B) to all the others. Both are of the ninth century A.D. One is in the National Library at Paris, and is generally known as the Paris A or A simply. ' Membranaceus, forma maxima, foliis 344, paginis bipartitis, scholiis minuto quodam uncialium genere scriptis.—Scriptus est seculo decimo' (nono) 'ineunte. ὠρθώθη ἡ βίβλος αὕτη ὑπὸ κωνσταντίνου μητροπολίτου ἱερᾶς πόλεως, τοῦ καὶ ὠνησαμένου.' (Turicenses). The other is in the Bodleian Library at Oxford, and is variously known as the Bodleian, Clarkian, or B. The two contain quite different parts of Plato's works, but nearly complete each other.

Here a word becomes necessary as to the ' tetralogies of Thrasyllus.' Thrasyllus was a rhetorician or ' *littérateur*,' who lived in the times of Augustus and Tiberius, and is said to have sometimes acted as travelling secretary to the former. He divided the works of Plato which he considered genuine into nine divisions of four each; and this arrangement, though occasionally somewhat dislocated, appears in all our MSS. It would seem to follow that none of these can be derived from any archetype earlier than the Christian era. B contains the first six tetralogies, or twenty-four dialogues. A contains the eighth and ninth, that is, the *Clitophon*, *Republic*, *Timaeus*, *Critias*, and the *Minos*, *Laws*, *Epinomis* and thirteen *Letters*, besides the *Definitions*, and seven dialogues which were not included in the tetralogies. But as the *Republic* and *Laws* are very much the longest of Plato's writings, the one volume is not much less bulky than the other. The seventh tetralogy, which thus falls between two stools, comprised the *Ion*, *Hippias*, First and Second, and *Menexenus*, of which only the Ion is undoubtedly genuine. Professor Schanz claims to have proved that A and B have been copied from one archetype, a codex in two volumes. It is certainly a striking fact that in two MSS. we find at the end of the *Menexenus* the words τέλος τοῦ πρώτου βιβλίου, although that dialogue does not complete either of these codices.

The Bodleian or Clarkian MS. (B) was brought from the island of Patmos by Dr. Edward Daniel Clarke, about the beginning of this century. Clarke's account of its acquisition is extremely amusing, and perhaps an Oxford editor may be forgiven for repeating it in brief. The monastery of St. John, said to have been founded by Alexius Comnenus, and the town of Patmos, stand on the highest point of a mountainous island. The library of the monastery was a chaos. The newest and best bound books occupied the best positions. ' A considerable number of old volumes of parchment, some with covers and some without, were heaped npon the floor in the utmost disorder : and there were evident proofs that these had been cast aside, and condemned to answer any purpose for which the parchment might be required. When we asked the Superior what they were? he replied, turning up his nose with an expression of indifference and contempt, χειρόγραφα !' Neither the Superior nor the Bursar could read. In this heap Dr. Clarke found the Plato and other MSS. A bargain was made, with the help of an Englishman in the Turkish service; but only two small volumes could be carried off at the time, as the Capitan Pasha would severely have taxed the monastery, had there been any suspicion of money passing. The day appointed for delivery of the books (11 October, 1801) went by in much anxiety; for the honour of the Caloyers (καλόγεροι) was scarcely to be depended on. At last appeared a monk with a huge basket of loaves, who, coming on board, desired the travellers, with a significant wink, to count the loaves, and see if they were all right. The precious MSS. were in the bottom of the basket, and were immediately concealed. Then, making a great parade of the loaves, Dr. Clarke and his friends dismissed the messenger with a handsome douceur.

'The monks told him' (Villoison) 'that twenty years before his arrival they had burnt from two to three thousand manuscripts.' Walpole's MS. journal *ap.* Clarke. (Clarke's Travels in Various Countries, vol. iii. chap. 9. pp. 334 sqq.)

The MS. thus rescued is a parchment quarto, beautifully written. At the end of the *Meno*, which terminates the sixth tetralogy, we find the epigraph (see the Greek in Schanz's *Novae Commentationes Platonicae*, p. 113). ' Written by the hand of John the scribe, εὐτυχῶς, for Arethas' ('Aρέθας) ' of Patrae, deacon, the price thirteen Byzantian nummi, in the month of November, the fourteenth year of the Indiction, the year of the world six thousand four hundred and four' (A.D. 896), ' in the reign of Leo, lover of Christ, son of Basileius the ever-memorable.' A subsequent line acknowledges receipt of the thirteen νομίσματα, about eight guineas of English money, according to Clarke. Two other MSS. exist purporting to be written for Arethas, from one of which we learn that he became Archbishop of Caesarea in Cappadocia.

One or two of the other MSS. may just be mentioned. Two volumes in the Vatican, Δ Θ of Bekker, Herr Schanz holds to be derived from the Clarkian, (or its archetype?), with some small exceptions. Θ also contains the *Republic* and *Timaeus*. The Crusian or Tübingen codex (C) has several dialogues. Bekker's Π, at Venice, gives the first four tetralogies, with the *Clitophon* and *Republic*. All these go very closely together with **B**. Other codices exhibit a different and inferior text, of which Schanz takes as an example the often quoted Venetian Ξ, which was written for the famous Cardinal Bessarion, and which contains all Plato except the spurious *Eryxias*.

The text here given is printed from the smaller Zürich recension in twenty one volumes, which has only been departed from in a few unimportant matters of spelling, etc. Unfortunately the different editions of this recension, when separate volumes have been reprinted, do not always agree. In such cases the latest has been followed. It is hoped that no material confusion can arise from this source, as the chief authorities have always been given in doubtful places, where also any readings disapproved of in the Zürich text have been criticised.

A word as to the editors of the third period of the text. It may be asked, How is recollation possible? What is done is surely done once for all. The answer is; A manuscript is not like a printed book. B for example is greatly damaged by moisture. It is also full of corrections upon erasure, which make it difficult or impossible to restore the original reading. Such corrections may be by several hands; and it is a work of much patience and time to disentangle them. But this laborious work once accomplished, it by no means follows that we are bound to accept the conjectures and alterations of those meritorious editors. Professor Schanz, for example, leans somewhat towards the methods of Cobet; methods most ingenious and learned, but not commanding general assent. He inclines upon the whole to cut out words from the text; although he sometimes inserts. Doubtless there are many glosses in the present text. The later the MS., the more it is interpolated. But we must not be rash to condemn. Nothing can be more useful than an examination of the peculiarities of MSS., classifying their blunders, and so on. But all this comes under the head of collation; and once this scrutiny terminated, we pass from certain data to conjecture. See notes on doubtful places below, especially in the *Apology* and *Crito*, and extracts from the *Phaedo*, *Cratylus*, and *Laws*.

The text here given rests upon good codices, and mainly on A and B, with corrections *variorum*. This remains to be amended by severe recollation, and reasonable alterations. But on the whole the Platonic text is good; better than that of some first-rate authors.

Those who wish for farther illustration, or more lengthened comment, than can be given here, will naturally turn to larger works. A brief list of such *subsidia* is given at the end of the volume, which it is hoped may be of use to teachers, or to any who wish to study the Platonic writings minutely.

CHARMIDES.

155 E—158 E.

Socrates, under cover of prescribing for a headache, impresses upon the beautiful Charmides that as the eyes cannot be well unless the head is so, nor the head unless the whole body, so neither can the body be well unless the soul also be in health.

Charmides was the maternal uncle of Plato. He was a favourite with Socrates (Xenophon, *Mem.* III. vi. 1), who thought highly of his abilities, and encouraged him to speak in public (III. vii.). He was one of the ten commanders of the Piraeus under the Thirty, and was killed in that neighbourhood, along with Critias, when striving to dislodge Thrasybulus from Munychia, B.C. 404. (Xenophon, *Hellenics,* II. iv. 19).

Critias, son of Callaeschrus, and near kinsman of Plato's mother, appears in the *Charmides, Timaeus,* and *Critias.* He was a man of great ability, and attained distinction both as an orator and as a poet. A few of his verses remain, and may be found in Bergk's *Lyrici Graeci.* In the year B.C. 404 the Spartans occupied Athens, and brought back the fugitives of the oligarchical party. Critias was the most prominent member of the Committee of Thirty, who composed the new government, and entered upon a wild series of executions and confiscations. One example of their doings we have below in the *Apology* (32 C), where we find Socrates defying their authority.

155 E. μόγις πως ἀπεκρινάμην] 'I did at last say that—.'

156 A. εἰ μὴ ἀδικῶ γε] 'I ought to know your name.' The same in sense as δίκαιός εἰμι ἀκριβοῦν. This form is not uncommon in Plato, *e. g. Republic* x. 608 E σὺ δὲ τοῦτ' ἔχεις λέγειν; Εἰ μὴ ἀδικῶ γε, ἔφην.

καλῶς γε σὺ—ποιῶν] 'that is well.'

B. Join αὐτοὺς μόνους—τοὺς ὀφθαλμούς.

C. διαίταις] 'treatment' or 'regimen.'

καὶ ἀποδέχει τὸν λόγον] 'and you approve the statement.'

D. ἐκεῖ] At Potidaea. In the beginning of the dialogue Socrates tells us that he had returned from Potidaea the evening before, just after an engagement. The siege of Potidaea, which had revolted from Athens, took place during the years 432-30 B.C. See note on *Apology* 28 E.

Ζάλμοξις is the spelling of the best MSS. of Plato, and also of Herodotus (see below). Ζάμολξις others. But we need not suppose the Greeks to have been rigorously consistent in writing foreign words, any more than we are in the spelling of such names as Mahomet

(Mahommed, Mohammed, Muhammad). The Turks again have made the name into Mehemet, assimilating the vowels after the fashion of their language.

ἀπαθανατίζειν] 'to confer immortality.' A remarkable passage in Herodotus (iv. 93, 94) is to be compared with this. Πρὶν δὲ ἀπικέσθαι ἐπὶ τὸν Ἴστρον, πρώτους αἱρέει Γέτας τοὺς ἀθανατίζοντας.—ἀθανατίζουσι δὲ τόνδε τὸν τρόπον. Every four years, Herodotus says, one of the Getae is chosen by lot, and put to death, to be a messenger to Zalmoxis. In the second clause quoted, then, ἀθανατίζουσι would seem to mean, 'they make the messenger immortal.' The meaning in the first clause might be more doubtful; perhaps we should understand the word in the same way. It has been taken to mean in both places 'pro immortalibus consecrare' (Gronovius), which comes to much the same thing; or 'immortalitatem hominibus tribuere,' 'animas immortales esse censere.' (Baehr *ad locum*).

How does all this bear upon our passage? The sense of 'who hold the doctrine of immortality' seems comparatively flat. Something striking and wonderful is wanted to point the sentence; and this is supplied by the interpretation given; 'those wonderful priests of Zalmoxis, who are said even to have the secret of life.' Only, as Stallbaum points out, we may well suppose Plato to have thought of the other meaning also. 'Itaque verbum liquet positum esse cum quadam ambiguitate ab ipso scriptore studiose quaesita.' See his note and Heindorf's. Ἀθανατίζειν is used in the sense of 'believe in immortality,' *Nicomachean Ethics*, X. vii. 8. 'We must not live after the advice of those who say that a man should not exceed human thoughts, nor a mortal mortal thoughts,' ἀλλ' ἐφ' ὅσον ἐνδέχεται ἀθανατίζειν, 'but hold fast to immortality and live according to the best that is in us.'

I have no instance of either the simple or compound verb occurring elsewhere in writers *optimae notae*, except in a curious fragment of Aristotle quoted by Athenaeus (697 A) from the Ἀπολογία τῆς ἀσεβείας πρὸς Εὐρυμέδοντα. Aristotle had been accused, according to the story, of addressing Hermeias in a paean as a god; see the whole chapter (xv. 51) in Athenaeus, who quotes the beginning of the poem. The fragment of the Ἀπολογία says, 'Had I sacrificed to Hermeias as a god, I had not given him the memorial (μνῆμα) of a man,' καὶ ἀθανατίζειν τὴν φύσιν βουλόμενος ἐπιταφίοις ἂν λόγοις ἐκόσμησα, 'and had I sought to deify his nature, I had not paid him the honour of funereal words.' The passage has a very poetical air. Fr. 601 in Rose's collection (Berlin Academy edition of Arist.).

ἰατροὶ οἱ Ἕλληνες, though a little striking, is strictly regular, Ἕλληνες being used as an adjective.

E. διαφεύγειν] 'escape the grasp of.'

ὥσπερ—ὄμματα] As the head influences the eyes, so the soul influences the body. Head : eyes :: soul : body.

157 A. μέλλει] The direct oration alternates with the indirect, as often.

ἐπῳδαῖς] 'spells,' 'incantations.' Cp. Euripides, *Hippolytus* 478, εἰσὶν δ' ἐπῳδαὶ καὶ λόγοι θελκτήριοι.

B. χωρὶς ἑκατέρου] 'of either separately.' Scil. of soul and body.

C. ποιοῖμέν σοι] 'with you,' 'to you.' Not quite the object of the verb, and not quite relative ('ethical').

ἕρμαιον] 'a happy chance.' *Banquet* 217 A ἕρμαιον ἡγησάμην εἶναι καὶ εὐτύχημα ἐμὸν θαυμαστόν. And other places.

D. εἰς ὅσον ἡλικίας ἥκει] 'for his age.' See on *Lysis* 209 A.

E. ἐκ τῶν εἰκότων] 'might fairly be expected to produce.'

Κριτίου] For this Critias see note on *Timaeus* 20 E.

158 A. Πυριλάμπους] Pyrilampes and Glaucon are otherwise unknown. The name of Glaucon was borne by Plato's brother, and that of Pyrilampes by his stepfather.

ἐν τῇ ἠπείρῳ] The mainland of Asia.

B. μακάριον.] 'Scita est haec Homericae simplicitatis imitatio. Conf. Odyss. γ. 95' (περὶ γάρ μιν ὀιζυρὸν τέκε μήτηρ). 'ζ. 25' (Ναυσικάα, τί νυ σ' ὧδε μεθήμονα γείνατο μήτηρ;) 'Il. δ. 399' (ἀλλὰ τὸν υἱὸν [Τυδεὺς] γείνατο εἷο χέρεια μάχῃ, ἀγορῇ δέ τ' ἀμείνω). Heindorf.

'Αβάριδος] The tale of Abaris was worked up variously in later times. What we have here is simple enough; and Herodotus (iv. 36) only says that the story was he travelled round the world, bearing an arrow, and never eating.

C. οὐκ ἀγεννῶς] 'like a man.' *Gorgias* 492 D οὐκ ἀγεννῶς γε, ὦ Καλλίκλεις, ἐπεξέρχει τῷ λόγῳ παρρησιαζόμενος. And elsewhere.

ἐξάρνῳ εἶναι] 'to say no to.'

D. ἐπαχθές] 'arrogant,' 'conceited.'

E. τούτου γε ἕνεκα] 'as far as that is concerned.'

LYSIS.

207 D—210 D.

Socrates converses with the young Lysis, who is not yet come to man's estate, using the simplest form of his accustomed manner. What is it that makes other people have trust in us, and liking for us? Knowledge.

Of Lysis, son of Democrates (209 A), we only know what the dialogue tells us (p. 205), that he was of a rich and noble family, famous for equestrian victories, and boasting a legendary descent. He is described as a handsome and ingenuous youth, 'like a fair vision,

and not less worthy of praise for his goodness than for his beauty'
(207 A).

Menexenus, son of Demophon, a young Athenian of noble family,
converses with Socrates in the dialogue, of doubtful authenticity, which
bears the name of *Menexenus*. Besides his share in the *Lysis*, he also
appears as one of the κωφὰ πρόσωπα of the *Phaedo* (59 B).

αὐτῶν] Of the two young friends, Lysis and Menexenus.

ἐδόκει—τυγχάνειν] 'for he was conducting a sacrifice, as I understood.'

E. εὐδαιμονοίης] The optative, expressing a remoter consequence,
is more general in sense than the subjunctive would be ; implying not
merely the present, but the future.

ἐμέ γε—καὶ μάλα γε] καὶ μάλα go together. Each γε qualifies the
words it stands immediately next ; so that there is no difficulty as to the
repetition.

208 B. πόθεν—ἐῷεν ;] ἄν is omitted, as the answer simply repeats
some words of the question. This use of πόθεν in a question to imply
a negative is not uncommon in Plato. 'How should they let me ?'
'Do you suppose they would let me ?' πόθεν, where πῶς might be
expected, seems at first strange ; but a passage like the following shows
how the usage is arrived at ; *Cratylus* 398 E σὺ ἔχεις εἰπεῖν ; Πόθεν, ὦ
'γαθέ, ἔχω ; 'My dear sir, whence am I to get an answer ?'

D. αὐτῇ] 'for her,' but really pleonastic. Cf. *Rep.* i. 343 A ὅς γε
αὐτῇ οὐδὲ πρόβατα οὐδὲ ποιμένα γιγνώσκεις. 'You, that cannot tell your
nurse the meaning of either "sheep" or "shepherd".' We have a
similar usage in English ; 'the Hotspur of the north, he that kills *me*
some six or seven dozen of Scots at a breakfast.' 1 Henry IV. ii. 4.

ἡ τῆς σπάθης—ὀργάνων] σπάθη and κερκίς are implements intended
for the same purpose, to drive home the thread of the woof each time it
is passed between the threads of the warp, so as to make the fabric
close. 'Reed,' 'lay,' or 'batten,' are given as names for the corresponding instrument in modern weaving. (Smith's Dict. Antiq. *s. v.* TELA).
'Shuttle,' therefore, though it may well pass as a translation when the
exact part of the loom is not important, is not the precise equivalent of
κερκίς or σπάθη, or κτείς, a third name for the same thing.

E. τρέφουσι has no particular force ; 'keep you,' as we say.

209 A. ἡλικίαν] The word denotes any particular age, even old
age, according to the context, but especially youth, or manhood, as
opposed to childhood. *Theaetetus* 142 D εἴπερ εἰς ἡλικίαν ἔλθοι, 'if he
lived,' 'if he came to age.' *Charmides* 154 A ἀλλ' οὔπω ἐν ἡλικίᾳ ἦν
πρίν σε ἀπιέναι, 'but he was only a child before you went away.'
Euthydemus 306 D ὁ μὲν οὖν νεώτερος ἔτι καὶ σμικρός ἐστι, Κριτόβουλος
δ' ἤδη ἡλικίαν ἔχει. *Cratylus* 440 D ἔτι γὰρ νέος εἶ καὶ ἡλικίαν ἔχεις,

'for you are young and able' (to study philosophy). We may understand here either 'I am not of an age,' or 'I am not grown up'; perhaps the first is simpler. For the sense of old age, see *e. g. Laches* 180 D ἅτε κατ' οἰκίαν τὰ πολλὰ διατρίβοντες, ὑπὸ τῆς ἡλικίας, 'we have to stay at home mostly, on account of our age.'

B. ἐπιτεῖναι—πλήκτρῳ] ἐπιτείνειν and ἀνιέναι are the regular words for tightening and slackening the strings, by turning the pegs on which their upper end was rolled. ψῆλαι is to 'play with the fingers,' as on a modern harp or guitar, instead of striking the string with the plectrum.

E. δραξάμενοι] 'taking a whole handful.'

210 A. ἐμπάσαι τῆς τέφρας] 'to sprinkle dust into his eyes,' partitive genitive.

ἐκείνων] This is an example of the usage by which, it is often said, ἐκεῖνος comes to be equivalent to αὐτός. Mr. Riddell puts it better (*Digest of Idioms*, § 49) when he says: 'Instances occur frequently in Plato, in which the same object is designated successively, in the same sentence or contiguous sentences, by οὗτος or the oblique cases of αὐτός, etc., and ἐκεῖνος. This mobility of language serves as an index of the onward movement of the thought, and helps and incites the hearer (or us the readers) to keep pace with it. As new objects are brought into the centre of the field of observation, the objects which were just now full in front drop behind.' He then gives a number of instances. In the present passage ἐκείνων is probably used to avoid clashing with αὐτῷ just before.

εἰς μὲν ταῦτα] Heindorf well explains that we may either understand this as meaning *quod attinet ad ea*, 'aut, quod equidem praefero, ταῦτα negligentius a Platone collocatum existimes'; *i. e.* the construction is really the same as in the corresponding clause below, εἰς ἃ δ' ἂν νοῦν μὴ κτησώμεθα: 'those things which we understand every one will intrust to us'; but the construction is complicated by the insertion of ταῦτα out of its strict grammatical position.

LACHES.

182 D—184 A.

The subject of the *Laches* is, 'What is Courage?' Laches thinks very little of the new art of ὁπλομαχία, or military gymnastics, a specimen of which he and his friends have been witnessing. If there were anything in this new drill, he thinks, the Lacedaemonians, whose whole study is in such matters, would be eager about it, which they are not. Besides, these gentlemen who call themselves 'masters-at-arms' are not much good in real service; nay, he has seen this very Stesileos, whose performances they have been looking at, make a pretty exhibition of himself on board a trireme in action.

Nicias and Laches are the two famous generals. Nicias is quite willing to hear reason about this new ὁπλομαχία; Laches is the blunt old-fashioned soldier, who is used to 'established ways, and has no faith in modern innovations.

Lysimachus (183 C), the son of Aristides the Just, was the fellow-demot and old friend of Sophroniscus, the father of Socrates, and in the preceding portion of the dialogue gracefully recognizes his son, whom he has not hitherto known.

τὸ ὁπλιτικὸν τοῦτο] The personages of the dialogue have been witnessing an 'assault of arms,' or exhibition of skill in the use of spear, shield, etc., by a professional teacher of the ὁπλομαχία, Stesileos. Laches is the speaker.

E. καὶ οἷον Νικίας λέγει] 'and if it be such an art as Nicias says it is.' Others understand simply 'and as Nicias says it is.'

μὴ μάθημα—μὴ μέντοι] μή on account of the supposition.

183 A. πλεονεκτοῖεν] 'might get the better,' 'have the advantage.'

παρ' ἐκείνοις ἄν—πλεῖστ' ἄν] The repetition of ἄν in the same clause is not uncommon. *Superflua non nocent.*

εἰς ταῦτα καὶ παρὰ τῶν ἄλλων] The two prepositional phrases do not go together; 'that professor who was esteemed among them ought to make a deal of money in other parts of the world.'

B. περὶ τὴν Ἀττικήν] i. e. outside of it.

εἰκότως] I should point off with Stallbaum and the Zürich editors; the omission of the stop with Hermann seems less idiomatic.

ἄβατον ἱερόν] 'a sacred place not to be approached.'

C. ἐν αὐτῷ τῷ ἔργῳ] 'in actual service.'

ὥσπερ γὰρ ἐπίτηδες] 'there has been a sort of fatality about this.' There is a play on the word ἐπιτηδευσάντων following.

ἐκ τούτων refer to the words that are coming.

παρὰ τοὺς ἄλλους οὕτω] 'beyond all others'; οὕτω, 'as I have just mentioned.'

D. ἐπιδεικνύμενον is a *vox signata*, 'making his exhibition.' ἐπιδεικνύμενον οὐχ ἑκόντα, 'making an involuntary exhibition of himself.'

ἐπεβάτευε] In which he was an ἐπιβάτης, a sort of marine; a regular soldier, and reckoned as a hoplite, but serving on shipboard. We learn from Thuc. vi. 43 that they were taken from the class of Thêtes, or the poorest sort of freemen. On one occasion we hear that a levy of ἐπιβάται was made among the higher classes (viii. 24); but this was on the special emergency of an attack upon Chios, and the epithet ἀναγκαστοί, 'conscripts,' is used.

διαφέρον] The regular Attic use; 'remarkable' or 'extraordinary.' 'A remarkable weapon, and proper for a remarkable man.'

E. οἷον ἀπέβη] 'intelligendum ἄξιον λέγειν.' Stallbaum. 'I want to tell you how it turned out.'

184 A. ἠφίει] -ειν, -εις, -ει is the form best supported in these imperfects. See Veitch, *Greek Verbs*, s. v. ἵημι. ἵη which he quotes from Homer is ἵει in La Roche's edition without any variant; and ἠφίην in *Euthydemus* 293 A is ἠφίειν in Zürich edition, Hermann, Stallbaum, cum codd. Hirschig has ἠφίην.

ἄκρου τοῦ στύρακος] 'the very end of the butt.'

ἴσως μὲν οὖν—ἄττα ἐστίν] 'perhaps there may be something in this accomplishment, as Nicias says; I can only tell you my own experience.'

Why should we put any date upon this charming anecdote? We know from a place in Thuc. (iii. 90) that Laches was admiral-general of an Athenian fleet which attacked Mylae of the Messenians (in Sicily), B.C. 426. But what of that?

PROTAGORAS.

310 A—316 A.

The young Hippocrates is eager to be introduced by Socrates to Protagoras, 'the sophist,' that he may learn wisdom from him. Socrates compels Hippocrates to confess that he would not like to be a 'sophist' himself, and that he does not know in what the wisdom of the sophists consists. They then go to the house of Callias, where they see Protagoras, Hippias, Prodicus, and other sophists.

Ἱπποκράτης] Of this Hippocrates nothing is known but from the dialogue. It is said below, 316 B, that he was of ' a great and prosperous house,' οἰκίας μεγάλης καὶ εὐδαίμονος. He is a young gentleman of good family, anxious to cut a figure in the state, and therefore desirous to learn from the sophists.

δέ] This use of δέ is very common, especially in Attic. See Kühner², ii. 520, note 1; Herodotus vii. 10 ἐγὼ δὲ καὶ πατρὶ τῷ σῷ, ἀδελφεῷ δὲ ἐμῷ, Δαρείῳ, ἠγόρεον μὴ στρατεύεσθαι ἐπὶ Σκύθας.

B. Ἱπποκράτης, ἔφην, οὗτος] 'Is that Hippocrates?' Not the same as ὦ οὗτος Ἱπποκράτης, but 'the person who is there (οὗτος) is Hippocrates.' 'That is Hippocrates?'

νεώτερον] 'no news, eh?' The commentators, looking to εἰ μὴ ἀγαθά γε which follows, understand νεώτερον to be used not without reference to its euphemistic meaning of something evil. This use of νέος is common from Pindar and Herodotus downward; but is not required here, and I do not know that it distinctly occurs elsewhere in Plato.

εὖ ἂν λέγοις] 'I am glad to hear it.'

Πρωταγόρας] Protagoras of Abdera in Thrace is with Plato the arch-sophist; and much of the *Theaetetus* is devoted to refuting him. In this dialogue (349 A) Socrates says that he has called himself σοφιστής, when other persons avoided the name, and has been the first to take fees for imparting his knowledge. In the introduction, given in this extract, he is represented as a very considerable personage, perhaps to point the representation of Socrates, who makes no pretensions, but before whose irresistible logic Protagoras falls prostrate.

C. Οἰνόης] There were two Attic demi of the name of Oenoë; one near Marathon, and one near Eleutherae. The first was an out-of-the-way country place; the other is frequently mentioned in the historians, being upon the high road to Thebes and Plataea.

ἦλθον] 'was returned.'

D. νυκτῶν] νύκτες in the plural, implying the hours or watches of the night, is a common Attic idiom, as in the first line of the *Clouds*, ὦ Ζεῦ πάτερ, τὸ χρῆμα τῶν νυκτῶν ὅσον.

ἐπειδὴ—ἀνῆκεν] 'as soon as ever I had slept off my fatigue.'

πτοίησιν] 'his impetuous eagerness.' 'I, who knew the very courageous madness of the man.'

E. εἰ γὰρ—εἴη] 'I wish that were all.'

τῶν φίλων] The article here performs a double duty, being at once the genitive of the neuter τά, and agreeing with φίλων. The omission is obviously to prevent the awkward recurrence of the same word twice.

οὐδ' ἀκήκοα οὐδέν] Scil. αὐτοῦ. For this construction after a verb, when there should strictly be two governments expressed, and only one case appears, compare below 313 C Πρωταγόρᾳ, ὃν οὔτε γιγνώσκεις, ὡς φῇς, οὔτε διείλεξαι πώποτε (supply αὐτῷ).

311 A. Καλλίᾳ] Callias, son of Hipponicus, was of one of the oldest and wealthiest families of Athens. His house is called the greatest and richest of the city (*Protagoras* 337 D), and is the scene of Xenophon's *Banquet.* He has spent a world of money on the Sophists (*Apology* 20 A). Lysias says (*De Bonis Aristophanis*, § 48) that when he came into his property he passed for being the richest man in Greece, and that his grandfather valued his estate at two hundred talents, say fifty thousand pounds English money. Athenaeus says (537 C), apparently quoting from Heraclides Ponticus, who was himself a hearer of Plato, that Callias reduced himself to poverty, and died in want of common necessaries. Certainly the distinction of the family ended with him.

ἐξαναστῶμεν] What is called a pregnant construction, two notions being expressed by the same word; 'let us rise and go out.' Cf. *Phaedo* 116 A (*infra*) ἀνίστατο εἰς οἴκημά τι.

B. ἀποπειρώμενος—ῥώμης] 'trying how far he would go.' ῥώμη is here 'the strength of his purpose.' Cf. Thuc. vii. 42 τῷ δὲ προτέρῳ στρατεύματι τῶν 'Αθηναίων ὡς ἐκ κακῶν ῥώμη τις ἐγεγένητο, 'they were heartened,' 'encouraged,' 'remoralized.'

τελῶν] future.

ὥσπερ ἂν εἰ] The ἄν in such constructions anticipates the ἄν of the apodosis; here we have τί ἂν ἀπεκρίνω following; but the ἄν is also used where no verb follows.

Ἱπποκράτη] Hippocrates of Cos, the most celebrated physician of antiquity, was a contemporary of Socrates and Plato, though the dates of his life are most uncertain. A great congeries of works remains bearing his name, although very few of these can certainly be referred to himself. To him we owe the doctrine of the four humours, blood, phlegm, yellow and black bile, the just proportion of which preserves health. The Asclepiadae were a distinguished *gens*, and the great Aristotle was one of them.

C. μέλλεις τελεῖν—ὡς τίνι ὄντι] Which is the interrogative word?

Πολύκλειτον—Φειδίαν] Pheidias of Athens and Polycleitus of Argos, or Sicyon, are mentioned as the chief of Hellenic sculptors. The masterpieces of Pheidias were the statue of Athene in the Parthenon, and that of Zeus at Olympia, both executed in ivory and gold. The former is said to have been forty feet high, the latter even more. Perhaps some of the Elgin marbles may come from the chisel of Pheidias himself; at all events they were executed under his immediate eye. The great work of Polycleitus was the colossal figure of Hera in her temple near Argos: but he is said to have portrayed rather human than divine figures.

D. ἐξικνῆται—αὐτόν] 'if it come within the compass of our purse.' The omission of the apodosis, 'well' or the like, is a common Greek idiom from Homer downwards; *e.g.* Thuc. iii. 3 καὶ ἢν μὲν ξυμβῇ ἡ πεῖρα· εἰ δὲ μή, Μυτιληναίοις εἰπεῖν ναῦς τε παραδοῦναι καὶ τείχη καθελεῖν. See Kühner², ii. 986.

E. ἄλλο γε] 'distinct,' 'separate,' 'further.'

312 A. εἰς τοὺς Ἕλληνας] 'to all the world.'

σοφιστήν] The Sophists of the time of Socrates and Plato were teachers of rhetoric; the art they taught was that of public speaking, then the only means by which public influence could be acquired; and to secure readiness in this, they supplied their pupils with a stock of commonplace dicta and arguments applicable to ordinary occasions, and with a number of rhetorical devices calculated to set out a case to advantage and throw dust in the eyes of the unpractised. Such a training, they easily persuaded themselves and their pupils, was really a course of mental and moral philosophy. The standing quarrel of

Plato with the Sophists is simply this; that their tendency is to promote, instead of philosophy, mere rhetoric and specious argument; that, upon the one hand, they usurp the place of the true philosophers in popular estimation, and so carry away the young men after them, while upon the other they bring on the philosophers, who are confounded with them, the bad reputation due to their own charlatanery and chicane; and, above all, that they sell wisdom for money. But we need not suppose that the Sophists of Plato are in all things the actual Sophists, any more than his Socrates is the actual Socrates; rather he attributes to them, as to a convenient impersonation, all inconsequent logic, all blundering or timeserving theories of society or morals, all baseless speculation. They are—for his purpose—the sum and embodiment of all that is bad in philosophy.

αἰσχύνοιο] Hippocrates shows the same kind of repugnance to the notion of becoming a sophist that a young gentleman of the present day might to the notion of becoming a professional actor.

αὐτόν] The reflexive of the third pronoun is used in Attic not unfrequently for those of the first and second; *e. g. Phaedo* 91 C ὅπως μὴ ἐγὼ—ἑαυτόν τε καὶ ὑμᾶς ἐξαπατήσας—οἰχήσομαι.

ἄρα—μή] μή implies the correction of a supposed mistake. 'But see, Hippocrates; perhaps you do not really think that Protagoras will teach you to be a sophist like himself, but that he will teach you an accomplishment such as may become a private gentleman?' The question begins with μή; and οὐ goes with τοιαύτην.

B. ὡς—πρέπει] 'as becomes an unprofessional gentleman.'

C. τὸν—ἐπιστήμονα] τῶν σοφῶν is neuter, as elsewhere. An example of the singular may be found in the *Banquet*, 175 D, ἵνα καὶ τοῦ σοφοῦ ἀπολαύσω, ὅ σοι προσέστη ἐν τοῖς προθύροις :—'I may partake of the wisdom.'

Hippocrates no doubt derives σοφιστής from σοφός and an imaginary ἴστης, from the root of εἰδέναι. Heindorf well compares the derivation of Ἥφαιστος in the Cratylus from φάεος ἴστωρ, 407 C, Ἦ τὸν γενναῖον τὸν φάεος ἴστορα ἐρωτᾷς;

D. τῶν τί σοφῶν] The adjective is here again and also below neuter. τί the relative accusative.

ἀποκριναίμεθα] A good example of an important variant. All the MSS. have ἀποκρινοίμεθα. Bekker altered the reading from conjecture, and so the Zürich editors, Hirschig, Stallbaum, and Wayte. Heindorf has οι without remark. The reason of the change is to have the aorist all through. But surely K. F. Hermann does well to keep the reading of the books. The irregularity is no more than if we were to say in English: 'Suppose one had asked us so and so; what are we to say to him?'

ἐπιστάτης] ἐπιστάτης is used where we might have expected ἐπιστήμων. Plato appears to regard the two words, for the moment, as convertible; and probably the word ἐπιστάτης is suggested by the mention of 'production' just before ; 'what manufacture does he direct ?'

313 A. οὔ] Wayte lays down that though in an independent disjunctive sentence we could only have μή, in a dependent one we may have either negative. See Kühner², ii. 749, note 1, and his additional cases. It may be doubted whether we do not over-refine in such delicate distinctions. Compare, for example, in English, the case of *shall* and *will*. The employment of these in literary language is supposed to be regulated by definite rules, and to differ considerably from colloquial or dialectical usage ; but when we come to examine the actual language of books, we shall find that, except in a few familiar cases, the use of *shall* and *will* is by no means fixed, and that in many instances they may be used, not exactly convertibly, but with a very slight difference of meaning.

B. τῷ ἀφικομένῳ τούτῳ ξένῳ] Stallbaum compares *Anabasis* IV. ii. 6 ἡ στενὴ αὕτη ὁδός. The correctness of the construction appears if we transpose the words into ξένῳ τῷ ἀφικομένῳ τούτῳ or ξένῳ τούτῳ τῷ ἀφικομένῳ. Heindorf proposed τῷ ξένῳ.

συνεστέον 'appears to be a solitary instance of the verbal adjective from εἰμί or any of its compounds.' Wayte. The word does not appear to be mentioned in Curtius' *Griechisches Verbum*.

διείλεξαι would require a dative, which however does not appear. The omission is softened by Πρωταγόρᾳ just before.

C. ἔμπορος ἢ κάπηλος] 'merchant or retailer.' Plato elsewhere draws the same distinction between the travelling merchant and the stationary huckster: *e.g. Rep.* ii. 371 D ἢ οὐ καπήλους καλοῦμεν τοὺς πρὸς ὠνήν τε καὶ πρᾶσιν διακονοῦντας, ἱδρυμένους ἐν ἀγορᾷ, τοὺς δὲ πλανητὰς ἐπὶ τὰς πόλεις ἐμπόρους ;

ὅπως γε μή] An example contravening the celebrated canon of Dawes, that ὅπως μή is never joined with the first aorist active or middle, see Jelf, Gr. Gr. § 812.

Richard Dawes, sometime Fellow of Emmanuel College, and head master of Newcastle Grammar School, published in 1745 his *Miscellanea Critica*, which contain *inter alia* a series of emendations upon the text of Aristophanes. One of these is upon line 824 (Dindorf⁸) of the *Clouds*, ὅπως δὲ τοῦτο μὴ διδάξῃς μηδένα. Dawes would read διδάξεις. So far well, though the correction is unnecessary. But he affirms, allowing that the saying will seem hard, in words which have perhaps received more attention than they deserved, 'Confirmo autem atque in me praestandum recipio ὅπως μὴ διδάξῃς soloecam esse loquendi rationem ; quippe Graeci sermonis ingenium exigere ὅπως μὴ διδάξεις. *Nunquamne igitur voc; lae ὅπως μὴ cum formae subjunctivae verbo construuntur?* Cum aoristo primo subjunctivo vocis vel activae vel mediae nunquam, si errores excipias,' etc. (p. 228. P. 459, given as a reference in Jelf, should be 329). He makes no mention of dependent sentences; all his examples are like the one quoted above; but the rule is laid down absolutely. The junction of ὅπως μή with the second or radical aorist, and with the passive aorists, he allows, with some notion that these forms are more akin in sense to the future than the first aorist. That the rule cannot stand has long been shown. The *prima facie* difficulty is almost enough. Why should there in this case be any difference between the two aorists, when no one pretends to find a difference elsewhere? And as to matter of fact, there are many places where the first aorist cannot be held an 'error.' See Kühner², ii. 899 (§ 553, note 5), where the question is discussed, and many negative instances given. One of the most striking is *Ecclesiazusae* 117 (Dind.⁵) ὅπως προμελετή-σωμεν ἀκεῖ δεῖ λέγειν, where the optative has been thrust in without necessity. As Kühner properly remarks, future or aorist is used according to the sense.

E. ὡς δ' αὔτως] The common Attic form; but ὡσαύτως is also found.

τυγχάνεις] The omission of the participle, though not common, is a recognised construction; *e.g. Gorgias* 502 B εἰ δέ τι τυγχάνει ἀηδὲς καὶ ὠφέλιμον.

314 A. παρὰ τοῦ καπήλου] 'from the merchant,' as we say ourselves. Genesis xxiii. 16 'silver, money current with the merchant.'

ἐπαίοντα] 'the expert.'

B. ἡμῶν] Gen. after πρεσβυτέρων, ' our elders.'

νέοι ὥστε] 'we are young to settle such a question,' as we might say in colloquial English. 'The raven himself is hoarse,' that is to say doubly hoarse, hoarse for a raven. (*Macbeth*, I. v. 377, where ingenious persons have proposed to read ' hoarser.')

Ἱππίας—Πρόδικον] Prodicus of Ceos, like Gorgias, is treated with considerable respect by Plato. He often came to Athens to transact business on behalf of his native city. Socrates talks of him as a teacher (*Meno* 96); and is very anxious to hear what he is saying (*Protagoras* 315); though he sarcastically distinguishes in the *Cratylus* (384) between his fifty-drachma course of lectures, which is ' a complete education in grammar and language,' and the single-drachma one, which is all the poor Socrates has been able to pay for.

To Hippias of Elis Plato is not so kind. If we suppose the two dialogues bearing the name of Hippias to be genuine, which is doubtful, especially as regards the former, he even took the trouble to satirize him. He describes him as bold in answer (*Protagoras* 315), and having the foible of omniscience.

C. δοκεῖ οὖν μοι] 'now, if I remember right.' Wayte.

D. οὐ σχολὴ αὐτῷ] 'not at home.' αὐτός, 'he' *par éminence*, 'my master.' So in the famous αὐτὸς ἔφα, and frequently. The regular use of αὐτός is adversative; in Homer it will be found almost always to imply some other noun or pronoun more or less contrasted.

ἀμφοῖν τοῖν χεροῖν] So the editions. τοῖν χεροῖν, like τὼ χεῖρε, the regular Attic form. The unfamiliar feminine has been thrust out by the masculine in common usage, but is found. τά is rare; τὰ δ' οὖν κόρα τάδ' οὐκ ἀπαλλάξει μύρου Soph. *Ant.* 769; ταῖν commoner, *e.g. Politicus* 260 C ταύταιν ταῖν τέχναιν. Kühner², i. 464. note 3. We may compare the inflexion of οὗτος, where τούτων is used for all genders, though we should have expected *τ*αυτῶν for the feminine. ταυτάων is found in an inscription of Thera. (Kühner², i. 466, note 3).

E. προστώῳ] A portico or cloister, running round the inner court of the house. See Heindorf.

ἐκ τοῦ ἐπὶ θάτερα] The phrase occurs in Thuc. vii. 37, καὶ οἱ ἱππῆς καὶ ἡ γυμνητεία τῶν Συρακοσίων ἐκ τοῦ ἐπὶ θάτερα προσῄει τῷ τείχει.

315 A. Πάραλος κ.τ.λ] In the *Meno*, 94 B, Paralus and Xanthippus are said to have been most carefully trained in all bodily and musical education; in the *Protagoras*, 328 D), it is hinted that they were not equal to their father; and in the *First Alcibiades* (118 E), if that be Plato's, Alcibiades says, 'But, Socrates, if the two sons of Pericles were simpletons, what has that to do with the matter?' Both are said to have died in the great plague, B.C. 429.

Philippides appears to be not otherwise known; and the illustrious name of Antimoerus would have been lost to posterity, but for this casual mention. Mende in Pallene was one of the revolting Athenian dependencies, but was afterwards reduced.

περιεσχίζοντο] 'fell back to right and left.'

τὸν δὲ μετ'] From Od. xi. 601, τὸν δὲ μετ' εἰσενόησα βίην Ἡρακληείην.

ἔφη Ὅμηρος] 'in the words of Homer.'

C. Ἐρυξίμαχος] Eryximachus, a physician like his father Acumenus, gives medical advice to Phaedrus (*Phaedrus* 227 A), and is one of the speakers in the *Banquet*.

Φαῖδρος κ.τ.λ.] Phaedrus we only know from the dialogue which bears his name.

Andron is mentioned in the *Gorgias* (487 C) as having studied philosophy along with Callicles and others.

αὐτοῦ] Of Hippias, strangers from Elis.

καὶ—εἰσεῖδον] Od. xi. 582 καὶ μὴν Τάνταλον εἰσεῖδον κρατέρ' ἄλγε ἔχοντα.

ἐπεδήμει γὰρ ἄρα] 'for Prodicus had arrived from abroad.' γάρ being a compound of γε and ἄρα, γὰρ ἄρα is strictly speaking pleonastic; but the combination is not uncommon. *Rep.* iv. 438 A πάντες γὰρ ἄρα τῶν ἀγαθῶν ἐπιθυμοῦσιν.

D. οἰκήματι] 'a closet' here; the word is used for a room of any kind. καὶ μάλα go closely together.

Παυσανίας] Pausanias appears also in the *Banquet*, and makes one of the speeches in honour of Love.

E. 'Ἀγάθωνα] Agathon was a darling of fortune; he was at once rich, well-born, handsome, accomplished, and a successful tragedian. The *Banquet* of Plato is supposed to be given on the occasion of his first victory, at the *Lenaea*, B.C. 416. A few graceful verses of his remain, and may be found in Nauck's *Tragicorum Graecorum Fragmenta*. Perhaps the most remarkable of these fragments is the one cited by Aristotle (or Eudemus), *Nicomachean Ethics*, VI. ii. 6 :—

μόνου γὰρ αὐτοῦ καὶ θεὸς στερίσκεται,

ἀγένητα ποιεῖν ἄσσ' ἂν ᾖ πεπραγμένα.

'Not heaven itself upon the past has power.'

τοῦτ' οὖν] The reading of the Zürich editors, after Heindorf, who says, not very decidedly, 'Itaque etiamnum suspicor, τοῦτό τ' οὖν τὸ μεῖρ.' Stallbaum and Hirschig, after some MSS. and Bekker, have τοῦτό τ' ἦν. But surely it is best to read with Hermann, after the Bodleian and other codices, τοῦτο ἦν. In the place generally quoted from the *Phaedo*, 59 B, ἦν δὲ καὶ Κτήσιππος, no difficulty is made ; ἦν is said to be used 'referentially' (ἀναφορικῶς), the simple verb after the compound παρῆν just before. We seem to have much the same thing here. ἦν might not have been used by itself for 'there was present,' but after παρεκάθηντο and the whole catalogue of 'assistants' it caused no difficulty. 'There was this youth Agathon.'

ION.

533 C—535 A.

Socrates questions Ion, the rhapsode, or reciter of Homer, as to his art, and finding that he can give no account of it, explains to him, not without irony, that poetry and similar arts are the immediate gift of the gods, and in no way depend upon the abilities of those who practise them.

533 C. καὶ ὁρῶ—εἶναι] Ion has just said, 'People say that I speak well about Homer, but not about other things. Think and tell me why this is?' καίτοι ὅρα τοῦτο τί ἐστι. Socrates answers, 'I am thinking, and I am going to begin and explain to you my view of the matter.'

ἔρχομαι most editions. Cp. *Phaedo* 100 B ἔρχομαι γὰρ δὴ ἐπιχειρῶν σοι
ἀποδείξασθαι. ἄρχομαι Stallbaum, which seems not so good. ἔρχομαι
means, 'I will proceed to tell you.' (The *Ion*, it should be remembered,
belongs to the seventh tetralogy, which is found neither in B nor Λ.)

D. οὐκ ὄν] The participle agrees with the subject, instead of the
predicate, as is rather more common.

τῇ λίθῳ] λίθος, when denoting a precious or remarkable stone, is
feminine. So of the βάσανος or Lydian stone, *Gorgias* 486 D, τούτων
τινὰ τῶν λίθων, ᾗ βασανίζουσι τὸν χρυσόν, τὴν ἀρίστην.

Μαγνῆτιν] The place in Euripides' *Oeneus* is preserved by Photius
and Suidas ; τὰς βροτῶν | γνώμας σκοπῶν ὥστε Μαγνῆτις λίθος | τὴν δόξαν
ἕλκει καὶ μεθίστησιν πάλιν. Nauck, Fr. 571. A syllable is wanting in
the second line. Stallbaum conj. ὅς, ὥστε ; Nauck ἐπωπῶν. Which
Magnesia, or which Heraclea, gave name to the stone, seems quite
uncertain. There was a Heraclea in Lydia, perhaps not far from
Magnesia ἡ ὑπὸ Σιπύλῳ, which is sometimes said to have furnished the
name of 'Ηρακλεία. Beside the two Magnesias, that of Lydia, beneath
Sipylus, and on the Hermus, and that of Caria, near the Maeander,
Pliny speaks of a third on the borders of Macedonia. (There were two
Heracleas in this neighbourhood). He quotes a certain Sotacus, who
knows five different kinds of loadstone. one of which comes ' a Magnesia
Macedoniae contermina ab Eione Bolben lacum petentibus dextra'
(xxxvi. 128). This brings us, at all events, near the territory of the ancient Magnêtes. Another kind, he says, comes from the Asian Magnesia ;
but by that he probably means Magnesia *ad Maeandrum*. The other
town was generally distinguished from its namesake. A coin, figured
in Smith's *Dictionary of Geography*, bears on the reverse ΜΑΓΝΗΤΩΝ ΠΟ
ΣΙΠΥΛΟΥ, and on the obverse a head of Cicero.

Ἡρακλείαν, surely. Stallb. Ἡράκλειαν with some codices.

E. σιδηρῶν δακτυλίων] Turr. after Jacobs. Codd. σιδήρων καὶ δακτυλίων or σιδηρίων κ. δ. The Zürich correction seems simplest. Stallb.
reads σιδηρίων καὶ δακτυλίων, ' of iron tools ' or ' of irons ' : but nothing
has been mentioned but rings.

A passage in Lucretius is very probably suggested by our text ; vi.
909 sqq. : —

> ' Hunc homines lapidem mirantur, quippe catenam
> Saepe ex annellis reddit pendentibus ex se.
> Quinque etenim licet interdum pluresque videre
> Ordine demisso levibus jactarier auris,
> Unus ubi ex uno dependet subter adhaerens,
> Ex alioque alius lapidis vim vinclaque noscit.'

534 Λ. κορυβαντιῶντες] A simile used several times by Plato.
which may be understood either of those who join in the Coryban-

tian worship of Cybele with its wild music and dancing. or of those who, like them, are possessed by some divine fury, breaking out into motion and song. *Crito* 54 D. In the *Laws*, vii. 790 D, the Corybantes are said to be cured by dancing and music.

καὶ κατεχόμενοι would imply a principal verb to follow in agreement; but the construction is changed into καὶ τῶν μελοποιῶν ἡ ψυχὴ τοῦτο ἐργάζεται.

B. κοῦφον γὰρ χρῆμα κ.τ.λ.] This reminds us somewhat of Shakspere's
  ' A lover may bestride the gossamer
   That idles in the wanton summer air,
   And yet not fall: so light is vanity.'
        Romeo and Juliet, ii. 6.

C. διθυράμβους—ἰάμβους] Three of these forms of Greek poetry are unfortunately known to us only by fragments. The dithyramb was a hymn addressed to or in honour of the gods, of a wild and bold character; the encomium a laudatory ode of men or heroes: the hyporchema is peculiarly associated with Apollo, and, as its name imports, it was accompanied by dancing and pantomimic gestures. Scraps of Pindar remain in all three kinds.

D. θείοις] 'holy' or 'reverend.' Compare *Laws* vii. 817 A (*infra*) τοῖς θείοις ἀνδράσιν.

μὴ πάρεστιν] μή marks the hypothesis: ' as we are to suppose.'

Τύννιχος] 'It is told of Aeschylus that his brothers wished him to compose a paean, but he said that the paean of Tynnichus was admirable; and that if his work were compared with his predecessor's, it would show like new statues of gods beside the old; the old, however simply fashioned, were esteemed divine; but the new, with their elaborate ornaments, although admired, had less of the semblance of divinity.' We seem to know nothing of Tynnichus but from this allusion in Porphyry *de Abstinentia* i. 18, (quoted by Stallbaum).

E. ἐξεπίτηδες] ' on purpose,' ' advisedly.'

APOLOGY.

(The whole).

The first question which presents itself with reference to the *Apology* is naturally, What relation does it bear to the actual defence of Socrates? There are no means of determining, except by internal evidence. The little tract called the Apology of Xenophon, but which is doubtless not from Xenophon's hand, is simply a clever rhetorical exercise, containing anecdotes of Socrates. Doubtless the *Apology* is in the main Plato's own. At all events we have there Plato's conception of his great master, who is also the representative of philosophy in general, and Plato's conception of the way in which he should be defended against the world. We have the whole of Socrates summed up; the search after knowledge, the interrogation of all persons pretending to have knowledge, the negative result, the irony, the indifference to popular opinion, the offence taken by those whose ignorance is exposed or their opinion despised, the dauntless courage, the almost defiance of those who administer the law as compared with the law itself

The *Apology* strictly conforms to the line of an ordinary speech in defence. We have the answer to the indictment; the production of witnesses (19 D 'Speak then, you who have heard me' etc. 21 A 'Chaerecrates will tell you, since his brother Chaerephon is dead,' and other places); the ἐρώτησις or cross-questioning of the prosecutor; the ἀντιτίμησις or counter-suggestion to the proposal of a punishment; and the last words after condemnation to death.

A few words as to the accusers of Socrates may be in place here.

Anytus, the most considerable of the three, was, or had been, a wealthy man (*Meno* 90 A), and had held high office (*ibid.*) He was a leading and esteemed member of the democratic party (his name is joined with that of Thrasybulus), was one of those who retreated to Phyle during the administration of the Thirty, and took a prominent part in the return from thence. Besides the notices of him in the *Apology*, he appears as one of the speakers in the *Meno*, where he exhibits much rancour against the sophists (*Meno* p. 92), and finally flies into a rage with Socrates, whom he warns to be careful how he speaks evil of people, a thing dangerous in Athens (94). 'As Anytus was the most influential accuser, so there is reason to think he was the most inflamed against Socrates' (Riddell). He seems to have been an honest, but thoroughly unintellectual, man; and his real complaint against Socrates is that he corrupts the youth by making them despise their elders and betters, not to say that he directly undermines the authority of these elders by showing them, in their own despite, that they can give no intelligent account of their ordinary avocations. 'And then, he has always friends about him like Alcibiades, or like Critias, from whose odious tyranny we are just escaped. What state can tolerate a fellow of this kind? We have enough to do to maintain the democracy as it is. Then his religious principles are still worse. The old gods are not good enough for him, but he must have a private deity of his own. Away with him from the earth!'

Meletus was nominally the chief accuser of Socrates, but probably only a tool of Anytus. In the *Apology* (23 E) he is said to be angry with Socrates on account of the poets. But we do not know, though the thing is very possible, that he was a poet himself. He cannot have been the Meletus mentioned in the *Frogs*, 1302; but he may have been his son. In the *Euthyphro*, the time of which is laid between the indictment and the trial of Socrates, Socrates says of him (p 2): ' My prosecutor is a young man who is little known, Euthyphro; and I hardly know him; his name is Meletus, and he is of the deme of Pitthos. Perhaps you may remember his appearance; he has a beak, and long straight hair, and a beard which is ill-grown.'

Of Lycon we know nothing but that he is said (*Apology* 23 E) to prosecute ὑπὲρ τῶν ῥητόρων. In the *Wasps* (1301) a Λύκων is mentioned along with Antiphon.

17 A. ὦ ἄνδρες ᾿Αθηναῖοι] So Socrates uniformly addresses the ἡλιασταί throughout his defence, except in 40 A, where he says that he may properly call those judges who have voted for his acquittal ἄνδρες δικασταί. He rather speaks to the general body of his fellow-citizens, and to the world at large, than to the individuals who may be before him.

καίτοι ἀληθές γε κ.τ.λ.] ' they spoke convincingly; and yet not one word, as I may say, of truth have they uttered.' ὡς ἔπος εἰπεῖν qualifies οὐδέν more particularly.

B. αὐτῶν ἓν ἐθαύμασα—αὐτῶν ἀναισχυντότατον] αὐτῶν masculine in both places.

οὐ κατὰ τούτους εἶναι ῥήτωρ] ' in that sense indeed I am an orator; but how differently from them!' I speak the truth, if that be oratory.

ὥσπερ ἐγὼ λέγω] ' as I was saying '; a common idiom.

ἢ τι ἢ οὐδέν inverts the English order; ' no truth, or next to none.' On the other hand we may compare ' seldom or never,' etc.

κεκαλλιεπημένους—ῥήμασί τε καὶ ὀνόμασιν] ῥῆμα is a phrase or sentence; ὄνομα a word. ' A set oration, duly ornamented with words and phrases.'

C. εἰκῇ] ' without study,' ' offhand.'

πλάττοντι] The accusative before εἰσιέναι would be more regular. But we must not be too precise in considering such constructions. We should look at them from the writer's point of view, and think only of the harmony of the sentence. Here the expression might have been varied in many ways. ' Like a lad telling a story.'

παρίεμαι] ' I must beg of you.' The word is used especially in the sense of begging that something may not be done. So *Republic* i. 341 B οὐδέν σου παρίεμαι, ' I ask no favour at your hands.' ' Do your worst.'

ἐπὶ τῶν τραπεζῶν] ἐπί descriptive of place; ' where the tables of the money-changers are.'

D. ἀναβέβηκα] *i. e.* to the tribune or platform for speaking, of which there were two, one for the accuser, and one for the accused. Cron and

Wagner understand this to refer to the high position of the δικαστήριον at Athens, close to the ἀγορά; which one finds very hard to believe. We have the word thrice again in the *Apology* (33 D, 36 A, 40 D), and ἀναβιβάζομαι twice (34 C. D). But in none of these, nor in the other Platonic passages where ἀναβαίνω occurs (see Ast), is there any necessity for thinking of anything but the βῆμα; and some of the places rather point the other way. There is no doubt an ambiguity in the word; the difference is only between 'coming up to the court' and 'coming up before the court.' In 40 B ἡνίκα ἀνέβαινον ἐνταυθ.ι ἐπὶ τὸ δικαστήριον might no doubt mean, 'when I was walking up to the court'; but the sense is as good or better if we understand 'while I was ascending the tribune.' If it be objected that ἐπὶ τὸ δικαστήριον or εἰς τ. δ. (*Euthydemus* 305 C) naturally means 'to the court,' one might answer that there is something pregnant in the sense of ἐπί; 'up to the bema, and so before the court.' In 31 C below we have ἀναβαίνων εἰς τὸ πλῆθος τὸ ὑμέτερον, which is explained in the same way of the high position of the Pnyx. Cron quotes Livy V. 50. 8 *in contionem escendere*; an illustration which tells against him; for there (and in II. vii. 7) the meaning is obviously that the speaker gets upon some place where he can be seen and heard.

ἑβδομήκοντα] So the Zürich editors with the Bodleian and other MSS. But most editors (Bekker, Stallbaum, Hirschig, Hermann, Riddell, Wagner) have πλείω ἑβδομήκοντα, 'although turned of seventy.' In the *Crito*, 52 E, we find it implied that Socrates was seventy, or a little more. Hermann would spare πλείω, as being too accurate for an interpolator; but perhaps we should rather expect the round number, as in the passage of the *Crito*. The difference in point of fact is immaterial, as Socrates cannot have been more than two years over seventy. See Hermann *ad locum* (in his critical prolegomena).

18 A. αὕτη ἀρετή] The construction would have been clearer if we had had τοῦτο ἡ ἀρετή; but the pronoun is attracted into the gender of the noun, and the article is omitted, possibly to mark that the two words stand to each other as subject and predicate.

δίκαιός εἰμι ἀπολογήσασθαι] 'I have to answer.'

[ψευδῆ] The word is bracketed also by Hirschig and Schanz; and its omission greatly improves the flow of the Greek. If retained, it would have to be joined closely with κατηγορημένα. 'Which are charged against me, and charged falsely.'

B. καὶ πάλαι πολλὰ ἤδη ἔτη] 'long ago, for years and years.'

τοὺς ἀμφὶ Ἄνυτον] 'Anytus and his company.' From this we may infer, as stated above, that Anytus was the chief accuser of Socrates.

μᾶλλον οὐδὲν ἀληθές] Hermann brackets these words. Schanz conjectures, very boldly, μὰ τὸν ——, the ὅρκος being unexpressed. There is a difficulty about μᾶλλον; but perhaps the word is right, and means 'more than my nominal accusers.'

σοφός and φροντιστής have an ironical force. 'A sage who speculates about the world above, and pries into all things which are under the earth, and makes the worse appear the better reason.'

C. οἱ—κατασκεδάσαντες] οἱ does not appear in the best manuscripts, and has been added, Schanz says by Heindorf, I know not where. The word seems absolutely required.

οὐδὲ θεοὺς νομίζειν] 'are atheists,' 'do not believe in the gods at all.'

ἀτεχνῶς ἐρήμην] Join. ἐρήμη, sc. δίκη, a trial where the accused does not appear.

πλὴν—ὧν] 'unless they happen to be known as the authors of comedies.' We naturally think of the *Clouds*, which is alluded to below, 19 C, but Cratinus, Ameipsias, and Eupolis are all said to have ridiculed Socrates.

D. φθόνῳ – χρώμενοι] 'in spite and detraction,' opposed to the αὐτοὶ πεπεισμένοι, who act in good faith. 'ὅσοι δέ includes all but the εἴ τις; that is, ὅσοι stands for ὅσοι ἄλλοι.'——'This ὅσοι [ἄλλοι] is then sub-divided into [οἱ μὲν] φθόνῳ χρώμενοι and οἱ δὲ—πείθοντες.' Riddell. In English we might say: 'But the rest of my accusers, whose real motive is spite and detraction—though some no doubt act in good faith upon what they believe—these gentlemen I find most difficult to deal with.'

ἀναβιβάσασθαι] 'bring up, produce,' i. e. upon the bema.

19 A. ἐξελέσθαι τὴν διαβολήν] 'to disabuse you of the prejudice.'

βουλοίμην—ἀπολογούμενον] 'I am willing to try and answer the calumny, if this is of any use to you or me, or is likely to do me any good in my defence.' με is subject.

B. ἀντωμοσίαν] Affidavit or sworn statement of facts. This was made both by the accuser and the accused; hence the ἀντί, implying their opposition.

περιεργάζεται] 'follows curious inquiries.' The word is here taken *in malam partem*: cf. the adjective in *Acts* xix. 19 ἱκανοὶ δὲ τῶν τὰ περίεργα πραξάντων, 'many of those who followed curious or magical arts.'

C. περιφερόμενον] 'swung round in a basket.' *Clouds* 218 sqq.

φύγοιμι] Be the accused, or defendant. Opposed to διώκω, 'prosecute.' This passage is usually understood to mean: 'But I speak not in disparagement of these arts, if such arts there be; I would not have Meletus fall foul of me with a new accusation.' This seems so simple, and all the words are so customary, that no difficulty has been found. But when we try to follow the thread of the reasoning, a very grave difficulty arises. The accusation of Meletus implies that these arts are either trivial or abominable; and in either case, what quarrel can he have with Socrates for saying he knows nothing of them? If the whole clause is omitted, the reasoning remains perfectly clear. Schanz says, ' Verba μή πως—φύγοιμι inclusi, quia sanam interpretationem spernunt.' Can they be a marginal addition, written by some lover of the physical sciences, who thought that Meletus might well have prosecuted himself? We should also expect the present rather than the aorist. Bessarion's codex (Ξ) has φεύγοιμι.

E. χρήματα] *Clouds* 98 sqq.

οἷός τ' ἐστίν] These words, which are like an echo of οἷός τ' εἴη just before, come in very awkwardly, and only confuse the sense. Schanz says: 'Equidem haec verba ad ὥσπερ a librario in margine addita puto'; and this is probably the way to explain them.

πείθουσι] The nominative being at some distance, the number of the verb is made to conform to the sense rather than the grammar.

20 A. ἐπεὶ καί] ἐπεί gives the proof in the form of an example. ' For there is another man.' ἄλλος, ' besides those I have mentioned.'

Καλλίᾳ] See the extract from the *Protagoras*, and note on 311 A.

B. ἀρετήν] ' excellence ' of animals as well as men.

Εὔηνος] So the best MSS. read. Εὐηνός would be more according to analogy, and the name is often so written. There is the same variation in the case of the river, or rather rivers. In *Iliad* ii. 693 we have a man Euenus; La Roche writes Εὐηνοῖο. Can we derive the word from the supposed stem ηνο, which appears in ὑπήνη, προσηνής, etc. (Curtius, *Grundzüge*, root 419), and understand the meaning to be ' fair-faced?' Euenus of Paros is mentioned again as a rhetorician in the *Phaedrus* (267 A), and as a poet in the *Phaedo* (60 D).

C. πέντε μνῶν] Rather more than £20 of our money. A small fee, compared with those sometimes charged by Protagoras, Gorgias, and other celebrities. Socrates is always making merry with the charges of the Sophists. In the *Cratylus* (*sub init.*) he excuses himself for his ignorance of the maker of names on the ground that he has not attended the fifty drachma course of Prodicus, but only the one drachma course.

ἐμμελῶς generally means ' suitably,' ' properly'; literally, ' harmoniously,' a metaphor taken from music; here ' moderately,' ' reasonably.' Cf. *Laws* vi. 776 B, where ἐμμελεστάτη οὐσία is ' the most convenient kind of property.' ' Happy Euenus, if he teaches so well and charges so modestly!'

περιττότερον] ' more out of the way,' ' more strange.'

[εἰ μή τι—πολλοί] Cobet, and Schanz after him, bracket these words, certainly without detriment to the sense. Cobet says (*Variae Lectiones*, ed. sec. p. 299), ' Sciolus nescio quis adscripsit εἰ μή τι ἔπραττες ἀλλοῖον ἢ οἱ πολλοί.'

D. αὐτοσχεδιάζωμεν] 'form a hasty conclusion.' 'How have I come by the evil reputation of being "wise"? Well, I must confess to a sort of wisdom; but then it is an every man's wisdom; these gentlemen claim a superhuman wisdom. which I know nothing about; and he who says I do, takes away my character.'

E. ἢ οὐκ ἔχω τι λέγω] 'they are either superhumanly wise, or—I know not how to describe them.'

μέγα λέγειν] In a bad sense, like the Homeric μέγα ἔργον; 'to speak arrogantly.'

εἰς ἀξιόχρεων] 'to a sufficient surety.'

εἰ—οἵα] The clause comes logically after μάρτυρα τῆς—ἐμῆς [σοφίας]; 'he will tell you whether I have wisdom, and of what manner it is.'

21 A. ἑταῖρός τε καί] ἑταῖρός τε is deleted by Cobet, ἑταῖρός τε καί by Schanz. The words are certainly awkward. There would be no difficulty about the expression in itself, but for the repetition.

τὴν φυγὴν ταύτην] 'This flight, as an event still vividly remembered, is called ταύτην, "the recent "' (Riddell). After the complete over-throw of the Athenian power by Lysander (B.C. 404), a board of thirty persons, commonly known as the Thirty Tyrants, was established at Athens as an executive under Lacedaemonian auspices. The partisans of democracy were in consequence compelled to retire from Athens, and this is the φυγή referred to.

Chaerephon was a prominent person in his own day. Aristophanes frequently ridicules him; e. g. *Birds* 1564, Χαιρεφῶν ἡ νυκτερίς, alluding to his dark complexion; and Eupolis and Cratinus are said to have done the same. He seems to have been thin, sallow, and excitable. In Xenophon's *Memorabilia*, II. iii., he is mentioned as having quarrelled with his brother Chaerecrates, who is mentioned here, though not by name. In the *Charmides* (153 B), he is called μανικός, 'a kind of madman.'

ὅπερ λέγω] 'as I was saying.'

B. Join οὔτε μέγα οὔτε σμικρὸν σοφὸς ὤν, 'I know very well that I am not wise in any degree, great or small.'

ἐπὶ ζήτησιν αὐτοῦ] αὐτοῦ masculine, as I understand. If we take the word as neuter, it seems feeble; and τούτου would seem more natural.

τῶν δοκούντων σοφῶν] 'those who had the name of wise.'

C. τοιοῦτόν τι seems to refer to what follows, as below 22 A.

καὶ διαλεγόμενος αὐτῷ] Schanz would reject these words; one scarcely sees why.

E. νὴ τὸν κύνα] Like νὴ τὸν χῆνα, is an evasive oath of Socrates. In the *Gorgias* 482 B we have μὰ τὸν κύνα τὸν Αἰγύπτιον θεόν, i.e. Anubis; where probably the reference to the 'god of Egypt' is a jest. In the *Phaedrus* 236 E Socrates swears by the plane-tree above his head.

The oath 'by the goose' does not occur in Plato; but old tradition connects it with Socrates. A fragment of Cratinus (238) gives the best explanation of such usages; οἷς ἦν μέγιστος ὅρκος ἅπαντι λόγῳ κύων, ἔπειτα χήν, θεοὺς δ' ἐσίγων. There should also be mentioned the curious note of the Scholiast upon our present passage: Ῥαδαμίνθυος ὅρκος οὗτος ὁ κατὰ κυνὸς ἢ χηνὸς ἢ πλατάνου ἢ κριοῦ ἤ τινος ἄλλου τοιούτου. See the commentators on the *Birds* of Aristophanes, l. 521, especially Theodor Kock (Weidmann, 1864), from whom the last two quotations are taken.

22 A. ἦ μήν is the regular formula of an oath.

ἵνα μοι κ.τ.λ.] These words are usually explained to mean either 'to prove the infallibility of the oracle'; or 'I laboured, only to find at last that the oracle was infallible.' The second of these explanations can hardly stand. But one is strongly tempted to adopt the suggestion of Stephanus, followed by Madvig and Schanz, ἵνα μή μοι κ.τ.λ. 'I took infinite labour to have the oracle thoroughly tested.' ἀνέλεγκτος then has its usual meaning, and the whole sense is greatly improved. The omission of μή is not at all remarkable.

B. πεπραγματεῦσθαι] 'to have had most pains spent on them,' 'their most laboured compositions.'

ὡς ἔπος γὰρ εἰπεῖν] This phrase expresses correction or qualification, guarding against misunderstanding. 'I must say that there is hardly a person who would not,' etc.

ἅπαντες οἱ παρόντες] 'any bystander.'

C. ἐν ὀλίγῳ] 'very soon.'

τῷ αὐτῷ οἰόμενος] τῷ αὐτῷ αὐτῶν Schanz after an old anonymous conjecture. It may be noted that B and Π have τὸ αὐτό.

D. δημιουργοί is the nominative to ἔδοξαν. καί, 'also,' 'as well.'

23 A. οἷαι χαλεπώταται] 'of the bitterest kind.'

ὄνομα δὲ τοῦτο λέγεσθαι] 'The subject of λέγεσθαι is [ἐμέ], not ὄνομα.' Riddell.

τὸ δέ] 'but for that matter.' τὸ δέ, referring to all the sentence following, is often used by Plato to introduce a counter-statement.

ὀλίγου—οὐδένος] 'is of little value, or rather of none.'

καὶ—Σωκράτη] 'and in saying this he is obviously referring not to Socrates.'

This is a good example of a place where we are almost forced upon an emendation. Twelve MSS, including the Bodleian, read τοῦτον; that is to say, if we went by authority, without regarding the sense, we should have no choice about τοῦτον. But τοῦτον τὸν Σωκράτη can hardly be right in itself; and the words προσκεχρῆσθαι δὲ τῷ ἐμῷ ὀνόματι seem to require an opposition. The celebrated F. A. Wolf proposed τοῦτ' οὐ λέγειν, which is adopted by the Zürich editors, Hirschig, Hermann, Schanz, etc. This makes admirable sense, and agrees much better with the use of φαίνεται. 'It is obvious that he, etc.' Stallbaum reads (from conjecture) τοῦτο λέγειν τὸν Σωκράτη, 'et manifesto hoc de me (Socrate) dicit.' There would be no difficulty about the double accusative.

B. ὥσπερ ἂν εἰ εἴποι] εἰ, which does not appear in the codices. was added by Stephanus. Cf. 27 A below. where εἰ (ὥσπερ ἂν εἰ εἴποι), which does not appear in B and Π, is added in both above the line.

ὅτι—σοφίαν] 'that he is good for nothing in respect of wisdom.'

ἀλλ'—εἰμί] 'I am in the extremest poverty.' Plato several times uses μύριος in the sense of 'infinite,' which usage will scarcely be found in any other Attic prose writer.

There are many allusions to the poverty of Socrates. Below (38 B) he says he could perhaps pay a fine of a mina, about £4. In Xenophon's *Oeconomicus* (ii. 3) he is made to say that all his property would fetch five minae.

C. εἶτα ἐπιχειροῦσιν] εἶτα and ἔπειτα are very frequently used thus, without any copula. The ἀσυνάρτησις adds a certain vivacity to the expression.

D. ὅτι—γῆς] This being a recapitulation of 19 B, the verbs are omitted.

E. ξυντεταγμένως] 'with one consent,' 'all in a body.' So B and Π. Bessarion's codex has ξυντεταμένως, which is adopted by Hermann, Wagner, and Schanz. The Zürich editors, Hirschig. and Stallbaum read ξυντεταγμένως. Were it not for the MSS, ξυντεταμένως would seem the better word; and perhaps we ought to accept it. 'With such force,' 'with such insistency.'

ὑπὲρ τῶν δημιουργῶν] Anytus is generally said to have been a βυρσοδέψης, or proprietor of a tanwork. This appears to be an inference from a passage in the so-called *Apology* of Xenophon (29 sqq.), where Socrates is made to say, 'He has compassed my death, because I told him that one who had been so highly honoured by the state ought not to bring up his son to be a tanner' (οὐκ ἔφην χρῆναι τὸν υἱὸν περὶ βύρσας παιδεύειν). The only independent anecdote in that little tractate.

24 A. ὑποστειλάμενος] Prop. drawing or shrinking back; often, as here, 'dissimulating.'

ὅτι τοῖς αὐτοῖς ἀπεχθάνομαι] 'that this is the very reason why I am so unpopular,' i. e. my plainness of speech.

B. αὕτη—ἀπολογία] αὕτη is subject, and ἀπολογία predicate ; 'let this be sufficient defence.' αὕτη is attracted into the gender of the predicate.

μετὰ ταῦτα] 'now.'

C. ὅτι σπουδῇ χαριεντίζεται] 'because he jests about a serious matter,' 'he is a practical joker.' His form of indictment is a joke.

ῥᾳδίως] 'he is too ready.'

εἰς ἀγῶνας] 'into court.'

Καί μοι δεῦρο κ.τ.λ.] 'The examination of Meletus by Socrates, which now follows, though it naturally affords scope for exhibiting Socrates' characteristic talent, is legally speaking the customary ἐρώτησις, to which either party was bound to submit at the requisition of the other.' Riddell.

D. εἰσάγεις] The regular word for 'bringing into court.'

E. νὴ τὴν "Ηραν] The Platonic Socrates swears by Hera frequently; e. g. *Gorgias* 449 D Νὴ τὴν "Ηραν, ὦ Γοργία, ἄγαμαί γε τὰς ἀποκρίσεις, ὅτι ἀποκρίνει ὡς οἷόν τε διὰ βραχυτάτων.

25 B. οὐ φῆτε] When this formula means, as here, ' to deny,' it keeps the οὐ, even where μή should regularly be used.

διαφθείρει is indicative, because Meletus gives this out as the actual state of things.

C. ὦ πρὸς Διὸς Μέλητε] Cf. *infra* 26 E ἀλλ' ὦ πρὸς Διός. *Meno* 71 D ὦ πρὸς θεῶν, Μένων.

ὦ 'τᾶν] 'my good friend.' The phrase is of doubtful origin. Those who write with an apostrophe suppose 'τᾶν to be a collateral form of ἔτης, ' friend,' a derivative of the reflexive pronoun, and meaning properly ' one's own man.' But Curtius says (*Griechische Etymologie*, 675⁴,) ' Whether the Attic form of address ὦ τᾶν (ὦ ταν) has anything to do with ἔτης is very doubtful.—Buttmann's notion—that τᾶν means ' thou," is supported by the Sanscrit *tvam* (thou) and τᾶν· σὺ 'Αττικῶς Hesychius.'

D. καὶ γὰρ ὁ νόμος κελεύει] The law is inserted in the second oration of Demosthenes against Stephanus, p 1131 τοῖν ἀντιδίκοιν ἐπάναγκες εἶναι ἀποκρίνασθαι ἀλλήλοις τὸ ἐρωτώμενον, μαρτυρεῖν δὲ μή.

E. ὑπ' αὐτοῦ] ὑπ' Ξ (Bessarion's MS.) and Cobet. ἀπ' B Π and other books, which surely is to be preferred.

οὐδένα] Supply ἂν πείθεσθαι, or something equivalent.

26 B. ἢ δῆλον δή] ἤ very frequently brings in the alternative or modification of statement which is meant to be accepted.

ὧν does not seem to be an attraction to the previous genitives, but the simple objective genitive instead of the usual περί ὧν. To this construction it is related as the rather unusual λέγειν τινά is to λέγειν περί τινος. Cf. *Charmides* 156 A οὐ γάρ τί σου ὀλίγος λόγος ἐστίν. Stallbaum.

C. ὦ θαυμάσιε Μέλητε] 'strange man!' It is often not easy to catch the exact force of such addresses as this and ὦ δαιμόνιε, ὦ μακάριε; but they generally express playful wonder or admiration. 'Wonderful man!' 'Happy man!'

. D. καταφρονεῖς] 'have you such a poor opinion of?'

οὐκ εἰδέναι] As in the case of οὐ φῆτε above, the two words combine into one expression = ἀγνοεῖν, and therefore the οὐ remains.

'Αναξαγόρου] l. 391. '᾽Αναξαγόρου delevit MS' (Martin Schanz) 'vide Studien p. 35, potius Σωκράτους postulavit Baiter.' Schanz. There is a difficulty. The rhetorical point is much damaged by bringing in the name of Anaxagoras before ὥστε οὐκ εἰδέναι κ.τ.λ. Either of the alterations would much improve the sense; and we can easily suppose 'Αναξαγόρου to be introduced from what follows.

'Αναξαγόρου] l. 394. Diogenes Laertius tells us (I. iii. iv. 8) Οὗτος ἔλεγε τὸν ἥλιον μύδρον εἶναι διάπυρον, καὶ μείζω τῆς Πελοποννήσου. Τὴν δὲ σελήνην οἰκήσεις ἔχειν, ἀλλὰ καὶ λόφους, καὶ φάραγγας. (Does οἰκήσεις mean 'flat inhabitable spots?')

Anaxagoras of Clazomenae, born about 499 B.C., resided at Athens for thirty years, where he became the friend of the most eminent men of the time, and notably of Pericles and Euripides. His reputation for daring speculation enabled the enemies of Pericles to strike a blow at that statesman, which they did by prosecuting Anaxagoras for impiety, and compelling him to leave Athens.

E. ἃ ἔξεστιν—καταγελᾶν] 'If I were to take the credit of these ideas, which really belong to Anaxagoras, every youth who goes to the theatre, and pays at the very utmost (εἰ πάνυ πολλοῦ) one single drachma for his seat—and that is more than the regular price—would know from what he hears there that I was a ridiculous impostor.' ἐκ τῆς ὀρχήστρας seems to mean 'getting his information from the orchestra,' *i. e.* from the chorus. Socrates means to say that the doctrines of Anaxagoras are expressed (or ridiculed) in the plays, as for example in those of Euripides. Such a passage is extant in the *Orestes*, line 982, μόλοιμι τὰν οὐρανοῦ | μέσον χθονός τε τεταμέναν | αἰωρήμασι μυρίαις | πέτραν ἁλύσεσι χρυσέαισι φερομέναν | δίναισι βῶλον ἐξ 'Ολύμπου κ.τ.λ. where the sun is called βῶλος, a 'lump' or 'clod.'

ἄλλως—ὄντα] 'especially considering that they are so striking,' 'singular.'

καὶ ταῦτα is regularly used, like our 'and that,' independently of the accompanying construction.

27 A. ἔοικε γάρ—διαπειρωμένῳ] One participial clause within another. 'Has he not compounded a riddle, thinking to try me?'

C. ὡς ὤνησας] 'you oblige me.'

ἀντιγραφῇ] Here = ἀντωμοσία.

D. δαίμονες] Here generally for inferior deities; all demigods or beings superior to man, although not regular inhabitants of Olympus.

ὧν δὴ καὶ λέγονται] 'as the case may be'; nearly pleonastic.

E. ἢ καὶ ὄνων κ.τ.λ.] The words can hardly be right as they stand.

If we delete either τοὺς ἡμιόνους, as in the text, or ἢ before ὧων, every-thing becomes regular. Schanz prefers the latter alternative, saying that the words τοὺς ἡμιόνους are recognized by Arrian (second century A.D.) 'Dissert. Epictet. 2, 5.' But it must be confessed that they have very much the air of a gloss, and that, as Wagner says, the passage is clearer without them. He follows Hermann and Cron in rejecting them. One scarcely sees why τὴν γραφὴν ταύτην should be bracketed. Schanz would retain the words, and reject ταῦτα. But why should not ἀποπειρώμενος govern the one word, and ἐγράψω the other two? So Wagner.

ὡς οὐ τοῦ αὐτοῦ κ.τ.λ.] This is a very provoking passage, and has caused much discussion. The difficulty lies in the οὐ. which is given in the best MSS. (B Π), but omitted in Ξ and Stephanus. Socrates is forcibly expressing the conclusion of his argument; but what is the precise form in which he puts this conclusion? The reasoning has been as follows: (1) 'It is absurd to say that one can believe in δαιμόνια, and not in δαίμονες; the one implies the other.' (2) 'But it is also absurd to say that one can believe in δαίμονες, and not in θεοί; they stand or fall together. Your accusation therefore involves a contradiction in terms; you say in one breath that I do and do not believe in the gods.' Now how are we to understand the concluding words? In what way does Socrates recapitulate the points he has made? (1) Let οὐ be retained. Riddell says, 'A confused anticipation of the coming negative οὐδεμία.' That is, οὐ is really *extra sensum*. 'You will never persuade us that a man can believe in divine things without believing in divinities.' But can we suppose that οὐ can be thus vaguely used? Cron suggests that if we keep the οὐ, the words might be taken to mean : 'You will never make out that a man can believe in δαιμόνια, and not in θεῖα; nor again will you make out that the man who believes in δαιμόνια (and therefore in θεῖα) disbelieves at the same time in δαίμονες, θεοί, and ἥρωες.' This would repeat the argument 'chiastically,' or in the inverted order, and would make fair sense. But, as Cron points out. this does not precisely correspond to what goes before, though pretty nearly; and the understanding of the second τοῦ αὐτοῦ in the sense of 'he who believes in δαιμόνια and θεῖα' does considerable violence to the Greek. (2) If the οὐ be omitted, with Stallbaum. Hirschig, Cron, Wagner (Turr. and Hermann retain οὐ), the sense is lucid : 'You will never persuade any person of common sense that a man who believes in things daemonic (and therefore in things divine) at the same time disbelieves in daemons and heroes (and conse-quently in gods). Your assertion about δαιμόνια involves the direct contradictory of your assertion about θεοί.' Schanz brackets the words μήτε ἥρωας. But one does not see why they should be disturbed. The point may be rather neater if we leave θεούs as the last of the four words indicating the series of the argument; but it is not the manner of Plato to express himself in the minimum of words; and this is just one of the places where the περικόπτοντες 'are not to be heard.' The heroes are mentioned as one of the most obvious examples of the demigods.

The omission of οὐ need cause no great difficulty. See *Phaedo* 59 C (*infra*) and 78 B καὶ ποίῳ τινὶ οὔ, in both of which places its insertion seems necessary.

Herr Schanz would read the whole passage as follows; ὅπως δὲ σύ τινα πείθοις ἂν καὶ σμικρὸν νοῦν ἔχοντα ἀνθρώπων, ὡς οὐ τοῦ αὐτοῦ ἐστὶ καὶ δαιμόνια καὶ θεῖα ἡγεῖσθαι, καὶ αὖ μήτε δαίμονας μήτε θεούς, οὐδεμία μηχανή ἐστιν. I presume this to mean; 'No man of sense will believe you, if you deny either that he who believes in δαιμόνια believes in θεῖα, or that he who believes in δαίμονες believes in θεοί.' This makes fair sense; but does it recapitulate the argument?

28 B. οὐδὲν δὲ δεινόν, μὴ ἐν ἐμοὶ στῇ] 'There is no danger of my being the last.' στῇ impersonal. This use of the word is common in Aristotle, and Riddell well quotes from the *Nicomachean Ethics*, VI. viii. 9, στήσεται γὰρ κἀκεῖ. 'We can go no further in that direction.'

C. προθυμουμένῳ] See *Iliad* xviii. 90 sqq.

D. κορωνίσιν] ἐτώσιον in our texts, l. 104. A variation in quoting from memory.

[ἢ] ἡγησάμενος] ἢ would more regularly come before ἑαυτὸν τάξῃ. Cf. above 18 D ἀπολογούμενόν τε, where τε is out of its strict position. The omission of ἢ seems to be needless.

E. Ποτιδαίᾳ] Potidaea, originally a Corinthian colony, had become one of the dependencies of Athens. It stood upon the isthmus connecting the most westerly of the three Chalcidic promontories with the main-land, and was a place of size and importance. In the year 432 B.C. the Potidaeans revolted from Athens to the Corinthians, and suffered a most severe siege (432–429) in which Socrates served. In the *Banquet* (219, 220) Alcibiades tells how Socrates rescued him at Potidaea, and afterwards resigned the prize of valour in his favour.

At Delium, on the coast of Boeotia, the Athenians suffered a severe defeat, B.C. 424. The cool behaviour of Socrates during the retreat is twice described by Plato (*Banquet* 221 (*infra*), *Laches* 181 B).

Plato does not again mention Socrates as having been at Amphipolis.

29 A. ἐνταῦθα δέ] There are two pairs of opposed particles, ὅτε μὲν —τοῦ δὲ θεοῦ, and τότε μὲν—ἐνταῦθα δέ.

B. καὶ τοῦτο κ.τ.λ.] 'This is ignorance, and the very ignorance we blamed.'

τούτῳ ἄν] supply φαίην or the like.

C. ἀπιστήσαντες] 'turning a deaf ear to Anytus.' The word migh
bear its more general sense of 'disbelieving.'

ἤδη ἄν] ἄν is several times in Plato joined with the indicative future
See Riddell on this place. A good example is *Republic* 615 D (*infra*
οὐχ ἥκει οὐδ᾽ ἂν ἥξει δεῦρο.

D. ἐνδεικνύμενος] 'demonstrating.'

E. ἀμφισβητῇ] 'dispute my words.'

το B. ταῦτ᾽ ἄν] 'this course of mine.'

D. οὐ θεμιτόν] 'impossible.' 'contrary to the divine ordering.'

ὑπὲρ ὑμῶν] Supply from ἀπολογεῖσθαι some verb in the sense of
'argue' or the like

31 A. προσκαθίζων] 'settling upon you.'

κρούσαντες] '"With a single tap," as you would a gnat.' Riddell

B. μέντα τι B Π.

C. τὸν μάρτυρα] The article is defined by ὡς ἀληθῆ λέγω. They
are not able to produce a witness, but I am able to produce the witness
that I speak the truth, to wit, poverty.

D. δαιμόνιον] This is the chief place in Plato about the δαιμόνιον
Socrates, and the others do not add much to it. Those who wish
have the δαιμόνιον rationalized may consult Mr. Riddell, in who
Excursus the passages are brought together, or Cardinal Manning,
his collected Essays. Their explanations do not greatly differ, and con
pretty much to this that the δαιμόνιον was a kind of unconscious co
science. Whatever may be the merits of this view, the representatio
of Plato is very different. He speaks of the δαιμόνιον much in the san
way, *mutatis mutandis*, in which Boswell speaks of some of Johnson
mysterious peculiarities. Though frequently alluding to the divine sig
he never dwells upon, or attaches much importance to it; he makes n
attempt at explanation: he seems to regard it as a personal tra,
peculiar to Socrates, just like his fits of deep and protracted reverie, suc
as are described in the *Banquet*, pp. 174, 5, and again in p. 220 (*infra*

At the beginning of the *Memorabilia* Xenophon explains that tl
δαιμόνιον stood to Socrates in the place of omens and auguries; and l
adds that Socrates often advised his friends to do or not do a thing, τ
τοῦ θεοῦ προσημαίνοντος, with invariable accuracy. In Plato the divi
sign meddles with no affairs but those of Socrates.

φωνή] 'Auctore Forstero delevit F. A. Wolf.' Schanz. The word
obviously introduced from φωνή immediately following. It is very pr
bable that πάλαι in line 610 should be ejected for the same reason.

ἐπικωμῳδῶν] 'caricaturing,' 'ridiculing.' He refers to the words '
the indictment, νομίζει δὲ ἕτερα δαιμόνια καινά.

33 A. ἵν᾽ εἰδῆτε—ἀπολοίμην] 'No one shall persuade me to d
anything unjust from fear of death; I will resist and die.' The gene

meaning is clear; but there is a great variety of reading at the end of the sentence. ἄμα καὶ ἄμα ἄν B Π. Schanz reads simply μὴ ὑπείκων δὲ ἄμα ἀπολοίμην. 'Plato scripsit ἄμα, quocum dittographia ἄμα ἄν conuncta est; inde lectionum varietas nata; ἄν ex antecedentibus posse suppleri notum ' Riddell (who reads simply ἄμα κἄν) says, 'It seems vain to find more than a shadowy justification for ἄμα καὶ ἄμα.' Stallbaum explains, after Fischer, that the first ἄμα belongs to μὴ ὑπείκων.

φορτικὰ—καὶ δικανικά] 'A tiresome story about law matters.'

ἄλλην μὲν ἀρχὴν – ἐβούλευσα δέ] ' I have never filled any office in the city, but I have been one of the βουλή.' The occasion referred to is he trial of the generals who had commanded at the battle off the Arginusae islands (more correctly Argennusae), where the Spartans vere defeated, B.C. 406. These generals were accused of gross negigence in picking up neither the men who were afloat on waterlogged essels and pieces of wreck, nor the bodies of the dead. A vehement prejudice prevailed against them at Athens, and led to the irregular proceedings detailed in the text.

B. ['Αντιοχίς] is probably a gloss.

τοὺς δέκα] Strictly speaking, only eight; for one of the ten was dead, nd Conon, the commander in chief, was not included in the accusation.

Apparently we are to understand that Socrates was ἐπιστάτης, or hairman of the council for the day, and therefore it depended upon him hether the question should be put or not. See the point discussed : much length in Mr. Riddell's note.

ὑμῖν is not found in B and Π. καὶ ἐναντία ἐψηφισάμην was ejected by ῾ermann (followed by Cron, Wagner, and Schanz) as a gloss or interpotion added by some one who did not understand the situation. The ιty of Socrates was not to vote (ψηφίζεσθαι), but to put questions to e vote (ἐπιψηφίζειν). This is very plausible.

ἐνδεικνύναι καὶ ἀπάγειν] 'To procure my suspension or arrest.' 'νδειξις was an interdictory procedure, ἀπαγωγή a procedure of summary rest.' R.

C. ὀλιγαρχία] The government of the Thirty, who were entrusted ith supreme power by the Lacedaemonians, after their taking posses-on of Athens, B.C. 404.

θόλον] 'rotunda.'—'The building where the prytanes, and while they bted the Thirty, daily banqueted and sacrificed. It was near the uncil chamber.' Riddell.

Λέοντα] From Xenophon's *Hellenics*, II. iii. 39, we learn that he was jt to death. Theramenes there describes him as a worthy man, and vll to do.

ἀναπλῆσαι] Not merely 'to fill,' but in the sense in which we find ts word and the cognate ἀνάπλεως used, 'to fill with infection.' Cf.

Phaedo 67 A μηδὲ ἀναπιμπλώμεθα τῆς τούτου φύσεως, 'and be not contaminated by the bodily nature.'

D. τούτου δὲ τὸ πᾶν μέλει] An emphatic resumption of τοῦ δὲ μηδέν.

E. μάρτυρες] As was pointed out before, the speech follows the regular order of a defence; and this would be the place for introducing witnesses in favour.

E. τοῖς δικαίοις] neuter.

33 B. τούτων] Such as Alcibiades and Critias, whose very names were hateful in Athens at this time.

μάθημα κ.τ.λ.] It is worth observing, as illustrating the defects of even the best MSS., that in B and Π the words μάθημα—πώποτε are omitted, the scribe having obviously slipped his eye from the one πώποτε to the other. A later hand has added them in Π.

C. θεία μοῖρα] 'divine providence,' 'the will of divine power.'

D. [καὶ τιμωρεῖσθαι] l. 689. The words have been rejected since Bekker.

Κρίτων κ τ.λ.] For Crito see the dialogue which bears his name.

Critobulus is mentioned several times in Plato and in the *Memorabilia* of Xenophon.

Aeschines, son of Lysanias, called ὁ Σωκρατικός, wrote dialogues; and three spurious compositions of this kind are extant under his name. Antiphon is not to be confounded with his celebrated namesake, the Rhamnusian. Epigenes appears in Xenophon (*Mem.* III. xii.), where Socrates impresses upon him the necessity of carefully attending to his health. Nicostratus, Theodotus, Paralus, and Acantodorus are mentioned only here. For Adeimantus see the *Republic*. Theages gives his name to one of the spurious dialogues, in which his father Demodocus also appears. Demodocus is said there (127 E) to have held the highest offices; Theages is said in the dialogue to be eager in the pursuit of philosophy; and in the *Republic* (vi. 496 B) to be debarred from politics, his natural sphere, by ill-health.

Apollodorus, nicknamed 'the madman,' ὁ μανικός, frequently appears in the Platonic dialogues, and in Xenophon. The narrative of the *Symposium* is put into his mouth.

Apollodorus, Crito, Critobulus, Epigenes, and Aeschines are among those mentioned as present at the death of Socrates. (*Phaedo* 59 B).

Of the life of Plato we know very little. There are abundant statements about him; but almost all are made by comparatively late writers, whose authority is of little value. What was his education; what he learned during his travels; what were his pursuits and tastes, other than philosophical; who were his intimate friends; what, in short, the man was, apart from his writings, we can, for the most part, only guess. (We assume the Epistles not to be genuine).

Plato was born about B.C. 427 (the year is uncertain), of an old and wealthy aristocratic family, claiming connection with Solon. After the death of Socrates (B.C. 399) he travelled to Egypt, Cyrene, Magna Graecia, and Sicily, where he visited the court of the elder Dionysius, and gave much offence by plain speaking. On the accession of the younger Dionysius (B.C. 367), Dion, the friend and connexion of both the Dionysii, induced him to visit Syracuse again. He also made a third voyage thither. He died about the year 347 B.C. Such are the bald facts of Plato's life. (Those who wish for details of the various stories about him will find them discussed *ad nauseam* in Zeller's History of Greek Philosophy; Grote's Plato; Grote's History of Greece; and most fully in Steinhart's *Platon's Leben*, forming vol. ix. of Müller and Steinhart's Plato).

E. ἐκεῖνός γε αὐτοῦ] ἐκεῖνος Theodotus, αὐτοῦ his brother. 'Theodotus is dead, and cannot interfere with his brother's evidence.'

34 A. ἐγὼ παραχωρῶ] Parenthetical; 'I yield him the bema.'

C. ἐγὼ δὲ—ἄρα] 'and then finds that I.' Riddell.

D. οὐκ ἀξιῶ] 'I do not expect.'

ἀπὸ δρυὸς κ.τ.λ.] *Odyssee* xix. 163 οὐ γὰρ ἀπὸ δρυὸς ἔσσι παλαιφάτου οὐδ' ἀπὸ πέτρης. 'Thou art no foundling, child of tree or stone.' There is some difficulty in reconciling this place with the other Homeric passage where the phrase is used (*Iliad* xxii. 126), οὐ μέν πως νῦν ἔστιν ἀπὸ δρυὸς οὐδ' ἀπὸ πέτρης τῷ ὀαριζέμεναι, ἅ τε παρθένος ἠίθεός τε κ.τ.λ. 'This is no time to chat from oak or stone, like maid and bachelor in amorous prate.' The writer there seems to take up the proverbial phrase and use it in a new way. Different again is the phrase of Hesiod (*Theogony* 35) ἀλλὰ τίη μοι ταῦτα περὶ δρῦν ἢ περὶ πέτρην; 'But why talk idly thus of stock or stone?'

υἱεῖς—τρεῖς] Xenophon tells us (*Mem.* II. ii. 1), that the name of the eldest was Lamprocles. Diogenes Laertius (end of second century A.D. or later) gives the names of the other two as Sophroniscus and Menexenus. (II. v. x.) But his account of Socrates is a mere jumble, and in flat contradiction to Plato.

E. τοῦτο τοὔνομα] The name of 'wise.'

τὸ Σωκράτη] So also read Hermann, Cron, and Wagner; but the expression seems strange. Riddell has τῷ Σωκράτει, following the Bodleian and three other MSS. Π has Σωκράτει and appears to have had originally τῷ (Schanz). Stallbaum and Hirschig give τόν, with no MSS. authority, which certainly is much the smoothest. τῷ, if a corruption of τόν, seems a strange one; and is the *lectio difficilior*. Schanz reads τῷ Σωκράτει. 'At any rate, the world has decided that Socrates is in some way superior to other men.'

35 B. οὔτε ἡμᾶς χρὴ] B and Π (with others) read ὑμᾶς, which may

be defended (Cron and Wagner), but ἡμᾶς is much simpler (so Schanz);
ἡμεῖς is then 'we who are on trial,' ὑμεῖς, 'you who are the judges.'
The confusion of the words is very frequent.

D. ἄλλως τε—πάντως go together, μέντοι νὴ Δία being interposed.
Both are familiar sequences of words. Schanz brackets πάντως.

36 A. τριάκοντα] So Stallbaum, Hirschig, Hermann, Riddell,
Cron, and Wagner, with the Bodleian and much authority; τρεῖς was
the old vulgate, it does not appear with what support. A curious
question arises, perhaps worth a little discussion, whether from this
passage we can calculate the number of δικασταί. Diogenes says (II. v.
xxi), and though he is not a *testis famosus*, perhaps we may believe him
this time, Ὅτ' οὖν κατεδικάσθη, διακοσίαις ὀγδοηκ ντα μιᾷ πλείοσι ψήφοις
τῶν ἀπολυουσῶν. This seems to be a loose or blundering expression for
'The number of the condemning majority was 281.' There is some
reason for supposing that the number of the court was 501. 500 was a
very common number of dicasts; and one seems to have been regularly
added. to make an even division impossible. If then the majority were
281, the minority would be 220. If we suppose 31 votes, (in round
numbers 30) to be transferred, we have 251 for, 250 against. See Mr.
Riddell's Introduction, where the authorities will be found.

ἀποπέφευγα] Socrates in his ironical way divides the condemning
votes among the three accusers, which would give ninety-three and a
fraction to each, according to the supposition of the last note. But the
fifth part of the total votes, the non-attainment of which entailed the
fine of a thousand drachmas, would have been one hundred and one.

B. ἀντιτιμήσωμαι] ἀντιτιμήσομαι B, and so Cron, Wagner, and
Schanz. Is there any necessity for the alteration into the subjunctive?

ξυνωμοσιῶν] Clubs or political societies.

C. ἰόντα] B and other MSS. have ὄντα, which Cron and Wagner
understand in the same sense as ἰόντα, by a 'pregnant construction.'
Cron candidly confesses that this would be perhaps a unique example.
Schanz has ἰόντα, which seems preferable even against the best books.

ἐνταῦθα ᾖα] Hermann ejected these words. Schanz again would keep
them and leave out ἰών, which is certainly better.

D. οὐκ ἔσθ' ὅτι κ.τ.λ.] Either μᾶλλον or οὕτως is grammatically
superfluous.

ζεύγει] ζεῦγος, which usually means 'a pair,' is here evidently used of
more than two horses. 'Team.'

εἶναι] Hermann, whom Schanz follows, bracketed εἶναι.

37 B. ὧν εὖ οἶδ' ὅτι κ.τ.λ.] Strict grammar would require either
the omission of ὅτι, or the substitution of κακά ἐστι for κακῶν ὄντων.
κακῶν is the genitive after a verb of knowing, when a participle is
added. Riddell, Digest of Idioms, § 26 C. We must understand ὧν

as attracted, and ὅτι as remaining unejected in a familiar combination of words.

τούτου τιμησάμενος] So B and others. C. Meiser, whom Wagner and Schanz follow, proposed the interrogative τοῦ; which certainly is neater. But τούτου is intelligible enough.

C. [τοῖς ἕνδεκα] The words were first ejected by Heindorf, as a gloss, and most succeeding editors have followed him.

38 B. ἐτιμησάμην—ἐκτίσειν] 'I should have laid the penalty at so and so, whatever it might have been.'

38 C. οὐ πολλοῦ γ' ἕνεκα χρόνου] 'It is but a brief span you have taken.'

39 B. θᾶττον γὰρ θανάτου θεῖ] The alliteration may be noticed.

ὄφλων and its conjugates are very often accented as paroxytones; but as they have every characteristic of aoristic forms, they should doubtless take the accent on the last syllable. Professor Schanz has ὄφλων in his text, but adds as a *corrigendum*, 'ὀφλών scribendum,' which excellent example I should wish to follow.

E. ὑπὲρ τοῦ γεγονότος κ.τ.λ.] ὑπέρ, 'in defence of,' as Wagner points out.

40 A. 'ἡ τοῦ δαιμονίου delevit Schleiermacher,' says Schanz, who follows him.

πάνυ—σμικροῖς go together.

B. 'ἐπὶ τὸ δικαστήριον inclusit Hirschig.' Schanz, who leaves the words, nor does one see why they should be disturbed. 'While I was ascending the bema, and about to address the court.'

C. 'τοῦ τόπου τοῦ om. codex C. Theodoreti, inclusit Hirschig.' Schanz, who brackets the words. We could certainly well spare them, although they may be defended with Wagner.

41 A. Μίνως κ.τ.λ.] Compare the passage in the *Gorgias*, 523 E (*infra*). Triptolemus of Eleusis, the mythical founder of husbandry, is said to have given three laws, to honour father and mother, to offer fruits to the gods, and not to injure animals. He does not appear elsewhere as a judge of the dead, and is doubtless mentioned here as peculiarly Athenian. See the account of him in Welcker (*Griechische Götterlehre*, ii. 471-3).

Μουσαίῳ] Musaeus is especially connected with the worship of Demeter. Pausanias says (I. xxii. 7) that the only certain work of Musaeus is a hymn to Demeter. That is, this was the oldest work extant bearing the name of the mythical Musaeus. This passage may have given a hint to Milton:—

> 'But. O sad virgin, that thy power
> Might raise Musaeus from his bower,' etc.

Il Penseroso.

B. Παλαμήδει] In Xenophon (*Mem.* IV. ii. 33) Socrates says that wisdom was the reason why Daedalus was enslaved by Minos, and why Palamedes incurred the fatal enmity of Odysseus.

D. οὐ πάνυ χαλεπαίνω] 'I am not indignant.' 'I cannot say that I am angry.' A word may be said here about the combination οὐ πάνυ, which is frequent in Plato. It has often been asserted, and notably by Buttmann and J. W. Donaldson, that the two words οὐ πάνυ coalesce into one, like οὔ φημι and similar junctions, and that the meaning is 'not at all.' The subject is discussed at length in an admirable note appended to the late Mr. Cope's translation of the *Gorgias.* His conclusion (with which I entirely agree) is, that each word retains its proper force, and that the whole means 'not quite,' 'not altogether.' I conceive Mr. Riddell to mean much the same thing when he says (Digest, § 139) 'The universal meaning of οὐ πάνυ is "hardly," "scarcely."' A good example, which I have not seen quoted, occurs in *Philebus* 16 C ἦν (ὁδὸν) δηλῶσαι μὲν οὐ πάνυ χαλεπόν, χρῆσθαι δὲ παγχάλεπον. 'To indicate the road is not very difficult; but to follow it is very difficult indeed.'

CRITO.

(The whole).

The *Crito* is perhaps the simplest of the genuine Platonic dialogues. Here we have Socrates, not as the philosopher, eager in the pursuit of truth, not as the questioner, making trial of all men, and finding them wanting in real knowledge, but as the good citizen, whose first and only duty is to obey the laws of his country. He has made his bargain with her, for better or worse; he has enjoyed the protection of her laws for seventy years; and if now they press unfairly upon him, that is but the losing side of the agreement. Perhaps the finest part of the dialogue is the personification of the Laws of Athens and the Laws of the world below.

Crito was of the same age and deme as Socrates (ἐμὸς ἡλικιώτης καὶ δημότης, *Apology* 33 E), and his attached and constant friend through life. He is in comfortable circumstances (*Crito* 45 B). He appears in the *Euthydemus,* where Socrates repeats to him the logical exploits of Euthydemus and his brother Dionysodorus. He is anxious (*Euth.* 306 D) about the education of his two sons; but very doubtful about the value of philosophy, especially when he considers the wonderful figure cut by its professors. He will be Socrates' surety (*Apology* 38 B). In this dialogue he offers Socrates the means of escape, and a refuge with his influential friends in Thessaly. In the *Phaedo* he receives the last commands of Socrates, and to him Socrates entrusts the care of his wife (see extracts below).

43 B. οὐ μὰ τὸν Δία κ.τ.λ.] 'far from waking you, I could have wished to be asleep myself.'

C. ἐν τοῖς βαρύτατα] The familiar phrase ἐν τοῖς replaces or enhances the superlative; but is difficult of explanation. Kühner (ii². 27, note 4) accounts for it by saying, 'To ἐν τοῖς we must repeat the superlative from the connection'; *i. e.* ἐν τοῖς βαρύτατα φέρουσιν ἐγὼ βαρύτατ' ἂν φέροιμι. But he goes on to point out that Thucydides uses it with a feminine adjective, *e.g.* iii. 81 ἐν τοῖς πρώτη (στάσις) ἐγένετο: in which case, he says, we must take ἐν τοῖς as neuter. Shall we rather suppose that ἐν τοῖς is a survival of the original use of the article, meaning 'among these things,' 'among things,' gradually crystallized into a quasi-adverb? We say, 'I should bear it very ill'; and we can also say, 'I should bear it ill of all things'; ἐν τοῖς πρώτη, 'first of all.'

D. ἀλλὰ δοκεῖ] ἀλλὰ δοκεῖν μέν μοι ἥξει τήμερον 'Buttmann: δοκεῖν—ἥξειν, quod probavit Winckelmann, BCD' (D is Π), 'sed ν verbi δοκεῖν punctis notata in B, δοκεῖ—ἥξειν, quod vulgo scribunt, E.' Schanz. One is strongly tempted to go with Buttmann (on Heindorf) and Schanz, who follows him. The Greek is better, and the variants are easily explained.

44 A. τῆς ἐπιούσης ἡμέρας] ἡ ἐπιοῦσα ἡ. generally means 'to-morrow,' but here is used of the same day, as below, 46 A, we have τῆς ἐπιούσης νυκτός, 'this very night.' As they are talking very early, the day may be said hardly to have arrived. 'The coming day' would cover both usages.

B. ἤματι κ.τ.λ.] See *Iliad* ix. 363, where Achilles says ἤματι κε τριτάτῳ Φθίην ἐρίβωλον ἱκοίμην.

τοῦ ἐστερῆσθαι *e conj.* B C Π Ξ all have σοῦ ἐστερῆσθαι.

D. [αὖ] does not appear in the best MSS. (BCΠΞ).

ποιοῦσι δέ κ.τ.λ.] 'they act at haphazard.' 'Whatever they do is the result of chance.'

45 A. δίκαιοί ἐσμεν] The regular Attic use instead of δίκαιόν ἐστιν ἡμᾶς etc., the adjective being attracted into the gender of the subject. 'We ought to run this risk, if running it will do you any good.'

B. ξένοι οὗτοι] 'those foreign friends you know of.' Schanz would strike out οὗτοι; one scarcely sees with what reason.

The Thebans Simmias and Cebes are generally mentioned together by Plato. They appear as the principal interlocutors in the *Phaedo*. They are described as eager young men, who have been acquaintances of the Pythagorean Philolaus. Simmias and Phaedrus (*Phaedrus* 242 B) have been the cause of more λόγοι than any others of their time. A little work called the 'Picture' (Πίναξ), bearing the name of Cebes, is still extant, and may have been originally from his hand. An old man explains a picture in which human life and its temptations are symbolically represented.

ὅτι χρῷο σαυτῷ] 'what you are to do with yourself.' ἀγαπήσουσί σε, ' will welcome you.'

D. καὶ τὸ σὸν μέρος κ.τ.λ.] 'as far as you are concerned, they will be left to themselves.' 'They will have to take their chance.'

E. ἡ εἴσοδος—ἐξὸν μὴ εἰσελθεῖν] 'εἰσῆλθεν, quod probavit F. A. Wolf. BCD' (*i.e.* Π) Schanz, who reads εἰσῆλθεν. The correction εἰσῆλθες (Ξ and late hand of B) is plausible, but unnecessary. 'The trial need never have come on, or might have been managed differently; and this last act, or crowning folly, will seem to have occurred through our negligence and cowardice.' ἐγένετο also supports the third person.

46 A. μία δὲ βουλή] 'and there is but one course to be taken.' Stallbaum quotes, to illustrate the variation of tense just before, *Charmides* 176 C οὗτοι, ἦν δ' ἐγώ, τί βουλεύεσθον ποιεῖν; Οὐδέν, ἔφη ὁ Χαρμίδης. ἀλλὰ βεβουλεύμεθα. The words μία δὲ βουλή might possibly be understood to mean 'you must choose now or never'; which would go well with what follows. But the former interpretation seems better; you have but one choice, that is, none at all.

χαλεπωτέρα] 'more dangerous.'

C. πλείω] acc. pl. neuter after μορμολύττηται. 'No, not even if the power of the multitude could inflict many more imprisonments, confiscations, deaths, frightening us like children with hobgoblin terrors.'

D. ἄλλως ἕνεκα λόγου] 'idle talk for talk's sake.'

47 A. οὐχὶ καλῶς *e conj.* and so Hirschig and Schanz. The books have οὐχ ἱκανῶς.

οὐδὲ πάντων, ἀλλὰ τῶν μέν, τῶν δ' οὔ;] These words are not found in BCΠ. 'Ea tam jejuna et supervacanea sunt, ut etiamsi omnes libri ea tuerentur, putarem ea delenda.' Schanz.

B. γυμναζόμενος ἀνὴρ καὶ τοῦτο πράττων] 'one who practises gymnastics, and makes this his business.'

C. ἡ βουλή] 'our deliberation.'

D. πειθόμενοι μή] Hirschig proposes to read τῇ τῶν μὴ ἐπαϊόντων δόξῃ, which is plausible, but seems not at all required.

E. ἆρ' οὖν βιωτόν κ.τ.λ.] 'is life worth living at such a price?' Compare the passage in the third book of the *Republic*, where this subject is treated at length, pp. 406-8 (*infra*).

ᾧ τὸ ἄδικον κ.τ.λ.] 'which injustice deteriorates.' λωβᾶσθαι with the dative, though an unusual, is a recognized construction, and is found in Aristophanes, *Knights*, the last line, ἵν' ἴδωσιν αὐτόν, οἷς ἐλωβᾶθ', οἱ ξένοι.

48 B. It seems much better to divide, with Schanz, ὦ Σώκρατες, ἀληθῆ λέγεις. He deletes φαίη γὰρ ἄν, reading ΚΡ. Δῆλα δὴ καὶ ταῦτα, ὦ Σώκρατες, ἀληθῆ λέγεις.

C. σκέμματα κ.τ.λ.] 'considerations not for us, but for the multitude, who lightly condemn to death, and would lightly recall to life, were it in their power.'

E. ὡς ἐγὼ περὶ πολλοῦ κ.τ.λ.] In this troublesome passage, if we read πεῖσαι with the books (BCΠΞ), the difficulty is to know what is the subject. The words would naturally be construed, 'I am anxious to persuade you, but not against your will.' But as this rendering does not suit the context, Socrates must be understood to refer to his whole drift in the previous conversation. And what does ταῦτα πράττειν mean? To do what? We seem forced to understand with the translators (Hirschig, Müller, Engelmann) that σε is the subject. 'I should be very glad if you could persuade me, but you must not do so whether I will or no.' 'I am extremely desirous to be persuaded by you, but not against my own better judgment.' In this case the absence of ἐμέ is remarkable; and in either case the genitive absolute ἄκοντος is abrupt.

πείσας, given in the text, is an emendation. 'πείσας Buttmanno auctore scripsit Hermann' Schanz, who himself adopts the participle. The alteration is so slight, and it is so natural to write the infinitive instead of the rather more difficult participle, that we may perhaps adopt the latter, seeing that it gives a lucid and much better sense. 'I am anxious, while I follow my own course (ταῦτα πράττειν), to take you with me; I would not have your conviction opposed to mine.'

49 A. [ὅπερ καὶ ἄρτι ἐλέγετο] The Zürich editors and Hermann retain the words; Stallbaum and Hirschig, with the smaller Zürich edition and Schanz, take them for a gloss.

ἐκκεχυμέναι] 'abandoned,' 'thrown away.' γέροντες is an obvious gloss.

D. παρὰ δόξαν] 'not what you really mean.'

κοινὴ βουλή] 'common ground of discussion.'

50 A. τὸ κοινὸν τῆς πόλεως] 'the community of the city,' 'the common weal.'

εἰπέ μοι] The Laws speak in the singular, as a tragic chorus does by its choragus. Perhaps also τὸ κοινὸν τῆς πόλεως partly suggests the singular.

D. ἐλάμβανε] 'took and had to wife.' The imperfect denotes the permanence of the connexion.

51 C. ἢ τὸ δίκαιον πέφυκε] 'he must either obey the command of his city and his country, or he must make them change their view of what is truly just.'

D. τῷ ἐξουσίαν πεποιηκέναι] 'inasmuch as we give (have given) opportunity.' 'We proclaim to each and every Athenian, and give him full licence, that when he has come to man's estate, and taken knowledge of us, he may depart from the city, if he do not like us.' ἐξεῖναι seems to stand in a double construction, both after ἐξουσίαν πεποιηκέναι and after προαγορεύομεν. It should be noticed that προαγορεύομεν is a conjecture for προαγορεύειν of the MSS (BC, Π corrected, Ξ, προσαγορεύειν Π), which seems unintelligible. δοκιμάσθη means 'after he has been approved and admitted a citizen,' has gone through the δοκιμασία εἰς ἄνδρας, or scrutiny of his claims to be a citizen of Athens. Stallbaum quotes a very apposite passage from Aeschines against Timarchus, (ix. 18. 44, according to the various divisions) ἐπειδὴ δὲ ἐγγραφῇ εἰς τὸ ληξιαρχικὸν γραμματεῖον (registration office) καὶ τοὺς νόμους γνῷ καὶ εἰδῇ τοὺς τῆς πόλεως καὶ ἤδη δύνηται διαλογίζεσθαι τὰ καλὰ καὶ τὰ μή, οὐκέτι ἑτέρῳ διαλέγεται (ὁ νομοθέτης), ἀλλ' ἤδη αὐτῷ τῷ Τιμάρχῳ. (Benseler).

52 A. ταύταις—ταῖς αἰτίαις ἐνέξεσθαι] 'such are the accusations to which you will be exposed,' 'under which you will allow yourself to fall,' lit. to be bound or implicated.

ἀλλ' ἐν τοῖς μάλιστα] See note on 43 C.

καθάπτοιντο] 'upbraid me,' 'catch me up,' 'retort upon me.'

B. [ὅτι μὴ ἅπαξ εἰς Ἰσθμόν] A fact mentioned only here. But the words are of the most dubious authenticity. They appear in none of the best books, but are added by very late hands in the margin of B and the Tübingen codex, and seem to have stood in the copy which Athenaeus had before him (v. 55). See Schanz *ad locum*, and *Novae Commentationes*, p. 162. 'Et ut concedamus Athenaeum legisse verba, quid aliud inde sequitur quam ut hominis cuiusdam docti adnotatio illa ὅτι μὴ εἰς Ἰσθμόν satis sit antiqua?'

D. ἂν φαῖεν] The pointing off of these words by the Zürich editors and by Hermann is to be observed. It does not seem at all necessary here, and most editions omit the commas. ἄν sometimes appears to come first in the clause; but this is more apparent than real. Kühner[2] says (ii. 212, note 7), 'The inclusion of such parentheses within commas is harsh; the ancients doubtless took them in immediate connexion with the context, and so made no difficulty as to putting ἄν first.' He quotes a good example from the *Greater Hippias* 299 D ταῦτα ἡμῶν λεγόντων, ὦ Ἱππία, Μανθάνω ἂν ἴσως φαίη καὶ ἐγὼ ὅτι πάλαι αἰσχύνεσθε ταύτας τὰς ἡδονὰς φάναι καλὰς εἶναι.

E. ἑκάστοτε = *identidem*. 'Which you are so fond of praising for their good constitutions.' Such praises are found all through Plato. A great part of the *Republic* looks unmistakeably towards Spartan institutions; and the scene of the *Laws* is laid in Crete.

53 A. Schanz brackets the words δῆλον ὅτι—ἄνευ νόμων. The excision is very tempting. The words have mightily the air of a gloss (δηλόνοτι is a regular glossator's word), and they only enfeeble the sense.

D. τύπων B and others. πόλεων Ξ.

Θετταλίαν] Thessaly, with its haughty and half civilized oligarchy, may well have been a great contrast to Athens.

διφθέραν] 'a peasant's coat of skins.' μεταλλάξας Ξ and the corrector of Π, καταλλάξας ΒCΠ. The change seems necessary.

E. γλίσχρως.] Schanz reads with B, the Tübingen codex, and the second hand of Π αἰσχρῶς, γλίσχρως Ξ and B in the margin. This is a very instructive passage. It may well be doubted whether we should defer even to the authority of B. γλίσχρως might easily be corrupted into αἰσχρῶς; but the reverse is hardly so likely. The sense of the former also seems better; 'to live in this pitiful, this sneaking way.'

ὑπερχόμενος] 'currying favour with,' 'fawning upon.' So also Plato uses ὑποτρέχω, *e. g. Republic* 426 C ὃς δ' ἂν σφᾶς οὕτω πολιτευομένους ἥδιστα θεραπεύῃ ὑποτρέχων κ.τ.λ. Schanz brackets ἐν Θετταλίᾳ, and the words can very well be spared.

54 D. οἱ κορυβαντιῶντες] In their sacred delirium they seem to hear the sound of flutes and other instruments. In the other Platonic passages (*e. g. Ion* 533 E *supra*) the word is used simply of 'the inspired reveller,' 'the orgiast' or 'mystic.' See Ruhnken on *Timaeus (sub verbo)* for the passages; but doubtless his interpretation is wrong.

PHAEDO.

(Beginning to 69 E; 114 D to end.)

The subject of the *Phaedo* is the immortality of the soul; but the beginning and end, which alone are given here, consist chiefly of an account of the last day of Socrates' life. The story has all the appearance of being in the main true to fact. In the second part of the first extract Socrates propounds the doctrine that the life of the philosopher should be a constant preparation for death; that he of all men should be most indifferent to death, and most ready to face it.

Phaedo is mentioned by Plato in this dialogue only. From 89 B we gather that he was a favourite with Socrates. The other stories about him come from the usual dubious authorities. He was of Elis, and wrote philosophical works, and possibly enough he may have been brought to Athens as a slave, and ransomed, which is one of the tales told of him.

Of Echecrates, Plato tells us nothing, except that he lived at Phlius. An Echecrates of Phlius is mentioned by Diogenes (VIII. i. 46) as one of the last of the Pythagoreans, and probably is the same person. Phlius lay high in the upper valley of the Asopus, which flows past Sicyon into the Corinthian Gulf, and would be an out-of-the-way place, as implied in the text. (See Kiepert, *Lehrbuch der Alten Geographie,* p. 272).

57 A. τῶν πολιτῶν Φλιασίων] Stallbaum seems to be right in his explanation that Φλιασίων is added by way of apposition, and being a proper name does not require the article. See his quotations, and especially *Meno*, sub init. καὶ οὐχ ἥκιστα οἱ τοῦ σοῦ ἑταίρου 'Αριστίππου πολῖται Λαρισσαῖοι, which is exactly parallel.

58 A. πολλῷ ὕστερον] Thirty days, says Xenophon, *Memorabilia*, IV. viii. 2 ἀνάγκη μὲν γὰρ ἐγένετο αὐτῷ μετὰ τὴν κρίσιν τριάκοντα ἡμέρας βιῶναι διὰ τὸ Δήλια μὲν ἐκείνου τοῦ μηνὸς εἶναι κ.τ.λ.

B. θεωρίαν ἀπάξειν] The translators understand this to mean simply 'would send a sacred mission'; to which the only objection is that it departs a little from the usual sense of ἀπάγω. May we not suppose (without excluding the first sense) that Plato thinks rather of the frequent usage of ἀπάγω, 'to pay in tribute'? 'They vowed a mission of thanksgiving' or 'recompense.' Plato does not appear to use the word again in either sense.

C. οἱ ἄρχοντες] Here in the general sense of 'the magistrates,' not the archons in the stricter sense. The Eleven are meant.

E. ἀνήρ] So Turicenses, Hirschig, Stallbaum, Schanz. Hermann with the codices ἀνήρ.

59 A. παρόντι πένθει] These words are to be taken separately; 'as would seem natural in one present on a melancholy occasion.'

B. τὸν τρόπον] Whence he had the name of μανικός. See *Banquet* 173 D καὶ ὁπόθεν ταύτην τὴν ἐπωνυμίαν ἔλαβες, τὸ μανικὸς καλεῖσθαι, οὐκ οἶδα ἔγωγε, and above, on *Apol.* 33 D.

Hermogenes is probably the same who appears in the Cratylus, the son of Hipponicus, and poor brother of the rich Callias. He is honourably mentioned by Xenophon (*Memorabilia* I. ii. 48) as one of those who frequented the society of Socrates not to learn rhetoric, but to improve themselves. The others specified by name are Crito, Chaerephon, Chaerecrates, Simmias, Cebes, and Phaedondas. None of these, says Xenophon, ever did, or was accused of doing, any evil thing.

Antisthenes, the founder of the Cynic school, is not elsewhere mentioned by Plato.

Ctesippus is a principal figure in the *Euthydemus*, where he is described (273 A) as νεανίσκος τις Παιανιεύς (Παιανία was the name of the deme) μάλα καλός τε κἀγαθὸς τὴν φύσιν ὅσον μέν, ὑβριστὴς δὲ διὰ τὸ νέος εἶναι.

C. Phaedondes, probably of Thebes, we only know from this passage, and that in the *Memorabilia* quoted as to Hermogenes. Schanz reads Φαιδωνίδης with B and the Tübingen MS. Φαιδώνδης is the reading of Ξ and B in the margin. Analogy would have led us to expect Φαιδώντας, as we have in Xenophon (*l. l.* L. Dindorf's edition).

Eucleides and Terpsion of Megara appear as persons in the introduction to the *Theaetetus.* 'On the death of Socrates Eucleides served for some time as a centre to his disciples' (Zeller). Diogenes, on the authority of Hermodorus, Plato's pupil, tells us that Plato and others retired with him to Megara. He was the founder of the Megarian school, whose chief peculiarity was 'eristic,' or formal argument.

Aristippus of Cyrene, the founder of the Epicurean philosophy, is not elsewhere mentioned by Plato. Diogenes will have it (III. i. 36) that Plato alludes to his absence here by way of reproach, which in no way appears upon the face of the passage; and that Xenophon had a grudge at him (II. viii. 65). In Xenophon (*Mem.* II. i) he certainly defends the cause of pleasure; but also argues generally (III. viii). Such inferences of too laborious students are valueless. We have a modern parallel in the fierce language of Landor as to the supposed absence of Plato from the death of Socrates. (*Imaginary Conversations, Chesterfield and Chatham, s. f.; Diogenes and Plato.*) Certainly, whether Plato tells the simple fact, when he says Πλάτων ἠσθένει, or whether, as seems more likely, this is a graceful way of withdrawing his own person from the dialogue, he does not mean to vilify himself; and Landor proceeds upon no other authority.

Cleombrotus is probably the celebrated Ambraciot who is said to have put an end to himself after reading this very dialogue. The story seems to rest upon no earlier authority than an epigram of Callimachus (xxiii. Meineke):—

> Εἶπας, "Ηλιε χαῖρε, Κλεόμβροτος ὡ'μβρακιώτης
> "Ηλατ' ἀφ' ὑψηλοῦ τείχεος εἰς 'Αίδην.
> "Αξιον οὐδὲν ἰδὼν θανάτου κακόν, ἀλλὰ Πλάτωνος
> "Εν τὸ περὶ ψυχῆς γράμμ' ἀναλεξάμενος.

> '"O Sun, farewell!" from the tall rampart's height,
> Cleombrotus exclaiming, plunged to night.
> Nor wasting care, nor fortune's adverse strife,
> Chilled his young hopes with weariness of life;
> But Plato's godlike page had fixed his eye,
> And made him long for immortality.'
>
> (J. H. Merivale.)

Milton puts him into the Limbo of Fools (*Paradise Lost*, iii. 471):—

> 'And he, who to enjoy
> Plato's Elysium, leapt into the sea,
> Cleombrotus.'

παρεγένοντο] οὐ παρεγένοντο Schanz, after Cobet, to the great improvement of the sense. One of the most useful labours of the present school of editors is the comparison of passages where small words like οὐ and καί have been omitted or inserted. Here Herr Schanz appeals to *Phaedo* 78 B τῷ ποίῳ τινὶ ἄρα προσήκει τοῦτο τὸ πάθος πάσχειν τοῦ διασκεδάννυσθαι,—καὶ τῷ ποίῳ τινὶ οὔ, where οὔ is not found in B C Π Ξ, but was added by Heindorf, the text being absolute nonsense without it.

D. διατρίβοντες] 'Talking,' lit. 'passing the time.'

E. οἱ ἕνδεκα] The Eleven were a board, consisting of a member of each of the ten tribes, with a ὑπηρέτης or secretary. Their especial office was to superintend the custody and execution of condemned persons; also the application of torture. They had besides to look after outlaws and other dangerous persons, and property that had been confiscated to the state.

καὶ παραγγέλλουσιν κ.τ.λ.] The translators for the most part strangely mistake the sense, rendering 'and are communicating to him that he must die this day.' How they reconcile this with ὅπως ἄν is hard to see. The meaning is obviously 'and are giving directions for his execution to-day.' I understand παραγγέλλουσιν to be used absolutely.

οὐ πολὺν—ἐπισχών] 'After a short interval.'

60 A. Xanthippe in Plato appears only in this passage, which speaks for itself. In Xenophon, *Memorabilia* II. ii. 1, 7, it is implied that she had a bad temper; and in Xenophon's *Banquet* (ii. 10) this is roundly affirmed. 'Why,' says Antisthenes, 'do you have a wife who has the worst temper that is or was or ever will be?' It must be remembered that the whole passage is jocular. This is really all we know about her. In the first passage of Xenophon her son admits that she never bit or kicked him; and that her intentions were good enough. (A humorous vindication of Xanthippe will be found in Dr. Zeller's *Vorträge und Abhandlungen geschichtlichen Inhalts*, p. 51 sqq.)

B. τῷ—μὴ ἐθέλειν παραγίγνεσθαι] 'inasmuch as they never come together.' We have had this construction before. See *Crito* 51 D.

D. ἐντείνας] 'putting into verse.' Cf. *Hipparchus* (a spurious dialogue) 228 D ἐντείνας εἰς ἐλεγεῖον. τὸ προοίμιον strictly speaking requires a different verb, such as ποιήσας, the προοίμιον of Socrates being doubtless an original composition. οἴμη is the regular Homeric word to express the song of a bard: and προοίμιον is the briefer hymn or address to some god which preceded such a recitation. Of these προοίμια there is no mention in Homer: but the shorter among the so-called Homeric hymns are obviously intended to be sung as prologues to something else.

To the mythical Aesop are ascribed fables such as are still conjoined with his name; but it is very doubtful whether any such were committed to writing in the time of Socrates. They were probably handed down from mouth to mouth, like modern fairy tales. The celebrated Demetrius of Phalerum, about a century later, is said by Diogenes (V. v. 80) to have made λόγων Αἰσωπείων συναγωγαί.

61 A. παρακελεύεσθαι κ.τ.λ.] Observe the three compounds of κελεύω all together. There is no great difference in the sense. Mr. Geddes' notion that διακελεύεσθαι = *alii alios hortari* is not borne out by the other passages of Plato, who frequently uses the word. Professor Wagner says, ' παρακελεύεσθαι is "to exhort to do a thing," ἐπικελεύειν, "to encourage when one is doing it" (ἐπί denoting here "after ").'

B. ἐποίησα (lines 156, 160)] 'made verses,' 'did into verse,' ποιέω being used in its technical sense of making poetry.

μύθους, ἀλλ' οὐ λόγους] 'tales, and not discourses.'

καὶ ἐρρῶσθαι] 'Greet him from me.' Any verb with the sense of 'tell' or the like, may be supplied to govern the infinitive.

D. Of Philolaus we only know that he was an Italian Greek who removed to Thebes, and that he was the first to publish a treatise upon the Pythagorean doctrine. This work was famous in ancient times, and was well known to Plato. Some fragments are extant.

62 A. ἁπλοῦν] 'absolutely true,' 'true without qualification.'

ἔστιν ὅτε καὶ οἷς] 'at some times and in some cases.' ἔστιν belongs also to οἷς, which is masculine. This passage has troubled the commentators; but the one obvious meaning is: 'Philolaus says that suicide is never right. Now you may think it strange if this is the only rule without exception; death, you will say, is sometimes better than life; why then should not a man choose the one state instead of the other?' τοῦτο then belongs, as it should, to what goes before, *i. e.* the law that self-destruction is never right. ἔστιν ὅτε καὶ οἷς are to be joined to the words that follow.

φωνῇ] His own Theban dialect. Ἴττω and the Attic ἴστω stand alike for *ἴδτω, a combination rejected by Greek euphony. In the one case the mute δ is softened into the sibilant, producing στ, a favourite Greek combination; in the other the sonant mute is assimilated to the surd. 'Gudeness kens.'

B. ἐν ἀπορρήτοις] 'as an esoteric doctrine.' Cf. *Theaetetus* 152 C, where it is said of Protagoras, καὶ τοῦτο ἡμῖν μὲν ᾐνίξατο τῷ πολλῷ συρφετῷ, τοῖς δὲ μαθηταῖς ἐν ἀπορρήτῳ τὴν ἀλήθειαν ἔλεγεν.

D. τῶν ὄντων] neuter: 'masters, the best in existence.' τὰ ὄντα, all things, the universe.

E. ἀγαθοῦ] Sc. δεσπότου.

63 A. πραγματείᾳ] 'earnestness,' 'sedulousness,' his keeping to the subject, and turning it over.

Join αὐτῷ μοι. The position of αὐτῷ is emphatic; 'to me, although I know him well.'

B. ἀνθρώπους] Cf. the end of the *Apology*, 41 A seqq.

64 A. ἀποθνήσκειν τε καὶ τεθνάναι] 'to die and to be in the state of death.'

T

B. οὐ πάνυ γέ με νῦν δή κ.τ.λ.] This is a passage which might be quoted by those who think that the two words οὐ πάνυ really coalesce into one. But they may just as well be taken separately; see note on *Apology* 41 D.

θανατῶσι] 'desire to die.' -άω is a rare desiderative termination. Curtius (*Das Verbum der Griechischen Sprache*, ii. 388) can only give, besides θανατάω, τομάω, φονάω (both in Sophocles), μαχάω (Hesychius), τοκῶσα (Cratinus), λοπάω (Theophrastus), of trees, 'to be ready to cast the bark.' -ιάω is commoner. The termination of -άω is simply the common -ya-, and we must regard its desiderative use as conventional.

C. ἡγούμεθά τι τὸν θάνατον εἶναι;] 'There is such a thing as death?' a frequent formula of question in the Platonic dialogues.

ἆρα μὴ ἄλλο τι κ.τ.λ. (lines 303–4)] The codices have ἆρα μὴ ἄλλο τι ᾖ ὁ θάνατος ἢ τοῦτο; perhaps from some remembrance of μὴ ἄλλο τι ἤ just before. 'Delevit Bekker; defendit Hermann,' etc., Schanz. The omission of ᾖ seems preferable.

D. ἱματίων διαφερόντων] 'fine clothes.'

65 A. ἐγγύς τι τείνειν] 'comes very near being dead,' 'is as good as dead.' Stallbaum compares for the phrase *Republic* viii. 548 D οἶμαι μὲν—ἐγγύς τι αὐτὸν Γλαύκωνος τουτουὶ τείνειν.

B. οἷον τὸ τοιόνδε λέγω] 'like this, I mean.'

ὅτι οὔτ' ἀκούομεν] He seems to refer to the well known line of Epicharmus, νοῦς ὁρῇ καὶ νοῦς ἀκούει, τἆλλα κωφὰ καὶ τυφλά.

C. καὶ ἐνταῦθα] ἐνταῦθα or ἐνθάδε, 'even in this world'; ἐκεῖ, 'in the other.' So Shakspere says—

'Here,

'But here, upon this bank and shoal of time.'

A line in the *Frogs* (where Sophocles is the person referred to) gives us both words together (v. 82) :—

ὁ δ' εὔκολος μὲν ἐνθάδ', εὔκολος δ' ἐκεῖ.

E. αὐτῶν τἀληθέστατον] Join.

παρατιθέμενος] 'employing in addition,' along with the mind.

66 C. διὰ γὰρ—γίγνονται] This is expanded in the *Republic*. See for instance the end of Book iii.; Book v. 464.

D. δέδεικται] 'we have proved.'

E. ὡς ὁ λόγος σημαίνει] 'as appears by our argument.'

67 A. ἀναπιμπλώμεθα] 'and are not infected.' Cf. *Philebus* 42 A, τότε μὲν αἱ δόξαι ψευδεῖς τε καὶ ἀληθεῖς αὗται γιγνόμεναι τὰς λύπας τε καὶ ἡδονὰς ἅμα τοῦ παρ' αὐταῖς παθήματος ἀνεπίμπλασαν.

μετὰ τοιούτων] With such as are καθαροί.

E. διαβέβληνται] 'are at variance.' *Rep.* vi. 498 C μὴ διάβαλλε— ἐμὲ καὶ Θρασύμαχον ἄρτι φίλους γεγονότας. 'Do not set us by the ears.'

68 E. τί δέ; οἱ κόσμιοι κ.τ.λ.] The meaning is clear; but there may

be doubts as to the best way of pointing. Professor Schanz, for instance, punctuates τί δὲ οἱ κόσμιοι αὐτῶν; οὐ ταὐτὸν τοῦτο πεπόνθασιν· ἀκολασίᾳ τινὶ σώφρονές εἰσιν; where I understand that all from οὐ ταὐτὸν to εἰσίν is one question.

69 B. σκιαγραφία] 'a mere show' or 'semblance,' 'an image.' From two places in Plato, *Theaetetus* 208 E and *Parmenides* 165 C, it appears that σκιαγραφία is something to be looked at from a distance. Aristotle, *Rhet.* III. xii. 5, implies the same. But how the compound σκιαγραφία comes to mean this remains very obscure. See Heindorf on *Theaetetus l. l.* The passage in Aristotle might seem to refer to scene-painting; ὅσῳ γὰρ ἂν πλείων ᾖ ὁ ὄχλος, πορρωτέρω ἡ θέα. The place in the *Parmenides* explains the word best; ἀποστάντι μὲν ἓν πάντα φαινόμενα—προσελθόντι δέ γε πολλὰ καὶ ἕτερα. Cf. also *Critias*, 107 C, σκιαγραφίᾳ δὲ ἀσαφεῖ καὶ ἀπατηλῷ χρώμεθα περὶ αὐτά.

C. τελετάς] With this passage corresponds the description in the *Frogs*, where the second chorus consists of μεμνημένοι or initiated persons, vv. 138 sqq., εἶτα βόρβορον πολύν κ.τ.λ. Cf. also *Republic* ii. p. 363 D, where Musaeus and his son τοὺς ἀνοσίους καὶ ἀδίκους εἰς πηλόν τινα κατορύττουσιν ἐν Ἅιδου. The word βόρβορος occurs also in *Republic* vii. 533 D ἐν βορβόρῳ βαρβαρικῷ τινὶ τὸ τῆς ψυχῆς ὄμμα κατορωρυγμένον, where probably Plato thinks of some such description as this.

ναρθηκοφόροι κ.τ.λ.] Obviously a hexameter verse transposed : πολλοὶ μὲν ναρθηκοφόροι, βάκχοι δέ τε παῦροι. Βάκχος is used in the tragedians to mean a Bacchanal, but in this line of one who is so in some higher sense. 'Many bear the fennel-rod, but few are votaries indeed.'

D. καί τι ἠνυσάμην] 'and was at all successful,' a common use of ἀνύτω. B, C, Π, Ξ read ἠνύσαμεν. Heindorf, the Zürich editors, Hirschig, Stallbaum, and Schanz read ἠνυσάμην from one codex. Hermann, Engelmann's editor, and Geddes keep ἠνύσαμεν, which is scarcely to be disturbed. The change of number is abrupt; but Socrates includes his friends as well as himself among those who have sought after truth.

E. τοῖς δὲ πολλοῖς κ.τ.λ.] 'Hirschig observes "est adnotatio praepostera scioli petita ex sequentibus his: τὰ δὲ περὶ τῆς ψυχῆς πολλὴν ἀπιστίαν παρέχει τοῖς ἀνθρώποις, verbis Cebetis, qui demum bene hanc dubitationem adfert, non ipse Socrates." It is very probable that Hirschig is right in his supposition.' Wagner. Schanz rejects the words. 'Inclusit Ast.' To me they appear incongruous, and obviously borrowed from the words of Cebes that follow (not given in this extract, but quoted by Hirschig above).

114 D to end.

114 D. οὐ πρέπει] So the account of the world's origin in the *Timaeus*, as is several times repeated, is only given as very probable. Socrates

T 2

here refers to the description of the earth and its interior, which he has been giving in the omitted portion of the dialogue.

ἐπᾴδειν] Repeat as a sort of charm or word of power: so 77 E ἀλλὰ χρή, ἔφη ὁ Σωκράτης, ἐπᾴδειν αὐτῷ ἐκαστῆς ἡμέρας, ἕως ἂν ἐξεπᾴσητε. 'Until you have charmed it away.' The notion of frequency is implied, as appears by the words following.

E. καὶ πλέον—ἀπεργάζεσθαι] 'and thinking them rather hurtful than useful.' ἕτερος for κακός is a common euphemism. ἕτερος δαίμων (Pindar, *P.* 3. 34), 'an unfriendly deity.'

115 D. ἐγγυήσασθε] 'Crito was my surety, that I would not go away, but appear for trial: be you my sureties to Crito, that I shall not remain here, but go away to some better place.'

E. προτίθεται] 'lays out'; ἐκφέρει, 'carries to the grave'; κατορύττει, 'buries.' Cremation and interment seem to have been equally common in ancient Greece, as appears both from passages in Greek writers, and from the excavation of actual graves. See Becker's *Charicles*, excursus on burials; Guhl and Koner, *Life of the Greeks and Romans*, p. 292, English translation.

116 D. εἰ τέτριπται] 'if it be pounded.'

E. ἔτι γὰρ ἐγχωρεῖ] 'there is plenty of time.'

117 A. φειδόμενος—ἐνόντος] 'beginning to save when the vessel is empty.' The phrase is evidently proverbial, and the verse of Hesiod may be referred to, *Works and Days* 369—

μεσσόθι φείδεσθαι, δειλὴ δ' ἐνὶ πυθμένι φειδώ.

B. Καὶ οὕτως αὐτὸ ποιήσει] 'And then the poison will work of itself,' 'without farther assistance.' Heindorf quotes from Dioscorides (first or second century A.D.), 'ποιεῖ πρὸς φάρμακα, *valet adversus venena*.'

οὐδὲν—διαφθείρας] οὐδέν in double construction, first as adverbial, then as accusative. διαφθείρας active, as always in good Greek. 'Hic tamen διαφθείρειν, ut ubique alias, *mutare in deterius* significat.' Heindorf.

ταυρηδὸν—ἄνθρωπον] 'looking sharply askance at the man.' This characteristic side look of Socrates is frequently alluded to. Cf. 86 D Διαβλέψας οὖν ὁ Σωκράτης, ὥσπερ τὰ πολλὰ εἰώθει. So Alcibiades says in the *Banquet*, 221 B (*infra*), that at the battle of Delium Socrates walked, in the phrase of Aristophanes,

βρενθυόμενος καὶ τὠφθαλμὼ παραβάλλων.

The quotation is from *Clouds* 362, which he then explains by ἠρέμα παρασκοπῶν (περισκοπῶν) καὶ τοὺς φιλίους καὶ τοὺς πολεμίους. That Socrates had projecting eyes, we learn both from Plato and from Xenophon. *Theaetetus* 143 E τὸ ἔξω τῶν ὀμμάτων, 'your projecting eyes'; 209 B ἐξόφθαλμον in the same sense. The place in Xenophon (*Banquet* v. 5) still better illustrates the present passage: Ὅτι οἱ μὲν σοὶ (ὀφθαλμοὶ) τὸ κατ' εὐθὺ

μόνον ὁρῶσιν, οἱ δὲ ἐμοὶ καὶ τὸ ἐκ πλαγίου διὰ τὸ ἐπιπόλαιοι εἶναι;   Eyes
à fleur de téte, as Mr. Geddes well puts it.

C. ἐπισχόμενος] 'putting the cup to his lips.'

D. ὦ θαυμάσιοι] 'you strange beings.'

118 A. πήγνυτο is the optative. For this rare form see Kühner[2], i. 643
(Jelf, i. 267). It is perhaps the only example in good Attic. There are
similar epic forms :—

$$\text{ἠὲ πεσὼν ἐκ νηὸς ἀποφθίμην ἐνὶ πόντῳ.}$$
Od. x. 51.

$$\text{τῇ δεκάτῃ δέ τε θάπτοιμεν δαινῦτό τε λαός.}$$
Il. xxiv. 665.

And others, not frequent. Schanz writes πηγνῦτο, as he writes διασκε-
δαννῦται (subjunctive) 77 B; rightly, one would think.

αὐτός can hardly be right, as it could refer only to Socrates himself.
καὶ αὖ Schanz, αὐτός B C Π Ξ.

τῷ 'Ασκληπιῷ ὀφείλομεν ἀλεκτρυόνα] In thankfulness for this εὐθα-
νασία.

B. καὶ ὃς τὰ ὄμματα ἔστησεν] 'and the eyes were fixed,' 'were set in
his head.' Heindorf quotes from Charito iii. 9 ἐμμανὴς γενομένη στήσασα
τοὺς ὀφθαλμοὺς ἀνέκραγε.

τῶν τότε] 'the men of that day.' 'Of my time,' as we should say
the time when I used to be in Athens.

SYMPOSIUM.

215 A—216 C; 220 C—222 A.

The *Banquet* is supposed to be given by Agathon in honour of his
tragic victory at the *Lenaea*, which happened, it is said, B.C. 416. After
all the other guests in turn have celebrated the praises of Love, Alcibiades, who has come in drunk, pronounces an encomium upon Socrates,
of which the first extract is the beginning, and the second a passage
following shortly afterwards.

215 A. Σειληνοῖς] For the personal appearance of Socrates, see the
passages quoted upon the *Phaedo* 117 B, and particularly the place in
Xenophon's *Banquet*. There, besides his projecting eyes, he is said to
have a snub nose, turned-up nostrils, and thick lips. 'Do you think
this no proof, Critobulus, of my being superior to you in beauty, that
the Naïdes, who are goddesses, bring forth the Sileni, who are more like
me than you?' (V. 7.)

B. οὖς τινας] 'such as.'

ἐὰν γάρ] γάρ refers to what is to be understood. 'Make haste and confess,' or the like.

C. ἃ γάρ—διδάξαντος] 'For the strains of Olympus I ascribe to Marsyas, who was the teacher of them.' We learn from this that airs passing under the name of Olympus were extant in Plato's time. They are elsewhere referred to; *e.g. Knights* l. 9 ξυναυλίαν κλαύσωμεν Οὐλύμπου νόμον, where *two* flutes are implied. According to Westphal (*Griechische Metrik*, ii. 285), this Phrygian music, which came in after the time of Archilochus, was for the most part purely instrumental, the instruments being the flute, and afterwards the lyre. It also introduced the major scale (Phrygian and Lydian modes). The name of Olympus is also connected with the enharmonic scale, and the hemiolian rhythm. The latter is still, though very rarely, used ($\frac{3}{4}$ time); the former brought into the scale intervals now hardly recognised ($\frac{3}{4}$ and $\frac{1}{4}$), which are however natural to some instruments. See Donkin's article *Music* in Smith's *Dictionary of Antiquities*; to whose remarks much might be added.

μόνα κατέχεσθαι ποιεῖ] 'they above all ravish the hearer.'

D. εἰ μὴ—μεθύειν] 'I would tell you, but you would think me drunk.'

E. κορυβαντιώντων] The Corybantes were the priests of the Great Mother, who danced and revelled, full of her inspirations. 'Unde κορυβαντιᾶν et laborare morbo, qui κορυβαντιασμός, morbus imaginosus, vocatur, quum aures videntur personare tibiarum cantu; qui morbus putabatur proficisci a Corybantibus.' Fischer ap. Stallb. on *Crito* 54 D (*supra*). See also *Ion* 534 A ὥσπερ οἱ κορυβαντιῶντες οὐκ ἔμφρονες ὄντες ὀρχοῦνται (*supra*).

216 A. βίᾳ] 'tearing myself away.' For the Sirens, see *Odyssee* xii. 39 *sqq.*

B. ὑπό] Cf. *Rep.* ii. 359 A τὸ ὑπὸ τοῦ νόμου ἐπίταγμα, and other passages.

220 C—222 A.

C. οἷον δ' αὖ] *Odyssee* iv. 242. ἀλλ' οἷον τόδ' ἔρεξε are the exact words of the passage.

ἐκεῖ] At Potidaea.

ξυννοήσας] 'having fallen into a meditation.' This habit of Socrates is mentioned before in the *Banquet*, 174 D *sqq.*, where it is said to be his way to turn aside and stand thinking.

D. ἀνέσχεν] 'rose.' *Od.* v. 320—

αἶψα μάλ' ἀνσχεθέειν μεγάλου ὑπὸ κύματος ὁρμῆς,

'to rise to the surface.' This intransitive use of ἀνέχω and ἀνίσχω is not uncommon, especially of the sun rising. Herodotus iii. 98 Ἰνδικῆς χώρης τὸ πρὸς ἥλιον ἀνίσχοντα. Compare another compound of ἔχω in *Odyssee* xiii. 93—

εὖτ' ἀστὴρ ὑπερέσχε φαάντατος κ. τ. λ.

'when the morning star rose.'

εἰ δὲ βούλεσθε κ.τ.λ.] A colloquial abridgment for 'Again, if you would like to know of his behaviour in battle, I will give you an instance.'

ἀποδοῦναι] To pay as a debt.

μάχη] This was also before Potidaea.

E. ἀξίωμα] 'my rank and position.'

221 A. Δηλίου] In the year 424 B.C. the Athenians suffered a heavy defeat at Delium, a small Boeotian town on the sea-coast, possessing a celebrated temple of the Delian Apollo, whence the place took its name. Thuc. iv. 96 *sqq.* See *Laches* 181 B, where Laches says that if every one had been as steady as Socrates, Athens would have escaped that heavy misfortune.

B. ἔμφρων] 'in keeping his head.'

τὸ σὸν δὴ τοῦτο] 'to quote you.' The clause stands in a loose apposition to the rest of the sentence. Aristophanes is one of its company.

βρενθυόμενος κ.τ.λ.] *Clouds* 362 Dind.[5] In *Phaedo* 117 B above, Socrates was said ταυρηδὸν βλέπειν.

περισκοπῶν is a conjecture of Bekker and Ast, adopted by Hermann and Hirschig. παρασκοπῶν the books, Stallbaum, and the Zürich larger edition. The παρά may possibly be a kind of 'attraction' of the scribe's eye from παραβάλλων just before.

ἀμυνεῖται] ἀμύνηται B and other codices.

σχεδὸν γάρ τι κ.τ.λ.] This is not unlike the sentiment of the *Iliad*, xv. 563-4 (and also v. 531-2):—

αἰδομένων δ' ἀνδρῶν πλέονες σόοι ἠὲ πέφανται·
φευγόντων δ' οὔτ' ἀρ κλέος ὄρνυται οὔτε τις ἀλκή.

E. τῶν Σωκράτους ἀκούειν λόγων] τὸν—λόγον B, Δ, and other books; a curious error, the plural being absolutely required. πάνυ does not appear in B etc.

ὀνόματα καὶ ῥήματα] See *Apology* 17 C, and note. Words, and the way in which they are put together.

Σατύρου δή] The vulgate reading is Σατύρου ἄν, retained by the Turicenses, Hirschig, Hermann, and Stallbaum. ἄν does not appear in B, Δ, and other books, and why it should be retained, as the construction is excessively harsh, not to say impossible, one does not quite see. 'Malim δή. BAIT.' (Quarto Zürich edition.) If ἄν be kept, we must explain with Stallbaum: 'Recte enim dici potuisse: Σατύρου ἄν τινα ὑβριστοῦ δορὰν οὖσαν, quilibet largietur.' But why not omit both ἄν and δή, and read with the best books Σατύρου τινὰ ὑβριστοῦ δοράν, which is easy and simple? ‘He clothes himself in language that is as the skin-of the wanton satyr.’

222 A. διοιγομένους κ.τ.λ.] ‘He who sees them opened, and gets behind the mask.’ ἰδὼν ἄν τις is the reading of all the books, and one does not see why it should be disturbed. ἄν τις Turr., Stallbaum. αὖ τις Bekker, Ast, Hermann, Hirschig. ἰδὼν ἄν is simply ‘were one to see,’ and quite different from the construction with ἄν of the last note.

μόνους] ‘above all others.’ So 215 C *supra*, μόνα κατέχεσθαι ποιεῖ.
τείνοντας] τείναντας B, Δ, etc., which can hardly be right.

PHAEDRUS.

228 A—230 E.   245 C—249 D.   258 D—259 D.   274 B—275 B.

The proper subject of the *Phaedrus* is Rhetoric, or the power of persuasion : but the subject of Love, out of the discussion of which the discussion of Rhetoric is made to spring, is handled at such length, that it may be regarded as a subordinate theme of the dialogue. Of the four extracts given here, the first is introductory ; the second arises out of the discussion of Love ; the third and fourth are beautiful digressions.

Phaedrus we only know from this dialogue and from the *Banquet*. He is represented as an amiable young gentleman, passionately fond of rhetoric and λόγοι. In the *Protagoras* (*supra* 315 C) we find him one of a company who are discussing physical and astronomical questions with Hippias.

228 A. Λυσίου] Lysias, the celebrated orator, was the son of Cephalus, in whose house the dialogue of the *Republic* is supposed to be held. Cephalus was a native of Syracuse. Lysias, though not an Athenian citizen (he once obtained the franchise, and was afterwards deprived of it), was an enthusiastic partisan of the democratic party in Athens, where he spent the most of his life.

ἐπαναλαμβάνων] ‘“Repeatedly,” “over and over again,” as τελευτῶν is presently used for εἰς τέλος.’ Thompson.
B. ἀπειπών] ‘having become weary.’
ἰδὼν μὲν ἰδών] A lively repetition, to express the delight of Phaedrus.
ἔξοι] So Hermann and Dr. Thompson ; ἔξει Stallbaum and Hirschig.
προάγειν] Intransitive, ‘to go with him.’ A list of similar intransitives may be found in Jelf’s Grammar, § 359 (Kühner², § 373).
C. ἐθρύπτετο] ‘he gave himself airs.’
τελευτῶν δέ] ‘but at the last.’

πάνυ γάρ σοι ἀληθῆ ἔοκῶ] 'Sed prorsus sic de Rep. viii. p. 567 D Κηφῆνας δοκεῖς αὖ τινάς μοι λέγειν ξενικούς τε καὶ παντοδαπούς. 'Αληθῆ γάρ — δοκῶ σοι. Intelligo igitur coartatam quotidiano usu dicendi formam pro πάνυ γάρ σοι ἀληθῆ δοκεῖ εἰ δοκῶ, etc.' Heindorf.

τὰ τοῦ ἐρῶντος κ.τ.λ.] 'The cases of the lover and the non-lover,' which are the themes of Lysias.

D. φιλότης] 'A form adopted by Plato's imitators, as Lucian, etc., but occurring nowhere else in extant Attic writers.' Thompson.

229 A. σὺ μὲν γὰρ δὴ ἀεί] A well-known trait of Socrates. See *e. g.* *Banquet* 174 A 'I found Socrates fresh from the bath, and wearing a pair of pumps, a thing he very seldom did,' on that occasion in honour of Agathon's banquet.

B. ἤ. ἂν βουλώμεθα] B ᾗ ἂν βουλόμεθα.

C. ᾖ—διαβαίνομεν] 'where one crosses to the temple of Artemis Agra,' or Agrotera, the goddess of the wild, or of the chase.

D. 'Αρείου πάγου] The Areopagus is a small hill or knob of rock, standing a little way from the west end of the Acropolis, which rises above it. 'ἤ ἐξ 'Αρείου πάγου—ἡρπάσθη] Haec verba Bastius—spuria censebat, assentientibus Krischio — et C. F. Hermanno.' Stallbaum. The editors retain the words. (Stallbaum, Hirschig, Turr., Thompson, and Heindorf, who had at first held them suspected.) Hermann says, very much to the point (*Praefatio* to the Teubner edition): 'Interpolationem id potissimum arguit, quod quae sequuntur non ad ipsam fabularum varietatem, sed ad interpretandi conamina spectant, quo Areopagi mentio nullo pacto pertinet.' Certainly, if the words had come before us as a marginal scholium, no one would have dreamt of their belonging to the text.

ἐπανορθοῦσθαι] 'to put right,' 'rehabilitate,' reduce to the real fundamental fact.

E. ἄγροικος σοφία is 'a wooden-headed wisdom,' painstaking, but without insight.

230 A. Τυφῶνος] Typhon, Typhōeus, or Typhōs, personifies the force of volcanic action. He is also connected with hurricanes and tornadoes, in which sense the word τυφώς is used in the poets, *e. g. Antigone* 418 (Dindorf[5]) τυφὼς ἀείρας σκηπτόν, οὐράνιον ἄχος. The name survives in our modern 'typhoon.'

ἐπιτεθυμμένου] 'enflamed,' 'enkindled,' like ἄτυφου below, is used with an etymological play on the name Τυφών.

This beautiful passage is well known as one of the few in which Greek writers describe natural scenery in detail. The place, according to Dr. Thompson, is still easily recognizable. 'On the left side, as one ascends the stream, the steep but not high banks retire and form an oval recess girt by rocks, in which are still visible certain small square niches, where doubtless stood the ἀγάλματα—little images of Pan and the Nymphs,' etc. See his long note *ad locum.*

B. καταγωγή] 'resting-place.'

πλάτανος] The plane is common in Greece. The agnus castus is a tall shrub, somewhat resembling the willow.

ἀμφιλαφής] 'spreading.' Timaeus *s. v.* says πολὺ καὶ ἄφθονον. ἔστιν δ' ὅτε καὶ ἐπίσκιον, evidently referring to this passage. But there is nothing about 'shadow' in the word; it belongs to the same root as λαμβάνω (which root appears to have been originally *labh = λαφ), and means 'embracing,' 'spacious.' For the φ we may compare λάφυρον, 'what is taken,' 'spoil.' See Curtius, *Griechische Etymologie,* 520⁴.

καὶ ὡς ἀκμήν κ.τ.λ.] The double ὡς has caused much difficulty to the commentators. I understand the place to mean : 'The height and shadow of the agnus castus, and its being in full bloom, will fill the place with fragrance'; which gives a not quite regular, but perfectly intelligible, sentence. The first ὡς is taken with ἔχει = τὸ ἀκμάζον, the second with εὐωδέστατον—' as fragrant as possible.' The optative παρέχοι ἄν is due to the Attic habit of softening direct statements : instead of 'it does make' we have 'it cannot but make,' 'it will always make.' 'The agnus castus, in its full bloom, fills the place with perfume.'

ὑπὸ τῆς πλατάνου] Cf. *Il.* ii. 307 καλῇ ὑπὸ πλατανίστῳ, ὅθεν ῥέει ἀγλαὸν ὕδωρ. Dr. Thompson says the tree grows by fountains and river-heads.

ὥστε γε τῷ ποδὶ τεκμήρασθαι] The Bodleian and best codices read ὥστε. So Turicenses, Hermann, Stallbaum. ὥς[τε] Hirschig, ὥς γε Dr. Thompson.

Ἀχελῴου] The Achelous, the only considerable river of southern Greece, stands as the representative of rivers in general.

C. ὦ θαυμάσιε] 'you curious being.'

D. σὺ μέντοι—ἐξόδου] The Bodleian has οὐ μέντοι δοκεῖ μοι τῆς ἐξόδου, which makes no sense. τῆς ἐμῆς ἐξόδου is often read after some codices. The best MSS. have οὐ, and omit the ἐμῆς.

ὥσπερ γὰρ—ἄγουσι] ' Ea recte statuit Astius posita esse pro ; ὥσπερ γὰρ οἱ τὰ πεινῶντα θρέμματα ἄγοντες θαλλὸν ἤ τινα καρπὸν προσείοντες ἄγουσι.' Stallbaum.

E. δοκῶ κατακεῖσθαι] '*Placet mihi recumbere.* Frequens est hic usus τοῦ δοκεῖν futuro juncti' (he has the vulgate reading κατακείσεσθαι). 'Protag. p. 339 c Δοκῶ οὖν μοι ἐγὼ παρακαλεῖν σε.' Heindorf. The best codices have the present : Dr. Thompson prefers the future.

245 C—249 C.

ψυχὴ πᾶσα ἀθάνατος] 'All soul is immortal.' Not any individual soul ; but soul in general. (Dr. Thompson.)

D. εἰ γὰρ ἔκ του ἀρχή κ.τ.λ.] This place has given expositors a great deal of trouble. *E. g.* Dr. Thompson says, 'as Fic. renders it, "ex principio utique non oriretur," *h. e.* a first principle must in that case derive its existence from something which is *not* a first principle; as if he had said, ἐξ οὐκ ἀρχῆς γίγνοιτ' ἄν, a perfect reductio ad absurdum.' One fails to see the cogency of the argument; why should not one ἀρχή arise from another? Surely the obvious meaning is, 'For if an original principle were derived from something else, the principle could not have subsisted from eternity.' ἀρχή changes its meaning, and the very simplicity of the sense has been misleading. Ficinus (as quoted by Stallbaum), though his words are ambiguous, may have meant the same thing, 'nam si principium oriretur ex aliquo, ex principio utique non oriretur.' But, if he meant this, no one seems to have followed him. The phrase ἐξ ἀρχῆς is so familiar that the ambiguity which we observe would hardly have struck a Greek writer. I take ἐξ ἀρχῆς immediately below (l. 126) in the same sense, and understand the reasoning to be; 'But having been from eternity, the principle must also subsist to eternity; for were it to be destroyed it could never again originate or be originated; and the effects of the principle would disappear; which is contrary to the doctrine that all things have subsisted from eternity:' or, as we should say, to the doctrine of the uniformity of nature. The question here is not what we are to think of the reasoning, which perhaps is not particularly convincing, but what is the point which Plato seeks to make?

E. λόγον] The 'account' or 'definition' of the soul. See Dr. Thompson's note, especially the quotation from the *Laws*, x. 895 D ἆρ' οὐκ ἂν ἐθέλοις περὶ ἕκαστον τρία νοεῖν—ἓν μὲν τὴν οἰσίαν, ἓν δὲ τῆς οὐσίας τὸν λόγον, ἓν δὲ τὸ ὄνομα ;

τοῦτο] i. e. the clause which follows, μὴ ἄλλο—ψυχήν.

246 A. ἰδέας] Its form; but the word may mean more generally kind or nature.

διηγήσεως] Plato's views are to be found *in extenso* in the *Republic* and *Timaeus*.

ὑποπτέρου] The charioteer and his two horses answer to the division of the soul in the *Republic* into the λογιστικόν, θυμοειδές, and ἐπιθυμητικόν—the rational, spirited, and concupiscent parts.

B. πῇ δὴ οὖν κ.τ.λ.] 'We must endeavour to explain in what sense the words mortal and immortal animal are used.'

πᾶσα ἡ ψυχή] 'Soul in its entirety.' Thompson.

C. κόσμον] The only attempt I know to find an etymology for this remarkable word is that of Fick (Dictionary), who derives it from the root καδ, 'to excel,' as in κέκαδμαι, Doric, for which the other dialects use κέκασμαι. This suits fairly well the older use of the word in the sense of 'decoration,' 'ornament.' κόσμος would stand for *κόδ-μος, cf. Κόδρος. Κάδμος, Κάστωρ are also referred to the same root. Curtius (*Griechische Etymologie*) does not notice any of these words.

ἡ δέ] Some part of soul, opposed to τελέα μὲν οὖν οὖσα.

ἀθάνατον κ.τ.λ.] A difficult passage. In point of grammar, what is to be supplied to ἀθάνατον? and in point of sense, what is the drift of the whole sentence? Does Plato mean the union of soul and body to extend to deities? or does he mean to reprehend such conceptions of divine natures altogether? The second explanation finds favour with Heindorf and Stallbaum; but when we think of the soul of the Cosmos in the *Timaeus*, and similar examples, we are not sure but that the former comes nearer Plato's intention. Perhaps it does not very much matter what we supply to ἀθάνατον (say ἔσχεν or ἔχει ἐπωνυμίαν or καλοῦμεν); for in any case the difficulty of sense remains. The words πῆ δὴ οὖν θνητόν κ.τ.λ. just before, 'Now we must explain how the names mortal and immortal animal are applied,' and the deprecation which follows our present passage, 'Let that, however. be as God approves,' etc., seem also to support the first explanation. Is the term 'immortal animal' brought in only to be denounced? and if the application of such a name be denounced, why is it also deprecated? One is therefore inclined to translate (with Hieronymus Müller), 'the name "immortal" we apply, not in consequence of any ratiocination, but, without vision or sufficient perception, we imagine deity as an immortal living being, possessed of soul and body conjoined in eternal union.'

247 A. The 'gods' of this passage more or less typify the heavenly bodies; and when Plato says that Hestia remains alone in the house of the gods, he seems to hint at the central fire of the Pythagoreans, about which the planets, including the sun, moon, and earth, were supposed to revolve. See Dr. Thompson's note.

The διέξοδοι, 'ways to and fro,' seem to be suggested by the orbits of the planets, and the description beginning at ἄκραν ὑπό by the Milky Way. διέξοδος is used of the sun's orbit, Herod. ii. 24.

πράττων ἕκαστος αὐτῶν τὸ αὑτοῦ] The same conception is one of the main themes of the *Republic*, where it is found, after much investigation (Book IV), that justice consists in every man having his own part to play.

φθόνος—ἵσταται] 'A bye-blow at the vulgar notion, ὅτι τὸ θεῖον πᾶν φθονερόν.' Thompson. Herodotus i. 32 τὸ θεῖον πᾶν ἐὸν φθονερόν τε καὶ ταραχῶδες.

B. ἄκραν—ἤδη] 'They mount to the top of the heavenly meridian by a road steep from the beginning.'

ᾧ μὴ—ἡνιόχων] 'for any driver whose horse is ill-broken.'

C. περὶ ἥν—τόπον] Heindorf, reading these words without any stop,

and having a comma before περί, explains, 'Circa hanc οὐσίαν, *i. e.* τὴν
τοῦ ὄντως εἶναι ἰδέαν, fingit ceteras ideas positas, ut δικαιοσύνην, σωφροσύνην etc.' I presume the reading of the text is intended to bear the
same meaning. But surely we should simply put a comma after νῷ and
after γένος, and understand the whole passage to mean, 'For the colourless and unembodied and impalpable very Reality, visible only to mind,
the governor of the soul, about which reality only we have very knowledge indeed, occupies this space.'

D. ἅτ' οὖν—τρεφομένη] ἅτ' οὖν is transposed to the beginning of the
sentence. 'For ἡ οὖν θ. διάνοια, ἅτε—τρεφομένη.' Thompson. ἀκήρατος
B and almost all MSS. Is the alteration into ἀκηράτῳ required?

καὶ ἀπάσης κ.τ.λ.] 'And the thought of every soul that is ready to
receive its portion.' 'Aoristum δέξασθαι tuentur plerique omnes,'
'codices' *scilicet.* Stallbaum. The other editors seem all to have the
future.

διὰ χρόνου] 'at long and last,' the regular meaning of the phrase.

E. ὄντων is a somewhat remarkable instance of attraction.

248 A. ὑποβρύχιαι] 'with their heads below,' not outside the celestial
sphere.

B. ἀτελεῖς] 'uninitiated.' τέλη and τελεταί are regular names for the
mysteries, viewed as an end or consummation of religious knowledge.
Cf. *infra* 249 C τελέους ἀεὶ τελετὰς τελούμενος, τέλεος ὄντως μόνος
γίγνεται.

τροφῇ δοξαστῇ] 'the husks of opinion,' δόξα; as opposed to the food
of exact knowledge, ἐπιστήμη.

οὗ δ' ἕνεχ'—τρέφεται] The Bodleian and other MSS. have οὐδὲν ἔχει
πολλὴ σπουδή. 'Verum primus restituit Bekker.' Stallbaum. 'And
the reason of their urgency to behold the Plain of Truth (is this); the
pasture which is proper for the noblest part of the soul is found in that
meadow, and with this food the pinions of the soul are nourished.'

C. 'Αδραστείας] Adrasteia is generally Nemesis, as in Aeschylus,
Prometheus 936—
οἱ προσκυνοῦντες τὴν 'Αδράστειαν σοφοί.
But Plato appears here rather to mean 'Ανάγκη, the divine Necessity,
perhaps borrowing the name from the Orphic mysteries. See Dr.
Thompson's note. The name seems to mean 'the Inescapable,' from
the root δρα of διδράσκω, etc. ἄδρηστος occurs in Herodotus, iv. 132, in
the active sense of 'not given to running away.'

χρησαμένη] Dr. Thompson, the Zürich editors, and Engelmann's
translator put a comma after this word, which only obscures the sense.

D. πέμπτην—ἕξουσαν] Observe the change of construction.

249 A. δικαιωτήρια] 'places of correction.' So κολαστήριον. Pollux
explains our word by βασανιστήρια. (Thompson.)

B. δεῖ γὰρ—ξυναιρούμενον] 'For man must understand through forms, as they are called, and forms proceed from many perceptions of sense to one whole compounded by reason.'

C. πρὸς γὰρ ἐκείνοις] *Phaedo* 84 C αὐτὸς πρὸς τῷ εἰρημένῳ λόγῳ ἦν ὁ Σωκράτης, 'was engaged upon,' 'was at it,' as we say colloquially.

πρὸς οἷσπερ θεὸς ὢν θεῖός ἐστι] 'by the contemplation of which deity is divine.' θεός is to be taken generally.

258 D—259 D.

Socrates gives as a playful reason for not yielding to sleep in so tempting a spot the legend of the Cicadae, which at once chimes in with the enthusiastic expressions of Phaedrus as to the delights of intellectual talk, and furnishes a transition to the remaining portion of the dialogue, which treats of rhetoric.

258 D. ἰδιωτικόν is rather strangely used in one sense, 'private' as opposed to 'public,' and ἰδιώτης in another, 'unskilled' or 'layman' as opposed to 'artist.' This latter antithesis is common in Plato, *e. g.* in the passage quoted by Heindorf *ad locum, Laws* x. 890 A ταῦτ' ἐστὶν—ἅπαντα ἀνδρῶν σοφῶν—ἰδιωτῶν τε καὶ ποιητῶν. Hirschig and Dr. Thompson bracket ὡς ποιητής, ὡς ἰδιώτης, surely without necessity. The MSS. give no variant. In the passage immediately preceding, laws, psephismata, and the like, have been explained to be really 'political compositions.'

E. οὐ γὰρ—ἡσθῆναι] 'It is not worth living for the sake of these pleasures which imply a previous pain, without which the pleasure does not arise.' Phaedrus speaks like a young student, full of the new-learned distinction between pure and mixed pleasures. In the *Philebus* the distinction is drawn out at great length, the result being that only the pleasures of the intellect, with a few others, such as the pleasures derived from painting, music, sweet smells, etc., are pure or unattended by pain, while all others follow upon a previous pain, as *e. g.* the pleasure of eating follows upon the pain of hunger.

ὡς ἐν τῷ πνίγει] 'as is their custom in the heat.'

'Sole sub ardenti resonant arbusta cicadis.'

Verg. *Ecl.* ii. 13.

259 A. καθορᾶν is said not to be used in the sense of 'looking down' by any good Attic prose writer, without a case following. 'Seem to be looking on.'

ἀκηλήτους] How to be construed?

B. τῶν πρὶν Μούσας γεγονέναι] From what would this be abbreviated?

C. γενόμενον] 'when once born,' opposed to τελευτήσῃ following.

The Cicadae, of which there are numerous species, are small insects, measuring say an inch and a half across the wings, widely diffused in southern Europe, but scarcely reaching beyond the limits of vine cultivation. They live on the sap of trees and plants. Only the males sing; the sound is produced by a vibrating membrane stretched across an aperture in the lower part of the belly. Our common house-cricket (*Gryllus* or *Achsta*), though emitting a similar sound, is entirely different.

274 B—275 B.

The point of this little episode lies in the suggestion that writing, instead of being an aid to the memory, really tends to weaken it.

274 C. ἀκοὴν—δοξασμάτων] 'You shall hear my story, but if it be true, antiquity only knows. Could we but discover the truth for ourselves, we should not be dependent on such traditions.' The first αὐτοί is a little remarkable.

Ναύκρατιν] Naucratis stood on the east side of the Canobic or west branch of the Nile, not far from the present Alexandria, and was the original Greek port of Egypt. See Herodotus ii. 178-9, and Baehr *ad locum*.

Θεῦθ] Theuth or Thoth was commonly identified by the Greeks with Hermes. In the *Philebus*, 18 B, he is credited with the distinction of vowels and consonants, the invention of letters, arithmetic, etc. 'He was one of the twelve gods of second rank, and called by the Egyptians "the scribe of the gods," "the lord of the divine word," "the writer of Truth." So Bunsen, *Aegypten* i. 462, from Lepsius. He was also the Moon-god.' Dr. Thompson.

D. Θαμοῦ] 'It is impossible to say where Plato found this word, which seems a corruption or variety of 'Αμοῦς, 'Αμοῦν, the Egyptian name, according to Herodotus, of Zeus (Her. ii 42).' Dr. Thompson.

Θήβας] Thebes, the capital of Upper Egypt, the Tāpē of the monuments, called by the Hebrews No Ammon, by the later Greeks Diospolis, stood on the right bank of the Nile, in an extensive plain, formed by the retiring of the desert hills on both sides of the river. On the opposite bank were the temples and tombs. The site upon the eastern bank is now occupied by the unimportant villages of Luxor and Karnak. Whoever wishes to have a vivid conception of Thebes in the time of the Pharaohs should read Ebers's *Uarda*.

καὶ τὸν θεὸν Ἄμμωνα] The construction is somewhat loose. 'The city the Hellenes call Thebes, and the god Thamus they call Ammon.'

ἀπέδειξε] ἐπέδειξε B and other codices, Stallbaum, Thompson, Hermann. ἀπέδειξε Hirschig.

E. τεκεῖν] The play on words in τεκεῖν—τέχνης is for once etymological. τέχνη is 'that which produces.'

275 A. ἢ δύναται] 'than their real effect.'

εὗρες] Almost 'have invented.' See note on *Cratylus* 426 C.

B. χαλεποὶ ξυνεῖναι] 'tiresome company,' 'bores.'

ὦ Σώκρατες—ποιεῖς] Plato here gives us a hint in what light we are to take the playful apologues of Socrates.

CRATYLUS.

425 B—428 D.

The *Cratylus* discusses the origin and nature of language, or, in the shape in which the question was put in Plato's time, Is language νόμῳ or φύσει, conventional or natural? In the following passage, Socrates, departing from his usual method, and speaking, as he says, by a kind of inspiration, advances the theory that every letter is imitative, and has a natural application to some class of ideas. The descriptions of the various letters, so far as they are mentioned, are forcible and exact.

For Hermogenes see the *Phaedo* (59 B).

Cratylus, a Heraclitean, was somewhat the senior of Plato, who, according to Aristotle (*Metaphysics* I. vi. 2), frequented his society. In the dialogue he maintains that words have their meaning naturally (φύσει); Hermogenes again that meanings are conventional (θέσει).

The analysis to which Socrates refers is that implied in the question; Can we classify and analyse the various letters, so as to find whether they have each a definite meaning, which is the reason why they are used in compounding such and such words? and do we find a corresponding division of things in nature?

425 B. σὺ πιστεύεις—διελέσθαι] 'Do you suppose that you will be able to analyse them in this way?'

ἢ βούλει οὕτως] 'or shall we rather—?'

C. ὥσπερ—τοῖς θεοῖς] προείπομεν scil. 400 E *supra*, where an etymology of the name Zeus has been given, and it is added that we know nothing of the gods, but that the names by which they call themselves must be true.

δόγματα—εἰκάζομεν] Somewhat briefly expressed; 'we can but conjecture about them, following the opinions of men.'

οὕτω δέ] 'Nihil isto δέ in comparatione frequentius.' Stallbaum on *Cratylus* 394 B.

τι χρηστόν] The sense must be something like this: 'Whoever would make a perfectly satisfactory analysis, must do it on the plan we have indicated.' But can τι χρηστόν be right? B and T have εἰ μέν τι χρηστὸν ἔδει. T (Bekker's t) is a codex of the second or inferior family of MSS. which contain this dialogue, and is chosen by Schanz to represent that family. He reads after Ast, εἰ μέν τι χρῆν, omitting ἔδει. If τι χρηστόν is retained, we must understand it to mean, 'to any purpose,' 'to any good result.' Heindorf, Buttmann, and Stallbaum have all felt a difficulty, and suggested various emendations.

νῦν δέ] 'as things are'; for the perfect analysis is beyond us.

τὸ λεγόμενον implies a reference to some proverbial expression; 'we must cut our coat according to our cloth,' we say. There is said to have been a line of Menander:—

ζῶμεν γὰρ οὐχ ὡς θέλομεν, ἀλλ' ὡς δυνάμεθα.

Caecilius, in a fragment (line 177 in Ribbeck's *Comicorum Latinorum Reliquiae*):—

'Vivas ut possis, quando non quis ut velis.' ,

Terence, *Andria* 805:—

'Ut quimus, aiunt, quando ut volumus non licet.'

Wagner on Terence, *l. c.*

D. κατάδηλα γιγνόμενα] These words form a predicate to the preceding γράμμασι—μεμιμημένα: 'when it turns out that actual things are imitated by letters and syllables.'

εἰ μὴ ἄρα δή] δεῖ B T, which makes no sense. δή appears as a correction in one MS., and presents a minimum of alteration. Schanz reads βούλει after Hermann. 'εἰ μὴ ἄρα βούλει Hermann; cf. *De Rep.* ii. 372 E,' that is, εἰ δ' αὖ βούλεσθε καὶ φλεγμαίνουσαν πόλιν θεωρήσωμεν. This is excellent in itself; but are we entitled to make so great a change?

ἐπειδάν τι ἀπορῶσιν] 'when they are in any perplexity.'

ἐπὶ τὰς μηχανὰς—αἴροντες] Such an appearance of a god we have at the end of Sophocles' *Philoctetes* (Heracles in this case), and frequently in Euripides. αἴροντες, 'elevating' or 'suspending' by means of machinery. 'To complete the skênê, a kind of ceiling of boards was necessary, traces of which can still be distinguished on the wall of the skênê of the theatre at Aspendos' [in Pamphylia]. 'On these boards stood the crane on which was suspended the flying apparatus.—By means of it gods and heroes and spectres entered and left the stage, or floated across it.' *The Life of the Greeks and Romans*, Guhl and Koner, p. 278, English translation.

ἀπαλλαγῶμεν following εἰ μὴ ἄρα is against Attic usage, which requires ἐάν, as Stallbaum would read. Perhaps the interval between the particles and verb may account for the unusual construction; as if the future or optative had been meant at first, and the subjunctive used instead. The subjunctive has also (Schneider on *Republic* ix. 579 D) been understood to have something of a cohortative force; which seems very unlikely. The reading βούλει would get over the difficulty.

E. εἰσὶ δὲ—βάρβαροι] 'and there were barbarians older than we.' Heindorf and Stallbaum would prefer οἱ βάρβαροι, which is plausible at first sight, but seems unnecessary. B T omit the article.

426 A. ἐκδύσεις] 'evasions.' B εἰσδύσεις, a manifest error. T and the second hand of B have ἐκδύσεις.

καὶ μάλα κομψαί] The words καὶ μάλα are to be joined.

τῶν γε ὑστέρων] ὀρθότητα scil.

φάσκοντα] 'who professes.'

B. ὕστερα—φλυαρήσει] Acc. of cognate sense. ὕστερα, 'all the rest of his exposition.'

ἃ—ἐγὼ ᾔσθημαι] 'my notion,' 'what occurs to me.'

πειρᾶσθαι] Infinitive for imperative, a common Platonic construction.

οὐδ' εἴπομεν] 'as to which (κίνησις) we quite omitted to say' in our previous etymologies.

ἵεσις like many words used in the dialogue, is formed *ad locum*, to show the derivation.

οὐ γὰρ ἦτα κ.τ.λ.] This may be seen in most of the older inscriptions still extant. εἶ and οὖ are the old names of ε and ο, and occur several times in the dialogue. The present Ionic alphabet, containing η and ω, which we use in writing Greek, is said to have been first formally brought into public use at Athens in the year 403 B.C., when Eucleides was *archon eponymus*.

ξενικόν] 'Dialectic,' 'non-Attic.' See 406 A, where a derivation of Λητώ is given; ἴσως δὲ ὡς οἱ ξένοι καλοῦσι· πολλοὶ γὰρ Ληθὼ καλοῦσιν. Ληθώ might fairly belong to some Greek dialect, unless indeed we suppose Socrates to invent his facts on the spot. Welcker (with many others) takes Λητώ to come from λανθάνω, a view which Curtius (*Griech. Etym.*[4] p. 119) very properly rejects. κίω, a poetical word, is used of the Attics only by Aeschylus; and therefore Socrates is entitled to call it 'dialectic.' 'The derivation of κίνησις is from κίειν, a dialectic word, signifying "to go".'

εἰ οὖν τις—καλοῖτο] 'Therefore, if one were to reconstruct the old form of the word κίνησις which corresponds to our pronunciation, he would be correct in giving this as ἵεσις.' εὕροι in the sense of 'discover,' or almost 'invent'; cf. *Phaedrus* 275 A (*supra*) οὔκουν μνήμης ἀλλ' ὑπομνήσεως φάρμακον εὗρες. φωνή may be 'dialect,' as in *Phaedo* 62 A (*supra*).

D. κιείνησιν—εἶσιν] These are the readings both of B and T. Stallbaum mentions as variants κιεικίνησιν—κιείνησιν—κιείνησις—κεκλῆσθαι ἢ ἴεισιν. All being obviously corrupt, we are reduced to conjecture. The strange forms, invented *ad tempus*, which are so frequent in the *Cratylus*, have sorely perplexed the scribes. Cornarius proposed to read here ἔδει δὲ κίεισιν—ἢ ἴεσιν, for which I would suggest, as still simpler, ἔδει δὲ κίεσιν—ἢ ἴεσιν. Heindorf is inclined to suspect the whole passage, and Ast and Schanz bracket from ἔδει δὲ to ὠνόμασται. This cuts the knot of course; and certainly the derivation of στάσις is very obscurely given. If we read ἔδει δὲ κίεσιν κεκλῆσθαι ἢ ἴεσιν, the connection is as follows. First of all there are ἰέναι and κίειν, from the first of which would naturally come ἴεσις. But anciently ε was used also for η. Substituting κι for ι, η for ε, and inserting ν, we get our modern κίνησις. But the corresponding ancient form would have been κίεσις or ἴεσις.

What is meant to be said about στάσις? Is it ἴεσις with στα prefixed? or is it δίεσις with στ as a καλλωπισμός? In either case the vagueness of the expression affords much ground for the suspicions of Heindorf. Besides, στάσις appears to be used in the sense of 'standing still,' a very rare meaning. Where Stallbaum gets his στᾶσις, a word otherwise unknown, I do not know. Whatever we think of the words ἡ δὲ στάσις—ὠνόμασται, they remind one strongly of that ingenious compilation, the *Etymologicon Magnum*.

ὥσπερ λέγω] 'as I was saying.'

πρὸς τὸ ἀφομοιοῦν τῇ φορᾷ] Sc. αὐτά. Stallbaum. 'For the purpose of assimilating the names of motion to motion itself.'

E. τραχεῖ] τρέχειν Hirschig and Schanz after one codex. Is the change required, especially looking at the list of words which follows?

ῥυμβεῖν] 'to spin' or 'twirl.' ῥέμβειν, ῥύμβειν, ῥύμβδειν are variants here; but ῥυμβεῖν, besides appearing in B and Π, is confirmed by the Lexicon of Timaeus (*s. v.*), who says: 'Ῥυμβεῖν· ῥομβεῖν. τοῦτο δὲ ἀπὸ τῆς κινήσεως τοῦ ῥόμβου. 'Ῥυμβεῖν Atticorum fuisse videtur, ῥομβεῖν ceterorum Graecorum.' Ruhnken's note on Timaeus *l. l.*, which see. No other example of either form is given in Liddell and Scott.

ἑώρα γάρ—σειομένην] ἑῶ BT and other MSS. We owe the certain emendation ἑώρα to Heindorf *ad locum*.

From this it appears that Plato's *r* was distinctly trilled, that is, the tip of the tongue (or of the uvula) was made to vibrate. Such a vibration is obviously very suggestive of motion. The South English *r*, even at the beginning of words, can scarcely be said to be trilled at all, although different varieties of trill may be heard in North England, Scotland, and Ireland. The French *r* is a firm trill of the point of the tongue, and the common German *r* of the uvula.

τῷ δ' αὖ ἰῶτα—πάντα] This again is an acute appreciation of ι. ι (as in English *see*, *tree*, when deprived of any tendency to diphthong) is at once the thinnest and the highest of all the vowels. The point of the tongue is brought as near the gum, and lifted as high, as can be done while still preserving the vocal effect; a nearer approximation passes into a *y*; and at the same time the oral passage is as much contracted as it can be for a vowel.

ἃ δή—ἴοι ἄν] 'which are the most penetrative.'

427 A. ἴεσθαι] There is no reason *à priori* against this present middle of εἶμι, especially as we have the Homeric εἴσομαι, εἴσατο; but it appears not to be used. ἴεσθαι would account for all passages in which ἴεσθαι has been supposed to occur (*e. g. Od.* xxii. 470) :—

αὖλιν ἐσιέμεναι, στυγερὸς δ' ὑπεδέξατο κοῖτος.

ἴεσθαι is the reading of T and the corrector of B; but B and Δ have ἱένεσθαι. ἴεσθαι Schanz.

πνευματώδη] That is, spirants or half-stops of the breath. φ, if we suppose it to have been, as is for many reasons probable, *p + h* (roughly), ψ and σ, being all surd, with the glottis open, are pronounced with a strong breath; ζ (*dz*), although sonant, with the glottis shut, has an effect of the same kind.

καὶ ὅλως σεισμόν can hardly be right. Why should this generalisation be used at all after σείεσθαι? And besides, though it is very well to say that shaking has a spirant or 'whiffling' effect, as in the English 'shake' itself, why should this be affirmed of all shaking? 'Non sane σεισμός generalem magis significatum habet quam τὸ σείεσθαι, ut admodum offendat verbum ὅλως. Fortasse scribendum σισμόν.' With Müller *in loco* one thankfully accepts this excellent emendation of Heindorf's, the meaning then being, 'and sibilation generally.' σισμός is found in the Lexicon of Suidas. The words in the modern or itacising pronunciation would be pronounced exactly alike. An example of such an itacism in the codices occurs a few lines back (426 E). ἐρύκειν was the old vulgate reading, for which the MSS. give the genuine ἐρείκειν. A modern Greek would not as a rule distinguish the two; though the pronunciation of υ as French *u* or the thinner German *ü* is said still to exist in parts of Greece.

συμπιέσεως —ἀπερείσεως] 'compression' and 'apposition' or 'application' of the tongue. In δ and τ, as in all the mutes, the contact of tongue and palate being perfect, the breath is stopped entirely; and if this position be held for a moment, we get an apt representation of fixity.

B. ὀλισθάνει] Apt again: in pronouncing any of the *l*'s (those of England, Scotland, the Highlands, Germany, for example, are all different) the breath is divided, passing on either side the tongue, and may fairly be said to 'slip' out.

ἡ δὲ—γλοιώδες] 'The heavier sound of γ detained the slipping tongue. and the union of the two gave the notion of a glutinous clammy nature, as in γλίσχρος, γλυκύς, γλοιῶδες.'

C. τοῦ νῦ] All the nasals, as being pronounced from the larynx up the nose, may well be said to have 'internality.'

τὸ δ' αὖ ἄλφα κ.τ.λ.] The broad *a*, as in *father, rather*, may be called the 'greatest' of the vowels; every part of the mouth is at the openest in pronouncing it, and the volume of sound is at the greatest. Hence the familiar fact of 'a' being used to sing musical notes to in the absence of words. This passage goes *pro tanto* to show that to Plato's ear the sound of η was not the thin English *a* in *say* (minus the diphthongising addition), but some sound more nearly related to full 'a,' such as English *a* in *hath, mad* prolonged, or better, very broad *e*, a sound common in English dialects ('Low front wide' and 'Low front primary' of Melville Bell). This would certainly be a μέγα γράμμα. The constant correspondence of *a* and η in the dialects points in the same direction.

οὖ] The o's of course are eminently the roundest of vowels, from the lips being pouted.

It is noticeable that Plato says nothing of the *u*'s, as in English *full, pull*, etc. (high back round, primary and wide). Now in the infinity of possible vowels there are three which may be called 'fixed' or 'terminal,' that is, the voice can go no farther in that direction. These are *a, i, u* (the last the 'primary' sound, without any aftersound or diphthongal effect). To the first two Plato has assigned a character; he passes over the third. Can we infer from this that *v* sounded to him, not as English *u*, but as something like French *u*, and that his *u* terminal was *ov*, a supposition otherwise probable?

αὐτῷ] Sc. τῷ γογγύλῳ.

προσβιβάζειν] To 'apply' or 'impose.'

ἤδη] εἴδη B T.

E. μαθεῖν τε καὶ διδάξαι] 'for one to impart, and another to receive knowledge.'

μέγιστον] So Ξ. B, T, and the second hand of Ξ, μεγίστοις μέγιστον, which is obviously wrong.

428 A. τὸ τοῦ Ἡσιόδου] *Works and Days* 361, Göttling :—

εἰ μὲν γὰρ καὶ σμικρὸν ἐπὶ σμικρῷ καταθεῖο,
καὶ θαμὰ τοῦτ' ἔρδοις, τάχα κεν μέγα καὶ τὸ γένοιτο.

'Many a little makes a mickle.'

B. γράφου] 'write me down,' 'enrol me,' 'register me.' The regular use of the middle is in the sense of registering an accusation; but with the present place may be compared *Laws* viii. 850 B ἀφ' ἧς ἂν γράψηται, 'from the day when he registers himself.' Γράφεσθαι in the sense of 'note down' is not uncommon, and may be found in Plato, *Theaet.* 143 A ἀλλ' ἐγραψάμην γὰρ τότ' εὐθὺς οἴκαδ' ἐλθὼν ἀπομνήματα.

C. ἐπέρχεται] 'it comes into my head.' *Banquet* 197 C ἐπέρχεται δέ μοι καί τι ἔμμετρον εἰπεῖν.

ἐν Λιταῖς] We see that the part of the *Iliad* which now appears as Book ix. was known at this time as the 'Supplications.' It must be remembered that our present division of books only dates from Aristarchus. The lines occur *Il.* ix. 644-5.

ἐπιεικῶς—κατὰ νοῦν] 'pretty much to my mind,' *i. e.* very much.

D. τὸ γὰρ ἐξαπατᾶσθαι κ.τ.λ.] Ignorance or mistaken conviction is with Plato the worst of evils. Compare *Republic* ii. 382 B ἀλλὰ μὴν ὀρθότατά γ' ἂν—τοῦτο ὡς ἀληθῶς ψεῦδος καλοῖτο, ἡ ἐν τῇ ψυχῇ ἄγνοια τοῦ ἐψευσμένου, and the whole passage. *Gorgias* 458 A 'For I imagine that there is no evil which a man can endure so great as an erroneous opinion about the matters of which we are speaking.'

ἐκείνου] As often. of the last mentioned; here Homer.

πρόσσω καὶ ὀπίσσω] The phrase occurs several times in Homer; *e. g. Il.* iii. 109—

οἷς δ' ὁ γέρων μετέῃσιν, ἅμα πρόσσω καὶ ὀπίσσω λεύσσει.

See also i. 343; xviii. 250; *Od.* xxiv. 452. 'Such large discourse, looking before and after.'

GORGIAS.

511 C—512 B.

A beautiful passage, in which rhetoric, which the Sophists think the be-all and the end-all of human life, is shown to be but a handmaid art, and compared with the art of the pilot.

Gorgias of Leontini, a city of Sicily, between Syracuse and Catana, was the most famous rhetorician of his time. He was born about the year 480 B.C., and in the year 427 B.C. he was sent by his native city as ambassador to Athens, to beg protection against Syracuse. Plato refers to him repeatedly, besides introducing him in the earlier part of the *Gorgias* as an old and prosperous gentleman, very well pleased with himself. Polus and he are auditors of the latter part of the dialogue, from which the extracts are taken.

Polus is a young and clever pupil of Gorgias. He has written a book on rhetoric (462 C). His long-tailed phraseology is ridiculed in the *Phaedrus* (267 B).

Callicles we only know from the dialogue. He is depicted as a finished gentleman and man of the world, but a thorough cynic, who has no belief in any objects of pursuit except power and pleasure, and laughs at the fools who talk of disinterestedness and virtue.

511 C. **εἰς τοιοῦτον** is relative to the words that follow, οὗ δεῖ ταύτης τῆς ἐπιστήμης.

D. **προσεσταλμένη**] 'modest,' not spreading abroad, but drawn tight. συνεσταλμένος is used in much the same way.

ἐσχηματισμένη] 'putting on an appearance,' 'making a show as if,' Plato's regular use of the word. Timaeus has: σχηματιζόμενος· προσποιούμενος ἢ συντατrόμενος, where Ruhnken collects the passages, wrongly interpreting in this place, *ornari, magnifice componi.* That meaning is conveyed rather by the whole combination of words. *Sophist,* p. 268 A (*s. fin.*), is a good example of the sense: φόβον ὡς ἀγνοεῖ ταῦτα ἃ πρὸς τοὺς ἄλλους ὡς εἰδὼς ἐσχημάτισται. 'He fears that he is ignorant of that which to the many he puts on an appearance of knowing.'

ἐξ Αἰγίνης] The voyage from the Piraeeus to the town of Aegina may be of some five and twenty miles.

ἐὰν—εὐεργεσίας] 'should she exact a high price for this great service, the preservation of all that I have mentioned.'

αὐτόν] 'the goodman.'

E. **ἐν μετρίῳ σχήματι**] 'like anybody else.'

512 A. **ἢ οἷοι ἐνέβησαν**] B and many books οἵ, an obvious mistake, arising doubtless from the repetition of the two letters οι. Turr., Hermann, Hirschig, Stallbaum οἷοι.

οὐκ refers to the whole proposition that follows. He does not think that the man hopelessly diseased ought to live, or the man of hopelessly corrupt mind : ἀλλ' οἶδεν, ὅτι οὐκ ἄμεινόν ἐστι ζῆν κ.τ.λ.

ὀνήσειεν] A sudden change to *oratio obliqua.*

521 C to end.

Socrates declares that if he be brought to trial, as Callicles says he may be, he will use no rhetoric in his defence except his ordinary mode of speech ; and that it matters not whether a man be condemned or not, if his soul be pure and just. 'No man fears death, except he be without reason and without courage ; but injustice is a fearful thing. For the supreme evil is to come to Hades with a soul full of injustice. And to show that this is so, I will tell you a tale.' The tale of the three judges of the dead follows, and is succeeded by the beautiful peroration of the dialogue, in which it is reasserted that not rhetoric, and not politics, is the first concern of every man, but his own soul.

521 C. **οὐκ ἂν εἰσαχθείς**] The participle not unfrequently takes ἄν, on the analogy of the moods. Stallbaum would refer ἄν to both participles ; but rather, the sentence, if resolved, would run thus: ὡς εἰ οἰκοίης καὶ οὐκ ἂν εἰσαχθείης.

ὅτι τύχοι] Oblique.

D. μόνος agrees with the subject, because not really governed by εἴπω.

E. οὐ πρὸς τὸ ἥδιστον] Plato often uses such repetitions; see *Gorgias* 452 E ὁ δὲ χρηματιστὴς οὗτος ἄλλῳ ἀναφανήσεται χρηματιζόμενος καὶ οὐχ αὑτῷ, ἀλλά σοι τῷ δυναμένῳ λέγειν καὶ πείθειν τὰ πλήθη.

ἥκει] 'becomes applicable to me,' 'is now come home to me.'

ἐν τούτοις may be neuter, but seems to be more naturally taken as masculine. The question is highly arguable. If we join ἐν τούτοις ληφθείς, τούτοις must be neuter; and this is strongly confirmed by ἐν τούτῳ τῷ κακῷ ἀποληφθέντα just below. Upon the other hand, ἐν τούτοις regularly means 'before these hearers,' and so the words have often been understood. They would then correspond to τοὺς τοιούτους δικαστάς l. 64.

καὶ αὐτούς κ.τ.λ.] 'he is doing his best to destroy you all, and notably the youngest of you.'

522 A. ἐν τούτῳ—ἀποληφθέντα] 'In has angustias adductum.' Heindorf.

ἢ εἰ εἴποι] 'V. εἰ deerat, quod iam Steph. vidit restitui oportere.' Stallbaum.

ὑγιεινῶς] 'for the good of your health.'

ἃς ἐκπεπόρικα] ἃς omitted in B Δ, evidently on account of repeated ας.

B. ἐγὼ δὲ—πορίζεται] 'although I do not envy either those who give or those who take them.' A parenthetical clause, not disturbing the construction.

C. τὸ ὑμέτερον δὴ τοῦτο] 'all this I do for your benefit.' *Apology* 31 B 'So many years have I neglected my own matters, and been content to let them go, while I was about your business.' τὸ δὲ ὑμέτερον πράττειν ἀεί.

ἐν αὐτῷ ὑπάρχοι] 'Quanquam fateor non suppetere mihi locum, in quo ὑπάρχει ἔν τινι dicatur.' Stallbaum. Yet one does not see how to construe except with him, 'If one thing were in him.' We could very well spare the preposition. ὑπάρχειν τινί is common and regular. the other strange. Heindorf says, 'Fortasse ἐν delendum,' and Hirschig and Dr. Thompson bracket. But the MSS. all have it, and there is no objection to it except the want of parallels.

E. ἀλλ' ἐπείπερ γε κ.τ.λ.] 'Since we have heard so much already, we may as well hear you out.'

523 A. φασί] 'as the phrase goes.' 'Listen then, Callicles, to a noble tale, which you may esteem a legend, but I hold to be very truth.'

Ὅμηρος] *Iliad* xv. 187 sqq.

B. **ἐs μακάρων νήσους**] The Islands of the Blest appear first in Hesiod (*Works and Days* 170 *sqq.*, Göttling²), as the habitations of the fourth race of men, the heroes. καὶ τοὶ μὲν ναίουσιν ἀκηδέα θυμὸν ἔχοντες ἐν μακάρων νήσοισι παρ᾽ ὠκεανὸν βαθυδίνην κ.τ.λ.

καὶ ἔτι—ἔχοντος] Heindorf is obviously right in explaining ' recenti adhuc Jovis imperio.' Stallbaum's ' et nuper etiam, Jove imperium tenente ' I cannot approve, though Mr. Cope follows him.

C. **ἐκατέρωσε**] Both to the Isles of the Blest and to Tartarus. σφιν poetical form.

D. **ἐπίπροσθεν**] ' obstruct their view.' Cf. *Banquet* 213 A καὶ περιαιρούμενον ἅμα τὰς ταινίας ὡς ἀναδήσοντα, ἐπίπροσθεν τῶν ὀφθαλμῶν ἔχοντα, οὐ κατιδεῖν τὸν Σωκράτη.

E. **ἔρημον—καταλιπόντα**] Both refer to the person who is to be judged. The gender is accommodated to the sense.

᾽Ασίας] Plato seems to give Crete to Asia; an arrangement probably unique.

524 A. λειμῶνι—τριόδῳ] One way leads to the meadow, and two others to the Islands and to Tartarus. In the myth at the end of the *Republic* (*infra*), the souls of the dead are in like manner assembled in a meadow. Perhaps this conception goes back to the ' asphodel meadow ' of the *Odyssee* (xi. 539, 573), although that appears to be simply a piece of rank and dismal vegetation, suitable to the melancholy gloom of the nether world.

πρεσβεῖα] ' the presidency,' ' primacy.'

B. **πραγμάτοιν**] πρᾶγμα in the sense of ' thing,' ' existing thing,' strikes one as very strange.

οὐ πολὺ ἧττον] ' very much in the same degree.'

C. **ἢ ἀμφότερα**] Used adverbially. Cf. *Laches* 187 A ἐπ᾽ ἐκείνους ἴωμεν καὶ πείθωμεν ἢ δώροις ἢ χάρισιν ἢ ἀμφότερα. The quotation is taken from Heindorf on *Charmides* 153 D ἢ σοφίᾳ ἢ κάλλει ἢ ἀμφότερα; but in that place the books and the editions unite in reading ἀμφοτέροις.

ὁ νεκρός] ' the corpse.'

ταὐτὰ ταῦτα ἔνδηλα] ταὐτὰ ταῦτα, which Stallbaum says is found only in one MS., is adopted by the editors (Turicenses, Stallbaum, Hermann; ταῦτὰ ταῦτ᾽ Hirschig). The omission of ταὐτά is easily accounted for.

E. **ἐπιστήσας**] ' setting them before him.'

κατεῖδεν] The ' gnomic ' aorist, of what happens frequently or regularly.

525 A. ἐκάστῳ] ἑκάστη ἡ πρᾶξις B Δ, Hermann, Hirschig, Stallbaum, Thompson. The feminine seems the better; but there is something to be said for both readings. ἑκάστη ἡ πρᾶξις, ' every several deed.' ἑκάστῳ certainly goes more neatly with αὐτοῦ; and we might imagine ἑκάστῃ induced by the feminines following.

ἐξωμόρξατο] 'has impressed,' 'stamped.'

ἀλαζονείας] 'false pretension,' 'dissimulation,' 'imposture.'

ἀκρατίας] Observe this older form. This and ἀκράτεια seem to have been the only forms used by Plato, although codices here and there often have ἀκρασίας, the common later form.

B. ἰάσιμα] The same distinction between curable and incurable offences appears also in the *Phaedo* and the *Republic*. *Phaedo* 113 E οἱ δ' ἂν δόξωσιν ἀνιάτως ἔχειν διὰ τὰ μεγέθη τῶν ἁμαρτημάτων—τούτους δὲ ἡ προσήκουσα μοῖρα ῥίπτει εἰς τὸν Τάρταρον, ὅθεν οὔποτε ἐκβαίνουσιν. *Republic* x. 615 E (*infra*).

D. 'Αρχέλαον] Archelaus, king of Macedonia, according to the account of Polus (p. 471), being himself the son of a slave-girl, had acquired the throne by murdering his uncle and cousin and his own legitimate brother. For this part of his history Plato appears to be the only authority. Thucydides (ii. 100) says that he made roads, built forts, improved the army, and did more for the military strength of Macedonia than the eight kings who had preceded him. He is said to have been a patron of literature and art, and to have entertained Euripides, Agathon, and others. In the *Rhetoric* (II. xxiii. 8) Aristotle says that Socrates declined to visit him, ὕβριν γὰρ ἔφη εἶναι τὸ μὴ δύνασθαι ἀμύνασθαι ὁμοίως εὖ παθόντα, ὥσπερ καὶ κακῶς.

εἶναι—γεγονότας] 'are such as have been.' Such combinations of the substantive verb, and participle are not uncommon, especially with ἔχω. *Politicus* 297 E καὶ τοῦτ' ἐστὶν ὀρθότατα καὶ κάλλιστ' ἔχον.

Ὅμηρος] *Odyssee* xi. 576 *sqq.*

E. ἐξῆν αὐτῷ] 'he had not the opportunity to sin greatly.'

ἀλλὰ γὰρ—καί] 'Yes, Callicles, it is too true,' etc. καί refers to ἐκ τῶν δυναμένων.

526 A. ἐπεὶ καὶ κ.τ.λ.] 'But there are such; for we find them now and again.'

B. ἄλλους] *Scil.* who are not Athenians.

'Αριστείδης] The famous Aristides.

ὡντινῶν] 'of what parents.'

C. τὰ αὑτοῦ πράξαντος] See *Phaedrus* 247 A (*supra*); *Republic* 433 A; *Timaeus* 72 A.

οὐ πολυπραγμονήσαντος] The words repeat the same idea negatively; 'who has not busied himself unprofitably with the work of others.'

D. χρύσεον κ.τ.λ.] *Odyssee* xi. 569.

E. ἀντιπαρακαλῶ] 'I exhort you in return.' Referring to the previous exhortations of Callicles. Cf. 521 A ἐπὶ ποτέραν οὖν με παρακαλεῖς τὴν θεραπείαν τῆς πόλεως; διόρισόν μοι.

ἀντί] 'as important as.'

ὅτι οὐχ οἷός τε] He turns Callicles' own words upon himself. See above, 486 A εἴ τίς σου λαβόμενος ἢ ἄλλου ὁτουοῦν τῶν τοιούτων εἰς τὸ δεσμωτήριον ἀπαγάγοι—οἶσθ' ὅτι οὐκ ἂν ἔχοις ὅ τι χρήσαιο σαυτῷ, ἀλλ' ἰλιγγιῴης ἂν καὶ χασμῷο οὐκ ἔχων ὅ τι εἴποις—τὸν δὲ τοιοῦτον (some paltry accuser) εἴ τι καὶ ἀγροικίτερον εἰρῆσθαι, ἔξεστιν ἐπὶ κόρρης τύπτοντα μὴ διδόναι δίκην.

527 A. τυπτήσει] It may be well to remind those whose paradigm of the Greek verb has been τύπτω, that τυπτήσω is the only future found in good writers. τύψω, according to Veitch, is first used by Nonnus, who lived in the sixth century A.D. See his 'Greek Verbs,' *s. v.*

B. ἐκεῖσε] 'for the other world.'

ἠρεμεῖ] 'remains undisturbed.'

οὐ τὸ δοκεῖν] Aeschylus has expressed the same feeling in a noble line, *Septem* 592 (Dind.⁵)—

οὐ γὰρ δοκεῖν ἄριστος, ἀλλ' εἶναι θέλει.

C. εἶναι—γίγνεσθαι] A good example of their contrasted senses, 'the being good' and 'the becoming good.'

ὡς ὁ λόγος σημαίνει] This, the reading of the Zürich editors, is perfectly easy and simple; but the MS. authority (B Δ and many more books) is strong for ὁ σὸς λόγος σημαίνει, which is adopted by Hirschig, Stallbaum, Hermann, Deuschle. If we read σός—which is certainly striking—the meaning will be, 'as your own argument shows,' 'as you have been compelled to admit,' 'even according to your own showing.' See *Gorgias* 511 A, and elsewhere.

D. πατάξαι] Inf. after ἔασον.

ἐπιθησόμεθα] 'we will apply ourselves.'

FIRST ALCIBIADES.

120 E—124 B.

The object of Socrates, in this dialogue, is to show Alcibiades the absurdity of his wish to direct the Athenian state, and be at the head of things, until he has first been educated. In the extract Socrates 'sets him down' by ironically pointing out how inferior he is in power and wealth to the Spartan, not to say the Persian monarchs. What a poor figure his mother would cut, if compared to the Queen of Persia!

It may fairly be doubted whether this dialogue is actually the work of Plato. Even in this short extract there are several things to excite suspicion. But if not proceeding from the master's hand, it still is an excellent imitation by a member of the School, and a work of high merit.

120 E. **Σκεψώμεθα δή**] 'Then let us compare our antecedents with those of the Lacedaemonian and Persian kings; are they inferior to us in descent?'

'Ηρακλέους] Herod. vi. 52 gives the genealogy of Eurysthenes and Procles, the first pair of the double kings of Sparta, according to the story. Their father was Aristodemus, the son of Aristodemus, the son of Cleodaeus, the son of Hyllus, the son of Heracles.

The sentence is incorrect as it stands; what has the genealogy of the Heracleid kings to do with that of the descendants of Perseus? The author doubtless meant to say, as the argument requires, that both lines go back to Zeus; but to give this sense the words *εἰς Δία* would require to be inserted after *γένος*, or some change made in the wording to the same effect. This curious omission, or confusion, which is probably due to the writer himself, does not seem to be observed by any of the editors. Stallbaum takes no notice. The translators (Müller, Schleiermacher, Engelmann) translate right on. Nor is any remark made in the editions (Hermann, Turr., Hirschig). Can any similar inaccuracy be found in Plato's undoubted works?

'Αχαιμένους] Herod. i. 125 'The Achaemenidae are a family of the Pasargadae, and the kings, the sons of Perseus, are of this family.' In vii. 11 Xerxes says that he is the son of Darius, the son of Hystaspes, the son of Arsames, the son of Ariaramnes, the son of Teïspes (the son of Cyrus, the son of Cambyses, the son of Teïspes), the son of Achaemenes. (The three generations in brackets appear to be a blunder, very likely of Herodotus himself: the other grades appear on one of the Bisutun inscriptions. See Bähr *ad locum.*) In Herod. vii. 61 we are told that Perseus and Andromeda had a son called Perses, the eponymus of the Persians. Cf. also vii. 150.

121 A. **καὶ γὰρ τὸ ἡμέτερον κ.τ.λ. 1. 7.**] Eurysaces, son of Ajax and Teemessa, who appears as a *κωφὸν πρόσωπον* in the *Ajax* of Sophocles. Ajax is descended from Aeacus, son of Zeus and Aegina.

εἰς Δαίδαλον] Socrates jocularly refers his pedigree to Daedalus, the inventor of sculpture, as being son of the sculptor Sophroniscus, and having himself some tincture of the art. There actually was an Attic deme called *Δαιδαλίδαι*, which may have claimed connexion with Daedalus.

ἀπ' αὐτῶν ἀρξάμενα go together.

οἱ μὲν "Αργους κ.τ.λ.] He means the *διοτρεφέες βασιλῆες* generally. The kings of Argos had long ceased to reign in Plato's time; but the

mention of Argos and Lacedaemon may be a reminiscence of the two
Atridae in Homer. Agamemnon however is not king of the town
Argos, which belongs to Diomedes, but king of Mycenae, and para-
mount of Argos in the larger sense, = Peloponnesus. The pedigree is;
Agamemnon, Atreus, Pelops, Tantalus, Zeus. But why should Argos
be lugged in at all?

B. προγόνους σε δέοι] σε does not appear in B Δ Π etc., but is
supplied by other books, and adopted by Turr., Hirschig, Stallbaum.
Hermann says (*Praefatio*) 'προγόνους δέοι O' (the Bodleian) 'cum aliis
bonis—quod interpolasse videntur, qui transitum a prima persona ad
secundam clare indicari vellent.' The word can well be spared.

ἐπιδεῖξαι] 'make a parade of.'

Ἀρτοξέρξη is the reading of most MSS., and is adopted by the Zürich
editors and Hermann. Ἀρταξέρξης is the form best supported in other
authors. See Bähr on Herod. vi. 98.

τῷ τε γένους ὄγκῳ] τῷ Turicenses, Hirschig; τοῦ Stallbaum and
Hermann, with B Δ Π Ξ and other books.

C. ἐν τῇ] ἀρχῇ scil.

εἰς τὸν ἄλλον χρόνον] 'in time following,' 'all the rest of his
life.'

γενέσια] So B Δ Π, Olympiodorus, and the Scholiast, Turicenses,
Hermann. γενέθλια Stallbaum, Hirschig. The grammarians, or some
of them, draw the distinction that γενέθλια were the festival of the
birth-day, γενέσια of the death-day; and so Stallbaum and Hirschig
here prefer γενέθλια. But we cannot suppose this to have been the
original meaning of γενέσια. In the place of Herodotus (iv. 26) the
word naturally means '*festa natalicia*,' as Bähr renders it. See his note
ad locum. Such distinctions are apt to be illusory.

τὸ τοῦ κωμῳδοποιοῦ] The Scholiast and Olympiodorus (whose notes
on a few of the dialogues we possess) ascribe the phrase to Plato the
comedian. Muretus ap. Stallb. well quotes Plutarch, *Phocion* 30 Ἐμοῦ
μέν, εἶπεν, ὦ παῖ, τὴν σὴν μητέρα γαμοῦντος οὐδ' ὁ γείτων ἤσθετο.
Meineke (*Comicorum Graecorum Fragmenta* ii. 686 and addenda) gives
the places without pretending to restore the line.

D. τροφοῦ] The Scholiast gives the name of Alcibiades' nurse;
αὕτη Λάκαινα τὸ γένος ἦν, Λανικὴ καλουμένη. Λανίκη surely, 'Tri-
victoria.'—Since making the above suggestion, I find that the nurse of
Alexander the Great, and sister of Cleitus, is said to have borne the
name of Lanice. The coincidence is rather too striking. Shall we
suppose the Scholiast to have transposed the nurse from Alexander to
Alcibiades? Those who receive the valuable information of the Scholiast
will doubtless think of the lines of Juvenal (vii. 232), where he says it is
expected of the wretched grammarian

> '*ut forte rogatus,*
> *Dum petit aut thermas aut Phoebi balnea, dicat*
> *Nutricem Anchisae, nomen patriamque novercae*
> *Anchemoli, dicat, quot Acestes vixerit annis,*
> *Quot Siculi Phrygibus vini donaverit urnas.*'

See Mr. Mayor's note for a collection of similar interesting questions.

ἐπιμέλεσθαι] So Turr., Hermann, after ἐπιμελέσθαι of Β Δ Π. Stallbaum and Hirschig ἐπιμελεῖσθαι. The words are perpetually confounded.

ὅ τι κάλλιστος] ὅτι is not found in B. Hermann omits.

E. ἐπτέτεις] Juv. xiv. 10—

> '*Cum septimus annus*
> *Transierit puerum.*'

(He will be already hopelessly corrupted.)

ἐν ἡλικίᾳ] See on *Lysis* 209 A. 'Of a proper age,' or 'in the prime of life.'

ὅ τε σοφώτατος κ.τ.λ.] We have here the four great virtues of the Republic, since known as the four cardinal virtues, wisdom, justice, temperance, and courage.

μαγείαν] The μάγοι we have in Herodotus; but this is probably the oldest place in which the abstract μαγεία occurs. Nor is the word found elsewhere in the works attributed to Plato; which Ast makes one proof that this dialogue is non-Platonic.

122 A. The writer introduces a Hellenic turn by describing Zoroaster πατρόθεν, making him the son of the god Horomazus, i. e. Ormuzd or Ahurâ-mazdâ, the Good Principle of Zoroaster's religious philosophy.

παρασκευάζων] Instead of the finite verb, we have a change into the participle.

ὡς ὅταν δείσῃ δοῦλον ὄντα] 'telling him that to be afraid is to be a slave.'

B. Ζώπυρον τὸν Θρᾷκα is not otherwise known.

ἀνταγωνιστῶν] 'those whom you consider yourself as good as.'

C. ἐθέλεις Baiter and Orelli, Hirschig. ἐθέλοις Winckelmann, Stallbaum, and Hermann, with Β Δ Π, which seems better.

ἕλξεις] Plut. *Alcib.* 198 E mentions this as characteristic of Alcibiades.

αἰσθόμενος] 'Unus solus Bodl. αἰσθανόμενος, quod Hermann non debebat recipere.' Stallbaum.

D. γῆν μὲν γάρ] Stallbaum wishes to read γῆς—one does not see why. ἀμφισβητήσειε] 'rival' or 'contend with.'

E. εἰσέρχεται κ.τ.λ.] The remark is acute. Stallbaum refers to Böckh's *Econ.* i. 32, ii. 138.

123 A. μῦθον] The fable appears again among those which bear the

name of Aesop. It was told by Lucilius in his *Saturae*, as appears from three fragments of his thirtieth book, quoted by Nonius (xxx. 2, 3, 4, ed. Gerlach). Then we find it in the well-known passage of Horace, *Epistles* I. i. 73 *sqq.*:—

> 'Olim quod volpes aegroto cauta leoni
> Respondit, referam : Quia me vestigia terrent,
> Omnia te adversum spectantia, nulla retrorsum.'

τετραμμένα] γεγραμμένα Β Δ Π, another instance of a glaring error in good MSS.

B. ἀξιοπίστου τῶν ἀναβεβηκότων] 'a man worthy of confidence, who had made the inland journey to Persia.' Olympiodorus and the Scholiast think he means Xenophon, who tells the story about 'the queen's girdle' (*Anab.* i. 4). The καλύπτρα might have been invented to match. If Xenophon be alluded to, this is *pro tanto* against the Platonic authorship of the dialogue; for Plato, for whatever reason, never refers to Xenophon or his very remarkable exploit.

C. μητρί] There is little regard to exact historical correspondence here. Xerxes was murdered B.C. 465, and Amestris is said to have survived him; but Alcibiades was not born till 450.

εἰ πάνυ πολλοῦ] 'at the outside.'

Ἐρχίασιν] Ἐρχία or Ἔρχεια was a deme of the tribe Aegeis; but its site appears not to be known.

124 A. Ἄγιδος] Agis the Second, of the Peloponnesian war.

ἠγμένος] 'brought up.' Ἄγω is not common in this sense; *Laws* vi. 782 D is alleged for it: δι' ὧν ἀρετή τε αὐτοῖς ἀγομένοις ὀρθῶς καὶ τοὐναντίον ἀποβαίνει κακῶς ἀχθεῖσι. But this rather means, 'as they are rightly or wrongly impelled by the three great appetites.' Hesychius has (i. 338. 31, Schmidt): ἄφορτος· οὐκ ἠγμένος τὴν Λυκουργείαν ἀγωγήν, 'not educated according to the precepts of Lycurgus.' And Plato has παιδεία μέν ἐσθ' ἡ παίδων ὁλκή τε καὶ ἀγωγὴ πρὸς τὸν ὑπὸ τοῦ λόγου νόμον ὀρθὸν εἰρημένον (*Laws* ii. 659 D). *Laws* vii. 819 A μετὰ κακῆς ἀγωγῆς. 'A drawing and directing of children.' 'Much experience, but misdirected.' In short, neither in the verb nor noun has Plato distinctly the sense of 'educate' or 'education,' something like which is required here; which again goes *pro tanto* to show that the *Alcibiades* is not Platonic.

αἱ τῶν πολεμίων] αἱ is omitted in Β Δ Π, and so Hermann. The Turicenses say that εἰ αἱ is omitted; is this a slip? 'εἰ τῶν O' (the Clarkian), 'εἰ αἱ τῶν V B S T; at insiticium articulum esse non optimorum tantum librorum silentium, sed aliorum quoque vacillatio suadet, qui eundem post πολεμίων ponunt.' Hermann.

τῷ ἐν Δελφοῖς γράμματι] Frequently mentioned in Plato, *e. g. Prota-*

goras 343 B (speaking of the Seven Sages) γράψαντες ταῦτα, ἃ δὴ πάντες
ὑμνοῦσι, Γνῶθι σαυτὸν καὶ Μηδὲν ἄγαν.

B. ἡμῖν εἰσὶν ἀντίπαλοι] 'ἡμῖν ante ἀντίπαλοι optimorum (B Δ Π)
'fide expuli ; iisdem vero ducibus mox εἰ μή περ pro vulg. εἰ μή scripsi,
sicut etiam sequente ἄν Aristoph. Nubb. 1184 : εἰ μή περ γ' ἅμα αὐτὴ
γένοιτ' ἂν γραῦς τε καὶ νέα γυνή.' Hermann. B Δ Π vary considerably,
but all give περ.

It may be worth while, with regard to the question of authenticity, to
bring together the points which make against Plato's authorship.
These are :—

The incorrect expression as to the descent of the Heraclidae (120 E).

The introduction of Argos *à propos des bottes* (121 A).

The word μαγεία (121 E), and the explanation, ἔστι δὲ τοῦτο θεῶν
θεραπεία, unless we consider this a marginal gloss.

The allusion to Xenophon, if Xenophon be intended (123 B).

The use of ἡγμένος (124 A).

And lastly—though it is easy to deceive oneself on this head—
a certain difference from Plato, not so much in the style, as in the
way the argument is put.

REPUBLIC.

Book I. Beginning—331 D.

The dialogue of the 'Republic,' as the work is generally called, or the
'State,' as we should rather say now-a-days, is supposed to take place
at the Piraeeus, in the house of the aged Cephalus, father of Polemarchus
and of Lysias the celebrated orator. He is an old family friend of
Socrates. The beginning, here given, speaks for itself. Socrates converses with Cephalus upon the inconveniences of age and the advantages
of wealth, and incidentally the question is started, What is Justice? An
answer to this is sought, until in the fourth Book Justice is determined
to be 'the doing of one's own business,' that is, the arrangement of the
State so that every man shall have his own sphere and his own duties.

It should be remembered that for the *Republic, Timaeus, Critias,* and
Laws, A is our chief MS. authority. For the *Republic* we have the
admirable editions of Schneider.

Cephalus, father of Polemarchus and of the celebrated orator Lysias,
was a native of Syracuse or Thurii. He is said to have come to Athens
at the instance of Pericles, and to have lived there thirty years.

Polemarchus is mentioned in the *Phaedrus* (257 B) as a student of
philosophy. He is said to have been put to death by the Thirty.

Glaucon and Adeimantus were the brothers of Plato. In the *Apology* (34 A) Adeimantus is adduced as a witness by Socrates, to prove that his brother Plato has not been corrupted by his teacher. From this Steinhart (*Platon's Leben*, p. 42) fairly infers that Adeimantus was the elder brother. At the beginning of the *Parmenides* both are mentioned casually. Throughout the *Republic* they alternately conduct the dialogue with Socrates, except in the first or introductory book.

From the place in the *Parmenides* it would appear that Perictione, the mother of Plato, had married a certain Pyrilampes (the name belongs to the family) after the death of Ariston, the father of Adeimantus, Glaucon, and Plato. Of this marriage nothing is otherwise known. This circumstance, and various chronological difficulties, led Schleiermacher, and others after him, to the hypothesis that Plato intended *two* different pairs, of each a Glaucon and an Adeimantus, that in the *Parmenides* belonging to an older generation. This entirely groundless supposition only leads to greater difficulties. We cannot here enter into the controversy, which may be found discussed in Steinhart, p. 45 *sqq.*

Glaucon and Adeimantus, though similar, are also contrasted. Glaucon is an impetuous youth, who knows the world, is full of wit and penetration into character, but does not always take the soberest view of things. ' The character of Adeimantus is deeper and graver, and the profounder objections are commonly put into his mouth. Glaucon is more demonstrative, and generally opens the game; Adeimantus pursues the argument further. Glaucon has more of the liveliness and quick sympathy of youth; Adeimantus has the maturer judgment of a grown-up man of the world.' Jowett, Introduction to *Republic*, p. 9.

Niceratus, son of the celebrated Nicias, 'was put to death by the thirty tyrants, to whom his great wealth was no doubt a temptation. Theramenes, in his defence, as reported by Xenophon, mentions the murder of Niceratus as one of the acts which tended necessarily to alienate all moderate men from the government.' (Smith's *Dictionary of Biography*.) His name has often been mentioned, since the publication of Wolf's *Prolegomena*, with reference to a curious passage in the *Banquet* of Xenophon (iii. 5), where he says; 'My father was anxious about my education, and compelled me to learn Homer off by heart; καὶ νῦν δυναίμην ἂν Ἰλιάδα ὅλην καὶ Ὀδύσσειαν ἀπὸ στόματος εἰπεῖν.' Antisthenes tells him, so can any blockhead of a rhapsodist. To a good memory the task would hardly be even difficult.

Thrasymachus is 'the sophist, madly vain of dubious lore.' In the First Book he expresses wild and cynical opinions, such as that force is the *ultima ratio* of all social and political arrangements. He is thoroughly put down by Socrates.

The Euthydemus here mentioned and Charmantides are otherwise obscure. Cleitophon lends a name to one of the spurious dialogues.

327 A. χθές] Socrates is supposed to repeat a conversation of the day before to Timaeus, Critias, Hermocrates, and a fourth unknown person, as appears from the beginning of the *Timaeus*, which forms a sequel to the *Republic*. The beginning of the dialogue is very abrupt; in the other works of Plato we are always informed who are the interlocutors. Here we should not know but for the *Timaeus*.

τῇ θεῷ] That is, as appears farther on (354 A), the Thracian Bendis, who was identified with Artemis. Timaeus says *s. v.* Βένδις· ἡ Ἄρτεμις· Θρακεῖα φωνή· καὶ Βενδίδια, Ἀρτέμιδος ἑορτὴ παρὰ Θρᾷξιν (p. 53 Ruhnken[2]).

νῦν πρῶτον] We need not be solicitous to fix a date for an imaginary dialogue, as many commentators are anxious to do. Plato, like all good writers of fiction, cares nothing for anachronisms, if they suit his convenience. The place where Amestris is mentioned in the extract from the *Alcibiades* would be a case in point, if the dialogue be Platonic. Any of Scott's historical novels will furnish similar examples. In the *Abbot*, for instance, Queen Mary, then newly arrived at Lochleven, is represented sometimes as prematurely aged by care and imprisonment, as she may have been in subsequent years; sometimes as what she really was, a woman in the height of her beauty and fascination, and about twenty-five years old. So in the *Fair Maid of Perth* the combat on the North Inch and the death of the Duke of Rothsay are brought together, to produce a fine dramatic effect; but Rothsay was not murdered till six years later, A.D. 1402. Similarly, in another place, Scott confesses to having ascribed, in *Ivanhoe*, an imaginary offspring to Edward the Confessor.

ἡ τῶν ἐπιχωρίων πομπή] 'The procession of the townsfolk,' *i.e.* of the people of the Piraceus. Such a procession, no doubt, as we see on the Panathenaic frieze of the Parthenon.

B. ἕ] 'him,' *scil.* Polemarchus.

μου—τοῦ ἱματίου] We have first the more general 'me,' without specifying how he is touched, and then the definition 'by the cloak,' both directly after λαβόμενος. Cf. *Parmenides* 126 A καί μου λαβόμενος τῆς χειρὸς ὁ Ἀδείμαντος.

αὐτός] Emphatic, 'his master.' See *Protagoras* 314 D *supra*.

C. ὅσοι ἐσμέν] Plato uses the same jest elsewhere, *e. g. Philebus* 16 A ἆρ', ὦ Σώκρατες, οὐχ ὁρᾷς ἡμῶν τὸ πλῆθος, ὅτι νέοι πάντες ἐσμέν, καὶ οὐ φοβεῖ, μή σοι μετὰ Φιλήβου ξυνεπιθώμεθα;

οὐκοῦν—ἀφεῖναι] Stallbaum and Hermann put the mark of interrogation after ἀφεῖναι. Turicenses and Schneider the full stop.

ἔτι ἐλλείπεται A and other books, and so Hermann. ἔτι ἓν λείπεται Turr., Stallbaum, Schneider.

ὡς—μὴ ἀκουσομένων] 'Then we are not going to listen; of that you may be assured.'

·328 A. λαμπάς] We are very much in the dark as to the precise manner of this race, and the information given in the text is not greatly supplemented by what we can gather from other passages. *Laws* vi. 776 B γεννῶντάς τε καὶ ἐκτρέφοντας παῖδας, καθάπερ λαμπάδα τὸν βίον παραδιδόντας ἄλλοις ἐξ ἄλλων. Lucretius ii. 78 (taken from the last passage evidently)—

> Inque brevi spatio mutantur saecla animantum,
> Et quasi cursores vitaï lampada tradunt.

'A little while, and all living things are changed; the torch of our race of life is passed from hand to hand.' To these should be added the whole description at the beginning of the *Agamemnon* of Aeschylus.

παννυχίδα] 'pervigilium,' such a nocturnal festivity as we find described in the *Pervigilium Veneris*, a beautiful poem of latish date, which may be found in Weber's *Corpus Poetarum Latinorum*, or Buecheler's separate edition.

B. διὰ χρόνου κ.τ.λ.] 'it was a long time since I had seen him;' the regular meaning of διὰ χρόνου.

C. ἐν τῇ αὐλῇ] The central court of a Greek house, round which the other buildings were grouped.

εὐθὺς—ἰδών] 'the moment he saw me.' Observe the force of the aorist.

οὐδὲ θαμίζεις] 'Amice expostulabundus cum Socrate senex hoc dicere videtur: tu neque alia facis, quae debebas, neque nostram domum frequentas.' Schneider. Why Baiter writes οὐ δέ I do not know. The words may have been suggested by *Iliad* xviii. 385-6—

> τίπτε Θέτι τανύπεπλε ἱκάνεις ἡμέτερον δῶ
> αἰδοίη τε φίλη τε; πάρος γε μὲν οὔ τι θαμίζεις.

There is a similar place in the *Laches*, 181 C, where the aged Lysimachus reproves Socrates for not keeping up old friendships (Sch.).

ἐν δυνάμει ᾖ] The editions have ἦν (Turicenses, Schneider, Stallbaum, Hirschig). ᾖ Bekker and the smaller Zürich edition (after Π). Both are genuine forms, and both stand for original *āsām. ᾖ for *εσα, with the terminal consonant dropped, as in the sigmatic aorist (ἔγραψα). See Curtius, *Das Verbum der Griechischen Sprache*, i. 172.

D. νεανίαις] νεανίσκοις Stallbaum with Π.

E. ὅ τί σοι φαίνεται τοῦτο] 'what you think on this point.' In this phrase τί is regularly neuter, whatever the gender of the subject. τί σοι φαίνεται ὁ νεανίσκος; *Charmides* 154 D.

ἐπὶ γήραος οὐδῷ] *Il.* xxii. 60 and elsewhere in Homer. (Me, Priam)—

δύσμορον, ὅν ῥα πατὴρ Κρονίδης ἐπὶ γήραος οὐδῷ
αἴσῃ ἐν ἀργαλέῃ φθίσει κακὰ πόλλ' ἐπιδόντα.

πότερον χαλεπὸν τοῦ βίου] There may be a little doubt as to the exact juncture of the words. Stallbaum translates '*etwas Schweres vom Leben,*' 'a hard part of life,' comparing *inter alia Apology* 41 C ἀμήχανον ἂν εἴη εὐδαιμονίας, but does not say whether he takes χαλεπόν as accusative after ἐξαγγέλλεις, or as nominative without a verb; perhaps the latter is preferable. He understands that his way differs from Schneider's; but I am not sure that there is any material difference; Schneider only says, 'Genitivus refertur ad τοῦτο eodem modo, quo dicebant; τοῦτο θαυμάζω τοῦ βίου seu θαυμάσιον ἡγοῦμαι τοῦ βίου.'

329 A. οἶόν γέ μοι] οἷόν γ' ἐμοί Bekker and Schneider.

διασώζοντες—παροιμίαν] The proverb ἧλιξ ἥλικα τέρπει. *Phaedrus* 240 C ἥλικα γὰρ καὶ ὁ παλαιὸς λόγος τέρπειν τὸν ἥλικα.

ξυνιόντες codices, Turicenses, Schneider, Hermann. ξυνόντες Stallbaum, from Ast's correction, approved by Buttmann. The second reading is perhaps smoother. But in such places, where there is no variety of reading, and no change pressed upon us, should we make any alteration? Perhaps those who read ξυνόντες have an idea that the other word may be suggested by συνερχόμεθα.

B. ἐπὶ τούτῳ] 'In hoc, dum in argumento sermone suo versantur; German. dabei.' Stallbaum. 'In hoc' Schneider, Latin version. 'Deswegen' (on that account) his German translation. 'And make this a ground for reproaching old age,' Davies and Vaughan. 'In dieser Beziehung' (in this respect = on that account), Müller. 'With that,' 'therewith,' is surely the meaning, which answers to Stallbaum's 'dabei.'

καὶ οἱ ἄλλοι πάντες] 'As,' we say, using a relative word, where the Greek has a simple copula.

C. ὦ ἄνθρωπε] Very much like our 'friend.'

ἀσμενέστατα] ἀσμεναίτατα Stallbaum, with Π.

αὐτό] 'that,' singular, answering to plural just before. 'Quod quidem in hac responsione tanto rectius fieri potuit, quod res venereae cum contemtione quadam commemorantur. Hipp. ma. p. 299 A τὰ δέ που περὶ τἀφροδίσια πάντες ἂν μάχοιντο ὡς ἥδιστον ὄν, δεῖ δὲ αὐτό—οὕτω πράττειν.' κ.τ.λ. Stallbaum.

ἐπειδὰν κ.τ.λ.] The meaning is clear, but there is some difficulty about the construction. ἐπειδὰν γάρ the inferior books, ἐπειδὰν A. 'At vide ne protasis per ἐπειδὰν instituta duplici apodosi includatur vel duo enunciata a παντάπασι incipientia velut appositione quadam inter se juncta sint.' Hermann (see his quotations).

D. ἔστι] Stallbaum wishes to expunge, and the words construe quite well without it; but we have only to put a colon after γίγνεται, and there is no need of alteration. Schneider in both editions, Turicenses, Hermann, and Baiter in his third edition (1858) retain.

τούτων πέρι] We have here something of the periphrastic use of περί with a word, the phrase scarcely meaning more than the word itself.

εὔκολοι] 'εὔκολος Sophocles vocatur ab Aristophane *Rann.* v. 82.' Stallbaum. The line is—

ὁ δ' εὔκολος μὲν ἐνθάδ', εὔκολος δ' ἐκεῖ.

μετρίως] 'not very,' 'not so.'

βουλόμενος—ἐκίνουν] 'wanting to draw him out.'

E. φασιν] Alluding to some proverbial phrase; Muretus suggests an iambic τοῖς πλουσίοις πόλλ' ἐστὶ τὰ παραμύθια, as I understand him (*apud* Stallbaum).

λέγουσι—τι] 'they are partly right.'

330 A. Σεριφίῳ] We have the story in Herodotus (viii. 125), but the carper there is one Timodemus of Aphidnae, one of the most northerly Attic demes, and the point is a little different. 'Had I been born in Belbina' (an insignificant islet off Sunium), 'I should not have been famous, nor you, if you had belonged to Athens itself.' Plato may be quoting from memory, or giving another version of the story.

οὔτ' ἂν ὁ ἐπιεικὴς πάνυ τι ῥᾳδίως] This passage goes much against the opinion of those who think that οὐ πάνυ is one consolidated phrase, and really positive in sense. We have here the words in the usual meaning, but separated. Schneider well says; 'De significatione nescio, an huiusmodi locos neglexerint, qui οὐ πάνυ sicut οὐ φάναι per conversionem dici statuunt; haec enim commodius ita intelliguntur, ut sonant.'

B. ποῖ' ἐπεκτησάμην;] 'Acquired, did you say?' See Heindorf on *Charmides* 174 B, and note on *Lysis* 208 B *supra*.

ὁμώνυμος] Such alternating repetitions of names were very common. 'Sic Nicias, Nicerati filius, Niceratum habuit filium. Sic in Lyside Lysis, Democratis filius, Lysidis nepos. Sic Aristoteles, Nicomachi filius, filium suum Nicomachum vocavit.' Muretus ap. Stallbaum.

οὗ τοι ἕνεκα] οὗ τοι A and other books.

C. καὶ κατὰ τὴν χρείαν] They love money as having made it, and also on account of its utility, like other people. Aristotle uses very similar language, possibly thinking of this place: *Eth. Nic.* iv. 1. 20 ἐλευθεριώτεροι δὲ εἶναι δοκοῦσιν οἱ μὴ κτησάμενοι ἀλλὰ παραλαβόντες τὴν οὐσίαν· ἄπειροί τε γὰρ τῆς ἐνδείας, καὶ πάντες ἀγαπῶσι μᾶλλον τὰ αὑτῶν ἔργα, ὥσπερ οἱ γονεῖς καὶ οἱ ποιηταί. And ix. 7. 3.

E. τέως] 'till then.' Timaeus s. v. explains πρὸ τοῦ, ἢ ἕως τινός. See Ruhnken's commentary, where many passages are given, *e. g. Phaedo*

117 C καὶ ἡμῶν οἱ πολλοὶ τέως μὲν ἐπιεικῶς οἷοί τε ἦσαν κατέχειν τὸ μὴ δακρύειν.

στρέφουσιν] 'begin to make him waver,' 'take hold upon him.'

δ' οὖν] 'But, however that may be, he becomes,' etc. This use of οὖν in the sense of 'but still' is not uncommon. *Timaeus* 28 B ὁ δὴ πᾶς οὐρανὸς ἢ κόσμος ἢ καὶ ἄλλο ὅ τι ποτὲ ὀνομαζόμενος—σκεπτέον δ' οὖν περὶ αὐτοῦ πρῶτον. Stallbaum.

331 A. Πίνδαρος] *Fr.* 198 Bergk³. Plato would seem to have given the words an application of his own, as the quotations of the same place by Plutarch and Synesius seem to show that the verses applied simply to one who had led a happy life. See Schneider's note. Bergk would divide the lines thus:—

> Γλυκεῖά οἱ καρδίαν ἀτάλλοισα γηροτρόφος συναορεῖ
> ἐλπίς, ἃ μάλιστα θνατῶν πολύστροφον γνώμαν κυβερνᾷ.
>
> 'Sweet Hope beside him walks, the nurse of age,
> The nourisher of the heart, chief piloteer
> Of mortals' wavering wishes.'

B. τὸ γὰρ—συμβάλλεται] 'Itaque τὸ cum infinitivis casu nominativo accipiendum, quae ratio per anacoluthiam explicanda est.' Stallbaum. The construction is not finished, but the whole clause is resumed in τοῦτο following. 'And the great blessing of riches, I do not say to every man, but to a good man, is, that he has had no occasion to deceive another, either intentionally or unintentionally; and when he departs to the other world he is not in any apprehension about offerings due to the gods or debts which he owes to men. Now the possession of wealth contributes greatly to truth and honesty.'

ἀλλά γε ἓν ἀνθ' ἑνός] So the codices and editions (Turr., Hirschig, Schneider) except Stallbaum, who would read ἕν γε, as the words appear in the commonplace-book or collection of fine passages of Stobaeus. Stallbaum's notion is that ἀλλά γε cannot go together; why? 'Nam ἀλλά γε nullo interposito vocabulo apud probos scriptores nusquam reperias.'

C. τὴν ἀλήθειαν] 'in very truth.' Adverbial accusative.

οἷον τοιόνδε λέγω] 'like this, I mean.'

εἰ μανεὶς ἀπαιτοῖ] Sc. ὁ φίλος. This sudden change of subject is common in all Greek, when the reference is clear. In Homer it is regular in the same line. *Od.* vii. 171—

> ὅς οἱ πλησίον ἷζε, μάλιστα δέ μιν φιλέεσκεν.

'Laodamas, who sat next to him, and was his favourite son.' *Gorgias* 510 B 'Were there a person in the city much superior to himself, οὐκοῦν φοβοῖτο ἂν αὐτὸν δήπου ὁ τύραννος καὶ τούτῳ ἐξ ἅπαντος τοῦ νοῦ οὐκ ἄν ποτε δύναιτο φίλος γενέσθαι;' That ὁ βελτίων is the nominative in the last clause appears from what follows.

ἐθέλων] One might expect the article; but we are to supply a subject (we have had ὁ ἀποδιδούς just before, which suggests one); 'nor would a person in such a position be justified if he were to tell the entire truth to the madman.' ἐθέλων therefore is only the qualificative.

D. οὗτος ὅρος] 'This is not the definition of justice.' We may regard either word as the predicate. The pronoun is attracted into the gender of the noun.

Σιμωνίδη] Polemarchus explains, in the passage immediately following, that Simonides said ὅτι τὰ ὀφειλόμενα ἑκάστῳ ἀποδιδόναι δίκαιόν ἐστι.

Book II. 376 E—end.

The discussion as to the nature of Justice has been continued. Glaucon and Adeimantus eloquently defend the cause of Justice, but cannot define wherein it consists. Socrates then proposes that Justice be sought, not in the individual, but in the State; and that to this end an ideal State be created in the discussion, and legislated for. Thus is introduced the main subject of the dialogue. After providing for the more pressing wants of the citizens, the question comes to be who are to fight their battles, and preserve the new State from extinction. This brings in the consideration of the φύλακες, or guardians, who are to be the dominant and warrior class of the community, and to whom the rest of the *Republic* is mainly devoted. What is to be the manner of their education? Pretty much the old manner, to which we have always been used: gymnastic and 'music.' But one thing important to be guarded against meets us at this point. We must not allow our guardians, in their youth, to have their minds corrupted by false tales concerning the gods; our poets must not speak in the manner of Homer and Aeschylus, but according to strict rules which we lay down. These τύποι or rules are discussed in the following extract.

Plato here only enforces what all the idealizing philosophers had said before him. Many of the myths were *prima facie* immoral; and no means existed of ascertaining their origin, or disentangling their primary meaning. The lines of Xenophanes are well known;

Πάντα θεοῖς ἀνέθηκαν Ὅμηρος θ' Ἡσίοδός τε
ὅσσα παρ' ἀνθρώποισιν ὀνείδεα καὶ ψόγος ἐστί,
καὶ πλεῖστ' ἐφθέγξαντο θεῶν ἀθεμίστια ἔργα,
κλέπτειν, μοιχεύειν τε καὶ ἀλλήλους ἀπατεύειν.

(Fr. vii. ed. Karsten. *quem vide*.)

E. μουσική is to be taken in the widest sense, and really implies the whole both of intellectual knowledge and of mental and moral cultivation.

εἰπών Schneider in both editions, Hermann, Turicenses, with most MSS. εἶπον Stallbaum after Ast with some MSS. Schneider seems right in retaining the participle; 'hujus musicae, inquit, quam dixisti, sermones esse statuis, an non?' The construction would be quite clear if we had μουσικὴν εἰπὼν μουσικῆς τίθης λόγους; 'when you say μουσική, you make λόγοι a part of this?' but for the sake of brevity and euphony the word is used only once, and then in the case which seems most required.

377 A. ὡς τὸ ὅλον εἰπεῖν κ.τ.λ.] 'The whole of these, you may say, are falsehood, yet there is a part of truth.'

τοῦτο δὴ ἔλεγον] 'that is what I was saying.'

B. πλάττεται—τύπος] 'is the shape fixed and assumed.' ἐνσημήνασθαι, 'to imprint.'

ἐπιστατητέον] 'we must be masters over,' 'we must take order with' the makers of fables.

C. καλόν sc. μῦθον, which is to be supplied from τοῖς μυθοποιοῖς.

ἐγκριτέον—ἀποκριτέον] 'must be accepted,' 'included,'—'rejected,' 'excluded.'

ἢ τὰ σώματα ταῖς χερσίν] One would like a parallel for this curious notion.

D. τὸν αὐτὸν τύπον εἶναι] The addition of αὐτῶν would make the construction complete.

οὐδέ] 'I do not understand you; no, not your major instances.'

E. τὸ μέγιστον—ψεῦδος] 'that greatest of all lies in high places.'

Οὐρανὸς κ.τ.λ.] Hesiod, *Theogony* 154 sqq. 178 sqq. The same tale is referred to in the *Euthyphron*, p. 5 E, where Euthyphron excuses his own conduct to his father by the example of that of Zeus to Cronus, and of Cronus to Uranus.

378 A. χοῖρον] The pig was the regular offering before initiation at Eleusis. Aristoph. *Peace* 373 sqq. ἐς χοιρίδιόν μοί νυν δάνεισον τρεῖς δραχμάς. δεῖ γὰρ μυηθῆναί με πρὶν τεθνηκέναι.

ὅπως—συνέβη] The want of the ἄν is noticeable. Are we to go back to the ἄν, misplaced in the usual manner, of οὐδ' ἄν εἰ ἦν ἀληθῆ, line 48?

B. πολεμοῦσί τε κ.τ.λ.] He has now passed from Hesiod to Homer.

C. ποικιλτέον] 'such things must not be represented in embroidery.' The best commentary, as Stallbaum well remarks, is the place in the *Euthyphron*, 6 B καὶ ὑπὸ τῶν ἀγαθῶν γραφέων τά τε ἄλλα ἱερὰ ἡμῖν καταπεποίκιλται, καὶ δὴ καὶ τοῖς μεγάλοις Παναθηναίοις ὁ πέπλος μεστὸς τῶν τοιούτων ποικιλμάτων ἀνάγεται εἰς τὴν ἀκρόπολιν. Similar tapestries are described in the *Ion* of Euripides, 1146 seqq.

[λεκτέα] 'Om. Par. A. Ven. Ξ. Vind. Φ. Vat. r. et pr. Vat. Θ.'

That is to say the best codices. 'Alii libri post μᾶλλον ponunt. Uncis secluserunt Turr. eiecit Hermann. Nobis genuinum videtur et per errorem transmissum.' Stallbaum. One can hardly agree with him. The word seems introduced to smooth the construction, which is a little rough without it, but perfectly intelligible.

D. εὐθὺς] from the beginning, from their youth up. 'Tales of that kind ought to be told to the young both by old men and by old women and by those who are getting up in years.'

ὑπὸ υἱέος] Hephaestus to wit. The story does not occur in any extant writer, but we are told it was found in Pindar and Epicharmus. The fullest version may be found in Pausanias, i. 20, 3. 'There is also a story among the Greeks, that Hera threw forth Hephaestus when he was born, and that he in revenge sent her a gift of a golden chair with invisible chains. She sat down, and was bound fast; and Hephaestus would listen to none of the gods, until Dionysus, his closest friend, intoxicated him and brought him to heaven.' (*ap.* Schneider.)

ῥίψεις] *Il.* i. 586 *sqq.*

ὑπονοίαις] lit. 'undermeanings,' *i.e.* allegorical interpretations. Only here in Plato, but found in his expositors. This allegorical explanation of the myths, the great resource of the earlier philosophers from things apparently shocking or impious, is especially connected with the name of Anaxagoras. In the *Ion*, 530 D, Metrodorus of Lampsacus, Stesimbrotus of Thasos, and a certain Glaucon, are mentioned as eminent Homeric expositors, and we know that their expositions were of this kind.

379 A. τύπους] 'models' or 'stiles.'

θεολογίας] 'the account of the gods,' the body of tales about the gods.

ἀποδοτέον] 'this must be ascribed to him.'

ἐάν τε ἐν μέλεσιν] These words do not appear in Α Θ Ξ etc. They have much the air of being added to make up the various possibilities of poetry.

B. τί δέ; ὠφέλιμον κ.τ.λ.] τί δαί; A. In such minute points, as we have seen from the example of B, we cannot trust even the good MSS.

C. οὐδ' ἄρα κ.τ.λ.] God cannot be the origin of evil. Stallbaum well compares x. 617 E (*infra*), where each soul chooses its own lot: αἰτία ἑλομένου· θεὸς ἀναίτιος. The same idea is to be found in the well-known lines of the *Odyssee* (i. 32–4),

> ὦ πόποι, οἷον δή νυ θεοὺς βροτοὶ αἰτιόωνται·
>
> ἐξ ἡμέων γάρ φασι κάκ' ἔμμεναι· οἱ δὲ καὶ αὐτοὶ
>
> σφῆσιν ἀτασθαλίῃσιν ὑπέρμορον ἄλγε' ἔχουσιν

αἰτιατέον] 'we must esteem the cause.' *Phaedo* 98 B ὁρῶ ἄνδρα— ἀέρας καὶ αἰθέρας καὶ ὕδατα αἰτιώμενον καὶ ἄλλα πολλὰ ἄτοπα, 'alleging as cause.'

D. δοιοὶ πίθοι] *Il.* xxiv. 527-8 *seqq.*; the words in Homer are considerably different ;

> δοιοὶ γάρ τε πίθοι κατακείαται ἐν Διὸς οὔδει
>
> δώρων οἷα δίδωσι, κακῶν, ἕτερος δὲ ἐάων.

See La Roche on the place.

E. ταμίας] No such passage occurs in our present Homer. Twice in the *Iliad* (iv. 84. xix. 224) we have the line,

> Ζεύς, ὅς τ' ἀνθρώποις ταμίης πολέμοιο τέτυκται.

In the *Odyssee* (iv. 392) we have the line,

> ὅττι τοι ἐν μεγάροισι κακόν τ' ἀγαθόν τε τέτυκται.

This, we are told by Diogenes Laertius (II. v. 21), on the authority of Demetrius (Phalereus?), was a favourite verse of Socrates, who applied it in the sense of ' Know thyself,' *Tecum habita.* Can we suppose that Plato, quoting from memory, mixes up these different places? The sentiment is Homeric enough : *e g.* besides the passages quoted,

> οὔ νύ τ' ἀοιδοὶ
>
> αἴτιοι, ἀλλά ποθι Ζεὺς αἴτιος, ὥστε δίδωσιν
>
> ἀνδράσιν ἀλφηστῇσιν, ὅπως ἐθέλῃσιν, ἑκάστῳ.

Od. i. 347-9. And other places.

δι' Ἀθηνᾶς κ.τ.λ.] *Il.* iv. 68 *sqq.*

380 A. Θέμιτος] *Il.* xx. 4 Themis is made to summon the meeting of the gods in which Zeus gives them permission to take sides in the battle below. The whole twentieth book, called Θεομαχία, is referred to. Observe the Attic form Θέμιτος. Pindar has θέμιτος (Krüger *s. v.* Grammar 1), Herodotus θέμιος.

Αἰσχύλος] *Fr.* 160 Dindorf (Νιόβη), 151 Nauck. Plato seems clearly to mean that these are verses of the *Niobe.*

τὰ Πελοπιδῶν ἢ τὰ Τρωϊκά] The legends of Troy, and of the house of Pelops, are often mentioned in Greek writers as the great centres of tradition. ' Presenting Thebes, or Pelops' line, Or the tale of Troy divine.'

αὐτοῖς] ' they (the poets) must look about for an explanation.'

B. ὅτι ἐδεήθησαν] comes in construction after ὡς ἄθλιοι οἱ κακοί.

διαμαχετέον] Schneider in both editions, Turicenses, Hermann. διαμαχητέον Stallbaum. Schneider well points out that, just as the vowel of the future and aorist fluctuates in quantity, so does that of the verbal, and that both forms are correct, the MSS. being to be followed in each case.

εὐνομήσεσθαι] πόλις is the subject.

D. ὁ δεύτερος ὅδε] *scil. δοκεῖ σοι.*

τοτὲ μέν—τοτὲ δὲ κ.τ.λ.] The opposition seems to be between an actual transformation and one which is only illusory. See below 381, E, 382 E.

νῦν γε οὕτως] 'offhand,' 'all at once.' *Phaedrus* 235 C νῦν μὲν οὕτως οὐκ ἔχω εἰπεῖν.

E. ὑπὸ μὲν ἄλλου] There is no clause strictly answering to this. We have two alternatives; a thing must be moved by something else or by itself. The first is here being considered, and is indicated by μέν; the second is taken up farther down, ἀλλ' ἆρα αὐτὸς αὐτὸν μεταβάλλοι etc. (l. 171).

εἰλήσεων] 'heats of the sun.' εἴλησις· ἔκκαυσις Timaeus *in Lexico.* A word may be said as to the etymology. εἴλη, 'the sun's heat,' is found in good authors. ἔλη, in the same sense, and εἰλεῖν, 'to be warm,' are given by Eustathius. Immediately related are ἐλάνη, 'a torch,' and probably Ἐλένη (*Svaranā), 'the bright one' = Bertha. The root is originally *svar, to be bright or burn, which appears in Σείριος, σέλας, σελήνη etc. (see Curtius, *Etymologie* R. 663, p. 541[4]). ἠέλιος, ἥλιος is from an entirely different root, *us, to burn (Curtius R. 612, p. 401[4]). ἀλέα, ἀλεάζω, ἀλεαίνω are doubtless related.

381 A. [καὶ ἀμφιέσματα] These words do not appear in A and other good MSS., and seem a manifest addition.

B. δῆλον—ὅτι, εἴπερ ἀλλοιοῦται] 'It is clear that this must be the case, if he changes at all.'

C. οὕτως ἔχοντος] neuter, 'this being the case.' Such absolute genitives, common in the case of persons, are also found even in the case of impersonal neuters. (Matthiae § 683. Kühner[2] § 486. 2. p. 641. vol. ii.) Xenophon, *Hipparchicus* iv. 2 ἀδήλου ὄντος εἰ πολεμίοις ἐντεύξει πορεύῃ ποι, κ.τ.λ. (K.) Thucydides i. 74 σαφῶς δηλωθέντος, and Krüger's note.

D. θεοὶ ξείνοισιν κ.τ.λ.] *Od.* xvii. 485-6.

Πρωτέως καὶ Θέτιδος] For Proteus see *Od.* iv. 417 *sqq.* There was also a satyric play of Aeschylus called Proteus, which was appended to the extant trilogy of the Oresteia. Two lines remain, and words are occasionally quoted from it by the glossators. Homer only says that Thetis was wedded against her will; *Il.* xviii. 433; but some story of her transformations may have been told in the Hesiodic Ἠοῖαι. The scholiast on Pindar, *Nemea* iii. 35 (καὶ ποντίαν Θέτιν κατέμαρψεν | ἐγ- κονητί sc. Πηλεύς) mentions these changes, and quotes from a satyric play of Sophocles (fr. 162 Dindorf[5]) the words (probably of Peleus),

> τίς γάρ με μόχθος οὐκ ἐπεστάτει; λέων
> δράκων τε, πῦρ, ὕδωρ.

For ἐπεστάτει ἐπεστρατεύετο Nauck. Some such correction seems required.

ἀγείρουσαν] 'collecting.' as we might say, going about as a mendicant priestess. Herodotus iv. 35 ὑμνέειν Ὦπίν τε καὶ Ἄργιν, οὐνομάζον- τάς τε καὶ ἀγείροντας. ἀγύρτης and ἀγύρτρια are well known words;

there are also μητραγύρτης, 'mendicant priest of Cybele,' and μηναγύρτης, 'monthly beggar.' There has been a great deal of disputing as to the authorship of the verse (see Schneider *ad locum* and Ruhnken's long note on *Timaeus, s. v.* ἀγείρουσαν), but it now appears that it was taken from the Ξάντριαι or 'Carderesses' of Aeschylus. The discussion will be found summed up in Dindorf⁵ (*Fr.* 170), who thus restores the passage from various quotations:

ὀρεσσιγύνοισι
Νύμφαις κρηνιάσιν κυδραῖσι θεαῖσιν ἀγείρω,
Ἰνάχου Ἀργείου ποταμοῦ παισὶν βιοδώροις.

E. ἐκδειματούντων] the imperative.

ἰνδαλλόμενοι] This epic word occurs in two other passages of Plato and once in Aristotle.

μὴ γὰρ] We are to supply the imperative again.

ἴσως] This is a good example of the force of the adverb, which varies in sense from 'doubtless' to 'the thing is possible.' Here we might render 'may be,' 'very likely,' the point in question being really admitted.

382 A. τῷ κυριωτάτῳ] 'in the most important part,' *i. e.* the soul, as is explained presently.

B. σεμνὸν] something grand and mysterious. Compare for the sense *Gorgias* 458 A οὐδὲν γὰρ οἶμαι τοσοῦτον κακὸν εἶναι ἀνθρώπῳ, ὅσον δόξα ψευδὴς περὶ ὧν τυγχάνει νῦν ἡμῖν ὁ λόγος ὤν. Aeschylus, *Prom. V.* 685-6

νόσημα γὰρ
αἴσχιστον εἶναί φημι συνθέτους λόγους.

C. πότε καὶ τῷ] τῷ = τίνι; So the best codices and our four editions. An old reading was τί χρήσιμον;

καὶ τῶν καλουμένων φίλων ὅταν] Hermann reads from his own conjecture οἳ ἄν, which no doubt makes the construction smooth. Schneider, Turicenses, Stallbaum ὅταν. Stallbaum explains the genitive as anticipating the ἕνεκα which is about to follow; but Schneider seems more right in removing the comma after φίλων, and understanding τινές. Perhaps the best way to put it is to say that ὅταν—ἐπιχειρῶσι is equivalent to τοὺς ἐπιχειροῦντας or οἳ ἂν ἐπιχειρῶσιν, and that φίλων is a partitive genitive; 'and against those of our friends who' etc. Hermann, from his reading, appears to understand the place so.

D. ταῖς μυθολογίαις] ταῖς best MSS. 'in legendary tales, of which we were speaking a little ago.' If it were omitted, as in old editions, and Ast, there would be a trifling difference of sense.

ποιητὴς κ.τ.λ.] 'Then there is no lying poet in God.' Cf. *Phaedo* 77 E ἀλλ' ἴσως ἔνι τις καὶ ἐν ἡμῖν παῖς, ὅστις τὰ τοιαῦτα φοβεῖται. 'But there is the child in us, who fears annihilation.'

E. τὸ δαιμόνιόν τε καὶ τὸ θεῖον] 'the superhuman and divine.' The words are hardly meant to be contrasted, but the use of both heightens the generalization. When they are distinguished, δαιμόνιον would belong to the lower rank of deities.

[οὔτε κατὰ φαντασίας] The words are not found in the best MSS. (A Θ etc.), and seem a marginal addition.

σημείων πομπὰς] 'the sending of portents.'

οὔθ' ὔπαρ οὔτ' ὄναρ] 'neither in waking vision nor in dream.' The opposition of these words dates from Homer (*Od.* xix. 547); 'Take courage, daughter of renowned Icarius; this is no dream, but a soothfast vision, which surely shall be fulfilled.' οὐδ' A and MSS. Turicenses, Schneider; οὔτ' Bekker, Stallbaum and Hermann with one MS. οὐδέ is doubtless to be preferred; see Schneider's long and acute note. 'Nor indeed.'

383 A. ποιεῖν] 'make poetry.'

ὡς μήτε αὐτοὺς γόητας ὄντας κ.τ λ.] The construction is free, but not really difficult. We have first an example of the so-called accusative absolute. Kühner² § 488 d. note 6, p. 653, explains such constructions with ὡς, which are common, by saying that the accusative with its participle may be regarded as the object of a verb *declarandi aut sentiendi*, which is implied in the ὡς. Here it would be 'we must think of them not as enchanters, by reason of transformations.' ὄντας does not appear in Paris A, although Θ Π Ξ and others have the word. Secondly, for παράγειν we should strictly have παράγοντας; but the writer changes from the construction he had adopted to the infinitive, which would have been perfectly regular in itself.

τὴν τοῦ ἐνυπνίου πομπὴν] See the beginning of the second book of the *Iliad*.

B. ἐνδατεῖσθαι κ.τ.λ.] Aesch. *Fr.* 281 Dindorf⁵. It is not known from what play these lines are taken; they have been referred to the Ὅπλων κρίσις, the 'Award' of Achilles' arms, in which we know that Thetis was a personage. A line remains (*Fr.* 175 D⁵), in which she is addressed as δέσποινα πεντήκοντα Νηρήδων χοροῦ. ἐνδατεῖσθαι seems here to mean 'to sing of, part by part,' *carmine perpetuo celebrare*, a use to which it would be hard to find a parallel. The quotation is at first incorporated with the words of the speaker, and afterwards continued independently; but so much is conceded to the tragic style, that ἑάς is used instead of the prose ἅς. We may suppose the first line to have run originally ὁ δ' ἐνεδατεῖτο τὰς ἐμὰς εὐπαιδίας. In Homer we find Apollo mentioned as singing at the marriage of Peleus and Thetis: *Il.* xxiv. 62-3. Hera says

πάντες δ' ἀντιάασθε θεοὶ γάμου· ἐν δὲ σὺ τοῖσι
δαίνυ' ἔχων φόρμιγγα, κακῶν ἕταρ', αἰὲν ἄπιστε.

These verses may have furnished a theme for Aeschylus. Perhaps they allude to some longer poem on the marriage of Thetis, such as is ascribed to Hesiod.

ξύμπαντά τ' εἰπὼν] If these words had not happened to scan, one would have been tempted to think them the prose of Plato; 'to cut a long story short, he said that no one was ever more the favourite of heaven.'

παιῶν] Doubtless Aeschylus had παιᾶν', the form he regularly uses, which appears in some MSS. A reads παίων.

τὸν παῖδα τὸν ἐμόν] Schneider ingeniously suggests that as Socrates began by weaving the quotation into his prose, so here in these words he passes over to prose again; but, as he himself confesses, this is not needful to be supposed.

Stallbaum gives several parallels to the repetition of αὐτός, *e.g.* Aeschylus, *Eumenides* 798 Dindorf⁵, αὐτός θ' ὁ χρήσας αὐτὸς ἦν ὁ μαρτυρῶν.

Book III. 405 C—408 C.

Gymnastic exercise, and plain living, will be all our art of medicine; our guardians are to be tough dogs, who have no leisure to be sick. Look at the surgery of the Asclepiads in Homer; there you have the true heroic practice. The wound is stanched, and simples applied, and there an end. We will have none of such life in death as Herodicus the trainer lived; he had no constitution, but contrived, by infinite doctoring, to live to a good old age, when by rights he ought to have been dead. The founder of medicine, Asclepius, was all for a kill or cure treatment; he was a politician, and would not keep alive persons who are useless, and who cannot think for five minutes without getting a headache. And they are not to be heard, who say that he brought a man back from the brink of the grave for a great fee.

C. ὅτι μὴ] 'unless indeed.'

D. ἐπετείων] 'seasonable' diseases, incidental to the time of year. The other Platonic passages are not quite similar; *Rep.* v. 470 B τὸν ἐπέτειον καρπόν, 'the year's corn.' *Laws* xii. 955 D τὴν ἐπέτειον ἐπικαρπίαν.

οἵαν διήλθομεν] Indulgence in sweet sauces, Syracusan cookery, and so on.

ῥευμάτων τε καὶ πνευμάτων] 'flowings and blowings,' a jocular description of colds and cholics, as appears from what follows. 'They get stuffed with wind and water, like standing ponds and give the ingenious sons of Asclepius the trouble of inventing new names like "flatulencies" and "catarrhs."' The 'marsh,' or 'quagmire,' is apparently supposed to be full both of water and gas; and so the translators understand.

ἐμπιπλαμένους] 'Platoni ubique ἐμπίμπλημι, ἐμπίμπρημι restituendum est.' Schanz, Preface to first six books of the *Laws*, p. xvii. His proofs do not admit of compression.

κομψούς] As usually in Plato, has a flavour of irony.

E. υἱεῖς] In the eleventh Iliad, Machaon (v. 507) and afterwards Eurypylus (583), are both wounded by the arrows of Alexander, the one in the shoulder, the other in the thigh. Nestor brings Machaon to his tent, where the slave Hecamede prepares a posset for them (638 *sqq.*), of Pramneian wine, goat's cheese, and barley; but Eurypylus is not present; Patroclus afterwards meets him (809), cuts out the arrowhead (844-8), and sprinkles simples on the wound (xv. 394). The quotation is therefore incorrect; or rather, Plato handles the passages as suits his convenience. In the *Ion*, 538 C, the giving of the posset by Hecamede to Machaon is mentioned as we have it in our Iliad. The other son of Asclepius in the Iliad is Podaleirius.

The construction is; ὅτι οἱ υἱεῖς αὐτοῦ οὐκ ἐμέμψαντο τῇ δούσῃ πιεῖν Εὐρυπύλῳ ἄλφιτα πολλὰ ἐπιπασθέντα κ.τ.λ. ἐπ' οἶνον Πράμνειον.

406 A. Πατρόκλῳ] Patroclus, *uti supra*, tends Eurypylus, but no son of Asclepius has anything to do with this.

παιδαγωγικῇ] 'nursing' or 'education' of diseases.

Of course we are not to take the account of Herodicus too literally. He was of Selybria, a Thracian town on the Propontis, not very far from Byzantium. His name occurs several times in Plato.

B. ἄλλους—πολλούς] His patients to wit.

παρακολουθῶν] 'humouring' or 'accommodating' himself to.

ἐν ἀσχολίᾳ—ἰατρευόμενος] 'never having leisure for anything but doctoring himself.'

καλὸν ἄρα—ἠνέγκατο] The words are half ironical.

C. δοκούντων] 'who are called,' 'who pass for.'

D. καύσει ἢ τομῇ χρησάμενος] 'by application of the hot iron or the knife.' Plato joins together cautery and excision as the main resources of Greek surgery.

μικρὰν δίαιταν] So Schneider and the Zürich editors, with A and the codices. Stallbaum and Hermann μακρὰν, with the correction of one MS. This is a good example of a case in which it might fairly be argued that the MSS. are not to be followed; μακράν is simple and tempting. But it is more easy to imagine μικράν corrupted to μακράν than reversely; μικράν is more difficult, and, as Schneider says, 'magis exquisitum et supra librariorum captum,' meaning, as I understand, 'a finicking regimen,' which interpretation is supported by 407 D below, διαίταις κατὰ σμικρὸν ἀπαντλοῦντα καὶ ἐπιχέοντα, 'by delicate processes of evacuation and infusion.'

εἶπεν] 'he says,' the aorist of repeated occurrence.

προκειμένης ἐργασίας] 'the work to hand,' 'the task before him.'

407 A. οὗ—ἀβίωτον] 'which if he does not, he ought to die.'

Φωκυλίδου] The line appears to have run, as restored from other citations (see Bergk, *Fragmenta*[3] fr. 10), Δίζησθαι βιοτήν, ἀρετὴν δ', ὅταν ᾖ βίος ἤδη. Plato, as often, has given the words of the poet a new sense.

οὐκ ἀκούεις] 'non audis, *i. e.* probas,' Stallbaum, and so Davies and Vaughan and Müller; but surely the sense is rather 'did you never hear of ?' So Schneider's German version. The use of the present is the same idiomatic use as in ὥσπερ ἐγὼ λέγω, 'as I was saying.' πῶς φησί supports this rendering.

τοῦτο] the practice of virtue.

B. τεκτονικῇ—τῇ προσέξει τοῦ νοῦ] the double dative after ἐμπόδιον need cause no difficulty, being a variation of the σχῆμα καθ' ὅλον καὶ μέρος, 'a hindrance to carpentering and the rest,' 'to giving attention to these.'

ναὶ μὰ τὸν Δία κ.τ.λ.] ἐμποδίζει or ἐμπόδιόν ἐστι is to be supplied to the whole sentence.

The repeated article (ἡ περιττή) is not uncommon in Plato; see Stallbaum's parallels, *e.g. Gorgias*, 502 B τί δὲ δὴ ἡ σεμνὴ αὕτη καὶ θαυμαστὴ ἡ τῆς τραγῳδίας ποίησις; (where the Zürich editors put a comma after θαυμαστή, making the phrase less notable).

ἑδραίους] 'continuous.' He cannot be depended upon for any long time. The other places where the word occurs, *Timaeus*, 64 B, 59 D, give the sense of 'steady,' 'immovable.' Schneider's Latin has 'stabiles,' his German 'die Führung eines öffentlichen Amtes daheim,' which is not like his usual severe closeness. Others (Müller, Davies and Vaughan) understand 'sedentary,' another common acceptation of the word, *e. g.* Xen. *Lac.* i. 3 οἱ πολλοὶ τῶν τὰς τέχνας ἐχόντων ἑδραῖοί εἰσι, 'most artificers are sedentary.'

δύσκολος] *i. e.* ἐπιμέλεια.

C. διαστάσεις with almost all the MSS. Schneider and the Zürich editors. διατάσεις Stallbaum and Hermann. διατάσεις would be 'over-straining,' 'tensions,' διαστάσεις 'splitting.' Schneider very clearly explains the state of the case. 'Sed διάτασις ipsam potius intentionem et contentionem (*Anspannung*) quam statum significare, διάστασις autem perturbationem et quasi dissidium capitis, cuius latera velut in diversas partes discedere moliantur, non inepte describere videtur. Harpocratio; διαστῆσαι· ἀντὶ τοῦ διαταράξαι καὶ οἷον ἀδύνατον ποιῆσαι. Ἀντιφῶν ἐν τῷ περὶ τῆς μεταστάσεως.' He goes on to say that διατάσεις might more easily have been corrupted into διαστάσεις than *vice versa*, and that he almost assents to the correction (Stephanus suggested διατάσεις). The question is interesting, because the MSS. are for the one reading, and Greek and sense rather for the other; and accordingly the best editors are divided.

It is not quite clear how these sentences are to be allotted to the two speakers. Is Socrates to begin again at καὶ γὰρ πρὸς οἰκονομίας, or τὸ δὲ δὴ μέγιστον? Perhaps it is best to suppose that Socrates speaks from καὶ γάρ.

ὅπῃ ταύτῃ] So A and others. 'Dein codd. meliores praeter Vat; ἀσκεῖται καὶ δοκιμάζεται,' as in the text. (Stallbaum.) Schneider, and Stallbaum with a trifling difference of pointing, read ὥστε ὅπη αὕτη, ἀρετῇ ἀσκεῖσθαι καὶ δοκιμάζεσθαι πάντη ἐμπόδιος.

ὠδίνοντα—λήγειν are to be closely joined. 'It keeps a man fancying that he is ill, and makes him live in perpetual solicitude about his body.'

νόσημα—ἐν αὑτοῖς] 'who have in their bodies some local malady.' ἀποκεκριμένον, 'partial,' 'separate' from the rest of the body. So Stallbaum. Or simply 'distinct.' *Vereinzelte* Müller. *Bestimmte* Schneider, 'certum aliquem et destinatum morbum' *id*. 'Specific' Davies and Vaughan.

D. τούτοις] Having begun with the accusative, as if ἰάσασθαι or θεραπεῦσαι were to follow, he changes to the dative on account of καταδεῖξαι.

καταδεῖξαι] 'Verbum de artium inventoribus proprium.' Stallbaum. 'revealed the healing art,' Davies and Vaughan; 'die Arzneikunst gelehrt hat,' Schneider.

φαρμάκοις—δίαιταν] 'Such as these he cured by purgations and operations, and bade them live as usual.'

τὰ δ' εἴσω κ.τ.λ.] The construction is quite regular, but instead of θεραπεύειν or ἰᾶσθαι we have the equivalent μακρὸν καὶ κακὸν βίον ἀνθρώπῳ ποιεῖν, after which the sentence goes on regularly.

κατὰ σμικρὸν—ἐπιχέοντα] The words have been cited already. 'By graduated processes of evacuation and infusion.'

E. περιόδῳ] the ordinary 'course' or 'tenor' of life. I do not know any passage where περίοδος occurs in exactly the same sense. The word is common in Plato, but always means a 'circuit' or 'revolution,' generally in a technical sense; and indeed here we might think of the 'round' of life.

οὔτε αὑτῷ οὔτε τῇ πόλει λυσιτελῆ] Is λυσιτελῆ singular or plural? If singular, αὑτῷ is to be read; and so Turicenses, Hermann, Stallbaum. If plural, then αὐτῷ, 'the man himself,' as Schneider, with Paris A and other MSS. (as I understand him), though this is not a case where the authority of codices would go for much; so Müller. Schneider puts the case with his usual admirable acuteness. 'Me, ut pluralem statuerem, duo moverunt ; primum, quod ex ista curatione potius, quam ex morbo, ad ipsum aegrotum pariter atque ad civitatem redundans damnum hoc loco commemorandum erat ; alterum, quod λυσιτελής, quanquam *Phaedr.* p. 239 B de homine dicitur (τὰ μὲν οὖν κατὰ διάνοιαν ἐπίτροπός τε καὶ κοινωνὸς οὐδαμῇ λυσιτελὴς ἀνὴρ ἔχων ἔρωτα) tamen multo frequentius res utiles operaeque pretium habentes indicat. Pluralem autem neutrius ad unam quidem, sed minime simplicem actionem verbo θεραπεύειν significatam referri posse nemo infitiabitur.' But in spite of this, one is tempted to think the singular more obvious.

καὶ οἱ παῖδες αὐτοῦ] After these words we have in Θ and other codices δεικνύοιεν ἄν, which seems an obvious interpolation. They have been added to make a construction for ὅτι τοιοῦτος ἦν. Something corresponding in meaning is to be understood. 'That he was such is clear, if you consider the qualities of his sons,' &c.

408 A. αἷμ' κ.τ.λ.] *Il.* iv. 218 αἷμ' ἐκμυζήσας ἐπ' ἄρ' ἤπια φάρμακα εἰδὼς πάσσε, sc. Μαχάων, who alone is spoken of in this passage. Podaleirius is twice mentioned in the *Iliad*, with his brother; ἰητῆρ' ἀγαθώ ii. 732, ἰητροί xi. 833.

B. αὐτοῖς l. 90] So Λ Π Turicenses, αὐτοῖς Stallbaum and others.

ἐπὶ τούτοις] 'for people of that sort.' The plural after the singular νοσώδη need cause no surprise.

Μίδου] The wealth of Midas, as of Gyges, was proverbial. Stallbaum quotes Tyrtaeus (12. 5 Bergk³) οὐδ' εἰ Τιθωνοῖο φυὴν χαριέστερος εἴη, πλουτοίη δὲ Μίδεω καὶ Κινύρεω μάλιον (formerly βάθιον, but merely on conjecture). The same lines are alluded to in *Laws* ii. 660 E ἐὰν δὲ ἄρα πλουτῇ μὲν Κινύρα τε καὶ Μίδα μᾶλλον, κ.τ.λ.

οἱ τραγῳδοποιοί] Aeschylus, *Agamemnon* 1022 Dindorf⁵,

> οὐδὲ τὸν ὀρθοδαῆ τῶν φθιμένων ἀνάγειν
> Ζεὺς αὖτ' ἔπαυσ' ἐπ' εὐλαβείᾳ,

where the readings vary much. The scholiast on that passage (ap. Dind.) says Hippolytus was the person restored to life, and this legend is followed by Vergil, *Aen.* vii. 765 *sqq.*

καὶ Πίνδαρος] *Pyth.* iii. 54

> ἀλλὰ κέρδει καὶ σοφίᾳ δέδεται.
> ἔτραπεν καὶ κεῖνον ἀγάνορι μισθῷ χρυσὸς ἐν χερσὶν φανείς
> ἄνδρ' ἐκ θανάτου κομίσαι
> ἤδη ἁλωκότα κ.τ.λ.

C. θανάσιμον one would prefer to understand 'at the point of death,' with most authorities, which is the ordinary use of the word. Others understand 'dead,' which occurs in Sophocles, *e. g. Ajax* 517

> Ἄιδου θανασίμους οἰκήτορας,

in conformity with the account of Aeschylus and Pindar; but Plato, as regularly, gives the story a turn to fit his own purpose; the moribund suits him better than the dead man.

Book III.   414 B—end.

We now come to the famous passage describing the 'noble lie.' All our fictions were to be strictly regulated by truth and morality: but one great exception we must have, one lie transcendant. We will impress upon our new citizens that their youth and education was all a dream, and that they are autochthonous, children of Earth, who has mingled various metals in their composition, according to the place each man is to fill in the state; and the position of each is to depend, not upon that of his parents, but upon the metal which predominates in his own commixture.

This false myth, or lie superlative, is really Plato's way of passing lightly over the subject in hand, without coming down to details. What he does enounce is really at bottom something like the principle of the 'open career,' '*la carrière ouverte aux talents,*' but no farther mention is made of it, and the lower classes of citizens are not at all considered in the remaining books of the Republic.

' We may now relinquish our fable to tradition. Our guardians are to be housed as becomes soldiers, and disciplined by education so as not to prey upon the community, of which they are the protectors. They must have no property, no private house ; they will receive from the State only such a modest stipend as may provide them with necessaries; they shall be interdicted the use of gold and silver; they themselves are framed of undefiled gold.'

414 B. τῶν ἐν δέοντι γιγνομένων] 'of necessary lies,' 'lies at a pinch.'

ὧν δὴ νῦν ἐλέγομεν] before, p. 389 B.

γενναῖόν τι] There is a certain equivoque in the word ; it means at once 'a noble lie,' 'a lie in which there is no baseness,' and 'a lie indeed,' 'a lie with a witness.'

C. Φοινικικόν τι] 'an old Phoenician story.' Φοινικικὸν ψεῦδος in later times became a common phrase ; but nothing of the kind need be understood here. Eustathius p. 1757, l. 59 (mixing up the two meanings) καὶ ψεῦδος δὲ Φοινικικόν, ἀπὸ τῶν κατὰ τὸν Κάδμον τὸν Φοίνικα καὶ τὸν δράκοντα καὶ τοὺς σπαρτοὺς μυθικῶς λεγομένων, ὥς φησι Παυσανίας. Plato seems to refer to the legend of the σπαρτοί, who sprang from the sown teeth of the dragon.

οὐδ' οἶδα εἰ γενόμενον ἄν] 'and not likely to happen.'   οὐδὲ γενόμενον ἄν would be regular, the participle for the optative in the indirect oration ; and so would οὐδ' οἶδ' ἂν εἰ γένοιτο ; the two are here compounded, or rather the οἶδα εἰ of the one is transplanted into the other, the main construction remaining unchanged.

συχνῆς πειθοῦς] 'Ad σ. π. int. ὄν.' Stallbaum.

D. ὁποίᾳ—ποίοις] 'Relativum cum interrogativo junctum non est quod mireris. *Gorg.* p. 500 A; ποῖα ἀγαθά—καὶ ὁποῖα κακά.' etc. Stallbaum.

ἃ—ἐτρέφομεν may be noticed ; ' our nurture of them.'

ὥσπερ ὀνείρατα—περὶ αὐτούς] 'They are to be informed that their youth was a dream, and the education and training which they received from us are appearances only.' The sense is clear, but there is a double construction which cannot be called grammatical. ἐδόκουν ταῦτα πάντα πάσχειν is quite regular, ταῦτα πάντα being in the accusative, but these two words must again be supplied as nominative to ἐδόκει (which must be repeated from ἐδόκουν) γίγνεσθαι. The expression is obviously abbreviated to avoid the repetition of the same words.

δημιουργουμένη, though in concord with the word nearest it, belongs in sense also to ὅπλα.

E. [καὶ] ἡ γῆ] Stallbaum after Ast would leave out the καί. Hermann writes *e suo* ὡς ἡ γῆ, which makes everything smooth. The Zürich editors leave the word, and Schneider with some doubt. καί is certainly very harsh, and perhaps can only be defended if we suppose a total change of structure after ἀνῆκε. Schneider's suggestion, that, if καί is to stand, we are to take it as correlative with καὶ νῦν following, does not commend itself to me.

πάλαι] 'a little ago.'

415 A. ἐπίκουροι] 'subsidiary.'

τὸ μὲν πολύ] Generally the offspring would be of the same class, golden, silver, and so on, as the parents ; but occasionally, as all are brothers and of one origin, gold would produce silver, silver gold, and so forth.

B. ὅτι αὐτοῖς—παραμέμικται] 'They must watch and see what proportion of each element is blended in each soul.'

C. φυῇ] This not very common aorist may be noted.

D. αὐτοὶ οὗτοι] ' this first generation.'

σχεδὸν γάρ—ἀγάγῃ] 'I see your difficulty ; and the creation of this belief we will leave to tradition.' 'Und wie es nun damit werden wird, das wird die Sage bestimmen.' Schneider. 'Enough of the fiction, which may now fly abroad upon the wings of rumour.' φήμη is the common report or tradition of men, *vox populi vox Dei*, which is believed because universal, much the same as the Homeric ὄσσα ; ἥ ὄσσαν ἀκούσῃς ἐκ Διός, ἥ τε μάλιστα φέρει κλέος ἀνθρώποισιν (*O.I.* i.

282). The sense of 'oracle' is quite out of place, though Müller (after Ficinus) seems to understand so; 'Doch Das will den Erfolg haben, den der Götterspruch ihm verleihen wird.' Davies and Vaughan are vague, not to say wrong; 'However, we will leave this fiction to its fate.'

416 A. κακουργεῖν has a great air of being either a gloss upon ἐπιχειρῆσαι, or the addition of some one who did not know ἐπιχειρεῖν in the sense of 'fall upon,' 'assault,' but took the word to mean simply 'attempt.' κακουργεῖν is regularly, and according to analogy, followed by an accusative. I do not find any mention of its being omitted in the books. (Baiter ed. 3 leaves the word.)

B. ἀντὶ ξυμμάχων κ.τ.λ.] The words seem at first abrupt; but Stallbaum well says: 'Deinde qui verbis ἀντὶ ξυμμάχων praefixerunt καί, ii non recordati sunt sententias explicationis gratia additas vulgari loquendi consuetudine copulam non additam habere.'

τὴν μεγίστην τῆς εὐλαβείας] 'Dictum pro τὴν μεγίστην εὐλάβειαν, ut ἡ ὀρθοτάτη τῆς φρονήσεως, ὁ πολὺς τοῦ χρόνου,' etc. Stallbaum.

τοῦτο—διϊσχυρίζεσθαι] 'We need not insist upon that point at present.'

C. παύσοι—ἐπαροῖ] So Stallbaum and Hermann. Turicenses and Schneider παύσοι—ἐπάρῃ.

D. μηδὲν belongs in sense also to οἴκησιν.

ἀθληταὶ πολέμου] 'Dictum ut p. 403. E: ἀθληταὶ μὲν γὰρ οἱ ἄνδρες τοῦ μεγίστου ἀγῶνος.' Stallbaum.

E. ταξαμένους] After δεῖ ζῆν some lines back.

ὅσια] This use of the plural is most frequent in the case of verbal adjectives, but is not confined to them. *E. g.* Thucydides, IV. i. 2 ἀδύνατα ἦν ἐν τῷ παρόντι τοὺς Λοκροὺς ἀμύνεσθαι. See Kühner² ii. 60.

417 A. τὸ—ἀκήρατον] The clause is added as a kind of after-thought.

B. πολιτῶν is genitive after ξυμμάχων.

Book V.   472 B—474 B.

Socrates has to face three great 'waves' of difficulty, which arise from the doctrine that all things are to be in common. The first is met by admitting that men and women of the guardian class must have common pursuits and common exercises; the second by instituting, under certain regulations, community of wives and children. 'The third and greatest wave now comes upon me, which I must face, although I be drowned in laughter and ridicule; "either philosophers must become kings, or kings philosophers." O Socrates, what a drubbing you will get from the respectable classes!'

472 B. **ἀλλὰ τί τοῦτό γ';**] Turicenses, Hermann, with Par. A. Stallbaum and Schneider omit γ' with most MSS. Stallbaum objects that γε is not used in this combination; but Schneider, though he does not put it in the text, well says that it is as defensible as many similar cases.

ἐὰν εὕρωμεν] 'If we have discovered the nature of justice.' In the Fourth Book it is elicited that justice is τὸ τὰ αὑτοῦ πράττειν.

C. **εἰ γένοιτο**] I should prefer to point off, with Schneider (as in the text), and understand 'supposing such a person can exist.' Stallbaum and the translators take it, 'We inquired whether he could exist.' But almost the next words are, that we made this inquiry for the sake of a παράδειγμα, an ideal, without considering its possibility. Stallbaum finds a difficulty in the καί before οἷος ἂν εἴη; but scarcely of necessity.

D. **τὴν ἐκείνοις**] l. 15. Turicenses, Stallbaum, Hermann. ἐκείνης Schneider with Par. A. and many others, which seems preferable. The genitive, though rarer, is perfectly legitimate after ὅμοιος.

φαμέν is often used in this interjected way, *e. g. Republic* ii. 368 E δικαιοσύνη, φαμέν, ἔστι μὲν ἀνδρὸς ἑνός, κ.τ.λ. The word is really pleonastic here, the sense being only 'do we say,' *i. e.* 'you remember' or the like. The French '*n'est-ce pas*' or the German '*nicht wahr*' would be fair equivalents. '*Wie nun ?*' says Schleiermacher.

E. **τὸ μὲν τοίνυν—διομολόγησαι**] The sense is; 'The fact is then, that my inventions are none the worse because I cannot show the possibility of their being realized; but suppose I am willing to stretch a point, and endeavour to prove this, to oblige you, you must readmit your former admissions.'

473 A. **ἆρ' οἷόν τε—τῳ δοκεῖ**] 'Can an idea be ever realized? Does it not rather stand to reason that the actual, whatever a man may think, can never come up to the conception?' φύσιν ἔχει, 'is it natural?' where our idiom would rather say, 'is it not natural?' An affirmative answer is implied. The phrase is common; *e. g. Rep.* vi. 489 B οὐ γὰρ ἔχει φύσιν κυβερνήτην ναυτῶν δεῖσθαι ἄρχεσθαι ὑφ' αὑτοῦ. 'We must not expect a pilot to run about asking sailors to be under his command.' Join the words πρᾶξιν ἐφάπτεσθαι ἀληθείας ἧττον λέξεως.

οὕτως l. 33] 'as I say.'

φάναι] Infinitive in the sense of imperative. This construction, common in the epic language (more rare in third person), is found not rarely in other poets, and even in Herodotus and the Attic prosators. (Kühner² § 474 a.) A good example is Thuc. V. ix. 5 σὺ δέ, Κλεαρίδα,— αἰφνιδίως τὰς πύλας ἀνοίξας ἐπεκθεῖν καὶ ἐπείγεσθαι ὡς τάχιστα συμμῖξαι.

B. **τοῦτον τὸν τρόπον**] the form we have been imagining, the best possible.

C. **τῷ μεγίστῳ—κύματι**] The three most startling features of the new polity are announced under the figure of three great waves, the last or τρικυμία being the greatest, *viz.* the doctrine that either the philosophers must be kings, or else the kings turn philosophers.

προσεικάζομεν (ll. 49, 50) Turicenses after Stobaeus. προσηκάζομεν Schneider. προεικάζομεν Paris A, and most codices, which Stallbaum and Hermann follow. προηκάζομεν Bekker. Schneider says: 'mihi verbum προεικάζομεν huic loco convenire non videtur;' he thinks the comparison was made so recently that the προ- is inappropriate; but the comparison may fairly be supposed to date from the first mention of a wave at all; 457 C. Either reading makes very good sense; but the authority is all for προ-.

κατακλύσειν] *sc. ἐμέ.* κῦμα ἐκγελῶν is a poetical phrase. 'Even though the overflowing of the laughing wave shall drown me in laughter and dishonour.'

D. ἢ οἱ βασιλῆς—ἱκανῶς] 'or the kings and princes of this world have the spirit and power of philosophy.'

τῶν δὲ νῦν—ἀποκλεισθῶσιν] 'and those commoner natures who follow either to the exclusion of the other are compelled to stand aside.'

οὐδὲ—μήποτε] Join the οὐ and μή of these two words, to make a compound negative.

E. ἄλλῃ τις] Turicenses and Hermann from one MS. ἄλλη τις Schneider, Stallbaum. The sense of course is much the same in either case; but ἄλλη need cause no difficulty if we remember that ἰδίᾳ καὶ δημοσίᾳ is a very common phrase, such as are often used somewhat carelessly, and that a state may well be said to be prosperous in its individual members. This is also the smoothest way of taking the words.

ῥῆμά τε καὶ λόγον] 'dictum and doctrine,' or 'expression and sentiment.' Perhaps no great distinction is intended.

474 A. οὕτως l. 67] 'at once,' 'without more ado.'

οἷον] 'as it were.'

θεῖν—ἐργασομένους] 'will run at you might and main, intending to do Heaven knows what.'

B. ἐμμελέστερον] 'perhaps I can accommodate you with a better answer than another.'

Book VI. 487 A—489 C.

Socrates, there is no answering you; but we have a notion that we are being circumvented all the same. We are like bad draught-players, who are driven into corners, and finally defeated, through unskilfulness. But one thing we do know, that philosophers in real life appear as very strange beings, not to say downright villains. You think you have got me into a difficulty; but I will answer you with one of my usual apologues. I will compare the philosopher to a pilot, who is a very good pilot, but rather deaf and parcel-blind, and so is unable to control his mutinous crew, who bind him fast, and manage matters their own way, and treat him with every kind of abuse and contumely.

487 A. πρὸς—ταῦτα] To the description of the philosophic character, which has preceded.

B. παραγόμενοι] A has παραγενόμενοι, an obvious error. 'Praeterea notanda est enuntiati anacoluthia, quandoquidem post ἡγοῦνται—παραγόμενοι, institutae orationis tenore derelicto infertur μέγα τὸ σφάλμα καὶ ἐναντίον τοῖς πρώτοις ἀναφαίνεσθαι.' Stallbaum.

ἐπὶ τελευτῆς τῶν λόγων] Join. We might possibly understand τῶν λόγων as also coming after σφάλμα, in a double construction.

φέρωσιν appears only in one MS. (Vind. E of Schneider), the other books all having φέρουσιν. The necessity of the change is obvious.

C. ἀποκλείεσθαι] 'can play no further.' φέρωσιν, 'move,' as we say. ἐπεὶ τό γε—ἔχειν] Yet all this, they are sure, is but juggling with words, and proves nothing as to the truth.

D. τοῦ πεπαιδεῦσθαι ἕνεκα κ.τ.λ.] Cf. the *Gorgias*, p. 485 A sqq., where Callicles, the fine gentleman and man of the world, says that philosophy is excellent, nay indispensable, for lads who are pursuing their education, but that it becomes ridiculous in a grown man.

ἀλλοκότους] 'strange beings.' The etymology of κότος is obscure. The simple word is only found in the sense of 'anger'; but if we suppose it to have meant originally 'temper,' 'mood' (in which case we might compare the double sense of ὀργή and of the English 'mood'), ἀλλόκοτος would mean 'of other temper,' which suits well with its ordinary use. παλίγκοτος would be 'of reverse mood,' 'contrary-minded,' as we see it in such phrases as κληδόνας παλιγκότους, 'conflicting rumours.' In Homer we have ζάκοτος, 'moody,' 'surly.' ἐπίκοτος (Aeschylus) means 'enraged.' ἔγκοτος means 'having a grudge,' or, as a substantive, 'a grudge.' νεόκοτος is generally understood to mean simply 'new'; but in the places of Aeschylus, who alone uses the word, it may well signify 'with new anger,' 'with new disaster.' The notion that -κοτος in compounds becomes a colourless termination is hardly borne out by the passages. (Pott, *Wurzelwörterbuch*, iv. 257 R. 1620 refers to Sanskrit *kvathati*, 'he boils,' which does not correspond according to Grimm's law. See his remarks.)

E. ἀκούοις ἄν really means 'I tell you.'

οὐκ εἴωθας κ.τ.λ.] Ironical, of course.

488 A. ὡς γλίσχρως εἰκάζω] 'you shall see the leanness of my

imagination,' 'see what a poor hand I am at a parable.' Schneider argues ingeniously for another rendering. 'γλίσχρως εἰκάζων est γλιχόμενος τοῦ εἰκάζειν (ut Phaedon. p. 117 A γλιχόμενος τοῦ ζῆν καὶ φειδόμενος οὐδένος ἔτι ὄντος, cl. Criton. p. 53 E γλίσχρως ἐπιθυμεῖν ζῆν),' etc. Socrates, he goes on to say, is so fond of a simile, that he will give you ever so bad a one, rather than none; which brings us almost to the first interpretation. But in the first place one is not prepared to admit that γλίχομαι has anything to do with γλίσχρος (root γλιτ); Curtius does not connect them (*Grundzüge*, R. 544). Secondly, the other Platonic passages are against Schneider. For *Crito* 53 E see note *supra* on the passage. 'To live in this pitiful manner.' *Cratylus* 414 C καὶ μάλα γε γλίσχρως. 'That is a very scrubby etymology, Socrates.' *Republic* viii. 553 C γλίσχρως καὶ κατὰ σμικρὸν φειδόμενος. 'By shabby and petty pinchings.' This way of taking γλίσχρως is also smoother than the other.

αὐτῶν] The philosophers.

γραφῆς] 'γραφεῖς. Sic libri. Bekkerus sine libris γραφῆς. Conf. p. 484 C.' Stallbaum. In that place the best books (A Θ Π Ξ) have γραφῆς. So in *Republic* v. 473 D (*supra*) A and Π have βασιλῆς.

B. ὑπόκωφον δὲ κ.τ.λ.] 'But somewhat deaf, and parcel-blind to match, and no great adept in navigation.' 'τοιαῦτα] h. e. item βραχύ τι.' Stallbaum.

C. κατατέμνειν] Not 'to cut down,' but 'to cut up,' *i. e.* into small pieces. Cf. *e. g. Republic* x. 609 B μηδ' εἴ τις ὅτι σμικρότατα ὅλον τὸ σῶμα κατατέμοι.

περικεχύσθαι] We pass from the participle to the infinitive, on account of the new series of participles which are about to be introduced. Both constructions come after νόησον.

τὸν δὲ γενναῖον—ξυμποδίσαντας] 'Having first chained up the noble captain's senses with drink or some narcotic drug.' The mandragora or mandrake (*Mandragora officinalis* or *Atropa mandragora*), a plant closely related to our British 'deadly nightshade' or belladonna (*Atropa belladonna*), from which the deadly poison atropine is extracted, furnishes a strong narcotic. The plant is very common in Greece.

D. ἐπαΐοντες] Schneider, Turicenses, Hermann, and so οἰόμενοι below, with Paris A, Θ Π Ξ, etc. The change into the nominative, though strictly speaking ungrammatical, is not without example. *Phaedrus* 241 D ἀλλ' ἤδη σοι τέλος ἐχέτω ὁ λόγος. ΦΑΙ. καίτοι ᾤμην γε μεσοῦν αὐτόν καὶ ἐρεῖν τὰ ἴσα περὶ τοῦ μὴ ἐρῶντος, ὡς δεῖ ἐκείνῳ χαρίζεσθαι μᾶλλον, λέγων ὅσα αὖ ἔχει ἀγαθά. Stallbaum reads ἐπαΐοντας and οἰομένους, without much authority.

ἀρχικὸς] 'one fit to command.'

ὅπως δὲ—κυβερνητικήν] The words ὅπως δὲ—ἐάν τε μή have often been misunderstood. They obviously refer to what follows. The meaning of the whole passage is: 'These mutineers are in a double ignorance. They have no conception of the art of the true pilot; and if they had, they deem such art incompatible with any art or practice of preserving order whether the ship's company consent or no.' τούτου refers to the whole preceding clause. 'They think it impossible to possess at once the pilot's art, and any art or practice of a compulsory maintenance of discipline.'

E. μετεωροσκόπον] Compare the extract from the *Theaetetus*, 173 E. 'A stargazer.'

σφισι I take to be the loose relative dative; see note on *Lysis* 208 D.

489 A. τὴν διάθεσιν comes in sense between πόλεσι and πρὸς τοὺς κ.τ.λ. 'It is like the case of cities in their relation to true philosophers.'

B. λέγει] λέγεις Schneider, Hermann, Turicenses, and almost all MSS. λέγειν some MSS. λέγει Stallbaum (after Bekker and Ast), who understands the nominative to be ἐκεῖνος ὁ θαυμάζων, taken from what precedes, or, if you like, the objector generally. This is very plausible; but almost all the MSS. have λέγεις, which presents no difficulty. τἀληθῆ λέγεις is the address of Adeimantus to the gentleman who makes difficulties. 'And tell him farther, "You say rightly that etc."; but impress upon him,' and so on. There is merely a passing change of person. So Schneider.

C. ὁ τοῦτο κομψευσάμενος] 'the author of that witty saying.' It is ascribed to Simonides by Aristotle (*Rhetoric* II. xvi. 2), and to Aristippus by later writers (Diogenes of Laerte II. iv. 69).

ἄρχεσθαι, line 87, I understand as passive.

Book VII. 514 A—520 E.

In this extract, which contains the celebrated simile of the 'Cave,' Plato describes the passage from ignorance to knowledge. The things of sense which we see are but shadows on the wall, cast by a great fire behind us; and to turn round, and learn to look upon the things themselves (that is, on the Ideas) in the light of day, is a work of the greatest difficulty. And not less painful is the return from light to darkness; but necessity is laid upon those who have seen to give instruction to their purblind brothers.

514 A. σπηλαιώδει] It is said that, before Plato, the Pythagoreans had talked of this life as led in a cave. We have also these words quoted from Empedocles, Ἠλύθομεν τόδ' ὑπ' ἄντρον ὑπόστεγον. (v. 31 ed. Karsten. See his note.)

ὥστε—ὁρᾶν is parenthetical, and does not affect the rest of the construction.

μένειν τε αὐτοῦ] αὐτοὺς Schneider and Turicenses with the books. αὐτοῦ Hermann, after the conjecture of Hirschig on *Wasps* p. 139; and Stallbaum seems to incline the same way. One scarcely sees what is gained by the change.

B. θαύματα] Cf. the extract from the *Laws*, 644 D. παραφράγματα are the barriers which conceal the performers who move the puppets.

515 A. εἰργασμένα goes with each of the preceding adjectives; ' wrought in stone, wood, or whatever it may be.'

οἷον εἰκός refers to what follows, 'some, as you might expect, talking,' etc.

τῶν παραφερόντων is bracketed in some editions of the minor Zürich recension, but not in the third.

ἑαυτῶν τε καὶ ἀλλήλων] ' of themselves individually, and of the rest of their number.'

B. παριόντα] παρόντα almost all MSS. (*e silentio*), Turicenses, and Schneider. Hermann and Stallbaum παριόντα, which necessitates the writing ταὐτά. (ταὐτὰ Paris A; but this is not a point where any MS. goes for much.) 'Sententia igitur haec est; vinctos illos nonne putas nomina rerum, quas conspicerent (conspicere sibi viderentur) ad umbras illarum praetereuntes esse de more translaturos?' Stallbaum. But, as Schneider acutely remarks, the point is not as to the difference between the real things and the shadows; how could they know anything of the distinction? He therefore understands, reading οὐ ταῦτα ἡγῇ ἂν τὰ παρόντα αὐτοὺς νομίζειν ὀνομάζειν, ἅπερ ὁρῷεν; ' Do you not think that they would suppose they were giving names to those things before them, which they saw, as to realities?' There remains a doubt about νομίζειν. The accurate Schneider understands in the sense of ' suppose,' as above. Davies and Vaughan, and Müller understand ' would be in the habit of.' The word in itself is ambiguous; but the context seems to me in favour of the former way. ὀνομάζειν is sometimes bracketed.

C. εἰ φύσει τοιάδε] ' like this in nature '=' a release of this sort,' I understand, φύσει not being at all emphatic. The translators mostly understand ' naturally' or ' in the course of nature,' which seems not at all required. Schneider reads τοιάδε plural.

D. ὀρθότερα βλέποι] Observe the plural and somewhat uncommon form of the comparative adverb. βλέποι Schneider, Turicenses, Hermann. βλέπει Stallbaum, which, although having some little MS. support, is not necessary.

516 A. αὐγῆς] αὐγή or αὐγαί regularly of ' the sunlight,' ' light of day,' from Homer downwards. *Iliad* xiii. 837

ἠχὴ δ' ἀμφοτέρων ἵκετ' αἰθέρα καὶ Διὸς αὐγάς.

Theognis 426 Bergk

μηδ' ἐσιδεῖν αὐγὰς ὀξέος ἠελίου.

Euripides, *Andromache* 935

βλέπουσ' ἂν αὐγάς, 'living.'

καθορῷ Α Θ Π etc. καθορῴη others.

B. μεθ' ἡμέραν] 'by day,' a common Attic phrase, in which μετά with the accusative retains its older sense of 'during.'

ἐπιτροπεύων] 'dominating.'

D. ἐπάρουρον κ.τ.λ.] *Od.* xi. 489 *sqq.* The insertion of a comma after ἄλλῳ makes the sense clearer.

ἢ 'κεῖνά τε Schneider, Hermann. ἢ κεῖνά τε A.

E. σκότους ἂν ἀνάπλεως] σκότους ἀνάπλεως seems to be the reading of all the authorities (*e silentio*). But the want of ἄν can hardly be excused. Schneider omits, but owns it may easily have fallen out, Turicenses omit. Stallbaum suggests σκότους ἂν πλέως, which Hermann puts in his text. Baiter's correction seems best (ἂν ἀνάπλεως). ἀνάπλεως may be 'filled up,' but more likely is 'contaminated.'

γνωματεύοντα] 'estimating,' 'forming an opinion about.' A rare word, perhaps not occurring elsewhere in classical Greek. We have γνῶμα both in the sense of 'sign' and in that of 'judgement.'

517 A. ἀμβλυώττει] Bekker and Stallbaum ἀμβλυώττοι with two MSS. The change seems needless.

καταστῆναι] 'had come round,' 'had become settled.'

τῆς συνηθείας] '*before* he becomes accustomed.'

καὶ ἀποκτείνειαν ἄν;] ἀποκτείνειν ἄν Α Θ Π and many others. κἂν ἀποκτείνειαν Hermann (after Ast). Stallbaum proposes καὶ ἀποκτείνοιεν ἄν. Turicenses and Schneider ἀποκτιννύναι ἄν (vulgate). I understand the latter to mean that εἰ—δύναιντο are parenthetical, and that the infinitive follows on some implied construction which would require that mood. But the correction of the text differs only by one letter from the reading of the best books; and the corruption is most easily explained.

τοῖς ἔμπροσθεν λεγομένοις] In the latter part of the Sixth Book.

B. ἕδραν] ἕδρα generally signifies 'place,' 'position,' 'space' in Plato, and seems here to be used by a kind of attraction of sense to the figure of the sitting prisoners.

θεὸς δέ που κ.τ.λ.] Compare the last words of the *Apology*.

ἐν τῷ γνωστῷ κ.τ.λ.] To make the construction quite regular we must supply φαίνεται before ὁρᾶσθαι.

ἡ τοῦ ἀγαθοῦ ἰδέα] The Idea of Good is the highest result of thought; and at the same time not easily to be distinguished from the Deity, viewed impersonally. See Zeller's *Plato*, p. 279 *sqq*, English version. 'The highest of all Ideas is the Idea of the Good.' 'He says clearly in the Philebus that the Divine Reason is none other than the Good' (p. 282). 'All things considered, we may say that the unity of the Platonic system can only be established on the supposition that Plato in his own belief never really separated the efficient from the logical cause, the Deity from the highest Idea, that of the Good' (p. 285).

C. συλλογιστέα] 'we are to infer about it.' Neuter plural, as appears from the εἶναι. If we had φαίνεται, or some word of the kind, the construction would be regular ; but we have συλλογιστέα εἶναι instead, which again naturally introduces ὡς.

D. σφόδρα γελοῖος] Compare the fine passage in the *Theaetetus*, pp. 173-4, etc., given in the extract *infra*.

περί—σκιαί] 'about the shadows of justice, or, at most, about the images which cast these shadows.'

518 A. σκότος, l. 130] The neuter is good Attic, but not so common as the masculine.

φανότερον—λαμπροτέρου] We may repeat βίον and βίου to these words ; but perhaps they should be more simply viewed as neuters.

B. περὶ αὐτῶν] 'the persons or souls described.' Müller is for omitting the comma after αὐτῶν, and joining the two words to what follows ; which is hardly necessary.

ἐπαγγελλόμενοι] 'giving out,' 'making profession,' a common Attic use. τὰ δὲ πολιτικὰ ἐπαγγέλλονται μὲν διδάσκειν οἱ σοφισταί, πράττει δ' αὐτῶν οὐδείς. *Nicomachean Ethics*, X. ix. 18.

C. ἑκάστου—ἐν τῇ ψύχῃ] 'Phaedon. p. 117 A : ἕως ἄν σου βάρος ἐν τοῖς σκέλεσι γένηται. Symp. p. 215 E : οὐδ' ἐτεθορύβητό μου ἡ ψυχή. quibus locis dativus aeque commodus erat, genitivus autem non pro eo positus aut eius vi praeditus videri debet, quemadmodum Stallbaumio visus est.' Schneider. That is, in all three places the genitive is governed by the noun following. Stallbaum wants these genitives to have also the sense of *dativi commodi*, which is not necessary in this place, or indeed in the two others.

δύναμιν—ὄργανον depend on περιακτέον following. Or perhaps we may say that the words are really in a double construction ; they come after σημαίνει until the phrase περιακτέον εἶναι appears, which at once replaces and confirms σημαίνει.

D. τοῦτο διαμηχανήσασθαι] τοῦτο refers back to τίνα τρόπον ὡς ῥᾷστά τε καὶ ἀνυσιμώτατα μεταστραφήσεται.

τῷ ὄντι γὰρ κ.τ.λ.] 'Parenthesis ita interposita, ut e verbo primarii enuntiati κινδυνεύουσιν pendeat.' Stallbaum.

E. παντὸς μᾶλλον goes together, as regularly.

519 A. πυνηρῶν μέν, σοφῶν δέ] 'rascals, but smart fellows.' ψυχάριον contemptuously, 'his bit of soul.'

ὡs οὐ φαύλην ἔχον] οὐ φαύλην go together.

ἐργαζόμενον] The somewhat unusual use of the participle, instead of the infinitive, may be explained by a kind of attraction to the participle preceding. Stallbaum. For the usage see Kühner [2] ii. p. 1015, note 3, who quotes among other parallels *Cyropaedia* VII. v. 46 τὰ τοῦ πολέμου τοιαῦτα ἐγίγνωσκον ὄντα, ὡs μὴ ὑστερίζειν δέον τὸν ἄρχοντα κ.τ.λ.

κοπτόμενον περιεκόπη] The repeated participle is a rather remarkable example of a construction not uncommon in Attic. A good example is *Apology* 19 B τί δὴ λέγοντες διέβαλλον οἱ διαβάλλοντες; See Kühner's *Grammar* [2] ii. § 490, 3. p. 657 (who gives the example). Here in the reduplication only the simple verb appears, to avoid the clumsy repetition of the compound. εἰ—κοπτόμενον are to be closely joined, and so περιεκύπη—ξυγγενῆ. 'Had this nature been docked at first, and shorn of its congenital infirmities.'

Neither the details of the grammar nor those of the metaphor are quite clear. Freely; 'If, I said, this visual part had in childhood been circumcised of these leaden scales of its nativity, which cling round it, these pleasures of eating and such like indulgences, which drag down the eye of the soul; if these had been removed, and the eye directed to the truth, the clever knave would have seen as keenly in truth as now in deceit.' τὰs τῆs γενέσεωs ξυγγενεῖs Schneider (Didot edition), Hermann, with Paris A. τὰ τῆs γενέσεωs ξυγγενῆ Bekker, Turicenses, Stallbaum, Schneider (edition of *Republic*), who has changed his mind since this his earlier work. The meaning is scarcely different. τὰs may be called an attraction; 'those parts of the eye which are as it were.' In the best MSS. (Paris A Π Ξ etc.) we find περὶ κάτω. Many books have περὶ τὸ κάτω. The authority for τὰ does not appear. The editors, Bekker, Schneider both edds. ('nisi forte etiam περὶ in dubitationem vocare volumus'), Turicenses, Stallbaum περὶ τὰ κάτω. Hermann would omit περὶ τὰ altogether, 'justo audacius,' says Stallbaum. περικάτω, the reading of the best books with the omission of one accent, appears in some of the minor Zürich editions; but the third (Baiter's) has [περὶ τὰ] κάτω.

How are we to take the words among these difficulties? ἐδωδαῖs τε καὶ τοιούτων ἡδοναῖs τε καὶ λιχνείαιs seem to be datives in a somewhat loose construction; 'these weights, in the shape of' etc. προσφυεῖs would seem to mean 'which are accretions to the eye,' comparing the famous passage about Glaucus (*Republic* x. 611 D) ἄλλα δὲ ὁρῶντες προσπεφυκέναι, ὄστρεά τε καὶ φυκία καὶ πέτρας. Those who read περὶ τὰ κάτω take the words with στρέφουσι, 'turn the eye of the soul upon things below,' which seems a strange use of περί. Surely, with that reading, περὶ τὰ κάτω would mean 'surrounding the lower part of the eye,' and στρέφουσι be used in the sense of 'distort,' 'misdirect.'

There is something very tempting in the bold word περικάτω; but it appears to be otherwise unknown. Yet, if ὑποκάτω, why not περικάτω? 'Those leaden weights of sensuality, which hang upon the eye of the soul, and divert its look from above towards the ground.'

C. Ἡμέτερον δὴ ἔργον—τῶν οἰκιστῶν] 'It is the business of us who are the founders of the state.' So Schneider (German and Latin), Schleiermacher. Others understand τῶν οἰκιστῶν to mean 'our colonists,' which seems less likely.

520 B. αὐτόματοι—τροφεῖα] 'They grow up at their own sweet will, and the government would rather not have them. Now the wild plant which owes culture to nobody, has nothing to pay for culture.'

ἡγεμόνας τε καὶ βασιλέας] Xenophon, *Cyropaedia* V. i. 24 βασιλεὺς γὰρ ἔμοιγε δοκεῖς φύσει πεφυκέναι οὐδὲν ἧττον ἢ ὁ ἐν τῷ σμήνει φυόμενος τῶν μελιττῶν ἡγεμών. When was it discovered that the queen bee, which, when young and unimpregnated, leads the 'swarming' of bees, becomes afterwards the mother of the hive? With this place cf. Shakspere, Hen. V. I. ii. 190, 196—

> 'They have a king, and officers of sorts.'
> 'To the tent-royal of their emperor.'

In Aristotle we have very copious notices of bees. He regularly uses the word βασιλεύς in speaking of the queen bee. (The places may be found in Bonitz's *Index*, Berlin Academy edition.) But he says candidly (*De Generatione Animalium*, Bekker 759 a 8), ἡ δὲ τῶν μελιττῶν γένεσις ἔχει πολλὴν ἀπορίαν, which words are succeeded by a very long discussion on the subject. Aristotle is rather in the dark upon the whole; he has not sufficient facts (οὐ μὴν εἴληπταί γε τὰ συμβαίνοντα ἱκανῶς 760 b 30); but he comes very near the true doctrine. 760 a 3 λείπεται τοὺς βασιλεῖς καὶ αὐτοὺς γεννᾶν καὶ τὰς μελίττας. This need not include the κηφῆνες. 760 b 7 εὖ δὲ καὶ τὸ τοὺς βασιλεῖς ὥσπερ πεποιημένους ἐπὶ τέκνωσιν ἔσω μένειν, ἀφειμένους τῶν ἀναγκαίων ἔργων, καὶ μέγεθος δὲ ἔχειν, ὥσπερ ἐπὶ τεκνοποιίαν συστάντος τοῦ σώματος αὐτῶν. Vergil seems not to have known the sex of the queens. (Conington on Geor. iv. 95.) For notices of bees in other ancient authors see Lenz, *Zoologie der alten Griechen und Römer*, p. 574 *sqq.*

C. ἐκείνων] 'the other members of the state,' I should understand. Stallbaum says 'quam illi, qui alibi αὐτόματοι φύονται,' which hardly makes such good sense.

ὡς νῦν—ὄντος] 'For in most states men are fighting a fight with shadows, and striving with one another for the possession of power, as if that were a very great good.'

D. ἐν πόλει ᾗ] The omission of the preposition is quite common, not to say regular, in Attic prose. Kühner² ii. 478, who quotes *Rep.* iii. 402 A ἐν ἅπασιν οἷς ἐστί, etc.

οἱ τρόφιμοι] 'our alumni.' The word is curious, as being used both in the active and the passive sense. Both are common.

ἐν τῷ καθαρῷ] 'in the heaven of ideas.' Literally, 'in the open air,' as opposed to the darkness of the cave.

Book VIII. 557 A—558 C.

A sarcastic description of the ideal democracy. This is the most beautiful of states, ornamented with varieties of every sort *ad libitum.* You can go as it were to the market, and buy a constitution to your fancy. Every one is free to do exactly what he pleases; and even the convict walks about, none the worse for his conviction. And the fine theories about education, with which we started, and which we thought so noble, are in no more esteem than anybody else's.

557 A. Δημοκρατία δὴ κ.τ.λ.] The remainder of this paragraph might furnish a text for a reviewer of Greek history, so often are each of the changes here supposed repeated in actual fact.

ἐν αὐτῇ γίγνονται] γίγνονται Schneider (both edd.), Turicenses. γίγνωνται Bekker and Stallbaum, with A and other good codices, which seems better. Hermann, and Baiter, as in the text take καὶ ὡς τὸ πολὺ—γίγνονται as a gloss or interpolation.

B. δῆλον γὰρ κ.τ.λ.] 'For as the government is such will be the man.'

ἕκαστον ἀρέσκοι] ἀρέσκω in this sense generally takes the dative, but the accusative also is quite common, especially in Attic, and was called by the grammarians the Attic construction. *Cratylus* 391 D ἀλλ' εἰ μὴ αὖ σε ταῦτα ἀρέσκει, where see Heindorf.

C. καὶ ἔστι γε κ.τ.λ.] 'Yes, my good sir, and this will be a very proper place in which to look for a constitution.'

E. ἧς] *scil.* ἀρχῆς.

ἐπιθυμῇς is smooth, and in agreement with the rest of the sentence; but Stallbaum gives no authority for it. ἐπιθυμῇ Α Θ Π and many other books, which is abrupt. but not intolerable.

558 A. ἐπίῃ] 'should come into your head.' A not uncommon use. Cf. *e. g. Rep.* iii. 388 D εἰ καὶ ἐπίοι αὐτῷ τοιοῦτον ἢ λέγειν ἢ ποιεῖν.

καὶ ἡδεῖα] Stallbaum wishes to read καὶ θεία, for which one sees no necessity. Hermann also takes offence at the phrase, and reads *de suo* θεσπεσία ὡς ἡδεῖα. But θ. καὶ ἡδεῖα means just the same thing, 'supremely delightful.'

ἐν τῷ παραυτίκα] 'for the time being.' ἔν γε τούτῳ, *scil.* ἐν τῷ παραυτίκα. This is a not inappropriate place to remark that ἴσως in Plato is regularly affirmative; 'no doubt,' 'doubtless,' almost 'yes.'

ἡ πραότης ἐνίων τῶν δικασθέντων] Stallbaum (followed by Davies and Vaughan) understands this to mean 'the coolness,' 'the easy-going way of some criminals.' Schneider cites *Crito* 43 B ὡς ῥᾳδίως αὐτὴν (τὴν συμφορὰν) καὶ πρᾴως φέρεις, where πρᾴως means 'how easily,' 'with what equanimity,' not quite the sense supposed here. But one is in. clined, although the construction is a little hard, to follow him in understanding rather 'their lenity towards some criminals.' So Müller. Schneider compares for the sense *Euthydemus* 303 D καὶ τόδε αὖ ἕτερον δημοτικόν τι καὶ πρᾷον ἐν τοῖς λόγοις, ὅτι κ.τ.λ. For the genitive cf. τὸ τῶν Μεγαρέων ψήφισμα, 'the decree against the Megarians,' Thucydides i. 140, 4. Sophocles, *Antigone* 632-3 τελείαν ψῆφον—τῆς μελλονύμφου, 'the final condemnation of thy bride.' (Kühner[2] ii. 287.)

μενόντων] Strictly, after εἶδες we should have the accusative; but the construction of the genitive participle is carried on.

καὶ ὡς οὔτε comes directly after εἶδες.

περινοστεῖ] The vulgate added ὁ καταψηφισθείς, an obvious gloss.

B. οὐδ' ὁπωστιοῦν σμικρολογία] 'the utter absence of pettiness.' 'The "don't care" about trifles.'

αὐτῆς] τῆς πόλεως or τῆς δημοκρατίας.

ὑπερβεβλημένην] 'surpassing,' 'remarkable.' So Euripides, *Alcestis* 153

> τί χρὴ γενέσθαι τὴν ὑπερβεβλημένην
> γυναῖκα;

ὡς μεγαλοπρεπῶς] We may call the construction here a 'resumption'; the preceding nominatives are not forgotten, but a fresh start is taken with ὡς μεγαλοπρεπῶς καταπατήσασα, the only doubt being whether a new subject is introduced, such as the πόλις of Stallbaum. Schneider would refer καταπατήσασα to συγγνώμη, carrying on one subject; and this is certainly supported by the πάνυ γενναία of Adeimantus's answer, which can hardly refer to anything else than ἡ συγγνώμη etc. Had ἡ πόλις been the subject, we should have expected γενναίως.

οὐδὲν φροντίζει, ἐξ ὁποίων] The editors insert the comma, but surely the sense is clearer without it.

562 A—563 E.

How does democracy degenerate into tyranny Oligarchy died of over-wealth; and so democracy dies of over-freedom. The subjects become rulers, and the rulers subjects; parent and child are on a level; so are teacher and pupil; the slave is as good as his master; the very horses and asses will get out of their way for nobody; and all these fine things are the beginning of tyranny.

562 A. λοιπά] Neuter after a feminine and a masculine.

τίς τρόπος—γίγνεται;] 'What is the origin of tyranny?' 'How does tyranny come about?' Literally, 'What is the manner that comes into being?'

B. προύθεντο Paris A and others, Schneider, Turicenses, Hermann. προύθετο Bekker and Stallbaum.

ὑπέρπλουτος] So Bekker and the Zürich editors. πλοῦτος Schneider, [ὑπερ]πλοῦτος Hermann. Stallbaum suggests ὑπέρπλουτος πλοῦτος. The difficulty is that ὑπέρπλουτος is elsewhere an adjective. *Rep.* viii. 552 B ὑπέρπλουτοι—πένητες. Aeschylus, *Prometheus V.* 466 Dindorf[5]—

Ἵππους, ἄγαλμα τῆς ὑπερπλούτου χλιδῆς.

One hardly sees why the word should not stand as a substantive. Phrynichus is quoted (ap. Schneider) to show that he did not know the word. He says that ὑπερθεμιστοκλῆς is a strange form (καινοτάτη ἡ φανή) like ὑπερπερικλῆς, ὑπερσωκράτης, or again ὑπερευρύβατος, 'a greater rascal than Eurybatus.' But his remark is confined to proper names.

C. καὶ πολὺ τοῦτο τὸ ῥῆμα] πολύ predicative.

ἦα νῦν δὴ ἐρῶν] like the English idiom, 'I was going to say.' See examples in Stallbaum, such as *Theaetetus* 180 C ὅπερ ἦα ἐρῶν. ἦα, Epic ἦια ('ἤειν first person rare,' Veitch) distinguished from ἦα, 'I was' (Homeric), by *iota subscriptum*, is the imperfect. The two forms represent original *āyām, *āsām respectively.

E. πᾶν τὸ τῆς ἐλευθερίας] 'the very superflux of freedom.'

καὶ καταδύεσθαί γε κ.τ.λ.] 'By degrees the anarchy finds a way into private houses, and ends by getting among the animals and infecting them.'

τὴν ἀναρχίαν is the subject of the sentence.

563 A. ἐν τῷ τοιούτῳ] 'in such a state of things.'

ξυγκαθιέντες] 'letting themselves down,' 'condescending to.'

εὐτραπελίας τε καὶ χαριεντισμοῦ] 'jocularity and facetiousness.'

C. Αἰσχύλον] *Fr.* 337 Dindorf[5], 341 Nauck. The latter makes ὅτι νῦν ἦλθ' ἐπὶ στόμα the end of a line; in haste, surely.

ἐλευθερώτερα] *scilicet* ταῦτα, i.e. τὰ θηρία.

γίγνονταί τε δὴ κ.τ.λ.] 'and not only that, but horses and asses become as good as their masters.' The Scholiast on this passage says; ἔστι δὲ ἡ ὅλη (παροιμία)· οἵαπερ ἡ δέσποινα, τοία χἀ κύων. 'As is my lady is my lady's brach.' Plato seems to have given the words a new turn, as usual.

ἐμβάλλοντες] 'charging,' 'falling foul of.'

Book IX.   588 A—592 B (end).

Did not some one say, a good while ago (Thrasymachus in the First
Book), that to be perfectly unjust, and have the name of just, was best ?
Now that we know something about justice and injustice, we may have
a word with him.   Let us imagine a beast with many and diverse
heads ; and a figure of a lion ; and a figure of a man ; and let us shut
them all up in a man, so as to be invisible from the outside.   These
represent the three parts of the soul, appetite, passion, and reason.
Our antagonist will be forced to confess that the many-headed beast
must be in every way suppressed and diminished, the lion guided
rightly, the man strengthened and increased ; we must 'move upward,
working out the man, and let the ape and tiger die.'   And to be un-
detected will be no good, but a great evil.   Our new man will keep
under his body, and attain and preserve the harmony of his soul ; and
with regard to the acquisition of wealth, he will make 'like healthful
music.'   Nor will he be a politician, except in his own city, the city of
our parable, which exists not on earth, but of which a pattern is laid up
in heaven, which the eye of the seer may see.

588 A. ἐνταῦθα λόγου] 'Frequentius dicitur addito articulo ἐνταῦθα
τοῦ λόγου.' Stallbaum.   A slight distinction might be made between
the two forms of expression, the one in the text being more general.
'Since we have proceeded so far in argument.'   'Since we have argued
so far.'

B. λεγόμενον] This was the doctrine laid down by Thrasymachus
in the First Book.

αὐτῷ διαλεγώμεθα] might be 'with Thrasymachus'; but this is not
necessary on account of the Greek, as αὐτός is used in this way by Plato
in reference to an unexpressed subject, e. g. *Gorgias* 469 C ὃ ἂν δοκῇ
αὐτῷ. where αὐτῷ is got out of τυραννεῖν preceding.   Probably Thrasymachus is supposed to be absent, as he only speaks in the First Book,
and as Glaucon answers for him a little below, 590 A.   αὐτῷ would
then mean 'with the author of the saying.'

πῶς ;] *i. e.* διαλεγώμεθα.

D. τὸ δεύτερον] These three figures represent the three parts of the
soul, as they have been before divided; the lower part, of appetites and
desires, the θυμοειδές, of courage and the nobler desires, and the wholly
rational part.

589 A. καὶ μηδὲν ἕτερον κ. τ. λ.] μηδέν is difficult *prima facie* ;
apparently it must be taken after λυσιτελεῖν αὐτῷ.   'It is the interest
of this creature (the total man) in no wise to reconcile the one
part to the other.'   μηδὲν μηδένι would be simple ; but instead of

μηδένι we have ἕτερον ἑτέρῳ. Literally, 'to reconcile no part one with another.'

C. οὐδὲν ὑγιές] 'Praestat ὑγιές ad ψέγει referre et hoc pro ψέγων λέγει accipere.' Schneider. I understand him to mean ; 'but he who impeaches justice does so without having a sound word to say, and in ignorance.' But perhaps the construction is really simpler, and we should join οὐδ' εἰδὼς οὐδὲν ὑγιές. 'But the person who finds fault finds fault in utter ignorance of right and truth.'

οὔ μοι δοκεῖ κ.τ.λ.] The only difficulty is to know what we are to supply. εἰδέναι ; or ἀληθεύειν ; or something of the kind.

τὰ μὲν καλά] Supp. εἶναι or the like. 'Because good is that which subjects the bestial nature to man, or rather to the divine in man.'

D. ἔστιν οὖν] 'Is it the case then, I said, that if,' etc. The construction then proceeds ιegularly.

ἢ εἰ μὲν λαβὼν κ.τ.λ.] 'Supposing he had sold a son or a daughter into slavery, into the hands of violent and savage men, we should allow that no price could possibly bring him profit; and if, without remorse, he sells the divinest part of himself into slavery, slavery to all in him that is atheistic and detestable, shall we not call him a wretch, many times more unhappy than Eriphyle, who took the necklace as the price of her husband's life ?'

The story of Eriphyle we have from Homer downwards; *Odyssee* xi. 326—

> Μαῖράν τε Κλυμένην τε ἴδον στυγερήν τ' Ἐριφύλην,
> ἣ χρυσὸν φίλου ἀνδρὸς ἐδέξατο τιμήεντα.

xi. 520—

> πολλοὶ δ' ἀμφ' αὐτὸν ἑταῖροι
> Κήτειοι κτείνοντο γυναίων εἵνεκα δώρων.

E. εἰς—ἀνδρῶν] Supply οἶκον or the like.

590 A. πολὺ ἐπὶ δεινοτέρῳ] The transposition is common in Plato. Cf. *Cratylus* 413 C πολὺ ἐν πλείονι ἀπορίᾳ, and Stallbaum's note here. 'He compasses a ruin, far far more terrible than that which Eriphyle wrought.'

ἐκείνου] As explained above, either Thrasymachus, or more generally, the maintainer of the position impugned.

ἐν τῷ τοιούτῳ] 'In such a person,' I understand.

B. συντείνηται] 'Is strung to the pitch,' 'is intensified.'

τῆς ἐκείνου ἀπληστίας] ἐκείνου = τοῦ θηρίου.

C. βαναυσία in literal sense of 'mean employment.'

τῶν ἐν αὐτῷ θρεμμάτων] So Stallbaum, Hermann, Turicenses. Schneider with many MSS. αὐτῷ. As often, it does not appear what A reads. αὐτῷ is perhaps better.

οἵουπερ ὁ βέλτιστος] 'h. e. ὑφ' οἵου καὶ ὁ βέλτιστος ἄρχεται.' Stallbaum.

D. οἰκεῖον ἔχοντος] Genitive absolute, though following παντί.
οἰκείου ἐνόντος some of the minor Zürich editions, without any authority,
apparently. 'Every man should be governed by the divine and the
reasonable; if they are to be found within himself, so much the better;
but if not, let a rule be imposed from without.'

E. βουλεύεται] Turicenses, Schneider, Hermann, with chief authorities; βούλεται Stallbaum. The sense is much the same, the difference
being nearly that between 'the law meditates' and 'the law wishes.'

καὶ ἡ τῶν παιδῶν ἀρχή] *Scil.* δηλοῖ.

591 A. τῷ παρ' ἡμῖν τοιούτῳ ἀντικαταστήσωμεν] 'have set up in
them a guardian corresponding to our own.'

ἐν αὐτῷ—ἐλεύθερον] Passing from the plural (αὐτοῖς etc.) to the
singular, by a not unusual construction.

B. τιμιωτέραν] More precious than anything belonging to the body.

C. ξυντείνας] 'concentrating.'

ἀπεργάσεται the editors. ἀπεργάζεται Α Π.

οὐχ ὅπως] What is the peculiarity of this idiom?

πρεσβεύων] 'making this his first care.'

ἀπ' αὐτῶν] ·from the possession of these qualities.'

D. [φαίνηται] φαίνηται Schneider, Turicenses. If this stands, we
must explain with Schneider, 'Coniunctivus pendet ex illo ὅπως post
πρεσβεύων et futurum excipit ut Tim. p. 18 E,' where the words are
ὅπως οἱ κακοὶ—ξυλλέξονται, καὶ μή τις—ἔχθρα—γίγνηται. Stallbaum
and Hermann bracket φαίνηται, which, or φαίνοιτο, φανεῖται appears in
all the authorities. The word can well be spared.

παντάπασι—εἶναι] 'Certainly he will, he replied, if he has true music
in him.'

οὐκοῦν—ξυμφωνίαν] 'Repetas apud animum τῆς ἐν τῇ ψυχῇ ἕνεκα
ξυμφωνίας ἁρμόσεται.' Stallbaum. Or anything to the same effect.
ξύνταξιν, 'arrangement,' ·order.'

οὐκ ἐκπληττόμενος κ.τ.λ.] 'οὐκ non cum ἐκπληττόμενος connecten-
dum, sed pertinet ad ἄπειρον αὐξήσει.' Stallbaum.

E. τιμάς γε] Again we must imagine some verb like διώξει or
μέτεισι. Or rather τιμάς begins with the anticipation of some governing
verb to follow, which is lost in the fresh start of the construction.

592 A. τούτου, l. 135] of this state of mind, of improving himself,
and admitting no deteriorating influence.

τῇ ἐν λόγοις κειμένῃ] 'the city of our parable.'

B. ἐν οὐρανῷ ἴσως παράδειγμα] 'Locus dici non potest quantopere a
scriptoribus posterioris aetatis celebratus sit.' Stallbaum. There is an
allusion, half playful, half serious, to the store of 'ideas' which are the
real essence of all existing things.

Book X.　613 E—621 D (end).

Justice has been vindicated. The just man is dear to the gods and wise in the esteem of men; but his reward here is nothing to that which awaits him hereafter. And I will tell you the tale of Er, the son of Armenius, who died, and lived again, and brought back an account of the other world. He saw the judgment of souls, and heard of the thousand years' journey of the good and bad above the heaven and beneath the earth, and the torments of the irreclaimable, and went with the spirits, and saw the light that holds the heavens together, and the spindle of Necessity, wherein the world is figured, and which produces the music of the spheres, and the choice of lives, the most important of all human concerns, and the plain of Forgetfulness, and the river of Indifference, 'whereof who drinks Forgets both joy and woe, pleasure and pain.' Wherefore let us hold fast to virtue in our present state and pass along the heavenly way in our journey of a thousand years, dear to the gods, and happy in ourselves.

614 A. ἑκάτερος line 7] AΘ, the first hand of Ξ, etc., have ἑκάτερον, which seems an obvious repetition from the line before.

ἀπειλήφῃ is an example of a rare form, the subjunctive perfect, the usual form being the circumlocution with the substantive verb. We have in the *Politicus*, 269 C, εἰλήφωσιν. εἰδῶ (formed as from a theme in -ε) is common; but then οἶδα is practically a present. Most of the other examples belong to similar present-perfects; *e. g.* τεθνήκωσι Thucydides viii. 74, 3. An example of a pure perfect is found in Aristophanes, *Knights* 1149 ἅττ' ἂν κεκλόφωσί μου. The instances are given in Curtius, *Das Verbum der griechischen Sprache*, ii. 224.

ἀκοῦσαι (line 8) is bracketed by Stephanus, Ast, and Stallbaum from conjecture, and retained by Turicenses, Hermann, Schneider. It might be dispensed with, but, as Schneider acutely remarks, the point is, that the account of the good man and the bad man is to be heard to an end.

λέγοις—ἀκούοντι] 'Speak, he said; there are few things I would more gladly hear.'

B. Ἀλκίνου κ.τ.λ.] The 'fable of Alcinoüs' is contained in books ix-xii of the Odyssee. Aristotle uses the same phrase twice. *Poetics* xvi. 8. p. 1455 a 2 ἐν Ἀλκίνου ἀπολόγῳ. *Rhetoric* III. xvi. 7. p. 1417 a 13 ὁ Ἀλκίνου ἀπόλογος.

ἀλκίμου μὲν ἀνδρός, Ἦρος τοῦ Ἀρμενίου] Observe the play upon words. The story is not traceable beyond Plato.

ὑγιής] 'uncorrupted.'

ἐκεῖ] 'yonder,' 'in the other world,' as regularly in Attic.

C. δαιμόνιον] 'mysterious.'

D. εἰπεῖν] *sc.* τοὺς δικαστάς. Stallbaum would make the construction first infinitive with (suppressed) accusative, and then optative. Perhaps with Schneider we had better omit the comma after ἐκεῖ, and refer both optatives to ὅτι; 'that he must be,' and 'that they straitly charged him.'

ταύτῃ μὲν—κατὰ δὲ τὼ ἑτέρω] The corresponding phrases are not exactly balanced. 'At the one place he saw the souls departing, whether for the upward or for the downward journey; and at the other two openings he saw them returning.'

μεστὰs—κόνεωs] 'full of dinge and dust.'

E. λειμῶνα] Compare the similar myth in the *Gorgias*, where it is said (524 A) that the three judges 'δικάσουσιν ἐν τῷ λειμῶνι,' as if the name of such a place were familiar.

615 A. τὰ μὲν οὖν—διηγήσασθαι] 'To be minute, Glaucon, would be tedious.'

ἐν μέρει] 'Suo quemque ordine, quemque deinceps.' Stallbaum. Do the words not rather mean *seriatim*, 'as the turn of each offence came round,' 'fault by fault?' They might possibly be understood of the ten times repeated punishment. 'Term after term.'

B. καὶ οἷον εἴ τινεs] Schneider, Turicenses, Hermann, with the books. Stallbaum wishes to read καὶ οἵτινες *e conj.*; without necessity. καὶ τοὺς αἰτίους—προδόντας κ.τ.λ. would be quite regular; instead of which we have οἷον εἴ τινες, a circumlocution with a changed construction.

κομίσαιντο, l. 52] If we are to distinguish between κομίσαιντο and κομίζοιντο, the difference will be that κομίσαιντο is 'they had received, and were done with,' which is rather confirmed by δεδωκέναι above (l. 45); and that κομίζοιντο is 'they had received, and were still enjoying.'

C. εὐθὺς γενομένων] Ast and Stallbaum, without authority, wish to add ἀποθανόντων, which is quite superfluous, and indeed excluded by the words καὶ ὀλίγον χρόνον βιούντων. Schneider, 'De mortuis hic agi in aperto est; nec nostrates, opinor offenderet *von denen, die eben erst geboren gewesen* etiam non addito *als sie starben*' ('those who were just born' 'when they died'). The words καὶ ὀλίγον χρόνον βιούντων in fact replace or correspond to such an expression as ἀποθανόντων. The simplest expression would be τῶν δὲ εὐθὺς γενομένων ἀποθανόντων πέρι; but as this would be awkward, καὶ ὀλίγον χρόνον βιούντων, which corresponds in sense, is substituted. The words εὐθὺς γενόμενοι may be found in the *Phaedo* 75 C ἠπιστάμεθα—εὐθὺς γενόμενοι—ξύμπαντα τὰ τοιαῦτα. 'We had this knowledge immediately after birth.'

C. ἀσεβείας τε] Genitive.

γονέας] Stallbaum wishes to insert εἰς before this word, without necessity.

αὐτόχειρος] αὐτόχειρας the books; the emendation of the text, αὐτόχειρος (though adopted by Hermann), seems for the worse. Schneider acutely says, 'Ne hoc quidem emendatione egere puto, quum praepositionem εἰς primum ad γονέας eadem significatione, quam ante θεούς habet, deinde ad αὐτόχειρας alia significatione subaudire liceat, si tamen alia dicenda est, quae ad eandem rerum rationem pertinet. Nam ἀσέβεια εἰς θεούς impietas est ad deos non aliter se habens, quam poenae, quas μισθοὺς εἰς αὐτόχειρας φόνου dicere videtur, ad interfectores.'

χιλιοστὸν ἔτος] -οστός, the same termination as in all the ordinals from εἰκοστός onwards, and in πολλοστός, ὀλιγοστός, ὁπόστος.

D. εἰπεῖν—φάναι] φάναι seems used of the narrator; 'Er said'; εἰπεῖν of the person who gives the answer, τὸν ἐρωτώμενον. This is very harsh: can we eject φάναι?

οὐδ' ἂν ἥξει δεῦρο] One of the most remarkable examples, in Attic prose, of the future indicative with ἄν. In Homer the future with κεν is very common; with ἄν much rarer. (Kühner².) Pindar has ἄν with future. The use in Attic prose, though rare, is well established. *Euthydemus* 287 D καὶ νῦν οὐδ' ἂν ὁτιοῦν ἀποκρινεῖ; One or two MSS. here have ἥξοι, which Baiter alone, of the three Zürich editors, would prefer. (ἥξει in his third minor edition.)

ἦσαν δὲ καὶ κ.τ.λ.] Schneider and the translators understand 'among the great sinners there were some private persons'; but surely Stallbaum's way is the more natural; 'there were there also some private persons, of the number of those who had been great sinners in life.' So Schleiermacher; 'nur einige darunter waren keine Staatsmänner, hatten aber sonst grosses verbrochen.'

E. τοὺς μέν, l. 75] The words refer to those who had not been sufficiently punished, but were not wholly incurable.

διαλαβόντες] The sense (a common one) of 'seizing round the waist,' which Stallbaum would give here, seems quite uncalled for. The word need not mean more than 'took,' 'arrested.' Cf. *Phaedo* 81 C διειλημμένην (ψυχὴν)—ὑπὸ τοῦ σωματοειδοῦς. Herodotus iv. 68 αὐτίκα διαλελαμμένος ἄγεται. Or it might be understood 'separated from the rest.' Müller understands 'divided among themselves,' which is certainly ingenious.

616 A. ἐκτός] 'aside,' 'off the road.'

ἐπ' ἀσπαλάθων κνάπτοντες] 'carding them, as it were, upon prickly branches of the aspalathus.' The ἀσπάλαθος is some shrub used for the same purposes as the English teasel (*Dipsacus silvestris* or *fullonum*). (According to Leunis, *Synopsis der drei Naturreiche, Botanik*, § 278, 8, *Spartium horridum*, a prickly plant, common on the hills of Greece, with strong fibres, suitable for making cordage, mats, etc.)

καὶ εἰς ὅτι [τὸν Τάρταρον] The whole passage is apparently corrupted by glosses. The most extended form of the place runs, ὧν ἔνεκά τε ταῦτα ὑπομένοιεν καὶ εἰς ὅ τι τὸν Τάρταρον ἐμπεσούμενοι ἄγοιντο. ἔνθα δὴ φόβων, ἔφη, πολλῶν καὶ παντοδαπῶν σφίσι γεγονότων τοῦτον ὑπερβάλλειν τὸν φόβον, κ.τ.λ. ταῦτα ὑπομένοιεν, τὸν Τάρταρον, τὸν φόβον appear to me (with Hermann) to be marginal additions. The two last, as I understand, are not found in A, although ταῦτα ὑπομένοιεν is. (It is much to be wished that editors would give the readings of codices in an unmistakeable form.) One's notion of the real reading would then be σημαίνοντες, ὧν ἔνεκα καὶ εἰς ὅ τι ἐμπεσούμενοι ἄγοιντο. ἔνθα δὴ φόβων, ἔφη. πολλῶν, καὶ παντοδαπῶν σφίσι γεγονότων τοῦτον ὑπερβάλλειν, μὴ γένοιτο κ.τ.λ. In late MSS. interpolations of the above kind become outrageous.

Stallbaum does not explain his reading καὶ εἰς ὅ τι εἰς τὸν Τάρταρον. Does he take εἰς ὅ τι as meaning 'to what end?' as Müller seems to understand. According to Schneider and others, εἰς ὅτι is an example of transposition, as it appears in the very best codices. *E. g.* above, 580 D, A and most MSS. have δευτέραν δεῖ δὲ instead of δευτέραν δὲ δεῖ.

B. ἑκάστοις] Each new set, as the seven days expire respectively.

προελθόντας] προελθόντες A.

φῶς εὐθύ, οἷον κίονα κ.τ.λ.] We now come to a difficult passage, (continuing to 617 D), brought in without any very apparent reason, as is indeed the manner of Plato. Compare the famous passage about the 'number' which presides over births (*Republic* viii. p. 546), and the two numbers of the *Timaeus* (pp. 35, 36). It amounts to a description of the universe or cosmos; but it is not so clear how far the pilgrims are supposed to see the actual cosmos, and how far it is represented in miniature. Perhaps first the one and then the other. We shall take the place upon its own merits, not holding it necessary to make everything square with the representations of the *Timaeus*.

The first difficulty of the description is that we only hear of a 'straight light, like a pillar,' and yet he seems to describe both a circle, or band of light, going round the heavens, *i. e.* the Milky Way, and also a straight beam of light passing through the centre of the earth (not to say of the universe) and furnishing an axis of revolution for the celestial bodies. This axis corresponds to the shaft of the spindle farther on. 'And they saw there in the midst of the light' (the circle or galaxy, we may perhaps understand) 'the extremities of the fastenings of heaven' (or 'of the straight light') 'stretched tight, for this light' (the circle again) 'was the girdle of heaven' (the universe), 'and like the frappings or undergirdings of a trireme, and held all the circumference fast together' (which last words shut us down to something circular), 'and from the extremities' (of whichever it is) 'was stretched the spindle of Necessity, which was the axis of all the circumvolvents.'

Here comes the second difficulty. We are told below (617 B) that the whorl of the spindle turns upon the knees of Necessity. If she be an actual figure, visible in the plain, how are the two descriptions to be reconciled? Plato seems to mix together the vision of the actual sphere (or hemisphere) and of a sort of representation or orrery; and the two do not cohere.

C. What is κατὰ μέσον τὸ φῶς? One does not clearly see how to understand these words. Any amount of conjectures may be made.

Ὑπόζωμα is well explained in Liddell and Scott's *Lexicon*, to which may be added from Admiral Smyth's *Sailor's Word-Book*, p. 321, ' Frapping a ship. The act of passing four or five turns of a large cable-laid rope round a ship's hull when it is apprehended that she is not strong enough to resist the violence of the sea.' See also Mr. Smith of Jordanhill, *Voyage and Shipwreck of St. Paul*, upon *Acts* xxvii. 17, ὑποζωννύντες τὸ πλοῖον (ed. 3. p. 106 sqq.). The place in the *Laws* (xii. 945 C), where the word ὑποζώματα occurs again, throws no particular light on this passage. οὓς ἐντόνους (Turicenses. The readings vary) καὶ ὑποζώματα καὶ νεύρων ἐπιτόνους—προσαγορεύομεν. The word refers to νεώς immediately preceding.

Guhl and Koner tell us (*Life of the Greeks and Romans*, p. 256 English version), ' as a further means of increasing their compactness, war-vessels were provided with a band consisting of four stout ropes (ὑποζώματα) laid horizontally round the hull below the water-line; in case of a dangerous voyage, the number of these ropes might be increased.' Athenaeus, 204 A, quoting the words of Callixenus, tells us of an immense ship built by Ptolemy Philopator, τεσσερακοντήρης. ὑποζώματα δὲ ἐλάμβανε δώδεκα· ἑξακοσίων δ' ἦν ἕκαστον πηχῶν. ἐλάμβανε, ' the ship required'? or rather 'took on board,' 'was supplied with,' 'the stock of ὑποζώματα was.' Our authors remark that this gigantic toy 'could only be used in smooth water' (p. 261). One hardly sees how supports applied lengthways could really strengthen any vessel. Whatever may be the exact comparison, the main point that the light holds the heavens together as the ropes hold the ship together remains the same.

ἄτρακτον] The spindle, an implement almost unknown now-a-days, is composed of two parts, a shaft and a whorl or verticil, to which two is here added a hook or catch (ἄγκιστρον). The carded wool, or tow, wrapped loosely round the distaff, is pulled out, and a part attached to the spindle, which is then made to revolve. The verticil, which may be of any heavy material, such as clay, or metal, serves the purpose of a fly-wheel, adding momentum to the revolution, and keeping it steady, while the finger and thumb regulate the size of the thread, and keep it as equal as possible. This explains the allusions here. The use of ἠλακάτη, which regularly means the 'distaff,' in the sense of 'shaft of the spindle,' appears to be unique.

τὰς περιφοράς] The 'circumferences' or 'revolutions' of the celestial bodies, or their representatives.

D. ἡ τοῦ ἐνθάδε] The shape must be supposed spherical, on account of the comparison. Actual examples of verticils are of any circular shape. The shape of the whole verticil is spherical; but at the same time somewhat of the upper part of each concentric hollow sphere is cut away, so as to show the one within.

διαμπερές] 'entirely.' 'all through.'

κάδοι] He seems to refer to some familiar toy.

E. κύκλους—ἀπεργαζομένους] 'showing their upper edges as circles, composing, when taken together, the surface of one continuous verticil.' κύκλους is predicative. The eight concentric verticils represent the revolutions of the seven planets and of the sphere of the fixed stars. The seven planets (as here given), taking them from the outside circle, or sphere of the fixed stars, are Saturn, Jupiter, Mars, Mercury, Venus, the Sun, the Moon. The place of Mercury is strange, when we remember that it has a very small orbit, and can rarely be seen at all by the naked eye, on account of its proximity to the Sun. Copernicus is said to have died without seeing it.

διὰ μέσου τοῦ ὀγδόου] 'through the middle of the eighth,' *i.e.* according to the context, the Moon; and so Stallbaum understands. But can we suppose Plato really to mean this? Shall we not rather think that he forgets his figures for the moment, and really means the Earth? Such certainly is the conception of the *Timaeus*, whether, according to a well-known controversy, we suppose this Earth to revolve upon its axis or not. (See Mr. Grote's pamphlet on the subject.)

πλατύτατον] 'broadest'; the edge exposed by the section is broader than that of any of the others. Plato does not explain what he means by this 'breadth.' He has been understood to refer to the relative distances of the planets. One would rather suppose the relative size to be meant.

The names of the planets are not here mentioned; but there can be no doubt what the series is intended to be. The word πλανῆται and the names Ἑωσφόρος and ὁ ἱερὸς Ἑρμοῦ λεγόμενος are found in the *Timaeus*, 38 C, where see Stallbaum's note. The order of the planets, and their names, may be found in Aristotle, περὶ κόσμου ii. p. 392 a Bekker. Within the sphere of the fixed stars a continuous space is occupied by ὁ τοῦ Φαίνοντος ἅμα καὶ Κρόνου λεγόμενος κύκλος, ἐφεξῆς δὲ ὁ τοῦ Φαέθοντος Διὸς λεγόμενος, εἶθ' ὁ Πυρόεις Ἡρακλέους τε καὶ Ἄρεος προσαγορευόμενος, ἑξῆς δὲ ὁ Στίλβων, ὃν ἱερὸν Ἑρμοῦ καλοῦσιν ἔνιοι, τινὲς δὲ Ἀπόλλωνος· μεθ' ὃν ὁ τοῦ Φωσφόρου, ὃν Ἀφροδίτης, οἱ δὲ Ἥρας προσαγορεύουσιν, εἶτα ὁ ἡλίου, καὶ τελευταῖος ὁ τῆς σελήνης μέχρι γῆς ὁρίζεται. Here again Mercury is placed outside Venus.

The circle of the fixed stars is broadest; after which the succession in diminishing breadth is Venus, Mars, the Moon, the Sun, Mercury, Jupiter, Saturn. Upon these two series follows the order of their various colours and rapidities. The whole may be represented in a simple table.

Names.		*Broadness.*	*Colour.*	*Rapidity.*
Circle of fixed stars	1	1	many-coloured	not counted.
Saturn	2	8	yellowish	5
Jupiter	3	7	whitest	4
Mars	4	3	reddish	3
Mercury	5	6	yellowish	{ 2
Venus	6	2	second in whiteness	
Sun	7	5	brightest	
Moon	8	4	light reflected	1

τὸν μὲν τοῦ μεγίστου] *i. e.* τὸν μὲν κύκλον τοῦ μεγίστου σφονδύλου.

τὸν δὲ—προσλάμποντος] *i. e.* the Moon receives her light from the Sun shining upon her.

617 A. Saturn and Mercury are similar, says the text, of a yellow or orange tint. Of Mercury Mr. George F. Chambers says (*Descriptive Astronomy*, Oxford, 1867, p. 52), 'It can never be seen free from strong sunlight—it may occasionally be detected after sunset and before sunrise, shining with a pale rosy hue.'

Jupiter has the whitest colour, says Plato; which may well be disputed ; one would say he was generally a little bluish   'The belts, distinguished from the general hue of the planet (often rose-coloured), are usually greyish.' Chambers, p. 106; but these colours are doubtless telescopic.

Mars, says Plato, is reddish.   He might have spoken more strongly ; 'Mars when in opposition is a very conspicuous object in the heavens, shining with a fiery red light.' Chambers, p. 85.

Venus is second in whiteness. This is a very curious statement. Venus, at its greatest effulgence, is, after the Sun and Moon, incomparably the brightest body in the sky, and, to any ordinary observer, of a dazzling white.

It is difficult to see upon what principles the breadth of the zones in section is fixed. Venus no doubt is very much the brightest of the planets; but as certainly Jupiter is second; yet Plato ranks it next to Saturn. And why are the Sun and Moon inserted in the middle of the scale? (The colours of the planets to the naked eye of different observers, and under different conditions, would furnish matter for an interesting

research. The few inquiries I have made induce me to believe that different persons see them differently).

τοὺς μὲν ἐντὸς κ.τ.λ.] The planets (viewed from the earth) appear,
upon the whole, to go round among the fixed stars the reverse way from
that in which the stars appear to move. All the bodies of the solar
system, with the exception of the satellites of Uranus, whose orbit is
almost perpendicular to the plane of the ecliptic, revolve round the Sun
in the same direction, from west to east, as is commonly said; or more
precisely, supposing we look from the north side of the ecliptic towards
the Earth, in the opposite direction to that in which the hands of a
clock move.

B. τάχιστα μὲν ἱέναι τὸν ὄγδοον κ.τ.λ.] The moon of course moves
much more rapidly upon the sphere of the fixed stars than any other
celestial body. She makes the circuit of the heavens, from any place
among the stars back to the meridian of the same, in about twenty-seven
days and a quarter; and in the course of every twenty-four hours moves
(not quite uniformly) over about thirteen degrees, or, roughly speaking,
something like her own breadth in an hour. The Sun again goes round
the sky in the time of one sidereal year at the mean rate of not quite
one degree a day, and he, Venus, and Mercury 'move with each other,'
that is, the planets, being inferior to us, are never seen at any great distance from the Sun. The three superior planets move among the stars
more slowly.

τὸν τρίτον δὲ φορᾷ κ.τ.λ.] The order is; τὸν δὲ τέταρτον ἰέναι
τὸν τρίτον ἐπανακυκλούμενον. 'And the fourth goes third in order of
rapidity as it revolves.' Most of the books have τόν; but surely the
sense would be clearer without it. Stallbaum supposes it repeated from
the last syllable of πέμπτον. Mars, Jupiter, and Saturn, go slower, in
the order of their mention.

We now come to the famous passage upon the 'music of the spheres.'

ἀνὰ τόνον] So some MSS. and Hermann. ἕνα τόνον A and most
books, and so Turicenses, Stallbaum, Schneider. The first reading
gives infinitely the better sense. 'Every Siren according to her proper
note (pitch).' We are clearly to think of the diatonic scale with its eight
notes. The other reading would mean, 'uttering one voice, one single
note.' ἁρμονίαν, as Stallbaum points out, is not to be understood of
harmony in the modern sense, but rather of a scale or 'diapason.' Does
Plato realise that the notes of the scale, taken together, produce a
horrible discord? Probably he is not thinking of the matter in this way.

δι' ἴσου] 'At equal intervals.'

C. διαλείπουσαν χρόνον] 'every now and then,' 'from time to time.'

τῇ δεξιᾷ] Because to one looking (from a point to the north of the
ecliptic) towards the sun, he in his daily revolution and the fixed stars

move from left to right ('with the clock'), while the movements of the planets among the fixed stars are in the reverse direction, and are said to be effected by Atropos with the left hand. If there be any distinct reference in the part assigned to Lachesis, it should be to the apparent stoppings and retrogressions of the planets; but this would not apply to the fixed stars.

D. προφήτην] 'an expounder' or 'intermediary.'

παραδείγματα] 'ensamples' or 'portraitures,' 'specifications' we might almost say. See below.

ἀρχὴ—θανατηφόρου] 'Now is the beginning of another letiferous cycle of mortal life.'

E. ἀδέσποτον] Virtue is not subject to arbitrary will. 'Love Virtue; she alone is free.'

ἒ δὲ οὐκ ἐᾶν] 'But they would not allow him to make a choice.'

618 A. ὁπόστος εἰλήχειν] 'what was the number which he had drawn.'

δοκίμων] 'men of mark.'

τοὺς μὲν—ἀγωνίαν] 'Some notable for presence and beauty, and others again for strength and endurance.' Instead of using an adverb, meaning 'again' or 'besides,' ἄλλος is used, and attracted into the case etc. of the word following.

B. ψυχῆς δὲ τάξιν κ.τ.λ.] 'But there was nothing fixed about the souls;' each soul was to become different according to the new conditions of its lot. 'Ueber die Seele aber sey nichts dabei bestimmt gewesen.' Schneider. Others understand τάξις in the sense of 'order,' 'series' (*Rangordnung* Schleiermacher, Müller); but this does not suit the rest of the sentence so well.

ἀλλήλοις τε, which the best editions have (Turicenses, Schneider, Hermann), is difficult at first sight, so that Stallbaum would almost read ἄλλοις with Dobree. But we have one construction on the top of another, so to speak. τὰ δ' ἄλλα ἀλλήλοις μεμῖχθαι would be perfectly simple. So would τὰ δ' ἄλλα καὶ πλούτοις κ.τ.λ. μεμῖχθαι. But the second is brought in as explanatory of the first, and τε is inserted, not very coherently, after ἀλλήλοις.

μεσοῦν] The infinitive.

C. τίς αὐτὸν κ.τ.λ.] It is not quite clear what is to be understood. 'What science' or 'what teacher?' ἐπιστάτης or ἐπιστήμη?

καὶ ξυντιθέμενα—διαιρούμενα] 'collectively and severally,' 'both in conjunction and in separation.'

D. τῶν φύσει—τῶν ἐπικτήτων] Natural and acquired qualities. .

τί—ἐργάζεται] τί is a kind of resumption; 'all these different qualities—what is their effect when combined?' τί accusative.

E. ἐάσει] Par. A and most codices, Schneider, Turicenses, Hermann.

Stallbaum would read ἐᾶν, which is intelligible enough; but why go against the MSS.? ἐάσει scil. ἕκαστος ἡμῶν line 171, or any general subject.

619 B. ὁ ἐκεῖθεν ἄγγελος must be Er; though the phrase strikes one as strange.

συντόνως] 'diligently,' 'with endeavour.'

C. βρώσεις] Such as we have in the tales of Thyestes, Harpagus, etc. τεταγμένῃ] 'regular,' 'sober.'

ἔθει—μετειληφότα] 'virtuous, but by custom, not by philosophy.'

D. ὡς δὲ καὶ εἰπεῖν] 'and in a word.'

οὐκ ἐλάττους εἶναι] 'there were perhaps more.'

καὶ διὰ τὴν τοῦ κλήρου τύχην] These words can only mean 'and according to the accident of the lot;' and so the translators understand. But the sense and connexion would be improved by their omission. The drift of the whole passage is that the order of choice is not of much importance. καὶ τελευταίῳ ἐπιόντι—κεῖται βίος ἀγαπητός, οὐ κακός.—μήτε ὁ τελευτῶν ἀθυμείτω. B above. μὴ ἐν τελευταίοις πίπτοι is one of those exceptions which are not really meant to be pressed; nor do we hear of any soul being compelled to make a bad choice. The reasoning would be clearest if instead of καί we had something like μᾶλλον ἤ. 'The change from happiness to misery, or the reverse, was not so much effected by the order of the lot as by individual choice.' Because, the speaker goes on to say, sound philosophy and anything but a most unfavourable lot will always secure happiness. But taking the words as we find them, they certainly present a difficulty.

ἐνθάδε] Here, in this world.

E. ἐκ—ἀπαγγελλομένων] 'according to the message from the other world.'

620 A. 'Ορφέως] For Orpheus see *Georgics* iv. 520 seqq., for Thamyras, or Thamyris, *Iliad* ii. 595 seqq.

μεταβάλλοντα εἰς—αἵρεσιν] The expression is somewhat curious. We may call it 'concentrated' from μεταβάλλοντα εἰς ἄνθρωπον καὶ τούτου βίον αἱρούμενον, or something of the kind.

B. εἰκοστήν] ὡσαύτως εἰκός· τήν Par. A and most codd., an obvious mistake for εἰκοστήν, which we know to have been the reading of Plutarch, and which appears in one MS. (εἰκοστήν Turicenses, Schneider, Hermann, Stallbaum.)

D. ὥσπερ ἔλαχον] In the order of the numbers that had fallen to them.

δαίμονα] Perhaps 'genius' is somewhat too personal and 'fate' rather too vague; we are not told very distinctly what the δαίμων is. There is no need to look for any precise agreement between the description here and those in similar Platonic passages, such as *Phaedo* 107 D.

' For after death, as they say, the genius of each individual, to whom he belonged in life, leads him to a certain place in which the dead are gathered together, whence after judgment they must go into the world below,' etc. Or *Phaedrus* 249 B.

ἑκάστῳ l. 258] 'each person,' for which in l. 260 is substituted αὐτήν, *scil.* ψυχήν, 'each soul.'

E. κυροῦντα ἣν λαχὼν εἵλετο μοῖραν] 'ratifying the destiny which he had chosen in the order of his lot.'

ἀμετάστροφα κ.τ.λ.] 'making the thread spun irreversible,' with an obvious allusion to the meaning of the name Atropos. ἀμεταστρεπτί, 'without turning round.'

621 A. τὸν Ἀμέλητα ποταμόν] 'The river of Indifference,' 'Unmindfulness.'

B. μέσας νύκτας] νύκτες is common in Attic of the 'night hours.' πόρρω τῶν νυκτῶν *Banquet* 217 D.

ἄττοντας the editions (Schneider, Turicenses, Hermann, Stallbaum), being the later Attic form for ᾄττω, ᾄσσω, ἀίσσω. 'Darting,' '*en filant.*'

ἀναβλέψας] 'opening his eyes,' 'awaking.'

καὶ οὕτως, ὦ Γλαύκων, κ.τ.λ.] καὶ οὗτος, ὦ Γλαύκων, μῦθος ἐσώθη Turicenses, Schneider in his earlier edition; which the latter explains as follows; '*Ecce fabulam, Glauco, non, quemadmodum vulgares, quarum leve et futile argumentum est, exstinctam sed salvam et victuram, quasi dicatur;* καὶ οὗτος, ὦ Γλαύκων, μῦθος σεσωσμένος καὶ οὐκ ἀπολωλώς ἐστι.' This makes very good sense; but is it the natural meaning of the Greek? His German translation corresponds; but in the interval between these works and the Didot edition he has changed his mind as to the reading, apparently yielding to the authority of A, which has ' οὕτως, non οὗτος' (see collation at beginning of Didot volume). The Latin translation *ad locum* is 'Salva est fabula neque emortua, et nos salvos praestabit.' This reading, which is also that of Hermann, seems best. οὕτως—ὁ μῦθος Stallbaum, from Paris K. The article, although appearing in other Platonic passages, is scarcely required, as the expressions μῦθος ἐσώθη, μῦθος ἀπώλετο, were doubtless familiar expressions. Photius (as quoted by Stallbaum on *Philebus* 14 A) says; Μῦθος ἐσώθη· ἐπίρρημα ἐστὶ λεγόμενον ἐπ' ἐσχάτῳ τοῖς λεγομένοις μύθοις τοῖς παιδίοις. ' And that's all of it.' The phrases occur several times in Plato. The place in the *Philebus* runs; κἄπειθ' ἡμῖν οὗτος ὁ λόγος ὥσπερ μῦθος ἀπολόμενος οἴχοιτο, αὐτοὶ δὲ σωζοίμεθα ἐπί τινος ἀλογίας. ' Would not the argument go from us like a tale that is forgotten, leaving us to escape by clinging to some fallacy?' Cf. *Laws* 645 B (*infra*), *Theaetetus* 164 D. We may render, 'Our tale is through,' 'Our tale is out.' ' And thus, Glaucon, our tale is told, and well told, and not a thing of naught.' Plato uses the familiar phrase with a slightly new turn, and then plays upon ἐσώθη in the σώσειεν following.

C. ψυχὴν line 285] τὴν ψυχὴν Turicenses, Schneider in large edition. τὴν omitted by Hermann, Stallbaum, Schneider in Didot edition, with Paris A and many MSS. Nor is the article necessary, being frequently omitted before ψυχή and σῶμα when used generically.

πάντα δὲ ἀγαθά] 'Intelligendum per zeugma est verbum ἀναιρεῖσθαι vel simile aliquod.' Stallbaum. ἵνα has a double reference; the principal clauses are φίλοι ὦμεν and καὶ ἐνθάδε—εὖ πράττωμεν, between which are interjected αὐτοῦ τε μένοντες—περιαγειρόμενοι. Even so the construction seems defective, and to require either another copula, or, as Stallbaum suggests, the understanding of ἵνα before ἐνθάδε καὶ ἐν τῇ χιλιετεῖ κ.τ.λ. This would make all easy; but why is the ἵνα not there? Perhaps the writer forgets that εὖ πράττωμεν is not in the same construction as κομιζώμεθα. One is tempted to say with Schneider; 'Ceterum quid alii sentiant, nescio; mihi haec extrema inde a verbis καὶ οὗτος, ὦ Γλαύκων rebus et sententiis aptissima, oratione et arte non ita, ut reliquae partes operis pulcherrimi, elaborata videntur.'

D. αὐτῆς] *scil.* δικαιοσύνης.

περιαγειρόμενοι cannot be better explained than in the words of Timaeus (*Lexicon s. v.*), περιαγειρόμενοι νικηφόροι· οἱ νικήσαντες ἐν δημοσίῳ ἀγῶνι καὶ δῶρα παρὰ τῶν φίλων καὶ οἰκείων λαμβάνοντες καὶ περιιόντες. We may compare the ἀγείρουσαν of Aeschylus (*supra*, Book II. 381 D).

'Thus shall we live dear to one another and to the gods, both while remaining here and when, like conquerors in the games who go round to gather gifts, we receive our reward. And it shall be well with us both in this life and in the pilgrimage of a thousand years which we have been reciting.'

TIMAEUS.

20 D — 26 E.

In the *Timaeus* we have the Platonic cosmogony; but the extract here given is from the introduction. The dialogue begins with a brief summary of the *Republic*. After this, Critias proceeds to tell an old tale, handed down from Solon, the friend of his house, which shows that such a state as Socrates had imagined has actually existed, and that in no other place than in this very Athens in which they are talking.

The *Timaeus* follows naturally upon the *Republic*. On the previous day Socrates is supposed to have recounted to Timaeus, Critias, Hermocrates, and a fourth unnamed person his conversation of the day before with Thrasymachus, Glaucon, Adeimantus, and others, which forms the *Republic*. He now calls the others to furnish their share of the feast of reason. Critias we know already (Introduction to *Charmides*). Timaeus, who farther on expounds his scheme of the universe, was of Locri in Italy, and a Pythagorean. A work bearing his name, but doubtless spurious, is often printed among the works of Plato. The speech of Critias, contained in the dialogue bearing his name, is a mere fragment; and that of Hermocrates, which was to follow, seems never to have been written.

20 D. ὡς ὁ τῶν—ἔφη] The meaning seems to be; 'The tale is strange, but quite true, according to the affirmation of Solon, the wisest of the Seven wise men.'

E. οἰκεῖος] 'a relation.'

πολλαχοῦ—ἐν τῇ ποιήσει] The name of Dropides does not occur in the verses of Solon which have come down to us; but eight of the Solonic fragments are addressed to Critias. In one of these, preserved by the scholiast upon this passage, Critias is told to follow his father's counsels ;

Εἰπέμεναι Κριτίῃ ξανθότριχι πατρὸς ἀκούειν·
οὐ γὰρ ἁμαρτινόῳ πείσεται ἡγεμόνι.

(*Frag.* 22 Bergk.) Aristotle (*Rhetoric* I. xv.) quotes the first line with the variant πυρρότριχι. Compare *Charmides* 157 E (*supra*) for the distinction of the family. We should remember that it was Plato's own.

φθορᾶς ἀνθρώπων] An extirpation of the race, here by a cataclysm. See 22 C *infra*, and the extract from the third book of the *Laws*, where the origin of society after such a catastrophe is imagined at length. We find a similar conception in the *Politicus*, 270 C.

21 A. πανηγύρει] The conversation of the *Timaeus* is supposed to take place two days after that of the *Republic*, and, according to Proclus, on the day of the lesser Panathenaea, so that we are to understand θεὸν of Athena. That Athena is meant is probable in itself; but it may be doubted whether the mystic philosopher of the fifth century A.D. was a good authority on the point of date.

λεγόμενον] Not a mere legend, but an actual fact. 'Non quidem celebratum,' says Stallbaum, following Proclus; which is surely wrong.

ἦν μὲν γὰρ δὴ τότε κ.τ.λ.] What are we to make of the chronological difficulty here? or is there anything beyond Plato's usual freedom of handling such matters? Solon is said to have been born about B.C. 638, and to have survived the usurpation of Peisistratus, B.C. 560. Critias was killed at Munychia, B.C. 404. We do not know his age; but sup-posing him to have been fifty, probably a large allowance, his tenth year goes back to B.C. 444. Adding ninety to this, the birth of the

elder Critias falls in B.C. 534, which is still a long way from Solon; but
it is expressly said (20 E) that Solon told the story to Critias. Either
Plato is not thinking of dates at all; or a generation has been left out;
or both.

B. **Κουρεῶτις**] The Apaturia, or common festival of the Athenian
(and Ionian) φρατρίαι, families or gentes, was held in Pyanepsion or
October, and lasted for three days, which were called respectively
δόρπεια, 'banquet,' ἀνάρρυσις, 'sacrifice,' κουρεῶτις, 'enrolment of the
κοῦροι and κοῦραι' among the phratries.

ᾔσαμεν is interesting, as it seems to show that poetry required for its
full effect at least some kind of intonation, if not singing proper. νέα is
very curious; can the word be right?

C. **'Αμύνανδρε**] Is the name significant? as it were 'supporter' or
'partisan'?

D. **'Η περὶ** is the reading of A, Bekker, Turicenses, Schneider, Hermann. Why should Stallbaum read περὶ simply?

ὀνομαστοτάτης—ἂν—οὔσης] ἄν with the participle. 'Which ought
to have been most glorious.'

E. **νομός**] Herodotus says, ii. 164, κατὰ γὰρ δὴ νομοὺς Αἴγυπτος
ἅπασα διαραίρηται, and immediately mentions the Saïte as one.

οἷς] The inhabitants of the νομός.

ἀρχηγός] 'foundress.'

τῶνδ'] Of the Athenians.

22 A. οὐδέν, ὡς ἔπος εἰπεῖν] ὡς ἔπος εἰπεῖν qualifies οὐδέν. 'Nothing, or next to nothing.' We may remember the place in the *Apology*,
17 A *supra*, ἀληθές γε, ὡς ἔπος εἰπεῖν, οὐδὲν εἰρήκασιν, which this
passage well illustrates.

τῇδε] Here at home in Hellas.

Φορωνέως] Phoroneus was associated in Argos with Hera, as the
introducer of husbandry. 'Phoroneus is said to have been the first who
offered sacrifices to Hera at Argos, and to have united the people, who
until then had lived in scattered habitations, into a city which was
called after him ἄστυ Φορωνικόν.—He is further said to have discovered
the use of fire.' Schmitz in Smith's *Dictionary of Biography*. τοῦ
πρώτου is remarkable.

ὡς διεγένοντο] 'Wie sie glücklich durchkamen,' Müller, 'how they
happily came off safe.' 'Wie sie erhalten wurden,' 'how they were
preserved,' Engelmann's translator. 'Ut superstites evaserint,' Schneider
(Didot edition). 'Et de tout ce qu'on en raconte,' Martin, who shirks
the difficulty. 'Escape' may seem the most obvious meaning to put
upon διαγίγνομαι; but where shall we find a parallel? The words by
themselves would naturally mean 'how they lived,' 'the tale of their
lives,' keeping to the common use of the verb. And then the words

μετὰ τὸν κατακλυσμὸν αὖ rather exclude the meaning of 'escaping' or 'being preserved through.' Perhaps we may translate; 'Then he proceeded to tell them of Deucaiion and Pyrrha, how they lived on after the flood,' etc. This implies their survival, without departing from the ordinary use of διαγίγνομαι. *Apology* 32 E ᾿Αρ' οὖν με οἴεσθε τοσάδε ἔτη διαγενέσθαι κ.τ.λ. 'Do you think I should have lived on so long?' Thucydides v. 16 ὄνομα ὡς οὐδὲν σφήλας τὴν πόλιν διεγένετο, said of Nicias, 'the reputation of having lived without bringing any harm upon the state.'

B. οἷς ἔλεγε] 'of the persons he enumerated.' So Stallbaum, as I understand him. Others take οἷς as neuter, with no great difference of meaning.

πῶς τί] Double question. We also have τί πῶς; *Philebus* 58 A σὺ δὲ τί πῶς—διακρίνοις ἄν; Euripides, *Helena* 873—

       'Ελένη, τί τἀμὰ πῶς ἔχει θεσπίσματα;

Stallbaum *ad Hipp. Maj.* 297 E πῶς τί ἄρ' ἂν ἀγωνιζοίμεθα;

D. παράλλαξις] 'mutation' or 'declension'; a change, especially for the worse. The best commentary on this passage is the beautiful myth in the *Politicus,* 269 sqq. The universe is at one time made to revolve by God; at another he lets it go, and it turns round of itself in the opposite direction, until he again resumes its guidance; and these changes are accompanied by a general destruction.

διὰ μακρῶν χρόνων] 'at long intervals.'

λυόμενος] 'releasing us.' The middle occurs once or twice in Plato; e.g. *Laws* i. 638 B καὶ οὐδ' ἂν Διονύσια πρόφασιν ἔχοντ' αὐτὸν λύσαιτο, 'he would not let a man go, if drunk and disorderly, because it was the time of the Dionysia.' Müller would understand 'letting himself loose,' 'durch sein Uebertreten,' λυόμενος τοὺς δεσμοὺς τῶν ὄχθων. ῥυόμενος some inferior books.

E. νομεῖς Turicenses, Hermann, Stallbaum. νομῆς Schneider, Stallbaum's folio.

ἐπιρρεῖ] Rain falls in Lower Egypt: but we must not spoil the story by inquiring too curiously into facts.

ἐπανιέναι] Turicenses, Schneider. Stallbaum and Hermann πᾶν ἐπανιέναι with A ('cum corr. A,' Turicenses).

ἐξαίσιος] 'extraordinary,' 'extreme.'

πλέον, τότε δὲ ἔλαττον] πλέον and ἔλαττον go closely together, 'a race of men subsists for ever, although in differing numbers.' Extreme heat or extreme cold makes some regions uninhabitable; but elsewhere the race continues, though varying from a maximum to a minimum, and reversely.

23 A. ἢ καὶ—ἔχον] 'or in any other way remarkable. Schol. παραδόξως ἐκβεβηκύς.

τὰ δὲ παρ' ὑμῖν—κατεσκευασμένα κ.τ.λ.] 'You, and all other nations except Egypt, are just beginning to be provided with letters and the other requisites of civilized life, when, at its accustomed period, the catastrophe recurs.' γράμμασι is specified, because the use of letters is the important point here; all record of the past is extinguished.

B. ἀγραμμάτους τε καὶ ἀμούσους] is best explained by *Laws* 677 B (*infra*), where such a φθορά or catastrophe is spoken of. 'The survivors of the catastrophe would be a handful of mountaineers and highland shepherds, a little gathering-coal of the human race; and such persons would be ignorant of arts and of the civilization of cities.'

ἐπ' ἀνθρώπους] The accusative seems to convey the notion of extension over. 'Through all the world.' Stallbaum well compares *Critias* 112 E ἐπὶ πᾶσαν Εὐρώπην ἐλλόγιμοι ἦσαν, and *Iliad* xxiv. 201—

> ὦ μοι, πῇ δή τοι φρένες οἴχονθ', ἧς τὸ πάρος περ
> ἔκλε' ἐπ' ἀνθρώπους.

Ib. 535—

> πάντας γὰρ ἐπ' ἀνθρώπους ἐκέκαστο
> ὄλβῳ τε πλούτῳ τε.

La Roche (school edition of *Iliad*, on x. 213, πάντας ἐπ' ἀνθρώπους) adds *Od.* i. 299, iii. 252, xix. 334, xxiii. 125, xxiv. 94, 201.

C. γράμμασι—ἀφώνους] join. 'They died, and left no record.'

ὑπέρ] 'beyond,' 'previously to.' Thuc. i. 41 πρὸς τὸν Αἰγινητῶν ὑπὲρ τὰ Μηδικὰ πόλεμον, 'the war between Athens and Aegina before the Persian invasion.' A rare usage.

D. ἀκούσας οὖν κ.τ.λ.] 'When Solon heard this, he said, he was astonished.'

ἐκ γῆς τε καὶ Ἡφαίστου] Cf. 31 B. 'Nothing can be seen without having igneousness, or touched without having solidity; wherefore God framed the body of the universe of fire and earth.'

E. ἐνθάδε Turicenses, Hermann. ἐνθαδί Stallbaum, Schneider, 'cum corr. A' (Turr.).

διακοσμήσεως] The 'constitution' appointed by the goddess.

ἐνακισχίλια] The meaning is clear, but the construction very strange, not to say impossible. We should expect some preposition, such as πρὸ—ἐτῶν, or ὑπέρ as just above. One is tempted to think that some preposition has fallen out. But the editions have γεγονότων ἔτη or ἔτη γεγονότων.

24 A. παραδείγματα] 'counterparts.'

. ὅτι καθ' αὑτὸ ἕκαστον] 'Each branch of handicraft by itself.'

καὶ τὸ τῶν θηρευτῶν A, Turicenses, Hermann, Schneider. καὶ τῶν Stallbaum.

σχέσις in same sense, *Republic* v. 452 C περὶ τὴν τῶν ὅπλων σχέσιν. To make the construction regular σχέσις must be taken twice; 'their

equipment is an equipment with spear and shield;' but since this would
be as awkward in the Greek as in the English, the word is used only
once. We might possibly understand 'Then again there is the manner
of their equipment, with spear and shield,' no verb being expressed; but
this seems hardly so good.

'Aσίαν] Observe that Egypt is counted a part of Asia.

καθάπερ—τόποις] I am inclined to understand with Stallbaum;
'the goddess appointed this equipment among you first in Europe, as
she afterwards did among us first in Asia.' Müller translates differently,
taking ἐκείνοις τ. τ. to be Attica and Europe. ἐκείνοις seems strange at
first in the meaning here given to it, but the speaker is thinking not so
much of Egypt as of Asia generally, in opposition to Europe.

C. εἰς τὰ ἀνθρώπινα] Supply ' what is useful,' ' what is needful,' or
something of the kind. ' The author's meaning appears to me to be,
that by the study of astronomy and the natural sciences, which partake
of something divine, because they have for object the contemplation of
the works of God, the laws of Egypt led on to practical sciences, useful
to men, such as divination and medicine.' Martin, note xi.

εὐκρασίαν] Euripides, *Fr.* 971 Nauck—

οὐρανὸν ὑπὲρ γῆς ἔχομεν εὖ κεκραμένον,
ἵν' οὔτ' ἄγαν πῦρ οὔτε χεῖμα συμπίτνει.

Said of Attica. Herodotus says of Greece generally, iii. 106 κατάπερ ἡ
'Ελλὰς τὰς ὥρας πολλόν τι κάλλιστα κεκραμένας ἔλαχε. Greece, to him,
is the central region of the world, and possesses the happiest mixture of
various qualities. "Attica has always been famous [for its mildness.
Though Herodotus gave the preference to the sky of Ionia on the
Asiatic coast (i. 142), yet both Plato and the Attic comedians always
speak with enthusiasm of their native climate, and the fineness of the
Athenian intellect was referred to the clearness of the Attic atmosphere.
The air of Athens was said to be the purest of all; it is this which
Euripides celebrates, when he speaks of the inhabitants as ' ever
walking gracefully through the most luminous aether '—

ἀεὶ διὰ λαμπροτάτου
βαίνοντες ἀβρῶς αἰθέρος—

(*Med.* 829) and another author says of Athens that a mist seems to
be lifted from the eyes as you approach it, and the light appears to
assume an unwonted brightness (Aristides, *Panath.* p. 97 ed. Jebb).
Those who approach this district from Boeotia almost always experience
a change of temperature as soon as they descend from Cithaeron or
Parnes; and in the summer the heat is lessened by the sea-breeze,
which in modern times is called ὁ ἐμβάτης, or that which sets towards
shore. Accordingly Xenophon is justified in saying ' one would not
err in thinking that this city is placed near the centre of Greece, nay

of the civilized world, because the farther removed persons are from it, the severer is the cold or heat they meet with.' (*Vectigal*, i. 6.)" Tozer, *Lectures on the Geography of Greece*, p. 140-141. Modern ἀφιλαθήναιοι say that Athens and the surrounding parts are the dustiest places in the known world.

E. πορεύσιμον] see below 25 D.

ὡς φατε ὑμεῖς] 'Intolerabilis haec est tautologia,' says Stallbaum; and so it seems at first. Most of the codices have καλεῖται. The words would be identical in the mouth of an itacizer. The Zürich editors and Hermann have καλεῖτε. Stallbaum would read ὁ καλεῖται--στῆλαι. Schneider has ὁ καλεῖται ὡς φατε ὑμεῖς Ἡρακλέους στήλας, and this is perhaps best; 'which is called in your phrase the Pillars of Heracles.' στήλας then would be governed by φατέ, by a somewhat free construction. ὡς φατε 'as you say' by itself may either mean 'as you tell us,' or 'as you use the words.'

ἐπιβατὸν is curious; 'from which there was a passage to' etc.

25 A. τὸν ἀληθινὸν ἐκεῖνον πόντον] What can Plato have known of the ocean beyond the Pillars of Hercules?

παντελῶς ἀληθῶς] It is not too clear how we are to join these words. Are we to take them with περιέχουσα, or with λέγοιτο? And we could do without three consecutive adverbs. Plato does not contemplate the possibility of the actual fact, that the water surrounds the earth. 'Wasser umfänget Ruhig das All.'

ἤπειρος] 'Ludit in vocabuli originatione.' St. That land may well be called 'boundless' which surrounds the great ocean of the world. The ordinary etymology from ἄπειρος is doubtless correct. The extension or 'increment' (*Steigerung*) of short α into η is remarkable, but finds analogy in such words as ἡγεμών, root ἀγ, ἠνεμόεις from ἄνεμος, ἤνυστρον from ἀνύω, 'the fourth stomach of a ruminant' Aristotle (Περὶ τὰ Ζῷα Ἱστοριῶν B p. 507 b 9 Bekker, etc.), 'the completer' or 'finisher' of digestion. An even more exact parallel, where the alpha privative is increased to η, is the Homeric ἤκεστος, 'ungoaded,' *Il.* vi. 94 etc. In the Homeric γρῆυς Ἀπειραίη we seem to find implied ἄπειρος without the augment.

τῶν ἐντὸς τῇδε] δεικτικῶς. τῶν partitive, and Λιβύης governed by ἦρχον. Here again Egypt is not reckoned to Libya: Libya is barbarous, except for its Greek colonies.

D. ἐλθούσης Turicenses, Schneider, ἐπελθούσης Stallbaum and Hermann with A.

παρ' ὑμῶν Turicenses. ὑμῖν Stallbaum, Schneider, Hermann, with A.

πηλοῦ] In *Critias* 108 E there is a similar passage, where mention is made of ἄπορος πηλός, 'impassable mud.'

βαθέος the Zürich editors after Bekker, and most codices, including

Paris A, which has however in the margin καταβραχέος. Schneider, Hermann, and Stallbaum read κάρτα βραχέος, no doubt rightly. 'βαθέος B T' (Bekker, Turicenses) 'cum Par. librisque plurimis, quos tamen hic mature ad blandam speciem correctos esse arbitror.' Hermann. 'A mud that makes the sea exceedingly shallow.' Those who wrote βαθέος have understood 'an abyss of mud'; but βραχέος makes better sense. The Scholiast tells us, 'They say that all the country there is τεναγώδης, and a τέναγος is mud with little water on the surface, and grass appearing on this.' This notion of an impassable outskirt of the inhabited world was very prevalent in ancient Greece. The subject is discussed in an interesting note to the eighteenth chapter of Grote's History (ii. 462-3 second edition) where many curious passages are given. The wildest of these is the description quoted by Strabo from the famous, or notorious, Pytheas, who flourished probably about the time of Alexander. In the neighbourhood of Thule there was neither air, land, nor water, but a mixture of all three, like a *pulmo marinus* (a sea-snail or a jelly-fish?) where they remained in suspension, and in which you could neither walk nor sail. (Grote, *l.l.*) We may also compare Milton (*Paradise Lost*, ii. 939) 'A boggy Syrtis, neither sea, Nor good dry land'; and the whole passage.

E. χθές] During the recital of the conversation which makes the *Republic*.

οὐκ ἀπὸ σκοποῦ] 'not fortuitously.' According to the grammarians, we are to write ἀπὸ σκοποῦ, ἀπὸ τρόπου. See Stallbaum on *Phaedrus* 278 D.

26 A. διὰ χρόνου κ.τ.λ.] 'Because, after so long a time, I did not remember the story very well.' Cf. *supra Republic* i. 328 B διὰ χρόνου γὰρ καὶ ἑωράκη αὐτόν.

ἀναλαβόντα] 'recovering,' 'recollecting.'

οὕτως we may call 'resumptive'; it sums up all that has gone before.

λόγον—ὑποθέσθαι] 'to provide a subject that hits the taste of the company.' The λόγος is the tale he has just been telling. Schneider renders 'argumentum proposito idoneum,' which is perhaps more accurate.

καθάπερ ὅδ' εἶπε] 'as Hermocrates has told you,' (above, 20 D.)

B. πρὸς τούσδε ἀνέφερον] 'I tried to recover the story, telling it as I did so to my friends here.'

τὸ λεγόμενον] 'As the proverb says, "Learn a thing young, and you will never forget it."'

οὐκ ἂν οἶδα εἰ δυναίμην] 'Quippe adhaesit in talibus ἄν principali enuntiati parti, ut statim a principio animadvertatur sententiam hypotheticam, quae infertur, aliunde esse suspensam.' Stallbaum. Demosthenes, *de Falsa Legatione*, p. 441, § 358 οὐδ' ἂν εἷς εὖ οἶδ' ὅτι φήσειε.

παμπολὺν χρόνον διακήκοα] The meaning is obviously 'what I heard a very long time ago'; but the use of the accusative is very strange. We should expect πρὸ παμπολλοῦ χρόνου, or διὰ παμπολλοῦ χρόνου, or ἤδη παμπολὺς χρόνος ἐπεί, or something similar. One is reminded of ἐνακισχίλια γεγονότων ἔτη above (23 E).

παιδικῆς (Turr., Hermann, Schneider) gives much better sense than παιδιᾶς of Stallbaum.

C. ἀνεκπλύτου] Cf. the passage in the *Republic* iv. 429 D, in which the effects of education are described. 'You know, I said, that the dyers, when they want to dye wool for making the true sea-purple, begin by selecting their white colour first ; this they prepare and dress with no slight circumstance, in order that the white ground may take the purple hue in full perfection. The dyeing then proceeds ; and whatever is dyed in this manner becomes a fast colour, and no washing with lyes or without lyes can take away the bloom of the colour.'

D. ὡς ἐκείνην τήνδε οὖσαν] 'as if the imaginary city were this our actual one.'

πάντως ἁρμόσουσι] ' Asyndeton, quod in asseveratione frequens est,' Stallbaum. Scarcely in any other place does Plato speak so warmly of, Athens.

PHILEBUS.

15 D—17 A.

' The discovery of Unity in Multiplicity, and Multiplicity in Unity, and the reduction of Multiplicity to Number, is the true process of Science.' Poste *in margine.*

Of Philebus we only know, from the dialogue, that he is a young gentleman, accompanied by young friends. Protarchus, perhaps a little older, is called the son of Callias (59 B), and says in 58 A that he has been a hearer of Gorgias.

'Locus plane divinus,' Stallbaum.

D. Φαμέν που—νῦν] 'We say that the unification of the One and the Many by ratiocination pervades all language and all thought.' 'Perhaps ὑπὸ λόγων alludes to the "magic words" by which the sorcerers of epic fable effect their transformations. As Plato has already dismissed the Eleatics and Megarici, he seems here to be ridiculing his own disciples for trifling with his Dialectical paradox.' Poste. Is it needful to put this sense upon ὑπὸ λόγων ?

πάντῃ] Words with this termination should doubtless be written without the *iota subscriptum,* as indeed we may see by the Doric παντᾷ etc. The η represents the instrumental case of the old Aryan language in -ā. τάχα, ἅμα, ἵνα, etc., have a short vowel instead of the long one. (Schleicher, Compendium der vergleichenden Grammatik² p. 579.) The remark might have been extended to the prepositions etc. which end in α.

ἀθάνατόν τι καὶ ἀγήρων] A Homeric collocation of words, *e. g. Iliad* viii. 539—

εἰ γὰρ ἐγὼν ὡς
εἴην ἀθάνατος καὶ ἀγήρως ἤματα πάντα,

and many other places.

ὁ δὲ πρῶτον αὐτοῦ γευσάμενος] Does this mean 'he who has tasted for the first time,' or 'from age to age the youth who first detects it' (Poste)? The second might seem simple ; but probably the first is right. Cf. the place in the *Republic*, viii. 539 B οἱ μειρακίσκοι, ὅταν τὸ πρῶτον λόγων γεύωνται. 'You must have observed, that young men, when first they have "tasted the blood" of logic, are so fascinated by this, that they make it their habitual pastime ; they are always contradicting somebody, and making a fool of him, as they have seen their master do ; they are like puppy dogs, who take a pleasure in pulling and tearing at everything they come across.'

16 A. ὀλίγου δὲ κ.τ.λ.] 'His merciless logic will not except shall I say the very cat and dog ; certainly a wild savage will find no quarter, if he can only come by an interpreter.'

εὐμενῶς πως ἀπελθεῖν] 'ταραχή ipsa tanquam dea aliqua dicitur εὐμενῶς κ.τ.λ.' Stallbaum. As if she were a somewhat maleficent deity, of whom it most concerns us to get rid with all proper respect.

B. ὦ παῖδες] Jocularly, 'my boys,' as Protarchus has just said they are all νέοι. Philebus does not use this phrase of address in the dialogue. See Stallbaum on 36 D.

γένοιτο, ἧς ἐγὼ κ.τ.λ.] The editors all put a comma after γένοιτο ; but surely the sense would be clearer without it. ἧς is at once the genitive after καλλίων, and the genitive after ἐραστής.

ἔρημον καὶ ἄπορον] 'desolate and helpless.'

C. δόσις I understand to be the predicate ; 'this was cast down from heaven, and was a gift of the gods.' This was one of the often-quoted Platonic passages. Stallbaum gives quotations from Julian, Damascius, Numenius, in all of which the words are more or less repeated.

ἐγγυτέρω θεῶν] who lived nearer to their great progenitors, the gods. *Odyssee* vii. 205—

οὔ τι κατακρύπτουσιν (θεοί), ἐπεί σφισιν ἐγγύθεν εἰμέν.

The gods disguise not themselves from the Phaeacians, for we are near

to them in blood.' *Republic* iii. 391 E, where a place is cited from the
Niobe of Aeschylus—

οἱ θεῶν ἀγχίσποροι
οἱ Ζηνὸς ἐγγύς, ὧν κατ' Ἰδαῖον πάγον
Διὸς πατρῴου βωμός ἐστ' ἐν αἰθέρι,
κοὔπω σφιν ἐξίτηλον αἷμα δαιμόνων.

(Nauck, *Fragmenta* 157.)

The 'most bright light' is to be taken figuratively.

ταύτην φήμην is the reading of the books : φήμην must then be
predicate; 'they have left this as their utterance.'

ὡς ἐξ ἑνὸς μὲν καὶ ἐκ πολλῶν ὄντων go together; and so again τῶν
ἀεὶ λεγομένων εἶναι. 'All things of which existence is predicated are
made up of the One and the Many.'

δεῖν οὖν—ζητεῖν] 'This being the constitution of things, we should
begin every inquiry by laying down one general conception.'

D. ἐὰν—μεταλάβωμεν] 'when we have obtained.'

καὶ τῶν ἐν ἐκείνων] So the MSS., which the Zürich editors, Hermann, and Hirschig, rightly follow. The words have often been misunderstood. Stallbaum in particular wishes to read, after Ast, τῶν ἐν
ἐκείνῳ ἕκαστον, which is intelligible, but very weak. There is not the
slightest necessity for change. Ἕν is obviously used as an indeclinable
plural, in the sense of 'unities,' its number being sufficiently indicated
by the inflections of the article. Plato declines the singular freely, but
shrinks from *ἕνα, *ἑνῶν, *ἑσί, especially as ἕν in a somewhat technical
sense is more striking and forcible when undeclined. Each of these
new 'ones,' these subdivisions, is to be again subdivided in the same
way. Just below, E, we have the phrase τὸ ἓν ἕκαστον, 'each unity.'
The same misunderstanding recurs in 17 E, where Stallbaum reads,
with most MSS., ὅταν τε ἄλλο τῶν ὄντων ὁτιοῦν ταύτῃ σκοπούμενος ἔλῃς.
So Hirschig. But the Bodleian, Vatican (Δ), Venetian Π, have τῶν ἐν
ὁτιοῦν. The Zürich editors and Hermann read τῶν ὄντων ἐν ὁτιοῦν.
But, in the first place, the best MSS. should have been followed ; and
secondly, they are obviously right, the meaning being 'any one of
unities,' 'any unity whatever.' 18 A ὥσπερ γὰρ ἓν ὁτιοῦν. ὄντων is
an attempt at correction by some one who could not make out ἕν. The
reading of the Turicenses and Hermann in 17 E gives *both* variants,
somewhat in the 'scholiastic' style of mentioning contradictory explanations without decision, or after the manner of the Septuagint,
when the same Hebrew words appear translated twice over.

πλῆθος—ἀριθμὸν] Unity and Multiplicity must be kept distinct,
until we know the number of the intervening stages.

E. τότε δὴ δεῖ] An instance of the importance of applying principles
to the fixing of the text. The three best MSS. (Bodleian, Vatican Δ,

Venice Π) read τότε δὴ δεῖ, which the Zürich editors adopt. This is at once very abrupt, and not much like Plato's usage. τότε δ' ἤδη is the vulgate reading, and is found in the margin of the Vatican MS. So Hermann, Hirschig, Stallbaum read, no doubt rightly, supposing an itacism to have occurred. One cannot but agree with Hermann when he says, 'Talia vel optimus liber passim confundit, nec si omnes manuscripti in eo consentirent, lenissimam pariter atque elegantissimam emendationem eorum auctoritati posthaberem.'

17 A. θᾶττον καὶ βραδύτερον] They are too ready with the extremes, and too slow with intermediate steps.

οἷς διακεχώρισται—λόγους] 'But all this, to repeat it again, is precisely the distinction between logical reasoning and that which is merely cristic.'

THEAETETUS.

172 C—177 C.

The main question of the *Theaetetus* is, What is Knowledge? but that subject is not discussed in the following passage, which is a digression. It contains a satirical description of the opposed characters of the philosopher, who proceeds by reason to the acquisition of knowledge, and of the litigious or demagoguic man, who seeks to attain some paltry end by rhetoric and chicanery. Each has his sphere. The philosopher is in a sad way when you bring him into law courts; he has no head for their details, and is unaccustomed to their servile way of subjection to times and forms. But how he has his revenge, when he gets his friend the pettifogger into the upper air of real knowledge! Frightened and dizzy, he loses his head and his tongue, and becomes ridiculous to all rational beings.

In the beautiful introduction of the dialogue Eucleides of Megara tells Terpsion of the same place that he has just seen Theaetetus being conveyed from the army at Corinth to Athens, and that his state is desperate both from wounds and disease. This suggests the remembrance of a remarkable conversation between Socrates, Theaetetus, and Theodorus, which Eucleides has heard repeated at Athens by Socrates, and which he has committed fully to writing. The notes are then read aloud.

Socrates had taken a great fancy to Theaetetus, and prophesied his future distinction (142 C, D). He is but a lad when the conversation takes place. He and Theodorus appear also in the *Sophist*, and Theodorus in the *Politicus*. Theodorus of Cyrene, a friend of Protagoras, was an eminent geometer. Theaetetus is his pupil, and a most intelligent one. 'Theaetetus is described by later writers as a great mathematician, who taught at Heraclea' (in Lucania?), 'after the time of the Peloponnesian war, and as the author of the first treatise on the five regular solids.' Campbell.

172 C. οὐκοῦν σχολὴν ἄγομεν] though put as a question, is really a statement—'We have plenty of time.'

ὡς εἰκότως] 'How natural it is,' 'how much to be expected.' Instead of an impersonal verb following, which we might use in English, the words are inserted adverbially in the principal sentence.

ἐν ταῖς φιλοσοφίαις] 'In scientific pursuits.' Campbell. Ast's *Lexicon* does not give any other example of the word in the plural.

κυλινδούμενοι] *volutantes*, 'who have been knocking about.' Cf. *Politicus* 309 A τοὺς δ' ἐν ἀμαθίᾳ τ' αὖ καὶ ταπεινότητι πολλῇ κυλινδουμένους εἰς τὸ δουλικὸν ὑποζεύγνυσι γένος, 'those who are wallowing.' *Republic* iii. 405 B ὅταν τις μὴ μόνον τὸ πολὺ τοῦ βίου ἐν δικαστηρίοις φεύγων τε καὶ διώκων κατατρίβηται.

D. Ἦι κ.τλ.] 'In this way, that to the one' etc.

τρίτον ἤδη λόγον] In the first λόγος, between Socrates and Theaetetus, Protagoras is criticized; in the second, the older Theodorus, who had before been silent, takes a part; and the third, from which the extract in the text is a digression, treats of some who partly agree with Protagoras, and partly depart from his views.

οὕτω κἀκεῖνοι] The editors put a comma before this; would not a colon be more appropriate?

ἀρέσῃ] 'please them,' 'be to their mind.' ἀρέσκω with the accusative is not uncommon in Plato, *e.g. Republic* viii. 557 D ὃς ἂν αὐτὸν ἀρέσκῃ τρόπος (*supra*), and note upon *ibid.* B.

ὕδωρ ῥέον] The water in the clepsydra, whose flowing determines the length of his speech.

E. ὑπογραφὴν] the signed statement of the opposite party.

ἣν ἀντωμοσίαν καλοῦσιν] 'which in their phraseology is termed the brief.' If we keep these words, we must understand Socrates to speak as an ἐλεύθερος, who is not too familiar with technical terms. (Turicenses, Hermann, Stallbaum retain.) But are they not simply a gloss upon the word ὑπογραφὴν? 'Verba ἣν ἀντωμοσίαν καλοῦσι glossema putant esse Alreschius (Auctar. Diluc. Thucyd. p. 425.), Heindorfius, Astius, alii.' Turicenses. Hirschig brackets. Heindorf quotes as 'simillimum glossema' *Phaedrus* 242 A ἡ δὴ καλουμένη σταθερά, which phrase certainly appears to be an echo of the words adjoining.

δεσπότην] 'Not simply the δικαστής, but rather δῆμος or νόμος, which he represents.' Campbell.

τὴν line 23] τὴν two of the Zürich editors, Stallbaum, Hirschig, Heimann. But surely we should read τινὰ with the best codices (Bodl., Vat., Ven. Π) as Winckelmann and Campbell do.

καὶ οἱ ἀγῶνες κ.τ.λ.] 'The trial is never about some indifferent matter, but always concerns himself.' περὶ αὑτοῦ Heindorf. But αὐτοῦ, which the editors have, gives really the same sense.

δρόμος] Cf. *Iliad* xxii. 161

ἀλλὰ περὶ ψυχῆς θέον Ἕκτορος ἱπποδάμοιο. (Campbell.)

173 A. ἔντονοι καὶ δριμεῖς] 'keen and shrewd.'

χαρίσασθαι would require a dative; perhaps we may take it absolutely.

οὓς οὐ δυνάμενοι κ.τ.λ.] 'which are too much for their truth and honesty.'

B. τοιοῦτοι is the predicate.

χοροῦ] 'brotherhood,' literally 'chorus.' 'The metaphor is continued in the words οἱ ἐν τῷ τοιῷδε χορεύοντες—οὔτε θεατὴς ὥσπερ ποιηταῖς—περὶ τῶν κορυφαίων.' Campbell. Cf. *Phaedrus* 247 A supra; φθόνος γὰρ ἔξω θείου χοροῦ ἵσταται.

διελθόντες line 39, for which we might rather have expected διέλθωμεν, is probably an attraction to the following participle ἐάσαντες.

C. οἱ ἡμέτεροι] Heindorf would have preferred οἱ omitted, so that we might understand 'are as it were our servants.' But it must be remembered that, not having a good text before him, he was often tempted to suspect the reading without occasion. Stallbaum and Hirschig reject the word; Turicenses and Hermann retain, with all the MSS. 'We are not at the bidding of the argument, but our arguments are as it were slaves, who have no will of their own.' Mr. Campbell thinks οἱ suspicious, but that, if genuine, it still belongs to the predicate; 'are as it were our servants;' οἱ ἡμέτεροι being put before ὥσπερ. It might be suggested that the two words stand in a double construction, with both λόγοι and οἰκέται.

ὡς ἔοικεν] as is proper or natural. οἱ κορυφαῖοι are the chiefs or leaders of our chorus. The beginning of the sixth Book of the *Republic*, where the philosopher is compared to a pilot who has no authority over his crew, is generally similar to this passage.

D. σπουδαὶ κ.τ.λ.] Instead of these words having a verb to agree with them, the construction is changed, and we have the impersonal προσίσταται. πράττειν also is not strictly applicable to σπουδαί, etc.

ἑταιριῶν Hermann (with B). ἑταιρειῶν the other editions. ἑταιρεῖαι are associations or societies, here ἐπ' ἀρχάς, to get their own candidates elected. We learn from Thucydides (viii. 54) that the ἑταιρεῖαι of Athens, in the time of the Peloponnesian war, were of an aristocratic kind, and dangerous both to order and liberty, *e. g.* by supporting their members in lawsuits without regard to justice, and promoting assassination as a means of political intimidation.

οὐδὲ—αὑτοῖς] 'They never even dream of meddling with such matters.'

τις γέγονεν] τι γέγονεν 'So the Bodleian and several other MSS.' Campbell. 'Vulgo inepte τι. Alterum revocavi e Clem. Alexandr. Strom. v. p. 249.' Heindorf, whom the editors follow. It is not easy to decide; perhaps the neuter is the simpler. εὖ γέγονεν ('Αλκιβιάδης) ἐν πόλει would surely be a harsh phrase.

αὐτόν] *ad sensum*, the singular instead of the plural.

χόες] The χοῦς was about three quarts English. 'He no more knows these things than he can tell the number of the sea.'

καὶ ταῦτα—οἶδεν] 'Neither is he conscious of his ignorance.'

E. ἡγησαμένη σμικρὰ καὶ οὐδέν] 'disdaining these pettinesses, not to say nullities.'

κατὰ Πίνδαρον] Plato seems to have somewhat altered the quotation, as is his manner, to accommodate it to a prose rhythm. See Bergk, *Poetae Lyrici*[3], *fr.* 277, who quotes passages from Clement of Alexandria and other late writers; but they seem to derive from Plato rather than from Pindar. 'Certe non licet Pindari versus instaurare.' 'Plato seems to have changed πέταται' (found in Clement) 'into the more prosaic φέρεται, (πέτεται occurs as a marginal reading)' (in the Bodleian etc.), 'and to have introduced the words καὶ τὰ ἐπίπεδα γεωμετροῦσα (perhaps also ἀστρονομοῦσα), in compliment to Theodorus, adding τῶν ὄντων ἑκάστου κ.τ.λ.' Campbell. Theodorus is a mathematician.

τὰ ἐπίπεδα] the surfaces (superficies) of the earth. 'ὅλου in its entirety.'

174 A. ἐμμελὴς καὶ χαρίεσσα] It is difficult to say whether we are to understand merely 'witty and clever' ('as the wise maiden of Thrace very wittily said'), or to suppose an antithesis between the slave's sharpness and Thales' absence of mind. The latter is rather favoured by τορῶς τε καὶ ὀξέως 175 E *infra*. 'A trim and dainty maiden.'

C. ἑκάστῳ] in company with any individual.

ὅπερ—ἔλεγον] 'These words refer only to δημοσίᾳ.' Campbell.

ἴδιον] 'fresh,' 'out of his own head,' 'supplied by himself.'

D. ληρώδης δοκεῖ εἶναι] 'he is taken for a booby.'

τύραννον κ.τ.λ.] 'Governed by ἀκούων, implied in ἀκούειν below.' Campbell.

The 'herdsman' is Plato's standing comparison for the ruler. 'The figure probably originated in some saying of Socrates.' C.

ἐκείνων] the various kinds of herdsmen, to wit.

E. σηκὸν—περιβεβλημένον] 'shut up in his castle, like a shepherd in his mountain-cote.' σηκὸν is in apposition with τεῖχος, so that a ὡς of comparison is not required.

ὑμνούντων] 'when they sing the praises of family.' The construction is free. We might suppose the genitive to be absolute; or we might think of ἔπαινον following. Perhaps the writer does not think of any strict construction, in our sense. ἀμβλὺ after ὁρώντων.

175 A. ἐπὶ—προγόνων] 'The order is ἐπὶ καταλόγῳ πέντε καὶ εἴκοσι προγόνων.' C.

ἀναφερόντων] without τὸ γένος, as we might say familiarly 'when they carry up to Heracles the son of Amphitryon.' Cf. *Alcibiades* I, 120 E *supra*.

B. οἷα—τύχη] 'was—whatever Fortune chose to make him.' ἀπ' αὐτοῦ, from this twenty-fifth progenitor again. For the sense, cf. Juvenal viii. 272

> 'Et tamen ut longe repetas longeque revolvas
> Nomen, ab infami gentem deducis asylo;
> Majorum primus quisquis fuit ille tuorum,
> Aut pastor fuit, aut illud quod dicere nolo.'

ἀπαλλάττειν] 'he laughs because they cannot do a short sum, which would cure them of their absurd pretension.'

αὐτός has a slightly adversative force, as is very common in all Greek. 'When he in his turn draws some one of his enemies into upper air, and gets him out of his pleas and rejoinders, and his commonplaces about the happiness of kings.'

C. τ' αὖ can hardly be right, unless it were part of the verbatim transference of some quotation, which is not Plato's manner, when it interferes with ordinary prose construction. Hermann reads [τ' αὖ] πολὺ χρυσίον, Hirschig πάμπολυ χρυσίον, Stallbaum seems to favour πάνυ πολὺ (Heinde and Buttmann in Heindorf.) The three best MSS (B Δ Π) omit πολὺ, from which τ' αὖ may be a corruption. In that case Hermann's κεκτημένος πολὺ χρυσίον would be best. Bekker, Stallbaum, Hirschig, omit εἰ before βασιλεὺς, with some MSS; but it is obviously a part of the quotation. Turicenses and Hermann retain.

D. δριμὺν] 'keen,' 'astute.'

τὰ ἀντίστροφα ἀποδίδωσιν] *correspondentia reddit*, 'he appears in the same ridiculous predicament.'

ὑπὸ ἀηθείας] with ἰλιγγιῶν? or rather with ἀδημονῶν &c. ? 'His head spins, because he is not used to be so high, or to look down; he is all abroad; he is dismayed, and lost, and stammers out broken words.'

ἀδημονῶν] 'being ill at ease,' 'being dismayed.'

ἀνδραπόδοις] by attraction.

E. ᾧ ἀνεμέσητον κ.τ.λ.] 'Who may, without any one's taking exception, figure as a simpleton and a nobody, when' etc.

στρωματόδεσμον—συσκευάσασθαι] 'who does not know how to pack up his baggage neatly.' στρώματα, or bedclothes, were regularly carried on journeys, so that the word is used for baggage generally. Cf. *Frogs* 165, *Birds* 656

ἄγε δή, Ξανθία,
καὶ Μανόδωρε, λαμβάνετε τὰ στρώματα,

and the places in Becker's *Charicles*, I. n. 8.

ὁ δ' αὖ] *scil.* τρόπος.

ἀναβάλλεσθαι seems to mean, 'how to cast his garment gracefully about him,' wear it like a gentleman. The best commentary is the place in the *Birds*, 1567

οὗτος, τί δρᾷς; ἐπ' ἀριστέρ' οὕτως ἀμπέχει;
οὐ μεταβαλεῖς θοἰμάτιον ὧδ' ἐπὶ δεξιά;

Poseidon is scandalized by the Triballian god, who is a low fellow, and has no idea how to dress himself. See *Charicles*, Exc. 1. Sc. xi. p. 418. 'The ἱμάτιον was first thrown over the left shoulder, and then round the back to the right side, and then above the right arm or below it, and again brought over the left shoulder or arm. This was called ἐπὶ δεξιὰ ἀναβάλλεσθαι or ἀμπισχνεῖσθαι.' This adjustment may often be seen in statues.

λαβόντος] 'There is an allusion to the well-known custom of taking the lyre in turn.' Campbell.

176 A. ὑπεναντίον] The ὑπ- appears to be one of those euphemistic qualifications in which the Attic delights. 'More or less' opposition, as we might say.

ἱδρύσθαι] 'have a fixed place,' as they would if they pertained to the gods. Cf.

ὅθι φασὶ θεῶν ἕδος ἀσφαλὲς αἰεὶ Ἔμμεναι

(*Odyss.* vi. 42), and innumerable places.

B. ἵνα δὴ μή] δή does not appear in B Δ, and the first hand of Π.

δοκῇ is the important word; 'that a man may be thought' etc.

λεγόμενος] probably best as H. Müller takes it ; 'this is, in my mind, but an old wives' fable, as we say,' like οἱ τῆς θαλάττης λεγόμενοι χόες above. Professor Campbell understands, 'This is what men commonly repeat.'

ὕθλος probably comes from the root ὑ- (original *su, to wet or sprinkle) (Curtius, *Etymologie* p. 512⁴), which appears in ὕει, ὑετός, and would then mean properly 'what is poured out,' and so 'babble.' Cf. Latin *futtilis* from the root of *fundo*, and the late Greek χυδαῖος, 'vulgar,' 'common,' from root χυ- (identical with root *fu- of fundo).

C. οὐδενία, or οὐδένεια, is a bold formation from οὐδέν direct. οὐδενία the best editions.

D. τὸ μὴ συγχωρεῖν] 'that it be not conceded him.' The unexpressed subject of the verb is really impersonal.

B b

καὶ οἴονται—σωθησομένους] 'And they fancy men say that they are no fools, no cumberers of the ground, but people who deserve to live.'

οὐδὲν ἀδικοῦντες do not go together, as one might suppose for a moment.

E. παραδειγμάτων] *Republic* ix. *s. f.* (*supra*). 'In heaven, I replied, there is laid up a pattern of such a city, and he who desires may behold this, and beholding govern himself accordingly.'

τοῦ ἀθέου] 'the undivine.'

177 A. οὗ δὴ τίνουσι Turicenses, Hermann, Stallbaum, Hirschig.

τὸν εἰκότα βίον] not 'the similar,' but 'the life you might expect from that to which they make themselves like.' This gives an abbreviated but intelligible construction. Both senses of the word are implied, though the word itself is used only once.

ἀνοήτων τινῶν] We should understand ὡς to refer to these words as well as to δεινοὶ καὶ πανοῦργοι.

B. ἀτόπως—τελευτῶντες] 'they come to a strange end.'

πάρεργα] 'as a digression' from the third branch of the discussion of the brocard of Protagoras, 'Man is the measure of all things.'

LAWS.

Book I. 644 D—645 C.

The *Laws*, the longest of Plato's compositions, are the work of his old age; and so different are they from his earlier writings, that their genuineness has sometimes been denied. The well-contrasted characters, the consecution of plan, the flowing and harmonious style, the endless play of intelligence and humour, have disappeared. Three old men, the nameless Athenian stranger, the Cretan Cleinias, and the Lacedaemonian Megillus, discuss, somewhat cynically, the conduct of human affairs. In a large part of the work the dialogue vanishes; the ideal city of the Republic is sobered down into one humanly possible; and for the principles merely suggested in the earlier work we have strict and definite laws. But the hand of Plato is very apparent in many noble passages. That from the First Book, where man is compared to a puppet or *fantoccino*, needs no comment.

The conversation of the *Laws* is supposed to happen in Crete. The speakers are three; a stranger of Athens, a Cretan, Cleinias, and a Lacedaemonian, Megillus. At the end of the Third Book (p. 702) Cleinias tells us that 'The greater part of Crete is going to send out a colony, and they have entrusted the management of the affair to the Cnosians; and the Cnosians to me and nine others.' This committee is to have an absolute power of legislation for the new colony. Let us therefore take advantage of the present discussion, and consider what laws they ought to have. Otherwise Cleinias and Megillus are mere names, except in so far as they refer to the usages of their respective countries.

Professor Schanz, in his critical edition of the first six books of the *Laws*, which has recently appeared (1879), says, 'Cum Leges a Parisino 1807 (olim 94 et 2087), quem A vocant, solo pendere notum sit (plura alibi), notarum exiguus sane usus est.' Accordingly he confines his notes to the readings of A and conjectures. If I understand him right, the MSS. called 'Vaticanus' (Ω of Bekker), 'Vossianus' or x, 'Riccardianus' (♭ of Bekker), 'Palatinus' (ƒ of Bekker) are all transcripts of A. He also mentions in passing that in the *Republic* he would rely solely on A and Π.

D. **θαῦμα**] A 'puppet' or 'marionnette.' We are reminded of the theories of our own day that the animals, or even man, may be no more than self-acting 'automata.' See *supra* in the famous simile of the cave, *Republic* vii. 514 B. *Laws* ii. 658 B οὐ θαυμαστὸν δέ, εἴ τις καὶ θαύματα ἐπιδεικνὺς μάλιστ' ἂν νικᾶν ἡγοῖτο. But in the latter place the meaning may very well be simply 'jugglers' tricks.' For the word see Ruhnken's *Timaeus*. Cf. Plautus, *Captivi*, Prologue 22

'Enim vero Di nos quasi pilas homines habent.'

More to the point is Horace, *Satires* II. vii. 82

'Duceris ut nervis alienis mobile lignum,'

in same sense as here. Apuleius, *De Mundo* (p. 351 Oudendorp. 408 Hildebrand) talks of 'illi qui in ligneolis hominum figuris gestus movent, quando filum membri quod agitare solent traxerint, torquebitur cervix, nutabit caput, oculi vibrabunt, manus ad *ministerium *praesto erunt, nec invenuste totus videbitur vivere.' The divine power exerts itself by instruments only. Marcus Aurelius x. 38 (Long): 'Remember that this which pulls the strings' (τὸ νευροσπαστοῦν) 'is the thing which is hidden within; this is the power of persuasion, this is life, this, if one may so say, is man.' See Ast upon the present passage. Favorinus in Gellius xiv. 1. 23, If the stars direct everything, it will happen 'ut plane homines non, quod dicitur, "λογικὰ ζῶα," sed ludicra et ridenda quaedam neurospasta esse videantur, si nihil sua sponte, nihil arbitratu suo faciunt, sed ducentibus stellis et aurigantibus.' Cf. also Persius V. 128

'Servitium acre

Te nihil impellit, nec quicquam extrinsecus intrat,

Quod nervos agitet,'

and Conington *ad locum*. 'Casaubon shows that the usage was a very common one, especially among the Stoics, occurring many times in Marcus Antoninus.'

τῶν ζῴων θεῖον] τῶν ζῴων θεῶν A, which, if awkward, is intelligible enough. τῶν [ζῴων] θεῶν Schanz. θείων and θεῖον are conjectural. The meaning is much the same in any case.

παίγνιον] So *Laws* vii. 803 C ἄνθρωπον δέ, ὅπερ εἴπομεν ἔμπροσθεν, θεοῦ τι παίγνιον εἶναι μεμηχανημένον, καὶ ὄντως τοῦτο αὐτοῦ τὸ βέλτιστον γεγονέναι.

E. ταῦτα τὰ πάθη] Pleasure and pain.

μήρινθοι] σμήρινθοι A al. Schanz.

οὗ δή—κεῖται] οὗ, *quasi* πράγματος, to be supplied from πράξεις, or it may be generally, ‘of whatever.’ The translators all take οὗ as the adverb; and so apparently Stallbaum. But surely the meaning must be, the expressions being somewhat elliptic, ‘We are drawn in different directions towards the opposite actions, with regard to every action as to which there is a fixed distinction of right and wrong.’ This agrees much better with the use of κεῖται, in such phrases as νόμος κεῖται or πρόκειται.

645 A. ἕκαστον] ‘every man.’

χρυσῆν] Plato may be thinking of Homer's σειρὴ χρυσέη (*Iliad* viii. 17 and context), which in the *Theaetetus* (153 C) is explained to mean the Sun.

χρυσῆν οὖσαν] ‘Post οὖσαν lacunam indicavi: οὖσαν καὶ μονοειδῆ apographum Riccardianum, οὖσαν καὶ μίαν μὲν Steinhart introduct. p. 372 n. 150.’ Schanz. We want something to balance παντοδαποῖς.

ξυλλαμβάνειν] ‘to give our aid.’

B. περὶ θαυμάτων ὡς ὄντων ἡμῶν] ‘H. e. περὶ ἡμῶν ὡς θαυμάτων ὄντων.’ Stallbaum.

ὁ μῦθος ἀρετῆς κ.τ.λ.] ‘Proverbii instar est ὁ μῦθος οἴχεται, ὁ μῦθος ἀπώλετο, et contrarium ὁ μῦθος ἐσώθη.’ Idem ad *Philebum* 14 A. In these frequently recurring phrases the meaning seems to vary between ‘the tale is remembered’ or ‘forgotten’ and ‘the argument is wrecked’ or ‘saved.’ See *supra* on *Republic* x. 621 B. The words in the *Philebus* are κἄπειθ' ἡμῖν οὗτος ὁ λόγος ὥσπερ μῦθος ἀπολόμενος οἴχοιτο. ‘And our argument would come to nothing and be lost, like a tale that is not told out.’ Here the author says, ‘And so the tale concerning virtue will not be out, which represents us as puppets.’

ὃ νοεῖ] ‘The meaning of the statement.’

τὸν μὲν] *scil.* the ἰδιώτης or individual, to which words are then added λόγον ἀληθῆ λαβόντα.

C. διηρθρωμένον] Observe the neuter. ‘And thus virtue and vice will come to be more clearly discriminated.’ αὐτοῦ then follows in agreement.

τὸ περὶ—διατριβῆς] This refers to the discourse a little way before. ‘The question of convivial entertainment.’

Book III.   676 A—682 E.

In the beginning of the Third Book is discussed the origin of society.
But the problem is no longer that of the *Republic*, to frame a state
wherein justice and all other good may be fully practised ; we rather
inquire what has actually happened. Tradition runs, that the human
race has been destroyed by deluges except some seed preserved of
shepherds in the mountain tops, who lived for ages a rude life, family
by family, like the Cyclopes. But by degrees they descended to the
slopes of the mountains, and began to practise husbandry, dwelling
in one great common habitation for security's sake, and living under
laws selected from the best of those belonging to each family. Such
an abode was Dardania. Then they came down, as Homer says, to
' Ilium, builded in the plain,' and near the sea, a city among other
cities, who made war against each other, until the time of the Achaean
war ; and from that we come to the tale of the returning Dorians, your
ancestors ; you know the rest.

A. ταῦτα μὲν οὖν δὴ ταύτῃ] 'So much for that subject.' Art or
'music,' with which the second book has been occupied. The transition is abrupt. Aristophanes *Plutus* 8

καὶ ταῦτα μὲν δὴ ταῦτα.

ἐπίδοσιν] 'progress' or 'development,' as several times in Plato.
Theaetetus 146 B ἡ νεότης εἰς πᾶν ἐπίδοσιν ἔχει. 'Youth can be de-
veloped in any direction.'

*B. οἶμαι μὲν] μέν without following δέ is common in Plato, the
adversative clause being understood. Here we may complete, ' I think,
but you may not agree with me.' The omission is especially common
after a negative statement, in which case the adversative clause has
in effect been expressed already. *Crito* 43 D (The ship) οὔτοι δὴ ἀφῖκται, ἀλλὰ δοκεῖν μέν μοι ἥξει τήμερον.

ἀπειρίας] 'infinity,' 'infinite time,' the less common use of the word.

κατὰ τὸν—λόγον] 'and by parity of number.'

C. ἑκασταχοῦ] 'in each case,' 'in each particular city.' Every city
has gone through all the stages in their turn.

εἰ δυναίμεθα] The optative should be remarked. It seems to imply
greater uncertainty than the subjunctive. ' Let us take the case of one
of these cities—if by any chance we could work such a problem
out.'

677 A. φθοράς] We have had the same conception of alternate
destructions and renewals of the human race before, in the extracts
from the *Timaeus*, p. 20 E, 22 C D. In the *Politics*, II. viii. 21,
Aristotle speaks of ' the first men, whether they were earth-born, or the

survivors of some catastrophe' (φθορά). Cicero, *Somnium Scipionis,*
VII. xvi. 'Propter eluviones exustionesque terrarum, quas accidere
tempore certo necesse est.' Censorinus *de Die Natali* c. 18 'Cujus
(magni) anni hiems summa est κατακλυσμός, quam nostri diluvionem
vocant, aestas autem ἐκπύρωσις, quod est mundi incendium ; nam his
alternis temporibus mundus tum exignescere, tum exaquescere videtur.'
See 'Ast's note for other passages. The idea was a very favourite one
with later philosophers. We may compare the words of a modern
poet ;

> 'An earth
> More fresh, more verdant than the last, with fruits
> Self-springing, and a seed of man preserved.'

(Matthew Arnold, *Balder Dead.*)

μίαν] πόλιν or πολιτείαν ?

B. εἴς τε πλεονεξίας] ἔκ τε Schanz after Cobet.

καὶ φιλονεικίας] φιλονικίας A Schanz. Are we to regard these forms
as simply different spellings ? or as different words ?

ἐπινοοῦσιν] Scil. οἱ ἐν τοῖς ἄστεσι.

Θῶμεν] So A. φῶμεν Schanz. Is this necessary ?

ἢ πολιτικῆς] substantive or adjective ?

D. καὶ ὁτιοῦν ; οὔτι μὲν γὰρ κ.τ λ.] This is a very troublesome
passage, and has much perplexed the interpreters, both as to the
reading and the sense. The Paris A has ὁτιοῦν τοῦτο ὅτι ; 'sed τοῦτο
punctis notavit a' (the later hand of Λ) 'γρ. ὁτιοῦν χωρὶς τοῦ τοῦτο in
marg.' Schanz. γὰρ does not appear in A and many MSS, and should
be omitted. But as neither τοῦτο ὅτι μὲν nor ὅτι μὲν can well be
right, we are reduced to conjecture; and no two editors write alike.
ταῦτ' οὔτι μὲν μυριάκις Schanz, omitting second γέγονεν. οὔτι μὲν γὰρ,
as in the text, Baiter's second edition. καὶ ὁτιοῦν ; τοῦτο [ὅτι] μὲν γὰρ
Hermann, omitting the first γέγονεν. In ὅτι he thinks οἴει may lie
concealed. καὶ ὁτιοῦν ; ὅτι μὲν γὰρ Turicenses. καὶ ὁτιοῦν ; [τοῦ ὅ τι
μὲν γὰρ] μυριάκις Ast, omitting the second γέγονεν. καὶ ὁτιοῦν ; ὅτι μὲν
μυριάκις μύρια ἔτη, διελάνθανεν ἄρα τοὺς τότε· Schneider (Didot). 'του
ὅτι μὲν γὰρ V' (vulgate of Stephanus) 'cum libris' (this is incorrect)
'nisi quod horum plerique γὰρ omittunt.' Hermann. Wagner (Engelmann's editor) suggests τοιοῦτό τι, putting the stop at ὁτιοῦν, as I
understand him. It is not easy to choose among these various lections.
Hermann's, omitting γὰρ, is nearest to the text of A, if we regard
τοῦτο as genuine. This would give us πῶς γὰρ ἄν—ἀνευρίσκετο καὶ
ὁτιοῦν ; τοῦτο μὲν—διελάνθανεν κ.τ.λ. Then follows a new difficulty as
to the connection of the sense. None of the translators seem to me to
give the right meaning ; but I conceive Baiter, Hermann, and Schanz
to understand the passage as I do. Whatever we read, the reasoning

appears to be something like this. *Athenian.* 'And we must suppose that all art and science, and all their instruments, perished in this deluge.' *Cleinias.* 'Certainly; for if the present constitution of things had subsisted since the beginning of time, how could discovery have been possible? At this rate we must suppose that inventions had remained undiscovered for myriads of myriads of years, until some trifle of a thousand or two thousand years ago Daedalus hit upon one discovery, and Palamedes on another, and so on. Such a supposition, that nature after an infinite lapse of time alters her order *per saltum*, we have no right to make; but if the last catastrophe swept away all art and science, and this happened not so long before the time of Daedalus, there is no difficulty.' ἄρα, 'according to this,' 'consequently,' its regular sense. The repeated γέγονεν might be defended, if with Stallbaum we understand ἀφ' οὗ γέγονεν to mean 'ex quo orta sunt,' 'their antiquity is.' But as the repetition is awkward, perhaps one of the words is better omitted.

The explanation of Stallbaum is; 'Nam dubitari certe non potest, quin artium illarum inventa, quibus nunc utimur, innumerabilia secula homines illius aetatis latuerint. Quae autem postea sunt inventa, ea admodum recentis memoriae sunt, ut vix millia aut summum duo millia annorum praeterierint, ex quo Daedalus, Orpheus, alii, sua inventa excogitaverint.' On this rendering I do not see the connexion of the reasoning. Schneider (reading καὶ ὁτιοῦν; ὅτι μὲν μυριάκις) translates; 'multis quidem millibus annorum ante fuisse haec, id scilicet fugiebat eos, qui illis temporibus erant;' which I presume to mean, 'The discoverers of our sciences did not know that these sciences had existed at infinite periods before; and they themselves are but of yesterday.' One is very loath to differ from Schneider; but does this give so good sense as the explanation above? And how does he defend his total omission of τοῦτο or του? The sense seems to me clear but the reading uncertain; perhaps the simplest change is, as we said above, to omit ὅτι; unless indeed we can make it into οἴει with Hermann. Misconception of the passage is ancient; for Theophilus (quoted by Ast), a bishop and Christian apologist of the second century, understood the words to mean that there was a prodigious interval between the κατακλυσμός and Daedalus.

Daedalus is the inventor of the plastic arts. To Palamedes are attributed all manner of inventions: *e. g.* in Aeschylus, *Frag.* 176 Nauck, he is said to have arranged the officers, and the meals, of the army before Troy; in Sophocles, *Frag.* 435 Nauck, he also invents πεσσοί and dice; Euripides further ascribes to him (*Frag.* 582 Nauck) mnemonics, writing, wills, and agreements. Each of the three great tragedians wrote a play concerning him, from which these scraps remain. Olympus is perhaps the most tangible of the mythical musicians mentioned here. He is ascribed to Thrace, and called the father of Greek music. See note on *Banquet* 215 C (p. 278).

χθὲς καὶ πρώην] A common combination. *Gorgias* 470 D τὰ γὰρ ἐχθές τε καὶ πρώην γεγονότα. From Homer downwards; *Iliad* ii. 303 χθιζά τε καὶ πρωιζά, where the time referred to is that of the meeting of the ships at Aulis. See Ast on this place.

οἶσθ'] ἴστ', (the plural), A, Schneider, Schanz. οἶσθ' Ast, Turicenses, Hermann, Stallbaum, Wagner.

'Επιμενίδην] Epimenides, who is here referred to in passing, was the ancient priest and sage of Crete; but his whole history is enveloped in myths. About the beginning of the sixth century B.C., he is said to have been invited to Athens, to undertake the purification of the city after the murder of Cylon. (Plutarch, Solon, c. 12, and Diogenes, i. 110.) This, however, does not tally with Plato. Cleinias has said before in the dialogue (i. 642 D) that Epimenides was of his family, and that he came to Athens ten years before the Persian war (*i. e.* about 500 B.C.), and delivered a prophecy as to the result of the war. We consequently have a discrepancy of a century, doubtless due to Plato. See the notes of Ast and Stallbaum on the place in Book I. The latter says, 'Relinqui ergo videtur, ut' Platonem 'imprudentem tempora neglexisse statuamus.'

To Epimenides is here referred the good old simple Cretan way of living, which was probably more imaginary than real. Crete is said to have resembled Sparta in the custom of συσσίτια, but in little else.

We are not told here what the μηχάνημα was, and the word might be taken in a general sense, as some of the translators do take it, though the use of the article would rather suggest some particular invention. The μαντεία of Hesiod is contained in the famous lines (*Works and Days*, 40)

νήπιοι, οὐδ' ἴσασιν ὅσῳ πλέον ἥμισυ παντός,
οὐδ' ὅσον ἐν μαλάχῃ τε καὶ ἀσφοδέλῳ μέγ' ὄνειαρ.

These words in themselves are simple enough; the plainest fare is the best; but at what time did the notion arise that Epimenides, or others, had invented some kind of concentrated food, known as ἡ ἄλιμος, of which a small quantity satisfied both hunger and thirst? Proclus (fifth century A. D.) in his commentary upon the place in Hesiod, gives first the simple explanation, adding, however, καὶ γὰρ ἐκ τούτων χυλὸν ἐσκεύαζον εἰς βρῶσιν. But a line farther on he continues: ἄλλως· ἢ τὸν ἐκ τοῦ ῥᾴστου βίου (βίον ?) λέγει, ἴσως δέ, καὶ ἀφ' ἱστορίας τοῦτο λέγει, "Ερμιππος γὰρ ἐν τῷ τῶν ἑπτὰ σοφῶν, περὶ τῆς ἀλίμου λέγει, μέμνηται δὲ τῆς ἀλίμου καὶ 'Ηρόδοτος ('Ηρόδωρος Boeckh), ἐν τῷ πέμπτῳ τοῦ καθ' 'Ηρακλέα λόγου. Hermippus is said to have been the pupil of Callimachus, which puts him late in the third century B.C.; but if the citation of Herodorus be really genuine, we have mention of the ἄλιμος long before Plato's time. The correction Ἡρόδωρος we may accept as certain, as his work upon Heracles is well known from other sources. He is said to have lived about the end of the sixth century B.C. But we do not know through how many hands the quotation may have come to Proclus; and he thoroughly damages his authority for exactness by the words which follow. Καὶ Πλάτων ἐν γ' τῶν νόμων. (sic) Ἐπιμενίδην φησὶ μικρόν τι ἐδεσμάτιον προσφερόμενον ὦδε τελεῖν τὴν ἡμέραν, ἦν δ' ἐξ ἀσφοδέλου καὶ μαλάχης. ὅπερ αὐτὸν ἄλιμον καὶ ἄδιψον ἐποίει. There is not a word about all this in Plato. If Proclus treated in this way Plato whom it was his business to know, how can we depend upon his citation of Herodorus, whom probably he did not know? John Tzetzes (twelfth century), in his note on the same passage, inserts some atrocious lines in which, after some round and most undeserved abuse of Proclus, a recipe is given for the preparation of the ἄλιμος. It is to be compounded of the bulb of the σκίλλα, and the branches of the mallow, minced, triturated, mixed with honey, and so forth. (I quote Proclus and Tzetzes from the edition of Trincavelli, Venice 1537.) Upon the whole, considering the use of the article, the possible authority of Herodorus, the certainty that the notion of some such food was abroad in antiquity (see the commentators), and the context down to φατέ, one is tempted to suppose that Plato alludes here to some more or less apocryphal concoctions ascribed to Epimenides. (A great deal more might be said on this question. See the commentaries of Ast and Stallbaum upon this passage (especially their quotations), and that of Göttling upon the place in Hesiod.)

σπάνια—κατ' ἀρχάς;] 'these remnants, which they made into their flocks, were but a scanty support for life at first.' νέμουσιν participle.

678 A. ὧν νῦν—παρέστηκεν] 'on the discussion of which we are now engaged.'

ὡς ἔπος εἰπεῖν only lends a little emphasis to the rest of the sentence; and may be said to anticipate or to qualify τὸ παράπαν. 'Can we really in the least suppose?' &c.

C. καὶ μάλα πρέπει τοῦθ' οὕτως] 'that is a very proper conception,' 'that is the way to put it.'

ἔναυλος] 'fresh,' 'still ringing in their ears.' Aeschines *in Ctesiphontem* § 192 ἔναυλον γὰρ ἦν ἔτι τότε πᾶσιν, ὅτι τηνικαῦτα ὁ δῆμος κατελύθη. (Ruhnken, *Timaeus, s.v.*)

ἐν τοῖς—χρόνον] 'in that age.' But are we to understand τοῖς of persons (ἀνθρώποις), or of times (χρόνοις)? Schanz, evidently feeling the difficulty, puts an obelus before τοῖς. One is inclined to think that the phrase is merely an expansion of ἐν ἐκείνῳ τῷ χρόνῳ.

πορεῖα] 'vehicles,' the correction of Stephanus for πόρεια. ** πόρεια A; that is, two letters are erased. τὰ πορεῖα Schanz.

ὡς ἔπος εἰπεῖν qualifies πάντα.

οὐκ ἦν—σφόδρα δυνατόν] 'was next to impossible.' 'Communication was extremely difficult.' The words οὐ—σφόδρα are here used much in the sense of οὐ πάνυ; and may be quoted in illustration of the contention that οὐ—πάνυ are to be taken separately. See note on *Apology* 41 D (*supra*).

D. μεταλλεῖα] The word μεταλλεῖον seems not to occur elsewhere. The common word is μέταλλον, 'a mine,' and here we are doubtless to understand 'everything metallic.'

συγκεχυμένα ἠφάνιστο] had been buried in a confused wreck by the deluge, and been lost to sight.

ἀνακαθαίρεσθαι] disentangling and separating from the mass.

κατατριβέντα] 'worn out,' as I understand, 'would have been worn away by use.' 'Contritum evanuit' Ast *ad locum*. So the translators (Müller, Schneider, Wagner). Stallbaum says 'nimirum aerugine corrupta ac depravata,' which surely is not the meaning.

679 A. διέζων] In this meaning from Herodotus downwards, iii. 25 ποιηφαγέοντες διέζωον. Compare διεγένοντο, *Timaeus* 22 A, and note.

ὅσαι πλεκτικαὶ τῶν τεχνῶν] The single art of πλεκτική, as appears from τούτω immediately following; but the phrase is put in the most general way.

οὐδὲ ἕν] 'not at all,' 'in no respect.' This unelided form is used for the sake of greater emphasis.

B. τούτω τὼ τέχνα] Most authorities take these words as the direct object of ἔδωκε; 'gave these two arts to men, so that they should provide,' 'for them to provide.' But I should rather understand the whole clause to be the object, ἔδωκε having the more general sense of 'grant'; 'granted that these two arts should furnish men,' etc.

τούτω τὼ] The want of uniformity in carrying out the use of the dual which is so general in Greek appears especially in the article, which generally uses τώ and τοῖν for the rarer τά, ταῖν. See note upon *Protagoras* 314 D. τούτω naturally goes with τώ. ταύταιν is rare, ταύτα very rare. *Oedipus Coloneus* 859 D⁵ ἐφάψομαι γὰρ οὐ ταύταιν μόναιν. For ταύτα Kühner quotes two passages, Aristophanes, *Peace*, 847 D⁵ πόθεν ἔλαβες ταύτα σύ; where however Dindorf with the best MSS (those of Ravenna and Venice) has ταύτας: and Isaeus vi. 49 (*Philoctemon*) καὶ πρὸς ταύτα (Demeter and Persephone) καὶ τοὺς ἄλλους θεοὺς εὐσεβεῖν, where Baiter and Sauppe have ταύτας. ταύτα was Reiske's correction, approved by Kühner. (*Ausführliche Grammatik*, ed. 2, i. 464, n. 3.) Both passages are therefore doubtful; but it would be strange if a word like ταύτα were not to occur sometimes.

ἵν' ὁπότε—γένος] 'that when the human race was reduced to this state of want after a deluge, it might nevertheless continue to grow and increase.'

βλάστην] An Attic form, the ordinary Greek rather affecting βλάστησις. Ast compares αὔξη, ἐπαύξη, πάθη, which are all found in the *Laws*.

διάφοροι ἑαυτοῖς] 'at variance with each other.'

ὃ τότε—παρῆν] 'which at that time was the state of matters among them.' ὃ has no strict antecedent; one must be supplied from the general sense of the preceding words; 'which want of gold and silver was at that time' etc. So Stallbaum, Schneider. Hermann, Turicenses, Schanz, also put the stop after παρῆν. Ast connects the words with what follows, and puts the stop at ὄντες. Wagner would insert them after γίγνοιτ' ἄν, making good sense. But the clause is very well where it is.

C. διὰ τὴν λεγομένην εὐήθειαν] 'in consequence of their "primitive simplicity," as the phrase is,' 'on account of their *sancta simplicitas*.'

διὰ σοφίαν] belongs to ὑπονοεῖν, 'they had not yet been educated to suspect a lie.'

D. τῷδε] 'our friend Megillus here,' the third interlocutor of the dialogue.

ἀτεχνότεροι] By a construction *ad sensum* we have the masculine, indicating the individuals of the generations, instead of the feminine. Join ὅτι μέλλουσιν εἶναι.

αὐτοῦ] The adverb apparently. The construction is clearer if we point with Schanz αὐτοῦ, δίκαι καὶ στάσεις λεγόμεναι.

E. τοῦδ' ἕνεκα] applies to what follows.

680 A. τὸ τοιοῦτον] τὸ νόμους τιθέναι or νομοθετεῖν.

τοῖς λεγομένοις πατρίοις νόμοις] 'the laws of their fathers,' 'their hereditary laws,' 'their ancestral laws, as the phrase is.' Par. A and others have πατρίοις. πατρικοῖς, the old vulgate reading, would give the same sense, though Plato appears to observe the distinction that πάτριος is 'ancestral,' πατρικός 'belonging to a father.' πατρικοὶ νόμοι occurs in a fragment of Cratinus, Νέμεσ. 6. (Liddell and Scott.)

B. δυναστείαν] must here be 'patriarchate' or 'paternal government;' but the regular use of the word is of a governing oligarchy of privileged citizens, of which there are many examples in the older history of Greece, such as the Cypselidae of Corinth, the Aleuadae and Scopadae of Thessaly, etc.

οἴκησιν] 'οἴκησις est gubernatio vel administratio, non habitatio.' Stallbaum. One would rather understand 'Homer says it prevailed among the settlements of the Cyclopes,' with the translators. So below 680 D κατὰ μίαν οἴκησιν.

τοῖσιν δ' οὔτ' ἀγοραί] *Odyssee* ix. 112 seqq.

C. It seems strange that the Cretan Megillus should disclaim any·

but a slight knowledge of Homer. Idomeneus and Meriones play a conspicuous part in the Iliad. Crete is alluded to more than once in the Odyssee, and the very curious passage in Od. iii. 293-6 looks like an adaptation from some cyclic poem about Crete.

καὶ γὰρ—ἀστεῖα] The sense is not too clear ; does Cleinias mean to speak only of himself? and is διεληλύθαμεν to be taken rather loosely ? ' I have come across some other passages of his, which were very fine ; but we Cretans have no great taste for the poetry of other dialects.'

τοιούτων] ' of his kind,' epic poets.

D. ἑκάστοτε] in each passage, as often as he treats of such matters.

αὐτῶν] ' of primitive men ' apparently, ' of the people we have been speaking of.'

μῶν οὖν κ.τ.λ.] The principal verb is to be repeated from γίγνονταί ποτε. ' And such societies spring from ' etc.

κατὰ μίαν—διεσπαρμένων] ' from survivors of the catastrophe scattered here and there by single houses and single families.'

ὑπὸ ἀπορίας] ' prae consilii inopia, qualis oriri solet inter istiusmodi devastationes.' Stallbaum. 'Their helplessness,' 'their unprovided state.' Ast (whom Wagner follows) understands the meaning to be ' propter defectum hominum ex eluvie ortum ;' but one would like to see a passage in which ἀπορία by itself is used in this sense. Plato seems to mean that all the appliances of civilization are swept away, and households or clans remain utterly unprovided, isolated, perhaps ignorant of each others' existence.

If ἀπορία could mean ' want of communication,' the sense would be good ; but the passage in Xenophon (*Anabasis* V. vi. 10) which is quoted for this meaning, scarcely requires it. ἐγὼ μὲν οὖν οὐ χαλεπὴν εἶναι νομίζω τὴν πορείαν ἀλλὰ παντάπασιν ἀδύνατον.—ἐξ 'Ηρακλείας δὲ οὔτε πεζῇ οὔτε κατὰ θάλατταν ἀπορία· πολλὰ γὰρ καὶ πλοῖα ἐστὶν ἐν 'Ηρακλείᾳ. ' A march from hence by land is impossible ; but you may go by sea to Sinope and Heraclea. After reaching Heraclea you will have no difficulty in proceeding either by sea or land.'

ἐν οἷς] Bekker, Turicenses, Stallbaum, Ast, Hermann, Wagner, Schanz. But Schneider with A and all the books reads ἐν αἷς ; nor perhaps need the text be disturbed. The masculine has been thought necessary, because it has been assumed that αἷς must belong to φθοραῖς, or is a corrupt reading produced by φθοραῖς. But does not αἷς refer to πολιτεῖαι ? ' Do not such constitutions arise from "fragments of forgotten peoples ?" And in these constitutions the oldest members rule, because the society began with father and mother,' etc. οἷς (l. 205) is generally referred to τὸ πρεσβύτατον ; perhaps it follows more naturally on πατρὸς and μητρός. Or it may refer generally to both ; the meaning in any case being much the same.

E. αὐτοῖς] I understand to mean 'these people' generally, and not to refer to τὸ πρεσβύτατον, as Stallbaum seems to understand. Schneider translates ἀρχὴν by 'originem,' and I suppose he means 'because their origin is from father and mother,' as if only one pair had been preserved, like Deucalion and Pyrrha. This is very ingenious; and we are not bound to take ἄρχει and ἀρχὴν in the same sense.

πατρονομούμενοι] living under a paternal or patriarchal government. So in xi. 927 E οὐ πολὺ διαφέρον ἡ παρ' ἡμῖν ὀρφανία κέκτηται τῆς πατρονομικῆς. 'In these respects the state of orphanhood under guardianship among us is not much worse off than that of those who enjoy a father's care.'

περιβόλους—ἐρύματα] 'enclosures of loose walls and works of defence.' αἱμασιά, a word of unknown origin, regularly means a rough wall, such as are built of stones gathered on the spot, without mortar. But the grammarians also explain the word as meaning 'a thorn hedge,' which appears to be unconfirmed by usage. τειχῶν ἐρύματα, 'protections which are walls.'

681 A. αὖ] 'as before.'

τὸ γοῦν εἰκὸs] Supply χρή or anything that carries an infinitive. We need not suppose that the writer thinks of any particular word.

μειζόνων αὐξανομένων] 'increasing to a greater size.' 'Dictum est cum prolepsi praedicati.' Cf. *Protagoras* 327 C οὗτος ἀν ἐλλόγιμος ηὐξήθη, 'he would have grown up to distinction.' *Republic* 424 E ἐννόμους τε καὶ σπουδαίους ἐξ αὐτῶν ἄνδρας αὐξάνεσθαι. 'That they should grow up into good and law-obeying men.' (Both from Stallbaum.)

B. κατὰ τρόπον] 'naturally.' Common in Plato, *e. g. Cratylus* 425 B εἴτε κατὰ τρόπον τά τε πρῶτα ὀνόματα κεῖται καὶ τὰ ὕστερα, 'in a natural manner,' 'as one might expect.'

ἀναιρέσεις] So A. The word is rejected by the modern editors except Stallbaum, and Baiter *e silentio;* for ἀναιρέσεις stands in the Zürich text, Messrs Orelli and Winckelmann dissenting. Stallbaum explains 'suscepta,' 'institutions,' literally, what one has taken up. But the difficulty is that, though ἀναίρεσις is a common word, no example of this use is produced. The senses of 'lifting up' and of 'rescission,' 'abrogation,' are often found. Ast would suggest αὐτῶν αἱρέσεις, omitting ἄν, and so Schanz; Orelli αὐτῶν ἀεὶ αἱρέσεις. Winckelmann κατὰ τρόπους οὕτως ἑκάστους τοὺς αὐτῶν ἀνευρήσεις, which is good sense, but departs widely from the books. ἂν αἱρέσεις is the reading of K. F. Hermann, Schneider, and Wagner. Perhaps ἀναιρέσεις is not quite indefensible; but, in the absence of all authority for such a word, I incline to write *divisim,* which can scarcely be called an alteration of the text, as a scribe might easily think he found the common word ἀναιρέσεις. The ἄν goes well with ἥκειν, and the only objection is that the particle has not been used in previous paragraphs.

ὁποτυπουμένους] 'impressing upon,' 'stamping upon,' as with a seal.

παίδων παῖδας, ὁ λέγομεν] 'and children's children, in the familiar phrase.' Cf. *Iliad* xx. 307, 8

νῦν δὲ δὴ Αἰνείαο βίη Τρώεσσιν ἀνάξει,
καὶ παίδων παῖδες, τοί κεν μετόπισθε γένωνται.

So in English. 'Children's children,' according to Cruden, occurs ten times in the Old Testament, *e. g. Genesis* xlv. 10. 'And thou shalt dwell in the land of Goshen, and thou shalt be near unto me, thou, and thy children, and thy children's children.'

C. ὑστέρους] 'in a less degree,' 'in the second place.' Schanz would delete τοὺς δὲ τῶν ἄλλων ὑστέρους.

ἐμβάντες] lit. 'having set foot upon,' *i. e.* having stumbled upon, or lighted upon.

κοινούς] 'certain persons in common,' almost = 'representatives.'

εἰς τὸ κοινόν] 'in publicum.' It seems to mean 'publicly,' like the common εἰς τὸ μέσον. The words are to be connected with what follows.

D. ἐν ταύτῃ—οἰκήσουσιν] 'in this altered form of the government they will live.'

οὕτω τε καὶ ταύτῃ seems pleonastic to a modern, but we have again iv. 714 D καὶ οὕτω καὶ ταύτῃ. xii. 947 D οὕτω τε καὶ ταύτῃ. Stallbaum quotes also κατὰ ταῦτα καὶ ταύτῃ, ταύτῃ καὶ κατὰ ταῦτα, ταύτῃ καὶ κατὰ ταῦτα οὕτω, all from the *Laws*. The following parallels are added from Ast upon i. 629 A, where the words are τάχ' ἂν ἴσως. ταῦτα—οὕτω, εἰς δύναμιν—ὅτι μάλιστα, ἐκ τοῦ παράχρημα—ἐξαίφνης, ὀρθῶς—μετὰ δίκης, all from the *Laws*, and παντάπασι—πάντως from the *Epinomis*.

τοίνυν] as Stallbaum well remarks, is not συλλογιστικόν 'inferential,' but μεταβατικόν 'connective,' not 'therefore,' but 'now then,' 'well then.'

E. κτίσσε κ.τ.λ.] *scil.* Dardanus, *Iliad* xx. 216–18, where the editions give πολυπίδακος, more correctly.

Ἴλιος ἰρὴ has generally been explained as 'holy Ilium,' a reference being supposed to the story that its walls were built for Laomedon by Poseidon and Apollo. See *Iliad* vii. 452–3 'And the wall shall be forgotten, which Phoebus Apollo builded about the city of warrior Laomedon with much labour.' Compare *Iliad* xxi. 443 and context. But the etymology of ἱερός generally received, that of Curtius, makes this very doubtful. The word corresponds to Sanskrit *ishiras*, 'vigorous,' 'fresh,' 'blooming.' This stands for original *isaras*, to which ἱερός or

Aeol. *ίαρός* answers letter for letter. Ἰερός therefore may well in Homer retain sometimes the sense of 'strong,' 'mighty.' Ἴλιος ἰρή, 'fastness Ilium,' ἱερὰ τείχεα, 'strong walls,' ἱερὴ ἴς Τηλεμάχοιο, 'the youthful might of Telemachus,' ἱερὸν μένος Ἀλκινόοιο, 'the vigorous might of Alcinous,' φυλάκων ἱερὸν τέλος, 'the vigorous band of watchers,' λαθὼν ἱεροὺς πυλαωρούς, Ἀργείων ἱερὸς στρατὸς αἰχμητάων (*Od.* 24. 81), ἱερὸς ἰχθύς in a description of fishing. In some of these phrases the word ἱερός cannot be understood in the sense of 'holy' without much straining. We are not bound to suppose that the composer of epic lays always understood the right sense of traditional words or combinations of words. Take the analogy of modern ballads (not that the Hellenic epics are really ballads); are we all of us quite certain as to the exact meaning of 'merry men,' 'lily lea,' 'men of mould,' 'a mile but barely three'? Did the reciter of 'Chevy Chase' always comprehend

> 'Then the wylde thorowe the woodes went on every side shear;
> Greahondes thorowe the grevis glent for to kyll thear dear'?

These and similar lines have all the air of regular commonplaces, of an older date, which might be inserted wherever they seemed moderately appropriate.

μερόπων is so familiar a word that we are apt to forget the utter uncertainty of its meaning. Perhaps it may not be unprofitable if we digress a little to illustrate this uncertainty, by mentioning some of the attempted explanations. The old derivation from R. μερ, 'divide,' and R. ὀπ, 'voice,' cannot hold, because of the well-preserved digamma of the latter in ὀπός, ὀπί, ὄπα. Analogy is for the word being a compound of ὀπ- in sense of 'face,' 'look.' Compare αἴθοψ, Αἰθίοψ, Φαῖνοψ, οἶνοψ, ἦνοψ, στέροψ, Πέλοψ, μῆλοψ, νῶροψ. It has been referred to R. σμερ, in actual Greek μαρ, μερ, 'think,' 'take care about,' as in μερμηρίζω, μάρτυρ, 'rememberer,' *memoria*, etc., in the sense of 'thoughtful-faced,' 'intelligent,' as opposed to the beasts. This is perhaps too far-fetched. Others understand 'mortal,' from R. of μαραίνω, μοῖρα, μόρτος, 'fate,' etc. Then the -οψ remains unaccounted for. Or could we refer the word to the R. μαρ of μαρμαίρω, μάρμαρος, etc., and understand 'bright-faced,' 'having a complexion,' as opposed to the hairy skins of animals? A parallel showing the root in this sense with the form μερ would be desirable. Perhaps the best etymology yet proposed is that of Fick, who connects the word with the root of μάρπτω, so that μέροψ would mean 'he who catches up,' 'understands,' 'der Begreifer.' μάρπτω is never used in a similar sense; but we have in Hesychius a gloss βρακεῖν· συνιέναι. For the connexion of μάρπτω and βρακεῖν see Curtius, *Etymologie*⁴, p. 456. It might be added that in that case the bird μέροψ, the 'bee-eater' (*Merops apiaster*), might be the 'snapper,' 'picker-up,' a very appropriate name, as it feeds on insects. Yet this derivation also is but a guess.

682 A. λέγει—εἰρημένα] Such pleonasms, real or apparent, are not uncommon in the *Laws.* Stallbaum compares *inter alia* iii. 689 E ταῦτα μὲν οὖν, καθάπερ εἴπομεν ἄρτι, λελεγμένα τεθήτω ταύτῃ.

θεῖον γὰρ οὖν δὴ κ.τ.λ.] 'Locus dubitari non potest quin labem aliquam susceperit.' Stallbaum. ἐνθεαστικός is a word not elsewhere found in Plato, and has been rejected here by many editors (Ast, Bekker, Stallbaum, Hermann, Wagner, Schanz). But it does not appear to be omitted in any MS., and is retained by Schneider and the Zürich editors, rightly, in all likelihood. The grounds of suspicion against the word have been, that it may be a gloss on θεῖον, and that Plato does not use it elsewhere. (We have ἐνθεάζων in the sense of 'inspiredly,' Herodotus i. 63.) Also Proclus thrice uses the place (see the passages in Stallbaum) without any mention of the word ἐνθεαστικόν; in a fourth passage he adds ἐνθεαστικόν. It is inferred that in the fourth place he may have inserted the word himself, for it is very common among the Neo-Platonists; but as he goes on to quote the words ὑμνῳδοῦν—σύν τισι χάρισι καὶ Μούσαις (which are not given in the other three places), this argument rather loses force. Winckelmann would read ἐνθουσιαστικόν, a received Platonic word; but if we read any such word at all, why depart from the manuscripts? If we keep the word, we may say that καί is transposed from after ποιητικὸν, or, if we like, that θεῖον γὰρ οὖν δὴ is a kind of anticipation, after which the construction goes on regularly.

μύθου] the tale of Troy.

βουλήσεως] 'our proposed design.' Cf. τοῖς βουλήμασιν *Timaeus* 26 A *supra.*

B. ἐπὶ λόφον τινά] Happily a discussion upon the precise site of Troy is unimportant to the argument. The description here (which is imaginary) agrees well enough with Hissarlik.

C. οὐ σφόδρα ὑψηλοῖς go together.

παντάπασί τινα μακρὸν] παντάπασί τι Bekker and Schneider with A and the books; παντάπασί τινα Stephanus (correction), Böckh, Ast, Stallbaum, Turicenses, Wagner, Schanz. The alteration is but slight,

d τις with χρόνος is common in Plato.

κατῴκουν] 'began to be settled.'

E. πάλιν ἐκπεσόντες κατῆλθον] 'who returned again from banishment.' πάλιν—κατῆλθον go together.

τὰς τότε φυγὰς] the exiles. Many examples of the use will be found in Stallbaum, of which two may suffice, one singular, and one plural. Thuc. viii. 64 καὶ γὰρ καὶ φυγὴ αὐτῶν ἔξω ἦν. Isocrates, 'p. 185 ed. Cor.' τὰς φυγὰς—οὐ διὰ τοὺς συκοφάντας κατελθούσας.

Book IV.   719 C—720 E.

Law is law; the legislator cannot have two voices. But the poet, who sits upon the tripod of the Muses, and sings he knows not what, may be allowed to contradict himself. Perhaps in some preamble the legislator may concede this much, and give advice, as well as lay down absolute enactment. You know there are two kinds of doctors; one, empirics who go about among their fellow slaves, and prescribe for them roughly by rule of thumb; the other, gentlemen doctors, who give advice to intelligent patients, and persuade them what is for their own good. Some corresponding division may be proper in our statutes.

τάδε. Cannot we make a representation to our legislator, and induce him to relax his severity somewhat towards poets? Well; what shall we say to him? This.

ξυνδεδογμένος] 'received,' 'accepted.'

D. ὑπὸ σοῦ] 'you' is the legislator, who has been laying down the law as to burial.

ἐν τῷ ποιήματι] The ingenious conjecture of Ast, ἐν τῷ γράμματι, 'in her will,' and that of Winckelmann, ἐν τῷ ἐπιστήματι, 'on her gravestone,',as also the suggestion of Stallbaum, 'Fortasse legendum ἐν τῷ μνήματι,' are not perhaps required. If we keep the word, the meaning would seem to be; Our state allows no burial except the μετρία; but my wife may have a mind to be buried handsomely in fiction, if she cannot be so in reality; 'there she sepulcred in much pomp may lie.' ἐν τῷ ποιήματι Schneider, Hermann, Turicenses, Müller. Wagner brackets, and Schanz puts an obelus after the word.

E. ἐπαινέσοι] 'Nonne ἐπαινέσαι.' Bekker *apud* Turicenses. They give ἐπαινέσοι. So Stallbaum, Hermann, Schneider, Ast. Bekker, Wagner, and Schanz would read ἐπαινέσαι, the regular construction. But if ἄν with the future indicative be Attic, as it confessedly is, why should ἄν not be used with the future optative? especially if ἄν ἐπαινέσοι here be regarded as a kind of compromise between ἐπαινέσαι ἄν and ἐπαινέσοι without the ἄν (as if the clause were put in the indirect oration). There are various passages (see Kühner² ii. p. 200, n. 2) in which ἄν appears with the optative future. Kühner is for emending them all; but it would require full examination of the authorities in each case to prove that we are right in doing so. He allows optative with ἄν in dependent sentences.

C C

σοὶ δ' οὐχ οὕτω κ.τ.λ.] 'Your part as legislator is not to use the bare word "moderate," but accurately to define what is the meaning of the word.'

μηδὲν τοιοῦτον] making no mention of μετριότης or the like.

προαγορεύῃ] So A, and also φράζῃ, τρέπηται. προαγορεύοι—φράζοι—τρέποιτο the correction of A, and other books. προαγορεύει some MSS. προσαγορεύῃ Turicenses, Hermann, Wagner. προσαγορεύῃ Stallbaum, Schneider, and Schanz. προσαγορεύοι ἄν Ast. 'It is difficult not to approve προαγορεύῃ, taken as a deliberative subjunctive; 'Shall then our legislator omit any such preface?' Compare *Meno* 92 E ἀλλὰ σύ —εἰπέ, παρὰ τίνας ἔλθῃ 'Αθηναίων; προσδιδῷ also favours this.

720 A. θεραπεύειν] The apodosis is not given, but the sense is obvious; 'Just as a physician may treat our case this way or that, so may the legislator lay down this law or that.'

ἀναμιμνησκώμεθα δὲ κ.τ.λ.] 'let us call to remembrance the two ways of treatment.'

οἷον δὴ τί λέγομεν;] 'But, you will say, what do you mean by this?'

B. δὲ l. 38] in apodosis.

θεωρίαν] 'observation' of their masters.

κατὰ φύσιν] Ast explains 'natura sua, per se s. proprio et studio et experientia.' Stallbaum 'secundum naturam, i. e. ratione, sicuti res ipsa videtur exigere et flagitare v. sect. D.' The words seem to mean, 'in a natural and proper way,' that is, by implication, not by mere rote, but by intelligence and self-development, things which come natural to a freeman, and which he would not think of exchanging for rule of thumb. In D below the force of κατὰ φύσιν is 'he investigates the disease from the beginning and in a rational way.' We have κατὰ φύσιν again in E. 'Will he not naturally begin with' etc.? (just after end of extract).

τοὺς—αὐτῶν—παῖδας] One does not see why we should go past the ordinary sense of 'their own children.' So the translators. Stallbaum will have it to be 'their pupils,' as we read in the Old Testament of 'the sons of the prophets,' comparing *Laws* vi. 769 B οἱ ζωγράφων παῖδες, etc. But it is one thing to say, οἱ παῖδες τῶν ἰατρῶν, which would naturally mean 'the schools of the doctors,' and another thing to say οἱ ἰατροὶ διδάσκουσι τοὺς ἑαυτῶν παῖδας, which would naturally mean 'the doctors teach their own children.'

C. ἑκάστου πέρι νοσήματος ἑκάστου τῶν οἰκετῶν] 'unum alterumve ἑκάστου delendum esse videtur.' Schanz. Why? and why should we write πέρι instead of περί? 'About each individual disease of each individual slave.'

τῷ δεσπότῃ] *Scil.* of the slave whom he is curing. So the translators; but is not the meaning rather; He is a slave himself, and saves his master, the real ἰατρός, the trouble of prescribing for slaves?

D. καὶ κατὰ φύσιν] 'in a rational way'; see above.

E. ἀποτελεῖν] 'to make a complete end of the case.' I should take the accusative after the participles, ἀποτελεῖν being used absolutely without a case.

διχῇ—ἀπεργαζόμενος] 'sanationi et praescriptioni adiungens persuasionem et admonitionem (c. 11' [721 E] 'τὸ πείθειν τε ἅμα καὶ ἀπειλεῖν); contra μοναχῇ est τῷ ἀπειλεῖν μόνον χρώμενος, ut infra dicitur' (*ibidem*). Ast.

Book VII. 816 D—817 D.

Comedy and farce we may put aside as servile. But what shall be said unto you, O 'lofty grave tragedians'? We too are poets; and the whole end and aim of our life and of our polity is to enact a tragedy indeed. Your competition we cannot admit. Go, tender souls, present yourselves before our magistrates; and if they prefer your songs to ours, you shall have your chorus; but if not, not.

D. οἴας] οἴα A.

Λέξις, ᾠδή and ὄρχησις are the three elements of scenic performance. I take κεκωμῳδημένα to come after the other words, 'when these things are made the elements of comedy.'

τὰ τούτων πάντων μιμήματα] as in scene, costume, and so forth.

E. καὶ πάντων τῶν ἐναντίων] The expression is somewhat abridged, perhaps to avoid the repetition of ἄνευ.

οὐκ ἂν δυνατόν] gives us a new construction.

αὐτῶν ἕνεκα τούτων—τοῦ μὴ] We have first the concrete in the plural, and then the abstract in the singular, referring to each other.

καινὸν δὲ ἀεί κ.τ.λ.] These comic imitations should always seem unusual and out of the way, and not become common. 'Nam cives, si eadem vel similia semper exhiberentur ridiculi genera, iis adsuescerent eaque moribus suis exprimerent.' Ast.

817 A. καὶ λόγῳ] λόγῳ might either be 'by reason,' 'reasoning,' 'argument,' or 'in our narrative'; the two senses need not exclude each other. The words are meant to be formal. 'Doctrina' Schneider, 'Rede' Müller, Wagner. But perhaps the best explanation is 'Let this be our law and our explanation of the law.'

φέρωμέν τε καὶ ἄγωμεν] 'shall we bring all our poetic gear with us?' Müller ingeniously suggests that they are to fetch not only their poetry, but all the 'properties' of the stage, masks, wigs, buskins, cloaks, etc., and that hence we have the two verbs instead of one. But we may

C C 2

doubt whether more than slight emphasis is intended. Compare in the prayer of Socrates at the end of the *Phaedrus* (279 C), τὸ δὲ χρυσοῦ πλῆθος εἴη μοι ὅσον μήτε φέρειν μήτε ἄγειν δύναιτ' ἄλλος ἢ ὁ σώφρων, where the words appear formulistic, and not to be pressed.

θείοις] Compare the place in the *Ion, supra*, 534 D.

B. παρ' ἡμῶν strikes one as curious. Ast ὥσπερ ἡμῶν. ἡ παρ' ἡμῶν A, Turicenses, Stallbaum, Hermann. ἡμῖν Schneider.

C. ἐπιτρέψειν] We have already had the principal verb ἐάσειν, which is now replaced, with a little departure from strict grammar, by another verb corresponding in sense.

δημηγορεῖν] *Gorgias* 502 D οὐκοῦν ῥητορικὴ δημηγορία ἂν εἴη (ἡ ποίησις); ἢ οὐ ῥητορεύειν δοκοῦσί σοι οἱ ποιηταὶ ἐν τοῖς θεάτροις;—Νῦν ἄρα ἡμεῖς εὑρήκαμεν ῥητορικήν τινα πρὸς δῆμον τοιοῦτον, οἷον παίδων τε ὁμοῦ καὶ γυναικῶν καὶ ἀνδρῶν, καὶ δούλων καὶ ἐλευθέρων, ἣν οὐ πάνυ ἀγάμεθα· κολακικὴν γὰρ αὐτήν φαμεν. (Ast.) From the present and similar places it would seem that women were allowed to be present at least at tragic representations. The passages bearing on the subject will be found in Becker's *Charicles*, Excursus to Scene X.

D. πρὶν—ἀρχὰς] 'previous to the decision of the magistrates.'

παρὰ τὰς ἡμετέρας] 'compared with ours.'

Book X.   887 C—891 A.

Who can keep his temper with those who will have it that there are no gods? who have been brought up in religion from their earliest youth, who have seen the sacrifices of their parents, and heard the litanies of all mankind, yet disbelieve without a reason? But we must not be mad with the mad; we will say temperately to each of them, 'Young man, you suffer under an old disease; but no one reaches age without thinking differently about the gods. Therefore wait, and offend not.' But in this, my friends, without intending it, we have touched upon a doctrine which many think to be the ultimum of philosophy; the doctrine that the world and all things about us are the work of nature and chance, without Gods and without mind; and that mind and art, working upon these materials, have produced comparatively little. And worst of all is the notion that the Gods are but the creations of law and custom, that the highest right is might, and justice an arbitrary convention. What shall be the remedy for these things? Persuasion and patience.

C εὐχήν] We are in deep waters of discussion, and I feel impelled to offer up a prayer for our deliverance. The prayer is implied in what follows.

σοῦ] Cleinias.

συντείνεις] 'are eager,' 'are thus in earnest.'

μέλλειν—λέγειν] The one infinitive after the other.

θυμῷ λέγοι] The simple dative is perhaps a little remarkable.

D. νῦν, οὐ πειθόμενοι κ.τ.λ.] The meaning of this long sentence is plain enough, but the construction is involved. The MSS. all read νῦν οὖν πειθόμενοι. It might be just possible, construing 'through a stone wall,' to make sense of this reading; but it is almost certain that the codices have been corrupted, some copyist failing (as he very well might) to remember the connection, and dropping into the familiar νῦν οὖν, instead of νῦν, οὐ πειθόμενοι, which is the reading of the editors, whether with Stallbaum we put a colon after νῦν, or a comma with Ast, Schneider, Hermann, Turicenses, Wagner. The apodosis, some way down, as often in Plato, does not precisely correspond in form to the protasis, but begins again resumptively τούτων δὴ πάντων ὅσοι καταφρονήσαντες.

ἐν γάλαξι] 'in their milk-days.' Euripides, *Hercules Furens*, v. 1266
ἔτ' ἐν γάλακτί τ' ὄντι.
One would like another example of the plural.

λεγομένων] I should understand as genitive absolute with Stallbaum, 'when these tales are told.' λεγομένους is the reading of Stephanus, Bekker and Ast, against A and other MSS. λεγομένων Schneider, Turicenses, Stallbaum, Hermann, Wagner.

αὐτούς] τοὺς μύθους.

θυόντων—ἐσπουδακότας] There is a great diversity of reading in these words, but A and others read as in the text, θυόντων ἐν σπουδῇ τῇ μεγίστῃ τοὺς αὑτῶν (codd. αὐτῶν) γονέας ὑπὲρ αὐτῶν τε καὶ ἐκείνων ἐσπουδακότας. θύοντας Ast, de suo. πραττομένας θυόντων, Hermann. πραττομένας, θυόντων Schneider, Turicenses, Stallbaum, Wagner. The general meaning is clear, but the construction almost desperate. Stallbaum would take θυόντων after σπουδῇ. But he says well, 'Videtur autem oratio utique manca esse atque hiulca.' Perhaps θυόντων may follow loosely upon ὄψεις, and ἐσπουδακότας upon ὁρᾷ, in which case we have a fine blending of constructions; while again, if θυόντων be taken absolutely, γονέας—ἐσπουδακότας may naturally enough be understood as in apposition with ὄψεις, or, if we choose, as accusative to the general notion of seeing which pervades the passage. We might say that in the frequent change of case and of construction what we call grammatical agreement is really lost.

ἐκείνων l. 13] the children, themselves.

E. ἐνδιδόντων] I understand ἐνδιδόντων, like the ὄντων's before, to agree with θεῶν understood. 'Not as if there were no gods, but as if their existence were patent, and no room whatever were left even for a suspicion of their non-existence.' ἐνδιδόναι may be either to 'yield,' 'leave as a possibility,' or 'to cause.' We might have had ὡs οὐκ ὄντων θεῶν ; but the repetition of οὐκ ὄντων would have been awkward. ὡs οὐκ εἰσὶ θεοί will then be a replacement.

τούτων δὴ πάντων κ.τ.λ.] 'The young people, who contemn all these traditions and observances, for no sufficient reason, as one may see without being remarkably wise, and compel us to say what we are saying,—how is one to keep his temper in remonstrating with them?'

καὶ σμικρὸν νοῦ] 'vel tantillum mentis seu prudentiae.' Stallbaum.

888 A. οὐ γὰρ ἅμα γε κ.τ.λ.] 'for it would be unseemly that one half of mankind should go mad with lust, and the other half in righteous indignation at them.'

ὑπὸ λαιμαργίας ἡδονῆς] 'from greediness of pleasure.' Such combinations of words similar in sense are not uncommon in the *Laws*; e. g. iv. 723 D μηκέτ', ὦ ξένε, διατριβὴν πλείω τῆς μελλήσεως ποιώμεθα.

ἴτω δὴ—ἄθυμος] 'Let us then address them dispassionately.' ἄθυμος 'without anger,' a sense of the word adapted *ad locum*.

B. τίθεσθαι] seems to have its very frequent meaning of 'deciding,' 'giving an opinion,' without any word being added to define the sense. We have it with ψῆφος in *Laws* ii. 674 A οὐκ ἂν τιθείμην ταύτην τὴν ψῆφον.

ταύτην τὴν δόξαν] So Ast, Wagner, and Baiter in minor ed. ταύτην δόξαν Schneider, Turicenses, Hermann, Stallbaum. The article only appears in one or two codices; not in A; though in a case like this, where the letters την are or are not repeated, we cannot depend on the best books. Stallbaum explains, (the article being omitted,) 'Nimirum ταύτην pro subjecto, δόξαν autem pro praedicato accipiendum est,' comparing iii. 702 C νῦν οὖν ἐμοί τε καὶ ὑμῖν ταύτην δῶμεν χάριν, and other places. ταύτην in that case should more strictly be τοῦτο, but the pronoun is attracted, as usual, into the gender of the noun. We might reverse the terms, and call δόξαν the subject, and ταύτην the predicate ; 'have held as an opinion about the gods this.'

πολλοῖσι] A and Bekker.

C. τὰ δύο—πάθη] 'the other two diseases.' The mention of a number of parts in such phrases implies that there is only one part besides.

εὐπαραμύθητοι] Was Plato thinking of Homer's phrase,

στρεπτοὶ δέ τε καὶ θεοὶ αὐτοί?

(*Iliad* ix. 497.) 'The gods themselves are exorable.' One might well have expected him to quote it.

τὸ δὴ σαφὲς—ἔχει] 'if you will be ruled by me, you will have patience, and enquire ripely, according to your ability, what may be the true doctrine about the gods.' 'τὸ σαφὲς ἂν γενόμενον, i. e. ὃ σαφὲς ἂν γένοιτο.' Stallbaum.

E. λέγουσί πού τινες] No particular person or school is indicated; but, besides many of the Sophists, we may suppose him to have been thinking of the materialist philosophers, such as Anaxagoras, Leucippus, Democritus.

γιγνόμενα κ.τ.λ.] The contrast of the tenses may be noted. We have the aorist participle used here distinctly of the *past*.

τύχῃ—τέχνην] A and most MSS have τέχνῃ—τύχην. So Ast, Wagner, Stallbaum, Schneider. τύχῃ—τέχνην Turicenses, Hermann. Those who choose the latter reading probably wish to put φύσις and τύχη on one side, against τέχνη on the other. This is not at all necessary for the argument; but it must be owned that in A—C following the corresponding order is adopted.

889 A. τοὺς ἐκεῖθεν] 'the men of that school.' Ast would read τὸ ἐκεῖθεν, 'what comes next,' very needlessly.

ἄστρων τε πέρι] περὶ in such cases forms a circumlocution nearly equivalent to the genitive, and might be omitted without altering the sense. *Timaeus* 35 A τρίτον ἐξ ἀμφοῖν ἐν μέσῳ ξυνεκεράσατο οὐσίας εἶδος, τῆς τε ταυτοῦ φύσεως αὖ πέρι καὶ τῆς θατέρου.

C. ταύτῃ καὶ κατὰ ταῦτα οὕτω] See note upon *Laws* iii. 681 D above.

οὐρανὸν] 'the universe.'

οὐδὲ διὰ νοῦν, φασίν] A etc.

ὃ λέγομεν] 'as we were saying.'

D. παιδιάς] παιδείας all the books, which does not make sense. The editors restore παιδιάς, 'triflings,' from Eusebius, *Praeparatio Evangelica* xii. 20, p. 621 A (Ast), which is obviously right.

ἑαυτῶν] 'Dein ἑαυτῶν ponitur perinde ac si pluralis τέχνας antecesserit, idque fieri potuit eo facilius, quod continuo artes plures enumerantur.' Stallbaum. The arts produce images resembling themselves respectively, ξυγγενῆ ἑαυτῶν, Ast, Stallbaum. 'Related to each other,' Schneider, Müller, of which I do not see the force.

συνέριθοι τέχναι] 'coöperant arts.' So in the fine passage of the *Republic* vii. 533 D. The dialectic method gently draws and leads upward the eye of the soul, which was buried in barbaric mud, συνερίθοις καὶ συμπεριαγωγοῖς χρωμένη αἷς διήλθομεν τέχναις. The word ἔριθος, according to Curtius (R. 488), naturally connects itself, as well as ἔρανος, with ἀρέσθαι, ἄρνυμαι, so that it would mean one who 'gains' or 'earns wages,' =μίσθαρνος.

φύσει ἐκοίνωσαν—κοινωνοῦν φύσει] 'whose power partly coincides with nature,' 'which goes along with nature.'

E. ἧς] refers to νομοθεσίας.

ἄλλῃ, ὅπῃ ἑκάστοι ἑαυτοῖσι, A etc., and so Schneider, Hermann,

Wagner. ἄλλοις, ὅπῃ ἕκαστοι ἑαυτοῖσι Ast, Stallbaum. ἄλλῃ, ὅπῃ ἕκαστοι ἑκάστοις Turicenses with some copies; but this hardly makes sense; ἕκαστοι ἑαυτοῖσι means 'each people among themselves.' ἄλλα —ἕτερα, just below, are scarcely distinguished.

τὰ δὲ [δὴ] δὴ does not appear in A, and so Hermann. Schneider, Wagner, Ast, Stallbaum, Turicenses insert the δή.

ἀμφισβητοῦντας] We must supply a general subject. 'men.'

890 A. ἅπαντα] Schneider suggests very ingeniously ἃ ἀπαντᾷ ἀνδρῶν σοφῶν πάρα νέοις ἀνθρώποις, and this is adopted by Stallbaum and Wagner. If the place were obviously corrupt, the change is almost nothing; but Plato is sometimes flat, like other people.

ἰδιωτῶν] 'prose writers,' 'prosators.' *Banquet* 178 B γονῆς γὰρ Ἔρωτος οὔτ' εἰσὶν οὔτε λέγονται ὑπ' οὐδένος οὔτε ἰδιώτου οὔτε ποιητοῦ.

B. After ὁ νόμος there is a break in the construction, or *aposiopesis*, which the editors express in different ways, Stallbaum by a dash and stop, —, the Turicenses by ·—, Hermann by the mark of interrogation;. Ast and Schneider have a simple comma. The apodosis is repressed to give greater force.

C. ὅσα τε] Turicenses, Stallbaum, Hermann, Wagner, who join these words with the previous clause. But I am inclined to follow Schneider with A and almost all the MSS, who read ὅσα δὲ. καὶ περὶ καλῶν—ὁ αὐτὸς λόγος is then the added generalization of what has preceded, and with ὅσα δὲ the Athenian comes to the main point, virtue and vice. This implies a colon after λόγος.

τὸν δέ τινα] Observe the indefinite pronoun added to the article. *Laws* ii. 658 B εἰκός που τὸν μέν τινα ἐπιδεικνύναι—ῥαψῳδίαν.

πειθὼ δὲ κ.τ λ.] 'Is the legislator not rather to persuade and soften (ἡμεροῦν) than to threaten?'

D. μηδαμῶς] refers not to the last sentence, but to the whole speech of the Athenian. 'Do not say so.'

πᾶσαν—ἱέντα] Cf. *Euthydemus* 293 A ἐπειδὴ ἐν ταύτῃ τῇ ἀπορίᾳ ἐνεπεπτώκη, πᾶσαν ἤδη φωνὴν ἡφίειν.

νόμῳ αὐτῷ go together.

οὐχ ἧττον] Hermann conjectures οὐχ ἧττονι, which has not found favour, nor does the alteration seem required. 'Which exist by nature, or no less than nature.'

ὃν σύ τε λέγειν] Stallbaum would read ὡς, *de suo*, which seems quite unnecessary. ὃν is, if we like to use the phrase, 'attracted' from the adverb into the pronoun. 'As you appear to me to mean' is the sense either way. The editions (Turicenses, Schneider, Hermann, Wagner) have ὃν.

E. τί δ' οὐ χαλεπά Turicenses, Schneider, Hermann. τί δ'; οὐ Stallbaum. τί δ', οὐ Ast. He practically corresponds with the first three editors. One cannot think that the elided δέ may end a sentence. The two expressions τί δέ and οὐ χαλεπά are run together.

ὦ προθυμότατε κ.τ.λ.] 'Yes, my enthusiastic Cleinias; but are not these things when spoken to a multitude hard to be understood, not to mention that they take up a dismal length of time?' λεγόμενα is striking; one would have expected λεγομένοις. Does the writer begin with οὐ χαλεπά; 'Is it not difficult?' and then complicate the construction by making λεγόμενα agree with χαλεπά?

διωλύγια] Timaeus, *Lexicon* s. v. (p. 75 Ruhnken [2]) διωλύγιον· ἐπὶ πολὺ ἀνῆκον· ἐπὶ φαύλου δὲ αὐτῷ κέχρηται· πολὺ καὶ ἄμετρον. The word occurs in Plato in only one other passage, *Theaetetus* 162 A οὐ μακρὰ μὲν καὶ διωλύγιος φλυαρία; 'a long interminable rigmarole.' The word was especially affected by the later Platonists; see Ruhnken *l. l.*

καὶ μὴν καὶ νομοθεσίᾳ κ.τ.λ.] The sense is; If our discussions are difficult, the results will remain fixed in written legislation, so that any one who finds them hard can return to them again and again; and if they are long, still, on account of their preeminent importance, it would be neither right nor pious not to devote to them whatever time may be needful.

891 A. διότι] seems to be used as equivalent to ὅτι; a usage of which Krüger says upon Herodotus ii. 43. 2 ; 'διότι für ὅτι dass, bei Attikern wenig üblich.' 'διότι for ὅτι = that, a rare usage in Attic.' In that place we have first ὅτι and then διότι, apparently in the same sense. But perhaps a better example is Herodotus ii. 50. 'I may say generally that the names of the Greek gods came from Egypt. διότι μὲν γὰρ ἐκ τῶν βαρβάρων ἧκει, πυνθανόμενος οὕτω εὑρίσκω ἐόν.'

ἠρεμεῖ] 'quum nihil respondeant.—*Phaedr.* p. 275 D δεινὸν γάρ που —τοῦτ' ἔχει γραφή, καὶ ὡς ἀληθῶς ὅμοιον ζωγραφίᾳ· καὶ γὰρ τὰ ἐκείνης ἔκγονα ἔστηκε μὲν ὡς ζῶντα, ἐὰν δ' ἀνέρῃ τι, σεμνῶς πάνυ σιγᾷ. ταὐτὸν δὲ καὶ οἱ λόγοι, κ.τ.λ.' Stallbaum.

LIST OF WORKS USEFUL FOR THE
STUDY OF PLATO.

THE following are some of the most useful works which may be employed in the study of Plato. Most of them have been quoted in the Notes. The list might be indefinitely increased.

General.

The Dialogues of Plato. Translated into English, with Analyses and Introductions. By B. Jowett, M.A., Master of Balliol College. Second Edition, Oxford, 1875. Five volumes. The Introductions prefixed to the several dialogues embody an account and criticism of the Platonic philosophy.

An admirable summary of the matter of Plato's works, digested into a systematic view, is to be found in the great work of Dr. Zeller, Die Philosophie der Griechen in ihren geschichtlichen Entwicklung dargestellt von Dr. Eduard Zeller. The part treating of Plato can now be had in English; Plato and the older Academy translated—by Sarah Frances Alleyne and Alfred Goodwin, M.A. Longmans, 1876.

See also the chapters in Grote's History of Greece upon Socrates and Plato, and his elaborate work, Plato and the other Companions of Socrates, in three large volumes.

Perhaps the best Greek Grammar is the Ausführliche Grammatik der Griechischen Sprache von Dr. Raphael Kühner. Zweite Auflage in durchaus neuer Bearbeitung, which has occasionally been quoted.

Indispensable in the study of Plato's language is the great work of Ast, Lexicon Platonicum sive vocum Platonicarum Index. Condidit D. Fridericus Astius.

There is unfortunately no special grammar for the language of Plato. The Digest of Idioms appended to Mr. Riddell's edition of the Apology (see below) is of great value.

Much valuable matter is to be found in Ruhnken's Notes on Timaeus, an author of uncertain date, who lived possibly in the third century A.D. Timaei Sophistae Lexicon Vocum Platonicarum. Ruhnken's second edition, republished by G. A. Koch. Leipzig, 1828. The Lexicon is very brief, but Ruhnken's notes are elaborate. The text may be found also at the end of the Zürich quarto edition, with additional glosses from other lexicographers.

Editions of the Text.

The text of Bekker, which first attempted to establish the text of Plato according to the best MSS., was published originally in 1816 and subsequent years (Reimer, Berlin). It has frequently been reprinted.

The following four editions, which have been regularly consulted and quoted, are all founded in the main upon Bekker.

Platonis Opera quae feruntur omnia. Recognoverunt Jo. Georgius Baiterus, Jo. Caspar Orellius, Aug. Guilielmus Winckelmannus. Commonly known as the Zürich edition. Title abbreviated as Turr. = Turicenses. In one large quarto, and also in 21 small volumes, many of which have passed through more than one edition. In consequence, there are occasional differences of reading. Where the 'Zürich text,' or 'Turicenses,' is quoted, the reference is always to the quarto.

Platonis Opera Omnia. Recensuit et commentariis instruxit Godofredus Stallbaum. See below. The text also in one folio volume.

Platonis Dialogi secundum Thrasylli tetralogias dispositi. Ex recognitione Caroli Friderici Hermanni. Teubner. 6 vols.

Platonis Opera ex recensione R. B. Hirschigii. 1 vol. Completed by Platonis Opera ex recensione C. E. Ch. Schneideri (see also below), containing Republic, Timaeus, Critias, Laws, etc. Vol. III contains the arguments of the dialogues, etc., and a valuable index by J. Hunziker. Latin translation in opposite columns. Paris, Didot.

To these succeeds a work still in progress. Platonis Opera quae feruntur omnia ad codices denuo collatos edid. M. Schanz. Leipzig, Teubner. This admirable edition has been available for a portion only of the present work. The following dialogues have appeared: Euthyphro, Apologia, Crito, Phaedo, Cratylus, Theaetetus, Symposium, Phaedrus, Euthydemus, Protagoras, Gorgias, Meno, Laws I–VI.

Professor Schanz had before published a critical edition of the Euthydemus, and a school edition with German notes.

There should also be mentioned two very important works of the same author: Novae Commentationes Platonicae and Studien zur Geschichte des Platonischen Textes.

Commentaries.

The notes *variorum* in the reprints of Bekker.

Stallbaum, as above, in Rost and Jacobs' Bibliotheca Graeca. Includes the received dialogues except the Parmenides, for which see below. A most valuable work, though sometimes unjustly depreciated; full of facts and sound interpretation.

Platonis Dialogi Selecti cura Lud. Frid. Heindorfii.   Berlin, Nauck, edited by the celebrated Buttmann.   4 vols., containing : i. Lysis, Charmides, Hippias Major, Phaedrus.   ii. Gorgias, Theaetetus.   iii. Cratylus, Parmenides, Euthydemus.   iv. Phaedo, Sophistes, Protagoras. Heindorf's acuteness and judgment have long been held in high repute. It should be remembered that he wrote before the publication of Bekker's edition, and had a bad text before him.

The Protagoras of Plato.   By William Wayte, B.A., Cambridge, 1854.   There is a second edition, which I have not seen.

Platons Protagoras.   Für den Schulgebrauch erklärt von Dr. Julius Deuschle.   Revised by Dr. C. W. J. Cron.   Teubner.

Protagoras, German notes by H. Sauppe.   Weidmann.

Protagoras, with notes by Dr. B. H. Kennedy, I regret I have not seen.

The Apology of Plato.   By the Rev. James Riddell, M.A. Oxford, 1867.   Mr. Riddell did not live to complete his work.   Appended is a most valuable Digest of Idioms, collected from the whole works of Plato.

Also by Cron, in Teubner's series as above, along with the Crito.   He has also edited the Laches.   The Teubner series farther includes the Symposium by Hug, and the Euthyphro by Wohlrab.

The Apology and Crito, by W. Wagner.   Cambridge.

The Phaedo of Plato.   By W. D. Geddes, M.A., Professor of Greek in the University of Aberdeen.   Williams & Norgate, 1863.

Phaedo, by W. Wagner.   Cambridge.

Phaedo, by Wohlrab.   Teubner.

The Phaedrus of Plato.   By W. H. Thompson, D.D.   Bibliotheca Classica, 1868.

The Gorgias of Plato.   By W. H. Thompson, D.D.   Ditto, 1871.

Also by Deuschle and Cron, as above.

Platonis Opera Graece.   Recensuit et adnotatione critica instruxit Car. Ern. Christoph. Schneider.   Leipzig, Teubner, 1830.   3 volumes, containing the Republic.   The best edition.   Schneider is so well informed, and so thoroughly clear-sighted, that we can only regret that his explanatory notes are not more numerous.

The Timaeus, with a French translation and notes, by T. Henri Martin.   The translation is not too correct; but M. Martin's notes and *excursus* are of the highest value.

Philebus, edited by E. Poste.   Oxford, 1860.

Platonis Parmenides cum quatuor libris prolegomenorum et commentario perpetuo.   Cura Godofr. Stallbaumi.   Gives also the Commentary of Proclus.   Leipzig. 1848.

The Theaetetus of Plato. By the Rev. Lewis Campbell, M.A. Second Edition. Oxford, 1883.

The Sophistes and Politicus of Plato. By the Rev. Lewis Campbell, M.A. Oxford, 1867.

Platonis Leges, edidit D. Frid. Ast. With copious and excellent Latin notes.

Translations.

Mr. Jowett's, as above.

Platon's sämmtliche Werke. Uebersetzt von Hieronymus Müller, mit Einleitungen begleitet von Karl Steinhart. 9 volumes, the last containing a life of Plato. A very useful book.

Platon's Werke. Griechisch und Deutsch mit kritischen und erklären-den Anmerkungen. Leipzig, Engelmann. Each dialogue separate, translator mostly anonymous. Very useful. The Republic, completing the work, has only just been published (1882), so that I have not been able to consult it.

Platon's Werke von F. Schleiermacher. Berlin, 1817-1828. 6 vols. Schleiermacher did not live to complete the work by adding the Timaeus, Critias, Laws.

The Latin versions in the Ast and Didot editions.

Plato's Gorgias, literally translated. By E. M. Cope. Cambridge, 1864. A great help.

Plato's Staat. Uebersetzt von Dr. C. E. Ch. Schneider. 2nd ed. Breslau, 1850.

The Republic of Plato, translated into English. By John Llewellyn Davies, M.A., and David James Vaughan, M.A. Second edition, Mac-millan, 1858. Since published in 'Golden Treasury' series. An excellent book.

The Philebus, translated by Edward Poste.

The Philebus of Plato, translated, with brief explanatory notes, by F. A. Paley, M.A. 1873.

INDICES TO NOTES.

I. GREEK.

ἀδικῶ, εἰ μὴ ἀδικῶ γε, 230.
ἀθανατίζειν, 231.
ἄθυμος, 'without anger,' 390.
αἱμασιά, 381.
ἀκούεις, οὐκ, 'did you never hear of?' 320.
ἀκρατία, 298.
ἄλιμος, ἡ, 376, 7.
Ἀλκίνου ἀπόλογος, 342.
ἀλλόκοτος. 328.
Ἀμέλης, the river, 352.
ἀμφιλαφής, etymology, 282.
ἄν with future indicative, 257, 344. With participle, 295, 355. Anticipative, 360.
ἀναβέβηκα, of mounting βῆμα, 247.
ἀναίρεσις, 381.
ἀναπίμπλημι, 'infect,' 259, 274.
ἀνάπλεως, 332.
ἀπαθανατίζειν, 231.
ἀπάξειν, 270.
ἀπειλήφῃ, 342.
ἄπο σκοποῦ, τρόπου, 360.
ἀπορία, 380.
ἀρέσκω with accusative, 336, 365.
ἁρμονία in sense of 'scale,' 349.
Ἀρτοξέρξης better supported spelling, 301.
ἀρχή, ἐξ ἀρχῆς, ambiguity, 283.
ἀσπάλαθος, 344.
ἄτρακτος, 346.
αὐγή, αὐγαί, 331.
αὐτός, 'the master,' 242, 306.

βλάστη, 379.

γάλαξι, ἐν, 389.
γενέσια, 301.
γενναῖος, ambiguous, 323.

γλίσχρως, reading and sense, 269; sense, 328.
γνῶθι σαυτόν, 303.
γνωματεύω, 332.
γράφομαι, 293.

δαιμόνιον of Socrates, 258.
δαίμων, 351.
δέ copulative (Φάσωνος δὲ ἀδελφός), 236.
διὰ χρόνου, 285, 307, 360.
διαγίγνομαι, 355.
διαζῆν, 378.
διαλαμβάνω, 344.
διαμαχετέον and -ητέον, 314.
δίκαιός εἰμι, 248, 265.
διότι = ὅτι, 393.
διωλύγιος, 393.
δοκιμασία εἰς ἄνδρας, 268.
δρῦς, ἀπὸ δρυὸς οὐδ' ἀπὺ πέτρης, 261.
δυναστεία, 379.

ἑδραῖος, 320.
εἴλησις, 315.
ἐκεῖνος 'equivalent to αὐτός,' 234.
ἔμπορος and κάπηλος, 240.
ἐν μέρει, 343.
ἐν τοῖς, 265.
ἐν τοῖς περί, 377.
ἔν indeclinable as plural, 363.
ἔναυλος, 377.
ἔνδεκα, οἱ, 272.
ἐνθεαστικός, 384.
ἐξαίρνῳ εἶναι, 232.
ἐπ' ἀνθρώπους, 357.
ἐπαγγέλλομαι, 333.
ἐπέτειος, 318.
ἐπὶ δεξιά, 369.
ἐπιβάτης, 235.

συνεστέον, 240.
σχηματίζομαι, 295.

τέχνη, of same root as τίκτω, 288.
τέως, 309.
τί—φαίνεται; 307.
τρόπαν, κατὰ, 381.
τυγχάνω without participle, 241.

ὕθλος, 369.
ὑμεῖς and ἡμεῖς confounded, 261.
ὕπαρ—ὄναρ, 317.
ὑπέρ, 'before,' 357.
ὑπέρπλουτος, 338.

ὑπόζωμα, 346.
ὑπόνοια, 313.

φαμέν, really pleonastic, = 'you remember,' 326.
φήμη, 324.
φθορά, -αί, 354, 357, 373.
Φοινικικός, 323.
φυγή, -αί, 'fugitives,' 384.
φύσιν, κατὰ, 386.

ὦ πρὸς Διός, with following vocative,
  254.
ὦ 'τᾶν or ὦ τᾶν, 254.

II. ENGLISH.

A, letter, full sound of, 293.
Abaris, 232.
Accusative, as if of time before—
  γεγονότων ἔτη, 357.
  πάμπολυν χρόνον, 361.
Achaemenes, 300.
Acheloüs, 282.
Adeimantus, 305, 260.
Adrasteia, 285.
Aeantodorus, 260.
Aegina, 295.
Aeschines (Socraticus), 260.
Aeschylus quoted—
  Ἀδράστεια, 285.
  σὺ γὰρ δοκεῖν ἄριστος, 299.
  Niobe, 314.
  Hera in Ξάντριαι, 316.
  speech of Thetis about Apollo,
    317.
  dead man recalled to life, 322.
  οἱ Ζηνὸς ἐγγύς, κ. τ. λ., 363.
Aesop, 272, 303.
Agathon, 243, 277; quoted (μόνου
  γὰρ αὐτοῦ), 243.
Agis II, 303.
Alcibiades, 277, 299, 300, 302.
Alcibiades I, doubts as to this dia-
  logue being the work of Plato,
  299-304.

Ammon, 287.
Amphipolis, 257.
Anaxagoras, 255, 313.
Andron, 242.
Animal, mortal and immortal, 284.
Antimoerus, 242.
Antiphon (not the orator), 260.
Antisthenes, 270.
Anytus, 246, 253.
Aorist participle, of past time, 391.
Apaturia, 355.
Apollodorus, 260, 270.
Archelaus, 298.
Areopagus, 281.
Arethas of Patrae, deacon, B written
  for, 228.
Arginusae (or rather Argennusae)
  islands, battle off, 259.
Argos, kings of, 300.
Aristippus, 271.
Aristotle on immortality (*Eth. Nic.*
  X. vii. 8), 231.
  his Ἀπολογία about Hermeias,
    ibid.
Artemis Agra, 281.
Article repeated, 320.
Asclepius, cock due to him, 277.
Asia, Crete given to, 297.
  Aegypt part of, 358.

THE END.

November, 1882.

BOOKS

PRINTED AT

𝕿𝖍𝖊 𝕮𝖑𝖆𝖗𝖊𝖓𝖉𝖔𝖓 𝕻𝖗𝖊𝖘𝖘, 𝕺𝖝𝖋𝖔𝖗𝖉,

AND PUBLISHED FOR THE UNIVERSITY BY

HENRY FROWDE,

AT THE OXFORD UNIVERSITY PRESS WAREHOUSE,

7 PATERNOSTER ROW, LONDON.

LEXICONS, GRAMMARS, &c.

A Greek-English Lexicon, by Henry George Liddell, D.D., and Robert Scott, D.D. *Sixth Edition.* 4to. *cloth,* 1*l.* 16*s.*

A Greek-English Lexicon, abridged from the above, chiefly for the use of Schools. 1881. square 12mo. *cloth,* 7*s.* 6*d.*

A copious Greek-English Vocabulary, compiled from the best authorities. 1850. 24mo. *bound,* 3*s.*

Graecae Grammaticae Rudimenta in usum Scholarum. Auctore Carolo Wordsworth. D.C.L. *Twentieth Edition,* 1882. 12mo. *cloth* 4*s.*

Scheller's Lexicon of the Latin Tongue, with the German explanations translated into English by J. E. Riddle, M.A. fol. *cloth,* 1*l.* 1*s.*

A Latin Dictionary, founded on Andrews' Edition of Freund's Latin Dictionary. Revised, enlarged, and in great part re-written, by Charlton T. Lewis, Ph.D., and Charles Short, LL.D. 4to. *cloth,* 1*l.* 5*s.*

A Practical Grammar of the Sanskrit Language, arranged with reference to the Classical Languages of Europe, for the use of English Students. By Monier Williams, M.A. *Fourth Edition.* 8vo. *cloth,* 15*s.*

A Sanskrit English Dictionary, Etymologically and Philologically arranged. By Monier Williams, M.A. 1872. 4to. *cloth,* 4*l.* 14*s.* 6*d.*

An Icelandic-English Dictionary, based on the MS. collections of the late R. Cleasby. Enlarged and completed by G. Vigfusson. 4to. *cloth,* 3*l.* 7*s.*

An Anglo-Saxon Dictionary, based on the MS. collections of the late Joseph Bosworth, D.D. Edited and enlarged by Professor T. N. Toller, M.A., Owens College, Manchester. Parts I and II, each 15*s.* *To be completed in four Parts.*

An Etymological Dictionary of the English Language, arranged on an Historical basis. By W. W. Skeat, M.A. 4to. *cloth,* 2*l.* 4*s.*

A Concise Etymological Dictionary of the English Language. By W. W. Skeat, M.A. Crown 8vo. *cloth,* 5*s.* 6*d.*

GREEK CLASSICS.

Aeschylus: Tragoediae et Fragmenta, ex recensione Guil.
Dindorfii. *Second Edition*, 1851. 8vo. *cloth*, 5s. 6d.

Sophocles : Tragoediae et Fragmenta, ex recensione et cum
commentariis Guil. Dindorfii. *Third Edition*. 2 vols. fcap. 8vo. *cloth*, 1l. 1s.
Each Play separately, *limp*, 2s. 6d.

The Text alone, printed on writing paper, with large
margin. royal 16mo. *cloth*, 8s.

The Text alone, square 16mo. *cloth*, 3s. 6d.
Each Play separately, *limp*, 6d. (See also page 11.)

Sophocles : Tragoediae et Fragmenta, cum Annotatt. Guil.
Dindorfii. Tomi II. 1849. 8vo. *cloth*, 10s.
The Text, Vol. I. 5s. 6d. The Notes, Vol. II. 4s. 6d.

Euripides : Tragoediae et Fragmenta, ex recensione Guil.
Dindorfii. Tomi II. 1834. 8vo. *cloth*, 10s.

Aristophanes: Comoediae et Fragmenta, ex recensione
Guil. Dindorfii. Tomi II. 1835. 8vo. *cloth*, 11s.

Aristoteles; ex recensione Immanuelis Bekkeri. Accedunt
Indices Sylburgiani. Tomi XI. 1837. 8vo. *cloth*, 2l. 10s.
The volumes may be had separately (except Vol. IX.). 5s. 6d. *each*.

Aristotelis Ethica Nicomachea, ex recensione Immanuelis
Bekkeri. Crown 8vo. *cloth*, 5s.

Demosthenes: ex recensione Guil. Dindorfii. Tomi IV.
1846. 8vo. *cloth*, 1l. 1s.

Homerus: Ilias, ex rec. Guil. Dindorfii. 8vo. *cloth*, 5s. 6d.

Homerus: Odyssea, ex rec. Guil. Dindorfii. 1855. 8vo.
cloth, 5s. 6d.

Plato: The Apology, with a revised Text and English
Notes, and a Digest of Platonic Idioms. by James Riddell, M.A. 1878. 8vo.
cloth, 8s. 6d.

Plato: Philebus, with a revised Text and English Notes,
by Edward Poste, M.A. 1860. 8vo. *cloth*, 7s. 6d.

Plato: Sophistes and Politicus, with a revised Text and
English Notes. by L. Campbell. M.A. 1866. 8vo. *cloth*, 18s.

Plato: Theaetetus, with a revised Text and English Notes,
by L. Campbell, M.A. 1861. 8vo. *cloth*, 9s.

Plato: The Dialogues, translated into English, with Analyses and Introductions. By B. Jowett, M.A. *A new Edition in five volumes*.
1875. Medium 8vo. *cloth*, 3l. 10s.

Plato: The Republic, translated into English, with an
Analysis and Introduction By B. Jowett, M.A. Medium 8vo *cloth*, 12s. 6d.

Thucydides: translated into English, with Introduction,
Marginal Analysis, Notes and Indices. By the same. 2 vols. 1881. Medium
8vo. *cloth*, 1l. 12s.

THE HOLY SCRIPTURES.

The Holy Bible in the Earliest English Versions, made from the Latin Vulgate by John Wycliffe and his followers: edited by the Rev. J. Forshall and Sir F. Madden. 4 vols. 1850. royal 4to. *cloth*, 3*l.* 3*s.*

Also reprinted from the above, with Introduction and Glossary by W. W. SKEAT, M.A.

(1) **The New Testament in English**, according to the Version by John Wycliffe, about A.D. 1380, and Revised by John Purvey, about A.D. 1388. 1879. Extra fcap. 8vo. *cloth*, 6*s.*

(2) **The Book of Job, Psalms, Proverbs, Ecclesiastes,** and Solomon's Song, according to the Version by John Wycliffe. Revised by John Purvey. Extra fcap. 8vo. *cloth*, 3*s.* 6*d.*

The Holy Bible: an exact reprint, page for page, of the Authorized Version published in the year 1611. Demy 4to. *half bound*, 1*l.* 1*s.*

Novum Testamentum Graece. Edidit Carolus Lloyd, S.T.P.R., necnon Episcopus Oxoniensis. 18mo. *cloth*, 3*s.*

The same on writing paper, small 4to. *cloth*, 10*s.* 6*d.*

Novum Testamentum Graece juxta Exemplar Millianum. 18mo. *cloth*, 2*s.* 6*d.*

The same on writing paper, small 4to. *cloth*, 9*s.*

The Greek Testament, with the Readings adopted by the Revisers of the Authorised Version :—

    (1) Pica type. *Second Edition, with Marginal References.* Demy 8vo. *cloth*, 10*s.* 6*d.*

    (2) Long Primer type. Fcap. 8vo. *cloth*, 4*s.* 6*d.*

    (3) The same, on writing paper, with wide margin, *cloth*, 15*s.*

Evangelia Sacra Graece. fcap. 8vo. *limp*, 1*s.* 6*d.*

Vetus Testamentum ex Versione Septuaginta Interpretum secundum exemplar Vaticanum Romae editum. Accedit potior varietas Codicis Alexandrini. *Editio Altera.* Tomi III. 1875. 18mo. *cloth*, 18*s.*

ECCLESIASTICAL HISTORY, &c.

Baedae Historia Ecclesiastica. Edited, with English Notes, by G. H. Moberly, M.A. Crown 8vo. *cloth*, 10*s.* 6*d.*

Chapters of Early English Church History. By William Bright, D.D. 8vo. *cloth*, 12*s.*

Eusebius' Ecclesiastical History, according to the Text of Burton. With an Introduction by William Bright, D.D. Crown 8vo. *cloth*, 8*s.* 6*d.*

Socrates' Ecclesiastical History, according to the Text of Hussey. With an Introduction by William Bright, D.D. Crown 8vo. *cloth*, 7*s.* 6*d.*

ENGLISH THEOLOGY.

Butler's Analogy, with an Index. 8vo. *cloth,* 5s. 6d.

Butler's Sermons. 8vo. *cloth,* 5s. 6d.

Hooker's Works, with his Life by Walton, arranged by
John Keble, M.A. *Sixth Edition,* 3 vols. 1874. 8vo. *cloth,* 1l. 11s. 6d.

Hooker's Works; the text as arranged by John Keble, M.A.
2 vols. 1875. 8vo. *cloth,* 11s.

Pearson's Exposition of the Creed. Revised and corrected
by E. Burton, D.D. *Sixth Edition.* 1877. 8vo. *cloth,* 10s. 6d.

Waterland's Review of the Doctrine of the Eucharist, with
a Preface by the present Bishop of London. 1868. crown 8vo. *cloth,* 6s. 6d.

ENGLISH HISTORY.

A History of England. Principally in the Seventeenth
Century. By Leopold Von Ranke. 6 vols. 8vo. *cloth,* 3l. 3s.

Clarendon's (Edw. Earl of) History of the Rebellion and
Civil Wars in England. To which are subjoined the Notes of Bishop War-
burton. 7 vols. 1849. medium 8vo. *cloth,* 2l. 10s.

Clarendon's (Edw. Earl of) History of the Rebellion and
Civil Wars in England. 7 vols. 1839. 18mo. *cloth,* 1l. 1s.

Freeman's (E. A.) History of the Norman Conquest of
England: its Causes and Results. *In Six Volumes.* 8vo. *cloth,* 5l. 9s. 6d.
    Vol. I. and II. together, *Third Edition,* 1877. 1l. 16s.
    Vol. III. *Second Edition,* 1874. 1l. 1s.
    Vol. IV. *Second Edition,* 1875. 1l. 1s.
    Vol. V. 1876. 1l. 1s.
    Vol. VI. Index, 1879. 10s. 6d.

Rogers's History of Agriculture and Prices in England, A.D.
1259—1793. Vols. I. and II. (1259—1400). 8vo. *cloth,* 2l. 2s.
    Vols. III. and IV. (1401-1582) 8vo. *cloth,* 2l. 10s.

MISCELLANEOUS.

An Introduction to the Principles of Morals and
Legislation. By Jeremy Bentham. Crown 8vo. *cloth,* 6s. 6d.

Bacon's Novum Organum. edited, with English Notes, by
G. W. Kitchin. M.A. 1855. 8vo. *cloth,* 9s. 6d. *See also page* 15.

Bacon's Novum Organum, translated by G. W. Kitchin,
M.A. 1855. 8vo. *cloth,* 9s. 6d.

Smith's Wealth of Nations. A new Edition, with Notes,
by J. E. Thorold Rogers, M.A. 2 vols. 8vo. *cloth,* 21s.

The Student's Handbook to the University and Col-
leges of Oxford. *Sixth Edition.* Extra fcap. 8vo. *cloth,* 2s. 6d.

𝕮𝖑𝖆𝖗𝖊𝖓𝖉𝖔𝖓 𝕻𝖗𝖊𝖘𝖘 𝕾𝖊𝖗𝖎𝖊𝖘.

The Delegates of the Clarendon Press having undertaken the publication of a series of works, chiefly educational, and entitled the 𝕮𝖑𝖆𝖗𝖊𝖓𝖉𝖔𝖓 𝕻𝖗𝖊𝖘𝖘 𝕾𝖊𝖗𝖎𝖊𝖘, have published, or have in preparation, the following.

Those to which prices are attached are already published; the others are in preparation.

I. ENGLISH.

A First Reading Book. By Marie Eichens of Berlin; and edited by Anne J. Clough. Ext. fcap. 8vo. *stiff covers,* 4d.

Oxford Reading Book, Part I. For Little Children. Ext. fcap. 8vo. *stiff covers,* 6d.

Oxford Reading Book, Part II. For Junior Classes. Ext. fcap. 8vo. *stiff covers,* 6d.

An Elementary English Grammar and Exercise Book. By O. W. Tancock, M.A. *Second Edition.* Ext. fcap. 8vo. 1s. 6d.

An English Grammar and Reading Book, for Lower Forms in Classical Schools. By the same Author. *Third Edition.* Ext. fcap. 8vo. *cloth,* 3s. 6d.

Typical Selections from the best English Writers, with Introductory Notices. In Two Volumes. Extra fcap. 8vo. *cloth,* 3s. 6d. each.

The Philology of the English Tongue. By J. Earle, M.A., formerly Fellow of Oriel College, and Professor of Anglo-Saxon, Oxford. *Third Edition.* Ext. fcap. 8vo. *cloth,* 7s. 6d.

A Book for Beginners in Anglosaxon. By John Earle, M.A. *Second Edition.* Extra fcap. 8vo. *cloth,* 2s. 6d.

An Anglo-Saxon Primer, with Grammar, Notes, and Glossary. By Henry Sweet, M.A. *Second Edition.* Extra fcap. 8vo. *cloth,* 2s. 6d.

An Anglo-Saxon Reader, in Prose and Verse, with Grammatical Introduction, Notes, and Glossary. By Henry Sweet, M.A. *Third Edition.* Extra fcap. 8vo. *cloth,* 8s. 6d.

The Ormulum; with the Notes and Glossary of Dr. R. M. White. Edited by R. Holt, M.A. 2 vols. Extra fcap. 8vo. *cloth,* 21s.

Specimens of Early English. A New and Revised Edition. With Introduction, Notes, and Glossarial Index. By R. Morris, LL.D., and W. W. Skeat M.A.

    Part I. From Old English Homilies to King Horn (A.D. 1150 to A.D. 1300). Extra fcap. 8vo. *cloth,* 9s.

    Part II. From Robert of Gloucester to Gower (A.D. 1298 to A.D. 1293). Extra fcap. 8vo. *cloth,* 7s. 6d.

Specimens of English Literature, from the 'Ploughmans Crede' to the 'Shepheardes Calender' (A.D. 1394 to A.D. 1579). With Introduction, Notes, and Glossarial Index. By W. W. Skeat, M.A. *Third Edition.* Ext. fcap. 8vo. *cloth,* 7s. 6d.

The Vision of William concerning Piers the Plowman, by William Langland. Edited, with Notes, by W. W. Skeat, M.A. *Third Edition.* Ext. fcap. 8vo. *cloth.* 4s. 6d.

Chaucer. The Prioresses Tale; Sire Thopas; The Monkes Tale; The Clerkes Tale; The Squieres Tale, &c. Edited by W. W. Skeat, M.A. *Second Edition.* Ext. fcap. 8vo. *cloth,* 4s. 6d.

Chaucer. The Tale of the Man of Lawe; The Par- doneres Tale; The Second Nonnes Tale; The Chanouns Yemannes Tale. By the same Editor. *Second Edition.* Extra fcap. 8vo. *cloth,* 4s. 6d.

Old English Drama. Marlowe's Tragical History of Doctor Faustus, and Greene's Honourable History of Friar Bacon and Friar Bungay. Edited by A. W. Ward, M.A. Extra fcap. 8vo. *cloth,* 5s. 6d.

Marlowe. Edward II. With Notes, &c. By O. W. Tancock, M.A., Head Master of Norwich School. Extra fcap. 8vo. *cloth,* 3s.

Shakespeare. Hamlet. Edited by W. G. Clark, M.A., and W. Aldis Wright, M.A. Extra fcap. 8vo. *stiff covers,* 2s.

Shakespeare. Select Plays. Edited by W. Aldis Wright, M.A. Extra fcap. 8vo. *stiff covers.*

The Tempest, 1s. 6d.	King Lear, 1s. 6d.
As You Like It, 1s. 6d.	A Midsummer Night's Dream, 1s. 6d.
Julius Cæsar, 2s.	Coriolanus, 2s. 6d.
Richard the Third, 2s. 6d.	Henry the Fifth, 2s.

(For other Plays, see p. 7.)

Milton. Areopagitica. With Introduction and Notes. By J. W. Hales, M.A. *Second Edition.* Extra fcap. 8vo. *cloth,* 3s.

Bunyan. Holy War. Edited by E. Venables, M.A. *In Preparation.* (See also p. 7.)

Addison. Selections from Papers in the Spectator. With Notes. By T. Arnold, M.A., University College. Extra fcap. 8vo. *cloth,* 4s. 6d.

Burke. Four Letters on the Proposals for Peace with the Regicide Directory of France. Edited, with Introduction and Notes, by E. J. Payne, M.A. Extra fcap. 8vo. *cloth,* 5s. See also page 7.

Also the following in paper covers.

Goldsmith. Deserted Village. 2d.

Gray. Elegy, and Ode on Eton College. 2d.

Johnson. Vanity of Human Wishes. With Notes by E. J. Payne, M.A. 4d.

Keats. Hyperion, Book I. With Notes by W. T. Arnold, B.A. 4d.

Milton. With Notes by R. C. Browne, M.A.

Lycidas, 3d.	L'Allegro, 3d.	Il Penseroso, 4d.
Comus, 6d.	Samson Agonistes, 6d.	

Parnell. The Hermit. 2d.

Scott. Lay of the Last Minstrel. Introduction and Canto I. With Notes by W. Minto, M.A. 6d.

A SERIES OF ENGLISH CLASSICS

Designed to meet the wants of Students in English Literature ; by the late J. S. BREWER, M.A., Professor of English Literature at King's College, London.

1. **Chaucer. The Prologue to the Canterbury Tales; The** Knightes Tale; The Nonne Prestes Tale. Edited by R. Morris, LL.D. *Sixth Edition.* Extra fcap. 8vo. *cloth,* 2s. 6d. See also p. 6.

2. **Spenser's Faery Queene. Books I and II. By G. W.** Kitchin, M.A. Extra fcap. 8vo. *cloth,* 2s. 6d. each.

3. **Hooker. Ecclesiastical Polity, Book I. Edited by R. W.** Church, M.A., Dean of St. Paul's. Extra fcap. 8vo. *cloth,* 2s.

4. **Shakespeare. Select Plays. Edited by W. G. Clark,** M.A., and W. Aldis Wright, M.A. Extra fcap. 8vo. *stiff covers.*
   I. The Merchant of Venice. 1s.   II. Richard the Second. 1s. 6d.
   III. Macbeth. 1s. 6d. (For other Plays, see p. 6.)

5. **Bacon.**
   I. Advancement of Learning. Edited by W. Aldis Wright, M.A. *Second Edition.* Extra fcap. 8vo. *cloth,* 4s. 6d.
   II. The Essays. With Introduction and Notes. By J. R. Thursfield, M.A.

6. **Milton. Poems. Edited by R. C. Browne, M.A. In** Two Volumes. *Fourth Edition.* Ext. fcap. 8vo. *cloth,* 6s. 6d.
   Sold separately, Vol. I. 4s., Vol. II. 3s.

7. **Dryden. Stanzas on the Death of Oliver Cromwell;** Astraea Redux; Annus Mirabilis; Absalom and Achitophel; Religio Laici; The Hind and the Panther. Edited by W. D. Christie, M.A., Trinity College, Cambridge. *Second Edition.* Extra fcap. 8vo. *cloth,* 3s. 6d.

8. **Bunyan. The Pilgrim's Progress, Grace Abounding, and** A Relation of his Imprisonment. Edited, with Biographical Introduction and Notes, by E. Venables, M.A., Precentor of Lincoln. Extra fcap. 8vo. *cloth,* 5s.

9. **Pope. With Introduction and Notes. By Mark Pattison,** B.D., Rector of Lincoln College, Oxford.
   I. Essay on Man. *Sixth Edition.* Extra fcap. 8vo. *stiff covers,* 1s. 6d.
   II. Satires and Epistles. *Second Edition.* Extra fcap. 8vo. *stiff covers,* 2s.

10. **Johnson. Select Works. Lives of Dryden and Pope,** and Rasselas. Edited by Alfred Milnes, B.A. (Lond.), late Scholar of Lincoln College, Oxford. Extra fcap. 8vo. *cloth,* 4s. 6d.

11. **Burke. Edited, with Introduction and Notes, by E. J.** Payne, M.A., Fellow of University College, Oxford.
   I. Thoughts on the Present Discontents; the Two Speeches on America, etc. *Second Edition.* Extra fcap. 8vo. *cloth,* 4s. 6d.
   II. Reflections on the French Revolution. *Second Edition.* Extra fcap. 8vo. *cloth,* 5s. See also p. 6.

12. **Cowper. Edited, with Life, Introductions, and Notes,** by H. T. Griffith, B.A., formerly Scholar of Pembroke College, Oxford.
   I. The Didactic Poems of 1782, with Selections from the Minor Pieces, A.D. 1779-1783. Ext. fcap. 8vo. *cloth,* 3s.
   II. The Task, with Tirocinium, and Selections from the Minor Poems, A.D. 1784-1799. Ext. fcap. 8vo. *cloth,* 3s.

II. LATIN.

An Elementary Latin Grammar. By John B. Allen, M.A.,
Head Master of Perse Grammar School, Cambridge. *Third Edition.* Extra
fcap. 8vo. *cloth*, 2s. 6d.

A First Latin Exercise Book. By the same Author.
Third Edition. Extra fcap. 8vo. *cloth*, 2s. 6d.

Anglice Reddenda, or Easy Extracts, Latin and Greek,
for Unseen Translation. By C. S. Jerram, M.A. Extra fcap. 8vo. *cloth*, 2s. 6d.

Passages for Translation into Latin. For the use of
Passmen and others. Selected by J. Y. Sargent, M.A. *Fifth Edition.* Ext.
fcap. 8vo. *cloth*, 2s. 6d.

First Latin Reader. By T. J. Nunns, M.A. *Third
Edition.* Extra fcap. 8vo. *cloth*, 2s.

Second Latin Reader. *In Preparation.*

Caesar. The Commentaries (for Schools). With Notes
and Maps, &c. By C. E. Moberly, M.A., Assistant Master in Rugby School.
> *The Gallic War.* Extra fcap. 8vo. *cloth*, 4s. 6d.
> *The Civil War.* Extra fcap. 8vo. *cloth*, 3s. 6d.
> *The Civil War.* Book I. Extra fcap. 8vo. *cloth*, 2s.

Cicero. Selection of interesting and descriptive passages.
With Notes. By Henry Walford, M.A. In Three Parts. *Third Edition.*
Ext. fcap. 8vo. *cloth*, 4s. 6d.
> *Each Part separately, in limp cloth,* 1s. 6d.

Cicero. Select Letters (for Schools). With Notes. By the
late C. E. Prichard, M.A., and E. R. Bernard, M.A. Extra fcap. 8vo. *cloth*, 3s.

Cicero. Select Orations (for Schools). With Notes. By
J. R. King, M.A. Ext. fcap. 8vo. *cloth*, 2s. 6d.

Cornelius Nepos. With Notes, by Oscar Browning, M.A.
Second Edition. Extra fcap. 8vo. *cloth*, 2s. 6d.

Livy. Selections (for Schools). With Notes and Maps.
By H. Lee Warner, M.A. *In Three Parts.* Ext. fcap. 8vo. *cloth*, 1s. 6d. each.

Livy. Books V—VII. By A. R. Cluer, B.A. Extra fcap.
8vo. *cloth*, 3s. 6d.

Ovid. Selections for the use of Schools. With Introductions and Notes, etc. By W. Ramsay, M.A. Edited by G. G. Ramsay, M.A.
Second Edition. Ext. fcap. 8vo. *cloth*, 5s. 6d.

Pliny. Select Letters (for Schools). With Notes. By the
late C. E. Prichard, M.A., and E. R. Bernard, M.A. *Second Edition.* Extra
fcap. 8vo. *cloth*, 3s.

Catulli Veronensis Liber. Iterum recognovit, apparatum
criticum prolegomena appendices addidit, Robinson Ellis, A.M. 8vo. *cloth*, 16s.

Catullus. A Commentary on Catullus. By Robinson
Ellis, M.A. Demy 8vo. *cloth*, 16s.

Catulli Veronensis Carmina Selecta, secundum recog-
nitionem Robinson Ellis, A.M. Extra fcap. 8vo. *cloth*, 3s. 6d.

Cicero de Oratore. With Introduction and Notes. By
A. S. Wilkins, M.A., Professor of Latin, Owens College. Manchester.
Book I. Demy 8vo. *cloth,* 6s. Book II. Demy 8vo. *cloth,* 5s.

Cicero's Philippic Orations. With Notes. By J. R. King,
M.A. *Second Edition.* Demy 8vo. *cloth,* 10s. 6d.

Cicero. Select Letters. With English Introductions,
Notes, and Appendices. By Albert Watson, M.A., Fellow and Lecturer of
Brasenose College, Oxford. *Third Edition.* Demy 8vo. *cloth,* 18s.

Cicero. Select Letters (Text). By the same Editor.
Extra fcap. 8vo. *cloth,* 4s.

Cicero pro Cluentio. With Introduction and Notes. By
W. Ramsay, M.A. Edited by G. G. Ramsay. M.A., Professor of Humanity,
Glasgow. *Second Edition.* Ext. fcap. 8vo. *cloth,* 3s. 6d.

Livy, Book I. By J. R. Seeley, M.A., Regius Professor
of Modern History, Cambridge. *Third Edition.* Demy 8vo. *cloth,* 6s.

Horace. With Introductions and Notes. By Edward C.
Wickham, M.A., Head Master of Wellington College.
Vol. I. The Odes, Carmen Seculare, and Epodes. *Second Edition.* Demy
8vo. *cloth,* 12s.

Horace. *A reprint of the above,* in a size suitable for the
use of Schools. Extra fcap. 8vo. *cloth,* 5s. 6d.

Persius. The Satires. With a Translation and Commentary. By John Conington, M.A. Edited by H. Nettleship, M.A. *Second
Edition.* 8vo. *cloth,* 7s. 6d.

Selections from the less known Latin Poets. By North
Pinder, M.A. Demy 8vo. *cloth,* 15s.

Fragments and Specimens of Early Latin. With Introduction and Notes. By John Wordsworth, M.A. Demy 8vo. *cloth,* 18s.

Tacitus. The Annals. With Essays and Notes. *Preparing.*

Virgil. With Introduction and Notes. By T. L. Papillon,
M.A., Fellow of New College. 2 vols. Crown 8vo. *cloth,* 10s. 6d.
The Text may be had separately, *cloth,* 4s. 6d.

A Manual of Comparative Philology, as applied to the
Illustration of Greek and Latin Inflections. By T. L. Papillon, M.A., Fellow
of New College. *Second Edition.* Crown 8vo. *cloth,* 6s.

The Roman Poets of the Augustan Age. *Virgil.* By
William Young Sellar, M.A. 8vo. *cloth,* 14s.

The Roman Poets of the Republic. By the same
Author. Extra fcap. 8vo. *cloth,* 14s.

III. GREEK.

A Greek Primer, for the use of beginners in that Language.
By the Right Rev. Charles Wordsworth, D.C.L., Bishop of St. Andrews. *Sixth
Edition. Revised and Enlarged.* Ext. fcap. 8vo. *cloth,* 1s. 6d.

Greek Verbs, Irregular and Defective; their forms,
meaning, and quantity; embracing all the Tenses used by Greek writers, with
references to the passages in which they are found. By W. Veitch. *Fourth
Edition.* Crown 8vo. *cloth,* 10s. 6d.

The Elements of Greek Accentuation (for Schools): abridged from his larger work by H. W. Chandler, M.A., Waynflete Professor of Moral and Metaphysical Philosophy, Oxford. Ext. fcap. 8vo. *cloth*, 2s. 6d.

A Series of Graduated Greek Readers :

First Greek Reader. By W. G. Rushbrooke, M.L., formerly Fellow of St. John's College, Cambridge, Second Classical Master at the City of London School. Ext. fcap. 8vo. *cloth*, 2s. 6d.

Second Greek Reader. By A. J. M. Bell, M.A. Extra fcap. 8vo. *cloth*, 3s. 6d.

Third Greek Reader.   *In Preparation.*

Fourth Greek Reader; being Specimens of Greek Dialects. By W. W. Merry, M.A. Ext. fcap. 8vo. *cloth*, 4s. 6d.

Fifth Greek Reader. Part I, Selections from Greek Epic and Dramatic Poetry. By E. Abbott, M.A. Ext. fcap. 8vo. *cloth*, 4s. 6d.

The Golden Treasury of Ancient Greek Poetry; with Introductory Notices and Notes. By R. S. Wright, M.A. Ext. fcap. 8vo. *cloth*, 8s. 6d.

A Golden Treasury of Greek Prose; with Introductory Notices and Notes. By R. S. Wright, M.A., and J. E. L. Shadwell, M.A. Ext. fcap. 8vo. *cloth*, 4s. 6d.

Aeschylus. Prometheus Bound (for Schools). With Notes. By A. O. Prickard, M.A. Ext. fcap. 8vo. *cloth*, 2s.

Aeschylus. Agamemnon. With Introduction and Notes. By Arthur Sidgwick. M.A., late Fellow of Trinity College, Cambridge, and Assistant Master of Rugby School. Ext. fcap. 8vo. *cloth*, 3s.

Aristophanes. In Single Plays, edited with English Notes, Introductions, &c. By W. W. Merry, M.A. Extra fcap. 8vo. The Clouds, 2s.   The Acharnians, 2s. *Other plays will follow.*

Arrian. Selections (for Schools). With Notes. By J. S. Phillpotts, B.C.L., Head Master of Bedford School.

Cebetis Tabula. With Introduction and Notes by C. S. Jerram, M.A. Ext. fcap. 8vo. *cloth*, 2s. 6d.

Euripides. Alcestis (for Schools). By C. S. Jerram, M.A. Ext. fcap. 8vo. *cloth*, 2s. 6d.

Euripides. Helena. Edited with Introduction, Notes, and Critical Appendix, for Upper and Middle Forms. By the same Editor. Extra fcap. 8vo. *cloth*, 3s.

Herodotus. Selections. With Introduction, Notes, and Map. By W. W. Merry, M.A. Ext. fcap. 8vo. *cloth*, 2s. 6d.

Homer. Odyssey, Books I-XII (for Schools). By W. W. Merry, M.A. *Twenty-fourth Thousand.* Ext. fcap. 8vo. *cloth*, 4s. 6d. Book II, separately, 1s. 6d.

Homer. Odyssey, Books XIII-XXIV (for Schools). By the same Editor. Ext. fcap. 8vo. *cloth*, 5s.

Homer. Iliad. Book I (for Schools). By D. B. Monro, M.A., Vice-Provost of Oriel College, Oxford. Ext. fcap. 8vo. *cloth*, 2s.

Homer. Iliad. Books VI and XXI. With Introduction
and Notes. By Herbert Hailstone, M.A., late Scholar of St. Peter's College,
Cambridge. Extra fcap. 8vo. *cloth*, 1s. 6d. each.

Lucian. Vera Historia (for Schools). By C. S. Jerram,
M.A. Extra fcap. 8vo. *cloth*, 1s. 6d.

Plato. Selections (for Schools). With Notes. By B. Jowett,
M.A., Regius Professor of Greek; and J. Purves, M.A. *In the Press.*

Sophocles. In Single Plays, with English Notes, &c. By
Lewis Campbell, M.A., and Evelyn Abbott, M.A. Extra fcap. 8vo.
Oedipus Rex, Oedipus Coloneus, Antigone, 1s. 9d. each.
Ajax, Electra, Trachiniae, Philoctetes, 2s. each.

Sophocles. Oedipus Rex: Dindorf's Text, with Notes by
the present Bishop of St. David's. Extra fcap. 8vo. *cloth*, 1s. 6d.

Theocritus (for Schools). With Notes. By H. Kynaston
(late Snow), M.A. *Third Edition.* Ext. fcap. 8vo. *cloth*, 4s. 6d.

Xenophon. Easy Selections (for Junior Classes). With a
Vocabulary, Notes, and Map. By J. S. Phillpotts, B.C.L., and C. S. Jerram,
M.A. *Third Edition.* Ext. fcap. 8vo. *cloth*, 3s. 6d.

Xenophon. Selections (for Schools). With Notes and
Maps. By J. S. Phillpotts, B.C.L., Head Master of Bedford School. *Fourth
Edition.* Ext. fcap. 8vo. *cloth*, 3s. 6d.

Xenophon. Anabasis, Book II. With Notes and Map.
By C. S. Jerram, M.A. Ext. fcap. 8vo. *cloth*, 2s.

Aristotle's Politics. By W. L. Newman, M.A., Fellow
of Balliol College, Oxford.

Demosthenes and Aeschines. The Orations on the
Crown. With Introductory Essays and Notes. By G. A. Simcox, M.A., and
W. H. Simcox, M.A. Demy 8vo. *cloth*, 12s.

Homer. Odyssey, Books I–XII. Edited with English
Notes, Appendices, &c. By W. W. Merry, M.A., and the late James Riddell,
M.A. Demy 8vo. *cloth*, 16s.

Homer. Iliad. With Introduction and Notes. By D. B.
Monro, M.A., Vice-Provost of Oriel College, Oxford. *Preparing.*

A Grammar of the Homeric Dialect. By D. B. Monro,
M.A. Demy 8vo. *cloth*, 10s. 6d.

Sophocles. With English Notes and Introductions. By
Lewis Campbell, M.A., Professor of Greek, St. Andrews. In Two Volumes.
8vo. *each* 16s.
Vol. I. Oedipus Tyrannus. Oedipus Coloneus. Antigone. *Second Edition.*
Vol. II. Ajax Electra. Trachiniae. Philoctetes. Fragments.

Sophocles. The Text of the Seven Plays. By the same
Editor. Ext. fcap. 8vo. *cloth*, 4s. 6d.

A Manual of Greek Historical Inscriptions. By E. L.
Hicks, M.A., formerly Fellow and Tutor of Corpus Christi College. Demy
8vo. *cloth*, 10s. 6d.

IV. FRENCH.

An Etymological Dictionary of the French Language, with
a Preface on the Principles of French Etymology. By A. Brachet. Translated
by G. W. Kitchin, M.A. *Second Edition.* Crown 8vo. *cloth,* 7s. 6d.

Brachet's Historical Grammar of the French Language.
Translated by G. W. Kitchin, M.A. *Fifth Edition.* Ext. fcap. 8vo. *cloth,* 3s. 6d.

A Short History of French Literature. By George
Saintsbury. Crown 8vo. *cloth,* 10s. 6d.

A Primer of French Literature. By George Saintsbury.
Second Edition, with Index. Extra fcap. 8vo. *cloth,* 2s.

French Classics, Edited by GUSTAVE MASSON, *B.A. Univ. Gallic.*
Extra fcap. 8vo. cloth, 2s. 6d. each.

Corneille's Cinna, and Molière's Les Femmes Savantes.

Racine's Andromaque, and Corneille's Le Menteur. With
Louis Racine's Life of his Father.

Molière's Les Fourberies de Scapin, and Racine's Athalie.
With Voltaire's Life of Molière.

Regnard's Le Joueur, and Brueys and Palaprat's Le
Grondeur.

A Selection of Tales by Modern Writers.

Selections from the Correspondence of Madame de Sévigné
and her chief Contemporaries. Intended more especially for Girls' Schools.
By the same Editor. Ext. fcap. 8vo. *cloth,* 3s.

Louis XIV and his Contemporaries; as described in
Extracts from the best Memoirs of the Seventeenth Century. With Notes,
Genealogical Tables, etc. By the same Editor. Extra fcap. 8vo. *cloth,* 2s. 6d.

V. GERMAN.

German Classics, Edited by C. A. BUCHHEIM, *Phil. Doc., Professor*
in King's College, London.

Goethe's Egmont. With a Life of Goethe, &c. *Third*
Edition. Ext. fcap. 8vo. *cloth,* 3s.

Schiller's Wilhelm Tell. With a Life of Schiller; an historical and critical Introduction, Arguments, and a complete Commentary.
Fifth Edition. Ext. fcap. 8vo. *cloth,* 3s. 6d.

Lessing's Minna von Barnhelm. A Comedy. With a Life
of Lessing, Critical Analysis, Complete Commentary, &c. *Fourth Edition.*
Extra fcap. 8vo. *cloth,* 3s. 6d.

Schiller's Historische Skizzen: Egmonts Leben und Tod,
and Belagerung von Antwerpen. *Second Edition.* Ext. fcap. 8vo. *cloth,* 2s. 6d.

Goethe's Iphigenie auf Tauris. A Drama. With a Critical
Introduction and Notes. Ext. fcap. 8vo. *cloth,* 3s.

Modern German Reader. A Graduated Collection of Prose
Extracts from Modern German Writers,—
Part I With English Notes, a Grammatical Appendix, and a complete Voca-
bulary. *Second Edition.* Extra fcap. 8vo. *cloth,* 2s. 6d.

Lessing's Nathan der Weise. With Introduction, Notes, etc.
Extra fcap. 8vo. *cloth,* 4s. 6d. *Just Published.*

LANGE's *German Course.*

The Germans at Home; a Practical Introduction to German Conversation, with an Appendix containing the Essentials of German Grammar. *Second Edition.* 8vo. *cloth, 2s. 6d.*

The German Manual; a German Grammar, a Reading Book, and a Handbook of German Conversation. 8vo. *cloth, 7s. 6d.*

A Grammar of the German Language. 8vo. *cloth, 3s. 6d.*

> *This 'Grammar' is a reprint of the Grammar contained in 'The German Manual,' and, in this separate form, is intended for the use of students who wish to make themselves acquainted with German Grammar chiefly for the purpose of being able to read German books.*

German Composition; Extracts from English and American writers for Translation into German, with Hints for Translation in foot-notes. *In the Press.*

Lessing's Laokoon. With Introduction, English Notes, &c. By A. Hamann, Phil. Doc., M.A., Taylorian Teacher of German in the University of Oxford. Ext. fcap. 8vo. *cloth, 4s. 6d.*

Wilhelm Tell. By Schiller. Translated into English Verse by Edward Massie, M.A. Ext. fcap. 8vo. *cloth, 5s.*

VI. MATHEMATICS, &o.

Figures made Easy: a first Arithmetic Book. (Introductory to 'The Scholar's Arithmetic.') By Lewis Hensley, M.A., formerly Fellow of Trinity College, Cambridge. Crown 8vo. *cloth, 6d.*

Answers to the Examples in Figures made Easy. By the same Author. Crown 8vo. *cloth, 1s.*

The Scholar's Arithmetic. By the same Author. Crown 8vo. *cloth, 4s. 6d.*

The Scholar's Algebra. By the same Author. Crown 8vo. *cloth, 4s. 6d.*

Book-keeping. By R. G. C. Hamilton and John Ball. *New and enlarged Edition.* Ext. fcap. 8vo. *limp cloth, 2s.*

Acoustics. By W. F. Donkin, M.A., F.R.S., Savilian Professor of Astronomy, Oxford. Crown 8vo. *cloth, 7s. 6d.*

A Treatise on Electricity and Magnetism. By J. Clerk Maxwell, M.A , F.R.S. A New Edition, edited by W. D. Niven, M.A. 2 vols. Demy 8vo. *cloth, 1l. 11s. 6d.*

An Elementary Treatise on Electricity. By James Clerk Maxwell, M.A. Edited by William Garnett, M.A. Demy 8vo. *cloth, 7s. 6d.*

A Treatise on Statics. By G. M. Minchin, M.A. *Second Edition, Revised and Enlarged.* Demy 8vo. *cloth, 14s.*

Geodesy. By Colonel Alexander Ross Clarke, R.E. Demy 8vo. *cloth, 12s. 6d.*

VII. PHYSICAL SCIENCE.

A Handbook of Descriptive Astronomy. By G. F. Chambers, F.R.A.S. *Third Edition.* Demy 8vo. *cloth,* 28s.

Chemistry for Students. By A. W. Williamson, Phil. Doc., F.R.S., Professor of Chemistry, University College, London. *A new Edition, with Solutions,* 1873. Ext. fcap. 8vo. *cloth,* 8s. 6d.

A Treatise on Heat, with numerous Woodcuts and Diagrams. By Balfour Stewart, LL.D., F.R.S., Professor of Physics, Owens College, Manchester. *Fourth Edition.* Ext. fcap. 8vo. *cloth,* 7s. 6d.

Lessons on Thermodynamics. By R. E. Baynes, M.A. Crown 8vo. *cloth,* 7s. 6d.

Forms of Animal Life. By G. Rolleston, M.D., F.R.S., Linacre Professor of Physiology, Oxford. *A New Edition in the Press.*

Exercises in Practical Chemistry. Vol. I. Elementary Exercises. By A. G Vernon Harcourt, M.A., and H. G. Madan, M.A. *Third Edition.* Revised by H. G. Madan, M.A. Crown 8vo. *cloth,* 9s.

Tables of Qualitative Analysis. Arranged by H. G. Madan, M.A. Large 4to. *stiff covers,* 4s. 6d.

Geology of Oxford and the Valley of the Thames. By John Phillips, M.A., F.R.S., Professor of Geology, Oxford. 8vo. *cloth,* 1l. 1s.

Crystallography. By M. H. N. Story-Maskelyne, M.A., Professor of Mineralogy, Oxford. *In the Press.*

VIII. HISTORY.

A Constitutional History of England. By W. Stubbs, D.D., Regius Professor of Modern History, Oxford. *Library Edition.* Three vols. demy 8vo. *cloth,* 2l. 8s.

    Also in Three Volumes, Crown 8vo., price 12s. each.

Select Charters and other Illustrations of English Constitutional History from the Earliest Times to the reign of Edward I. By the same Author. *Third Edition.* Crown 8vo. *cloth,* 8s. 6d.

A Short History of the Norman Conquest. By E. A. Freeman, M.A. Extra fcap. 8vo. *cloth,* 2s. 6d.

Genealogical Tables illustrative of Modern History. By H. B. George, M.A. Small 4to. *cloth* 12s.

A History of France, down to the year 1793. With numerous Maps, Plans, and Tables. By G. W. Kitchin, M.A. In 3 vols. Crown 8vo. *cloth,* price 10s. 6d. each.

Selections from the Despatches, Treaties, and other Papers of the Marquess Wellesley, K.G., during his Government of India. Edited by S. J. Owen, M.A. 8vo. *cloth,* 1l. 4s.

Selections from the Wellington Despatches. By the same Editor. 8vo. *cloth,* 24s.

A History of the United States of America. By E. J. Payne, M.A., Fellow of University College, Oxford. *In the Press.*

A Manual of Ancient History. By George Rawlinson, M.A., Camden Professor of Ancient History, Oxford. Demy 8vo. *cloth,* 14s.

A History of Greece. By E. A. Freeman, M.A., formerly
Fellow of Trinity College, Oxford.

Italy and her Invaders. A.D. 376–476. By T. Hodgkin,
Fellow of University College, London. Illustrated with Plates and Maps. 2 vols.
demy 8vo. *cloth,* 1*l.* 12*s.*

IX. LAW.

The Elements of Jurisprudence. By Thomas Erskine
Holland, D.C.L. *Second Edition.* Demy 8vo. *cloth,* 10*s.* 6*d.*

The Institutes of Justinian, edited as a Recension of the
Institutes of Gaius. By the same Editor. Extra fcap. 8vo. *cloth,* 5*s.*

Gaii Institutionum Juris Civilis Commentarii Quatuor;
or, Elements of Roman Law by Gaius. With a Translation and Commentary.
By Edward Poste, M.A., Barrister-at-Law. *Second Edition.* 8vo. *cloth,* 18*s.*

Select Titles from the Digest of Justinian. By T. E.
Holland, D.C.L., and C. L. Shadwell, B.C.L. Demy 8vo. *cloth,* 14*s.*

Also in separate parts :—

Part I. Introductory Titles. 2*s.* 6*d.*   Part II. Family Law. 1*s.*
Part III. Property Law. 2*s.* 6*d.*
Part IV. Law of Obligations (No. 1). 3*s.* 6*d.*   (No. 2). 4*s.* 6*d.*

Elements of Law considered with reference to Principles
of General Jurisprudence. By William Markby, M.A. *Second Edition, with
Supplement.* Crown 8vo. *cloth,* 7*s.* 6*d.*

International Law. By W. E. Hall, M.A., Barrister-at-Law.
Demy 8vo., *cloth,* 21*s.*

An Introduction to the History of the Law of Real
Property, with Original Authorities. By Kenelm E. Digby, M.A. *Second
Edition.* Crown 8vo. *cloth,* 7*s.* 6*d.*

Principles of the English Law of Contract, etc. By Sir
William R. Anson, Bart., D.C.L. *Second Edition.* Demy 8vo. *cloth,* 10*s.* 6*d.*

X. MENTAL AND MORAL PHILOSOPHY.

Bacon. Novum Organum. Edited, with Introduction,
Notes, etc., by T. Fowler, M.A. 1878. 8vo. *cloth,* 14*s.*

Locke's Conduct of the Understanding. Edited, with
Introduction, Notes, etc., by T. Fowler, M.A. Extra fcap. 8vo. *cloth,* 2*s.*

Selections from Berkeley. With an Introduction and
Notes. By Alexander Campbell Fraser, LL.D. *Second Edition.* Crown 8vo.
cloth, 7*s.* 6*d.*

The Elements of Deductive Logic, designed mainly for
the use of Junior Students in the Universities. By T. Fowler, M.A. *Seventh
Edition.* with a Collection of Examples. Ext. fcap. 8vo. *cloth,* 3*s.* 6*d.*

The Elements of Inductive Logic, designed mainly for
the use of Students in the Universities. By the same Author. *Third Edition.*
Ext. fcap. 8vo. *cloth,* 6*s.*

A Manual of Political Economy, for the use of Schools.
By J. E. Thorold Rogers, M.A. *Third Edition.* Ext. fcap. 8vo. *cloth,* 4*s.* 6*d.*

XI. ART, &c.

A Handbook of Pictorial Art. By R. St. J. Tyrwhitt, M.A. *Second Edition.* 8vo. *half morocco,* 18*s.*

A Treatise on Harmony. By Sir F. A. Gore Ouseley, Bart., M.A., Mus. Doc. *Second Edition.* 4to. *cloth,* 10*s.*

A Treatise on Counterpoint, Canon, and Fugue, based upon that of Cherubini. By the same Author. *Second Edition.* 4to. *cloth,* 16*s.*

A Treatise on Musical Form, and General Composition. By the same Author. 4to. *cloth,* 10*s.*

A Music Primer for Schools. By J. Troutbeck, M.A., and R. F. Dale, M.A., B. Mus. *Second Edition.* Crown 8vo. *cloth,* 1*s.* 6*d.*

The Cultivation of the Speaking Voice. By John Hullah. *Second Edition.* Extra fcap. 8vo. *cloth,* 2*s.* 6*d.*

XII. MISCELLANEOUS.

Text-Book of Botany, Morphological and Physiological. By Dr. Julius Sachs, Professor of Botany in the University of Würzburg. *Second Edition.* Edited, with an Appendix, by Sydney H. Vines, M.A. Royal 8vo. *half morocco,* 1*l.* 11*s.* 6*d.*

A System of Physical Education : Theoretical and Practical. By Archibald Maclaren, The Gymnasium, Oxford. Extra fcap. 8vo. *cloth,* 7*s.* 6*d.*

An Icelandic Prose Reader, with Notes, Grammar, and Glossary. By Dr. Gudbrand Vigfusson and F. York Powell, M.A. Extra fcap. 8vo. *cloth,* 10*s.* 6*d.*

Dante. Selections from the Inferno. With Introduction and Notes. By H. B. Cotterill, B.A. Extra fcap. 8vo. *cloth,* 4*s.* 6*d.*

Tasso. La Gerusalemme Liberata. Cantos I, II. By the same Editor. Extra fcap. 8vo. *cloth,* 2*s.* 6*d.*

A Treatise on the Use of the Tenses in Hebrew. By S. R. Driver, M.A., Fellow of New College. *New and Enlarged Edition.* Extra fcap. 8vo. *cloth,* 7*s.* 6*d.*

Outlines of Textual Criticism applied to the New Testament. By C. E. Hammond, M.A., Fellow and Tutor of Exeter College, Oxford. *Third Edition.* Extra fcap. 8vo. *cloth,* 3*s.* 6*d.*

A Handbook of Phonetics, including a Popular Exposition of the Principles of Spelling Reform. By Henry Sweet, M.A. Extra fcap. 8vo. *cloth,* 4*s.* 6*d.*

The DELEGATES OF THE PRESS *invite suggestions and advice from all persons interested in education; and will be thankful for hints, &c., addressed to the* SECRETARY TO THE DELEGATES, *Clarendon Press, Oxford.*

9 783337 007720